More praise for Ben Kiernan's *The Pol Pot Regime*

"Ben Kiernan's first book focused on Pol Pot's rise to power. In this long awaited sequel, Kiernan describes what happened once Pol Pot was in power, from 1975 to 1979. Its strength lies in its wealth of detailed information, most of it gathered through his hundreds of interviews; and in the patience with which he has fitted it together to give a clear overview of a period as bewildering as it was brutal. . . . No other writer has listened to so many Cambodians describe what they did, and what was done to them, in those four years. Everyone who wants to understand what actually happened under the Pol Pot regime must read Kiernan's exhaustive, absorbing and thoroughly depressing account."—Kelvin Rowley, *Asia-Pacific Magazine*

"A detailed and chilling history."—*Asiaweek*

"Making effective use of the new information that continues to surface, Kiernan weaves a convincing history of the regime and its impact on Cambodian society."
—Jeffrey M. Chwieroth, *History*

"In this authoritative work, Ben Kiernan . . . explores the reasons why Pol Pot's Khmer Rouge revolution became a Cambodian nightmare."—Richard Gough, *Times Higher Education Supplement*

"A crucial contribution to the existing historical literature on the subject."—Hélène Lambert, *International Affairs*

" For anyone interested in Cambodia, this is . . . required reading."—Martin Stuart-Fox, *Australian Journal of Politics and History*

THE POL POT REGIME

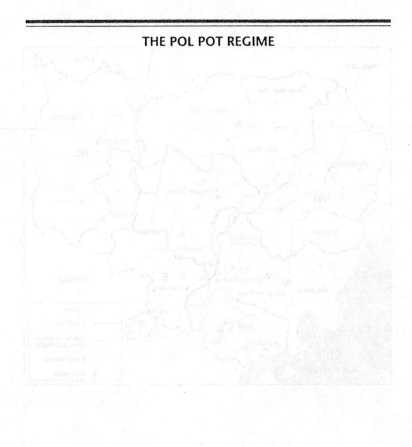

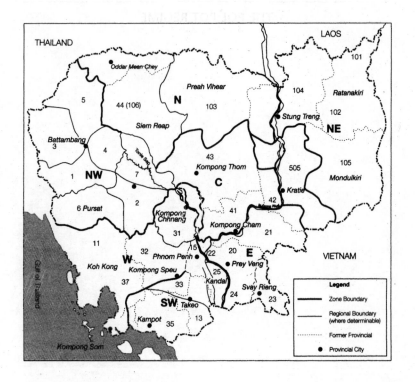

BEN KIERNAN

The Pol Pot Regime

Race, Power, and Genocide
in Cambodia
under the Khmer Rouge, 1975–79

SECOND EDITION

SILKWORM BOOKS

ISBN 974-9575-71-7

This Southeast Asia edition is first published in 2005 by
Silkworm Books
6 SukkasemRoad, Suthep, Muang, Chiang Mai 50200
E-mail: silkworm@silkwormbooks.info
http://www.silkwormbooks.info

Printed in Thailand by O. S. Printing House

8 7 6 5 4 3 2 1

For Mia-lia and Derry

The Samlaut Rebellion and its Aftermath, 1967–70

Peasants and Politics in Kampuchea, 1942–1981
(co-author)

*How Pol Pot Came To Power: A History of Communism
in Kampuchea, 1930–1975*

Cambodia: The Eastern Zone Massacres

Burchett: Reporting the Other Side of the World, 1939–1983 (editor)

*Genocide and Democracy in Cambodia: The Khmer Rouge,
the United Nations, and the International Community* (editor)

Le Génocide au Cambodge, 1975–1979: race, idéologie et pouvoir

Contents

Preface to the Second Edition   ix
Acknowledgments   xvii
List of Acronyms   xxi
Glossary   xxiii

CHAPTER ONE Introduction: The Making of the 1975 Khmer Rouge
Victory   1

Part I: Wiping the Slate Clean: The Regime Takes Shape

CHAPTER TWO Cleansing the Cities: The Quest for Total Power   31

CHAPTER THREE Cleansing the Countryside:
Race, Power, and the Party, 1973–75   65

CHAPTER FOUR Cleansing the Frontiers:
Neighbors, Friends, and Enemies, 1975–76   102

Part II: Writing on the Slate, 1975–77: The CPK Project

CHAPTER FIVE An Indentured Agrarian State, 1975–77 (I):
The Base Areas—The Southwest and the East   159

CHAPTER SIX An Indentured Agrarian State, 1975–77 (II):
Peasants and Deportees in the Northwest   216

CHAPTER SEVEN Ethnic Cleansing:
The CPK and Cambodia's Minorities, 1975–77   251

Part III: The Slate Crumbles, 1977–79: Convulsion and Destruction

CHAPTER EIGHT Power Politics, 1976–77   313

CHAPTER NINE Foreign Relations, 1977–78:
Warfare, Weapons, and Wildlife   357

CHAPTER TEN "Thunder without Rain":
Race and Power in Cambodia, 1978   386

CHAPTER ELEVEN The End of the Pol Pot Regime   440

Select Bibliography   467
Index   471

Photos and maps follow page 250.

Preface to the Second Edition

While the first edition of this book was in press in 1995, the Khmer Rouge, in a clandestine radio announcement, "indicted" its author as an "arch war criminal." Driven from Phnom Penh by the Vietnamese invasion of 1979 and having boycotted the United Nations–organized elections in 1993, the Khmer Rouge forces were still holding out along the Thai–Cambodian border. Referring to the Cambodian Genocide Program, a Yale research project I founded with a State Department grant to document the Khmer Rouge era,[1] Pol Pot's radio station alleged that "the Australian Ben Kiernan, who is an accessory executioner of the U.S. imperialists," was "prosecuting and terrorizing the Cambodian resistance patriots."[2] In another broadcast two days later, a Khmer Rouge spokesman called me a "vile and odious hireling of the communist Vietnamese and the Allies." Apparently in the forty-eight hours from the announcement of my "indictment," I was "tried by humanity" and "sentenced" as a "war criminal." With this demonstration of legal process, the Khmer Rouge claimed to "continue to stand tall, displaying their most lofty heroism" and to be "able to defend and forever maintain their nation, people, and race."[3]

A popular Khmer saying has it, "Cambodia will never disappear," but the

1. Ben Kiernan, "Bringing the Khmer Rouge to Justice," *Human Rights Review* 1, 3, April–June 2000, pp. 92–108.

2. Radio of the Provisional Government of National Union and National Salvation of Cambodia (Khmer Rouge), in Cambodian, 14 August 1995. A translated transcript of the broadcast can be found in United States, Central Intelligence Agency, *Foreign Broadcast Information Service* (FBIS), Daily Report, FBIS-EAS-95-157, 15 August 1995, "Commentary Views Prosecution of Khmer Rouge," pp. 67–68. See also "Khmer threat to kill Aussies," *Age* (Melbourne), 8 August 1994.

3. "Khmer Rouge 'Communique' on Alliance, Vietnam's Crimes," Radio of the Provisional Government of National Union and National Salvation of Cambodia (Khmer Rouge), in Cambodian, 16 August 1995. A translated transcript of the broadcast was declassified by the CIA on May 8, 2000.

Khmer Rouge enjoyed less longevity. In 1996, Pol Pot's former brother-in-law and deputy prime minister, Ieng Sary, defected to the Cambodian government of Hun Sen, bringing with him the Khmer Rouge military units under his command. Sary received a "pardon" for his opposition since the Khmer Rouge defeat, and for his new loyalty retained autonomous authority over Pailin province.[4] Other Khmer Rouge leaders soon jockeyed for similar treatment from Phnom Penh. In June 1997, fearing further defections and possible betrayal, Pol Pot murdered Son Sen, another deputy prime minister of his Democratic Kampuchea (DK) regime and its defense and security chief from 1975 to 1979. In the jungle of northern Cambodia, as the last military forces still loyal to Pol Pot fled their headquarters at Anlong Veng, they drove their trucks over the bodies of their final victims: Son Sen, his wife Yun Yat, the DK minister of culture, and a dozen of their family members. The Khmer Rouge army commander, Chhit Choeun (alias Mok), turned in pursuit and arrested Pol Pot. His former accomplices quickly subjected Pol Pot to a show trial in the jungle for the murder of Son Sen. But in March 1998, the former DK deputy army commander, Ke Pauk, led a new mutiny against Mok and defected to the government. The next month, as the various factions slugged it out, Pol Pot died in his sleep. He may have committed suicide in order to evade capture. U.S. officials had been negotiating with Mok's forces to take custody of Pol Pot at the Thai border.

In December 1998, the top surviving Khmer Rouge leaders—Nuon Chea, formerly deputy party secretary under Pol Pot, and Khieu Samphan, former DK head of state—abandoned Mok's border hideout and surrendered to the Cambodian government. They said they were now sorry for the crimes they had perpetrated.[5] Alone in the jungle, Mok did not hold out long either. Cambodian troops captured him in March 1999. And the next month, Kang Khek Iev, alias Deuch, the former commandant of Tuol Sleng prison, DK's nerve center, was discovered by the British journalist Nic Dunlop wearing a T-shirt with the logo of the American Refugee Committee and proclaiming himself born again. "I had a difficult life and I decided to be a Christian. It is God's will that you are here. I have done very bad things," Deuch told Dunlop in a confession more genuine than those he had routinely tortured from his prisoners two decades earlier. "I'm only interested in my children, my stomach, and God. There is no future for the Khmer Rouge, they're finished." Deuch left his own fate "up to Hun Sen and Jesus."[6] He too was quickly arrested by Hun

---

4. Ben Kiernan, "Ieng Sary's Role in the Pol Pot Regime," *Phnom Penh Post*, 24 January 1997, and "Pol Pot's Brothers in Crime," *New York Times*, 20 June 1997.

5. Ben Kiernan, Dith Pran, and Youk Chhang, "Désolés pour le génocide," *Le Monde*, 5 January 1999.

6. Nic Dunlop, "KR Torture Chief Admits to Mass Murder," *Phnom Penh Post*, 30 April–13

Sen's police.[7] Phnom Penh prosecutors announced that Deuch and Mok would be charged with genocide, and that both Nuon Chea and Khieu Samphan would be summoned to testify and also charged with genocide.[8]

In July 1997, Cambodia's two prime ministers, Hun Sen and King Sihanouk's son Norodom Ranariddh, had appealed to the United Nations to establish an international tribunal to judge the crimes of the Khmer Rouge. The next year the UN created a Group of Experts to examine the evidence, including the documents collected by the Cambodian Genocide Program and its now-independent offshoot, the Documentation Center of Cambodia. The UN experts concluded that the Khmer Rouge should face charges "for crimes against humanity and genocide."[9] They wrote that the events of 1975–79 fit the definition of the crime outlawed by the United Nations Genocide Convention of 1948. In their view, the Khmer Rouge regime had "subjected the people of Cambodia to almost all of the acts enumerated in the Convention. The more difficult task is determining whether the Khmer Rouge carried out these acts with the requisite intent and against groups protected by the Convention." The experts' response to this challenge was affirmative:

> In the view of the Group of Experts, the existing historical research justifies including genocide within the jurisdiction of a tribunal to prosecute Khmer Rouge leaders. In particular, evidence suggests the need for prosecutors to investigate the commission of genocide against the Cham, Vietnamese and other minority groups, and the Buddhist monkhood. The Khmer Rouge subjected these groups to an especially harsh and extensive measure of the acts enumerated in the Convention. The requisite intent has support in direct and indirect evidence, including Khmer Rouge statements, eyewitness accounts and the nature and numbers of victims in each group, both in absolute terms and in proportion to each group's total population. These groups qualify as protected groups under the Convention: the Muslim Cham as an ethnic and religious group, the Vietnamese communities as an ethnic and, perhaps, a racial group; and the Buddhist monkhood as a religious group.

May 1999, pp. 1, 10; Ben Kiernan, "Notes from a Slaughterhouse," *Bangkok Post* Perspective, 30 May 1999, pp. 1, 3.

7. "Duch murder, treason charges confirmed," DPA, *South China Morning Post*, 15 May 1999.

8. "Khmer Rouge leaders to be summoned for Ta Mok trial," Reuters, Phnom Penh, 23 April 1999; "Rebel pair set to face genocide charges," *South China Morning Post*, DPA, 26 April 1999; "K. Rouge chief said implicates up to 30 comrades," Reuters, Phnom Penh, 27 April 1999.

9. United Nations, AS, General Assembly, Security Council, A/53/850, S/1999/231, March 16, 1999, Annex, *Report of the Group of Experts for Cambodia established pursuant to General Assembly resolution 52/135*, pp. 19–20, 57. The UN experts also concluded that the Khmer Rouge regime had committed "war crimes" against Vietnam and Thailand (p. 23).

Specifically, in the case of the Buddhist monkhood, their intent is evidenced by the Khmer Rouge's intensely hostile statements towards religion, and the monkhood in particular; the Khmer Rouge's policies to eradicate the physical and ritualistic aspects of the Buddhist religion; the disrobing of monks and abolition of the monkhood; the number of victims; and the executions of Buddhist leaders and recalcitrant monks. Likewise, in addition to the number of victims, the intent to destroy the Cham and other ethnic minorities appears evidenced by such Khmer Rouge actions as their announced policy of homogenization, the total prohibition of these groups' distinctive cultural traits, their dispersal among the general population and the execution of their leadership.[10]

From 1999 to 2002 the UN pursued negotiations with the Cambodian government with a view to establishing a joint tribunal to ensure legal accountability for the Cambodian genocide and the Khmer Rouge's other crimes against humanity. The UN withdrawal from the process in February 2002 placed responsibility squarely on Cambodia, as a signatory to the Genocide Convention, to provide a fair trial. The international community should help. In 1991, U.S. Secretary of State James A. Baker promised such assistance: "Cambodia and the US are both signatories to the Genocide Convention and we will support efforts to bring to justice those responsible for the mass murders of the 1970s if the new Cambodian government chooses to pursue this path."[11]

A scholarly consensus on the genocide had already emerged,[12] and new evidence continued to accumulate.[13] An archive of fifty thousand pages ob-

10. *Report of the Group of Experts*, pp. 19–20. Stephen Heder and Brian Tittemore portray the UN report as hesitant on the genocide issue: "The Group of Experts concluded that while the CPK was in power the people of Cambodia had been 'subjected . . . to almost all of the acts enumerated in the [Genocide] Convention,' citing evidence of acts of genocide 'against the Cham, Vietnamese and other minority groups, and the Buddhist monkhood.' However, they cautioned that it might be a 'difficult task' to prove that the CPK carried out acts 'with the requisite intent' to destroy such ethnic and religious groups 'as such.'" Heder and Tittemore, "Seven Candidates for Prosecution: Accountability for the Crimes of the Khmer Rouge," War Crimes Research Office, American University, 2001, p. 14n24.

11. *New York Times*, 24 October 1991, p. A16. Australia's Foreign Minister Gareth Evans added: "We would give strong support to an incoming Cambodian government to set in train such a war crimes process." *Age* (Melbourne), 24 October 1991, p. 1.

12. See Steven Ratner and Jason Abrams, *Accountability for Human Rights Atrocities in International Law: Beyond the Nuremberg Legacy* (Oxford: Clarendon, 1997), p. 244: "The existing literature presents a strong *prima facie* case that the Khmer Rouge committed acts of genocide against the Cham minority group, the ethnic Vietnamese, Chinese, and Thai minority groups, and the Buddhist monkhood. While some commentators suggest otherwise, virtually every author on the subject has reached this conclusion."

13. The Cambodian Genocide Program (CGP) website (www.yale.edu/cgp) contains the Cambodian Genocide Data Bases, which include nineteen thousand biographical records of

tained by the Cambodian Genocide Program in 1996 includes a vast amount of secret correspondence and other documents from the highest levels of the Khmer Rouge regime, including its security organ, the *Santebal*.[14] For example, a handwritten document dated April 17, 1978, includes a list of names of relatives and associates of a prisoner named San Eap. The commander of Zone 801 sent the list to "Committee 870," a title reminiscent of the royal plural, used by Pol Pot.[15] Using a similar personal alias, Angkar ("the Organization"), Pol Pot scribbled on the cover letter in thick red pencil, "A/k 19/4/78 Follow up." This was an order to arrest those named in the list.[16]

The *Santebal* archives also document the ethnic purges and the regime's genocidal intent. For example, in November 1975, a Khmer Rouge official in the Eastern Zone, where Muslim Chams had recently revolted, complained to Pol Pot of his inability to implement "the dispersal strategy according to the decision that you, Brother, had discussed with us." Pol Pot had ordered 150,000 Chams from the east dispersed across the Northern and Northwest Zones. But officials in Ke Pauk's Northern Zone had barred the way to the initial 50,000 Cham arrivals. They "absolutely refused to accept Islamic people," preferring "only pure Khmer people." The Eastern Zone would take them back, the official said, but, he asked, how did Pol Pot plan to reach his target of 150,000 deportees? "More than one hundred thousand Islamic people remain in the Eastern Zone. We only withdrew the people in important places."[17] In another message to Pol Pot two months later, Ke Pauk himself referred to "enemies" such as "Islamic people."[18] Both he and Pol Pot engaged in racist

---

Khmer Rouge figures from Pol Pot to local district chiefs, five thousand photographs of victims, and three thousand catalogue records on Khmer Rouge–era documents, many of them digitally displayed.

14. This archive, now held at the Documentation Center of Cambodia, has been microfilmed by Yale University's Sterling Library Southeast Asia Collection.

15. For Pol Pot's use of *Angkar* as a personal pseudonym, see Document VIII, "Introduction," in *Pol Pot Plans the Future: Confidential Leadership Documents from Democratic Kampuchea, 1976–1977*, ed. D. P. Chandler, Ben Kiernan, and Chanthou Boua, New Haven, Yale Southeast Asia Studies Monograph no. 33, 1988, p. 232.

16. *Santebal* collection, Documentation Center of Cambodia, Phnom Penh, bbkkh 117, *Som courup kana 870 ceati snaeha*, signed by Sae (Kang Chap), 17 April 1978. For extensive translations of further documents, see "The Pol Pot Files," on the CGP website. In another case of top-down political repression, Son Sen, writing to Pol Pot, requested that local authorities "follow up the suspects." *Chhuun bang ceati courup*, handwritten letter to Pol Pot from "Khieu" (Son Sen), 24 September 1977, forwarding a typed letter from Deuch dated 20 September 1977. See also "The Son Sen Files," extensive translations on the CGP website.

17. "To Comrade Brother Pol with respect," signed Chhon, 30 November 1975. Original held at the Documentation Center of Cambodia, Phnom Penh, DC-Cam Document No. N0001045 (01 bbk).

18. "To Brother Pol with respect," signed "Comrade Pauk," 4 February 1976. DC-Cam Document No. N0001187 (02 bbk).

repression and forced dispersal of the Chams. In legal terms, this constituted destruction of an ethnic group "as such"—genocide.

What was the nature of the ideology that drove this genocide?[19] The phenomenon is notable for its explosive combination of totalitarian political ambition and a racialist project of ethnic purification.[20] Democratic Kampuchea, unlike the communist regimes of the USSR, China, and Vietnam, never created "autonomous zones" for its national minorities. From September 1975, DK even refused public recognition of Cambodia's specific minorities and asserted that they totaled a nominal 1 percent of the population rather than their actual 15–20 percent.[21] DK was the only communist regime systematically to disperse its minorities by force and to make punishable by death the use of minority and foreign languages. DK distinguished itself even from its Stalinist predecessors, Mao's China and Enver Hoxha's Albania.[22] Only Kim Il Sung's North Korea pursued no minority policy, but unlike other communist states it had no ethnic minority populations.[23] A close ally of Democratic Kampuchea, North Korea may have provided Pol Pot a model of ethnic as well as ideological purity, one that disregarded Korea's distinct ethnic homogeneity.[24] The Khmer Rouge similarly dismissed material facts of history in their economic program, setting production targets, for instance, without data on existing productivity.[25]

Thus, racialist and ideological strands intertwined in a tapestry of tragedy. On the one hand, DK labeled all Muslim Chams, although they came from a variety of social classes, as petit bourgeois "whose lives are not so difficult."

19. See Ben Kiernan, "Penser le génocide au Cambodge," *Le Monde*, 14 May 1998, and "Le communisme racial des Khmers rouges," *Esprit*, no. 252, May 1999, pp. 93–127.

20. For a comparison with Rwanda, see Scott Straus, "Organic purity and the role of anthropology in Cambodia and Rwanda," in *Patterns of Prejudice*, Institute for Jewish Policy Research, 35, 2, 2001, pp. 47–62.

21. See p. 251, below, and Stephen Heder, *Southeast Asia Research*, 5, 2, July 1997, p. 113n23.

22. These states also repressed religion. But China formally established large minority "Autonomous Zones." Albania, home to fifty-nine thousand Greeks in "one of the most ethnically homogeneous populations in the world," enforced atheism, purged Christian names, and removed crosses from graves but formally recognized its Greek minority's existence and published the tightly controlled Greek-language periodical *Tavima*. Tirana also eschewed irredentism toward Kosovo. See Elez Biberaj, *Albania: A Socialist Maverick* (Boulder, 1990), pp. 5, 89, 98–99, 95–96; R. Zickel et al., *Albania* (Washington, 1994), pp. 68–69.

23. "There are no non-Korean ethnic or cultural minorities of any significance on the peninsula. The population is one of the most homogeneous in the world." *North Korea: A Country Study*, ed. Frederica M. Bunge (Washington, D.C., 1981), p. 56.

24. "Cultural and linguistic variation was not on the scale of China or even Japan." Stewart Lone and Gavan McCormack, *Korea since 1850* (New York: St. Martin's, 1993), p. 3.

25. See Document II, and "Introduction," in *Pol Pot Plans the Future*, p. 12. On Khmer Rouge antimaterialist ideology, see Kiernan, "Kampuchea and Stalinism," in *Marxism in Asia*, ed. Colin Mackerras and Nick Knight (London: Croom Helm, 1985), pp. 232–49.

DK considered Chams the only nationality with no laborer class. This clearcut racial stereotype disguised as class discrimination served a policy of targeted ethnic repression. Conversely, DK often justified the liquidation of majority Khmer political opponents and potential dissidents by a slogan with strong racialist overtones, in the name of wiping out those with "Khmer bodies and Vietnamese minds." The tragedy was twofold. In absolute numbers most of DK's victims were from the Khmer majority, but the ethnic minorities suffered in severe disproportion (see table 4, p. 458). Political repression and genocide reinforced one another to exact a toll unique in the history of communist regimes: over a fifth of a nation's population perished in less than four years.

Pol Pot, Son Sen, and Ke Pauk are dead, but their leading associates can and should be held accountable for some of the heinous crimes of "the century of genocide." The Cambodian genocide was accompanied and followed by comparable atrocities in East Timor, Guatemala, Bosnia, and Rwanda, committed by perpetrators across the political spectrum in Asia, Latin America, Europe, and Africa. In the first year of a new millennium, another outbreak of mass murder took some three thousand lives in North America. Genocide has not been consigned to the past or confined to the undeveloped world. It must be punished, and future crimes prevented, by strengthening international criminal law.

New Haven
February 2002

Acknowledgments

In his 1946 work *The Idea of History*, R. G. Collingwood remarked that "historians do not fit out expeditions to countries where wars and revolutions are going on." But history has a way of catching up with the times, including the emergence of oral history. Cambodia today is largely a product of recent revolution and continuing war. Although thousands of its citizens fled abroad, their accounts could be carefully corroborated only by interviews with others remaining behind. And those archives not destroyed can be found only on the spot.

This book is not the outcome of expeditions. Yet it was impossible to study the country's history without gaining years of familiarity with its suffering and conflict. Readers will have to assess my success at maintaining sound judgment and determine whether Collingwood rightly predicted that fact-finding at sites of war and revolution "would not teach historians anything they want to know." He saw such knowledge as useful only for comparison of "wars and revolutions as such," whereas the historian's priority was "a general study" of the society and era of a specific conflict. My view is that comparative history is just as important. I plan another work on twentieth-century revolution, nationalism, and genocide. But I believe this book already outlines, besides the violent origins, social context, and course of the Cambodian revolution, the role played in it by factors recognizable worldwide: racialist ideology and the quest for total power.

Twenty years of research accumulate vast intellectual debts. Ian Black, Prescott Clark, Ian Copland, Jamie Mackie, John Ingleson, John Legge, and Ian Mabbett introduced me to Asian history and inspired me to pursue it professionally. So did David Chandler, an excellent teacher and colleague. Like all scholars of modern Cambodian history, I am deeply indebted to the senior historians in the field: David Chandler, Milton Osborne, and Michael Vickery. Fellow postgraduate students at the Centre of Southeast Asian Studies at Monash University, in Melbourne, Australia, particularly Phuwadon Songprasert, Chalong Soontranavich, and Somkiat Wanthana, shared their valuable knowledge, insights, and experiences with me. Chanthou Boua, La'or Rampaneenin, and Jean-Louis Clavaud taught me to speak and read Khmer. Colleagues in the history departments at Monash, the University of New South Wales, the University of Wollongong, and Yale University all helped me in ways too numerous to mention. Grants from Monash, Wollongong, Yale, the Christopher Reynolds Foundation, and the Federation of American Scientists enabled me to research and write this book. The Frederick W. Hilles Fund assisted in its publication and in the production of maps 2 to 5.

I first visited Cambodia in early 1975. None of the Cambodians I knew then survived the next four years. I cherish the generosity and memory of Kong Aun, Pan Sothi, In Hoeurng, and Duong Chantha. Survivors Chum Bunrong, Khieu Kanharith, Heng Sovannary, Ly Kimsok, Nil Sa'unn, Nong Rom, Sar Sambath, Soeung Kung, Sok Sokhun, Sorn Samnang, Thun Saray, Ung Pech, and Vandy Kaon have been fountains of experience, knowledge, and friendship over fifteen years. Poeu San, who died as this book neared completion, is sadly missed.

From 1975 to 1979, in a political prison known as Tuol Sleng, many other Cambodians left invaluable traces of their struggles in autobiographical "confessions," not so difficult to interpret as they were to compose—under torture before execution. The staff of the Tuol Sleng Museum of Genocide were always friendly and helpful; thanks go especially to Ung Pech, Chea Samaun, Chey Sopheara, and Lor Chandara. The National Archives of Cambodia provided valuable access and assistance in 1981 and 1992; I particularly wish to thank Sin Khin and Lim Ky.

Five hundred Cambodians aided this project immeasurably by granting long interviews that often revived painful memories. I was able to compare the accounts of a hundred refugees in France with those of four hundred Cambodians interviewed in their homes and workplaces in their own country. As many again told me their stories more informally. Some requested anonymity. Most cannot safely be identified: since the 1991 return of the Khmer Rouge to Phnom Penh and subsequent military resurgence, they are again threatened, and I have altered their names.

James C. Scott has long provided patient encouragement, keen advice, and unfailing support. I also thank Michael Adas, Abbas Amanat, George Andreopoulos, Ivo Banac, Doron Ben-Atar, Melanie Beresford, John Bresnan, Paul Bushkovitch, Lyn Caldwell, Linda Colley, Harold Conklin, Deborah Davis Friedman, Donald Dingsdag, Bradon Ellem, J. Joseph Errington, Herbert Feith, Michael Godley, Jon Halliday, Valerie Hansen, Robert Harms, Thomas Head, Stephen Henningham, Helen Hill, George Kahin, Deborah Kaspin, Paul Kennedy, Charles Keyes, Howard Lamar, Daniel Lev, David G. Marr, Gavan

McCormack, Val Noone, Michael N. Pearson, Anthony Reid, Merle Ricklefs, Kelvin Rowley, Peter M. Sales, Mark Shulman, Gaddis Smith, Jonathan Spence, Jeremy Stone, Joanna Waley-Cohen, Andrew D. Wells, Robin Winks, and Diana Wylie. Many colleagues shared information with me, including Anthony Barnett, Eileen Blumenthal, Nayan Chanda, David Chandler, Sara Colm, May Ebihara, Kate Frieson, Denis Gray, David Hawk, Stephen Heder, Patrick Hughes, Helen Jarvis, Gareth Porter, Kelvin Rowley, Toni Shapiro, Gregory Stanton, Keng Vannsak, and Michael Vickery. I am most grateful to Talya and Jonathan Berger, Darryl and Jantu Bullen, Nguyen Dien and Paula Simcocks, Ulla Kasten, Tinuk and Philip Yampolski, Sheri Prasso, Laurie Sears, Anne Weills, and Haynie Lowrey Wheeler. Lydia Breckon was an able research assistant during the final two years of writing. I also learned much about Southeast Asia from working with other graduate students, including Gene Ammarelle, James Carter, Susan E. Cook, George Dutton, Daniel Fineman, Heng Samnang, Eugenie Jenkins, Kim Ninh, Puangthong Rungswasdisab, Brett Seaman, and Eric Tagliacozzo. Charles Grench, my editor at Yale University Press, shepherded the book through various stages of writing and production.

In all my endeavors, Joan and Peter Kiernan have been loving guides and intimate friends. This book is dedicated to Mia-lia Boua Kiernan and Derry Reuben Kiernan, in memory of the extended family they never knew.

Acronyms

BBC SWB	British Broadcasting Corporation *Summary of World Broadcasts*
BCAS	*Bulletin of Concerned Asian Scholars*
CCP	Chinese Communist Party
CNA	Cambodian National Archives
CNRS	Centre National de la Recherche Scientifique
CPK	Communist Party of Kampuchea (1966–)
CPRA	Cambodian People's Representative Assembly (1976–79)
CPT	Communist Party of Thailand
DK	Democratic Kampuchea (1976–79)
FBIS	*Foreign Broadcast Information Service*
FEER	*Far Eastern Economic Review*
FLPH	Foreign Languages Publishing House
FULRO	Front Uni de Libération des Races Opprimées (Vietnam)
IHT	*International Herald Tribune*
KC	"Khmer Communists" (U.S. official usage for insurgents, 1970–75)
KK	Khmer Krahom (Red Khmer, or Khmer Rouge)
KKK	Khmer Kampuchea Krom (U.S.-trained Khmer troops in Vietnam)
KPRP	Khmer People's Revolutionary Party (1951–60)
KR	Khmer Rumdos (Khmer Liberation, 1970–75)
MC-DK	Ministry of Commerce of Democratic Kampuchea
NUFK	National United Front of Kampuchea (led by CPK, 1970–75)
NVA	North Vietnamese Army
PRK	People's Republic of Kampuchea (1979–89)
UFNSK	United Front for National Salvation of Kampuchea (anti-DK, 1978–)
UPI	United Press International

USAID   United States Agency for International Development
VC   "Viet Cong" (U.S. usage)
V/N   Vietnam
VODK   *Voice of Democratic Kampuchea*
VWP   Vietnam Workers' Party (1951–76)

Glossary

Angkar	the "Organization" (CPK)
Angkar Loeu	the "High Organization" (CPK "Center")
chalat	DK mobile work brigade, mostly composed of young workers
damban	Region (DK usage)
hakkem	Islamic community leader
Khmer Krahom	"Red Khmers" (Khmer Rouge)
Khmer Krom	"Lower Khmers," ethnic Cambodians from southern Vietnam
Khmer Loeu	"Upper Khmers," ethnic minority hill peoples of Cambodia
Khmer Rumdos	"Khmer Liberation"
khum	subdistrict
krom	work team
neak moultanh	"base" people
neak penh sith	"full-rights" people
neak phñoe	"depositees" (deportees)
neak thmei	"new" people
neak triem	"candidates"
phum	village, hamlet
phumipeak	Zone (DK usage); Region (U.S. usage)
prahoc	Cambodian preserved fish paste
srok	district
trokuon	water morning glory, a nutritious Cambodian plant
wat	Buddhist monastery

THE POL POT REGIME

CHAPTER ONE

Introduction: The Making of the 1975 Khmer Rouge Victory

Sixty-eight long-haired soldiers trudged across the border from southern Vietnam. In their American uniforms they looked like troops of the defeated Saigon regime. It was April, the hottest time of the year in Cambodia, and they must have been relieved to get there. Dressed in khaki uniforms and U.S. army boots, white sweat bands on their wrists, they dripped with grenades and firearms. Some carried U.S.-made M-16 rifles, others M-79 grenade launchers and packs of rice rations. They were all in their twenties, except for the leader, who was over fifty but also wore his hair long. He carried a Chinese-made AK-47 rifle and an automatic pistol.

Not far inside the border a crowd of workers, dressed all in black, labored in the sun, apparently digging earthworks for irrigation. Unbeknown to the newcomers, they were deportees from the now-empty city of Phnom Penh, mute testimony to the nature of the revolution unfolding in Cambodia. Around them the parched lower Mekong plain stretched for miles in every direction, broken only by a few hillocks, their rocky slopes plunging into ring-shaped verdant oases of fruit trees and coconut palms. Here were Cambodian villages. The newcomers headed for the nearest patch of shade, the village of Svay Sor, and asked to meet local officials.

The soldiers were Khmer Krom, or Lowland Khmers, members of Vietnam's million-strong ethnic Khmer minority. Recruited by U.S. Special Forces in the 1960s to fight communism in the Mekong Delta of south Vietnam, these troops had developed into an independent force opposed to all Vietnamese. Trained for the American unit known as Mike Force, they became instead "White Scarves." They described themselves as the liberation movement of Kampuchea Krom, or Lower Cambodia, as many Khmers called Vietnam's Mekong Delta. In this cause they had even turned their guns on Americans. For a year now, they had held out doggedly against the communist victors in the Vietnam War. Finally driven across the border, they had come to make common cause with the Pol Pot regime in what they considered their Cambodian motherland.

Local officials quickly arrived, headed by the subdistrict chief, Ngaol. They listened to the newcomers' story and asked them what they wanted. Replying in his native Khmer, the commander told Ngaol he wished to see "brother Khieu Samphan," the new president of "Democratic Kampuchea" (DK). "Right, but let's eat first," was the answer. "And please put down your weapons." They did. Nen, chief of the youth movement of Kirivong district, spoke some words of welcome. He agreed that they were all fighting a common fight against the Vietnamese. Peasants brought coconuts for the soldiers, and a pig and a cow were slaughtered for them to eat. President Samphan would be notified of their arrival. They all sat down to a hearty meal.

Khieu Samphan was busy. Following Prince Norodom Sihanouk's resignation as head of state on 4 April 1976, a new cabinet had just been announced in Phnom Penh. On 14 April, Samphan had replaced Sihanouk, becoming "Chairman of the State Presidium." And a certain Pol Pot had been named Democratic Kampuchea's new prime minister. The next day, Samphan addressed a mass meeting to celebrate the first anniversary of the revolutionary victory against "the U.S. imperialists and their lackeys of all stripes," including "the Saigon puppet forces." This victory, he said, was a "masterpiece written with fresh blood and achieved through the sacrifices of flesh and bones of our people." It was also "a new and brilliant page of history for our race."[1]

Samphan did not mention other races. At this very time, just downriver from Cambodia's seat of government, local DK officials were suppressing one of Cambodia's significant ethnic minorities, the Muslim Chams. As the White Scarves waited in the neighboring province for a response from Samphan, DK officials banned Islam, closed the local mosque, and dispersed the Cham population as far as the northwest provinces. Some Muslims were forced to eat pork, on pain of death. On 11 April, local officials also arrested fifty-seven Arabs, Pakistanis, and Indians, including forty women and children, who were sent to their deaths in the capital.[2] In order to emphasize that this was no mere assault against Islam, Cham was now banned as "a foreign language." The officials began killing any who infringed these regulations. One local peasant recalls: "Some Cham villages completely disappeared; only two or three people remained. We were persecuted much more than Khmers." Half a

---

1. Khieu Samphan on Phnom Penh Radio, 15 April 1976, in U.S. Central Intelligence Agency, *Foreign Broadcast Information Service* (*FBIS*) IV (Asia-Pacific), 16 April 1976, pp. H1–5.

2. List of foreign prisoners, compiled by Ung Pech from Tuol Sleng prison records, 1980. These fifty-seven Muslims were all arrested in DK's Region 25, southern Kandal province, and sent to Takhmau, site of the predecessor of Tuol Sleng, on 29 April 1976.

dozen Cham families escaped across the border into Vietnam. Relatives left behind were singled out for punishment.[3]

It was not long before the White Scarves received their reply from Phnom Penh. Their leader was discreetly taken aside. Then his troops were loaded onto seven small Daihatsu trucks. They drove a short distance to a nearby rice field. The first truck pulled up, and as the long-haired soldiers disembarked from the rear, a waiting Khmer Rouge squad quickly opened fire, cutting them down. The soldiers on the remaining trucks saw what was happening. They all jumped to the ground and scattered for their lives. But the Khmer Rouge troops pursued each one of them across the dry rice fields. It was over within minutes. All sixty-seven of the disarmed men were massacred.

Several days after the slaughter of his soldiers, the Khmer Krom commander reached the notorious Tuol Sleng prison in Phnom Penh. Before his execution, he "confessed" under torture that he was an "internal enemy" of Democratic Kampuchea.

Back in Kirivong district, fighting had broken out with Vietnamese troops across the border. A local DK village chief announced that "Cambodian forces were attacking and were going to liberate Kampuchea Krom." The troops penetrated ten kilometers inside Vietnam.[4] A couple of months later, in mid-1976, subdistrict chief Ngaol proclaimed at a military parade: "We have to take back the territory of Kampuchea Krom." But other local officials boasted that they had now killed over two thousand Khmer Krom, remnants of Mike Force. The head of the district security forces claimed that "American slaves" were identifiable because they "had milk to drink."[5]

The fate of the sixty-eight White Scarves showed the colors of the Pol Pot regime. Its two major enemies, U.S. imperialism and Vietnam, were embodied in this pathetic group. Born in Vietnam, country of the "hereditary enemy," they wore long hair in the "imperialist" fashion. Despite their ethnicity and their new, racially driven embrace of Democratic Kampuchea, the regime considered them dangerous. They were "Khmer bodies with Vietnamese minds." This slogan, which was to echo throughout the DK experience, suggests the readiness of the Pol Pot regime to suppress not only ethnic minorities like the Cham, but also huge numbers of the Khmer majority. This readiness was justified on the racial grounds that they were not really Khmer, evidently

3. Author's interviews with surviving Chams in Cham Leu village, Koh Thom district, 1 August 1980. They dated this repression as beginning in April 1976.
4. Michael Vickery, *Cambodia 1975–1982*, Boston: South End, 1984, p. 190.
5. This account is based on the author's interview with one of those working in the fields at Svay Sor in April 1976. He saw the newcomers cross the border and was later told of their fate by local Khmer Rouge supporters. Interview, 26 August 1980, Preah Bat Chuon Chum, Kirivong district.

because their minds could not be controlled. Racial ideology expressed political suspicion.

The White Scarves were dispatched in a manner that was to make Democratic Kampuchea infamous: cynical deception and stupefying violence.[6] Given DK's aim of "retaking Kampuchea Krom," no political group could have been a better candidate to become the innocent ally of Pol Pot. But Democratic Kampuchea did not favor allies. It could not trust those outside its creation or control. It distinguished territory from people, race from citizens. The long-haired soldiers were destroyed because of the presumption that they might one day become enemies. In a way, this was well founded. Though dedicated to Cambodia's independence, they would have reeled at the transformation it was undergoing. Such newcomers could not be expected to marvel at the "correct and clear-sighted policies and leadership" of Pol Pot's Democratic Kampuchea once they had seen it from the inside. Among Cambodians, racial preference rarely provoked reflection, but the *practical* cost to them of any political or territorial windfall for their "race" was discouraging. And then, the White Scarves' American and Vietnamese background may have told against the revolution. The risk was too great. It was a case, in DK parlance, of "spare them, no profit; remove them, no loss."[7]

The DK regime believed the transformation of Cambodia to be both a necessity for and a guarantee of its independence. It would eventually destroy it.

The Cambodian Scene

At first glance, mid-twentieth-century Cambodia seems a society resistant to transformation. Compared to neighboring Thailand and Vietnam, it was geographically compact, demographically dispersed, linguistically unified, ethnically homogeneous, socially undifferentiated, culturally uniform, administratively unitary, politically undeveloped, economically undiversified, and educationally deprived. Cambodia was more isolated and landlocked than any other Southeast Asian country except Laos. It had also been mummified by ninety years of a French colonial protectorate, which preserved,

6. For descriptions of the fate of others regarded by the Pol Pot regime as having "Khmer bodies with Vietnamese minds," see Kiernan, "Wild Chickens, Farm Chickens and Cormorants: Kampuchea's Eastern Zone under Pol Pot," in David P. Chandler and Ben Kiernan, eds., *Revolution and Its Aftermath in Kampuchea: Eight Essays*, Yale Southeast Asia Studies Monograph No. 25, 1983, pp. 136–211; and Kiernan, *Cambodia: The Eastern Zone Massacres*, Columbia University Center for the Study of Human Rights, Documentation Series No. 1, 1986.

7. Joan D. Criddle and Teeda Butt Mam, *To Destroy You Is No Loss: The Odyssey of a Cambodian Family*, New York: Atlantic Monthly Press, 1987; Y Phandara, *Retour à Phnom Penh*, Paris: Métailié, 1982, p. 74, says he heard this slogan in 1978 "from the mouths of Khmer Rouge leaders."

even enhanced the country's traditional monarchy and social structure. France walled Cambodia off from other foreign influences, especially Vietnamese ones and especially communism, until French rule in Indochina broke down under the impact of—precisely—Vietnamese communism, and Cambodia found itself with a new neighbor.

Prerevolutionary Cambodia was 80 percent peasant, 80 percent Khmer, and 80 percent Buddhist. First, it was an overwhelmingly rural economy. Its village society was decentralized, its economy unintegrated, dominated by subsistence rice cultivation. Compared to Vietnam's, its villagers participated much less in village-organized activities. They were often described as individualistic; the nuclear family was the social core. May Ebihara, the only American anthropologist to study a Khmer village in Cambodia, wrote: "In village society there are no larger, organised kin groups beyond the family or household. . . . The family and the household are the only enduring and clearly defined units." The broader kindred did not "crystallize as a group." Most villagers usually did not recall their grandparents' names.[8] Subsistence was usually a personal or a family matter.

The only Cambodians who participated in the international economy were garden farmers along the riverbanks and rubber plantation workers in the country's east, totaling at most 10 percent of the rural population, and the 15 percent of the population who lived in towns. Therefore Cambodia nearly comprised two separate societies, with little exchange between them: one rural, producing for subsistence, the other largely urban, producing a few goods for the world market and consuming mostly international commodities. Rice growers provided food for the city dwellers, but the cities offered little for rural consumption.

Second, Cambodia was ethnically quite homogeneous, as were Thailand and Vietnam. But unlike its two neighbors, Cambodia had had much less exposure to external cultural influence, which, when it came, was potentially destabilizing. Mostly as a result of French colonial policy in Indochina, Cambodia acquired substantial but unintegrated minority populations of Vietnamese, Chinese, and Lao, as well as Thais, the large Cham Islamic community, and approximately sixteen other small tribal groups. Eighty percent of Cambodia's residents were Khmer, but Chinese and Vietnamese dominated the cities.[9] And the rural Khmers' geographic dispersal often made concentrations of non-

8. May Ebihara, "A Khmer Village in Cambodia," Ph.D. diss., Columbia University, Ann Arbor, Mich.: University Microfilms, 1968, pp. 148, 186, 171, 153.

9. Peter Kunstadter, ed., *Southeast Asian Tribes, Minorities and Nations*, Princeton University Press, 1967, considers the national figure of 86 percent Khmer an overestimate (p. 4 n. *c*). Phnom Penh was 42 percent Khmer, 30 percent Chinese, 27 percent Vietnamese; Ruth Tooze, *Cambodia: Land of Contrasts*, New York: Viking, 1962, p. 90.

Khmer populations regionally significant, especially in strategic areas of Cambodia's periphery but also, in the case of the Chams, along the riverine arteries on which Cambodia depended for lack of a modern road grid. Moreover, the legacies of medieval Cambodia, the resurgence of its neighbors, and the map-making of the French colonial authorities left ethnic Khmer minorities of a million each in both Vietnam and Thailand.

Third, Cambodia was overwhelmingly Buddhist. The Khmer, Lao, and Thai are all Theravada Buddhist, while Chinese and Vietnamese are usually Mahayana Buddhist. Of the two Theravada monastic orders, the reformist Thommayuth never rivaled the Mohanikay order for Khmer adherents, as it did in Thailand. Cambodia's non-Buddhist communities are limited to Catholic Vietnamese, Islamic Cham, and animist highland tribes. The Vietnamese Cao Dai sect, which did enjoy popularity among Khmers in the 1920s, was banned by French officials, and Christian missionaries never converted more than a few thousand Khmers.

Yet the country had already undergone major transformations by the middle of the twentieth century.[10] Under French colonial rule from 1863, traditional Cambodian intellectual institutions, such as Buddhist pagoda schools, had severely declined, but the authorities provided no modern education system to take their place. By 1954 elementary schools enrolled only a small proportion of school-age children. A full secondary education only became available in the country from 1933, and only 144 Cambodians had completed the *baccalauréat* by 1954. The number in secondary schools was fewer than three thousand. Cambodia had no tertiary education at all. In the 1940s, the tasks of modern nationalism, and even communist organizing, fell to those with a traditional, religious education.

There was rapid change in the Sihanouk period (1954–70). The number of high schools rose from eight in 1953 to two hundred by 1967, with 150,000 students. Another eleven thousand students were attending nine new universities. Nearly all Khmers now had the opportunity of achieving basic literacy, and the country produced over one million educated youth, 20 percent of the population. A mass of politically aware teachers and students comprised an entirely new Cambodian phenomenon, and the Paris-educated Pol Pot group was able to capitalize on their grievances. Even after the disappearance of the last veteran communist leader with a traditional religious education, they probably felt it unnecessary, as well as inadvisable, for communism to rely on its former sources of recruitment such as the Buddhist monkhood.

They did see the peasantry as key. But by 1970 there were two peasantries in Cambodia. Most were poor and indebted, but a majority were small landowners.

10. Information in this section is documented in Ben Kiernan, *How Pol Pot Came to Power*, London: Verso, 1985, pp. xii–xvi.

A minority were landless. (There was a tiny landlord class.) This was the result of another, more ominous transformation of the Sihanouk period. Between 1950 and 1970, the proportion of landless farmers increased from 4 to 20 percent, and the number of dispossessed no doubt increased greatly during the war and the U.S. bombardment. They probably never formed a majority in the Cambodian countryside. But they *were* numerous enough for Pol Pot to build a viable recruitment strategy targeting poor peasants, and particularly their teenage children, who had no enduring ties to land or traditional village community.

Fish and Rice

Five thousand years ago the land of Cambodia did not exist. It lay submerged beneath the South China Sea, between two peninsulas. At its mouth the Mekong River poured silt into the ocean near what is now Cambodia's northern border. The silt gradually filled up the bay, and Cambodia emerged, a country so flat that what had once been islands still stand out prominently as hillocks in a vast alluvial sea. Owing to the large volume of silt, and the great speed of the Mekong when the vast flow from Tibet's melted snows is supplemented by the heavy tropical rainfall in mainland Southeast Asia, the bay filled up relatively quickly.

The land outflanked the sea. Now landlocked, an arm of the bay gradually became an inland lake. The saltwater fish, some of enormous size, slowly adapted to a new freshwater ecology. This is now known as the Tonle Sap, or Freshwater River. It is the world's richest fishing ground, yielding up to thirty times as much per square kilometer as the North Atlantic.[11] The reason for the abundance of fish is that the great volume of water in the Mekong still heads in two directions: to the sea and to the lake that once was an arm of the sea. Each September the Tonle Sap reverses its flow as the Mekong pours into it at Phnom Penh. Upriver, the lake triples its size, inundating most of the vast flat plain of Cambodia. "You can sail across Cambodia," wrote a Chinese visitor to late-thirteenth-century Angkor. "In no other part of the world have I ever had the sensation of being surrounded by fish in whatever direction I turned," wrote an Australian visitor to mid-twentieth-century Cambodia.[12] Fish swim across the country from September to November. They nibble the grasses and spawn in the shallows.

As the skies clear and the flood retreats, peasants trap fish in ponds and pluck them from shrubs. The waters speed past Phnom Penh, back into the

11. P. Chevey, "The Great Lake of Cambodia: The Underlying Causes of Its Richness in Fish," *Proceedings of the Fifth Pacific Science Congress,* Canada, 1933, vol. 5, p. 3812.
12. Chinese quoted in A. Barnett, "Sabotage of the Defeated," *New Statesman,* 25 September 1981, p. 14; Wilfred Burchett, *Mekong Upstream,* Hanoi: Red River, 1957, p. 29.

Mekong and on to the sea. Fisherfolk dam the Tonle Sap river with massive nets at one-kilometer intervals. At full moon the nets are drawn up, the air comes to life, and the city flaps for days. "Elephants fished from the water, fishes trapped in trees," the Australian wrote of "the advance and retreat of the waters, which play such a vital role in the rhythm of Cambodian life."[13]

Control of the waters has always been crucial. Wet rice cultivation is "the fabrication of an aquarium."[14] Paddy fields are bunded with low walls of mud, and their water levels are carefully manipulated to obtain the best results from the growing plant. But for over half the year the country is dry, the rice fields bare. If supplied with water stored during the rainy season, could they produce another crop each year, or even two more? It was long thought that this had been the key to the prosperity and power of the old Angkor kingdom, an economic high point from which Cambodia had apparently declined. This was the view of French archaeologists and scholars who pioneered study of the "lost world" of the medieval Khmers. The "intensive irrigation" theory was accepted as fact until the 1980s.

The evidence for it has crumbled under scrutiny, however.[15] Dry season irrigation "was just not possible at Angkor."[16] In the heyday of the Khmer empire, it now seems, the canal network had two major purposes: transportation and flood control to enable *extensive* wet season irrigation. The second, dry season rice crop was not grown on the same plot of land, but only on more low-lying plots closer to water. The intensive, nonseasonal "permanent irrigation" of vast areas by means of storing water throughout the year proved to be a myth—a costly one for Cambodia's people. "Return" to it was an impossibility and yet a major economic goal of the Pol Pot regime.

In the first few days after Cambodia became Democratic Kampuchea, all cities were evacuated, hospitals cleared, schools closed, factories emptied, money abolished, monasteries shut, libraries scattered. For nearly four years freedom of the press, of movement, of worship, of organization, and of association, and of discussion all completely disappeared. So did everyday family life. A whole nation was kidnapped and then besieged from within. By 1977,

---

13. Burchett, *Mekong Upstream*, p. 33.

14. Clifford Geertz, *Agricultural Involution: The Process of Agricultural Change in Indonesia*, Berkeley: University of California Press, 1963, p. 31.

15. W. J. van Liere, "Traditional Water Management in the Lower Mekong Basin," *World Archaeology*, 2(3) 1980, pp. 265–80; B. P. Groslier, "La cité hydraulique angkorienne: exploitation ou surexploitation du sol?," *Bulletin de l'Ecole Française de l'Extrême-Orient*, 1979, p. 161: "It is not evident that they were trying for or that they might have achieved a permanent irrigation." Compare Groslier's earlier "The Angkorian Civilisation and Water Control," *Etudes Cambodgiennes*, no. 11, 1967, pp. 22–31.

16. Van Liere, "Traditional Water Management," p. 279.

parents ate breakfast in sittings; if they were lucky their sons and daughters waited their turn outside the mess hall. Human communication almost disappeared. Democratic Kampuchea was a prison camp state, and the eight million prisoners served most of their time in solitary confinement. And 1.5 million of the inmates were worked, starved, and beaten to death. Why?

The vicious silence of Democratic Kampuchea tolled in the late twentieth century, well into the era of mass communications. For Cambodia was sealed off. The borders were closed, foreign embassies and press agencies expelled, newspapers and television stations shut down, radios confiscated, mail and telephone use suppressed, the speaking of foreign languages punished. Worse, Cambodians could tell each other little. They quickly learned that any display of knowledge or skill, if "contaminated" by foreign influence (as is normal in twentieth-century societies), was folly in Democratic Kampuchea. So people were reduced to their daily instructions. Memory was as dangerous as drinking milk.

What kind of regime would enforce such a revolution? And what were the conditions of its emergence ?

Pol Pot's Rise to Power

The shadowy leaders of this closed country gave few clues to their personal lives. The first journalists to enter Democratic Kampuchea came from Yugoslavia in 1978. They had to ask the prime minister, "Who are you, comrade Pol Pot?"[17] He was evasive.

The story begins in a large, red-tiled timber house on stilts overlooking a broad, brown river, downstream from the town of Kompong Thom. The river teemed with fish, its lush banks lined by coconut and mango trees. Behind the houses along the bank stretched large rice fields. A small Chinese shop sold a few consumables.

On May 19, 1928, Pol Pot was born Saloth Sar, the youngest of seven children. His parents owned nine hectares of rice land, three of garden land, and six buffalo. Pol Pot's father Saloth, with two sons and adopted nephews, harvested enough rice for about twenty people. In later years the family would have been "class enemies." But few villagers thought so then. Rich or poor, everyone tilled the fields, fished the river, cooked tasty soups, raised children, propitiated local spirits and French colonial officials, or thronged Buddhist festivities in Kompong Thom's pagoda. In 1929, a French official described Kom-

---

17. *Interview of Comrade Pol Pot . . . to the Delegation of Yugoslav Journalists in Visit to Democratic Kampuchea,* DK Ministry of Foreign Affairs, 1978. In his reply, Pol Pot did not mention his real name (Saloth Sar) or his education in the palace in Phnom Penh, falsely claiming to have "been a monk for two years" in the countryside (pp. 20–21).

pong Thom people as "the most deeply Cambodian and the least susceptible to our influence."[18]

But the Saloth family were Khmer peasants with a difference. They had royal connections. Pol Pot's cousin had grown up a palace dancer, becoming one of King Monivong's principal wives. At fifteen, his eldest sister, Saroeung, was chosen as a consort. In 1928, the eldest brother, Loth Suong, began a career in palace protocol. Pol Pot joined him in 1934, at the age of six.

The country boy Saloth Sar never worked a rice field or knew much of village life. A year in the royal monastery was followed by six in an elite Catholic school. His upbringing was strict. The girl next door, Saksi Sbong, recalls that Suong "was very serious and would not gamble or allow children to play near his home." The palace compound was closeted and conservative, the old king a French puppet. Outside, Phnom Penh's 100,000 inhabitants were mostly Chinese shopkeepers and Vietnamese workers. Few Cambodian childhoods were so removed from their vernacular culture.

At fourteen, Pol Pot went off to high school in the bustling Khmer market town of Kompong Cham. He missed World War II's tumultuous end in Phnom Penh, where nationalist youths forced the new boy king Norodom Sihanouk to briefly declare independence from France and Buddhist monks led Cambodian nationalists in common cause with Vietnamese communists. In 1948, back in the capital learning carpentry, Pol Pot's life changed. He received a scholarship to study radioelectricity in Paris. He set out with another youth, Mey Mann. The first stop was Saigon, the largest town they had ever seen. In the heart of commercial Vietnam, the two young Cambodians felt "like dark monkeys from the mountains." They were relieved to board ship for Marseilles, arriving in September 1949.[19]

Two other young Cambodians with palace connections, Thiounn Thioeunn and Thiounn Chum, had been sent to study in Hanoi from 1942 to 1945; according to their 1979 account, they found that "Vietnamese intellectuals spoke of Angkor as their own." After the war the two men went on to Paris; Thioeunn completed a degree in medicine and Chum a doctorate in law. Their brother Mumm gained a doctorate in science, and the fourth brother, Prasith, was also sent to study in France, where he lived for over twenty years. The Thiounns all developed left-wing contacts, but their nationalism was so fierce that they refused to meet the Vietnamese communist leader, Ho Chi Minh. Chum recalls: "In Paris during the Fontainebleu Conference, in

18. Archives d'Outre-Mer, Aix-en-Provence, Cambodge 3E 6(2), report from Kompong Thom, 1929.

19. Toni Stadler, personal communication, New Haven, 1991. Mey Mann gave Stadler his account of the voyage in numerous meetings in Site 8, on the Thai-Cambodian border, in 1989–90.

July 1946, we were called to the Vietnamese delegation. 'You will pay your respects to Uncle Ho,' they said. But we answered, 'He is not our "Uncle Ho."' Then they said, 'We are brothers. You should pay your respects.' But we did not do it. . . . We said to the representatives of the Yugoslavian Youth Federation: 'It is not right that a country as fertile as Kampuchea should have such a small population.' "[20]

Saloth Sar wrote his brother Suong occasionally, asking for money. But one day a letter arrived asking for the official biography of King Sihanouk. Suong sent back advice: Don't get involved in politics. But Pol Pot was already a member of the Cambodian section of the French Communist Party, then in its Stalinist heyday. Those who knew him then insist that "he would not have killed a chicken"; he was self-effacing, charming. He kept company with Khieu Ponnary, eight years his senior, the first Khmer woman to get the *baccalauréat*. The couple chose Bastille Day for their wedding back home in 1956.

Most of Pol Pot's Paris friends, like the Thiounn brothers, Khieu Samphan, and two Khmer Krom students, Ieng Sary and Son Sen, remained in his circle for over forty years. Sary married Khieu Ponnary's sister, Shakespeare studies major Khieu Thirith. Pol Pot had disagreements in Paris with Hou Yuon, later a popular marxist intellectual who would be one of the first victims after Pol Pot's seizure of power in 1975. But Pot stood out in his choice of *nom de plume*: the Original Cambodian (*khmaer da'em*).[21] Others preferred less racial, modernist code names, such as Free Khmer or Khmer Worker. Pol Pot's scholarship ended after he failed his course three years in a row. His ship arrived home in January 1953.[22]

The previous day, King Sihanouk had declared martial law in order to suppress Cambodia's independence movement, which was becoming radicalized by French colonial force. Pol Pot's closest brother, Saloth Chhay, joined the Cambodian and Vietnamese communists and took him along. In this first contact, Vietnamese communists began teaching him, as one of them later put it, how to "work with the masses at the base, to build up the independence committees at the village level, member by member." It seemed a patronizing slight; he did not quickly rise to leadership, despite overseas training. A former Cambodian comrade claims that Pol Pot "said that everything should be done

20. Quoted in Jan Myrdal, "Why Is There Famine in Kampuchea?," *Southeast Asia Chronicle*, no. 77, February 1981, p. 17.

21. *Khmaer da'em* is the pseudonym Saloth Sar used in his handwritten contribution to a Khmer student magazine in Paris. *Khemara Nisit*, no. 14, August 1952. Keng Vennsak, personal communication. Translations from the Khmer and the French are mine unless otherwise noted.

22. Kiernan, *How Pol Pot*, pp. 30–32, 119–22.

on the basis of self-reliance, independence and mastery. The Khmers should do everything on their own."[23]

Cambodia's transformation into Democratic Kampuchea began in 1945. Having lost their colonial authority to the Japanese in March of that year, in September the French tried to reestablish control. But the nationalist genie had escaped from the bottle.

Pressure had been building. When the French arrested two Buddhist monks for preaching nationalist sermons in July 1942, they provoked Cambodia's first modern political demonstration. Seven hundred monks from all but one of Phnom Penh's pagodas and two thousand civilian supporters poured onto the streets of the sleepy capital. A Japanese plane flew over the crowd in an apparent show of support.[24] Otherwise Tokyo did little to help the Cambodian protestors. French police arrested the leading nationalists, but only succeeded in creating more. A riot ensued. Some monks fought back; some died later in French jails. Others fled and joined up with anti-French nationalists in nearby Vietnam.[25]

For the future of Cambodia, the most important of these new nationalists were two Khmer Krom, named Son Ngoc Minh and Tou Samouth. Both had started their careers as monks, and while studying in Phnom Penh they participated in the 1942 demonstration.[26] After the French reimposed their control in 1945, both left the monastic life to pursue political careers. In 1946 they joined the Indochina Communist Party, led by Ho Chi Minh. The longer France tried to hang onto its colony, and the more backing Paris got from the USA, the more Cambodians embraced an alliance based on mutual interest with their Vietnamese neighbors, disregarding historical animosities.[27]

By 1954, when the French abandoned their Indochinese colonial war and withdrew from Cambodia and Vietnam, Son Ngoc Minh and Tou Samouth

23. Ibid., p. 123.

24. Author's interview with the Venerable Chhun Chem, age 86, at Wat Svay Att, Prey Veng district, Prey Veng Province, 17 January 1986. Chem was then probably the only surviving witness to the 1942 demonstration; he is the only one to have provided an estimate of the size of the crowd. He studied at the Higher Pali School in Wat Unnalom from 1939 to 1944.

25. The only account of the demonstration written by a participant is Bunchan Mul, "The Umbrella War of 1942," in Ben Kiernan and Chanthou Boua, eds., *Peasants and Politics in Kampuchea, 1942–1981*, New York: M. E. Sharpe, 1982, pp. 114–26, a partial translation of Mul's *Kuk Noyobay* (Political Prison), Phnom Penh, 1971.

26. On Son Ngoc Minh's participation in the 1942 demonstration and other activities see Kiernan, *How Pol Pot*, p. 44; on Tou Samouth and the 1942 demonstration see Archives d'Outre-Mer, Aix-en-Provence, *Indochine*, C.P. 34, "Propagande rebelle," DPSR 27 June 1949, doc. 5, n.5.

27. This and the following sections are based on Kiernan, *How Pol Pot*, chs. 1–4.

had built up a formidable Issarak, or "independence" movement. It had an army of five thousand Cambodian fighters (and numerous village militias), backed by an alliance with the Vietnamese victors of Dien Bien Phu. The movement, called the Khmer Issarak Association,[28] was spearheaded by its communist organizational backbone, the Khmer People's Revolutionary Party. Minh and Samouth had established the KPRP in 1951 under the supervision of Vietnamese communists. In three years it recruited over one thousand members, mainly from the two largest sectors of Cambodian life: the peasantry and the monkhood. Out of this nationalist struggle for independence, the first precondition for Pol Pot's Democratic Kampuchea had been realized: a viable communist party had emerged on the Cambodian political scene.

The KPRP's influence among sections of the peasantry was one reason Prince Sihanouk, after the Geneva Conference of 1954, adopted a new policy of neutrality in foreign affairs. Party leaders Tou Samouth and Son Ngoc Minh, like their Vietnamese mentors, welcomed this departure from the previous procolonial policies of the prince. After all, their own conversion to communism had been provoked by their nationalist awakening. But this left the party open to criticism by younger militants, such as Saloth Sar, who had been students in France during the anticolonial war. Whatever the prince's stand on independence or neutrality, these younger communists aimed to confront his feudalist autocracy. Indeed, Sihanouk's initial repression of democrats and leftists only fueled their case. It drove Son Ngoc Minh, a third of the KPRP's members, and hundreds of Issarak supporters into exile in Hanoi. Sihanouk's government rigged the 1955 general election, denying any seats to either the winner of all previous elections, the Democratic Party, or the KPRP's new legal organ, the Pracheachon Party. Ominously, the middle ground, along with the left, was now unrepresented on the open political stage.[29]

Later Sihanouk relaxed the pressure on some dissidents. But his erratic repression of the left played into the hands of the younger party group. Sihanouk's secret police suppressed the orthodox grassroots KPRP veterans, partly because of their historical affinity with Hanoi, while sparing younger, educated militants with more privileged backgrounds. The former Paris students grew in importance with police harassment and silencing of their party elders. Their own greater familiarity with the urban political scene, and their apparent murder of Tou Samouth in 1962,[30] eventually enabled the Pol Pot group to take over leadership of the communist party in early 1963.

28. *Samakhum Khmer Issarak*. In *How Pol Pot Came to Power*, I used the incorrect French official translation of this Khmer title, "Unified Issarak Front."

29. See Kiernan, *How Pol Pot*, ch. 5, for detailed discussion of the fraudulent 1955 elections.

30. Although the evidence is circumstantial, it all points in the same direction: that the Pol Pot group was involved in Samouth's murder, even if only by tipping off Sihanouk's police

The new leaders quickly went underground, forestalling any serious party debate while preparing a rebellion against Sihanouk. This meant a party break not only with Hanoi, but also with the Khmer Issarak such as Son Ngoc Minh and half the party's membership who remained in Vietnam, and with their policy of accommodation to the prince's neutralism. But propaganda from Pol Pot's rebels in the bush carefully encouraged Sihanouk's erroneous presumption that the pro-Vietnamese left, the old KPRP leadership, was behind the unrest. This provoked him to crack down on the remaining above-ground Khmer leftists, who in accord with Hanoi's strategy had been trying to work within the framework of the prince's regime. His repression *drove* them to rebellion and into Pol Pot's emerging guerrilla movement in the countryside. This strengthened these orthodox communist veterans' acceptance of party discipline, even though their position was now subordinate. Stage Two of Pol Pot's rise to power had been accomplished. From 1967, he found himself at the head of an authentic communist insurgency.[31]

In 1954 the Cambodian communist party had been largely rural, Buddhist, moderate, and pro-Vietnamese. By 1970 its leadership was urban, French-educated, radical, and anti-Vietnamese. A major factor in this "changing of the vanguard" was the rivalry between Chinese and Vietnamese communists for influence in this part of Southeast Asia. While China supported Sihanouk, it also encouraged a formerly pro-Vietnamese communist movement whose new leaders were preparing to distance themselves from Hanoi. Thus Beijing's sponsorship provided Pol Pot's faction with manueverability that it would not otherwise have enjoyed.

But the party's membership, unlike its Center, or national leadership, had not abandoned the tradition of solidarity with the Vietnamese communists. And the party's regional committees, or Zones, were mostly strongholds of these Issarak veterans. The most orthodox and effective was the Eastern Zone, led by So Phim, who had worked closely with the Vietnamese since the 1946–1954 war. He was more reluctant than Pol Pot to force a violent con-

---

to his whereabouts. (See Kiernan, *How Pol Pot*, pp. 198, 241 n.135.) No evidence suggests that Sihanouk's police were solely responsible. David Chandler reports a 1980 DK defector's claim that "Pol Pot ordered the execution" (*The Tragedy of Cambodian History,* New Haven, 1991, p. 338 n.98) and notes Pol Pot's 1962–63 police connections and "double-dealing" (*Brother Number One: A Political Biography of Pol Pot,* Boulder, 1992, pp. 64, 207 n.42), yet resists "reading Pol Pot's power and villainy back into 1960." He clears Pol Pot of the murder, attributing it to the police only (p. 206 n. 37). Chandler also overlooks Pol Pot's hostility to Samouth, and his attempt to disguise it, after Samouth's killing became public knowledge (*How Pol Pot,* p. 241). Chandler gives the impression that Pol Pot's secret 1977–78 torture and murder of two formerly trusted CPK cadres for involvement in the killing—in order to "tidy up the file"—was an effort to protect Sihanouk (p. 64).

31. See Kiernan, *How Pol Pot*, ch. 6.

frontation with Sihanouk's forces or a political break with Hanoi.[32] By January 1970, So Phim's eastern branch of the Cambodian communist insurgency was described by U.S. intelligence as being "in close liaison with the Viet Cong," who sheltered them on Vietnamese soil when they were attacked by government forces. They were considered "the most ideologically communist-oriented of all the Khmers Rouges," but they were also "much better educated," "the best organized," and "the most immediate insurgent threat." So Phim's Eastern Zone insurgency had a potential "far and away greater than that of a combination of the others." The other Khmer Rouge groups, the American intelligence report went on, "have more of a bandit flavour than an ideological one."[33]

The rebellion's political success was also limited by its confrontation with Sihanouk's nationalism. Meanwhile, however, Sihanouk began to face a challenge from the right. By 1969 Pol Pot had to abandon his claim that Sihanouk was "a secret agent of the United States." As the party later put it, "when the storm came [he] had to come and take shelter in our refuge."[34] In March 1970, the Vietnam War engulfed the country. The prince was overthrown by General Lon Nol, who enjoyed American support.[35] From exile in Beijing, Sihanouk now aligned himself with the continuing insurgency. And from their own exile in Hanoi, about one thousand veteran Issaraks returned home after a sixteen-year absence. Working with them and with Sihanouk's supporters, Vietnamese communists successfully mobilized Khmer peasant support for the second time since World War II.[36]

32. Vorn Vet wrote in his 1978 confession of a conversation with So Phim in mid-1966, when the Pol Pot leadership was preparing for armed struggle against Sihanouk. "Phim raised with me the question of the armed struggle—it had to be resisted [he said], the people did not want to spill blood. . . . In the Eastern bases, there would be real difficulties in the event of an armed struggle." See Kiernan, *How Pol Pot*, p. 230.

33. "Viet Cong Khmer Rouge Threat to Cambodia" and "General Location/Strength Khmers Rouges," U.S. Army Field Activities Command, 5 and 6 January 1970, declassified by U.S. Army, 2 April and 14 May 1987.

34. Kiernan *How Pol Pot*, ch. 7, and quotations on pp. 224, 297. See also Kiernan, "The Samlaut Rebellion, 1967–1968," in Kiernan and Boua, *Peasants and Politics*, pp. 166–205.

35. For evidence of U.S. involvement in the 1970 coup, see Ben Kiernan, "The Impact on Cambodia of the U.S. Intervention in Vietnam," in Jayne S. Werner and Luu Doan Huynh, eds., *The Vietnam War: Vietnamese and American Perspectives*, Armonk, New York: M. E. Sharpe, 1993, pp. 219–21. In March 1965, the U.S. chief of staff in Vietnam, General Richard Stillwell, had raised with a *New York Times* journalist "the possibility that Sihanouk might have to be overthrown in Cambodia." C. L. Sulzberger, *An Age of Mediocrity: Memoirs and Diaries, 1963–1972*, New York: Macmillan, 1973, p. 166. I am grateful to Jon Halliday for this reference. See also R. Smith, "Coup Questions," *Far Eastern Economic Review (FEER)*, 13 January 1994, pp. 30–31, and Justin Corfield, "Khmers Stand Up!" Ph.D. diss., Monash University Department of History, Victoria, Australia, 1992.

36. Kiernan, *How Pol Pot*, ch. 8, is a history of the 1970–75 war.

With regional autonomy persisting in the Cambodian party,[37] all this necessitated a long series of secret purges and executions if the party Center was to secure organizational control and pursue its extremist domestic and foreign policies. These purges were begun in 1971, but most of the country, although in the hands of the insurgents, remained untouched by the Center for several years. (Meanwhile, former party leader Son Ngoc Minh died of illness in 1972, after eighteen years in exile.)

The Center eclipsed and nearly destroyed its Sihanoukist and moderate communist rivals, including the one thousand Issarak returnees from Hanoi, in most regions between 1973 and 1975. Even in the East, where the intact Zone Party branch remained dedicated to more moderate goals, So Phim was required by 1974 to abandon his longstanding cooperation with the Vietnamese communists. The next year the party triumphed over Lon Nol's U.S.-backed regime, two weeks before the Vietnamese communists won in their own country.

U.S. Intervention

Although it was indigenous, Pol Pot's revolution would not have won power without U.S. economic and military destabilization of Cambodia, which began in 1966 after the American escalation in next-door Vietnam and peaked in 1969–73 with the carpet bombing of Cambodia's countryside by American B-52s. This was probably the most important single factor in Pol Pot's rise.

At least from 1950, the United States had backed French efforts to reestablish colonial rule in Vietnam and Cambodia.[38] In 1954, U.S. attempts to partially encircle China had aggravated differences between Vietnamese communists (who wished to fight on to certain victory) and their Chinese allies (who feared continuing war would bring American troops to their southern border). From 1960, U.S. escalation of the war in Vietnam made Sihanouk's neutrality increasingly precarious, provoking him to lean toward Hanoi and Beijing in foreign policy while taking ever more repressive measures against the grassroots and rural domestic left. This cleared the field for the urban, middle-class, pro-Chinese party elite, which was almost untouched by the repression until 1967.

In 1963, Cambodia had a record rice harvest. In 1964, that record was

37. In 1970 the Eastern Zone CPK branch and the party Center used different Khmer terms for their united front (ibid., pp. 298, 312); the existence of two Region 3's (in the Northwest and Northeast Zones) and two Region 31's (in the Southwest and North) also suggests autonomous Zone organizations.

38. See for instance ibid., p. 102, and George McT. Kahin, *Intervention: How America Became Involved in Vietnam*, New York: Knopf, 1986.

broken. Rice exports soared, and the country's balance of trade was positive for the first time since 1955. Nineteen sixty-five saw another good crop, and National Bank deposits recovered from a long decline.[39] But in the same year, the Vietnam War escalated. American troop levels rose from 20,000 to 300,000 in the year to mid-1966.[40] Saigon's forces also increased. In response, recruitment and conscription by the National Liberation Front quadrupled. The 1964 tally of 45,000 new recruits increased to 160,000 in 1965.[41] All these additional soldiers had to be fed; more important, they were doing greater damage than ever to Vietnam's rice production. Large amounts of Cambodian rice began to be smuggled across the Vietnamese border to the armies of both sides.

Prince Sihanouk's Cambodia depended for its revenue on taxing rice exports. It now plunged towards bankruptcy. In December 1965, U.S. intelligence noted that Sihanouk was already complaining privately about "considerable loss of revenue" as a result of "the illicit traffic in rice from Cambodia to Vietnam."[42] Over the next year, taxable rice exports fell by two-thirds, from 490,000 tons in 1965 to only 170,000 in 1966. (Later figures are not available.) About 130,000 tons of rice, 40 percent of rice exports for 1966,[43] were smuggled to Vietnamese communist agents and to black market circles in Saigon.

Equally important, the Vietnamese communists were resorting increasingly to the use of Cambodian territory for sanctuary from American attack. By the end of 1965, according to the U.S. intelligence report, they had established "clandestine and probably temporary facilities" there, but that year had already seen "eight instances of fire fights between Cambodian border forces and the Viet Cong." And U.S. aircraft in hot pursuit bombed and strafed Cambodia's border areas. Sihanouk's government claimed in 1966 that "hundreds of our people" had already died in American attacks.[44]

The U.S. intervention in Vietnam also produced a wave of Khmer refugees. From the early 1960s, Khmer Krom began fleeing to Cambodia to escape the Saigon government's repression in the countryside. In 1962 a Khmer Buddhist monk who had fled the Diem regime with four hundred others claimed: "Our

---

39. For the data, see L. Summers, "Introduction," in Khieu Samphan, *Cambodia's Economy and Industrial Development*, Ithaca, Cornell Southeast Asia Program Data Paper No. 111, 1979, p. 13. For a different view see M. Vickery, *Kampuchea: Politics, Economics and Society*, London: Pinter, 1986, p. 177, n. 22.

40. Michael Maclear, *Vietnam: The Ten Thousand Day War*, London: Methuen, 1981, pp. 129–30.

41. Noam Chomsky, *American Power and the New Mandarins*, London, 1969, p. 221, n. 11, citing "official Pentagon figures." See also Maclear, p. 130, for another U.S. estimate: that guerrilla strength in 1965 had shown "an increase of thirty-three percent over 1964."

42. Kiernan, *How Pol Pot*, p. 228.

43. Rémy Prud'homme, *L'Economie du Cambodge*, Paris, 1969, p. 255, table 12, note a.

44. Kiernan, *How Pol Pot*, pp. 228–29, 285.

schools have all been closed. . . . With the slaughter of our people, the destruction of our villages, the repression of our culture and language, it seems our people are to be exterminated." In 1965–68 over seventeen thousand Khmers, including over twenty-three hundred Buddhist monks, fled South Vietnam for Cambodia.[45]

Since the early 1960s, U.S. Special Forces teams, too, had been making secret reconnaissance and mine-laying incursions into Cambodian territory. In 1967 and 1968, in Operation Salem House, about eight hundred such missions were mounted, usually by several American personnel and up to ten local mercenaries, in most cases dressed as Viet Cong. One Green Beret team "inadvertently blew up a Cambodian civilian bus, causing heavy casualties." The code name of the operation was changed to Daniel Boone, and from early 1969, the number of these secret missions doubled. By the time of the 18 March 1970 coup against Sihanouk, over a thousand more had been mounted. In a total of 1,835 missions, twenty-four prisoners were taken, and an unknown number of people were killed or wounded by the "sanitized self-destruct antipersonnel" mines that Daniel Boone teams were authorized to lay up to thirty kilometers inside Cambodia.[46]

Another U.S. Special Forces operation was the highly secret Project Gamma, which was formally listed as Detachment B57 but not mentioned under either name in an official Army history of the Green Berets. Unlike Salem House and Daniel Boone, Project Gamma, according to a former member, "utilized only ethnic Cambodians in its operations, which were designed to gather tactical intelligence from deep inside Cambodia."[47]

Starting exactly a year before the coup (on 18 March 1969), over thirty-six hundred secret B-52 raids were also conducted over Cambodian territory. These were codenamed Menu; the various target areas were labeled Breakfast, Snack, Lunch, Dinner, Dessert, and Supper.[48] About 100,000 tons of bombs were dropped; the civilian toll is unknown. The U.S. aim was to destroy Vietnamese communist forces in Cambodia or drive them back into Vietnam. But in September 1969, Lon Nol reported an *increase* in the number of communist troops in the sanctuaries, an increase that he said was partly motivated by "the cleaning-up operation" of the U.S.-Saigon forces. He added ominously, "In this period, nothing suggests that these foreign units will soon leave our terri-

45. Ben Kiernan, "Put Not Thy Trust in Princes: Burchett on Kampuchea," in Kiernan, ed., *Burchett: Reporting the Other Side of the World, 1939–1983*, London: Quartet, 1986, pp. 252–69.

46. W. Shawcross, *Sideshow: Kissinger, Nixon and the Destruction of Cambodia*, London: Deutsch, 1979, pp. 65, 24; S. Hersh, *The Price of Power: Henry Kissinger in the Nixon White House*, New York: Summit Books, 1983, pp. 177–78.

47. Hersh, pp. 178–79.

48. Shawcross, p. 27.

tory."[49] Like the failing economy, this was one of the major factors in Sihanouk's downfall at Lon Nol's hands. Both factors were exacerbated by the U.S. escalation of the Vietnam War.

By 1970 Cambodia's frontier with Vietnam was breaking down. It was unable to withstand the pressure exerted by the two mighty contending forces that had been expanding and straining against one another in the limited space of southern Vietnam since the escalation of 1965. The pressure was economic, demographic, political, and military. Cambodia's rice crop drained into devastated Vietnam, while both Khmers and Vietnamese fled into Cambodia, with the U.S. military and air force in pursuit.

Richard Nixon's May 1970 invasion of Cambodia (undertaken without informing Lon Nol's new government) followed simultaneous invasions by Saigon and Vietnamese communist forces. It created 130,000 new Khmer refugees, according to the Pentagon.[50] By 1971, 60 percent of refugees surveyed in Cambodia's towns gave U.S. bombing as the main cause of their displacement.[51] The U.S. bombardment of the Cambodian countryside continued until 1973, when Congress imposed a halt. Nearly half of the 540,000 tons of bombs were dropped in the last six months.[52]

From the ashes of rural Cambodia arose Pol Pot's Communist Party of Kampuchea (CPK). It used the bombing's devastation and massacre of civilians as recruitment propaganda and as an excuse for its brutal, radical policies and its purge of moderate communists and Sihanoukists.[53] This is clear from contemporary U.S. government documents and from interviews in Cambodia with peasant survivors of the bombing.

In the early years of the Cambodian war, Sihanoukists, moderates, and pro-Vietnamese communists predominated in a factionalized insurgency. The CPK Center admitted it still needed to "get a tight grasp, filter into every corner."[54] Before defeating Lon Nol, it needed to eclipse its revolutionary rivals and allies.

49. Kiernan, *How Pol Pot*, p. 286.

50. Hersh, p. 202.

51. G. C. Hildebrand and G. Porter, *Cambodia: Starvation and Revolution*, New York: Monthly Review Press, 1976, p. 109, n. 83. The authors cite interviews conducted with Khmer refugees in 1971 by the General Accounting Office, Congressional Record, 18 April 1973, p. S7812.

52. A fully documented version of this section appears in Ben Kiernan, "The American Bombardment of Kampuchea, 1969–1973," *Vietnam Generation*, vol. 1, no. 1, Winter 1989, pp. 4–41.

53. Kate Frieson writes, "The Red Khmer forces grew because the CPK leadership took advantage of events that were outside its control, such as the American bombing, by appealing to Cambodian nationalism, and at the most basic level, people's desire to survive, in order to recruit members into its army." Kate G. Frieson, *The Impact of Revolution on Cambodian Peasants, 1970–1975*, Ph.D. diss., Department of Politics, Monash University, Australia, 1991, p. 188.

54. See Kiernan, *How Pol Pot*, p. 323, for the full quotation.

In 1973 the United States withdrew its troops from Vietnam and trained its air force on Cambodia. The secretary of the air force later said that Nixon "wanted to send a hundred more B-52s. This was appalling. You couldn't even figure out where you were going to put them all."[55]

The early bombing had been disastrous enough. In 1970 a combined U.S. aerial and tank attack in Kompong Cham province had taken the lives of two hundred people. When another raid killed seven people nearby, a local peasant recalls, "some people ran away . . . others joined the revolution."[56] In 1971, the town of Angkor Borei in southwest Cambodia was heavily bombed by American B-52s and Lon Nol's U.S.-supplied T-28s. It was burnt and leveled. Whole families were trapped in trenches they had dug for protection underneath their homes. Over one hundred people were killed and two hundred houses destroyed, leaving only two or three standing, local residents say. In the same year, Sihanouk's former advisor, Charles Meyer, accused the U.S. air force of "systematic pillage" of "peaceful and captivating villages, which are disappearing one after another under bombs or napalm," and ended with a prescient observation: "According to direct testimonies, peasants are taking refuge in forest encampments and are maintaining their smiles and their humour, but one might add that it is difficult to imagine the intensity of their hatred towards those who are destroying their villages and their property. Perhaps we should remember that the Cambodians have the deserved reputation for being the most spiteful and vindictive people in all Southeast Asia, and this should in any case hold the attention of President Nixon."[57]

U.S. intelligence soon discovered that many "training camps" against which Lon Nol had requested air strikes "were in fact merely political indoctrination sessions held in village halls and pagodas." Lon Nol intelligence noted that "aerial bombardments against the villagers have caused civilian loss on a large scale" and that the peasant survivors of the U.S. bombing were turning to the cpk for support.[58]

One young Khmer joined the communists a few days after an aerial attack took the lives of fifty people in his village.[59] Not far away, bombs fell on O Reang Au market for the first time in 1972, killing twenty people, and twice more in 1973, killing another twenty-five people, including two Buddhist monks.[60] When bombs hit Boeng village, it was burnt to the ground, and

55. Shawcross, *Sideshow*, pp. 218–9.
56. See Kiernan, *How Pol Pot*, pp. 349–57, for further details.
57. Charles Meyer, *Derrière le sourire khmer*, Paris: Plon, 1971, pp. 405–6.
58. "Cambodia: Can the Vietnamese Communists Export Insurgency?," *Research Study*, Bureau of Intelligence and Research, US Department of State, 25 September 1970, pp. 4, 6.
59. B. Baczynskyj, "Bombing Turns Cambodian Villagers into Refugees," *Asian Reports*, 21 February 1972.
60. Author's interviews with Yan and others, O Reang Au, 6 October 1980.

according to peasants, many people were caught in their houses and burnt to death. Nearby Chalong village counted over twenty dead. An inhabitant told me: "Many monasteries were destroyed by bombs. People in our village were furious with the Americans; they did not know why the Americans had bombed them. Seventy people from Chalong joined the fight against Lon Nol after the bombing."[61]

The B-52s scored a direct hit on Trapeang Krapeu village. Twenty people died. Anlong Trea was napalmed and bombed, killing three and driving over sixty people to join the Khmer communist army "out of anger at the bombing," locals recall.[62]

In March 1973, the bombardment spread west to envelop the whole country. Around Phnom Penh, three thousand civilians were killed in three weeks. At the time UPI reported: "Refugees swarming into the capital from target areas report dozens of villages . . . have been destroyed and as much as *half their population killed or maimed* in the current bombing raids."[63]

Days later, the U.S. bombardment intensified, reaching a level of thirty-six hundred tons per day.[64] As William Shawcross reported in *Sideshow,* the "wholesale carnage" shocked the chief of the political section in the U.S. embassy, William Harben. One night, Harben said, "a mass of peasants" went out on a funeral procession and "walked straight into" a bombing raid. "Hundreds were slaughtered." And Donald Dawson, a young air force captain, flew twenty-five B-52 missions but refused to fly again when he heard that a Cambodian wedding party had been razed by B-52s.[65]

One Cambodian villager lamented in April 1973: "The bombers may kill some Communists but they kill everyone else, too." The next month the *New York Times* reported that "extensive" destruction had wiped out "a whole series of villages" along the main highway, including seven villages in the eastern part of the country, with many people killed. Nothing was left standing for miles: "A few people wander forlornly through the rubble, stunned by what has happened, skirting the craters, picking at the debris." Correspondent Sidney Schanberg noted: "The frightened villagers uprooted by the bombing have a great deal to say." One refugee requested politely, "I would be very glad if the Government would stop sending the planes to

61. Author's interviews with four villagers at Ampil Tapork, 6 October 1980, and with Sang, O Reang Au, 6 October 1980.
62. Author's interviews, Prek Chrey, 7 October 1980.
63. United Press International dispatch, Boston, 1 April 1973. Emphasis added.
64. Dana Adams Schmidt, *Christian Science Monitor,* 5 April 1973.
65. Shawcross, *Sideshow,* pp. 272, 291.

bomb," while a Buddhist monk pleaded with the U.S. government, "Don't destroy everything in Cambodia."[66]

But in July and August 1973 the Southwest Zone of Cambodia was carpet bombed. It was the most intensive B-52 campaign yet. Its impact in the Southwest was not simply to destroy many more civilian lives. Politically, it tipped what had been a delicate CPK factional balance there[67] in favor of Pol Pot's "Center."

The political effect reached the highest level of the CPK in the Southwest Zone, its ruling party committee. In 1973–74, four of the eight leaders of this zone committee were purged. Two of these CPK moderates were murdered by Pol Pot allies Mok and Vorn Vet. The other two were killed after 1975, when the Southwest became the stronghold of the Pol Pot regime and Mok went on to purge all other Zones in the country.

During the 1973 bombardment, a similar process occurred at the local level. In one village in the southwest, eighty people died when B-52s hit the village and its pagoda.[68] Nearby Wat Angrun village was annihilated; a single family survived. Peasants claimed that 120 houses were destroyed in the air raid. This part of the Southwest was one of the strongholds of the CPK Center. In 1973 Mok's son-in-law, the local deputy CPK secretary, was promoted to chief of a new Southwest Zone Division, and his wife became district chief.[69]

The CPK was now able to recruit many peasants by highlighting the damage done by air strikes. The CIA's Directorate of Operations, after investigations in the Southwest Zone, reported on 2 May 1973, that the CPK had launched a new recruiting drive:

> *They are using damage caused by B-52 strikes as the main theme of their propaganda.* The cadre tell the people that the Government of Lon Nol has requested the airstrikes and is responsible for the damage and the "suffering of innocent villagers" . . . The only way to stop "the massive destruction of the country" is to . . . defeat Lon Nol and stop the bombing.
>
> This approach has resulted in the successful recruitment of a number of young men . . . Residents . . . say that *the propaganda campaign has been effective* with refugees and in areas . . . which have been subject to B-52 strikes.[70]

66. *New York Times*, 11 April, 24 and 27 May 1973, quoted in E. Herman and N. Chomsky, *Manufacturing Consent: The Political Economy of the Mass Media*, New York: Pantheon, 1988, pp. 277–78.

67. Kiernan, *How Pol Pot*, ch. 8, esp. pp. 314 ff., 331 ff., 340–47.

68. Author's interviews with Kus villagers, 16 July 1980.

69. Kus interviews, and author's interview with Ieng Thon, Tram Kak, 16 July 1980.

70. "Efforts of Khmer Insurgents to Exploit for Propaganda Purposes Damage Done by Airstrikes in Kandal Province," *Intelligence Information Cable*, 2 May 1973, declassified by the CIA on 19 February 1987 (emphasis added). For an example of politically inspired deletions

Mam Lon, a CPK cadre in the Southwest, says that when T-28s and B-52s bombed his village, more than one hundred people were killed and wounded. "The people were very angry at the imperialists," he adds. Soon afterwards the CPK's political line hardened, and a number of cadres, including Lon himself, were dismissed.[71] Early in 1973, the CPK began a new purge of Sihanoukists, pro-Vietnamese communists, and other dissidents. Mok rounded up hundreds from all over the Southwest Zone. They were forced to perform hard labor before being executed.[72]

In the Northern Zone of the country, where Pol Pot was based, B-52s struck Stung Kambot village one morning in February 1973. They killed fifty villagers and seriously wounded thirty others. Then, in March, B-52s and F-111s bombarded an oxcart caravan in the same district, killing ten peasants. A local says that "often people were made angry by the bombing and went to join the revolution." One peasant youth recalled B-52s bombing his village three to six times per day for three months. Over one thousand people were killed, nearly a third of the population. Afterwards, "there were few people left . . . and it was quiet."[73]

Chhit Do was a CPK leader near Angkor Wat in northern Cambodia. In 1979, he fled the country. Journalist Bruce Palling asked him if the Khmer Rouge had made use of the bombing for anti-U.S. propaganda:

Chhit Do: Oh yes, they did. Every time after there had been bombing, they would take the people to see the craters, to see how big and deep the craters were, to see how the earth had been gouged out and scorched. . . . The ordinary people . . . sometimes literally shit in their pants when the big bombs and shells came. . . . Their minds just froze up and they would wander around mute for three or four days. Terrified and half-crazy, the people were ready to believe what they were told. . . . That was what made it so easy for the Khmer Rouge to win the people over. . . . It was because of their dissatisfaction with the bombing that they kept on cooperating with the Khmer Rouge, joining up with the Khmer Rouge, sending their children off to go with them . . .

Palling: So the American bombing was a kind of help to the Khmer Rouge?

Chhit Do: Yes, that's right . . . , sometimes the bombs fell and hit little children, and their fathers would be all for the Khmer Rouge . . .

---

from documents declassified by the CIA in 1987, see "The CIA's El Salvador," *New York Times*, 17 December 1993, p. 39.

71. See Kiernan, *How Pol Pot*, pp. 354–55, for references.

72. Author's interview with Nou Mouk, Oudong, 26 August 1981.

73. Author's interview with Thoun Cheng, Ubon, 13–14 March 1979. For Cheng's full account, see Kiernan and Boua, *Peasants and Politics in Kampuchea: 1942–1981*, London: Zed, 1982, pp. 330–34.

On 3 August 1973, U.S. aircraft bombed the hill village of Plei Loh in north-eastern Cambodia, home of *montagnard* tribal people known as Khmer Loeu, or Upland Khmers. An American agent reported that "the village was totally destroyed, with 28 civilians and five VC guerrillas killed."[74] The next day, B-52s attacked nearby Plei Lom village, "killing twenty people, including children."[75] On 10 August, Plei Lom was bombed again, killing thirty montagnards.[76] On the same day B-52s struck nearby Plei Blah village: fifty died. The U.S. army report on this event noted that "the Communists intend to use this incident for propaganda purposes."[77]

Another report to the U.S. army in July 1973 stated that "the civilian population fears U.S. air attacks far more than they do Communist rocket attacks or scorched-earch tactics."[78] Up to 150,000 civilian deaths resulted from the U.S. bombing campaigns in Cambodia from 1969 to 1973.

In 1991, accused of having been "not very candid" about the 1969–70 bombings, former U.S. secretary of state Henry Kissinger replied: "My quick response is that journalists keep saying 'bombing Cambodia.' We were bombing four Vietnamese divisions that were killing 500 Americans a week."[79] In a longer response, Kissinger made the sarcastic claim, "We destabilised Cambodia the way Britain destabilised Poland in 1939."[80] His memoirs state: "It was Hanoi—animated by an insatiable drive to dominate Indochina—that organised the Khmer Rouge long before *any* American bombs fell on Cambodian soil."[81]

Kissinger's view *at the time* was more perceptive. In a 1974 cable to Phnom Penh's U.S. embassy, he had pointed out that in areas like southwest Cambodia the Vietnamese were actually in conflict with Khmer communists, who "not only had little training abroad but probably resent and compete with the

74. *U.S. Army Bomb Damage Assessment*, 20 August 1973. Declassified 1987.
75. U.S. Department of Defense, *Intelligence Information Report*, No. 2 724 2014 73, 16 August 1973.
76. U.S. Department of Defense, *Intelligence Information Report*, No. 2 724 2083 73, 23 August 1973.
77. U.S. Department of Defense, *Intelligence Information Report*, No. 2 724 2116 73, 27 August 1973.
78. "Effectiveness of US Bombing in Cambodia," U.S. Army document dated 21 August 1973, p. 2. Declassified 7 April 1987.
79. Kissinger replied to this query by UPI's Helen Thomas: "I think that Dr. Kissinger should remember that, when we were bombing Cambodia for fourteen months, that his White House was not very candid on that subject." Cable News Network, Bill Moyers Program, 19 January 1991. Besides Kissinger's implicit denial of "bombing Cambodia," his figure falsely suggests that four Vietnamese divisions based in Cambodia killed up to 30,000 Americans in 1969–70: "And we were informing major leaders of Congress of that event. And we were waiting for somebody to protest, so that we could ask for a UN investigation."
80. Bruce Page, "The Pornography of Power," in Anthony Barnett and John Pilger, *Aftermath: The Struggle of Cambodia and Vietnam, New Statesman* (London), 1982, p. 51.
81. Quoted in Page, p. 45.

better-trained men from North Vietnam." "The Khmer communists, such as Saloth Sar," he said with prescience, "are probably xenophobic . . . when it comes to Vietnamese."

In 1974, Kissinger was unsure if the Cambodian insurgency was "regional" and "factionalized" with only "a veneer of central control" or whether "the real power" lay with Pol Pot's center.[82] The tragedy is that the former had been largely true in 1972, the latter was largely true in 1974, and Kissinger and Nixon were largely responsible for the change. Attempts on their part to rewrite the record are not surprising.

Communist Party cadres told young peasant victims of the bombing that "the killing birds" had come "from Phnom Penh" (not Guam), and that Phnom Penh must pay for its assault on rural Cambodia.[83] On the day the bombing ended, CPK propaganda leaflets found in bomb craters attacked the "Phnom Penh warriors" who were, they vowed, soon to be defeated.[84] The popular outrage over the U.S. bombing, predictably manipulated by the CPK, was as fatal for the two million inhabitants of Phnom Penh as it was for moderate Khmer Rouge and for Lon Nol's regime.

In April 1975, when CPK troops took the country's second largest city, Battambang, they headed straight for the airport. Finding two T-28s, they tore the planes apart with their bare hands, according to a witness. "They would have eaten them if they could," he added.[85] Refugees reported "the lynching of hated bomber pilots."[86] When they forcibly evacuated Battambang and Phnom Penh, CPK forces told the urban populations that the exodus was necessary because "American B-52s" were about to bomb the city. The second phase of the Cambodian tragedy had begun.

The Key Issues

Interpretations of the Pol Pot regime vary. Democratic Kampuchea claimed to be "the Number 1 Communist state." In the early 1970s, the CPK had ranked Albania first, followed by China and then itself, whereas Vietnam was described then as "Comrade Number 7."[87] In 1976, DK proclaimed itself "four

82. "Emergence of Khmer Insurgent Leader Khieu Samphan on the International Scene," cable from secretary of state to U.S. Embassy, Phnom Penh, April 1974.

83. Staffan Hildebrand, personal communication.

84. U.S. Army, *Intelligence Information Report*, "Bomb Damage Assessment, Cambodia," No. 2 725 1716 73, 22 August 1973, p. 2.

85. David Chandler, Ben Kiernan, and Muy Hong Lim, *The Early Phases of Liberation in Northwestern Cambodia: Conversations with Peang Sophi*, Monash University Centre for Southeast Asian Studies, Working Paper no. 10, 1976, p. 3.

86. W. J. Sampson, letter to *The Economist*, 26 March 1977.

87. Author's interview with Kong Aun, minister of refugee affairs in the Khmer Republic, Phnom Penh, February 1975. Aun cited Lon Nol regime intelligence.

to ten years ahead" of the other Asian communist states, having "leaped" from feudalism "to a socialist society straight away."[88] Interestingly, from a conventional anticommunist perspective, historian David Chandler concurs, asserting that the CPK was "the purest and most thoroughgoing Marxist-Leninist movement" and that "what happened in Cambodia, although more intense, was standard operating procedure" in China and the USSR, a case of "socialist practice."[89] By contrast, another historian, Michael Vickery, characterizes DK as an anti-Marxist "peasant revolution," whereas Hanoi's publicists and their Cambodian protégés saw it as a Maoist deviation from orthodox Marxism.[90]

The two most important themes in the history of the Pol Pot regime are the race question and the struggle for central control. In this book I shall show, first, that Khmer Rouge conceptions of race overshadowed those of class. The leaders of the CPK Center—from elite backgrounds and without experience of peasant life—privileged themselves and each other, to the detriment of alternative leaders from grassroots backgrounds, whether of Khmer or ethnic minority origin. (I use the terms "race" and "ethnicity" interchangeably, because of the emerging scholarly consensus that racial boundaries have no biological basis.) Over time the membership of the top CPK circle became increasingly restricted to the French-educated Pol Pot group. Race also overshadowed organizational imperatives. Non-Khmer Cambodians with extensive revolutionary experience and CPK seniority were removed from the leadership and usually murdered.

At the other extreme—the bottom of the social ladder—non-Khmers, who comprised a significant part of the supposedly favored segment of the peasantry, were singled out for persecution because of their race. This was neither a communist proletarian revolution that privileged the working class nor a peasant revolution that favored all farmers. Favors in DK, such as they were, were reserved for approved Khmers.

Membership in the single approved race was a condition, but not a sufficient one, of official approval. Like the Lon Nol regime, the White Scarves discovered that to their cost. The second theme of this book, therefore, is the CPK Center's unceasing, and increasingly successful, struggle for top-down domination. The political diversity and ethnic heterogeneity of Cambodia's modern history, equally characteristic of its communist movement, challenged a CPK leadership aiming to "get a tight grasp [and] filter into every corner." Enemies

88. Chanthou Boua, David Chandler, and Ben Kiernan, eds., *Pol Pot Plans the Future: Confidential Leadership Documents from Democratic Kampuchea, 1976–1977,* New Haven: Yale University Southeast Asia Council, 1988, pp. 45–46.

89. Chandler, *Brother Number One,* pp. 3, 4, 49.

90. Vickery, *Cambodia 1975–1982;* Vladimir Simonov, *Kampuchea: Crimes of Maoists and Their Rout,* Moscow: Novosti, 1979.

were thus, by definition, everywhere. In Chapters 2 and 3 we will see how the Center tackled this problem in its establishment of Democratic Kampuchea, in both the cities and the countryside. These early successes, though militarily resounding, only provoked further struggles. The large numbers of intended victims increased the likelihood that some, previously sympathetic or neutral but now driven by hatred, would escape to fight, in some way, another day. The struggle for total central control was therefore self-defeating. The more absolute the control sought, and the more successful the search, the greater its harmful impact on people's lives, the larger the numbers of people affected, and the greater the numbers driven to resistance. In the end, it was enemies created by the regime itself—foreign and domestic, armed and unarmed, political operatives and sullen survivors—people alienated by the regime's attempt to destroy perceived enemies, who brought about its downfall. So the struggle for central control frames this book, dominating both the beginning and the end of the Khmer Rouge political revolution. It also helps explain the broader social history of Democratic Kampuchea.

The power accumulated by the CPK Center was unprecedented in history. Yet its revolution failed. Much of the horror of DK resulted from the goals of true reactionaries: their attempts to turn back the clock. The regime was confronted with the human and material forces of history, in an endeavor to destroy existing social groups (for instance, those of foreign origin, education, or employment). In terms of population as well as of territory, history was to be undone. Here Maoism proved a useful ideological tool, for it stresses the capacity of human willpower to triumph over material conditions and so reverse historical trends. Orthodox Marxism, with its faith in history as inevitable progression, was doubly inappropriate for DK's goals. The CPK Center saw Cambodian history up to 1975 neither as progress nor as inevitable. The Cambodian people and their neighbors paid the price of the attempt to reverse it.

I

**Wiping the Slate Clean:
The Regime Takes Shape**

CHAPTER TWO

Cleansing the Cities: The Quest for Total Power

"Beloved brothers, sisters, workers, youths, students, teachers and functionaries," announced the clandestine CPK radio on 16 April 1975. "Now is the time! Here are our Cambodian People's National Liberation Armed Forces, brothers! . . . Rebel! . . . It is time for you to rise up and liberate Phnom Penh."[1] But to most Cambodians, it was the time of the traditional Khmer New Year festival. Seng Horl, then a student at Phnom Penh's Faculty of Law, remembers: "On 15 and 16 April, the whole city of Phnom Penh were playing gambling games all over town."[2] Another Khmer recalls that on the night of the sixteenth, "at around seven, the whole city exploded with small-arms fire. It was like popcorn in a hot pan. People were celebrating the New Year, firing off any weapon they had."[3] But there was little to celebrate.

During February and March 1975, the Mekong River town of Neak Leung, southeast of Phnom Penh, had been encircled by the 126th Regiment of the Eastern Zone insurgents. Its commander, Heng Samrin, says his regiment closed in on Neak Leung "from east and west, and on the water."[4] On 1 April, the town fell. The Mekong had been Phnom Penh's lifeline. Lon Nol left for the United States the same day.

The Surrender

Heng Samrin was ordered to send his troops "to fight their way into Phnom Penh." They led one of three thrusts from the east. The 126th,

1. Voice of the National United Front of Cambodia (Clandestine), 16 April 1975, in U.S. Central Intelligence Agency, Foreign Broadcast Information Service [henceforth FBIS], Asia Pacific, 16 April 1975, p. H6.
2. Author's interview with Seng Horl, Creteil, 3 December 1979.
3. Someth May, *Cambodian Witness: The Autobiography of Someth May,* London: Faber and Faber, 1986, p. 102.
4. Author's interview with Heng Samrin, Phnom Penh, 2 December 1991.

along with the 173rd and 160th regiments, made up the Eastern Zone's 1st Division,[5] deployed southeast of Phnom Penh. Its commander was a veteran revolutionary, the 173rd's Chan Chakrey. Samrin was his deputy. The 2nd Zone Division, commanded by Samrin's younger brother, Heng Thal, fought through to the east bank of the Mekong, opposite the capital. The 3rd, which included marines, advanced along the west bank under the command of a former teacher named Chhien. These Eastern Zone divisions would soon distinguish themselves from other CPK units. Their more moderate behavior won them the reputation of "Sihanoukists."

The CPK insurgency had built at least twelve divisions. A hundred battalions moved against Phnom Penh, including the 11th and 12th Divisions of the Special Zone, which was run by the Center's Vorn Vet and Son Sen.[6] The 12th, which included women's battalions, commanded by Nath, had launched rocket attacks on Phnom Penh in 1974, killing many civilians.[7] The Special Zone forces now attacked the city's southern outskirts. Other forces involved in the offensive were the 3rd Southwest Zone Division, commanded by Muth, son-in-law of the Zone CPK secretary Mok, and the 1st Southwest, commanded by Paet Soeung, which approached Pochentong airport from the west, along Highway 4. Northern Zone forces, for their part, moved down the Sap River along Highway 5.[8] They were hurriedly brought into position, many units covering over one hundred kilometers on foot for the start of the final attack on 14 April. They then advanced so quickly that their command lost contact with them for twenty-four hours.[9]

On 4 April 1975, Chakrey was called to an Eastern Zone meeting to receive

5. Here I use the title *Division* assumed in the military reorganization following victory in 1975. During the 1970–75 war the 1st Eastern Division was actually called the "Region 25 Front Committee." Heng Samrin interview, 1991.

6. Timothy Carney, "The Unexpected Victory," in Karl Jackson, ed., *Cambodia 1975–1978: Rendezvous with Death,* Princeton: Princeton University Press, 1989, p. 26; Heng Samrin interview, 1991.

7. Chap Lonh, interview with Stephen Heder, 11–12 March 1980. In the DK period, Lonh was a member of the standing committee of the CPK in Kompong Som city.

8. Chap Lonh interview, 1980. Therefore, all major Zones except the Northeast and Northwest participated in the capture of Phnom Penh. Varying accounts have left out the role of one or the other Zone, however. A Northern Zone official ignored the Eastern Zone althogether in an early account to a Westerner in Phnom Penh. (Henri Becker, "Les Evénements de Phnom Penh," typescript dated "Singapour, 15 mai 1975," p. 4. The late M. Becker kindly allowed the author to copy his original, published in Switzerland in 1975.) The first DK account had mentioned only the "Northern and Eastern" Zone contributions (Carney, "The Unexpected Victory," p. 13), and Lonh recalls, "In the 1975 offensive, the East reached its objective first, namely Neak Leung. . . . The key battlefields for the capture of Phnom Penh were considered the Mekong and Pochentong. . . . Pochentong was the responsibility of Division One, Southwest. . . . Division Three of Ta Muth was defeated" (p. 58).

9. Becker, Les Evénements, p. 8.

instructions from the Center. Heng Samrin says: "The plan was announced at the meeting to attack and liberate Phnom Penh, and to evacuate the people out of Phnom Penh, temporarily." Chakrey passed the order to his officers. He also secretly told Samrin that at an earlier Center meeting, a prominent revolutionary intellectual, Hou Yuon, had spoken out against the proposed evacuation. Yuon, a cabinet minister in the Sihanouk regime in 1962–63, was now minister for the interior, communal reforms, and cooperatives of the CPK's front, the pro-Sihanouk royal government. He was also on the CPK central committee. Samrin was interested to hear of Yuon's stance, partly because Yuon had recently congratulated Samrin's troops on the capture of Neak Leung. But the evacuation of the capital was another matter. "Hou Yuon struggled against it. He got up and said that it was not the right situation to evacuate the people from the cities. At that time, Pol Pot accused Hou Yuon of not agreeing to implement the Center's plan." This was the second occasion on which Yuon had dissented from the evacuation proposal.[10] Tainted with the charge of oppositionism, Samrin claims, "Hou Yuon disappeared for ever."[11]

Pol Pot referred to this Center conference when he said, two years later, that "the evacuation of city residents" was decided in February 1975.[12] But even members of the revolutionary leadership remained in the dark. Information Minister Hu Nim recalled that "the Organization" (*Angkar*), which he defined as "Brother No. 1 and Brother No. 2," the secret code names for Pol Pot and CPK deputy secretary-general Nuon Chea, had informed him of "the plan to evacuate the people" on 19 April.[13] This was two days after the evacuation started. The Organization, a small circle, kept its secrets.

So transmission of the evacuation order took time, and it reached different Zone units in different versions. Troops in an artillery unit attacking the city from the Northern Zone, where Pol Pot's Center headquarters was located,

10. Author's interview with Nou Mouk, Oudong, 26 August 1981. Mouk says he was told in 1974 by a company commander named Mat that Hou Yuon had opposed the proposed evacuation of the capital. (Later Mat was himself arrested and jailed with the Khmers who had returned from Hanoi. He later died.) On an earlier occasion, during a visit to the Northwest Zone districts of Maung and Leach in 1973, Hou Yuon had "opposed destruction of people's houses," according to the man who commanded the zone army in the early 1970s. Author's interview with Heng Teav, Phnom Penh, 14 January 1986.

11. Heng Samrin interview, 1991.

12. Quoted in Kenneth M. Quinn, "The Pattern and Scope of Violence," in Karl Jackson, ed., *Cambodia 1975–1978*, p. 181. Pol Pot was presumably referring to the NUFK "Second National Congress," held on 24 and 25 February 1975. (Phnom Penh Radio, 29 April 1975, in FBIS, Asia Pacific, 30 April 1975, p. H1.)

13. Hu Nim, "Planning the Past: The Forced Confessions of Hu Nim," in Chanthou Boua, David P. Chandler, and Ben Kiernan, eds., *Pol Pot Plans the Future: Confidential Leadership Documents from Democratic Kampuchea, 1976–1977*, New Haven: Yale University Southeast Asia Council Monograph No. 33, 1988, p. 276.

"knew all along that Phnom Penh was to be evacuated."[14] A senior Southwest Zone cadre recalled in 1980 that the evacuation of Phnom Penh "had been a long-standing plan." However, it was promulgated to the troops only "about ten days before the liberation." He partly corroborates Heng Samrin's account: "This came after the fall of Neak Leung. There was no set period in which people were supposed to be gotten out of the city but each unit and [Zone] was to make its own decision. People were supposed to go wherever they could."[15] Some Southwest Zone troops, told of the order no earlier than 15 April, were also warned that the pretext of a "temporary" evacuation would be a lie.[16] Some Eastern Zone forces were informed in the first week of April but were led to believe the evacuation would be temporary. Heng Samrin says he only discovered a month later that the townspeople would be forbidden to return to their homes.[17] Further, while Samrin was aware of Hou Yuon's opposition, the Southwest cadre knew of "no opposition to this plan within the Party and Army."[18] The occupation and evacuation of the city were therefore chaotic. The various Khmer Rouge forces often contradicted one another, misleading the residents. They even engaged in skirmishes.

Seng Horl recalls that on the night of 16 April, a heavy barrage of rockets, artillery fire, and M-79 grenades was launched from the south. At 6 P.M., word spread that Khmer Rouge forces had taken Takhmau, on the capital's southwestern outskirts. Thousands of people, including defeated Lon Nol soldiers, fled their advance.[19]

At 7:30 the next morning, the Lon Nol command ordered all its troops to surrender at 9 A.M. At 8:30, Lon Nol's replacement as president of the Khmer Republic, General Sak Sutsakhan, called the ministry of information with instructions for the surrender to be announced by radio at nine o'clock. However, he was told by the only person at the ministry, expatriate technician Henri Becker, that all the Cambodian employees had left at 7:45. Becker raised a white flag over the ministry and dismissed the building's sentries.[20]

14. Michael Vickery, *Cambodia 1975–1982*, Boston: South End, 1984, p. 70.
15. Chap Lonh, Heder interview, 1980.
16. Vickery, *Cambodia 1975–1982*, p. 70.
17. Chea Sim, then the crk's secretary of Ponhea Krek district in the Eastern Zone, adds: "After 17 April, the orders from the Center were to evacuate the people temporarily. After liberation, they said, for fear that American planes would come and bomb, creating danger for the people who were in the city. It was for a short period. Then the people would be allowed back. This was declared by radio." Interview with author, Phnom Penh, 3 December 1991. Stephen Heder's interview with a former Special Zone courier confirms the "temporary" evacuation order (Sakeo, 7 March 1980).
18. "At least there was no open opposition. I don't know what people felt in their hearts." Chap Lonh interview, with Stephen Heder, 11–12 March 1980.
19. Seng Horl interview, 1979.
20. Becker, *Les Evénements*, p. 1.

Veasna, a former schoolteacher, is a lithe, frizzy-haired man with a ready smile and a sharp eye.[21] Then thirty-one years old, Veasna was working as an official at Phnom Penh's Olympic Stadium, organizing sports events for the city's youth. He was living in a room at the top of the Hotel Hawaii, crammed in with thirty refugees from the west of Phnom Penh. At 9 A.M., he saw the first Khmer Rouge forces arrive in the city center. All were very young, he says; some were riding bicycles, and several drove trucks. They immediately set about seizing medicine from downtown shops and carrying it off.

At the same time, in a southern suburb, Horl heard that white flags were going up everywhere. An hour later truckloads of troops (almost certainly Southwest or Special Zone forces) arrived at Tuol Tampuong market. As people lined the streets to watch, the troops quickly moved to block off all roads, preventing access to the western part of the city. Transgressors risked being shot. Forced evacuation to the south began immediately. Horl saw young Khmer Rouge soldiers kill three people who refused to leave.[22]

Meanwhile, the 126th Regiment and other Eastern Zone forces had also arrived, from the southeast. At the precise moment of the surrender, Heng Samrin reached the Independence Monument in south-central Phnom Penh.[23] Citizens of the capital quickly noticed the difference between the Eastern troops and those entering the town from other zones; the Easterners wore khaki or green military fatigues, the rest peasant black.[24]

At first the victors concentrated on disarming their enemies. At O Russei marketplace, they fired into the air above crowds of looters. They instructed surrendering Lon Nol soldiers to disarm and to remove their uniforms. They stopped the looting and told people to leave. Near the central market, victorious troops had taken possession of Lon Nol military vehicles. With Lon Nol rank-and-file beside them, they were driving around in circles, crashing into buildings. At the Olympic Stadium market, a female Khmer Rouge soldier forced defeated troops to disarm and strip off their uniforms. In front of Santhor Mok high school, six Khmer Rouge in their mid-teens stopped a jeep carrying a Lon Nol general and forced him to undress on the spot.[25]

In his detailed memoir, Pin Yathay tells of a first "wave" of Khmer Rouge,

21. Author's interview with Veasna, Caen, 7 October 1979.
22. Seng Horl interview, 1979.
23. Heng Samrin interview, 1991.
24. Author's interview with Yun, Creteil, France, 12 November 1979. Yun said: "I saw two groups of Khmer Rouge; the ones from the west wore black, the ones from the east green fatigues. Those in black were mostly younger." See also Pin Yathay, L'Utopie Meurtrière, Paris: Laffont, 1980, pp. 33–44; and author's interview with Chhin Phoeun, Kong Pisei, 17 September 1980.
25. Author's interviews with Tan Peng Sen, Alençon, 3 October 1979, and Khieu Sisavoun, Paris, 30 November 1979.

whom he saw stop the driver of a Lon Nol military truck. The man ran away. "Instead of firing and shooting him down without warning, the Khmer Rouge ran after him and caught him. We thought that he was going to be executed on the spot. The Khmer Rouge calmly ordered him to remove his military uniform, leave his truck, and go home. That scene reassured me." However, soon a second wave of Khmer Rouge arrived "from the Southwest," and began ordering the evacuation of the city.[26]

Events became even more chaotic. Not long after 9 A.M., a self-proclaimed army general named Hem Keth Dara, brother of a Lon Nol official, arrived at the ministry of information, with about forty soldiers. He claimed to have liberated Phnom Penh with his own troops and said he was preparing to form a "coalition government." Henri Becker, who was there to witness this, later discovered that Keth Dara was in league with Lon Nol's brother, Lon Non. At 11:30, the first Khmer Rouge soldiers arrived on the scene. They challenged him. "Keth Dara, very sure of himself, upbraided them and ordered them to make off, which they did rather reluctantly." By 12:10 he had found two radio technicians; they broadcast his prerecorded appeal to the Khmer Rouge: "We, your younger brothers, invite all our elder brothers to meet with us and discuss a settlement."[27]

Meanwhile Veasna noticed a crowd approaching from the west, along Kampuchea Krom street toward the central market. It was a demonstration by students and some teachers and officials, who had assembled to welcome the Khmer Rouge victors. Veasna saw a banner proclaiming "Peace Is Here Now." He quickly joined in the march. He soon heard that the demonstration had been sponsored by Hem Keth Dara "to help the Khmer Rouge" and perhaps win their sympathy. The crowd paraded through the central market to the National Bank, made its way past the old Buddhist pagoda on the city's only hillock, known as Wat Phnom, and then headed west again, stopping in front of the ministry of information in the early afternoon.[28]

The leaders of both of Cambodia's orders of Buddhist monks were there as well. A microphone was ready to broadcast the proceedings over the radio. Many of Phnom Penh's residents, still closeted in their homes, were listening in anticipation. As Veasna watched from the crowd, the chief monks announced that they were "preparing the country" for a return to "easy" times. They called for the cooperation of officials of the ministry, students, doctors, Lon Non, and army general Mey Sichan (who was present, having removed his signs of rank). The Venerable Huot Tat, chief of the Mohanikay Order, said: "Now we

26. Yathay, *L'Utopie Meurtrière*, pp. 32–33.

27. Becker, *Les Événements*, pp. 1–2, 19; Phnom Penh Radio, 17 April 1975, in FBIS, Asia Pacific, 17 April 1975, p. H4.

28. Veasna interview, 1979.

have peace: put down your guns." It was Mey Sichan's turn to speak; he called on all soldiers to lay down their arms. The chief monk had a sheaf of papers in his hands and was preparing to read from it.

Suddenly, a Khmer Rouge officer burst onto the scene. He immediately grabbed the papers from the hands of the chief monk. Veasna, taken with fright, began to pace up and down nervously. Pin Yathay, listening to the radio, could not tell what was happening. He heard only a series of "unintelligible discussions." Then "the confusion ended abruptly." The newcomer took the microphone and told the crowd, in what Yathay found "a serious and threatening voice": "I hereby inform the contemptible, traitorous Lon Nol clique and all its commanders that we are not coming here for negotiations: We are entering the capital through force of arms." He ordered Lon Nol's officials to "lay down weapons and surrender." Then he left. The radio transmission was cut off, and listeners were suspended in silence.[29]

Veasna quickly made himself scarce. According to Becker, "about 100 Khmer Rouge with their chiefs" now demanded the surrender of all of Keth Dara's men. "He sought to negotiate and explain, but in vain. The Khmer Rouge, automatic weapons in hand, were ready to fire at the least resistance. . . . They were all immediately disarmed."[30] At 1 P.M., the Khmer Rouge "northern sector command" secured the ministry and the national radio station. It called on all ministers, generals, and high officials of the defeated government to report to the ministry at 2 P.M., to "be given all respect due to their rank."[31]

The Venerable Huot Tat, who had meanwhile gone to Unnalom pagoda, sent a leading monk, So Hay, to attend this meeting. He wanted to know if the city was to be evacuated. Southwest Zone forces were forcibly emptying parts of the city, whereas the Eastern forces occupying the riverbank near the pagoda were not. At the information ministry, So Hay met a "high-ranking Khmer Rouge officer" who courteously denied the whole thing: "I can give you my word of honor that I know nothing of that order," which he described as "an imperialist maneuver" to "sow panic."[32] So Hay returned to Unnalom pagoda at 6 P.M. with an "optimistic report."

But his informant had almost certainly lied. Why? The officer was probably Nhiem, the vice president of the Northern Zone command, whom Becker

---

29. Ibid.; Phnom Penh Radio, 17 April 1975, in FBIS, Asia Pacific, 17 April 1975, p. H5; Yathay, L'Utopie Meurtrière, p. 30; Var Hong Ashe, From Phnom Penh to Paradise, London: Hodder and Stoughton, 1988, p. 21.

30. Becker, Les Evénements, p. 2.

31. Ibid. Pin Yathay, five years later, recalled that the officials were asked to report at 4 P.M. (p. 35).

32. Yathay, L'Utopie Meurtrière, p. 36.

would soon meet at the ministry.[33] Nhiem likely lied to encourage the leading officials of the defeated regime, such as Lon Nol's former aide-de-camp, General Chhim Chuon, who was waiting at Unnalom pagoda, to give themselves up.[34] Had Nhiem or the other Northern Zone officials occupying the ministry conceded that Phnom Penh was to be evacuated, their ousted opponents may have tried to escape to the countryside in the exodus. Most did not, and forty-three civilian and military leaders of the Lon Nol regime, including Chhim Chuon, presented themselves at the ministry.[35] They were probably executed soon after. At 6:30 the next morning, Northern Zone troops began the immediate evacuation of their sector of the city. They gave people only ten minutes' notice, and their orders included, according to Becker, who was present as they were given: "The inhabitants who put up resistance or refuse to take to the road will be liquidated, as enemies of the people."[36] The Northerners soon became known for their use of methods even more brutal than those of the Southwest and Special Zone forces. They delayed their evacuation by a day in order to round up the leaders of the defeated regime first. The "Northern Zone command" must have had the confidence of Pol Pot to be entrusted with such an important task.[37]

33. Michael Vickery suggests that the officer who gave his "word of honour" may have been from the East, but there is no evidence for this. Vickery says the incident "seems to show" that the Eastern Zone forces "had a different attitude toward evacuation than the other Zonal forces" and at least that "there were DK officers in Phnom Penh on April 17 who neither knew of nor approved of the policy" (p. 74). The latter point may be true, but this incident is not corroboration. Pin Yathay (p. 36) does not specify that this man belonged to the Northern Zone, though "nothing distinguished him, apart from the quality of his manners and his good language, from the other Khmer Rouge soldiers," which appears to rule out the fatigue uniform of the east. The evidence that he was from the north is that he gave his "word" to So Hay at the ministry of information between 4 and 6 P.M. on 17 April, and Becker (pp. 2, 3) makes clear that at 1 P.M. the ministry's radio had been taken over by "the Khmer Rouge northern sector command," which installed itself next door. In later discussions with Becker, Nhiem minimized the role of the Eastern forces (Becker, pp. 10, 8).

34. He had also told So Hay: "We have soldiers with guns to win the war but not enough cadres and technicians to build the peace." Yathay, *L'Utopie Meurtrière*, p. 36.

35. Becker, Les Événements, p. 4; Yathay, *L'Utopie Meurtrière*, p. 34. Ponchaud points out that Chhim Chuon "was held to be one of the most corrupt officers of the Republic." F. Ponchaud, *Cambodia Year Zero*, London: Allen Lane, 1978, p. 46.

36. Becker, Les Événements, p. 5.

37. Nhiem was also appointed "vice-president of the Committee of Phnom Penh, in charge of relations with foreigners," and entrusted with escorting the first column of twenty-six trucks carrying the foreigners, who had been confined in the French embassy compound, across the country to the Thai border (Becker, Les Événements, p. 13). Ponchaud describes "Nhem" losing his generally even temper on 27 April: "Consider yourselves fortunate that we are letting you go. We could perfectly well have disposed of you otherwise!" *Cambodia Year Zero*, pp. 51, 53.

The surrender of the defeated was so complete that the victors quickly turned on other enemies. On the Monivong Boulevard, an American journalist watched a young Khmer Rouge soldier attempting to ride a motorcycle. He could not get it started. In apparent frustration, he took out a pistol and dispatched the motorcycle. Other Khmer Rouge went to the city's only communist embassy buildings, forced their staff to leave for the French embassy, where all foreigners were being gathered for expulsion, and fired a B-40 rocket through the front gate of the Soviet embassy.[38]

The Evacuation

Nearby, at the National Library, Veasna saw young troops from the Southwest Zone that afternoon carrying out stacks of what they called "imperialist" books, throwing them into the street, and burning them.[39] Passing by the Preah Khet Mealea Hospital, Veasna came upon more troops, who were expelling patients into the street. Nearby, city residents were also being violently driven out, "not knowing where to go," Veasna says. The Khmer Rouge shot several of them dead.[40]

The behavior of the soldiers entering the city was far from consistent, however. Many reports tell of Eastern Zone forces in khaki uniforms playing divergent roles. The afternoon of 17 April saw armed clashes between different

38. Ponchaud, *Cambodia Year Zero,* p. 29.
39. Veasna interview, 1979. This is confirmed by another witness, interviewed by officials of the U.S. embassy in Thailand while Veasna was a refugee in Vietnam (until December 1977): "A Phnom Penh schoolteacher has described the book burnings which he saw take place there at the time of the takeover. In one of these, the entire contents of the National Library in the capital city were destroyed." See "Life Inside Cambodia," Extracts from an airgram report by an officer of the American Embassy at Bangkok, 31 March 1976 (declassified in 1978), p. 2. Though not all the contents were in fact destroyed in 1975, these accounts cast doubt on David Chandler's claim that a Cambodian was "hired by the Vietnamese in 1979 to assist with pulping" newspapers "held in Cambodia's National Library." (*The Tragedy of Cambodian History,* New Haven: Yale University Press, pp. 91, 332 n. 13.) Other libraries were also scattered during the 1975 evacuation. On 19 April, Teeda Mam saw that the Law Library had been destroyed. At her English school next door, "stacks of books had been simply tossed out library windows and set afire." And later, "looking down into the Bassac River, I saw books and magazines by the hundreds floating in lazy eddies; the river was awash with soggy French literature." J. D. Criddle and Teeda B. Mam, *To Destroy You Is No Loss: The Odyssey of a Cambodian Family,* New York: Atlantic Monthly Press, 1987, pp. 30–32.
40. Veasna interview, 1979. Ponchaud, p. 22, gives an account of the evacuation of Preah Khet Mealea Hospital. May, p. 107, saw the evacuees from the Khmero-Soviet Hospital. Seng Horl gave the author an account of the expulsion of patients from the Chinese Hospital. Vickery, challenging the "Standard Total View" of the evacuation of hospitals, shows that some medical care continued to be administered (p. 77). But thousands of patients died when most hospitals were emptied.

units trespassing in each other's sectors of the city.[41] Another clash occurred near the Monk's Hospital when a group of Khmer Rouge forcibly "requested" a motorcycle from a civilian. A second squad opened fire on the first, killing at least three.[42] It is not clear which groups were involved in these particular skirmishes, but there is abundant evidence of conflict between Eastern and other units. There is also evidence that easterners could be ruthless. Pin Yathay reports that a khaki-clad officer confiscated bicycles from monks at Wat Unnalom with "brutal and impudent naiveté."[43] Another account reports "officers in fatigue dress" evacuating a hospital.[44] But in those cases in which Eastern troops can be identified, they are reported to have either insisted that the evacuation was temporary[45] or opposed it altogether.

Tam Eng, who ran a tailor shop at O Russei market, tells of her experience that day.[46] With five children of her own, she was also looking after nine others. She recalls seeing the Khmer Rouge notice her shop. "I was closed that day. They walked in and took some material. . . . They said: 'Aunt, why don't you go?' I asked: 'Where do my friends want me to go to?' They said: 'You must leave, leave your house.' . . . I said: 'Leave today? I can't leave yet. I haven't got my things ready.' They said: 'No need to take anything, but just a little food, no need to take clothes or goods. . . . Soon Angkar will bring you things.' I dared not say anything. Then another one the same age came in. I asked him: 'Do we really have to leave for the countryside?' He said: 'Aunt, where do you want to go? Just stay in your house. Just keep some food with you and stay in the house. Don't go outside.' The two Khmer Rouge asked one another where they came from. The one said he came from the East, and he asked the others. They replied: 'The Southwest.'[47] They did not smile at one another. They did not get on. . . . I shut the doors and made all the children stay inside, like piglets."

41. Becker, Les Événements, p. 4.
42. Author's interview with Hul Yem, Strasbourg, 31 October 1979. Chap Lonh, of the Southwest, minimizes these incidents: "There was a little fighting in Phnom Penh but not much. There were some disputes between troops from different [Zones] over their fronts of control, but no fighting" (interview with Heder, March 1980).
43. Yathay, L'Utopie Meurtrière, pp. 37-38.
44. Molyda Szymusiak, The Stones Cry Out: A Cambodian Childhood, 1975-1980, trans. Linda Coverdale, London: Jonathan Cape, 1987, pp. 16-17.
45. Heng Samrin's statement that he believed the evacuation to be temporary is supported by other sources. For instance, Szymusiak's account, given her by her grandmother who was evacuated at gunpoint from an unnamed hospital in Phnom Penh by "officers in fatigue dress," quotes one of them, who found her "a hospital cart loaded with ten big loaves of bread, some grilled fish, and some pork," as telling her: "You should go outside of the city, not far. You'll be back in two days. First we have to empty out the hospital and kill off the stubborn ones." Szymusiak, The Stones Cry Out, pp. 16-17.
46. Author's interview with Tam Eng, Paris, 24 January 1980.
47. Tam Eng recalls the reply as "Southeast" (akhnei), but there was no such Zone, and this seems a mistake for the Southwest (niredei) on her part.

On 19 April, however, "a 14-or 15-year-old youngster carrying a grenade" entered Eng's house in O Russei market. "He asked me: 'Why don't you leave your house? . . . If you don't leave, I'll throw the grenade in here.' I said: 'Okay, I'll leave if you want me to, but I don't know where to go.' He said: 'Just leave your house and go anywhere. Wherever you go, *Angkar* will watch over you. . . .*Angkar* will be there.' I had no idea what *Angkar* was. All I could do was get us together and go."[48] Tam Eng headed south.

Lor Chandara was then a first-year student at Phnom Penh's Faculty of Law. He had spent the last days of the war hiding in the cellar of his home to avoid rockets and shelling. The first group of Khmer Rouge he saw comprised eight young men, wearing white handkerchiefs (*konsaing*) on their heads. They came up "and began digging trenches" near his house. Chandara spoke with them. They called themselves "the Great East" (*Moha Bophea*). What should he do? "They said, 'Stay home.' If anyone asked why I should stay, I was told to say that the 'Eastern group' said I could stay."

Ignoring this advice, Chandara went out to search the town for his parents. On the riverbank, however, he met another group of Khmer Rouge soldiers. This group was "from the hills and forests" to the west. They told him to leave the city. "When I mentioned the instructions of the first group, they said: '*Angkar* has changed direction.'" Then they questioned him: "Who allowed you to meet the ones with white handkerchiefs?" The latter may not have been aware even of the "temporary" evacuation order (though they appear to have expected their instructions to be challenged). Chandara concluded that "there were different groups out of contact with one another."[49]

Another man, ordered to leave home on 18 April, got only five hundred yards before meeting a second group of Khmer Rouge. These "spoke nicely to me, and asked where I was going." When the man told them he had been driven out of his home, they said: "Don't be afraid, just go home. Don't worry, things will soon be all right again." The next day a third group of Khmer Rouge violently expelled him from his home.[50]

The same morning, Molyda Szymusiak and her family left home after a Khmer Rouge told them: "If you're not gone by nine o'clock, I'll blow up your house!" Later that day, after her father helped two Khmer Rouge start a truck,

48. Tam Eng interview, January 1980.

49. Author's interview with Lor Chandara, Phnom Penh, 21 September 1980. This "Eastern group," Chandara says, had come from Tuol Kork in the western part of the city. But Ping Ling provides corroboration that Eastern Zone forces ("wearing khaki uniform") were present in the Tuol Kork area on 18 April (*Cambodia: 1,360 Days!*, an account of life in DK, typescript, 1981, at pp. 17–18). At any rate, their status and statements are intriguing and certainly suggest differences within the Khmer Rouge. They may have been a scouting patrol of Chhien's 3rd Eastern Division.

50. Author's interview with Sum, Toul, France, 28 October 1979.

they offered to give his family a ride out of town. "My father was at the back with the two Khmer Rouge. 'Why did you take us with you?' he asked them. 'We're Sihanouk Khmer,' said one of them, looking at his companion. 'You're not all the same?' 'Yes, but there are different groups. We're from the East. Here, the North is in command, under Khieu Samphan.'"

That evening, by the roadside south of Phnom Penh, one of these Khmer Rouge introduced Molyda's group to a man named Sakhron, who had been "in the forest with Pol Pot's men for ten years." Sakhron told them: "My heart is not with the Khmer Rouge. If you like, I'll take you into Prey Veng province, on the Vietnamese border. . . . If you're related to the royal family, you won't survive here [in the Special Zone]." The next morning he added: "There are Sihanouk Khmer in Prey Veng, it's your only chance." This was a recommendation to go to the Eastern Zone. Molyda's parents dithered. Sakhron offered to help find their missing relatives in Phnom Penh, but Khmer Rouge guards there fired at him. "He had escaped only by throwing himself into the Mekong, where he swam all night." The next day Sakhron left: "I'm going to report this to general headquarters in Prey Veng."[51] His disillusionment with the Khmer Rouge did not seem to include the Eastern Zone administration, which he considered allied to Sihanouk.

Ping Ling, an ethnic Chinese engineer, left his Phnom Penh home at noon on 18 April, "with bullets whooshing past from everywhere." A large group of Khmer Rouge stopped him and his companions and began searching their belongings. Then another group approached and yelled, "Let them move on!" Ping Ling comments: "Those surrounding us stared at this second group with defiance in their eyes. . . . It seems there is restrained conflict between these two groups. It seems the second group [was] keen on our leaving the city fast." Later that day, in the city's northern suburbs, "we came across another group of Khmer Rouge this time wearing khaki uniform. . . . We were told by them to return back to the city." Unsure what to do, Ling and his companions waited, "trying to catch our breath." But soon afterwards, "out of nowhere a loud-speaker blared out at us, ordering everyone to move on, followed by machine-gun firing."

Later a friend of Ling's was told by Khmer Rouge that "a fight started between Sihanouk's troop and Hu Nim's people, then of course the Khieu Samphan blackshirts joined in the fight later on. . . . [O]ne side wanted this area, the other side wanted the same area so the fighting broke out." The "Sihanouk" group were telling people "to stay at their home," whereas the "Khieu Samphan and Hu Nim" forces ordered "everybody out of the city." Ling's informant added, "Some say the Sihanouk troop wears khaki uniform

51. Szymusiak, *The Stones Cry Out*, pp. 7–10.

while the blackshirts belong to Khieu Samphan's side."[52] The "Sihanouk troop" were easterners.

Chey Sopheara, a medical student at Phnom Penh University, and his family were forced out of their home at 10 P.M. on 17 April by Southwest Zone forces in black uniforms. They moved people along by firing over the heads of the crowd. "Once I crossed the Monivong Bridge I saw the Eastern Zone forces, in fatigue uniforms. The Easterners used kind methods along the road. They gave out medicine and rice." Unlike the Southwesterners, they did not open fire. "But people were not allowed to go back."[53]

The 11th Special Zone Division, commanded by Saroeun, entered the city in full strength. Chhin Phoeun, a member of its 32nd Regiment, recalls: "We went to Phnom Penh to search for enemies hidden there, and drive the people out. . . . We were told to tell people to leave for three days, and that then they could return. We were told to shoot people who refused. Our group shot 2 or 3 families north of Daeum Thkou market."[54] A passerby saw "two piles of bodies in civilian clothes, as if two whole families had been killed, babies and all. Two pieces of hardboard stuck out of the pile, and someone had scrawled in charcoal: For refusing to leave as they were told."[55]

The Eastern Zone forces were generally much better behaved. But all Khmer Rouge units in the capital eventually implemented the order to evacuate the population. Had they reflected on their orders, it is likely that many Khmer Rouge (unlike Hou Yuon) initially saw prudence in evacuating the town, for fear of enemy air bombardment after its change of hands. This was the reason given to most city dwellers. Like them, few Khmer Rouge expected a practiced, defensive, wartime tactic to become a permanent strategy—an offensive weapon against a city's people in peacetime. Few expected it to be maintained after the emergency ended. Given recent Cambodian history, many on both sides believed in at least the possibility of retaliatory U.S. bombardment.[56]

Early in the morning of 18 April, Ly Veasna watched from the top of the Hotel Hawaii as four very young Khmer Rouge rained shells and bullets onto a French-style house and a Peugeot outside. Other victorious soldiers broke into shops and pharmacies, loading medicine onto trucks and heading off

52. Ling, *Cambodia: 1,360 Days!*, pp. 14, 18, 69–70.
53. Author's interview with Chey Sopheara, Phnom Penh, 23 September 1980.
54. Author's interview with Chhin Phoeun, Kong Pisei, 17 September 1980.
55. May, *Cambodian Witness*, p. 107.
56. One man recalled the night of 17 April: "The town was very quiet, everyone was in their houses. There was a fear of U.S. bombing of the cities. There was the sound of planes flying over the city incessantly. I couldn't see any. But there were planes, for sure." Tan Peng Sen interview, 1979.

towards the west. Troops wearing black rubber sandals told the people in Veasna's area to take their cooking pots and some rice and move out. Those who stayed would be shot. Many were evacuated from their homes at gunpoint. In other parts of the city, people were given time to pack or to search for relatives; others were shot dead for refusing to leave immediately. Many, but not all, were advised to go to their native villages in the countryside. Passing by the *Paradis* restaurant later in the morning, Veasna noticed "a lot of confused people on the tops of buildings and in the street, not knowing where to go." Four or five soldiers were firing shots, ordering them along, calling everyone out into the street. Enormous crowds filled the roadways, swaying en masse under the pressure. At one point, Khmer Rouge fired an M-79 grenade into the crowd. Veasna saw three or four people cut down. The crowd panicked, and people ran in all directions.[57]

Ouch Sruy, thirty-four, a mechanic in charge of the agriculture ministry's warehouse, was evacuated on 19 April. His family of six slowly made their way south with the crowd, passing the Bokor cinema. Suddenly, grenades abandoned on the street by Lon Nol soldiers began to explode, killing nearly a hundred people.[58]

Someth May describes the scene: "We moved very slowly in the heat of the day. Some people were carrying their possessions on their backs or on bicycles. Others had handcarts which they pushed and pulled. There were overloaded *cyclos* [bicycle pedicabs] with families balancing on them and parents pushing. Those of us with cars were the lucky ones. Children cried out that they were being squashed in the crowd. Everywhere people were losing their relatives." Patients driven out of the hospitals were pushed in their hospital beds by relatives, who "struggled with the beds, like ants with a beetle," some "with their plasma and drip bumping alongside." Limbless Lon Nol soldiers hobbled and crawled with the crowd. "I shall never forget one cripple who had neither hands nor feet, writhing along the ground like a severed worm, or a weeping father carrying his ten-year-old daughter wrapped in a sheet tied round his neck like a sling, or the man with his foot dangling at the end of a leg to which it was attached by nothing but the skin."[59]

The Trek

It took Veasna a full day to get across town. At the Monks' Hospital, a sign forbade people from taking Highway 5 north to Battambang, so he

---

57. Veasna interview, 1979.

58. Author's interview with Ouch Sruy, Stains, 11 August 1979.

59. May, *Cambodian Witness*, p. 106; Ponchaud, *Cambodia Year Zero*, p. 22; Seng Horl interview, 1979.

took Highway 3, southwest towards Kampot. Tens of thousands of evacuees filled the road.

Along the way the Khmer Rouge began asking people's occupations. Seng Huot says: "The sorting center was at Kompong Kantuot; civilians were allowed to pass but the military were led away and shots were heard soon afterward."[60] Kem Hong Hav, his family of ten traveling on a motorcycle and bicycles, admitted that he had been a military medic. "The Khmer Rouge said: 'Come with us.' I said I could not, I had my family. They said: 'You must. *Angkar Loeu* [the high organization] needs officials.' I cried, my wife cried." Soon a number of cars pulled up, and Hav quickly saw his chance. He sped off on his motorcycle, with the Khmer Rouge firing shots after him. He changed into a new set of clothes by the river, threw off his pursuers, and even managed to rejoin his family later.[61]

At the same place, the Khmer Rouge were appealing for skilled workers. One man, traveling with his uncle, who was a railway worker, brought his family along. Over two hundred evacuees—factory, electrical, and railway workers—were taken back to Phnom Penh and put to work.[62]

On Highway 5, leading north from Phnom Penh, the Khmer Rouge were also calling on officers and officials of the defeated regime to identify themselves. Near Prek Phneou, Bounchan Sameth met her brother-in-law, who urged her and her family to go back. She was suspicious of the Khmer Rouge, and they did not return. But others volunteered, including her cousin, who had served in the Lon Nol air force; he took his family back to Phnom Penh. Two weeks later, one of the returnees arrived in Prek Phneou suffering from a bullet wound. He told Sameth that her cousin and all the others were dead, and he advised them to move on quickly, since all their names were being recorded. He said that when his group was returning to the capital, the men had been loaded onto one truck, the women onto another. That night, each man had been forced to face accusations of service in the Lon Nol army. Then they were taken to a ditch and shot. This man, wounded but not killed, fell in, with bodies collapsing on him. The next morning he escaped back to Prek Phneou.[63]

On the same highway, Ping Ling wrote, "the girls were gathering up the dishes" after a roadside evening meal when "nine blackshirts strode into camp ordering everybody to leave immediately." This was too much for one youth of twenty-three, who "jumped up in front of those blackshirts yelling his head

60. Ponchaud, *Cambodia Year Zero*, p. 44, corroborated by May, *Cambodian Witness*, p. 107.
61. Author's interview with Kem Hong Hav, Stains, 13 October 1979.
62. Author's interview with Muk Chot, Toul, 18 October 1979.
63. Author's interview with Bunchan Samedh, Melun, 17 November 1979.

off and hitting at his own chest with his two open palms, then moving upward to tear at his own hair." Then, Ping Ling recounts, "he begins to strip off all his clothing revealing himself completely naked. All the time, jumping up and down yelling. Then dropping on all fours and pointing at his bottom with one hand, daring those blackshirts to kick him there." The youth stood up and cursed the Khmer Rouge, proclaiming that they would "die in hell" and that "the devil is his angel, protecting him right now, that he can fight all of them with only one hand." Hammering his chest, he began "a boxing dance." A teenage Khmer Rouge pointed his M-79 at the youth's stomach. A bystander begged him to hold his fire. The crowd began to scatter. "An older blackshirt with a Mao cap" placed a restraining hand on the shoulder of the young Khmer Rouge. He "calmly drew out his .45 U.S. Army pistol and shot the poor mad man through the head."[64]

South of the capital, Ouch Sruy watched Khmer Rouge soldiers shoot people climbing coconut trees and kill others who entered houses seeking provisions for the journey. "They said this was against morality, stealing the property of others."[65] The executions carried out in the city and along the route at various checkpoints like Kompong Kantuot probably number in the thousands. Up to a thousand were probably killed in Phnom Penh itself, including the surrendering officials. One man says he saw a body every hundred meters along the road to Pochentong, possibly a hundred in all. Some would have been Lon Nol soldiers killed in the last fighting for the city, but another man confirms seeing several soldiers executed at Pochentong.[66]

Many others were treated as well as could be expected given the circumstances and the resources available. According to Pin Yathay, "The majority of the Khmer Rouge used reassuring language. They tried to console us. They did not smile but their voices did not betray the slightest nuance of threat. They promised to protect our houses."[67] Sopheara's testimony that "the Easterners used kind methods along the road" is corroborated by other deportees. Thida Mam writes that ten miles east of Phnom Penh, after a week of walking, her young niece Tevi "was little more than skin and bones. Death seemed imminent." However, "a Communist officer noticed Tevi's illness. In an inexplicable humane gesture, he used his influence to secure the streptomycin that saved Tevi."[68] Ly Chhiv Ha recalled that during her trek to Prey Veng, her family was fed along the way. "The Khmer Rouge were good, they asked for food for us

64. Ling, *Cambodia: 1,360 Days!*, pp. 70–71.
65. Ouch Sruy interview, 1979.
66. Author's interviews with Poeu Mek, Phnom Penh, 5 July 1980; and Muk Chot interview, 1979.
67. Pin Yathay, *L'Utopie Meurtrière*, p. 43.
68. Criddle and Mam, *To Destroy You Is No Loss*, p. 32.

from the local people. . . . The locals . . . were told by cadres to help us, to give us things that we lacked."[69]

Ping Ling, meanwhile, continued his trek north. Like most who took Highway 5, he found the Northern Zone "blackshirts" very harsh to the refugees; at the same time these Khmer Rouge were very critical of the Khmer Rouge across the river, in the Eastern Zone. Ping Ling crossed the river. Disembarking at a small wharf, he found "greenshirts" instead of blackshirts. "They were at the end of the planks where the passengers were descending, helping everyone who was overloaded with things in their arms. Carrying babies for the mothers, they even helped to carry the invalid ashore. So much for those blackshirts' propaganda on the other side. They even tried to steady me by holding on to my arms loaded with bundles. They were helpful . . . good commie soldiers."[70] They were probably part of Chhien's 3rd Eastern Division.[71]

Another contrast between the Northern and Eastern Zone forces was their use of money, which had been abolished in the Northern Zone in mid-1974.[72] A new national currency, printed in January 1975, was announced in February.[73] But on 18 April, Northern troops threw bills into the air, shouting, "The revolutionary *Angkar* has put an end to money."[74] But in the East three weeks later, Thida Mam recalls, "In Prek Po we saw for the first time the new Khmer Rouge money. Garish posters advertised the colorful bills, which depicted idealized soldiers in combat, peasants harvesting rice, and various scenes of 'true laborers' at work."[75] Differences over the use of currency festered for months.

69. Author's interview with Ly Chhiv Ha, Toulouse, 9 December 1979.

70. Ling, *Cambodia, 1,360 Days!*, pp. 115–22. For a fuller quotation, see Kiernan, "Wild Chickens, Farm Chickens, and Cormorants: Kampuchea's Eastern Zone under Pol Pot," in D. P. Chandler and B. Kiernan, eds., *Revolution and Its Aftermath in Kampuchea*, New Haven: Yale Southeast Asia Studies Monograph No. 25, 1983, p. 136.

71. This statement is based on the testimony of Heng Samrin (1991 interview) that Chhien's 3rd Division had advanced on the north bank of the Mekong to Chrui Changvar and on the fact that this area, Muk Kampoul District, formed part of Region 22 of the Eastern Zone, of which Chhien was party secretary.

72. Author's interviews in Kompong Svay, 16 October 1980.

73. Kate G. Frieson, *The Impact of Revolution on Cambodian Peasants, 1970–1975*, Ph.D.diss., Department of Politics, Monash University, Australia, 1991, p. 244.

74. Ponchaud, *Cambodia Year Zero*, p. 41, quoting Suon Phal's account of his journey on Highway 5 to Prek Phnoeu. Poeu San Bopha confirms that "the Khmer Rouge were throwing away money, up in the air" at Prek Phnoeu (Author's interview, Paris, 26 September 1979).

75. Criddle and Mam, *To Destroy You Is No Loss*, p. 50. The new CPK currency was dated January 1975.

The Toll

The population of the capital was nearly two million. During a visit to Cambodia in early February 1975, I was given the figure of 1.8 million by a New Zealander working on an official census of Phnom Penh. There is no evidence that the city's population had reached three million, the figure cited by Ieng Sary when he attempted to emphasize the problems faced by the new administration[76] and accepted by foreign observers because it actually seemed to be an admission of the evacuation of such a large number. The victorious Khmer Rouge had no way of knowing the true figure.[77]

Of the one hundred or more people I have interviewed about the evacuation of Phnom Penh, I asked thirty-six exactly how many members of their family or group had left the city together, and also how many of each group arrived safely in a rural community where they chose or were told to settle. They told of a total of 376 people. The thirty-six groups set out from the city and walked west, south, and east into the countryside for various lengths of time ranging from several days to six weeks. Only seven groups walked less than a week; four traveled for one to two weeks; another six for two to four weeks; and twelve families walked for more than one month. During these treks, two people died, a month-old baby and an elderly woman. The other 374 people arrived safely at their destinations. That suggests a death rate on the trek of approximately 0.53 percent, or a toll of 10,600 deaths in an evacuated population of two million.[78]

This figure seems reasonable in light of the fact that many people report having seen bodies along the way, especially on Highway 5. Veasna, who took Highway 3 through the Southwest Zone for six weeks, saw fifteen bodies by the roadside, mostly children and others who had died of illness.[79] Chandara, who walked south for two weeks along Highway 3, says he saw no killings on the road and no deaths from starvation, though he heard of several women dying in childbirth.[80] Hul Yem, who traveled forty-eight kilometers south, says more than twenty children, as well as several elderly people, died on the road in just over two weeks. Further, he saw land mines in the road past Kompong Kantuot take three more lives: "A sign gave warning but there were too many people being driven along." Yem also saw two people shot by

76. Ieng Sary interviewed by James Pringle, 4 September 1975, quoted in Ponchaud, *Cambodia Year Zero*, p. 36.

77. An erroneous report claimed that they carried out "a complete census" during the evacuation.

78. Pin Yathay's family of 18 also survived the trek (*L'Utopie Meurtrière*, p. 133), though only Yathay himself was to survive the next two years.

79. Veasna interview 1979.

80. Lor Chandara interview, 1980.

Khmer Rouge for not handing over their motorcycle when "requested" to do so.[81]

Executions in the city and during the exodus, mostly of Lon Nol officers, police officers, and high-ranking officials, but also of civilians who disobeyed orders from their new masters, would probably bring the death toll from the evacuation of the city to around twenty thousand. As Khieu Samphan remarked on 21 April, "the enemy died in agony."[82]

The Other Cities

All other towns in Cambodia, including those in the East, were also evacuated. The major port, Kompong Som, fell on 18 April. There were "white flags on every house and car." As the Khmer Rouge came in, they announced on loudspeakers that everyone would have to leave for three days to avoid possible U.S. bombardment. The city's population of one hundred thousand moved out. Engineer Ung Pech left from the airfield with his colleagues in five cars loaded with belongings. Friends told them to buy up supplies as well, because money would soon be useless. "We did not believe it. We even thought that perhaps we could go to Phnom Penh." But the cars were soon confiscated. They transferred all their belongings to oxcarts, but then their belongings were confiscated as well. According to a participant, "The Khmer Rouge who evacuated Kompong Som were as tough as those in Phnom Penh. Whoever resisted would be killed; the rest, no problem."[83]

Samon, a high school student in Prey Veng, was evacuated from her home at gunpoint, along with her father, a Lon Nol policeman, her husband, and ten other family members. Some people refused to leave their houses; the houses were demolished with grenades and set on fire. Samon heard that the patients in Prey Veng Hospital were also evacuated, and that those who could not walk were killed. Her family walked for two days without rest, passing bodies along the road. Six to eight families of evacuees would be sent to one village, another group to another, and so on. Two days after her arrival, Khmer Rouge shot Samon's husband dead, and later her father and brother as well.[84]

In northwest Cambodia, the evacuation of towns was delayed a week. The CPK deputy secretary of the Northwest Zone, Khek Penn, led the troops down the main street of the major northwestern city, Battambang, on 17 April. They proceeded cautiously. "Some of the young CPK soldiers had never seen a market

81. Hul Yem interview, 1979.

82. Phnom Penh Radio, 21 April 1975, in FBIS, Asia Pacific, 22 April 1975, p. H1.

83. Author's interviews with Ung Pech, Tuol Sleng, 7 September 1980, and Moeung Sonn, Sarcelles, 25 October 1979.

84. Author's interview with Samon, Prey Veng, 14 July 1980.

before."[85] A factory worker reported that they were "real country people, from *far away,"* and that they "were scared of anything" in a bottle or a tin. "Something in a tin [perhaps insecticide] had made one of them sick, so they mistook a can of sardines, with a picture of a fish on it, for fish poison, and one of them asked a friend of mine to throw it out. I saw them eating toothpaste once, and as for reading, I remember them looking at documents upside down."[86]

Khmer Rouge troops also entered the town of Pursat on 17 April. They went to the market, overturned the stalls, and drove around in vehicles with loudspeakers blaring, telling those who had taken refuge from the fighting in the countryside to go back to their native villages. Shopkeepers were ordered to stay a while and "assist" the victorious army.[87]

San, thirty, was a teacher in Sisophon when the Khmer Rouge took over. At first, "the people were very happy . . . singing all over the place." Only after some days did the Khmer Rouge begin to evacuate the town, telling people to go wherever they wished and "to grow rice." San saw no killing on his trek. "At first they did not make us suffer. . . . We did not get the impression that the Khmer Rouge hated the townspeople."[88]

Then Battambang was evacuated. "On 24 April, around 6 o'clock, loudspeaker cars ordered the civilian population to leave Battambang within three hours."[89] Workers in the textile factory were excepted.[90] On the same day, the market in Pursat was fired on; people were ordered to leave immediately, without taking time to prepare or pack. People screamed and ran in many directions amid the sound of gunfire.[91] The Thai border town of Pailin soon followed: "On the 26th, loudspeaker cars drove through Pailin and ordered everybody to get out of town within three days."[92]

What was the reason for this weeklong delay in the Northwest Zone? Poor communications between the Center and the distant Northwest Zone, perhaps a loss of radio contact, may have kept the Zone ignorant of Center policy. But there is a suggestion of Northwestern recalcitrance. A member of the Zone CPK committee, Heng Teav, asserts that "before the liberation of Phnom Penh, we

85. Frieson, *The Impact of Revolution*, p. 243.

86. See Ben Kiernan and Chanthou Boua, *Peasants and Politics in Kampuchea, 1942–1981*, London: Zed, 1982, p. 320. For a similar story, see Frieson, *The Impact of Revolution*, p. 243: "One woman soldier looked puzzled when she saw a can of sardines." Someone joked that it was motor oil. She believed this.

87. Author's interview with Tae Hui Lang, Chatenay-Malabry, 10 August 1979. For a full account of her story, see Kiernan and Boua, *Peasants and Politics*, pp. 358–62.

88. Author's interview with San, Paris, 29 May 1980.

89. Ponchaud, *Cambodia Year Zero*, p. 62.

90. Kiernan and Boua, *Peasants and Politics*, p. 319.

91. Tae Hui Lang interview, 1979.

92. Ponchaud, *Cambodia Year Zero*, p. 66.

did not know there was a plan" to evacuate the towns. "Our relatives were all there" in Battambang, he says. But after the capture of Phnom Penh, the Center "summoned the Zone chief, the military commander," Ros Nhim. Nhim declined to go. Keu, his deputy, went off instead. The Center ordered Keu "to go back and evacuate the people."[93]

But meanwhile, in Battambang, one of the first actions of the new occupiers (besides executing hundreds of officers of the defeated army) was to force prices down in the city. "There was a stampede, everybody trying to buy as much as they could." Large-denomination banknotes were banned, but not those worth less than fifty riels. As in Pursat, "loudspeaker cars drove through the streets asking people to return to their native villages; but it wasn't an order."[94] In Sisophon, schoolteacher San reports, "the first few days were normal. They lowered prices: beef, fish, rice." San, who then worked with the Khmer Rouge for a year, attributes the price deflation effort to orders from Battambang coming from Khek Penn, whom he describes as a "reasonable" CPK leader.[95]

This program again contrasts with that of the Northern forces occupying Phnom Penh, who had been forewarned that both money and cities were to be abolished. The weeklong window that opened on the Khmer Rouge in the Northwest as a result of the distance from the party Center shows how a Zone could receive orders in recognizable form but interpret them idiosyncratically, or even devise policy on its own, before being pulled back into line.

Back in Phnom Penh

On 18 April around 1 P.M., Son Sen arrived in Phnom Penh, in a convoy of two grey Peugeot 404s and a black Mercedes. From the crowd, Yathay saw him pass by, "talking and looking at us," with "an ironic smile" on his lips.[96] The next morning, a DC-3 landed at Pochentong. It brought "military political commissars" who were to form a "Phnom Penh Committee" for the military administration of the capital. Northerner Nhiem, who was named vice president of this committee, told Henri Becker that the plane had come

93. Author's interview with Heng Teav, Phnom Penh, 14 January 1986.
94. Ponchaud, *Cambodia Year Zero*, p. 57.
95. San interview, 1980. For a different view of Khek Penn's policy in April 1975, see Frieson, *The Impact of Revolution*, p. 243, where another teacher reports offering Penn 50,000 *riels* (U.S.$30) "as a gesture of good will" on 17 April, but says Penn replied that in the future, "money would have no value and would not be used." Penn is likely to have wished to dispel any suspicion of bribery. For his promise that money would be reintroduced, see Chapter 3.
96. Yathay does not name Son Sen but accurately describes him as bespectacled and "thinly built" (p. 45). The convoy came from the south, like the troops of the Special Zone, of which Sen was deputy secretary.

from Krek, in the Eastern Zone. One passenger was an unnamed man in "a new Khmer Rouge uniform," a high-ranking officer who gave the impression of being "a chief sure of himself." Becker described him as "uncontestably impressive": "A commissar with a certain fine bearing, an elegant hair cut, a very free and open countenance. A bursting smile." In a speech to information ministry technicians, this officer defended the evacuation as a necessary measure to avoid exposing the population to U.S. bombardment and promised the workers that they would be treated well (though no "sabotage" would be tolerated), that their families would be able to join them soon, and that they would receive daily rations. And he "used in his speech for the first time the name of Norodom Sihanouk as Head of State." Becker says this distinguished the newcomer from the Northern Zone command: "The soldiers never pronounce the word 'Sihanouk' and never refer to him. During discussions, Nhiem manifestly avoided the subject 'Norodom Sihanouk.' It was a subject to be avoided if one did not wish to be labelled 'Sihanoukist.' Moreover, Nhiem had told me on the morning of 18 April that 'the speeches of Sihanouk do not interest the soldiers.'"[97] The commissar from the East did not share their view.

In the late afternoon of 21 April, another leader, named Suon, arrived at the ministry in a yellow Peugeot preceded by an M-113 armored personnel carrier with about twenty soldiers. Becker watched: "All the northern sector command was in the street to receive him." Becker describes him as a rather corpulent man just over forty. He seemed an important figure, but remains a mystery. Becker dined with Suon for two hours that evening, "in a big room lit by fifty candles." "The atmosphere was full of gaiety, with Suon's loud bursts of laughter." Becker thought he recognized him from somewhere; Suon claimed to have been a district chief in Kompong Cham province in 1957, but said he had secretly left for Hanoi the next year, returning to Cambodia in 1962 to organize the underground. When Becker asked him about Western journalists who had disappeared in communist zones, he claimed that most had gone missing in areas then controlled by the Vietcong. Suon claimed that Hu Nim was one of his closest associates. However, in contrast to the unnamed commissar from Krek (who was also present at the dinner), questions about Sihanouk and Khieu Samphan "did not particularly please Suon; he answered briefly and immediately led the discussion onto another subject."[98]

Meanwhile, on 20 April, the Northern Zone leaders arranged for a car to travel the streets of Phnom Penh, broadcasting an appeal to the soldiers searching houses for signs of enemies. The troops were ordered to "respect personal objects, such as spectacles, watches, *pièces d'identité*, and jewellery."

97. Becker, Les Evénements, p. 10.
98. Ibid., pp. 17–19.

Becker comments: "This appeal made no sense, given that on the third day of operation 'evacuation,' Phnom Penh was practically empty. The car was still going around on 21 April."[99]

But it does make sense. The point was not to reassure departed civilians, but to forbid soldiers from looting. There was probably an ideological rationale: to prevent the troops from being "contaminated" by urban materialism. And a hierarchical one: watches, in particular, would become a sign of rank in the new society. But the loudspeakers blaring in the empty streets served yet another purpose: maintaining the fiction, among troops from other zones, that the residents would at some point be allowed to return home. Revealing at this stage that the evacuation was permanent could have risked confrontation with the Eastern Zone forces, who had been told otherwise.

On the evening of 21 April, Nhiem escorted Becker from the information ministry to the French embassy, where he joined most other foreigners. But one Western relief worker was still at large in the city. The manager of an orphanage, he had decided to stay with the children rather than abandon them to the evacuation. From 17 April, he watched from the orphanage as a constant stream of people crowded past on their way out of the capital. His view is that it was very efficiently done, and as for brutality, "I saw none of that. That happened later, when the Westerners had all been expelled from the country." Interviewed in 1980, this man remained struck by the apparent lack of brutality, particularly because he was able to see a lot of the town. From 17 to 29 April, he had on several occasions ridden a bicycle or driven a car through the streets. When stopped by Khmer Rouge, he says, he would tell them that he was on his way to the French Embassy. Since they knew that was where he was supposed to go but they did not know where it was, they would let him pass. Finally, on 29 April, a cadre came and told him politely but firmly that he would have to go to the Embassy. The convoy of foreigners left the city the next day.[100] The orphans may well have been sent into the countryside unaccompanied.

The city was rigorously divided between the various zonal forces. Norodom Boulevard was the line between areas held by the Eastern Zone and the Spe-

99. Ibid., p. 7.

100. Author's interview with an anonymous British relief worker, September 1980. Corroboration comes from a young man studying to be a mechanic at Pochentong airport when the Khmer Rouge arrived there at 7.00 A.M. on 17 April. "Two or three of them asked me to come over, and asked me how I was, saying that we had joined hands now that they had taken over Phnom Penh. . . . They asked six or seven of us to drive them to the New Market where we helped them load goods they had confiscated. . . . I worked with them for a week, organizing vehicles, towing, etc., and teaching the Khmer Rouge to drive. . . . I saw no killings in the week in Phnom Penh. They did not terrorize people, just tried to make us loyal." Interview with the author, Strasbourg, 31 October 1979.

cial Zone forces. The road was divided "along the white line." Heng Samrin recalls that on the Special Zone side, women stood guard. "And [if] my troops crossed over the white line to the west—that was their territory. They stopped us. If we insisted they would arrest us." This happened to many of Samrin's subordinates, and he had to work hard to get his men back. Another soldier recalls Southwest Zone forces arresting the "more liberal" Eastern Zone troops.[101]

Bernard Gaude, a Frenchman, had lived in Cambodia for twenty-six years. Before his expulsion with other Westerners in May 1975, Gaude spent two weeks with the Khmer Rouge in Phnom Penh and its vicinity. He reported that "along a single Phnom Penh street there might be two or three different groups, each controlling its own sector and separated from one another by much more than just military unit distinctions." He added, "There was a certain feeling that all was not right among the various groups, that there was a powder keg that might explode into still further fighting."[102]

Pol Pot did not reach Phnom Penh until 24 April.[103] Nothing is known of the manner of his arrival. Ieng Sary landed in a Chinese Boeing 707 at Pochentong airport the same day.[104] The brothers-in-law were right on time for a three-day, celebratory "Special National Congress" in the city. Phnom Penh Radio listed those attending as "125 representatives of people's organizations," 112 military delegates, "20 representatives of the Buddhist clergy," and 54 representatives of the National United Front and the Royal Government. On 27 April, Khieu Samphan announced their "unanimous" decisions: that "the important winners are the people," that the country would be "an independent, peaceful, neutral, sovereign, nonaligned Cambodia with territorial integrity," and that Prince Sihanouk "is a great, high-ranking patriotic personality" who would "remain chief of state."[105] But this was only the curtain-raiser for a much more important CPK gathering.

101. Heng Samrin interview, 1991; S. Heder's with Um Samang, Sakeo, 10 March 1980. Samang was describing the situation in Phnom Penh in May 1975.

102. Quoted in Denis Gray, "A Lifestyle of Austerity," *Bangkok Post*, 13 May 1975. Refugee Hav reported that friends who drove trucks to Phnom Penh from the Northwest Zone, apparently as late as 1976 or 1977, confirmed that the city remained "divided": "The Eastern Zone were in charge from the Royal Palace along the Mekong River. The Southwest had from Phnom Penh to the Chinese Hospital. The North had from Kilometer 6." Kem Hong Hav interview, 1979.

103. "Interview of Comrade Pol Pot . . . to the Delegation of Yugoslav Journalists in Visit to Democratic Kampuchea," Phnom Penh: Ministry of Foreign Affairs of Democratic Kampuchea, March 1978, p. 22.

104. Nayan Chanda, *Brother Enemy*, New York: Harcourt Brace Jovanovich, 1986, p. 12.

105. Phnom Penh Radio, 27 April 1975, in FBIS, Asia Pacific, 28 April 1975, p. H1.

Consolidation: The 20 May 1975 Conference

All military and civilian officials of the new regime were summoned to a special meeting on 20 May 1975. "District and region secretaries came from all over the country, and representatives from all armed forces and units and regions, so there were thousands." The assembly was held in the old sports center in the northern part of Phnom Penh.[106] Its purpose was "to receive the plan distributed by the Center" and then return home to "implement the plan." The meeting lasted five days.

This was the Center's first major attempt to run its political writ throughout Cambodia. No documents from the meeting, and very few members of its audience, appear to have survived. But it has been possible to reconstruct some of the event through interviews with three of those present and with two others whose superiors attended and gave them accounts of it. (Later they were arrested; both disappeared.) The accounts are not only rare but modulated, informative despite lapses of memory, and, as we shall see, mutually corroborative without indication of prearrangement.[107]

The earliest account dates from mid-1980. It comes from Sin Song, who in 1975 was political commissar of the 3rd Battalion of Chakrey's 1st Eastern Division. Song was stationed in Prey Veng. He did not attend the May assembly, but his immediate superior, Chhouk, the Region 24 CPK secretary, did. On his return, Chhouk told Song that Pol Pot had made eight points:

1. Evacuate people from all towns.
2. Abolish all markets.
3. Abolish Lon Nol regime currency and withhold the revolutionary currency that had been printed.
4. Defrock all Buddhist monks and put them to work growing rice.
5. Execute all leaders of the Lon Nol regime beginning with the top leaders.
6. Establish high-level cooperatives throughout the country, with communal eating.
7. Expel the entire Vietnamese minority population.
8. Dispatch troops to the borders, particularly the Vietnamese border.[108]

106. This is Heng Samrin's 1991 account. Chea Sim thought the meeting took place at the Khmero-Soviet University. In 1992, Heng Samrin insisted he was right, saying that he was living in the city at the time.

107. Four of the five sources, it should be noted, were from the Eastern Zone and later rebelled against Pol Pot. They may be treated with caution. Readers can decide cause and effect—whether damning accounts are explained by the rebels' politics, or vice versa.

108. Author's interview with Sin Song, Phnom Penh, 12 August 1980. See Kiernan, "Wild Chickens," in Chandler and Kiernan, eds., *Revolution and Its Aftermath in Kampuchea*, pp. 178–79.

The second source is an officer named Ret, a Center battalion commander from the Northern Zone who attended the meeting. Before his arrest in 1977, he told colleagues in the north of a large meeting in Phnom Penh around 27 May 1975. Ret said that "eleven points" were discussed, but his colleagues, interviewed in 1980, could recall his mentioning only the leadership's orders to "kill Lon Nol soldiers, kill the monks, [and] expel the Vietnamese population" and its opposition to "money, schools, and hospitals."[109]

Mat Ly, a CPK district committee member in Region 21, attended the meeting. In 1991 he agreed with Sin Song that there were eight points. He started his list with five of the first six points recalled by Song (1, 2, 3, 4, and 6). He added the following: close schools, close hospitals, and "uproot spies root and branch."[110] Chea Sim, CPK secretary of Ponhea Krek district on the Vietnam border and a member of the Region 20 Committee, confirms Sin Song's list.[111]

To get to the meeting, Sim traveled along Highway 7 from the border to Tonle Bet, then took a ferry down the Mekong. He arrived in the capital on 19 May, spending the night with hundreds of other participants at the Phnom Penh Technical School, west of the city center. The next morning the meeting began at 8 A.M. The assembly lasted five days. Nuon Chea spoke on the first day, Pol Pot on the second. Chea Sim recalled some of the details in a 1991 interview.

"Nuon Chea said that building socialism in Kampuchea consisted of two parts, agriculture and industry. He said agriculture would be modernized in ten to fifteen years by scientific methods, by preparing irrigation dams and canals all over the country. And the dams and canals had to be started in the coming year, 1976. Industry would be modernized in a similar period of ten to fifteen years."

"And the second issue: in order to achieve the construction of socialism progressively and advance all together in the set period, we must take care to carefully screen internal agents (*samrit samrainh phtey khnong*) in the party, in the armed forces, in the various organizations and ministries, in the government, and among the masses of the people. We have to carefully screen them, Nuon Chea said. He mentioned 'the line of carefully screening internal agents to improve and purify, in order to implement the line of building socialism so that it advances to modernization by new scientific technology.'"

"This was a very important order to kill. Their careful screening was to take all measures so that people were pure (*borisot*). The line laid down must be fol-

109. Author's interview with Kun Chhay, Kompong Svay, 16 October 1980.
110. In an interview with the author on 21 January 1986, Mat Ly had begun with Song's point no. 1: "Expel people from the cities." In an interview with Jeremy Stone and Gregory Stanton on 11 July 1991, Ly recalled the points in a different order from Sin Song (6, 1, 4, 3, 2).
111. Chea Sim interview, 1991.

lowed at all costs. . . . If people could not do it, they would be taken away and killed. This was called the line of 'careful screening.' It came out in concrete specifics in the eight points. . . . These came from the broad lines, the strategic principles. Socialist construction can only succeed under the line of careful screening of internal agents. The words 'carefully screen' were the killing principle . . . and were stated strongly on 20 May. It was to be done." This recalls Mat Ly's description of the slogan, "Uproot spies root and branch."

Heng Samrin, then studying military affairs under Son Sen, was also at the meeting.[112] He recalls the use of yet another term: "They did not say 'kill,' they said 'scatter the people of the old government.' Scatter (*komchat*) them away, don't allow them to remain in the framework. It does not mean 'smash' (*komtec*). . . . Smash means 'kill' but they used a general word, 'scatter.' Nuon Chea used this phrase." This appears to be Sin Song's point number 5, though the use of varied euphemisms is an important qualification.

Samrin agrees that "mostly, it was Nuon Chea who did the talking," explaining the new Center policies in detail. Samrin did not recall eight points, but mentioned permanent evacuation of the cities (Sin Song's no. 1); the decisions to withhold the new currency and abolish the circulation of money (no. 3); establishment of "medium-level cooperatives" in the countryside (not quite no. 6); evacuation of the foreign embassies; and the division of the population into two groups: "full rights" citizens (*neak penh sith*, those who had lived in Khmer Rouge zones before 17 April); and "candidates" (*neak triem*) for such status, especially the newly evacuated deportees or "depositees" (*neak phñoe*) from the towns.

Samrin continues: "Nuon Chea talked of wiping out markets, not allowing money. If there were markets and money, there was property. The important, heavy pressure was against property. Where there was money there were markets, and if there were markets there would be people with money and those people would have property. So they wanted to wipe out property, not allow private property to exist." This is Sin Song's point number 2.

"It was Pol Pot who distributed this plan personally," says Samrin, who quoted him as saying, "Don't use money, don't let the people live in the cities." There was, however, "no mention of closing schools or hospitals." Chea Sim agrees. On the other hand, Samrin adds: "Monks, they said, were to be disbanded, put aside as a 'special class,' the most important to fight. They had to be wiped out (*lup bombat*). . . . I heard Pol Pot say this myself. . . . He said no monks were to be allowed, no festivals were to be allowed any more, meaning 'wipe out religion.' " Nuon Chea affirmed this, adding that "wats would not be allowed." This is Song's point number 4.

112. Heng Samrin interview, 1991.

Samrin claims that the two leaders' views were "clearly the same." But their manner was different. I asked Chea Sim if Pol Pot spoke of killing people, or if he ever used the word *kill*. He replied, "It is difficult for us to understand. We saw Pol Pot's behavior and heard his words, and he did not seem to us to be a killer. He seemed kindly. He did not speak very much. He just smiled and smiled. . . . And his words were light, not strong. In general, you would estimate that Pol Pot was a kindly person, simple, with a mass view. But his methods were confrontational; he was just a killer."

On the other hand, Sim continued, "Nuon Chea's behavior was somewhat coarse, different from Pol Pot's. It could be observed. . . . People always say that Nuon Chea is somewhat cruel. His behavior is stronger. And they always praise Pol Pot as the kindliest person of all."

Heng Samrin adds, "Nuon Chea was the one who did the consciousness work, the propaganda." Chea elucidated official positions: "Only the very special documents would be introduced by Pol Pot. . . . As a rule Pol Pot spoke little, and about broad general principles: lines, vanguard views, socialism, Great Leaps Forward, great whatevers. . . . While [Nuon Chea] was speaking the two of them were right there together, presiding side by side, but only Nuon Chea spoke about the documents. Pol Pot was the listener. Pol Pot did not offer many personal opinions."

The party secretary did make one strong, specific point. According to Chea Sim, "Pol Pot spoke a lot about the question of Vietnam. He stressed the importance of the issue of evacuating all of the Vietnamese people out of Cambodian territory." Heng Samrin recalls Nuon Chea's adding, "We cannot allow any Vietnamese minority" to live in Cambodia. This is Sin Song's point number 7. Pol Pot also noted that Vietnam's Mekong Delta had been Cambodian territory in the past. But Chea Sim recalls no order sending troops to the borders to attack Vietnam. That came later, he says.

We are now in a position to list the major decisions announced at that 20–24 May 1975 meeting. Chhouk's account, as told through Sin Song, holds up reasonably well. The evacuation of the cities was declared to be permanent. Money, markets, and Buddhism were now prohibited. Song seems to have been right (and Chea Sim less well-informed) about the dispatching of troops to the Vietnamese border. But Song predates the order establishing "*high-level* cooperatives throughout the country, with communal eating." Communal eating was probably foreshadowed in May 1975, but it was not ordered until 1976. Medium-level cooperatives were now formed. In August 1975, the CPK's monthly internal magazine, *Tung Padevat* (Revolutionary Flags), announced that "the party has decided to upgrade the cooperatives into village-cooperatives." Replacing small groups of fifteen to thirty families in which "the strength of the party members was thinly spread," cooperatives consisting of entire villages now ensured that "the leadership has a more centralized character." It added, "The party branches have grasped the leadership of the village-cooperatives more firmly than before."[113] The party Center was slowly asserting its power.

Dissent

Contrary to Heng Samrin's account, Hou Yuon did not "disappear forever" after opposing the Center's evacuation plan in February. Monks saw him at their wat in his home district in Kompong Cham province on 8 March.[114] An ex-monk also recognized Hou Yuon at Oudong, north of Phnom Penh, on 17 April. Yuon, escorted by soldiers, was traveling in a jeep heading very fast towards the surrendered capital.[115] The next month Yuon's wife, Ung Yok Leang, returned to the couple's native village. According to relatives, she came to collect her daughter and take her "to live with her father and mother" now that the war was over.[116] It is unlikely she would have done this had Hou Yuon already disappeared or been killed. But he was certainly under a cloud. Hu Nim recorded in his "confession" that "after liberation, when the Party abolished money and wages and evacuated the people, Hou Yuon again boldly took a stand against the Party line."[117]

Chhouk told Sin Song that at the May meeting Hou Yuon had publicly dissented from some of eight points. According to Song, "There was some disagreement with these points at the Assembly, especially over the creation of high-level cooperatives because three million city people and others were not familiar with revolutionary politics. And also, the country had just emerged from a war, so there were great shortages and a lack of capital and facilities. Communal eating cooperatives throughout the country was not a feasible proposition. Hou Yuon, for one, said that this was just not possible, Chhouk reported to me. . . . After that, Hou Yuon was sacked from the cabinet."[118]

113. "Another Important Victory of Our Cooperatives and Revolutionary Movement," *Tung Padevat*, August 1975, pp. 71ff.

114. "Khmer Refugee Walks Out from Phnom Penh," Extracts from a Cabled Report from the American Embassy in Bangkok, 5 June 1975 (declassified in June 1978), p. 3.

115. Author's interview with Long, Oudong, 18 September 1980. Long said he was absolutely sure this was Hou Yuon. Long had been a monk for 18 years before the town of Oudong was captured by Mok's forces in March 1974, when he was evacuated along with its other residents. Locals hid him from the CPK.

116. Author's interview with relatives of Hou Yuon, Sambor Meas, 5 August 1980. These relatives included his mother and two of his sisters.

117. *Chamlaiy Hu Nim*, confession in Tuol Sleng prison dated 28 May and 16 June 1977, translated in Chanthou Boua, David P. Chandler, and Ben Kiernan, eds., *Pol Pot Plans the Future: Confidential Leadership Documents from Democratic Kampuchea, 1976–77*, New Haven: Yale Southeast Asia Studies Monograph No. 33, 1988, p. 304.

118. In June 1975, Hing, the CPK Secretary of Region 5, in the northwest, secretly

Song continues, "Some people also disagreed with the policy of execution, preferring reeducation so that the victims could then play a useful role. And there was disagreement with the abolition of money and markets. Chhouk and the secretary of the Northeast Zone, Ney Sarann, were among the main dissidents. On his return, Chhouk called a meeting of over thirty Region 24 cadres, including myself. He told us he disagreed with these policies; if the party went ahead along this road, he would not yet follow."

Battalion commander Ret, for his part, claimed that Northern Zone Secretary Koy Thuon, himself, and others had argued in favor of "money, schools and religion." Hu Nim, too, probably found himself in a difficult position in May 1975. Seng Horl, who had taken Highway 1 out of the city, was camping at Prek Eng, "waiting for news" of what would be allowed next. There he heard that Hu Nim had come to Prek Eng "to talk to the people." Another refugee saw Hu Nim in black clothes, traveling in a jeep with several soldiers; he had stopped along the way and was "asking the people how they were going." Horl says Hu Nim told the waiting evacuees that "*Angkar Loeu* had got the people to leave Phnom Penh for only three months, then they could go back again."[119] Heng Samrin put it this way: "The people were evacuated into the environs of the city. They were not yet evacuated to distant regions. Then, after receiving the plan on the twentieth [of May], the people were evacuated to the remote countryside. . . . From that time, they were evacuated forever, not allowed to live in cities again."[120] Thus, Horl stayed at Prek Eng for a month, until after the 20–24 May meeting. Then, forbidden to go back to Phnom Penh, he had to move further into the countryside. As Chea Sim recalled, "They just sent people on and distributed them permanently. They did not announce it, they just sent people on."

There were a few exceptions. Skilled workers were being recalled at the same checkpoints where Lon Nol's soldiers were being rounded up for execution. Nop, a railway worker who volunteered to go back, was given a house in the suburb of Tuk La'ak for his family. He was put to work on the railway line south of Phnom Penh. Factory and electrical workers went back to their jobs as well.[121] After a month in the countryside, Tran Heng, a former textile worker, responded to a call for all textile and metal workers to go back to work. About six ferryloads of workers were taken back to the capital by river. But

---

told San, one of his trusted workers, that Hou Yuon had "departed from the line and had been sent by *Angkar* to a cooperative for reeducation and would come back and be a leader again after living with the people for a period" (author's interview with San, Paris, 29 May 1980.)

119. Author's interviews with Seng Horl, 1979, and Nhek Davy, Melun, 20 November 1979.

120. Heng Samrin interview, 1991.

121. Author's interview with Nop, Toul, 28 October 1979.

only fifteen workers went back to Heng's factory, of which his father had been director. They included Heng and his wife, his parents, his three older sisters and three brothers. Three hundred female Khmer Rouge soldiers were brought in to take the place of those workers who had presumably not trusted in the regime's call to return to work.[122]

Two fairly similar accounts indicate what happened to Hou Yuon. French journalist Jean Lacouture writes that Yuon "was killed by one of his bodyguards a few days after the capture of Phnom Penh, as he was departing on a motorcycle from a public meeting where he had criticized the plan to turn pagodas into stables."[123] If this is true, it is more likely to have occurred after the May meeting, where Pol Pot urged people to "wipe out religion." The second account, bearing a date of August 1975, is consistent with this inference. A CPK cadre in Kompong Cham reported that Hou Yuon addressed a large gathering of evacuees and others by the Mekong River at Prek Po. He spoke out strongly against the evacuation and was applauded by the crowd. Soon after leaving this meeting, Hou Yuon was shot dead by a CPK squad, and his body was thrown into the Mekong.[124] A confidential CPK report later confirmed that he had been murdered in 1975.[125] His name was never officially mentioned by DK, though its representatives told foreigners Yuon was alive, "tending to organization."[126] In September 1975, a Vietnamese official asked Koy Thuon what had happened to Yuon, and was told that Hou Yuon suffered from "heart disease."[127]

122. Author's interview with Tran Heng, Hagenau, 2 November 1979.

123. Jean Lacouture, *Survive le peuple cambodgien!*, Paris: Seuil, 1978, p. 117. In 1979, I wrote to Lacouture inquiring about the source of his story, but received no reply.

124. Author's interview with Ros Kann, Surin, 3 March 1979. Kann said he was told of this in Kompong Cham Province by a CPK cadre named Pen Kimsruong, among others, who disapproved of what was happening and advised Kann to flee.

125. The notebook of Eng Hei, alias Ly, a CPK *Santebal* (security) cadre, entry dated 18 August 1978, says: "In 1975 we killed the contemptible Hou Yuon."

126. See *Far Eastern Economic Review,* 13 May 1977, p. 5; St. Louis *Post-Dispatch,* 15 January 1979, p. 7B.

127. Author's interview with Kieu Minh, Phnom Penh, 22 October 1980. (Minh speaks Khmer.) San, a Northwest Zone teacher working with Hing, CPK secretary of Region 5, was told, apparently by Hing after Yuon's death, that "Hou Yuon wanted to circulate money, [and allow] Buddhism, and opposed the evacuation of the towns. The extremists regarded this as revisionism. Hou Yuon could not be spared" (San interview, 1980. See note 118, above). Evidence suggesting that Yuon might have survived into 1976 is fragile. A brother-in-law in Australia, Ung Bunhuor, claims to have heard Yuon's unannounced voice over Phnom Penh Radio in 1976 (*Far Eastern Economic Review,* 24 June 1977, p. 7). In early 1977 a woman in the Northern Zone was told by a man named Khon, Hou Yuon's bodyguard from 1967, that Yuon was then "not very far away, but that his freedom was restricted greatly and that he was under very close surveillance. Khon said Hou Yuon was raising pigs." (In late 1977 Khon himself was arrested and disappeared, as did his wife. Interview with Hing Sopanya, Creteil, 14 November 1979.) As late as December 1978, DK officials claimed Yuon and other known victims were alive, an outright lie (R. Dudman, St. Louis *Post-Dispatch,* 15 January 1979, p. 7B).

Rationales for the Evacuation

Ouch Bun Chhoeun, then the cpk's deputy secretary of Region 21, recalls "the propaganda line" passed down from the party Center after the evacuation of Phnom Penh: "1. The city people have had an easy life, whereas the rural people have had a very hard time. 2. The city people were exploiters. 3. The morality of the cities under Lon Nol was not pure and clean like in the liberated areas. 4. The city people shirked productive work."[128] Their real problem was that they were not trusted to remain in their homes. A Southwest Zone cadre later recalled, "The main thing was that we could not be assured who the people in Phnom Penh were."[129] Some were known political enemies, many others were members of unapproved racial groups, even more were ethnic Khmer but apolitical. If the Khmer Rouge applied their class analysis to the urban population, they found no allies.

This play for total power was highlighted in an article in *Tung Padevat* in August 1975. Referring to the earlier wartime evacuation of Kratie, the magazine was answering or anticipating questions about the emptying of Phnom Penh. In the cpk zones before 1973, the article said, the party "was to some extent in control of commerce." But the private sector remained active: "Kratie township showed the same signs as in the old society. Honda motorcycles were speeding up and down the streets like before, while our ragged guerrillas walked in the dust. This showed that they were still the masters. . . . They could go wherever they wanted. *Our state was their satellite.*"[130] This was the cpk's description of a situation in which it had achieved political and military domination. That was not enough. The cpk still considered itself suppressed. The passage highlights the new state's extreme sensitivity to the freedoms of others, viewing them as threats to its own ambition to acquire total power.

Others have suggested that the city dwellers were evacuated in 1975 to bring them closer to food sources in the countryside.[131] Stocks were low, U.S. and other foreign aid supplies could not have been expected to continue, starvation was already affecting the city's poorest inhabitants, and predictions of famine were rife. The U.S. Agency for International Development (usaid) draft end-of-term report noted that when U.S. rice aid stopped in April 1975, Cambodia was "on the brink of starvation." The bulk of the rice production now

128. Author's interview with Ouch Bun Chhoeun, Phnom Penh, 30 September 1980.
129. S. Heder's interview with a Region 13 cadre, 8 March 1980.
130. *Tung Padevat*, no. 8, August 1975, pp. 8–9. Emphasis added. For further quotations from this document see Ben Kiernan, *How Pol Pot Came to Power*, London: Verso, 1985, pp. 368–69, and Carney, "The Unexpected Victory," in Jackson, ed., *Cambodia 1975–1978*, p. 28. I am grateful to Carney for a U.S. government draft translation.
131. This argument is advanced in G. C. Hildebrand and G. Porter, *Cambodia: Starvation and Revolution*, New York: Monthly Review Press, 1976.

depended on "the hard labor of seriously malnourished people." Thus, "to avert a major food disaster, Cambodia needs from 175,000 to 250,000 metric tons of milled rice to cover the period July 1 to mid-February 1976." The USAID report went on:

> Even with completely favorable natural conditions, the prospects for a harvest this year good enough to move Cambodia very far back toward rice self-sufficiency are not good. . . . If ever a country needed to beat its swords into plowshares in a race to save itself from hunger, it is Cambodia. The prospects that it can or will do so are poor. Therefore, without large scale external food and equipment assistance there will be widespread starvation between now and next February and probably more of the same next year. . . . Slave labor and starvation rations for almost half the nation's people. . . . will be a cruel necessity for this year and general deprivation and suffering will stretch over the next two to three years before Cambodia can get back to rice self-sufficiency.[132]

But the deportation was devised neither as a punishment for the city dwellers nor as a solution to their problems. It was a calculated, strategic move in an ongoing military contest. The USAID report was correct to doubt that Cambodia would "beat its swords into plowshares." The first and last of Sin Song's eight points, evacuation of the cities and dispatching of troops to the Vietnamese border, were related. In February 1975, as the Lon Nol regime entered its death throes, the CPK Center decided on the evacuation of Phnom Penh. At this point few predicted that the war in neighboring south Vietnam would soon end in a communist victory there as well. Saigon still seemed certain to hold out. So after the CPK's victory, war in the region would probably continue. This was something of a threat to Cambodia, but also an opportunity. Khmer Rouge troops were dispatched to the Vietnamese border immediately after Phnom Penh's surrender. Detailed evidence suggests that their mission was to attempt to seize territory from the weakening Saigon regime before Vietnamese communists could.[133] This part of Vietnam, CPK commanders said, was Kampuchea Krom, "Lower Cambodia." The emptying of the cities was part of a strategy of continuing warfare to reunify the country's ancient territories on the basis of racial homogeneity. For this campaign, Cambodia would be in better fighting shape without vulnerable population centers.[134]

---

132. U.S. Agency for International Development, draft Termination Report for Cambodia, April 1975, Part Six, "Cambodia's Food and Fibre Needs: The PL 480 Assistance Program to Cambodia for Rice and Other Commodities," pp. 16–17. William Shawcross provided the author with a copy of this document.

133. See Kiernan, How Pol Pot, pp. 414–16, 422 n. 14, and Chapter 4, below.

134. The second evacuation of Phnom Penh (1979) was described by the CPK in such

The evacuation was important not only for the lives of those evacuated, which were transformed forever; it was also a sea change in Cambodia's political demography, facilitating both ethnic cleansing and the acquisition of totalitarian power. Not only were the cities effectively Khmerized when their ethnic Chinese and Vietnamese majorities were dispersed;[135] without towns, too, citizens became far more easy to control. From now on, there would be no assembled constituency to whom dissident or underground political activists could appeal or among whom they could quietly work. No human agglomeration facilitating private communication between individuals. Nowhere that the exchange of news and ideas could escape tight monitoring that reduced it to a minimum. No venue for a large crowd to assemble except on CPK initiative, no audience for someone like Sihanouk to address. No possibility of pressuring the nerve center of the regime by means of popular demonstrations in the capital. And no chance for an orthodox marxist or other dissident faction to develop a base among a proletariat. A CPK subdistrict committee member in the Eastern Zone comments on the emptying of the cities: "After 17 April 1975 the party stopped saying that the workers were the base."[136] Indeed, a CPK magazine the next year would claim, in precise inversion of the dictatorship of the proletariat, "We evacuated the people from the cities which is our class struggle."[137]

The CPK Center's quest for absolute power in Cambodia had been waged at a cost. The goal was so comprehensive as to provoke unease even among the tools used for its achievement, CPK members and troops. If they did not imagine it eventually threatening themselves, some felt this awesome concentration and deployment of power to be distinct from the cause they had fought for. The evacuation was the first major trauma of the Khmer Rouge period, not only for Phnom Penh's population, but also for the Khmer Rouge army. The divisions and contradictions that surfaced in the organization during the exodus would only widen and fester in the years ahead. But the evacuation was not the first major trauma for the rural population, many of whom had been living under Khmer Rouge rule for some time. Divisions in the countryside were already wider.

terms. "The departures were presented as a guerrilla tactic to dissuade the Vietnamese from bombarding the capital." Laurence Picq, *Au-delà du ciel: Cinq ans chez les Khmers Rouges*, Paris: Barrault, 1984, p. 151.

135. In the 1960s, Phnom Penh's population had been only 42 percent Khmer; 57 percent were Chinese and Vietnamese. Ruth Tooze, *Cambodia: Land of Contrasts*, New York, Viking, 1962, p. 90.

136. Author's interview with Chan Mon, Suong, 7 August 1980.

137. Quoted in Jackson, *Cambodia 1975–1978*, p. 279.

CHAPTER THREE

Cleansing the Countryside: Race, Power, and the Party, 1973–75

Confrontation in the East, 1973–75

In 1973–74, U.S. State Department officer Kenneth Quinn carried out one of the first studies of the Khmer Rouge. Reporting the testimony of refugees on the Cambodia-South Vietnam border, Quinn showed how Cambodia's insurgency was split between the hard-line *Khmer Krahom* (Red Khmer, or K.K.) and the moderate, pro-Sihanouk, pro-Vietnamese *Khmer Rumdos* (Khmer Liberation, or K.R.). Quinn noted that the Khmer Rumdos "control the KC [Khmer Communist] movement in Prey Veng," in the Eastern Zone. But across the Mekong River was Vorn Vet's Special Zone and beyond it, Mok's Southwest. Here the Center-sponsored K.K. faction ran the insurgency. By November 1973, Quinn wrote, "the two factions were at each other's throats."[1]

In his 1991 interview with the author, Heng Samrin said that in 1973 he had taken command of the Eastern Zone's 126th Regiment. Attacking Lon Nol's forces, the 126th advanced across the Mekong, leaving Prey Veng for Kandal province and the Southwest Zone. There, however, Samrin's forces came into conflict with Mok's. In late 1973, he claimed, "My troops went to climb Chisor mountain to look for traditional medicine to cure soldiers with malaria. The Southwesterners arrested twelve of my troops and took them away and killed them. I assigned a representative to go and argue with Mok, who was the Zone secretary, to confront him." Samrin said he even got his superior, Eastern Zone leader So Phim, to write Mok asking for the soldiers' release, "but Mok resisted and said he didn't know anything about it. . . . We requested a meeting of representatives, for negotiations between the Eastern Zone and the Southwest." The Southwest officials denied responsibility. "They said that region was a rebellious region, and our forces entered; they didn't know whether it was their armed forces or others who had arrested them. We

1. Kenneth Quinn, "The Khmer Krahom Program to Create a Communist Society in Southern Cambodia," US Department of State Airgram, 19 February 1974, pp. 1, 8, 7.

said it doesn't matter whether they had been arrested or not, but we asked for them to be released. . . . They said they wouldn't release them, and that they had been taken away and disappeared. This meant that they had been taken to be killed." The twelve were never seen again. Samrin believes they were killed on Mok's orders, and he dates the bitter relations between Mok and Phim from that point. He adds: "From 1974 we resisted Pol Pot on the question of Vietnam."[2]

Now here is what Quinn, using quite different sources, was able to report at the time: "On November 3 [1973], the KK kidnapped three KR cadre[s] near Angkor Borei Mountain who have not been seen since and were presumably executed." The next day, K.K. cadres from Region 25 (Kandal Province) met with K.R. from Region 24 (Prey Veng). "The KK demanded that the KR (who control the KC movement in Prey Veng) terminate their policy of cooperating with the VC and NVA [Vietcong and North Vietnamese Army] in Area 24. The KR refused, the discussion grew heated, and a firefight ensued. The KR, supported by a nearby VC/NVA unit, killed 42 KK and drove the rest off. Since that time, the KK and KR have conducted raids across the Mekong into each other's territory."[3] If this was not the same incident, it at least confirms that Eastern Zone Khmer Rumdos units were the victims of attacks by CPK forces from other Zones, and that they fought back.

Heng Samrin continues: "From that time on, my troops . . . never again crossed the boundary." The Southwest forces "even brought up guns and set up artillery facing us on the border of Region 25 and the Southwest. There was conflict between us. Not fighting but threatening each other." Samrin also asserts that the CPK secretary of Region 25, Chey (alias Non Suon), "worked with my group, no problem; but he was not in accord with their side. Mok and Chey were not very friendly." In the confession extracted after his arrest in November 1976, Suon indeed recalled that he and Mok "were not close friends": "I never interfered in the Southwest outside Region 25 because I was afraid of Mok."[4] A former member of the Special Zone's 11th Brigade said in 1980 that his units had also been stationed in the area and had clashed with Eastern Zone troops. "They wore green, not black like us, with different caps, and they called us 'cormorants.' . . . They shot two of us in a boat on the river, and after that there were constant reprisal raids, back and forth, day and night." These clashes, the soldier said, had continued right up to the war's end

2. Author's interview with Heng Samrin, Phnom Penh, 2 December 1991.
3. Quinn, The Khmer Krahom Program, pp. 7–8.
4. Non Suon, Phnaek ti pi: royea mun rotpraha 18.3.70, Tuol Sleng confession dated 7 November 1976, p. 3, and Sekkedey sarapeap rebos dop pi (The Confessional Report of No. 12), Tuol Sleng confession dated 28 November 1976, p. 7. Vorn Vet, in his confession, corroborates Suon's disagreement with and fear of Mok. Untitled confession, December 1978, p. 31.

in April 1975.[5] Heng Samrin belonged to the K.R., which Quinn considered a moderate, pro-Sihanouk, communist faction. So did most of the Eastern Zone communists. In 1975, for instance, Chhien's Region 22 troops also displayed antagonism toward the CPK Center, reporting further skirmishes with Center troops.[6]

Heng Samrin was born in 1934, the third of eight children. He is a dark-skinned, round-faced, small but strongly built man with tiny stubs of fingers on his hands. His parents farmed three acres of rice fields with a pair of buffalo and one oxcart. As a poor peasant, Heng Samrin served only a three-month candidacy in 1961 when he joined the underground party. His brothers, Heng Samkai and Heng Thal, also joined the revolution, as did two brothers-in-law. Samrin initially worked as a secret courier for So Phim's Eastern Zone office, taking messages between Phim's headquarters near the Vietnamese border and Phnom Penh. In 1962–63, he met Pol Pot in both locations. He also infiltrated the Sihanouk militia, becoming chief of his village platoon. But in March 1968, Samrin was called in for questioning by his colonel. The Sihanouk regime was cracking down hard. Samrin handed over his platoon's weapons to the district office and, on So Phim's instructions, took to the forest with several hundred Eastern Zone comrades. Three truckloads of soldiers came looking for him, burnt down his house and barn, and threw three village boys into a well, killing them. Samrin served as a medic in the jungle until Sihanouk's overthrow in 1970. He then volunteered for the officer corps of the burgeoning revolutionary army and became a company commander. In 1971–72 he commanded the Eastern Zone's 12th Battalion. His promotion to command of the 126th Regiment, and his prominent role in the capture of Neak Leung and Phnom Penh, would not end his opposition to forces aligned with the Center. Samrin was probably influenced by his Division commander, Chakrey, who was "unhappy with developments" in the CPK, according to reports received by the U.S. embassy in Phnom Penh before the war ended.[7]

Others in the East were even more recalcitrant. In 1974, the CPK disbanded its Muslim Cham front there, the Eastern Zone Islamic Movement. Its head, Sos Man, was a Cham who had spent 1954–70 in Hanoi. He now retired, though his son, Mat Ly, remained a member of a CPK district committee in

5. Author's interview with former 11th Brigade soldier Chhin Phoeun, Kong Pisei, 17 September 1980. See Ben Kiernan, "Wild Chickens, Farm Chickens, and Cormorants: Kampuchea's Eastern Zone under Pol Pot," in David P. Chandler and Ben Kiernan, eds., *Revolution and Its Aftermath in Kampuchea*, New Haven: Yale Southeast Asia Studies Monograph No. 25, 1983, p. 177. In *How Pol Pot Came to Power*, London: Verso, 1985, pp. 388, 400 n. 156, and 416, I mis-described the 11th as a Southwest Division rather than a Special Zone unit.

6. Author's interview with Khieu Sisavoun, a former Lon Nol military policeman who went to Region 22 in 1975. Paris, 30 November 1979.

7. Timothy Carney, personal communication, Bangkok, November 1980.

Region 21. The East was the only CPK Zone that had ever allowed an autonomous Cham organization. Not all Chams took its dissolution lying down. At the end of 1974, James Fenton, who interviewed refugees from Region 21, reported in the *Washington Post*: "A group called the *Khmer Saor*, or 'White Khmers,' had broken away from the Khmer Rouge and taken to the forests. The White Khmers, whose leaders are former Communist officials, are mostly Cham Moslems. They support Sihanouk and oppose collectivization of property. They believe simply in the abolition of middlemen."[8] Further south, in Svay Rieng province, large numbers of communist troops went over to the Khmer Saor, in one case after a CPK unit commander had arrested one of his men. These troops now fought alongside the Vietnamese communists in the border zones, mostly against South Vietnamese forces, but they also commonly clashed with CPK units.[9]

Like Quinn's Khmer Rumdos, Fenton's Khmer Saor were supporters and allies of Prince Sihanouk. But they were also communists. This was not a contradiction, but merely the strategy Hanoi had been pursuing since 1956: supporting Sihanouk's neutralism and nationalism. Whereas the Khmer Saor broke with the CPK before 1975 to continue working with the Vietnamese, the Khmer Rumdos in Prey Veng remained within the CPK fold when Phnom Penh was captured, participating in its evacuation. The Easterners were still seen as closer to Sihanouk than the other CPK forces, but their name, Rumdos, is actually a direct Khmer translation of the Vietnamese *bo doi*, or "liberation" forces.

So the Lon Nol regime was not the only opposition to the CPK. But neither were the various Eastern Zone units the only dissident communists. In April 1975 other groups of rebels, along with large numbers of civilians, held out against the Khmer Rouge in remote parts of the country. These had to be dealt with as Lon Nol and Phnom Penh had been.

Cleansing the West, 1973–75

In January 1974, a telegram arrived at the CPK headquarters in Koh Kong province, on Cambodia's rugged western border with Thailand. The message summoned local CPK leader Prasith to a meeting of the Central Committee. It instructed him to set out without delay.[10] Prasith, codenamed "Chong," ranked seventh in the Central Committee hierarchy. He was also deputy CPK secretary of the Southwest Zone. But the leading position of Zone Secretary was held by his nominal inferior, Mok, who ranked ninth in the Cen-

---

8. *Washington Post,* 24 November 1974.
9. Donald Kirk, "The Khmer Rouge: Revolutionaries or Terrorists?," unpublished 1974 paper, p. 17. Kirk kindly provided me with a copy of this paper.
10. Author's interview with Tea Banh, Phnom Penh, 4 January 1986.

tral Committee. The two had clashed. Mok may have owed his seniority on the Zone Committee to Prasith's ethnic minority status.

A light-skinned ethnic Thai whose father was part Vietnamese, Prasith had led the 1946–54 Issarak anti-French resistance in Koh Kong.[11] The Issarak forces in the province mustered two hundred troops by 1954. After the Geneva Conference, eight of them regrouped to North Vietnam, where they would spend the next sixteen years. These eight Thais included the local Issarak deputy military commander, Sae Phuthang, and two others, Prasath and Oudon. After taking courses in Vietnamese, they studied various military, industrial, and economic subjects. Phuthang trained as a military specialist, mainly on the Chinese-Vietnamese border. Prasath went on to China and trained as a pilot for five years.[12]

Meanwhile, in 1962 Prasith had again taken to the jungle, this time in opposition to Sihanouk's regime. Tea Banh, who followed him then, describes Prasith as "deeply educated." Banh, a thin, wiry, dark ethnic Thai, recalls joining the communist movement at the age of seventeen, in protest at *corvée* labor obligations enforced by Sihanouk's officials in Koh Kong. "So in 1965," he says, "the soldiers came to arrest me." He was jailed with three others and interrogated for a month. Banh escaped. He claims the Sihanouk regime killed over one hundred suspected revolutionaries in Koh Kong that year, mostly by throwing them into the sea.

Three years later, Prasith led an armed uprising. A rebel force of three hundred fighters mustered in the forest, attacked government positions, and ambushed roads. The military repression recommenced. Hundreds of people fled to Thailand, some returning only after Sihanouk's 1970 overthrow by Lon Nol, when the rebels began taking over the countryside.[13] Within a month of

11. Author's interview with Udom Meanchey, Kompong Speu, 6 July 1980. (I am grateful to Chanthou Boua for her notes of this interview, in which Meanchey said: "The struggle began in 1948, in Kampot, Koh Kong, the Northeast, and Stung Treng. In Koh Kong the leaders were Prasith, Prasath, and Oudon. There was a division of thousands of Issarak troops there. In Stung Treng the leader was Sida." Udom Meanchey was born in Koh Kong.) In an interview with the author in Phnom Penh on 8 December 1992, Sae Phuthang said that Prasith had headed the Khmer Issarak administration in Koh Kong, then a district of Kampot province, during the anti-French resistance. He and Tea Banh (1986) both said that another Thai, Nava, was Issarak military commander there. Nava was killed by Sihanouk's forces in 1968.

12. Tea Banh interview, 1986; author's interview with Sae Phuthang, Phnom Penh, 8 December 1992. Phuthang lists the five other Thais from Koh Kong who went to Hanoi in 1954: Somloui, who studied banking and finance; Bunsong, who also went to China for five years to study industry; Amphan and Thom, who studied industry in Vietnam; and Daeng, who became a military officer. All eight returned to Cambodia in 1970–71, but Bunsom, Thom, and Daeng did not go to Koh Kong, and they subsequently disappeared, presumably killed in Pol Pot's purge of Hanoi-trained Cambodians.

13. Tea Banh interview, 1986.

the coup, Sae Phuthang, Prasath, and Oudon set out from Hanoi on the long journey home. Phuthang reached Koh Kong first, in mid-1971.[14] They joined forces with Prasith, who was running a successful insurgency in Koh Kong. By 1973, the Lon Nol regime controlled only the small provincial capital, its airstrip, and four nearby villages. The majority of the province's population of seventy thousand lived in the countryside, home to over forty thousand Thai-speaking fisherfolk and peasants as well as thousands of Khmers. These rural areas of Koh Kong were in the hands of the CPK. The revolutionaries had set up a sophisticated administrative network in the province, which they called Region 11. Prasith supervised a Region CPK committee of seven, headed by a former Issarak subdistrict chief named Von (Tea Banh's father-in-law), and a Region administrative committee of five, headed by Prasath. Most members of the committees were ethnic Thais. Each of the Region's four districts had its administrative committee.

The armed forces were organized at three levels: there were regional forces, district forces, and village militia. The Region chief of staff was Sae Phuthang. Tea Banh recalls: "He went up and down, preparing, observing living conditions, uniforms, ammunition supplies . . . going everywhere and inspecting. He was the person who took the military's plans to the province committee, took the province committee's orders and issued commands to the armed forces." Phuthang, however, declined to serve on the Region 11 Committee, which therefore included no military representative.[15]

The armed forces mustered over one thousand, but Banh's Region 11 battalion contained the only regular units. The battalion was oversized, comprising four companies of 130 to 140 troops, each equipped with six mortars. Two company commanders were Thai, two Khmer. A company of female troops and special forces completed the order of battle. A political commissariat, headed by Rong Chream Kaysone, managed CPK affairs in the battalion and recruited party members among the ranks. Local district forces (forty to sixty troops each) and village militias were separated by ethnic group, with units made up of Chinese, Vietnamese, Thais and Khmers. Organizations of farmers, women, and youth, led by cadres based at the Region headquarters at the river town of Trapeang Roung, brought villagers into the CPK's political network.[16]

One of the differences between Prasith and Zone Secretary Mok concerned

14. Sae Phuthang interview, 1992.

15. "So the enemy did not have his name. . . . It was because he was not on the province committee that he survived," Banh adds. Phuthang agreed that there was no military representative on the Region 11 Committee.

16. Author's interviews: Tea Banh (1986), Sae Phuthang (1992), and Tan Hao, 4 October 1979.

the divergent policies employed by Khmer Rouge forces in Region 11 and neighboring Region 37, both in the Southwest Zone. Tan Hao, an ethnic Chinese woman who lived in both areas, testifies to this. Prasith's Region 11, she recalls, was run by "the free Khmer Rouge" (*khmaer krohom serei*), whereas in Region 37 the Khmer Rouge were "strict." In Region 11, shops remained open, and trade continued with Thailand and Vietnam, mostly in locally caught seafood. In Region 37, "life was difficult," exchange was forbidden, and permission was required to travel. So in late 1972, Hao's family, with "many" others, fled from Region 37 to Region 11. They took up fishing in a more amenable environment. Here, she found, the Khmer Rouge forces "helped the people in the fields." In Thmar Sar, where she lived, the CPK "would ask the people to support them and give them chickens, ducks, fish, rice and money. If we had anything we gave it to them; they didn't force us."

Another source of friction between Prasith and Mok was the presence of Vietnamese communist troops in the area in 1973. In Region 11, Tan Hao continues, "the Khmer Rouge and the Vietnamese cooperated with each other. Some of the local people liked the Vietnamese a lot, because they did many good things. . . . They visited from house to house, and occasionally called the people to meetings and taught them about the use of medicine and how to do injections. They didn't kill anybody; they liked the Khmer people like their own people. They liked the ethnic Chinese too." Members of different ethnic groups usually attended separate meetings. Ethnic Chinese revolutionaries told Hao's group "about struggle and communism, and about the benefits the poor people could gain," if oppression by the rich were ended. "It was appealing; they were trying to change our way of thinking. Some people who had come from China ran away because, they said, the Communist system is hard, but most people went to work with the revolutionaries." In late 1973, Hao says, the Vietnamese troops departed, the ethnic Chinese cadres also disappeared, and the Chinese unit was dissolved.[17] The departure of the Vietnamese following the 1973 Paris Agreement now brought the differences between Prasith and Mok into the open.

Tea Banh takes up the story. "The conflict arose because in Region 37 they were killing people on a large scale and the people of that Region were fleeing to Koh Kong." About five hundred people took refuge in Region 11. Then Prasath "made enquiries and saw that they had done nothing wrong, and asked that they go back to their villages. But those people refused to go. They said if they went they would die. We did not know what to do." In the end the Region 11 administration allowed the refugees to stay, recruiting some of them into its armed forces. But, Tea Banh says, the Khmer Rouge in Region 37

17. Tan Hao interview, 1979.

"feared that Koh Kong had joined hands with the enemy." "This was the start of it. And we resisted. We said that was not true. When the Party Committee of the Southwest Zone could not resolve it, it went to the Center. It was wartime, and we still had no grasp. We placed our hopes in the wisdom of the Center!"

In January 1974, Prasith left Koh Kong for the Central Committee meeting. He was never seen again. Tea Banh recalls: "When they summoned Prasith, they sent forces to arrest him along the way. And he disappeared from that time. . . . " A CPK Center official later boasted that "in 1974 we killed the contemptible Chong."[18] The CPK deputy secretary of Region 37 at the time revealed that Prasith had been "accused of being a Thai spy."[19]

Three weeks later, before Prasith's fate became known to his comrades, another message arrived. The Center announced: "The Central Committee is now in agreement with your stand and views. There is no problem. Would the [Region] committee please come to a meeting at the Zone headquarters in order to discuss and resolve this among ourselves as to who is right and who is wrong." Banh recalls that the message noted the names, "1, 2, 3, . . . " of those summoned.

There were seven names on the list, all ethnic Thais. Prasath, Oudon, and the Region's CPK secretary, Von, Banh's father-in-law, had all been Issarak district chiefs during the struggle against the French. Oudon and Prasath had been trained in Vietnam and China. The message named three other members of the Region Committee and Prachha, head of the Region's commercial branch.[20]

As commander of the Region battalion, Tea Banh assigned a unit to escort the province committee. He recalls: "I was curious. I asked: 'Why have they summoned the whole province committee like this? In the middle of a war, why don't they leave one or two people to take charge of the work?' I was told that this was an order from above. 'We can't refuse, and we all have to go.'" At the halfway point, Banh's escort turned back, and the committee continued on their way. Soon afterwards, other Khmer Rouge forces appeared: "They were waiting to take them away. . . . The seven of them all disappeared, and so did their ten bodyguards. They were all veterans."

18. This statement appears in the diary of a CPK cadre found in Tuol Sleng prison in 1979. The entry is dated 18 August 1978.
19. Chap Lonh, interview with S. Heder, 11–12 March 1980.
20. Tea Banh named two others: Thieu (a.k.a. Boua) and Chanong (a.k.a. Men), "a resistance veteran." Banh does not give the seventh name on the list, possibly suggesting that it may have been Prasith's, which would have been a clever tactic allowing his colleagues to assume, wrongly, that he was still alive and free. Sae Phuthang (1992) named the Region 11 Committee as Chhem (a.k.a. Von, the chairman), Prachha, Oudon, Prasath, and Boua (a.k.a. Thieu). None were military officers.

A month later, Tea Banh remained unaware of what had happened to his father-in-law and the others. Three regiments of the 13th Division now arrived in Region 11. Commanders Prak and Saron, from the Southwest Zone, proclaimed themselves "Center armed forces."[21] The 401st battalion, commanded by Soeun, took up positions at Trapeang Roung, asking Sae Phuthang's forces to feed them.[22]

Tea Banh recalls: "They said they had come down to help us" liberate the region from Lon Nol. "And, as a member of the province command, I came to discuss plans . . . to work with them. . . . I met with them twice. They had us report on the general situation in our province, how much we had liberated, where the enemy still was, and in what areas there were only civilians, and no enemy. We reported on the general situation. Second, we asked them to help us launch a quick final attack. They praised us a good deal. They said we had not received guns from higher up . . . but we had risen up and struggled, and liberated that much already. . . . Then they requested me to accompany their troops to the front. But their aim was to inspect our troops. . . . I showed them."

Still unaware of the newcomers' aim, Banh was quickly caught in a trap. A Center regiment surrounded his battalion. "At my command post they even stationed their Special Forces to block any commands. They surrounded us everywhere." The locals, mustering fewer than two thousand troops throughout Region 11, were outnumbered.

Region chief-of-staff Sae Phuthang decided to fight back. Phuthang secretly visited Tea Banh to discuss the predicament. Banh concedes that "at first I did not grasp it," and he failed to act decisively. But then defectors from the Center camp came to warn him that Prak and Saron intended to arrest "all the leaders" of Region 11. The sweep was planned for 29 April 1974.[23] Now, Banh says, "I knew [but] they knew I knew." Prak and Saron had first tried to convince a member of Banh's bodyguard to shoot him, but the agent changed his mind. Banh brought in a platoon of Special Forces to protect his command post. Then, on the night of April 28, as Center troops moved in for the attack, Banh took to the forest. The attackers found his camp empty the next morning. "At first I did not go far," Banh says; he was hoping to follow events from close by. Others were finding themselves in the same position.

21. *Thoap mocchim*; Tea Banh, 1986 interview. Tan Hao says the new units were called *kang damban* or *kang peak*, "Region [37] forces" or "[Southwest] Zone forces." 1979 interview.
22. Author's interview with Sae Phuthang, 1992.
23. Tea Banh actually said "29 February 1974," but that is impossible. His 1981 official biography says he broke with the Khmer Rouge in April 1974; Sae Phuthang's says *he* did so on 29 April 1974. But to increase the confusion, Sae Phuthang in 1992 said resistance began on "29 May 1974"; this may have been the date of Tea Banh's first attack on the Center forces.

"When they started to arrest and tie people up and kill them," cadres and others "started to break away in small groups." Most took to the forest near their villages.

Meanwhile, Sae Phuthang had begun to organize resistance. A dozen of his troops carried out their first attack on 29 April, storming a post of the 401st battalion at Trapeang Roung. The next group to join him was led by Koy Luon, the Region official in charge of agriculture and mass organizations. They made for the Thai border area, and from there started to contact the scattered survivors and bring them together. Tea Banh and Rong Chream Kaysone, head of the Region 11 military's political commissariat, joined up with them, as did Cha Rieng, chief of the Region supply department. Most of the rebels were ethnic Thais. Exceptions included the two Khmer company commanders in Tea Banh's battalion and Yay Soeui, a battalion medic.[24]

Tea Banh claims that "hundreds . . . perhaps over a thousand" troops and cadres soon took to the forest. Sae Phuthang gives the same figure, noting that over four hundred came from Banh's battalion alone, though fewer members of other Region 11 units joined the rebels.[25] However, Banh says, "Our stars were really inauspicious because our forces were thinly spread." Closest to the Thai border and in the best position to escape the Center troops was a company commanded by Rong Chream Kaysone that had been besieging Koh Kong city from the west. A large force approaching battalion strength and equipped with mortars, Kaysone's unit now moved further west across the rugged border to the Thai village of Cham Yeam, which served as its base from then on.

"At first we thought about the people," Tea Banh claims, "thinking that if we took up arms the enemy might be provoked into even greater anger and could persecute and torture the people. We suspected this, but before we even took up arms, the enemy was already killing the people all the time." The rebels determined to deny the Center a free hand. "We did not yet know where to go," however. "We were very angry."

After preparations in the forest, the Region 11 rebels began to attack. Tea Banh led twenty men in an assault on Dong village, their first battle against a Center unit. He says, "We killed most of them. They retreated." Sae Phuthang's rebels attacked again at Thmar Sar, killing seven Center troops. Fighting continued throughout 1974. "I can't say how many of the enemy we killed. We couldn't go in and count them. But in some places we would find, on one occasion, four or five dead, on another, two or three. We mostly shot at their boats. They would travel by boat and we would shoot at the boats, and they would

24. Sae Phuthang, 1992 interview, and Tea Banh, 1986 interview.

25. Wilfred Burchett, *The China-Cambodia-Vietnam Triangle*, New York: Vanguard Books, 1981, pp. 195–96, puts the figure at only about 200 troops. This may refer to the surviving forces in 1979, though Sae Phuthang (1992) puts that figure at "over 300."

capsize. That would be our victory. . . . We also shot a lot of them dead. . . . Sometimes we would get their guns as well." Sae Phuthang claims his forces killed over ten soldiers of the 401st battalion in the first year. A female CPK officer, wounded and surrounded in Ta Ok village, fired a pistol from the ground as rebels moved in to seize her. They shot the woman dead and discovered U.S.$20,000 on her body. In late 1974, the CPK Center had to send in two companies of reinforcements.[26] The challenge they faced was partly a result of their failure to incapacitate the Region 11 military. Since none of the military commanders had served on the ill-fated Region Committee, virtually all the officers had escaped.

But the Region 11 political administration was cut down in a harvest of death. Center forces took over the countryside, executed local officials, evacuated villages, and transferred populations out of Koh Kong. Sae Phuthang states that during April 1974, his enemies "succeeded in annihilating all the cadres of the Thai minority group and their wives and children, totaling 600 persons."[27] Tan Hao recalls the disappearance of Prachha: "Everybody in Koh Kong was afraid, because their leader had been taken away. . . . Many people fled to Kompong Som, and many others like us wanted to flee but couldn't. From now on, everyone in the village had to go and work together, and it got harder and harder. The Khmer Rouge began killing people; those who did anything wrong were taken away and shot. In 1974 they recruited every youth of sixteen years old or more into the army. If you didn't go they asked you why you didn't love your country and fight for it. Some who didn't go were killed. They were hard."

Remaining members of the Region 11 CPK committee were executed. The last Hanoi-trained cadres still at their posts were killed in May. Sae Phuthang was now the only survivor of the group of ten.[28] Also captured was Region 11's company of female troops. Its members, and a contingent of female medics, were marched to Prey Nup in Kampot province, where they were massacred.

26. Tea Banh, 1986, and Sae Phuthang, 1992. The latter's account of the $20,000 is credible, though it may have occurred after April 1975. Errol de Silva, the first Western journalist to enter Cambodia after April 1975, traveled to Battambang that September. He met Pouvong, one of the three top Khmer Rouge leaders in Battambang, and noticed that Pouvong was carrying about $20,000 in 100-dollar bills. De Silva wrote in the *Bangkok Post*: "I was told the Khmer Rouge have an abundant supply of American dollars all seized when Phnom Penh fell" (24 September 1975).

27. "Report on Some Typical Cases of the Genocidal Crime Committed by the Pol Pot-Ieng Sary Clique against National Minorities in General and the Cham Muslims in Particular," in "A Group of Cambodian Jurists," *People's Revolutionary Tribunal Held in Phnom Penh for the Trial of the Genocide Crime of the Pol Pot-Ieng Sary Clique: Documents (August 1979)*, FLPH, Phnom Penh, 1990, pp. 180–81.

28. Apart from Prasath, Oudon, Somloui, and Amphan, Tea Banh names two other ethnic Thais who had spent the years 1954–1970 in north Vietnam and who were now killed:

Two civilian escapees who made their way to Thailand told Tea Banh that Center units had rounded up their entire village by force. "They tied people up, all together, young and old." Prefiguring the tactics used in the evacuation of Phnom Penh, Center forces told the villagers "that they could not stay there in wartime, due to the shelling and bombing, and so on. They said they were moving them to 'another village,' and along the way they killed them. . . . They killed five hundred people, using one hundred troops who were escorting them. There were so many people . . . they sprayed arcs of fire at them. The bullets cut the rope tying some of them up, and the two escaped and survived." Around mid-1974, another four to five thousand Koh Kong residents fled to the border seeking the protection of the rebels.[29] Many others were killed and wounded attempting to escape. Tea Banh claims: "We sent some troops to meet the people. The enemy followed and we shot at them to liberate the people."[30]

These refugees and the resistance forces, camped along the remote Thai border, all had to be fed. A large new village sprung up at Cham Yeam, out of reach of the Khmer Rouge on the eastern border of Thailand's Khlong Yai province. It had over five thousand inhabitants. Tea Banh explains: "We found shelter there because we had some money, and we contacted Thais who helped us buy food. They would quickly supply us there, after finding out how many of us lived there. . . . The history of the struggle is complicated!" He claims, however, that Thailand provided no aid. "We were self-reliant, exchanging what we could, secretly. We assigned trusted people to tell [Thai traders] to come and sell to us, and we paid them. And we also exchanged some goods with them, commodities we could collect." Jungle products were traded for rice.

Maintaining this existence eventually became the rebels' major concern. After the initial burst of fighting, the rebels committed few forces to the military effort, according to Tea Banh. "Just enough to fend them off, to track them, or pin them down. And we used our main forces to collect timber, beeswax, and rattan. We collected them all in one place and assigned a representative to sell them to the traders . . . so that they would bring us rice."

Sae Phuthang exaggerated when he claimed in 1979 that the resistance

---

Sup and Phum. Bunsong, Thom, and Daeng were apparently killed in other provinces in this period. Udom Meanchey, who also was not in Koh Kong at the time, but had already defected from the Khmer Rouge in Stung Treng province, was a seventh ethnic Thai trained in Hanoi, though Tea Banh did not seem to know his background.

29. This figure, given by both Tea Banh and Sae Phuthang, is corroborated by Thai sources. After the rebels sent the refugees further across the border into Thailand in April 1975 (see below), the *Bangkok Post* reported on 27 August 1975 that 5,093 refugees of Thai origin had arrived in Trat province from Cambodia.

30. Tea Banh, 1986 interview.

had "fully liberated" Koh Kong province in 1974–75.[31] But it is true that Region 11 survived in microcosm. The "free Khmer Rouge" fought on. The leaders—Sae Phuthang, Rong Chream Kaysone, and Cha Rieng—were all second-rank region cadres in their forties. The other rebel commanders were ethnic Thais with one exception.[32] They managed to establish a resistance base that, while not a serious threat to the Center forces in Koh Kong, denied them control of a large section of the population, and also promised continuing military harassment. It was a struggle ignored in the outside world. When I visited Koh Kong in February 1975, a Lon Nol officer explained that Nava, Prachha, and Prasith "have all been killed"; he seemed to claim the credit for the Lon Nol regime. Perhaps he did not know that Nava had been killed by Sihanouk's regime, the others by the CPK Center.

But in April 1975, word came of the Khmer Rouge seizure of Phnom Penh. Koh Kong city was also quickly occupied and evacuated. Lon Nol officers and wealthy people were executed. In late April some units were still holding out on Koh Kong island, opposite the city, but from 16 to 18 May the Khmer Rouge cleared the island. "Well-to-do families were taken out first to trawlers which headed toward the mainland," the Thai press reported.[33] Their fate was unknown.

Within a week of capturing Phnom Penh, the CPK also launched attacks against Sae Phuthang's rebels on the border, posing a serious problem for them and the five thousand people living under their protection. Now free to concentrate on wiping them out, on 25 May 1975 (right after the national meeting in Phnom Penh), the Center launched a new offensive in Koh Kong. The rebels faced a decision. Banh recalls: "We saw that to keep the people living there like that would be disastrous." So on 29 May 1975, "the people all went into Thailand, we sent them[34] . . . We just kept only the resistance fighters who could easily escape into the forest. . . . We entered into a phase of preserving our forces."

But they retained some influence even behind enemy lines. In August 1975 the U.S. embassy in Bangkok, reporting the rebellion of the previous year, said an "astute press observer" believed members of the moderate "local faction" were "now controlling part of the province," under the "direction" of the new rulers. "Indeed, there have been some indications that the Khmer Commu-

31. "Report on Some Typical Cases" in "A Group of Cambodian Jurists," *People's Revolutionary Tribunal*, p. 181.

32. These were Tea Banh, Thong Chan, Koy Luon, and the Khmer, Yay Seuy, who was the youngest and had had the least revolutionary experience; he had joined the communist movement in 1970 at age 21.

33. Bangkok *Nation*, 24 April and 22 May 1975.

34. As noted above, by August 1975 a total of 5,093 Cambodian refugees of Thai origin had arrived in Thailand's Trat province. *Bangkok Post*, 27 August 1975.

nists are hard pressed to protect their convoys" on Highway 4 from Kompong Som port through Koh Kong province to the capital.[35] In 1975–76, according to Tea Banh, the fighting subsided: "We continued to attack but only to a small extent, choosing our targets." Five small military bases were established along the border, each of platoon strength or more.[36]

Important news came in 1975 with a group of refugees, one of whom had died on the trek to the border. Three men had escaped from the CPK troops who had forcibly evacuated the Thai population of Koh Kong, to the north of Kompong Speu.[37] Other ethnic Thai villagers were being moved down the coast to Kampot. Evacuees from the port of Kompong Som were in turn resettled in Koh Kong, with newcomers from Takeo and Kompong Speu. But refugees from Koh Kong "claimed that much of the province has been kept purposely empty."[38]

Villagers like Tan Hao, remaining in Koh Kong, found that the CPK now "communalized everything: pots, pans, tomahawks, axes" and imposed a strenuous twelve-hour workday. In mid-1975, obligatory communal eating was introduced, with over two hundred families using a single mess hall.[39] Rebels could no longer get food from their families at night. Fisherfolk stranded in the mountain air, the ethnic Thai survivors of Region 11 were cut off from their population base; the fish now had no water in which to swim.

Who had ordered this? Information on events inside the country was difficult to obtain. Isolated on the Thai border, Tea Banh did not know who had replaced his murdered father-in-law Von as CPK secretary of Region 11.[40] In Bangkok, the U.S. Embassy knew by mid-1975. "The Chief of the Koh Kong Region is a former sandalwood merchant from the district town of Thmar Bang named Ky (probably an alias), who likes to wear a white uniform. With a group of female Khmer Communists as bodyguards for his vehicle, he is alleged to drink Hennessy cognac and smoke '555' cigarettes."[41]

At a higher level, Tea Banh blames Chou Chet. A member of the Standing

35. "The New Cambodia: Life in the Provinces," Extracts from an Airgram Report by an Officer of the American Embassy at Bangkok, 26 August 1975 (declassified 1978), p. 3.

36. Burchett, *The China-Cambodia-Vietnam Triangle*, pp. 195–96.

37. Charles Twining reports the story of a man who escaped to Thailand in March 1977: "After the town of Koh Kong was emptied in 1975, he was moved three times. . . . The man's family was 200 kilometres inland." See Karl Jackson, ed., *Cambodia 1975–1978: Rendezvous with Death*, Princeton University Press, 1989, p. 136.

38. "Life in Southern Cambodia," Extracts from an Airgram Report by an Officer of the American Embassy at Bangkok, 25 January 1977 (declassified 1978), p. 4.

39. Author's interview with Tan Hao, 4 October 1979.

40. In 1986, Tea Banh still knew only the names of the Center military commanders he had met before his early 1974 flight. Sae Phuthang in 1992 could name only the battalion commander *he* had met.

41. "The New Cambodia: Life in the Provinces," 26 August 1975, p. 3.

Committee of the Southwest Zone CPK Committee, Chet replaced Prasith as deputy Zone secretary.[42] "From what I know, he was the one who was responsible for the strongest conflict with Koh Kong province. And for the order to suppress my group." Chou Chet had previously visited Region 37. Banh had met him in Kompong Seila before the arrest of Prasith. "I went there to meet him. He had the aim to ask me to come take command on Highway 4, but [Region 11] did not let me go."

Chou Chet's role remains unclear. There is no evidence that he visited Koh Kong or that he sent the 13th Division, who announced themselves as "Center" units. We have Banh's testimony that the Southwest Zone CPK Committee "could not resolve" the dispute between Regions 11 and 37, as a result of which the issue "went to the Center." On the Zone Committee, it is not known which side Chou Chet might have taken in the struggle between Mok and Prasith, though presumably there was a deadlock. But we do know from Quinn's report that in 1973 Chou Chet "had his authority and influence reduced because of his pro-NVA and pro-Sihanouk stands, and in fact, was even ambushed and slightly wounded by the KK forces once in late November while travelling with some NVA soldiers on Route 16," in Kampot province.[43] This was just prior to the execution of Prasith. The two victims may have shared political views. Chet may even have genuinely wanted to promote Banh, Prasith's acolyte, to the command of the Highway 4 front at Kompong Seila, though Banh is skeptical: "Had I gone, I don't know what would have happened!"

At any rate it is unlikely that Chet was in a position to move against Prasith, unless under extreme pressure from Mok and the Center to do so. In mid-March 1974, when the repression in Koh Kong was at its height, Chet was in Kampot.[44] Lon Nol intelligence reported that it was Vorn Vet who assumed control of Region 11 in mid-1974.[45] We know that Vet's Special Zone forces included the 11th and 12th Divisions;[46] Prak and Saron's 13th Division probably belonged to the Special Zone as well, which would explain why they announced themselves as "Center" troops. (Southwest Zone forces in 1974 were called the 1st, 2nd and 3rd Divisions.) In August 1975, the U.S. embassy

42. Chap Lonh, interview with Stephen R. Heder, 11–12 March 1980.

43. Quinn, "The Khmer Krahom Program," p. 7.

44. Author's interview with Nou Mouk, Oudong, 26 August 1981.

45. Khmer Republic, Deuxième Bureau, "Evolution de l'Organisation Politico-Administrative et Militaire des K.C. depuis Mars 1970," Feb.-Mar. 1975, p. 5. Vorn Vet is identified here as "Ta Van" (Vorn). Vorn was the code name Sok Thuok used from 1970 to 1975, before assuming the name Vorn Vet in 1976. See Timothy M. Carney, *Communist Party Power in Kampuchea (Cambodia): Documents and Discussion,* Cornell University Southeast Asia Program Data Paper No. 106, 1977, p. 43.

46. Author's interview with Heng Samrin, Phnom Penh, 2 December 1991.

in Bangkok confirmed that Koh Kong province "is said to be firmly in the hands of center-oriented Khmer Communists."[47]

In his 1978 confession, Vorn Vet recalled noticing in 1970 that Region 25 chief Non Suon and Chou Chet were "very friendly" and "in agreement to fight Ta Mok."[48] In March 1974, CPK forces captured Cambodia's nineteenth-century capital, Oudong. On Mok's orders, it was immediately evacuated. A participant recalls: "Forty thousand people were sent in all directions. The Khmer Rouge burnt houses everywhere. . . . Uniformed Lon Nol soldiers were executed along the way."[49] Chou Chet visited the area later in 1974 and dissented from the proposal to evacuate Phnom Penh. A cadre from Oudong recalls: "Chou Chet told us in lectures that when we take Phnom Penh city, there will be no need to evacuate the people from it. All we needed to do was fight the Lon Nol system and the Lon Nol army, and gather up the high-ranking Lon Nol people for reeducation. . . . " Mok and Khieu Samphan had already declared themselves for evacuation.[50] The cadre who in 1974 was deputy secretary of Region 37, launching pad for the attack on Region 11, later stated: "If we had captured Phnom Penh in 1974 there would also have been an evacuation. This had been a long-standing plan; the slogan was 'Dry up the people from the enemy.'"[51] If Chet was in league with Center and Region 37 forces in the suppression of Region 11, it would seem an anomaly. More likely are parallel chains of command. But the destruction of Prasith's Region 11 undermined Chet's position in the Southwest Zone as well as that of any of Prasith's network still in place in Koh Kong. Chet's dissent was weaker than that of Heng Samrin and the *Khmer Rumdos* leaders of the Eastern Zone.

Imposing Central Control in the Northeast

Diagonally across the country from coastal Koh Kong is the most remote highland area of Cambodia. Ending in "the Naga's Tail," a tapered promontory curling into the hills of the Annamite Cordillera between Laos and Vietnam, the northeast is home to an array of national minorities. In Stung Treng province alone the 1986 population of fifty thousand was divided among twelve of Cambodia's twenty-two nationalities.[52] The provinces of Rattanakiri

47. "The New Cambodia: Life in the Provinces," 26 August 1975 (declassified 1978), p. 3.

48. Vorn Vet, untitled confession, December 1978, p. 31.

49. Author's interview with Tim, Oudong, 18 September 1980.

50. Author's interview with Nou Mouk, Oudong, 26 August 1981. Mouk had been a CPK subdistrict cadre.

51. Chap Lonh, interview with Stephen R. Heder, 11–12 March 1980.

52. Speech by Kham Teuang, Stung Treng province president of the United Front for Construction and Defence of the Motherland, to the Fifth Congress of the Front's National Council, Phnom Penh, 21 January 1986. In "The Survival of Cambodia's Ethnic Minorities,"

and Mondolkiri are also ethnolinguistic patchworks. The minority populations of the three provinces in 1975 numbered around ninety thousand. Buddhist, rice-farming Khmer and Lao inhabit the river valleys, and animist upland groups such as Brou, Kravet, Kreung, Kachak, Phnong, and Tapuon hunt game and tend jungle clearings.

The Northeast Zone is of interest not only as a test of the importance of race in cpk politics. It is also the only Zone to have been run directly by Pol Pot, as cpk Zone secretary, from 1968 to 1970, and then by his deputies Ieng Sary and Son Sen. In 1972–3, the Northeast was still "under the direct administration" of the Center.[53]

Kham Teuang is a sixty-three-year-old member of the Brou (or Prov) nationality. Small in stature, his earlobes are elongated and slit in traditional tribal fashion. Besides his native Brou and related tribal dialects, he also speaks Lao and an accented Khmer resembling that of the Cambodian minority in Thailand. He was born in Ta Veng, on the San River, whose watershed shapes the curves of the Naga's Tail. Ta Veng is in Voeunsai district of Rattanakiri province, the far northeast of Cambodia. In 1950, at the age of twenty-one Teuang joined the Indochinese revolutionary movement in Champassak, across the border in Laos, and later became a member of the Lao People's Party. When the French left Indochina in 1954, Vietnamese communists offered to take him to Hanoi for training. "But I did not dare go . . . I said my mother was too old, and there was no one to look after her." Had he gone, he would have been the only Brou to do so. Teuang says about thirty members of minority groups from Cambodia did go to Hanoi then, mostly Lao but also Tapuon, Kreung, and Jarai. In 1958, after a stint as a coolie on a coffee plantation, Teuang recommenced his political activities in Ta Veng. In the late 1950s, he asserts, "the Sihanouk soldiers came killing." Teuang lost his elder brother and a brother-in-law in the repression of 1962. Two years later he joined the underground communist party.

In June 1967, Teuang first met Ieng Sary, who came accompanied by an ethnic Jarai named Thoeun, his interpreter.[54] "Ieng Sary was good then," Teuang recalls. He took Teuang and several others for a political course, held in the secret base of Voeunsai district cpk leader Khliem, a Kreung related to

Cultural Survival, 14, 3, 1990, p. 66, I mistakenly wrote that Teuang had said there were twenty-two nationalities, rather than twelve, in Stung Treng.

53. On Pol Pot, Ieng Sary, and Son Sen's leadership of the Northeast Zone up to at least 1970, see Kiernan, How Pol Pot, pp. 268, 273–5, 308–9, 374. On the Center's continuing "direct administration" of the Zone in 1972–3, see Carney, Communist Party Power, p. 43.

54. Thoeun is described as a Jarai "cadre" accompanying Pol Pot in August 1966 in the untitled confession of Kheang Sim Hon (a.k.a. But), 18 December 1978, p. 10, copy provided by David Chandler.

Teuang. Then they returned together to Ta Veng. Several months later, Pol Pot arrived, with Thoeun and a Jarai bodyguard.[55] He had just been to Vietnam and China. "He came to propagandize in all the subdistricts and villages. At that time he did good things, but he hid [other] things. He was close to the people, young and old. Everyone believed in him." Pol Pot gave a nine-day political course to 150 people, at least three from each subdistrict in the Zone. "From 1967 to 1970 Pol Pot and Ieng Sary kept coming and going" between their headquarters at Andaung Meas ("the golden well"), in Bokeo district, and Ta Pok village in Voeunsai.

In 1969 and 1970, Pol Pot revisited Vietnam and China. He was in Beijing when Sihanouk was overthrown by Lon Nol. He returned home down the Ho Chi Minh Trail. Arriving in the Northeast Zone in mid-1970, Pol Pot joined up with Ieng Sary again. With their entourage of fifty bodyguards, the two CPK leaders stayed two months in Teuang's village, Ta Veng. Pol Pot reorganized political affairs in the Naga's Tail, now a safe liberated area, creating a new administrative unit, Ta Veng district. Its first CPK secretary was Bun Mi, a member of a local minority and one of seventy Hanoi-trained Cambodian cadres who arrived in Ta Veng in 1970.[56] By 1971, all of the thousand Cambodians in north Vietnam since 1954 would return to Cambodia. Pol Pot distrusted this group. He told Teuang: "We are the masters, masters of the territory, because our relatives who have come from foreign countries are under our leadership. This group are not going to command us."

By 1973, Bun Mi had risen to become deputy chief of the Zone's Region 3, under the Region CPK secretary, a man named Kon, whom Teuang describes as an ethnic Khmer appointed "from the network of Pol Pot and Ieng Sary." Region 4 was also headed by a Khmer, Region 1 by a Jarai, and Region 2 by Teuang's Kreung relative. Stung Treng province was run by Chea Keo, another returnee from north Vietnam. The Zone military commander, Bou Thang, and his staff assistant, Seuy Keo, had also spent the years 1954–70 in Hanoi.

On Bun Phan, an ethnic Lao then serving in the Voeunsai district militia, recalls that starting from from 1971, the CPK "collected all the people into one place," ending their dispersed, semi-nomadic way of life. They "gathered everyone to dig dams and grow only rice." The hill people had to put four-fifths of their labor time into rice cultivation. "And religion was made to disappear completely. Anyone who believed in it was killed." Lao were affected by the

55. Pol Pot's Jarai bodyguard was named Chan. Author's interview with Kham Teuang, Phnom Penh, 15 January 1986.

56. Kham Teuang names some of the 70 returnees from Hanoi who came to his village in Ta Veng Subdistrict in 1970 and who later died or were killed: Khliem, Pre, Pheua. According to On Bun Phan, those who survived included Bou Thang, Seuy Keo, Nou Beng, Dy Phin, Kong, Thong Chan, Om Chhuong, Sivung. Author's interview with On Bun Phan, Phnom Penh, 15 January 1986.

destruction of Buddhist wats, but animist shrines were also targeted. "From 1970 they came and propagandized the people not to believe in anything at all. They wiped it all out. . . . Pol Pot personally spoke about wiping out religion."[57] Teuang, like Heng Samrin (see page 57), confirms that Pol Pot did use this language.

At first, small-scale production groups were established to work the land. But in 1971 and 1972, the Khmer Rouge organized "cooperative groups" (*krom sahakor*). Bun Phan says that in Voeunsai, "they collectivized everything, from houses to cattle, buffalo, plates, and pots." In 1972, communal eating was enforced. Teuang's village of Phao consisted of seventy families. "There were two cooperatives. Everything was collectivized: spoons, pots, plates, everything. Each person kept only one plate and one spoon, to be master of. All other goods were taken." For this Teuang blames Kon, the Khmer secretary of Region 3.

On Bun Phan relates that in 1973, the CPK began large-scale killings to enforce their rule. He singles out Vong, the Khmer chief of Region 4, for "spilling a lot of the people's blood." Most vulnerable were the members of ethnic minorities trained in Hanoi. "They searched out those regroupees from north Vietnam. Some were taken to be killed, and [soon] none were left." In 1973 two of them, Zone military commander Bou Thong, an ethnic Tapuon, and his ethnic Kachak staff assistant, Seuy Keo, staged a mutiny in Voeunsai. Thousands of tribal people rose in rebellion, and many fled to the Vietnamese border, where Thong and Keo joined Dy Phin, a Hanoi-trained ethnic Lao military technician who had defected from the CPK in 1971.[58] The CPK political leadership responded with repression, according to Kham Teuang, who was now an official in Ta Veng subdistrict. The authorities alleged that "Ta Veng subdistrict . . . was all 'a CIA group, a Vietnamese contact network.' . . . They talked of 'the Vietnamese enemy,' and were always complaining. At that time they wanted to kill off our group first, before everyone else."

But the CPK targeted other parts of the northeast as well, particularly its ethnic Lao leadership, and especially in neighboring Voeunsai. Those executed included Ta Kien, Voeunsai district CPK secretary, and Thong Nam, Voeunsai's chief of staff, both of whom were Lao; and Nam's assistant Khvong, also of ethnic minority origin. Other Lao to be executed included Kham Phay, a member of the Stung Treng CPK committee, who was accused of being a CIA agent and "massacred together with his family." Higher-level purges took the

---

57. Author's 1986 interview with On Bun Phan.

58. This information comes from Dy Phin's 1981 campaign biography. His 1971 defection from the Khmer Rouge followed that of Udom Meanchey, an ethnic Thai from Koh Kong who had also been trained in Hanoi from 1954 to 1970 and who had then traveled to Stung Treng. Then, he told the author and Chanthou Boua in an interview on 6 July 1980, he "went into the jungle at the end of 1970 with ten others."

lives of Chan Den, an ethnic Lao member of the Northeast Zone Committee, and Thong Samey, "Assistant to the Political Department of the Northeast Zone."[59] In Kratie province in 1974, a CPK district secretary was killed as a "traitor."[60]

Meanwhile, a new Zone secretary was appointed. He was Ney Sarann, a former anti-French leader who had been a schoolteacher in the Sihanouk period. Since 1970 he had been running the office of the CPK Central Committee, at Pol Pot's headquarters in northern Cambodia. Teuang describes him as "big, fat, and pale." Sarann arrived in the Northeast in July 1973 and attempted to smooth over the problem. He made a good impression. He met with Bun Mi and other local officials and invited Teuang to a political course in Stung Treng province. Teuang declined this invitation as he had the one to Hanoi in 1954, saying: "Oh, I dare not go. You go." But Sarann returned to Ta Veng in September 1973.[61] He organized a festival, inviting locals to question him about whatever exercised their curiosity. Teuang stood to speak. He acknowledged the Center's right to make decisions and to resolve conflicts between Regions, districts, and subdistricts. But Teuang added: "As for the future, if anyone makes accusations or claims, or kills people, breaking solidarity and affection . . . I will kill them. But whoever is pure, we'll love each other. In solidarity, we'll live or die together." A blunt message for Ney Sarann.

"Then he asked me to go to study. But I still dared not go. Twelve people went." They included Teuang's nephew, Kham Len, brother-in-law of Bun Mi, and other minority local officials.[62] Teuang was so fearful for them that he escorted them part of the way with sixty troops. "They went to study for a month, then came back." Teuang remained distrustful. "Salt, cloth, medicine, everything [was provided] to cover up their trick, so we could not see it. But my group were also looking for methods to prevent them from knowing that we wanted to flee the country." Bun Mi soon defected to Vietnam, joining Bou Thong and Seuy Keo on the border.

In early 1974, Teuang claims, Pol Pot assigned three Brou men to find and arrest him.[63] "I nearly died. . . . But I had a little luck. . . . When I was in the

59. "Report on Some Typical Cases" in "A Group of Cambodian Jurists," *People's Revolutionary Tribunal*, p. 179.

60. Timothy Carney, personal communication to Stephen Heder, 24 March 1980. The secretary's name was Chhun Yong (a.k.a. Chek); he was killed in 1974 and replaced by Ny Phan.

61. Teuang says September 1974, but this is unlikely, for reasons made clear below. I have assumed it was 1973, when Ney Sarann reportedly took up the post of CPK secretary of the Northeast Zone. Kiernan, *How Pol Pot*, p. 407, n. 331.

62. Of the twelve, Teuang names Kham Len, Veng Khuon, Thav Ngon, Khim Sai, Chreng, Suon, Kham Teu, and Kota. At least the first three were Brou. (According to Sae Phuthang, Bun Mi married Kham Len's younger sister. Interview with the author, Phnom Penh, 8 December 1992.)

63. The men's names were Chen Ven, Chhoeun, and Ut.

office, they did not come. . . . When I left the office to go to the district office
. . . they came to the subdistrict office to arrest me. They came and went, came
and went, and did not get me." On 20 March 1974, with his family and with
four other local officials who had all taken Ney Sarann's political course,
Teuang quit his post.[64] He returned briefly to his native village, where he met
up with On Bun Phan, who claims that by then he had already led the troops
from the Voeunsai district military post en route to the border. The dissidents
now numbered about five hundred troops and civilians, from seven nationalities.[65] They all joined forces and trekked for a week through the jungles of the
Naga's Tail. "The Pol Pot forces came after us, and shot five people dead on the
way, a militiaman and four civilians," Teuang says.

At the border, they met up with Bun Mi, Bou Thong, and Seuy Keo's rebel
forces and a large number of other dissidents. The refugees now totaled five
thousand civilians and five hundred armed troops from Regional, district, and
subdistrict units. The largest group were Brou, but there were also ethnic Lao,
Lun, Kreung, Tapuon, Kravet, and Kachak and a few Chinese. Interestingly,
ethnic Khmer and Jarai seem to have been missing from this muster. Nearly
all the refugees were from Voeunsai and Ta Veng districts in Rattanakiri, but
some came from Stung Treng and Mondolkiri provinces.[66]

The problem now, according to Teuang, was "Who would accept us? Laos
and Vietnam did not yet accept us. The world did not yet accept us." More
refugees kept arriving at the border.[67] The months went by with no prospect of
a solution. As the anticommunist regimes tottered in Vietnam and Laos, and
the CPK began to close in on Phnom Penh, the dissidents on Cambodia's northeastern border faced the same problem as those at the Thai border. After victory over Lon Nol, the new regime would turn to complete suppression of its
other opponents. The rebels decided to split up and leave Cambodia. Teuang
recalls the choices: "We didn't know the language in Vietnam, but we had

64. 20 March 1974 is the date given in Veng Khuon's official biography for his flight from
the Khmer Rouge. Kham Teuang gives no specific date in 1974, but says the two fled together,
along with Khim Sai, Chreng, and Suon. Chreng died in 1974.

65. On Bun Phan says they included Kravet, Kachak, Kreung, Tampuon, Brou, Lao, and
four Chinese.

66. Nou Beng, a Hanoi-trained ethnic Lao doctor, came from Stung Treng. Teuang names
one man, Chhoeun, from Mondolkiri. Teuang and On Bun Phan both say that "everyone,"
"all of Voeunsai district" joined the exodus. Teuang says there were "no Khmer" among the
refugees. He and On Bun Phan (see previous note) both provide lists of ethnic groups represented, but neither cites any Jarai.

67. On 27 December 1974, probably the most senior ethnic minority cadre, Thong Bai, a
Tapuon who had joined the Indochinese communist movement in 1941 at the age of nineteen, defected to the border. In 1975, Brou cadres Thav Ngon and Kham Len followed suit.
This information comes from official biographies published during the 1981 election campaign. Thong Bai died in 1984.

many relatives in Attopeu, in Laos. So we changed course and went there. Veng Khuon and I went to Attopeu with 2,999 people. . . . And 2,000 went to Vietnam [with] Bun Mi, Bou Thong, and Seuy Keo." Teuang's group left in April 1975 and reached Attopeu on 25 May. A new order began for the minority peoples of Cambodia's Northeast Zone.[68]

Teuang looks back on this period with relief informed by hindsight. "We had observed the enemy's ruse . . . and escaped. Had we not seen it, we'd be all gone now." Significantly, though, Teuang retains some admiration for Ney Sarann (alias Ya), the Zone secretary, whom he says Pol Pot now held responsible for having allegedly "organized our group to flee the country." On Bun Phan even suggests that "Ya's aim was to take refuge on the border too," following "frequent contacts" with Bun Mi in 1973. Pol Pot's charge really betrays an accusation of excessive tolerance, with which Teuang might agree: "Ya did not kill people. He was good." On Bun Phan adds: "Ya used to be a member of Pol Pot's Center. But Ya could not go this way, or come that way. . . . He didn't jail and kill people. . . . The majority of the people had nothing against him. They liked him."[69]

By 1975, the CPK Center had effectively Khmerized the administration of the areas with significant minority populations: the Eastern, Western and Northeast Zones of Cambodia. It had destroyed the autonomous Cham, Thai, and northeastern tribal minority organizations and administrations in those Zones. But as with the defeat, evacuation, and Khmerization of Phnom Penh, the purges created many new enemies. And the CPK itself contained a substantial body of dissident opinion.

The New Regional Administrations

At the time of the April 1975 victory, the country was divided into six Zones: the Southwest, the East, the Northeast, the North, the Northwest Zones and the Special Zone around Phnom Penh. *The Special Zone* spearheaded the Center's pursuit of direct military and political power in the countryside, a process begun with Pol Pot's, Ieng Sary's, and Son Sen's personal command

68. Meanwhile, Kea, another of Pol Pot's former bodyguards from a northeastern ethnic minority, slipped out of Phnom Penh and fled back to his village in Mondolkiri.

69. In February 1993 interviews with Sara Colm, Rattanakiri's State of Cambodia governor, Lak Aun, a provincial official in the Sihanouk period, agreed: "From 1970 to 1975, the Khmer Rouge did not kill people. Even though my father had been a policeman under Sihanouk, they didn't kill him. At the time, the Khmer Rouge helped the people . . . while the Americans were bombing here and hurting the people. The people stayed on the side of the Khmer Rouge and thought the Americans were bad." On Bun Phan blames CPK cadres Vong, Khmau, and Phainh for the repression. "It was only the Regional chiefs who mistreated the people, especially chiefs of the cooperatives. District, subdistrict, village and Region [officials] reported to their superiors, who decided to arrest people and kill them."

of the Northeast from 1968 to 1973. The Special Zone had been carved out of the East and Southwest Zones in 1971. Region 25 south of Phnom Penh was taken from the East, Regions 15 and 33 from the Southwest. The Special Zone's secretary was Vorn Vet; Son Sen was his deputy. They controlled the 11th, 12th and 13th Divisions. The 11th and 12th were commanded by Saroeun and Tith Nath, Son Sen's nephew.[70]

The Southwest Zone initially comprised the provinces of Takeo, Kampot, Kompong Chhnang, Koh Kong, and Kompong Speu. Mok was the Zone secretary. Mok, a tall, thin, light-skinned, grey-haired, balding man, had been a guerrilla leader near his home in western Tram Kak district, Takeo province, during the anti-French war. French officials accused rebels there of "exactions against the population," and a former monk concurs that Mok would "kill ordinary people" as well as political enemies.[71] Mok met Pol Pot in the early 1960s, apparently while attending Phnom Penh's Buddhist institute of learning, the Higher School of Pali, at Wat Unnalom.[72] Promoted to the Party Central Committee in 1963, he became Southwest Zone secretary in 1968 after his predecessor died in the jungle.[73]

Mok carefully placed a network of family members in various important positions in his Zone. These included two brothers-in-law, four sons, two daughters, and five sons-in-law. They were all promoted through the ranks, most after serving time in Mok's home district, Tram Kak, known as District 105 of Region 13. As we saw in Chapter 1, Mok's son-in-law, Khe Muth, had begun his career as CPK secretary of Tram Kak and had also become deputy secretary of Region 13. In 1973 Muth rose to become secretary of the 3rd Southwest Division. Mok's daughter, Khom, replaced her husband Muth as CPK secretary of Tram Kak District. In 1975 another daughter, Ho, became director of the Region 13 hospital. Two sons, Cham and Chay, also served on the Tram Kak CPK district committee, and a brother-in-law, San, a former schoolteacher, was a leading CPK official. A second brother-in-law, Tith, was CPK secretary of Kirivong (District 109). A third son, Chong, was CPK secretary of District 55 (Prey Krabas). A fourth son, Kol, was a leading official in Kampot province, or Region 35 of the Southwest Zone. A second son-in-law, Boran, began his career as a courier for the CPK Center and then in 1975 took charge of a new factory in Tram Kak. A third son-in-law, Soeun, commander of Region 13's

70. Laurence Picq, Au-delà du ciel: Cinq ans chez les Khmers Rouges, Paris: Bernard Barrault, 1984, p. 163, says Nath (alias Ny Kân) is Son Sen's brother.

71. Picq, Au-delà du ciel, p. 133; Kiernan, How Pol Pot, p. 86.

72. Author's interviews with Yusof, Kompong Tralach, 5 September 1980, and Nou Mouk, Oudong, 26 August 1981.

73. The first Southwest Zone secretary was Mar (a.k.a. Nhim) (a.k.a. Moong?). His death from illness was reported to Tea Banh by Prasith at the time. (Author's interview with Banh, 1986.)

120th Regiment, was promoted to division commander in 1975. A fourth, Ren, was a brigade commander in 1975.

Tram Kak was the most "ideologically advanced" district in Cambodia. Muth and Khom introduced communal eating there as early as May 1973, bringing the district official cpk praise as the pioneer of collective mess halls.[74] But the project failed. People ate "banana leaves, sugar-palm roots, coconuts, and finally weeds." Then, a Southwest trooper recalls, "people rebelled, killing cadres." The cpk gave in, again permitting private eating.[75] But Region 13 cadres announced plans to build "a new capital," adding that the "old one, Phnom Penh, would be destroyed."[76]

Mok also managed to get family members promoted to positions outside the Zone, through his connections with the Center. In 1975, Ho's husband Vin, Mok's fifth son-in-law, became a commander at Pochentong Airport outside Phnom Penh. Son-in-law Khe Muth retained command of the 3rd Southwest Division and also became cpk secretary of Kompong Som city and commander of the DK navy.[77]

Chou Chet, Mok's deputy and rival, was a thin, short, dark-skinned revolutionary. In 1954 he had been an Issarak delegate to the Joint Commission for the Implementation of the Geneva Accords in Cambodia. He edited leftist newspapers in Phnom Penh and was jailed by Sihanouk in 1960 and again from 1962 to 1963. During his second prison term, he was overlooked for promotion to the cpk Central Committee in favor of Mok. Chet took to the jungle in the mid-1960s. In a 1973 defector's account he was named as "Chairman" of the Southwest Zone.[78] This may have been a temporary compromise between Chet and Mok. Kang Chap, cpk secretary of Region 35 (Kampot province), was the third member of the Zone Standing Committee. Candidate members included Sem Pal and Thuch Rin.

In mid-1975, the Southwest Zone was divided between Mok and Chet. Mok retained the bulk of the populous areas, Takeo and Kampot in particular.

74. Author's interview with Chhin Phoeun, Kong Pisei, 17 September 1980.

75. Author's interview with Ieng Thon, Tram Kak, 16 July 1980.

76. Donald Kirk, "Communism and Political Violence in Cambodia," in J. J. Zasloff and MacAlister Brown, eds., *Communism in Indochina: New Perspectives*, Lexington, Mass.: Lexington Books, 1975, pp. 222–23; and Kirk's draft paper, "The Khmer Rouge: Revolutionaries or Terrorists?," presented at the conference that led to the volume.

77. Information on Mok, his family, and their positions comes from the author's interviews with a cpk member from 1973 and DK subdistrict chief, Kirivong, 25 August 1980; a cpk member since 1973 and DK subdistrict committee member, Kong Pisei, 17 September 1980; and Chon, Takeo, 16 July 1980; author's interviews in Kampot, 29 August 1980; and Stephen Heder's interview with a Region 13 cadre, Sakeo, 8 March 1980. (On Soeun, see Kiernan, *How Pol Pot*, p. 415, and "Orphans of Genocide," *Bulletin of Concerned Asian Scholars*, 20, 4, 1988, p. 26.)

78. Carney, *Communist Party Power*, p. 43.

The Special Zone was also divided, with most of it, Regions 33 and 25, going to the Southwest. Chou Chet came off second best. With Region 15 and the largely barren, hilly areas of Koh Kong, Kompong Speu, and Kompong Chhnang, he got what the Center called "our poorest Zone, having poor soil and little water."[79] Mountains, forests, and inhospitable coastline in the west dominate low-rainfall, sandy-soil plains in Kompong Speu and Kompong Chhnang. The latter province is watered by the Sap River, which has great fishing potential but floods large areas for several months each year. Chou Chet became CPK secretary of the new *Western Zone*, with Pal as his deputy. Paet Soeung became Zone military commander and the member of the CPK Zone committee in charge of security.[80]

Chou Chet's wife, Li, held an important position in the Western Zone, but Chet did not pepper his Zone administration with close relatives as Mok did. Chet lived in a village of thatch huts surrounded by coconut trees a few miles north of Highway 4 in Kompong Speu. By contrast, Mok began building himself a large new three-story brick headquarters on an island in a lake just north of the city of Takeo. It was linked to the shore by an earthen causeway. (See photos 7, 8.)

The Eastern Zone comprised the former provinces of Svay Rieng, Prey Veng, and eastern Kompong Cham, plus Chhlong district of Kratie. The Zone bordered Vietnam in the east and the Mekong River in the west. Most of it is rice land, watered by the Mekong and Tauch Rivers. Prey Veng, Cambodia's second largest rice-growing province in the 1960s, probably retained this position in DK. Except for some large forests in the north of the Zone near Kratie, the East is well populated.

Like other Zones (*phumipeak*) the East was divided into Regions (*damban*), numbered twenty to twenty-four. The Regions were divided into thirty districts (*srok*),[81] each district into subdistricts (*khum*), and each subdistrict into villages (*phum*). Unlike in other Zones, Eastern districts were known by their traditional names, not by numbers. CPK local committees, usually of three members each, controlled the administration at every level.

The Eastern Zone was headed by So Phim, its CPK secretary. Phim was a round-faced, stocky man, about 1.8 meters tall, with dark brown skin and

79. Phnom Penh Radio, in United States Central Intelligence Agency, Foreign Broadcast Information Service [FBIS], Asia Pacific, 31 January 1978, p. H11. Pol Pot said in a speech to Western Zone cadres in June 1976 that "there are mountains everywhere and the soil does not have much fertility." See Boua, Chandler, and Kiernan, eds., *Pol Pot Plans the Future: Confidential Leadership Documents from Democratic Kampuchea, 1976–77*, New Haven: Yale Southeast Asia Studies Monograph no. 33, 1988, Document No. 2.

80. Author's interview with Moeung Sonn, Sarcelles, 25 October 1979.

81. Author's interview with Heng Samrin, Phnom Penh, 7 December 1992.

straight black hair. He was a former Issarak officer with the curt, peremptory voice of a soldier.[82] Phuong, his deputy, and Suas Nau, alias Chhouk, secretary of Region 24 (Quinn's *Khmer Rumdos* stronghold), completed the Zone Standing Committee. Candidate members included Sin So, secretary of Region 23 (Svay Rieng), and Chhien, commander of the 3rd Zone Division. In September 1975, the Eastern Zone Committee was revamped by the Center. Phuong was dropped as deputy secretary and replaced by Chan (Seng Hong), up to that time CPK secretary of Region 21 (eastern Kompong Cham). Chhouk was dropped from the Standing Committee and replaced by Chhien. Two new members, Sin and Piem, joined Chhouk and Sin So as candidate members.[83]

So Phim's wife, Kirou, a familiar figure to many Eastern Zone cadres, did not occupy a leading position. There are no reports of nepotism on So Phim's part. Several of his nephews trained in Hanoi from 1954 to 1970, including an artillery officer named Kim Teng who became a brigade commander. In 1974, Teng was arrested and killed by Center forces. So Phim could not save him.[84] Phim had a national kin connection: his daughter married the son of the Northwest Zone CPK secretary, Moul Sambath.[85] But his position in the Eastern Zone was a function of his political organization, not clan loyalty.

The Northeast Zone was headed by Ney Sarann. His deputy and military commander, Um Neng (alias Vy), and the three other members of the Zone Committee, were all ethnic Khmers.[86] So were at least two of the six Region chiefs.[87] Unlike in other Zones, however, minority people retained some authority. The new head of Region 1 was the Jarai, Thin, who had served as Pol Pot's interpreter in 1967 and had replaced another Jarai, Loeun, who had been executed; and Phoi, a Brou, had replaced Bun Mi as military commander of Region 3.[88] In 1975, Ney Sarann was transferred to Phnom Penh

82. Ibid. Nayan Chanda, *Brother Enemy: The War after the War. A History of Indochina Since the Fall of Saigon*, New York: Harcourt Brace Jovanovich, 1986, calls Phim "a pudgy, round-faced peasant" (p. 250).

83. Author's interview with Ouch Bun Chhoeun, Phnom Penh, 30 September 1980.

84. See Kiernan, "Wild Chickens," in Chandler and Kiernan, eds., *Revolution and Its Aftermath*, pp. 158–60, for details.

85. Author's interview with Heng Teav, Phnom Penh, 14 January 1986. Moul Sambath's son was named Khnang, alias Kriel or Chiel. Teav did not know the name of So Phim's daughter. The East did have political marriages: Phuong's daughter married Region 21 security chief Yin Sophi, and Heng Samrin's sister was the wife of Region 21 committee member Chen Sot.

86. Their names were Khen, Vung, and Khmau.

87. These were the CPK secretary of Region 4, Vong, and the head of Kratie province (Region 505), Sim Son. Author's interviews with Kham Teuang and On Bun Phan, 1986; and U.S. Central Intelligence Agency, 23 April 1975, p. H3, quotes Phnom Penh Radio as describing Sim Son as "chairman of the NUFC Committee of Kratie province." He was later appointed D.K. ambassador to Pyongyang. He was killed by a falling tree near the Thai border in 1989.

88. Author's interviews with Kham Teuang and On Bun Phan, 1986. Timothy Carney

and replaced by Um Neng. The next year the Zone was reduced in size, with Kratie becoming "autonomous" Region 505, under more direct Center control. *The Northern Zone* CPK secretary was Koy Thuon, and Ke Vin (Ke Pauk), Zone military commander, was deputy. Like Mok and Chou Chet, these two were rivals, and after 1975 Pauk won out in the North. Like Mok, his fellow warlord in the Southwest, Pauk was able to take advantage of his command of the Zone military forces and of his ability to appoint relatives to leading administrative positions.

Pauk was born in Baray, Kompong Thom, in 1935. His parents had thirteen other children from previous marriages; he was the only child they had together. His father Keo Ke, a "lower middle peasant" with three to four hectares of rice land, died in the 1940s when Pauk was about fifteen. A year in Buddhist *wats* gave Pauk his only schooling. In 1950 he joined the anti-French Issarak movement. He was arrested in 1954 and sentenced to six years in jail. Released after three years in Kompong Thom and Phnom Penh prisons, he returned home, married a woman from a nearby village, and started a family there. They had at least six children. In his late twenties, Pauk remained almost illiterate, supplementing the income from one hectare of rice land, according to a local, by "selling alcohol, buying chickens, and doing political work." But in 1964 he was "attacked by police and driven into the forest." His career as a CPK warlord now began.

Koy Thuon, a former journalist and schoolteacher who joined the party in 1960, took to the forest in the same period. He was appointed CPK secretary of the Northern Zone, with Pauk as his deputy and military chief of staff. Opinions differ on their qualities. A Pauk supporter claimed in 1980: "Pauk and Koy Thuon did not get along. Pauk was good at commanding troops and fighting the enemy whereas Koy Thuon was good at theory but afraid of going down into the battlefield. So the troops liked Pauk better."[89] By contrast, an admirer of Koy Thuon recalls him as "a good man, [who] allowed the people to trade," established village associations and mutual aid teams, and "favored money, schools, and religion." And, though Pauk may have been popular with the troops, the commanders of three Northern Zone divisions were all protégés of Koy Thuon.[90] In 1975, however, Thuon was transferred to Phnom Penh, and Pauk replaced him as CPK Zone secretary. Cho Chhan (alias Sreng) became Pauk's deputy.

---

offers the names of two later members of the Northeast Zone CPK committee: Tim, alias Chhean Chuon (arrested 1978), and Bun Than, alias Chan (arrested February 1977). These two may possibly have been Thin and Chan, who Teuang says had been Pol Pot's Jarai interpreter and bodyguard, respectively, in 1967.

89. Interview with Stephen Heder in Sakeo, 9 March 1980.

90. Author's interview in Kompong Svay, 16 October 1980; and Heder interview, Sakeo, 9 March 1980.

The Northwest Zone consisted of Battambang and Pursat provinces, far from the major battlefields of the 1970–75 war. Batttambang was the country's biggest rice-exporting region. The Zone secretary was Ros Nhim (Moul Sambath), and Keu was his deputy. Members of the Zone Committee included Khek Penn (Sou) and Heng Teav.

The Struggle for Control at the Center: 1975

Hong was twenty-seven when the war ended. His father, a trader, had been a Lon Nol soldier in his home village outside Sisophon, near the Thai border in Battambang. Khmer Rouge entered the village on 17 April 1975. Eighteen families of urban evacuees soon followed. The men, all soldiers, were quickly arrested, tied up, told they were being taken to another village, and massacred a kilometer away. On 1 May, fifty-nine villagers were arrested, including Hong, his parents, and five brothers and sisters. They too were told they were moving to another village, for former "big officials." Hong lied to the troops, saying that he was only a cousin. They let him go home, but Hong's family and the other fifty-one people were killed that day. Hong estimates that one hundred people were executed in his village in 1975, mostly former soldiers and officials.[91] Similar massacres, particularly of former military officers, occurred elsewhere in Battambang and other provinces in the same period. By late August 1975, however, the U.S. embassy concluded in Bangkok from refugee testimony that with the exception of the Pailin area, after "the first month" of Khmer Rouge rule, "reports of the willful killing of former government officials and soldiers more or less ended."[92]

Indeed, a few months after the evacuation of the cities, independent sources reported that central authorities had ordered an end to killings. According to an account in the *Bangkok Post* on 25 June 1975: "A former diplomat who escaped with 11 members of his family reported that on May 31 a Khmer Rouge official stopped him about 30 miles from the Thai border and told him: 'You are lucky. Three days ago we received instructions not to kill any more people of the old government.'" The same newspaper reported on 23 July that, according to "a Vietnamese in Phnom Penh on official business," "soldiers have been ordered to stop killing people without proper investigations and authority."[93] A refugee who escaped in 1976 reported being told by local

---

91. Author's interview with Hong, Alençon, 3 October 1979.

92. "The New Cambodia: Life in the Provinces," Extracts from an Airgram Report by an Officer of the American Embassy at Bangkok, 26 August 1975 (declassified in 1978), p. 8.

93. The Vietnamese official, whose identity is unknown, added that "thousands had been shot dead by the Cambodian communist soldiers" and that some killings continued even after the order to stop. *Bangkok Post*, 23 July 1975.

cadres of their executions of former government officials, but said they added that in May 1975 the regime had ordered an end to these killings.[94] The wife of a Lon Nol trooper in Battambang concurred, saying that orders came from Phnom Penh "in April or May" to stop killing members of the defeated army and administration.[95] In 1980 Michael Vickery interviewed a refugee from southwest Cambodia: "Van, one of the most careful reporters I met among the refugees, and who was relatively positive toward life in Democratic Kampuchea, claimed that during the first six months after April 1975, orders had been issued from Phnom Penh to kill urban evacuees indiscriminately. He had obtained this information from an elder brother, a base peasant, whose son and Van's nephew was a high-ranking DK officer who worked at the Phnom Penh airport after the war. Later, during a trip home to visit his family, he mentioned the execution order and said that it had been countermanded in October 1975 by another order forbidding lower levels of cadre to kill at all without instructions from above." A village chief in the northwest, an "old revolutionary," corroborated this, reporting that "in April indiscriminate killing was allowed, but in October an order came forbidding it."[96]

So in Phnom Penh from May to October 1975, several attempts were made to end or at least limit the killing, not entirely successfully. The CPK Center[97] was either struggling to maintain control or temporarily outmaneuvred by different government organs or factions. The Center, different Zone administrations, the mysterious commissar who arrived in the capital on the plane from the East, the unidentified "Suon," and the military-dominated "Phnom Penh Committee" of which Nhiem was vice president are all possible authors of the series of orders. Their drift was clear: to limit the number of executions and the ability of lower levels to carry them out. A closer look at this period highlights the Center's careful approach to consolidating its power.

94. *The Early Phases of Liberation in Northwest Cambodia: Conversations with Peang Sophi*, by David P. Chandler, Ben Kiernan, and Muy Hong Lim, Monash University Centre of Southeast Asian Studies, Working Paper No. 11, 1976, p. 9. I cited this and the two 1975 *Bangkok Post* accounts in "Social Cohesion in Revolutionary Cambodia," *Australian Outlook*, 30, 3, 1976, p. 34, n. 13, as evidence for my view at the time that the violence was mostly spontaneous, consisting of postwar, local revenge killings.

95. Her husband was put to work in the fields with over 3,000 other Lon Nol soldiers in Battambang village, where she joined him in September 1975 before their December escape to Thailand. Interview with the author, Flers, 9 October 1979.

96. Vickery, *Cambodia 1975–1982*, pp. 98–99, 112.

97. Whereas the term *Center* technically invokes the authority of the CPK Central Committee, there is no evidence that such a body met, in plenary session or as a body on any other occasion during the life of DK. The term *Party Center* thus refers to members of the Standing Committee of the Central Committee with national responsibility, not specifically responsible for a *regional* area such as one of the Zones of the country. These people included Pol Pot, Nuon Chea, Vorn Vet, Ieng Sary, Son Sen, and Khieu Samphan.

First, the Special Zone was abolished. Its leaders, Vorn Vet and Son Sen, moved their headquarters to Phnom Penh and brought Non Suon. Suon's Region 25 was not returned to the Eastern Zone, but transferred to the Southwest. Suon took up a position at the National Bank, with a seemingly limited future given the May decision to abolish the *riel*. A subsequent decision reversed the order, however. A September 1975 Center document reveals the following: "Will we use this new *riel* or not? At the last meeting we decided to use it so that the people see our new state power, because finance is the instrument of state power." The newly minted currency was therefore "given to a number of large Zones to use it gradually."[98] Who was behind this new decision remains a mystery. Presumably Non Suon's presence in Phnom Penh had some influence.

On 22 July 1975, another important meeting was held in the capital. This marked "the founding of the Revolutionary Army of Kampuchea throughout the country, that is, the ceremony where the different Zones handed over their armed forces to the Central Committee."[99] So the Special Zone, geographically dissolved, simply expanded its command of CPK regular units. Non Suon recalled this meeting in his prison confession the next year: "I was very disappointed not to see Achar Sieng [Ney Sarann] in the Politburo as I had hoped. . . . I was worried that the Organization did not trust me, because it had taken me away from my base area."[100]

At the 22 July meeting, Pol Pot made a long speech to "3,000 Revolutionary Army unit representatives of the CPK Central Committee." He asserted: "We have won total, definitive, and *clean* victory, meaning that we have won it without any foreign connection or involvement. We dared to wage a struggle on a stand completely different from that of the world revolution. . . . In the whole world, since the advent of the revolutionary war and since the birth of U.S. imperialism, no country, no people, and no army has been able to drive the imperialists out to the last man and score total victory over them [as we have]. Nobody could." Revolutionary elation was high: "The U.S. imperialist retreat in panic from Kampuchea was filmed and shown to the whole world." This victory was "a precious model for the world's people." Not all was yet in order, however. Pol Pot announced that "the immediate missions that you comrades

98. "Pinit kar kdap ning anuvatt meakea noyobay sdar settekec ning reap com khosang prates krup phnaek" ("Examine the Control and Implement the Political Line to Save the Economy and Prepare to Build the Country in Every Field"), "Document no. 3," dated 19 September 1975, p. 22. Translation by Chanthou Boua.

99. *Livre Noir: Faits et preuves des actes d'agression et d'annexion du Vietnam contre le Kampuchéa*. Phnom Penh: Département de la Presse et de l'Information du Ministère des Affaires Etrangères du Kampuchéa Démocratique, Sept. 1978, p. 97. (Henceforth *Livre Noir*. This is a different version from a later English translation published under the title *Black Paper*.)

100. Non Suon, *Chamlaiy XII* (2), Tuol Sleng confession dated 22 November 1976, pp. 3–4.

are fulfilling at present, such as the defence of Phnom Penh, . . . are meant to
. . . wipe out intelligence networks and eliminate saboteurs who attempt to
destroy our revolution."[101] It was later claimed that during this meeting, "the
enemy plotted to assassinate the leaders of the Communist Party."[102]

After the July ceremony, Heng Samrin went back to Prey Veng. In late May,
the Eastern Zone had withdrawn the 2nd and 3rd Divisions from the capital,
leaving only Chakrey and Samrin's 1st Division.[103] For three months Samrin
studied military matters under Son Sen, who lectured about "building the
army, making the army tough and strong." At the July meeting, the 1st Division was officially handed over to the Center, and renamed the 170th. It came
under the command of Son Sen, who was named deputy prime minister in
charge of national defense.[104] But Sen did not retain Heng Samrin. He sent him
back to the East without his troops, who were ordered "to grow rice at Prek
Eng," south of Phnom Penh. Samrin's unit had to abandon its equipment in
the capital. Each soldier could take two bundles of possessions. The army confiscated everything but monosodium glutamate, toothpaste, and hoe heads.[105]
Agriculture seemed the new battlefield for Chakrey's division. Samrin was
given command of the Eastern Zone's 4th Division, based in Prey Veng. His
brother Thal and his 2nd Division were brought into the Center army along
with the 1st. Meanwhile, units of three Center divisions from the North "were
put into the East patrolling the border from Rattanakiri to Svay Rieng."[106] This
established the first strong Center presence in the Eastern Zone.

Pol Pot visited the East on 5 September. So Phim traveled to Chhouk's
Region 24 office to meet him. Non Suon, who had also come from Phnom
Penh, recalled the meeting in his confession. He gives the impression of having
been intimidated by Pol Pot's presence, because Chhouk asked him about Sok
and Chamroeun, two Region 25 officials Suon had described as "the men I
trusted." His reply was apparently insincere. "I said they had been 'taken care
of.' They were immoral." Soon after, a member of Suon's staff revisited Region
25, and returned with the news that "the cadres were discouraged because one
by one they were being called in by the Organization and disappearing."[107]

101. Pol Pot, "Long Live the Great Revolutionary Army of the Communist Party of Kampuchea," *Tung Padevat* [Revolutionary Flags], no. 8, August 1975, pp. 24–66, esp. pp. 24–30
(emphasis in original).

102. *Livre Noir*, pp. 97–98.

103. Heng Samrin added that his 1st Division now had responsibility for the eastern side
of the road running from Wat Phnom to Chbar Ampeou to Prek Eng.

104. Phnom Penh Radio, 13 August 1975, cited in *Bangkok Post*, 14 August 1975.

105. Author's interview with Heng Samrin, 1991.

106. S. Heder's interview with a former DK official, Sakeo, 9 March 1980. These were the
310th, 450th and 520th Divisions, formerly Northern divisions.

107. Non Suon's confession of 3 November 1976, pp. 8–9; and "The Affair of Comrade
Heang," Non Suon's confession of 25 November 1976. Tuol Sleng Museum archives.

The political situation remained fluid. In early September, a Northwest Zone official named Pouvong, described as one of the three leading cadres in Battambang province, had told a Thai reporter: "There is no central government for another six months."[108] Three weeks later he reiterated his assessment and complained about "the confusion as to who was the real power in Cambodia."[109] On 16 September, Phnom Penh Radio stopped broadcasting for two days.[110] In 1978 DK claimed that there had been a "coup attempt" in the capital that month.[111] "In September 1975, the enemy plotted once again to assassinate the leaders of the Communist Party of Kampuchea. They organized 3 to 4 fighters of a unit of the Eastern Zone . . . to carry out the plot, but these fighters did not know the leaders and consequently did not know whom to fire at."[112] Some top-level gathering had taken place. The week following 16 September seems to have been a crucial period.[113]

Abandoning the People

One issue being discussed was a new series of deportations, mostly to the Northwest Zone. These had begun in some places in July, but division reigned. In August Khek Penn, a member of the Northwest Zone Committee, apologized to a crowd of six hundred peasants and urban evacuees in Battambang for their diet of rice porridge, promising that city people could return home in eight months' time and that schools and currency would be reintroduced.[114] Each of Penn's points ran directly against Center policy.

The August 1975 issue of *Tung Padevat* (Revolutionary Flags), a secret CPK monthly journal, claimed the evacuation of the cities had dealt a blow to "private property." The lead article said: "If we had kept Phnom Penh, it would have had much strength. It was true that we were stronger and had more influence than the private sector when we were in the countryside. But, in Phnom Penh we would have become their satellite. However, we did not keep them in Phnom Penh." Thus, "the bourgeoisie have nowhere to go. They have become satellite to the worker-peasant power. They have been forced into car-

---

108. Bangkok *Nation*, 2 September 1975.
109. *Bangkok Post*, 24 September 1975.
110. F. Ponchaud, "Kampuchéa: Un peuple dynamisé. Essai d'analyse de Radio Phnom Penh," *L'Afrique et l'Asie modernes*, no. 108, first trimester, 1976, p. 3.
111. Ieng Sary, official statement, 17 March 1978.
112. *Livre Noir*, p. 98.
113. Two of at least six secret Center documents from this period are extant. One is headed "19-9-75, Document No. 3," the other "Document No. 6, 22-9-75."
114. Author's interview with Thuy Bounsovanny, Creteil, 14 October 1979. She heard Khek Penn's speech at Boeng Thom village, Anlong Vil district, Battambang province, in August 1975.

rying out manual labor as peasants. . . . Their classes have already collapsed, but THEIR VIEWS STILL REMAIN, THEIR ASPIRATIONS STILL REMAIN. Therefore, they continue to conflict with the revolution. Whether they can carry out activities against us is the concrete condition which prompts us to continue the revolution."[115]

Progress was rapid. A secret Center document dated 19 September 1975 asserted that "compared with the revolutions in China, Korea, and Vietnam, we are thirty years ahead of them."[116] This document continued: "In some places we gather the people's force to be active in production day and night, regardless of rain or wind. So the people, new and old, work hard with no hesitation." An example was made of the Western Zone's Region 15, which was directed to bring "30,000 or 40,000 laborers to work along Highway 5." But, the document continues, "we must divide the people according to the needs of production. . . . The Northwest needs 500,000 additional forces. Preah Vihear has made a request for 50,000 for now[;] . . . 20,000 are provided to start with. The North also needs people. . . . So each Zone must organize carefully, and avoid taking sides. What is left over the Center will distribute to other places."[117]

City dwellers who had been evacuated to the Southwest and East were now rounded up again and sent to the more thinly populated Northern and Northwest Zones. One hundred thousand people from Region 22 in the East were sent across the Mekong to the North.[118] Five thousand more traveled by boat to Kompong Thom and then walked northward to Preah Vihear.[119] They brought the North's population to around one million.[120] In the Northwest, Region 5, which had a population of 170,000, saw another 200,000 to 210,000 people arrive in early 1976.[121] The Northwest Zone's population reached 1.79 million by March 1976, up from 908,000 in 1968. About 800,000 former city dwellers were sent to the Northwest alone.[122]

Disaster was in the making. All these people needed food, but the national export goal was now to "sell 2 million tons of rice" in 1977. "From 1980," soothed the Center, "there must be machinery to help the people" with agri-

115. "Cadres, Party Members, People and the Revolutionary Army Must Be Unanimous with the Party in Examining and Assessing Conditions in Order to Carry out the New Tasks with Soaring Success," *Tung Padevat*, no. 8, August 1975, pp. 1–23. Emphasis in original.

116. "Examine the Control," p. 2.

117. Ibid., pp. 4–5, 16, 30–31.

118. Kong Samrach, testimony at the "Cambodia Hearing," Oslo, April 1978, typescript.

119. Charles H. Twining, "The Economy," in Karl D. Jackson, ed., *Cambodia 1975–1978: Rendezvous with Death*, Princeton, N.J.: Princeton University Press, 1989, p. 138.

120. See the table "Population and Riceland in Kampuchea, 1977," based on DK's March 1976 count, in Boua, Chandler, and Kiernan, eds., *Pol Pot Plans*, p. 52.

121. Author's interview with San, a former Region 5 statistician, Paris, 29 May 1980.

122. See Boua, Chandler, and Kiernan, eds., *Pol Pot Plans*, p. 52.

culture. "Our people are working very hard, 15 hours per day. It could disturb their health." But they should expect no relief for five years.[123] The Center's attitude toward labor emerges in its discussion of profit in the provision of commodities to the population. It asks, "Should the state exchange for profit?" The example is given of clothing purchased by the state for 1 riel, with transport costs of 0.5 riels, and sold to the people at 1.5 riels. "What do we gain from this ? We do not build our country quickly, and *the people do not overuse their labor power.*" "If we do not make profit, we only move one step forward and stop there, unable to proceed. If we make profit we build one and a half steps. . . . There is a little friction with the people, but *we can abandon the people, there is no problem.*"[124]

The 19 September document made two other important points. First, "since the war we have been very busy. Neither children nor youth have received much education." It claimed that "in some places schooling has started gradually." But the Center gave little encouragement. It suggested that when people "arrange to study at twelve noon," such part-time education "gives quite good results." The proposition that "the state must organize to have exercise books and pencils for schools" seems tokenistic. "Later on" expert teachers would be needed, but they would have "to educate themselves among the people's movement first."[125] This amounted to indefinite abandonment of national education.

Second, in a new twist, the abolition of money was now reaffirmed. The new currency had been distributed. "But, so far, many places have not yet used it because there is nothing to spend it on. Because our state has not got enough to sell. . . . Next year our state will have more goods. Will we sell or give them to the people freely? Will we use money or not?" The answer was no. Three reasons were given. First, "we are not yet masters" and are unskilled in "protection" of the currency from theft or counterfeiting. Second, "enemies . . . act to destroy our money." The United States was an "important" enemy, "the Vietnamese can only act in cooperation with Russia," and the Thais "have international bandits for this type of activity." Therefore, "we shouldn't be in a hurry."

But these were practical considerations. A more basic objection involved political principle. "According to the Marxist-Leninist system, the state body is to be gradually abolished, not to be strengthened any further. . . . So the top structure disappears. . . . We must reduce it." The next step in the argument was difficult: to elide the state with private and individual interests. "Money leads to private ownership. . . . So if we use money it will fall into the hands

123. "Examine the Control," pp. 9, 10–11.
124. Ibid., pp. 26–27. Emphasis added.
125. Ibid., p. 32.

of individuals. . . . If the money falls into the hands of bad people or enemies, they will use it to destroy our cadres by bribing them with this or that. . . . They have the money to bribe and trap people's sentiment. Then in one year, ten years, twenty years, our clean society of Kampuchea will become Vietnam." The alleged Vietnamese threat delivered the coup de grâce. It only remained to turn on its head the earlier argument for the withering away of the state. "When they have money they can use it as a means to destroy our state power." Thus the document concludes, "Will we decide to use it or not? The standpoint is not to use it. . . . It is dangerous to use it. Because it creates individual and private ownership." Previous dithering on the issue was a "point to think about": the cpk both lacked experience and "had no clear stand. What would be the easy way out?"[126] Money now joined education in the dustbin of history, along with the withering of the state—but not the profit motive.

Errol de Silva, the first Western journalist to enter Cambodia after the war ended, visited Battambang in September 1975. He wrote in the *Bangkok Post*: "I was told the Khmer Rouge have an abundant supply of American dollars all seized when Phnom Penh fell." However, de Silva also heard that "the people are not allowed to have money" and that "anyone found with any type of money is shot. The old *riel* notes are no longer legal tender. . . . Inside the provincial administrative base camp in Battambang, I saw these notes being burnt to cook food."[127]

On 22 September, another Center appraisal was drawn up. Interestingly, this document appears to relax the pressure. Confidence in the achievements of the previous five months is evident. "From liberation until today there have been many changes. It is the first step of our Kampuchean society. In reality, its class composition comprises workers and peasants, old and new. The new peasants consist of public servants, the petty bourgeoisie, businessmen, national and comprador capitalists, aristocrats, etc." There is no mention of the urban working class. "These new peasants have no old political system, no economic base as before, especially in our rural areas. So now, it is all our zone. In the city, there are only workers, youth, and our army. In the rural areas, there are old peasants and new peasants. That is all, nothing else. The economic base of all classes is limited to peasants." Cooperatives had been established, and private farming or mutual aid teams were "very few." In this context, "we must not see them as before, as capitalists, professors, public servants, students, petty bourgeois, traders, national and comprador

126. Ibid., pp. 22–25.

127. Errol de Silva, "Where they burn money to cook the food," *Bangkok Post,* 24 September 1975.

capitalists, because they have entered our circle. We have full capacity to control them."[128]

Other social groups were also under control. Buddhist monks "have disappeared from 90 to 95 percent," the rest being "nothing to worry about." As for other political forces, "we also control Sihanouk as he has nothing at all," and "he has to be totally under us materially and politically." Sihanouk visited Phnom Penh briefly in September, then left for the U.N. Now, "we have everything, everything is up to us, even the palace. It is our palace. But we have worked with him well. . . . He likes it as it is. . . . If he changes later, we compare him to a scab that drops off by itself, with nobody doing anything and no pain."[129]

With Sihanouk and his followers under control, a CPK government could now be built. On 9 October, the Standing Committee met and "allocated tasks and operational matters." Technically a party meeting, this gathering showed its power in all spheres. It produced a CPK Center government of Cambodia, hierarchically ranked. Pol Pot was given "overall charge of the military and the economy." Next came CPK deputy secretary Nuon Chea, in charge of "Party work; social welfare, culture, propaganda and formal education." Ieng Sary headed "both Party and State foreign relations." Khieu Samphan was "in charge of the Front and the Royal Government" and of "the accountancy and pricing aspects of commerce." Koy Thuon had "domestic and foreign trade"; Son Sen was "in charge of the General Staff and security"; Vorn Vet, "industry, railways and fishing"; Khieu Thirith was "in charge of culture, social welfare and foreign affairs," sharing the last field with her husband Ieng Sary; Non Suon moved to agriculture; and other leaders were given responsibility for the various offices of the party Center.[130]

A notable omission was Eastern Zone leader So Phim, formally fourth in the Standing Committee hierarchy.[131] But a more direct target was the Eastern

128. "Ompi kar kdap ning anuvatt meakea noyobay promoul komlang renaksei pracheacheat pracheathipathaiy rebos paks" ("On the Control and Implementation of the Political Line to Gather Forces for the Party's National Democratic Front"), "Document No. 6," dated 22 September 1975, pp. 2–3, 5–6. Translation by Chanthou Boua.

129. Ibid., pp. 3–4.

130. "Kar prochum ajentraiy thngai 9–10–75" ("Meeting of the Standing [Committee] on 9 October 1975"), pp. 1–2. David Chandler provided a copy of the original. See also S. Heder, *Pol Pot and Khieu Samphan*, Monash University, Centre of Southeast Asian Studies, Working Paper No. 70, 1991, p. 10.

131. The CPK secretaries of the Northwest and Southwest Zones, Nhim and Mok (who ranked fifth and seventh), were also given no responsibility beyond their Zones. Vietnamese general Nguyen Xuan Hoang learned the ranking of the seven members of the Standing Committee during a visit to Cambodia in August 1975. He stated, however, that "we were told nothing about the other 13 Central Committee members." Author's interview, Hanoi, 4 October 1980.

general Chan Chakrey. At the 9 October meeting, Pol Pot warned that although Chakrey's division was "the strongest of all," its members' political education was "not very deep." Chakrey was "new," and owed his rank to "V/N" (Vietnam). "We must pay attention to what he says, to see [whether] he is a traitor who will deprive himself of any future." With Chakrey's deputy, Phan, too, "we must be totally silent. . . . We must watch their activities." Pol Pot removed Chakrey from his division command and brought him under close Center supervision as deputy chief of the general staff.[132] The Center's governing committee remained both secret and controversial. "This question of setting up a government" would not be resolved until March 1976, when the Center acknowledged that "we have repeatedly discussed [it] back and forth among ourselves ever since May [1975]."[133]

In November and December 1975, seven hundred party officials from all over the country were summoned to a Center political course. Members of Zone, Region, and district committees, and all officers from battalion commanders up, arrived for six weeks' study at Phnom Penh's Olympic Stadium. Mat Ly, who attended, says that Nuon Chea proclaimed that Cambodia now had two "universities." One taught productive labor; the other was "the fight against the Vietnamese enemy." Hun Sen recalls hearing Chea and Pol Pot retell a nineteenth-century story of Vietnamese burying Khmers up to their necks, using their heads to support a teapot, and lighting a fire under it, warning the tortured Khmers not to "spill the master's tea." Chea Sim, in the capital for the second time that year, says that as in May, Nuon Chea and Pol Pot seemed to be in full agreement. "The important point was the move to construction of cooperatives, from low-level cooperatives to high-level cooperatives."[134] Money was once again off the agenda, and a national system of communal mess halls would be imposed. The countryside would soon be free of contamination. As the meeting ended in mid-December, the CPK project went into full swing. On 5 January 1976, a constitution was proclaimed, christening the new state Democratic Kampuchea.[135]

132. "Meeting of the Standing [Committee] on 9 October 1975," pp. 14ff. Chakrey's code name was "Mean." Pol Pot referred to him by the derogatory pronoun *via.*

133. "Decision of the Central Committee on a Variety of Questions," 30 March 1976, in Boua, Chandler and Kiernan, eds., *Pol Pot Plans the Future*, p. 7.

134. Author's interviews in Phnom Penh with Hun Sen, 21 October 1980; Mat Ly, 21 January 1986; and Chea Sim, 3 December 1991.

135. The text of the constitution is in Ponchaud, *Cambodia Year Zero*, pp. 219–26. See D. Chandler, "The Constitution of Democratic Kampuchea: The Semantics of Revolutionary Change," *Pacific Affairs*, Fall 1976. Party records from 1975 refer to the state as *Prates* ["country"] *Kampuchea.*

CHAPTER FOUR

Cleansing the Frontiers:
Neighbors, Friends, and Enemies,
1975–76

Pol Pot's assertion that he had won a *"clean* victory," a triumph "without any foreign connection or involvement," is difficult to defend. The CIA's chief strategy analyst in Saigon, Frank Snepp, reported that Phnom Penh's fall was hastened by the CPK's "ultimate weapon . . . captured U.S. 105 mm. howitzers that were undoubtedly a gift of the North Vietnamese."[1] A Chinese official added in 1977 that "in the battle of liberation for Phnom Penh, Vietnam sent more than two army divisions into the war. As a result, Phnom Penh was liberated even before Saigon."[2] There is no evidence to support the assertion that two divisions were sent, but Vietnam claims to have provided artillery support.[3] Also, with credits obtained from China in return for promised supplies of Cambodian rubber, the CPK had obtained Chinese water mines. They strung the mines along cables across the Mekong River, drawing them up as boats passed, scuttling dozens and suffocating the Lon Nol regime. These and other arms had been delivered down the Ho Chi Minh Trail by the Vietnamese.

But the collaboration between China and Vietnam was already coming unstuck. Tensions went back as far as the 1954 Geneva Conference, when

1. Frank Snepp, *Decent Interval*, Harmondsworth: Penguin, 1977, p. 135.
2. Huang Hua, "Problems with Indochina, Albania, and Yugoslavia," in King C. Chen, ed., *China and the Three Worlds*, New York: 1979, p. 269. (Irene Nørlund provided a copy of this work.) A slightly different version is "Huang Hua's Report on the World Situation," *Issues and Studies* (Taipei), December 1977, pp. 76ff.
3. Author's interview with Vo Dong Giang, deputy foreign minister of Vietnam, Hanoi, 1 November 1980: "At the liberation of Phnom Penh in April 1975, the mortar operators were all Vietnamese." (Wilfred Burchett also notes "the role that Vietnamese artillerymen played in the final offensive." *The China-Cambodia-Vietnam Triangle*, New York: Vanguard, 1981, p. 143.) U.S. State Department specialist T. Carney also points out that from 1970 to 1972, "the People's Army of Vietnam formed a two-year shield in eastern Cambodia behind which the party [the CPK] developed its infrastructure and the army trained its troops." "The Unexpected Victory," in Karl D. Jackson, ed., *Cambodia 1975–1978: Rendezvous with Death*, Princeton, N.J.: Princeton University Press, 1989, p. 13.

China had conceded the division of Vietnam despite the French defeat at Dien Bien Phu. At that time, China had published a map of its "lost territories," including much of Southeast Asia and even the South China Sea. There were also tensions over the citizenship of the ethnic Chinese in Vietnam.[4] But in January 1974, China took the first military step, when its navy seized the Paracel Islands from the Saigon regime. The next year, as Hanoi began its final push toward the South Vietnamese capital, North Vietnamese seaborne troops overwhelmed Saigon's forces on the more southerly Spratly Islands, which China also claimed. "I tasted ash in my mouth," recalled a *Xinhua* journalist visiting Vietnam at the time.[5] The third round of the Indochina Wars had commenced.

Meanwhile, the second round raged on. On 12 May, the new CPK navy commandeered the U.S. military supply vessel *Mayaguez* in the Gulf of Thailand. Three days later American marines were back in action in Indochina. Eleven helicopters stormed Cambodia's Tang island in the belief that the thirty-nine members of the *Mayaguez* were being held there. They were not; Cambodia had already agreed to release them.[6] Fifteen marines were killed by CPK troops. President Ford called in the air force which destroyed Cambodia's only oil refinery, in Kompong Som, and its nearby fleet of military aircraft based at Ream. Nayan Chanda comments: "This last fling of American power in Indochina helped to hide the making of a new war."[7] According to the CPK, "as soon as the battle cries faded, while their bodies still smelled of gunpowder, our combatants in some units moved to the areas along the border and to various bases to set up positions."[8]

The Black Dragon: Conflict with Vietnam

Just before the fall of Phnom Penh, the CPK's 120th Regiment, besieging Takeo city, received a large consignment of Chinese arms: B-40 rockets, machine guns, AK-47 rifles, and ammunition. The new supplies encouraged the troops, and they took Takeo on 18 April. The victorious Region

---

4. Ben Kiernan, *How Pol Pot Came to Power*, London: Verso, 1985, pp. 148–51. The map, from *A Brief History of Modern China* (Beijing, 1954), is reproduced in the *Hong Kong Star*, 5 July 1968, and *New York Times*, 11 January 1992, p. A8. On ethnic Chinese in Vietnam, see Charles Benoit, "Vietnam's 'Boat People,'" in David W. P. Elliott, ed., *The Third Indochina Conflict*, Boulder: Westview, 1981, pp. 139–62.

5. Nayan Chanda, *Brother Enemy*, New York: Harcourt Brace Jovanovich, 1986, p. 19. See also pp. 29–30.

6. Roy Rowan, *The Four Days of Mayaguez*, New York: Norton, 1975.

7. Chanda, *Brother Enemy*, pp. 9–10.

8. Phnom Penh Radio, 14 May 1977, translated in United States Central Intelligence Agency, Foreign Broadcast Information Service (henceforth FBIS), Asia-Pacific, 18 May 1977, p. H2.

13 forces were immediately deployed to the Vietnamese border. The commander of the 120th Regiment, Mok's son-in-law Soeun, ordered his troops "to liberate Vietnamese territory because it is all our territory." Ten miles from the border, other commanders announced that "we have to fight Vietnam because there are eighteen of our provinces there, including Prey Nokor [Saigon]." One member of the 120th Regiment heard such exhortations from three different DK military leaders in this period.⁹ Two cpk district secretaries from neighboring Region 33, Mok's son Chong and his colleague Khim, also announced that "Kampuchea Krom" was Cambodian territory.¹⁰ On 30 April, Saigon fell to the Vietnamese communists. Hanoi claims that the next day cpk forces attacked across the land border between the two countries, "causing great human and material losses to the border populations."¹¹

Meanwhile, another of Mok's sons-in-law, Khe Muth, commander of the DK navy, launched an offensive by sea soon after occupying Kompong Som. As early as 19 April, Muth's forces shelled the large Vietnamese island of Phu Quoc.¹² Muth quickly landed six boatloads of his 3rd Southwest Zone Division troops on a Saigon-held island in the Gulf of Siam, and then a smaller force on Phu Quoc.¹³ South Vietnamese forces recaptured the first island before Saigon's fall, but fighting continued into the peace. From 10 to 25 May, the Khmer Rouge occupied Vietnam's Tho Chu island and, according to Hanoi, "destroyed villages, killed many people, and abducted 515 inhabitants of the island." Vietnamese communists retaliated, capturing six hundred Khmer Rouge and also, on 6 June, taking Cambodia's Wai island.¹⁴

These attacks on Vietnam benefited from cpk Center acquiescence and probable direction. In interviews given in 1981, some former members of the 3rd Division (which became the 164th in July 1975) agreed that the new

9. Author's interview with Ieng Thon, Tram Kak, 16 July 1980. Thon had joined the Khmer Rouge in July 1973 and had become a member of the 2nd Battalion of the 120th (Region 13) Regiment, commanded by Soeun. Soeun was promoted to brigade commander before the 120th reached the border in mid-1975; his replacement, Pien, reiterated the irredentist claim.
10. Author's interview with Chap Hen, Kong Pisei, 17 September 1980. Khim was cpk secretary of Kong Pisei (District 54). "Kampuchea Krom" is the Mekong Delta.
11. Kampuchea Dossier, Hanoi, 1978, vol. I, p. 125.
12. Snepp, Decent Interval, p. 299, attributing the shelling to unidentified "Communist artillerymen."
13. David P. Chandler, The Tragedy of Cambodian History, New Haven: Yale University Press, 1991, p. 256. Inexplicably, Chandler prefaces his description of these events as follows: "The need to defend the country arose immediately after liberation when Cambodian troops were dispatched to the Thai and Vietnamese frontiers to guard against a (South) Vietnamese offensive or a Thai incursion." There is no evidence for either; it is clear from Chandler's and other sources that the aggressor was Cambodian—the cpk.
14. Kampuchea Dossier, I, pp. 125–26.

regime's goal in these attacks had been to capture Vietnamese territory both in the Mekong Delta and on Phu Quoc.[15] Along with the clear involvement of Mok's family, we also know that Pol Pot discussed the conflict with Vietnam at the 20–24 May meeting in Phnom Penh, stating that the Mekong Delta was once Cambodian.

Events, however, worked against retaking Kampuchea Krom now. By the time of the May meeting, the Vietnamese communists had already occupied the Mekong Delta and were on the offensive in the Gulf of Siam. A window of opportunity—the overlap between the new Cambodian regime and a weakened Saigon—slammed shut with Hanoi's victory. Pol Pot was now forced to make a quick tactical retreat, to patch up relations with Vietnam—at least temporarily. Delegations scurried back and forth. On 18 May, Khieu Samphan traveled to Ho Chi Minh City to attend the celebration of Vietnam's victory in his capacity as president of the "Cambodia-Vietnam Friendship Association."[16] As Nuon Chea later told the CPK Standing Committee, "soon after victory" the Vietnamese had been "very brash," but "at the ceremony in Prey Nokor [Ho Chi Minh City], they spoke normally and were not brash."[17] Six days later, Radio Phnom Penh announced that the Mekong River was open for ships to travel to Cambodia through Vietnam.[18]

On 2 June, a high-ranking representative of the ruling Vietnam Workers' Party (VWP), Nguyen Van Linh, was permitted to travel by car from Ho Chi Minh City to Phnom Penh. Pol Pot told Linh that the clashes had occurred because of Cambodian troops' "ignorance of local geography."[19] Vietnam's deputy foreign minister, Phan Hien, met Cambodian officials at a border town, offered to return Wai Island, and proposed the mutual creation of provincial committees to resolve local issues. This was soon done by both sides.[20] On 12 June, a top-heavy CPK delegation consisting of Pol Pot, Nuon Chea, Ieng Sary, and other Central Committee members, visited Hanoi. Pot proposed "a treaty of friendship

15. Stephen Heder, personal communication, 2 February 1981. When questioned closely by Heder "on the issue of Kampuchea Krom and more particularly Phu Quoc," these former 164th Division troops, then in Mai Rud camp in Thailand, told Heder: "Yes, these areas were considered Khmer territory and were to be brought under DK control." Others he interviewed denied this claim. Heder adds, "A number of people, moreover, say that in '75–76 policy was irredentist," claiming that in 1977 it was "reversed."

16. *Bangkok Post*, 19 May 1975.

17. "Pinit ompi pratekamm vietnam khnong ong prochum leuk ti 5 prik thngai 14-5-76" ("Examining Vietnamese Reactions at the Fifth Meeting on the Morning of 14 May 1976"), minutes of the meeting of the Standing Committee of the CPK Central Committee, 14 May 1976, at p. 8.

18. Bangkok *Nation*, 27 May 1975.

19. Kiernan, *How Pol Pot*, p. 414; Chanda, *Brother Enemy*, p. 14.

20. Gareth Porter, "Vietnamese Policy and the Indochina Crisis," in Elliott, ed., *The Third Indochina Conflict*, p. 94.

and non-aggression based on mutual respect for independence, sovereignty and territorial integrity."[21] His aim, if not a bluff, was to get the Vietnamese formally to agree to a boundary demarcation known as the Brevié Line as the sea border between the two countries. But the Vietnamese demurred, preferring to negotiate a border agreement rather than implicitly accept the Brevié Line. If Pol Pot was bluffing, it worked. With no border agreement, Cambodia reserved the right to pursue territorial conquests beyond the Brevié Line later. Like boxers, the leaders of the two countries were quietly circling each other.

On 2 August, VWP secretary-general Le Duan flew to Phnom Penh with a high-level return delegation. Chanda reports, "A joint communiqué was signed, pledging to settle differences peacefully, but it was never published. Neither was there any banquet or speech." Both sides announced unanimity of views "on all questions raised." On 10 August, Nuon Chea again visited Hanoi. Nguyen Van Linh said Vietnam had withdrawn its forces from Cambodia's Wai Island. Chea reiterated Pol Pot's assertion that "unawareness of the border problem" had caused the dispute.[22]

On the surface, all seemed well again. The announcement on 13 August of the appointments of Ieng Sary and Son Sen as Cambodia's new deputy prime ministers was interpreted in the West as a sign of Hanoi's influence.[23] But below the surface, tension wrenched the relationship. Privately, DK asserted that Vietnamese troops remained in remote Cambodian sections of the Ho Chi Minh Trail.[24] According to both Chinese and U.S. sources, these Vietnamese forces in fact withdrew from Cambodia within six months of the twin victories of April 1975.[25] In 1978, the DK regime publicly claimed that, at first, "only one part of the Vietnamese withdrew." But it then conceded that those who remained were "much less numerous than before," mostly in Rattanakiri,

21. *Livre Noir: Faits et preuves des actes d'agression et d'annexion du Vietnam contre le Kampuchéa*, Phnom Penh: Département de la Presse et de l'Information du Ministère des Affaires Etrangères du Kampuchéa Démocratique, septembre 1978, pp. 95–96. (Henceforth *Livre Noir*. This is significantly different from a later English translation published under the title *Black Paper*.)

22. Chanda, *Brother Enemy*, pp. 14–15; *Kampuchea Dossier*, I, pp. 125–26.

23. Phnom Penh Radio, 13 August 1975, cited in *Bangkok Post*, 14 August 1975.

24. "Komnot haet nei ang prochum kana ajentraiy thngai 11 minaa 1976" ("Minutes of the Standing [Committee] Meeting of 11 March 1976"), p. 1.

25. Geng Biao, secretary-general of the CCP Military Commission, "Geng Biao's Report on the Situation in the Indochinese Peninsula," 16 January 1979, in *Journal of Contemporary Asia*, 11, 3, 1981, p. 381: "Following the liberation of Phnom Penh . . . , Vietnamese troops hung around and refused to clear out. . . . China exerted repeated pressure on Vietnam and resolutely supported the new Cambodian Government. Vietnam finally withdrew all its troops from Cambodia six months later." Huang Hua, in "Problems with Indochina," in Chen, ed., *China and the Three Worlds*, said in July 1977, "After the liberation, Cambodia had to ask repeatedly for Vietnam to withdraw its troops. . . . Vietnam eventually acceded to the request" (p. 269). Information on U.S. intelligence sources for Vietnam's withdrawal came from

totaling "more than 1,000 scattered here and there." Soon, the DK version goes, CPK troops threatened these units and they also withdrew to Vietnam.[26] The Vietnamese made other concessions. They even returned to Cambodia some of the many refugees who had escaped into Vietnam. Though Hanoi accepted ethnic Vietnamese refugees from Cambodia, at first "refugees of Chinese and Khmer descent were forced back to Cambodia."[27] Some of these the Khmer Rouge massacred soon after they crossed the border. A similar fate awaited the families of Cambodians who had spent the years 1954–70 in Vietnam who went to rejoin their husbands and fathers.[28] Vietnamese officials soon realized what was happening and stopped sending refugees back.[29] At least three thousand Khmers who in 1972 had fled across the border from the CPK's Southwest Zone were permitted to remain in Vietnam.[30] And new Cambodian refugees soon received a far warmer welcome in Vietnam than in Thailand.[31]

Though beating a tactical retreat on the military front, both Pol Pot and Nuon Chea had announced at the May 1975 meeting their plans to remove the entire Vietnamese minority from Cambodia. A later DK account calls them "Vietnamese residents whom Vietnam had secretly infiltrated into Kampuchea and who lived hidden, mixed with the population." The CPK ordered them out before July 1975.[32] By late September, over 150,000 Vietnamese residents of Cambodia had been rounded up and sent to Vietnam.[33]

Gareth Porter, Washington, D.C., May 1978; and *Time*, 16 January 1978. Hanoi's deputy foreign minister, Vo Dong Giang, told me, "After liberation they asked us to leave, and we left" (1 November 1980).

26. *Livre Noir*, pp. 93–94.

27. Chanda, *Brother Enemy*, p. 16. These included about seven thousand Khmers from Takeo Province who had fled to Vietnam in 1974 and were now exchanged for ethnic Vietnamese residents of Cambodia. Three thousand others from Takeo were permitted to remain in Vietnam. Author's interview, Phnom Den, 26 August 1980.

28. Shawcross, *Sideshow*, p. 386.

29. Author's interview with Vong Heng, a Cambodian refugee then in Vietnam, Flers, 8 October 1979.

30. Author's interview with a Khmer peasant who had fled to Vietnam in 1974, Phnom Den, 26 August 1980.

31. William Shawcross wrote in late 1975, "Ironically, those who flee in the other direction—to South Vietnam—appear to be guaranteed a better future. They are being almost welcomed (there are even reports of South Vietnamese border guards giving them covering fire as they cross into the country); they are not housed to camps; and those with connections abroad are being allowed to leave on evacuation flights." "The Khmer Rouge's Iron Grip on Cambodia," *Far Eastern Economic Review* (henceforth FEER), 2 January 1976, p. 9. Two years later this was still the case. See Chapter 9.

32. *Livre Noir*, p. 93.

33. Chanda, *Brother Enemy*, p. 16. Ignoring the 1970 exodus of 310,000 ethnic Vietnamese from Cambodia after pogroms sponsored by the Lon Nol regime, *Time* magazine described this movement as "the largest mass uprooting since Stalin sent 500,000 Volga Germans to Siberia in 1941." *Time*, 26 April 1976.

A Center document drawn up at this time suggests the idiosyncrasy of the CPK's assessment of Vietnam. 'In North Vietnam they said they will not have 100 percent mastery over water for ten years. Compared with us, what takes us 10 years takes Vietnam 30 years. So Vietnam cannot catch up with us. They are also slow in harvesting rice. We can harvest 10 bunches to Vietnam's only 2."[34] This does not suggest a rational approach to foreign policy. But the Center was holding its fire for the time being. According to Prince Sihanouk, who had just returned to Phnom Penh, "In September 1975, I was indeed surprised to hear Khieu Samphan, Son Sen and company say, smiling and very pleased with themselves, that their soldiers were 'displeased' with 'the Party,' because the latter did not give them the green light to go and take back Kampuchea Krom as well as the border districts of Thailand which belonged to Kampuchea in the past (Aranya, Surin, etc.)."[35] When the green light did flash, priority would go to a campaign against Vietnam. After a visit to Thailand, Ieng Sary reported to the CPK Standing Committee on 2 November, "We want the countries of the world to see that our foreign policy is just for contact with all countries without distinction of political regime. On this basis we want to pressure the east."[36]

But first, the Center's purge of the Hanoi-trained Khmer communists was renewed. On 30 September, their most senior survivor, Mey Pho, was arrested in Phnom Penh at the party's twenty-fourth anniversary ceremony. The next month, the first of a number of Hanoi-trained CPK cadres who had been working for the party's foreign affairs branch for several years was arrested and handed over to the *Santebal*, or Special Branch, for imprisonment and interrogation. Two more followed in November and December, and eight more in January 1976.[37]

After being evacuated from Phnom Penh, Vong Heng arrived in Svay Rieng (Region 23), on the Vietnamese border, in May 1975. Many local Vietnamese residents had already left the country. Only a few remained, and some of these were soon expelled to Vietnam, several dying of disease on the way. Heng says the CPK specified that if a Khmer husband had a Vietnamese wife, she had to go. "They could not stay and live together in Cambodia."[38] Heng Samrin concurs, saying that "if the wife stayed she would be killed," adding that some

---

34. "Examine the Control and Implementation of Policy to Save the Economy and Prepare to Build the Country in Every Field," "Document no. 3," dated 19 September 1975, p. 8. Translation by Chanthou Boua.

35. Norodom Sihanouk, *Chroniques de guerre . . . et d'espoir,* Paris: Hachette-Stock, 1979, p. 79.

36. "Kar prochum ajentraiy thngai 2–11–75 maong 7 yup" ("The Standing [Committee] Meeting on 2 November 1975 at 7 P.M."), p. 2.

37. Kiernan, *How Pol Pot,* p. 418; Benchhi neak tous (List of Prisoners), S-21, undated, p. 6.

38. Author's interview with Vong Heng, 1979.

Khmer men decided to go with their spouses.[39] But hundreds of couples took the risk and remained in Cambodia rather than separate,[40] because not all Cambodian men could pose as Vietnamese. Ngoy Taing Heng, an ethnic Chinese, decided in September 1975 to escape from Cambodia because of the lack of food. When the CPK announced that "anyone with Vietnamese or Chinese blood who wanted to leave the country could go," Heng volunteered. He reached the border in November, but Vietnam would not take him because he could not speak Vietnamese. Another three thousand people were also rejected.[41]

Vong Heng was luckier. In October he managed an overnight escape to Vietnam. The authorities there gave him permission to stay, saying he could do whatever work he could find. There were no food rations for Khmer refugees, but there were no camps or further expulsions back to Cambodia either. Ostensibly, cross-border relations remained good. Local officials described the Khmer Rouge as "friends" and even "brothers." Vietnamese took salt into Cambodia by the truckload, in return for pigs, beans, car engines, and tires. The trucks returned with ethnic Vietnamese from Cambodia. Heng reports no fighting along the border in 1975 or 1976.[42]

The CPK assessment tends to corroborate Heng's perception. In September 1975, a Vietnamese embassy was established in Phnom Penh.[43] Two days later the Center was planning to sell Cambodian cigarettes abroad, "especially to South Vietnam."[44] In early October, a boatload of Vietnamese rice arrived in Phnom Penh.[45] U.S. analysts received "several reports in 1975 and early 1976

39. Author's interview with Heng Samrin, Phnom Penh, 2 December 1991: "After liberation those [ethnic Vietnamese] who remained had to go. Even those who stayed the longest of all, Vietnamese wives of Khmer husbands, had to go, and those who did not go were killed. . . . They started to kill them in 1976." Prak Voa, a peasant from Region 24, says that Vietnamese men married to Khmers were expelled in 1975, but that in her village ten Vietnamese wives stayed with their Khmer spouses. Author's interview, Kompong Trabek, 9 October 1980.

40. Author's interview with Mau Met, Kompong Cham, 5 October 1980. Met's wife, who was part Vietnamese, stayed with him in Memut District, Region 21. He says that over two hundred other mixed couples also stayed.

41. Author's interview with Ngoy Taing Heng, Caen, 6 October 1979.

42. Author's interview with Vong Heng, 1979.

43. Author's interview with Kieu Minh, who arrived in Phnom Penh on 17 September 1975 as a member of the embassy staff; Phnom Penh, 22 October 1980. On 19 May 1976, Vietnamese deputy foreign minister Phan Hien, in a conversation with Ieng Sary, referred to "the two Vietnamese embassies in Cambodia." "Conversation between Deputy Prime Minister Ieng Sary and the Deputy Minister of Foreign Affairs of the Democratic Republic of Vietnam, Comrade Phan Hien, on 19 May 1976," p. 1.

44. "Examine the Control," p. 17.

45. The pilot reported that "there was no sign of life in the capital city until, after a three-hour wait, an official came to yell at them to unload the rice themselves and depart." "Life in Cambodia," three-page extract from a cabled report from the American embassy, Bangkok, 19 December 1975, p. 2, citing the pilot's interview with "another embassy here."

of Vietnamese barges moving up the Bassac River, and perhaps the Mekong River, hauling petroleum or rice" to Phnom Penh.[46] In June 1976, the secret cpk magazine *Tung Padevat* remarked that border incidents were few: "The enemy carried out several activities along the land and sea border from the months of November and December [1975] to January and February [1976]. From March onwards, the situation has softened maximally."[47]

In April 1976, at Vietnam's initiative, the two Communist Parties agreed to negotiate a border treaty in June of that year. Preparatory talks were held in Phnom Penh from 4 to 18 May. At the meetings, Vietnamese delegates charged DK with "initiating clashes eight times since March," including two "serious incursions" from Mondolkiri province as recently as 7 May. Vietnamese were killed and wounded.[48] Democratic Kampuchea denied these allegations, but as we have seen it had few complaints about Vietnamese behavior since at least March. The most serious incident was reported by Nuon Chea to the cpk Standing Committee on 14 May: "When four Chinese ships were sent to us, across the Vietnamese sea," Chea charged, Hanoi's gunboats and airplanes trailed them, firing shots "for five nights and five days" (from 2 to 7 May, just as the negotiations began). The shots, however, "did not hit the ships, just around them."[49]

Pol Pot was still trying to maintain cordial relations with Vietnam without committing DK to concessions. This led to a series of contradictions. On 30 March 1976, at a cpk Center meeting, he found "a way out" of an invitation to visit Vietnam. The minutes say, "The Comrade Secretary need not go. In the interest of solidarity, arrange for the State Presidium or the President of the Assembly to go."[50] But neither did. The Standing Committee decided in a 19–21 April meeting to "invite journalists for one-month visits" from the "socialist nations" China, North Korea, Vietnam, and Laos, and to "prepare to receive the Vietnamese for negotiations" in June.[51] These resolutions were time bombs. Pol Pot himself "reminded" the Standing Committee that it had "set about resolving the eastern border and the sea border with Vietnam." But next, under the

---

46. Charles Twining, "The Economy," in Jackson, ed., *Cambodia 1975–1978*, p. 138.

47. *Tung Padevat*, June 1976. The magazine continued: "Even now the enemy cannot persist in trying to have his way with us. . . . The enemy is hesitant towards us. . . . It is impossible for the enemy to attack us."

48. "Examining Vietnamese Reactions," p. 1.

49. Ibid., p. 4.

50. "Sekkedei somrac rebos kanak mocchim ompi pahnyaha pseng pseng muoi chumnuon" ("Decisions of the Central Committee on a Variety of Questions"), in *Pol Pot Plans the Future*, p. 8.

51. "Sarop sekkedei somrac rebos kanak ajentraiy khnong ong prochum thngai 19–20–21 mesaa 1976" ("Summary of Decisions Made by the Standing Committee on 19–20–21 April 1976"), p. 3.

agenda item "Other Problems with Vietnam," came the decision: "*Indochina Problem*: We want to end this story for ever."[52] Tension was palpable.

In a speech the next day at the first meeting of Democratic Kampuchea's cabinet, Pol Pot let fly. "Vietnam is a black dragon," he said, that "spits its poison." But it was "in difficulties," particularly economic ones, and had "no force to attack Southeast Asia." Using a succession of metaphors, Pol Pot illustrated his point: "If they have 100 horsepower, they can attack only at 10 horsepower. But their hands are full in Laos, they have to help Laos with 3 horsepower. So there is only 7 horsepower left to attack Southeast Asia. . . . Vietnam will not be successful in attacking us. . . . On average they walk at a 1-year speed; we walk at a 3-year speed. If we walk fast, they hold on to our tail." Carried away, Pol Pot now mixed his metaphors. "No matter how it spits its poison," Vietnam was "a performing dragon with only 7 ["horsepower"] poison which it uses to attack us as well as Southeast Asia."[53]

It is clear that Democratic Kampuchea went into the negotiations with Vietnam without much commitment. The talk of "solidarity" was empty. In Kirivong district, in the Southwest (Region 13), which was run by Mok's brother-in-law Tith and tended to reflect Center policy, DK troops attacked ten kilometers into Vietnam during April, and several local officials announced their intention to "liberate Kampuchea Krom."[54] In Phnom Penh on 1 May, three days before the negotiations with Vietnam began, thirteen more Hanoi-trained Khmer communists were taken from the DK foreign ministry's re-education camp and transferred to the authority of the *Santebal*.[55] Like the Khmer Krom soldiers who had crossed the border at Kirivong a few weeks earlier, none survived.

The May 1976 Negotiations

The negotiations foundered on the "Brevié Line," a subject of much misunderstanding. In 1939 the French governor-general of Indochina, Jules Brevié, had determined administrative and police boundaries between the French protectorate of Cambodia and the colony of Cochinchina (southern Vietnam). The land border was fairly clear, but no sea boundary had ever been demarcated. Brevié did not create one, but he drew a line from the sea coast at an angle of 140 degrees out into the Gulf of Siam, deviating north to skirt the

52. Ibid., p. 5.
53. "Bot ateseniem rebos samamit lekha khnong samay prochum kanak rottmuntrei leuk ti muoi thngai 22 mesaa 1976" ("Speech of the Comrade Secretary at the First Ministerial Committee Meeting, 22 April 1976"), p. 7.
54. See Introduction, and Vickery, *Cambodia 1975–1982*, p. 190.
55. List of Prisoners, S-21, p. 6.

large Vietnamese island of Phu Quoc. Islands south of this line were to be under the administrative and police control of southern Vietnam; those north of it, under Cambodian control. But Brevié dodged the issue of sovereignty: "The question of whose territory these islands are remains outstanding." Even further from resolution was the question of ownership of the seas between the islands on both sides of the line.[56] A secret 1977 DK foreign ministry document conceded the point: "This border was of an 'administrative' character, but Democratic Kampuchea considers it as the state border between Kampuchea and Vietnam which was left by history."[57]

In 1967, the Vietnamese communists had recognized Cambodia's "existing borders." But no sea border, delimiting territorial waters, was included in this agreement.[58] In June 1977, Vietnamese deputy foreign minister Phien Hien was asked whether Hanoi had accepted the Brevié Line. He responded: "Yes, we did, but at the time we agreed to the Brevié Line, we were not aware of problems of territorial waters, continental shelf, etc.—those new phenomena."[59] This constituted an admission that in 1967 Hanoi had agreed to use the Brevié Line to demarcate sovereignty over the islands. But there is no evidence to contradict Phan Hien or to indicate that the question of "territorial waters" even came up in 1967. It remained to be negotiated.[60] Sihanouk's

56. Chanda, *Brother Enemy,* pp. 32–33. See the text of Brevié's decision in *Kampuchea Dossier,* I, Hanoi 1978, pp. 139–41.

57. "Provatt prumdaen Kampuchea-Vietnam" ("The History of the Kampuchea-Vietnam Border"), Foreign Ministry of Democratic Kampuchea, Internal Document, 15-6-1977, 5th copy, p. 16.

58. The agreement is reproduced in S. Heder, "Kampuchea's Armed Struggle," *Bulletin of Concerned Asian Scholars* (henceforth BCAS), 11, 1, 1979, p. 24. Heder wrongly suggests the Vietnamese had recognized the Brevié Line in 1967 because it was "the only 'existing' maritime frontier" (in Elliott, ed., *The Third Indochina Conflict,* p. 26). It was not a frontier at all, and there was no maritime frontier at the time. Cambodian diplomat Sarin Chhak wrote in 1965, in a book endorsed by a preface from Sihanouk, "The measure taken concerns only the administration. As for the question of sovereignty, it was reserved. But if it was reserved, this does not mean that any advantage was already presumed for one country or the other. It was in suspension, totally in suspension." Chhak claimed to have demonstrated that "the islands of the Gulf of Siam have always been Cambodian, even those which were only administratively connected to Vietnam by the Brevié note and in particular the island of Phu Quoc" (S. Chhak, *Les Frontières du Cambodge,* Paris: Dalloz, 1966, pp. 158–59). In other words, Cambodia still claimed the islands *south* of the Brevié Line, which it neither recognized nor claimed as a national border.

59. Chanda, *Brother Enemy,* p. 33.

60. A precise map on the cover of Democratic Kampuchea's *Phumisas Kampuchea Pracheathipathaiy* (*Geography of Democratic Kampuchea*), the "first edition" of a "first grade" text published by the DK "Education Ministry" dated 1976, shows Cambodia without a sea border. Only in August 1977 did Democratic Kampuchea produce a map (unilaterally) claiming the Brevié Line as the sea border (*Democratic Kampuchea Is Moving Forward,* Phnom Penh, August 1977).

Cambodia never claimed the Brevié Line, even with respect to sovereignty over the islands. In 1969, significantly, Sihanouk had declined to acknowledge the line, still hoping to get additional islands to its south.[61] His regime and, from 1970, Lon Nol's Khmer Republic both patrolled sea borders with South Vietnam that fell far short of the Brevié Line.[62] Thus, there had never been an agreement. Hanoi's 1967 offer to Cambodia vis-à-vis sovereignty over the islands did not amount to a proposed *sea* border, matched no Cambodian claim, was not acknowledged by Phnom Penh, and was never published or documented by either side. So in 1976, when Democratic Kampuchea claimed the Brevié Line as the nonnegotiable sea border, the Vietnamese insisted on negotiating the border. Democratic Kampuchea claimed Hanoi was backtracking. It refused to parley. The talks were doomed.

Yet Pham Van Ba, who participated in the negotiations on the Vietnamese side, recalls the May 1976 meetings as "rather positive." Deputy foreign minister Phan Hien headed the Vietnamese delegation. A Khmer-speaking delegation member, Kieu Minh, agrees that the negotiations proceeded for two weeks in a "reasonably amicable" atmosphere.[63] The Cambodian team was headed by Ney Sarann, former cpk secretary of the Northeast Zone (see Chapter 3), whom Ba describes as "neither distrustful nor generous," a stance he found "normal" for such negotiations.[64] The two had known each other as anti-French fighters in the early 1950s. Ba even knew Pol Pot, having once smuggled him into Phnom Penh, disguised as his own aide-de-camp, at the war's end in 1954. From 1975 to 1977 Ba served as Hanoi's ambassador in the Cambodian capital. On several occasions he met Pol Pot, who addressed Ba as "comrade."

Neither Pol Pot nor DK foreign minister Ieng Sary participated in the talks. But the three Zones bordering Vietnam were all represented. Sarann, from the

61. S. Heder, "The Kampuchean-Vietnamese Conflict," in Elliott, ed., *The Third Indochina Conflict*, p. 26. Heder reveals that in 1969, "Sihanouk instructed his cartographers to . . . omit the Brevié line. Sihanouk apparently hoped to renew Kampuchea's historical claims on several small and more distant islands south of the Brevié line at some future point, and wanted to leave the maritime situation ambiguous in order not to rule out such claims." In 1977, a DK foreign ministry document asserted that as a result of Brevié's 1939 decision, "Kampuchea lost a number of its islands, especially Koh Tral [Phu Quoc]." "The History of the Kampuchea-Vietnam Border," Foreign Ministry of Democratic Kampuchea, Internal Document, 15-6-1977, 5th copy, p. 6.

62. See the map dated 14 November 1973, from the archives of the Saigon navy, in *Kampuchea Dossier*, Hanoi, 1978, p. 142.

63. Author's interview with Kieu Minh, Phnom Penh, 22 October 1980. When asked, Minh conceded that Sihanouk's former diplomat Sarin Chhak, a specialist on Cambodia's borders, "might have been behind the scenes." The Vietnamese side seemed to fear manipulation. Pham Van Ba says that "Ieng Sary was really controlling the negotiations," though the DK foreign minister was not present, "and I saw the hand of the Chinese preventing a reconciliation."

64. Author's interview with Pham Van Ba, Ho Chi Minh City, 28 October 1980.

Northeast, had a number two, Chan (Seng Hong), the new deputy secretary of the Eastern Zone. Kang Chap from the Southwest completed the delegation. Chap, "a soldier slightly over 40 years of age, who wears black pajamas,"[65] was rising fast in Democratic Kampuchea. He had recently been named president of the national "Judiciary Committee." The delegation's secretaries, Keat Chhon and Touch Khamdoeun, were intellectuals.

In a 1978 interview, Phan Hien recalled that "the Vietnamese proposed to use the last French map before 1954" to demarcate the land border. But Democratic Kampuchea "would agree only to use the map as the basis for discussion, demanding the right to make some amendments." Hien claimed the Cambodians then "refused to specify in advance all the changes they wished to make, offering only one or two examples."[66] Hanoi politburo member Xuan Thuy has said, however, that Democratic Kampuchea proposed eleven specific changes.[67] Pham Van Ba claimed that the issue was resolved anyway: "We all agreed to cede territory to the other side if there was a majority of the other's race living there." Ba was quick to point out that this did not involve large tracts of territory like "Kampuchea Krom," which Democratic Kampuchea ostensibly did not claim. The agreement applied only to discrepancies along the land border. Nevertheless, Ba adds, "we thought this was positive, and took into account the local people's interests. This was the principle; it showed mutual goodwill, though it could only be worked out in practice in actual negotiations to be held later."[68] If true, this was a Vietnamese concession, because the CPK had already expelled or dispersed all concentrations of Vietnamese residents that might have allowed Hanoi to now claim border readjustments in its favor. Khmer populations remained along the Vietnamese side of the border.

According to Kieu Minh, the "one or two bitter words" that were exchanged concerned the sea border. The Vietnamese, he said, acknowledged the Brevié Line only insofar as it determined ownership of islands, "since for navigation purposes the line did not allow enough water to the Vietnamese around Phu Quoc."[69] There was no compelling technical reason to rule out a compromise. But politics intervened. The record of the CPK Standing Committee's discussion of the issue, during the afternoon and evening of 14 May 1976, not only reveals that the Vietnamese reports of the negotiations are sub-

---

65. "Life in Southern Cambodia," Extracts from an Airgram Report by an Officer of the American Embassy at Bangkok, 25 January 1977 (declassified in 1978), p. 3.

66. Gareth Porter, "Vietnamese Policy and the Indochina Crisis," in Elliott, ed., *The Third Indochina Conflict*, p. 94, based on Porter's interview with Phan Hien on 2 November 1978.

67. Porter, p. 126 n. 139, citing his interview with Xuan Thuy, 2 November 1978.

68. Author's interview with Pham Van Ba, 1980.

69. Author's interview with Kieu Minh, 1980.

stantially accurate, but also shows how the Cambodian side decided to break off the talks after five meetings, thus canceling the June summit with Vietnam.

The Transcripts of Conflict

Here is what happened.[70] Ney Sarann opened the Standing Committee meeting with a report on Vietnam's position. He paraphrased Phan Hien's assertions that morning: that Cambodian troops had recently attacked Vietnamese territory, that the Brevié Line was baseless, that accepting it "would infringe their sovereignty," and that previous Vietnamese positions had "no legal meaning" without signatures. "They stressed that the sea border must be a median line to be reasonable. They said that we said that the median dividing line would leave us with no room to get out. They said that there would be no problem with that; once the border is set there would be an agreement on movements."

Sarann commented: "They tried to keep the atmosphere happy. But . . . because the gist of the declarations was weighty, the situation was rather tense, though there were no clashes." Sarann then summarized his own response to Hien. First, he had claimed that the Brevié Line was "unquestionable because the French drew the line and it had been respected since then." Second, Sarann had asserted that "half each is not just," to which the Vietnamese "reacted quite strongly; they were not happy." Third, Sarann pointed out that with respect to the land border, the Cambodians accepted the French map only "as a document for discussion by requesting changes at some points." Thus the Cambodian positions on the land and sea borders were contradictory. (But it was Phan Hien who, in his reply, stated that "the land map and the sea line cannot be compared with one another," apparently meaning that no sea border existed, whereas a land border map did exist even if it had to be carefully negotiated on the ground.) Sarann concluded that "they absolutely do not recognize our Brevié line. The insist on dividing the sea in the middle." Finally, the Vietnamese queried which land map the Cambodians were using and asked to show the Cambodian delegation a film the next evening.

Then the Standing Committee discussion commenced. First, Chan commented: "If we cannot resolve the sea border it could cause trouble in the future." Kang Chap suggested that the Vietnamese were fishing for, if not demanding, a new Cambodian position. Then a digression occurred. Nuon Chea brought up the Vietnamese naval harassment of the four Chinese ships tra-

70. What follows is from the minutes of the CPK Standing Committee meeting on 14 May 1976, recorded in "Examining Vietnamese Reactions."

versing their waters. Son Sen denied the Vietnamese charges: "They encroach into our border non-stop. We do not infringe them." (As we have seen, his accusation was contradicted in *Tung Padevat* the next month.)

At this point, Pol Pot "asked for clarification." He wanted to know whether the Vietnamese were willing to extend the negotiations, "not wanting to break them off yet, or do they ?" This was the first suggestion of ending the talks. Pol Pot speculated that the Vietnamese negotiators may have been exceeding their instructions and fishing for a change in Cambodia's position. He asked if there had been "any interesting incidents."

Ney Sarann replied that the Vietnamese "can extend the time and chew on it." He repeated, "This morning the atmosphere was tense but did not reach a breakdown. . . . The two organizations [parties] will meet in June." Sarann noted that the Vietnamese had said "whatever happens they must have our delegation visit their country," so they could "show us around like we did them." He concluded that "this atmosphere shows that they need us in order for us to make concessions so that they gain on the border." Kang Chap volunteered, "Today's discussion shows that they still think they are a big country with many people; they still want to oppress us and think we are scared of them. They say we interfere with their sovereignty. They want to show off their power. But this is their method of attack, to have us look for a way out."

Chan agreed with Sarann that the Vietnamese "do not want to break off the negotiations yet." However, the atmosphere was worsening. "Phan Hien's expression was different, like copper. Even when he smiled it was not fresh. The reasons: 1. The events at the border. We rejected their accusations. 2. Our strong standpoint which shows that their request and the line they drew were not just." Kang Chap, of the Southwest, was suspicious: "There are many of them; their composition is unknown. I suspect some are cia elements. They look like cattle traders." The discussion was careering off course. Nuon Chea now drew the conclusion that no progress was possible: "They maintain their standpoint and we maintain our standpoint." He then focused on "the important point," the sea border. "Is this going to be a tough problem?," he asked. Such bargaining was "quite normal," and there had been "sea clashes before." However, Cambodia now knew that the Vietnamese "want to divide the sea into two." Chea asserted, "We cannot give them any concession on the sea." This was Democratic Kampuchea's bottom line. The negotiations could be extended to discover Hanoi's. However, Chea said his priority was to maintain "the same atmosphere of solidarity and friendship." He was concerned that "if the negotiation situation stayed the same like this, the atmosphere could become tense." Phan Hien was "not a very experienced politician" and was "playing with law, capitalist law. Negotiating with us like with the Americans." Perhaps Hien did not understand the importance of solidarity, Chea said. "He wants to suppress us by the method of negotiations." Therefore, even though "the negotiation today was not terribly tense," Chea argued, "we could find ways to ease it, to stop the negotiations in order to maintain the same situation." Accepting the status quo, an unresolved border, would be preferable to pursuing conflicting claims.

Now Vorn Vet had his say. He said it seemed "unlikely that they will concede." Further talk may not produce results. "It is their philosophy that they are a big country and don't want to submit to our requests." While Cambodia wants to "defend our interest," Vietnam "wants to profit from us." Vet also plumbed for breaking off the talks. "So the negotiations can be postponed but [we can] maintain a stable situation, and avoid clashes in order to preserve peaceful coexistence and for us to strengthen our self-sufficiency." Nevertheless, "this is not easily done." The future would surely bring "clashes at the border." That prospect did not alter his recommendation.

Son Sen weighed in again, noting that "each side has an absolute standpoint." He concurred that Vietnam wanted to keep talking: "Even though their expression was more vulgar this time, they do not want to break it off yet." But it was a zero sum game: "If we concede and are soft, they profit from it." Sen predicted that "we won't achieve our requests Nos. 2, 3, and 4," which are not specified, though this suggests that Cambodia's first request, "No. 1," was within sight of acceptance. "If the negotiations are extended, it would lead to tension. . . . I agree with comrade Nuon [Chea] that we should find some method . . . to end the negotiations by maintaining a normal atmosphere."

Son Sen then detailed his reasons. "We have investigated carefully, and we could lose tremendously if we apply international law." A 1969 case had decided that a country's territorial sea rights depended on the length of its coastline. "Our land is large, but with a small opening to the sea. . . . The Vietnamese and the Thai take all the sea. So we can not solve the problem with this standpoint. We postpone this problem in order to build our self-sufficiency and explain to our friends on the international stage." Which friends? "Vietnam does not gain. If they quarrel with the Chinese it would be even more complicated." Nuon Chea agreed that "the Vietnamese need for us has not faded, especially with the Non-Aligned Nations meeting coming up. . . . If the negotiations are postponed, we gain." Sen again stressed the Chinese role, describing Vietnam's situation as "difficult."

By this time, Ney Sarann must have seen the writing on the wall. He gave ground with a Maoist dismissal of the Vietnamese: "I agree with brother Nuon that they are not politicians, they are experts." But he went over the issues again. Each side, he said, had clarified its position. "They were ambitious and wanted to achieve their request. They need us but they also want concessions from us. So far the atmosphere is still relaxed. We tried, and they also tried.

They still show a happy manner." He agreed that "if we could find a way to end it we should. . . . But as hosts, we might not profit politically if we end it. We want them to leave, . . . [but] it seems they won't be leaving easily." Sarann's position suggested his ambivalence about forcing a break with Vietnam.

The discussions up to this point take up eight pages of the minutes. Pol Pot has said almost nothing except to introduce the idea of breaking off the negotiations. Various nuances have been expressed, and no single speaker has predominated. Pol Pot now takes over. The "Comrade Secretary" makes a speech that takes up the next eight pages. On the final (the seventeenth) page, the minutes of the meeting record a brief exchange limited to Pol Pot, Nuon Chea, and Ieng Sary—numbers one, two, and three in the CPK hierarchy. The roundtable discussion ended before the meeting's halfway mark.

Pol Pot begins by stating that his view is "nothing different from what we have heard so far." He merely wants to add something. His first point is that "negotiation with Vietnam to resolve the border problem is our current revolutionary task." There is "a chronic conflict with Vietnam," and "we are not idealists who say there should not be any conflict." Pol Pot does not envision a resolution. "At present and in the future there will always be conflict. We must strengthen our standpoint. . . . In the future if we stand on this experience we can negotiate with anybody. So it is a big lesson. . . . Even if we don't resolve the problem, we still have the experience." The purpose of negotiating is not pragmatic, but didactic. The lesson seems to be the impossibility of negotiating with Vietnam.

Second, Pol Pot discusses "more complicated" conflicts in other parts of the world. Yugoslavia and Romania have more difficulties with "Russia" than Cambodia does with Vietnam. And "the same goes for Albania," which "is in difficulties with the East as well as with the West." Yet "these countries preserve their independence," even though they are geographically "in the Russian horde." They are Slavs, and even "speak Slav," but despite its strength, "Russia can still not do anything." Now in comparison, Pol Pot continues, "We are in a better position. Our situation has improved a great deal." Moreover, Scandinavian, Southeast Asian, and African countries "also want independence." Even in the Middle East, "the U.S. and Russian imperialists are not in control." Among the nonaligned nations, the forces resisting imperialism and colonialism are "very strong." Border conflicts exist, but do not result in war, unless a state faces "internal" resistance as well. "Attacking from outside is not easy . . . unless the internal force is strong enough" to support external aggression. Crushing internal opposition is an important priority.

Third, Pol Pot analyzes "the negotiation problem." It is normal, he says, for Vietnam to defend its interests. Cambodia does the same. "We give them some peel. This is where they disagree. We stand on the Brevié line to give them the peel. They draw the Phan Hien and the Viet Minh line to give us the peel. The problem is: they do not accept the Brevié line. Because if they accept that line they will have given us the core. So it is normal that they want the advantage." But normality in Pol Pot's eyes argues for ending the talks, not pursuing them with a readiness to tackle problems along the way. Normality does not apply to Cambodia; it is a feature of Vietnamese history. "We don't go back to old times. We use old documents just to maintain the existing situation. We don't claim anything new." Vietnam does. Moreover, its drive for gain is a result of normal Vietnamese actions: "In their party, they have educated their youth for a long time . . . about the concept of Indochina, the concept of the federation." Hanoi's ingrained "expansionist strategy" prevents it from accepting "our Brevié line." Vietnam, presenting itself as "a big country" to intimidate Cambodia, has "pulled a gun to threaten us."

Pol Pot advises "solving those problems that can be solved," postponing others, and telling the Vietnamese that "there have been frictions in past experience but our two parties, standing on friendship and solidarity, could always resolve problems. As for this problem, we'll definitely resolve it." This answer, he suggests, would keep Cambodia on the same level as the Vietnamese. It is a "winning" tactic. Moreover, it "conforms with our request to ease the atmosphere." Here Pol Pot presumably refers to ending negotiations, with the ostensible goal of improving relations. By contrast, he says, the Vietnamese wish to prolong the talks "so we would become bored" and "to profit from these negotiations." The Vietnamese proposal "to divide the sea equally" is "a very dumb trick."

Finally, Pol Pot draws conclusions and proposes action. "We have arrived at a standstill." Further negotiations are risky because Hanoi wants concessions. "If we follow this direction we would be tricked and led into tension. It is a loss to continue. It is better to end it. But how are we going to end it? Let's discuss that." He reminds the Standing Committee that this will "only be a break," but one that will offend Hanoi. "In the future when we ask them to start negotiations they will not come again. They'll ask us to go to them." He does not point out that Democratic Kampuchea's leaders would retain the initiative only if they refuse to go.

Pol Pot's proposed method of breaking off the negotiations begins and ends with sweet talk. "In our answer the day after tomorrow, we'll stress that we stand on friendship and solidarity." Ney Sarann's delegation should say that Cambodia's relations with Vietnam "must be cared for, enriched and further beautified" and should tell the Vietnamese that "upon this standpoint we believe that we'll definitely solve the problem." The Cambodians should also add that "both delegations have expressed their opinions" and that "we have largely agreed on the land." They should then announce that the Brevié Line "was drawn a long time ago in history and both sides have respected it since." They should point out that all borders were created by the French and add that "we do not accept two lines to divide the sea and the islands. We accept only one line." Ney Sarann should then conclude, 'We'll report further to our Organization. . . . Even though we have different standpoints, I think there'll be new light after it is examined by our Party. And according to our experience, time will lead us to understand and have solidarity with each other, and we will definitely solve the problem. . . . We consider friendship and solidarity with Vietnam as our sacred object." In this vein, the bilateral liaison committees along the border should keep "in constant contact."Pol Pot ended his speech: "Tell them that enemies are active. [Say that] it could be that the enemy starts conflicts in order to destroy our negotiations."

No dissent from Pol Pot's instructions was expressed. The only recorded comments are from Nuon Chea and Ieng Sary, who expressed concern. Nuon Chea worried, "It is possible they won't go." They "insist" on a June summit. He thought a break could create problems, for as he admitted, "we only negotiate when they accept our points." For his part, Ieng Sary wondered if "after a long time they might accept" the Brevié Line. Pol Pot reassured them that there was no need to continue negotiations: "I observe they are not in a better position than us." He pointed out that clarity, moderation, reason, and gentleness characterized the Cambodian position. It did not look unfriendly. And it would do no harm, because "they need us for a summit conference," whether in June or later. Nuon Chea was convinced. "Le Duan himself wrote twice that he wanted to meet us. . . . He really needs us." The matter was resolved. Pol Pot ended the meeting, and the Cambodia-Vietnam negotiations, in perfect rectitude: "So we act kindly. Let's go and see their film. They have no reason to cut us off because we are still smiling, we have never abused them. If they cut us off they have nothing to gain, only to lose." Cambodia was in a position of strength, and talks could be held any time. Noone present is recorded as having disputed this or argued forcefully for continuation of the meetings for any other reason. If Cambodia had a fallback position, which seems unlikely, no one present referred to it.

On 19 May, the day after the last session, Ieng Sary met with Phan Hien. Ney Sarann and the other members of the DK negotiating team were not present. After a short chat, Hien read a letter from Hanoi's foreign minister, Nguyen Duy Trinh. Trinh asked that the two countries' delegations to the August nonaligned Summit Conference in Colombo exchange views beforehand. He also suggested to Ieng Sary that Cambodia, Vietnam, and Laos consider coordinating their policies on international aid, "in order to have the best application and in order to show the Conference that the three countries are in good solidarity."[71] Turning to the bilateral talks, Hien noted that Sarann had "requested a rest." The resumption of talks was related to the date of the planned bilateral summit. Hien now offered his agreement on a break "for two weeks in order to do the necessary work." The talks could resume on 5 or 10 June, or later, depending on the date set for the summit. Hien added, "We will call comrade Ney Sarann."

Ieng Sary took "a little rest" before responding. He first thanked the Vietnamese delegation, "which has worked in Cambodia with good results." Shortcomings and mix-ups were inevitable, he said, after war in each country. But the Vietnamese should consider that they are "visiting relatives." The Cambodian side would "do whatever we can to further expand and strengthen solidarity." There had been no "great result," but "the meetings allowed us to understand each other." Now, "we see that solidarity and friendship between the two countries is necessary."

The Cambodian side would "need time to think further." As to Hien's suggested resumption, Sary responded with, Don't call us, we'll call you. He told Hien: "The real work is for a later date to be communicated by telegram. We'll let you know the date, the month, and the venue." Sary likewise deferred Nguyen Duy Trinh's requests.[72] Sary said he feared that raising funds among the nonaligned nations for aid to Kampuchea, Vietnam, and Laos might damage nonaligned unity. "It must be done so that other countries are not jealous that our three countries are the only ones being considered." Study was required to distinguish "good and bad outcomes." Sary did not reveal that the CPK Standing Committee had already decided a month before to dispose of the "Indochina" notion "forever" and to find a way to "explain to the Non-Aligned Nations."[73] Or that two weeks earlier it had also decided that the only initiative Democratic Kampuchea would pursue at the nonaligned meetings would be to "keep close contact with Senegal."[74] The Vietnamese proposals were still-born.

According to a Vietnamese embassy official, the Cambodians asked to

71. "Santeneakar rebos opaneayok rottmuntrei Ieng Sary chumpouh samamett Phan Hien anurottmuntrei krosuong karboretes sathearonarott procheathipathely Vietnam thngai 19 osophea 1976" ("Conversation between Deputy Prime Minister Ieng Sary and Comrade Phan Hien, Deputy Minister of Foreign Affairs of the Democratic Republic of Vietnam, on 19 May 1976"), p. 4. What follows is also from these minutes.

72. Sary stated that diplomatic cooperation between the two countries depended on "each country to make it close." So, he nodded vaguely, "there will be a continuous exchange of opinions as necessary." And "we will report to the Standing Committee about the Conference in Colombo. . . . As for the big problems in the world, we are collecting more documents."

73. "Summary of Decisions Made by the Standing Committee on 19–20–21 April 1976," p. 5.

74. "Minutes of the Standing Committee Meeting on 3–5-76," 2 pp.

break off the negotiations so that they could report on the Vietnamese position to the CPK Central Committee and await its decision. No decision was ever announced.[75] The June summit never took place, nor did any further negotiations between Democratic Kampuchea and Vietnam. If Pol Pot ever had any intention of reopening talks, he abandoned it. But he maintained the facade of friendship for the rest of the year. Ieng Sary asked Phan Hien to send "three to five journalists and photographers from both North and South for a period of one week to ten days." This was substantially less than the "one-month visit" decided on by the Standing Committee on 21 April. But he also invited a delegation from Air Vietnam.[76] Four days later Nuon Chea wrote to a Vietnamese counterpart that the May meetings had been "very successful in further consolidating and strengthening our militant solidarity" and that the two sides had been "extremely sincere with each other, as the comrades-in-arms and revolutionary brothers they are."[77]

But internal DK propaganda was frank. Cadres in the border district of Kirivong (Region 13) proclaimed that Cambodia and Vietnam were "big enemies" who "could not look at each other or speak to one another."[78] Once again, CPK policy in Region 13, heart of the Southwest Zone, quickly reflected that of the Center.

The Vietnam News Agency's director, Tran Thanh Xuan, had been waiting a year for permission to go to Cambodia. In July 1976, he led a delegation of journalists on a two-week visit.[79] In Phnom Penh they stayed near the Vietnamese embassy in a guest house whose former owner, their hosts said, had been "driven away."[80] The DK minister of information, Hu Nim, officially welcomed them. Xuan recalled having met Nim in 1964, when he visited the Vietnamese capital.[81] Nim did not recognize him, but later mumbled, "I think I know you from somewhere." Xuan recalls, "I could see Hu Nim had no power any more. He was not at ease; he was very friendly, but not his own master. Everything was arranged by Ieng Sary. Hu Nim just implemented it and played the official role." The Vietnamese visited Kompong Cham, Kompong Thom, Siemreap and Angkor, and Battambang. But they were allowed to travel only

75. Author's interview with Kieu Minh, 1980.

76. "Conversation," 19 May 1976, p. 9.

77. Letter from Nuon Chea to Pham Hung, dated 23 May 1976, quoted in *Kampuchea Dossier*, I, Hanoi 1978, pp. 130–31.

78. Author's interview with a woman deported to Kirivong district in early 1976. She said the cadres made these statements in 1976. Tram Kak, 16 July 1980.

79. Author's interview with Tran Thanh Xuan, Ho Chi Minh City, 26 October 1980. The following report on Xuan's visit to Cambodia is based on this interview and on Nayan Chanda's 1981 interview with Xuan, recounted in Chanda, *Brother Enemy*, p. 34.

80. Author's interview with Ha Thi Que, Hanoi, 4 November 1980.

81. Hu Nim's confessional account is reproduced in Boua, Chandler, and Kiernan, eds., *Pol Pot Plans the Future*, p. 243.

on the roads, not through villages, and they were prevented from interviewing the people. "Our camera crew had great difficulty finding smiling peasants building the country. They all looked so sullen and sad," Xuan says. "Things did not seem normal, but I did not write about that." His report merely stated, "While the cities are empty, the people are working in the fields," a line excised by his Hanoi editor, Hoang Tung. Xuan did not ask after Hou Yuon. "I did not want to interfere," he says, hinting he had suspected problems. Xuan had known Ieng Sary, Khieu Samphan, and Pol Pot from their days as students in France together. When the three Cambodian leaders received him "solemnly" in Cambodia's royal palace, Khieu Samphan said to him, "We have struggled together against the United States." Xuan got the impression that Samphan was moved to see him. Ieng Sary also hosted a reception. Xuan found them friendly and failed to distinguish any nuances in their attitudes toward Vietnam. On 20 July Pol Pot granted Xuan an interview, but he wrote the text of the interview himself. "I did not write it," says Xuan. "I let him say what he wanted. He talked about solidarity with Vietnam as a strategic question, and also a sentiment, from the heart!"[82] Pot sent Xuan off with a gift for Hoang Tung—a baby crocodile.[83]

This was a period of peace along the border. Hanoi says that following the May meetings, "border incidents decreased in number."[84] On the Cambodian side, *Tung Padevat* reported that "even now the enemy cannot persist in trying to have his way with us. . . . The enemy is hesitant towards us. . . . It is impossible for the enemy to attack us."[85] On 21 September a Vietnamese civil aircraft arrived at Pochentong airport, inaugurating a regular but rarely used fortnightly Air Vietnam service.[86] Delegations were not criss-crossing one another as in mid-1975, but there was more traffic than at any time since. Vietnamese ships sailed to Phnom Penh with cargoes of salt.[87] Cambodia imported five hundred thousand meters of Vietnamese cloth.[88]

The journalists had left Phnom Penh with a Cambodian request for per-

82. Author's interview with Tran Thanh Xuan, 1980. The text of the interview was published in *Vietnam Courier*, no. 52, September 1976, pp. 5–7. Pol Pot's statement was that solidarity "between Kampuchea and Vietnam is both a strategic question and a sacred feeling" (p. 7).

83. Chanda, *Brother Enemy*, p. 34, citing Hoang Tung's interview with James Burnet on 12 January 1986.

84. *White Paper*, Hanoi, 20 January 1978.

85. *Tung Padevat*, June 1976.

86. British Broadcasting Corporation, *Summary of World Broadcasts* (BBC *SWB*), FE/5320/A3/2, 24 September 1976; Twining, in Jackson, ed., *Cambodia 1975–1978*, p. 137.

87. "Life in Southern Cambodia," 25 January 1977, p. 4.

88. Cambodian National Archives, records of the Ministry of Commerce of Democratic Kampuchea, Box 4, Dossier 16, "Benchhi khleang pholitphol borotes kit trim thngai 30-9-76" ("Warehouse list: foreign products as of 30-9-76").

mission to send a return women's delegation to Vietnam. Hanoi saw this as a welcome gesture, since the Cambodian side had broken off relations with the Vietnamese Women's Union at the end of 1975.[89] The delegation of five Cambodian women, who also visited Albania, North Korea, and Laos,[90] toured Vietnam from 28 August to 4 September 1976.

The official president of the DK Women's Association, Pol Pot's wife Khieu Ponnary, was not a member of the delegation. Its leader was Leng Sei, thirty-five, a former teacher at the same Phnom Penh school Ponnary's sister, Ieng Thirith, taught at. Sei, whose real name was Leng Sim Hak, was married to Deputy Information Minister Tiv Ol. She was CPK secretary of the ministry of social welfare and director of the April 17 Hospital,[91] but since the CPK remained secret she was described as "a member of the Standing Committee of the Women's Association of Phnom Penh."[92] Two delegation members were officials of Northern and Eastern Zone Women's Associations, and one was a "textile worker." The fifth, a soldier named Ren, was a member of a regimental staff and of the Standing Committee of the DK Women's Association.[93] Thus the delegation's senior Association official was ranked last. It was the CPK hierarchy that counted.

The Cambodians flew first to Ho Chi Minh City. On arrival, they told their Vietnamese counterparts that they did not want to discuss "Indochina" and preferred to treat Vietnam, Laos, and Cambodia separately. Ha Thi Que, president of the Vietnamese Women's Union and a member of the VWP Central Committee, recalls: "We said that we were willing to agree to this."[94] This seems to have satisfied Leng Sei, who later said in a public speech in Hanoi,

89. In Hanoi in 1975, the Cambodian ambassador's wife had complained to Lao women's union officials that Vietnam was trying to annex her country and was supporting Sihanouk, even though he had killed many Cambodian communists. The Vietnamese Women's Union replied that they supported the united front, not Sihanouk's anticommunist killings, but Democratic Kampuchea broke off relations with the Vietnamese women's organization in late 1975 or early 1976. Author's interview with Ha Thi Que, Hanoi, 4 November 1980.

90. FBIS, Asia Pacific, 20 September 1976, p. H10, quoting Phnom Penh Radio of 18 September 1976.

91. People's Republic of Kampuchea, *People's Revolutionary Tribunal Held in Phnom Penh for the Trial of the Genocide Crime of the Pol Pot-Ieng Sary Clique*, August 1979, Document no. 2.5.24, DK S-21 document, "Important Culprits (Arrested from 1976 to April 9, 1978)," English translation, p. 7.

92. FBIS, Asia Pacific, 2 September 1976, p. K10, quoting Hanoi Radio of 31 August 1976.

93. The particulars of the Cambodian delegation were provided to the author by the Vietnamese Women's Union in Hanoi on 5 November 1980. The members were named as Leng Sei, Bo Ven, So Se, Vuon, and Ren, respectively. They were accompanied by Yek Srun, wife of Sok Kheang, the DK ambassador in Hanoi.

94. Author's interview with Ha Thi Que, Hanoi, 4 November 1980. She added, "We wanted peace and freedom for their country." Other details of the women's delegations are also taken from this interview.

"We pledge to tend to our militant solidarity" and to "oppose all divisive acts in any form. . . . and to make our relations evergreen."[95] From Vung Tau (a beach resort) and cooperatives in the south, the guests went to scenic Ha Long Bay and factories in the north. Throughout, they "spoke very few words," apart from Leng Sei, who introduced herself to Ha Thi Que as a teacher. "They were a little reticent, which was difficult for us, but we talked when they asked us anything," Que recalls. "They were very surprised to see the way of life in Ho Chi Minh City. Cambodia and Vietnam seemed like two different worlds. You could see on their faces that they liked the life in Ho Chi Minh City, but they did not dare say so. They called Ho Chi Minh City "capitalist." After Vietnam, they went on to Laos. There, they refused to join in dancing, as was the Lao and Khmer custom, or to participate with the Lao women in their traditional show of friendship, which is to tie threads around your wrists." Que claims the Lao women were rather disappointed.[96] As the Cambodians returned home, Democratic Kampuchea's relations with Vietnam and Laos were about to reach a crisis point.

The China Connection

Demographers agree that at least thirteen million people, and probably twenty to thirty million people, starved to death in China between 1958 and 1961.[97] In 1959, Mao Zedong nevertheless claimed that 30 percent of the Chinese people supported the "Great Leap Forward" and that 30 percent were neutral. Mao called this a 60-percent majority in favor. In 1965, Indonesian communist leader D. N. Aidit, a frequent visitor to China, used the same figures to "prove" that Indonesia's armed forces supported revolution.[98] The results of that miscalculation were equally disastrous: in 1965–66, over half a million Indonesian communists perished in an army-instigated bloodbath.[99]

Pol Pot, on his first visit to China, watched from Beijing. In 1965 China's foreign minister told another visiting delegation about the Great Leap. "The country was very tense," Chen Yi said. "There were very many chimneys from which no smoke came; factories didn't have machines; our money had

95. FBIS, Asia Pacific, 2 September 1976, p. K10, quoting Hanoi Radio of 31 August 1976.
96. Author's interview with Ha Thi Que, 1980.
97. Edward Friedman, "After Mao: Maoism and Post-Mao China", *Telos*, no. 65, Fall 1985, p. 26, citing Basil Ashton et al., "Famine in China 1958–1961," *Population and Development Review*, Spring 1985, pp. 613–645.
98. John Gittings, "The Black Hole of Bali," *Guardian* (London), September 8–9, 1990, pp. 4–6.
99. See Robert Cribb, ed., *The Indonesian Killings, 1965–66*, Monash University, Clayton, Victoria, Centre for Southeast Asian Studies, 1991.

gone."[100] Perhaps Pol Pot heard an equally frank account. But from his later policies it is not clear that he would have taken Chen Yi's words as *criticism* of the Great Leap Forward. Life in Democratic Kampuchea from 1975 to 1979 was certainly "tense," and favored features of its economy excluded factories, machinery, and money.

Pol Pot left China before the Great Proletarian Cultural Revolution broke out. Interestingly, at the time of his visit, the person in the CCP responsible for relationships with communist parties in other countries was Kang Sheng, and Pol Pot probably worked with him more closely than any other Chinese leader. Sheng has been called "a truly faithful follower of Mao," though he had worked as a Comintern official and lived in Moscow at the height of the Stalinist purges, from 1932 to 1937. In 1965 Kang Sheng was an alternate member of the CCP politburo, and in 1966 was promoted to its Standing Committee.[101]

In 1966 Pol Pot returned to Cambodia and began planning the 1967 uprising against Prince Norodom Sihanouk's regime.[102] In September 1966, he changed the party's name from "Workers' Party" to "Communist Party of Kampuchea."[103] This signaled a move away from the Vietnam Workers' Party and towards the Chinese Communist Party. In the same year the CPK established two new underground journals. One was called *Tung Krahom*, the Cambodian version of the name of the Chinese Communist journal *Red Flag*, which had been launched in 1958 during the Great Leap Forward.[104] The other was *Reaksmei Krahom* (Red Light), Cambodian for the name of a Chinese student newspaper established in France in the 1920s by Pol Pot's counterpart, the sec-

100. Roderick MacFarquhar, *The Origins of the Cultural Revolution*, vol. 2, *The Great Leap Forward, 1958–1960*, Royal Institute of International Affairs/Columbia University Press, 1983, p. 218.

101. J. Daubier, *A History of the Chinese Cultural Revolution*, New York: Vintage, 1974, pp. 76, 37, 259. Kang Sheng died in December 1975.

102. That the CPK sponsored the 1967 uprising is attested to by the party's internal history, written a few months later: "'Samlaut' and 'Pailin' in Battambang, etc. . . . show the great strength of our people under the leadership of the Party which dares fight and defeat the enemy." "Provatt pak songkep" ("Short History of the Party"), special issue of *Tung Krahom*, Sept.-Oct. 1967, p. 71. This undercuts the 1977 Pol Pot assertion, accepted by Heder, Vickery, and Chandler, that the 1967 rebellion was spontaneous. (S. Heder, "Kampuchea's Armed Struggle," *BCAS*, 11, 1, 1979; M. Vickery, "Cambodia," *BCAS*, 21, 2–4, 1989, p. 44, n. 26; D. Chandler, *Brother Number One*, p. 81.)

103. "A Short Guide for Application of Party Statutes," in T. Carney, *Communist Party Power in Kampuchea*, Cornell Southeast Asia Program Data Paper, 1977, p. 56; and Kiernan, *How Pol Pot*, p. 190.

104. Kiernan, *How Pol Pot*, p. 226. Daubier, *A History of the Chinese Cultural Revolution*, p. 226, notes that in 1967 Chen Boda was still director of *Red Flag*, which he had launched in 1958.

retary-general of the ccp Deng Xiaoping,[105] whom Pol Pot had also met in China.[106]

In late 1967, Pol Pot ran a cpk training school in the jungle of Cambodia's northeast. In nine days of political lectures, he rarely mentioned China, and never the Cultural Revolution raging there. "China is a big country," he remarked at one point. "But," he added, "it is not only us who are struggling. All over Southeast Asia people are taking responsibility."[107] He meant that Cambodia had friends not only in China but also among the pro-Chinese communist insurgencies of Thailand, Burma, Malaya, and the Philippines. This comment betrays a number of the strains of Pol Pot's motley ideology. First is the pragmatic Cambodian view, long shared by Sihanouk, of China as a weighty ally. Second is the Chinese geopolitical strategy of treating the insurgencies in Southeast Asia as rivaling the Vietnam War in importance, a view dovetailing with Cambodian anti-Vietnamese feeling. Third is a Maoist emphasis on self-reliance. Fourth is that Pol Pot's exhortation echoes Lin Biao's "Long Live the Victory of People's War," a strategy spelled out dramatically in September 1965, when Pol Pot was still in China. Neither Pol Pot, nor Ieng Sary, Son Sen, Khieu Samphan, or anyone else in the cpk Center, however, is known to have expressed sympathy with the Cultural Revolution while it was occurring.

Not all Great Leap Forward policies resurfaced in the Cultural Revolution, when the influence of Mao and his closest supporters was at its height. Crash collectivization and communalization were not repeated in China. No second attempt was made at reinstituting communal eating. This is how a leader of the Cultural Revolution, "Gang of Four" member Zhang Chunqiao, put it in April 1975, at the very time the cpk was seizing power:

> The wind of "communization" as stirred up by Liu Shaoqi and Chen Boda shall never be allowed to rise again. We have always held that, instead of having too big a supply of commodities, our country does not yet have a great abundance of them. So long as the communes cannot yet offer much to be "communized" . . . and enterprises under ownership by the whole people cannot offer a great abundance of products for distribution according to need among our 800 million people, we will have to continue with commodity production, exchange through money and distribution according to work.[108]

105. For details see Kiernan, *How Pol Pot*, p. 224.
106. Ibid., pp. 219–224; Carney, "Cambodia: The Unexpected Victory," in Jackson, ed., *Cambodia 1975–1978*, p. 24; Daubier, *A History of the Chinese Cultural Revolution*.
107. Kham Teuang, interview with the author, Phnom Penh, 21 January 1986. Teuang was a witness and a participant in the Rattanakiri province cadre training school run by Pol Pot.
108. Zhang Chunqiao, "On Exercising All-Round Dictatorship over the Bourgeoisie," *Red Flag*, 4, 1975.

Cambodia's new relationship with China was bound to be complex. Though some in the CPK admired the Great Leap Forward, and others the Cultural Revolution, in neither case was Chinese advice easily swallowed. It's important to note, however, that some saw China predominantly as a powerful strategic ally.

Aid from China

When the U.S. mission was evacuated from Cambodia on 12 April 1975, Ieng Sary was heading there by jeep, through the newly liberated parts of southern Vietnam. He received a cable from Hanoi reporting what had happened. Sary turned around and flew back to Hanoi, and then on to Beijing. According to Nayan Chanda, "he requested that his hosts stop delivering weapons and other supplies through the normal conduit—the Vietnamese." By the time he arrived by plane in Phnom Penh on 24 April, Sary had negotiated "an end to the era of the Ho Chi Minh Trail."[109] He also negotiated a Chinese military aid package for Cambodia of 13,300 tons of weapons.[110] But the first Chinese supplies were already on the way. They arrived in Kompong Som on 20 April on the *Hongi* (Red Flag), a three-thousand-ton military vessel bearing the number 153 and flying China's flag. CPK troops unloaded several hundred tons of salt, and the ship left empty.[111]

Pol Pot made a secret visit to China in June, following his firefighting trip to Hanoi. He met Mao on 21 June. Soon after, Chinese Boeing 707s began flights to Phnom Penh.[112] In August, Khieu Samphan visited Beijing and "signed a joint communiqué reflecting the current Chinese international line

109. Chanda, *Brother Enemy*, p. 12.

110. Speech by Wang Shangrong, deputy chief of the general staff of the Chinese People's Liberation Army, at talks with Son Sen, Phnom Penh, 6 February 1976, in the proceedings of the *People's Revolutionary Tribunal*, August 1979, Document no. 2.5.05 (translation), p. 5. Chanda, *Brother Enemy*, pp. 18 and 416 n. 14, argues persuasively for the authenticity of this document.

111. Author's interview with Sok Sam, a former navy pilot who worked as a docker in Kompong Som from 1975 to 1978 (Kompong Som, 18 July 1980). There is some doubt as to the date of the first arrival of the *Honqi 153*. DK ministry of commerce archives note its arrival on 15 May, but this could have been its second visit. A document listing its cargo on the 15 May shipment mentions no salt (Cambodian National Archives, records of the Ministry of Commerce of Democratic Kampuchea, Box 7, Dossier 32, "Sarop sompearea chumnui krup phnaek taam kpal nimuoi nimuoi" ("List of aid materials of all kinds on each ship"), March 1976 [?]), but a "Report on the Materials on the First Ship" dated 2 October 1975 lists the same cargo but adds "202 tons of salt" (Box 1, Dossier 5). This may have been a consolidation of two shipments, and I have accepted Sok Sam's date for the first; he correctly identified the ship's name and cargo of "several hundred tons of salt" as well as a July 1975 weapons shipment.

112. Chanda, *Brother Enemy*, p. 16; Twining, in Jackson, ed., *Cambodia 1975–1978*, p. 137.

completely."[113] In the same month, "experts from China's defense ministry conducted an extensive survey in Cambodia to assess defense needs."[114] By mid-September, China was prepared to extend to Cambodia a total of U.S.$1 billion in interest-free economic and military aid, including an immediate $20 million gift. This was "the biggest aid ever given to any one country by China."[115] At the same time, Beijing cut its aid to Vietnam. According to the U.S. government's Cambodia watcher in Thailand, "refugees reported seeing rice in the summer of 1975 in bags from the People's Republic of China."[116] A Kompong Som dock worker says that two- to four-thousand-ton Chinese ships arrived every month from mid-1975. They brought mostly rice but in July 1975 brought a cargo of weapons. North Korean convoys came once or twice a month, and there were occasional Yugoslav ships, but none from Vietnam. The ships went back empty, the docker says.[117]

In September 1975, engineer Ung Pech was recalled from the countryside, where he had gone when Kompong Som was evacuated in April. The Khmer Rouge needed technicians and engineers to help drive the cranes and forklifts used to unload the Chinese ships. When Pech arrived back in the port, he was recruited into the commerce ministry's Kompong Som branch, headed by Prum Nhiem, the same man who had taken over the information ministry building during the capture of Phnom Penh. Nhiem seems to have mellowed in the months following his round-up and execution of leaders of the defeated regime. Pech describes Nhiem as "a former worker, who got on well with us, in a cooperative manner." The town was divided between the port and the commerce ministry section. Unloading was slow: when Pech arrived there were six Chinese ships in the port. Some were oil tankers, others had brought agricultural equipment, but none carried arms.[118] A railway worker on the line to Phnom Penh adds that in late 1975 trains passed several times a day, each with twenty-five to thirty carriages, usually loaded with Chinese rice.[119]

The accounts of these workers are amplified by the archives of the DK min-

113. Porter, in Elliott, ed., *The Third Indochina Conflict*, p. 78. Samphan pledged "common struggle" against "colonialism, imperialism, and hegemonism," the last meaning the USSR. Porter cites Beijing's *New China News Agency* in English, 19 August 1975, in FBIS, PRC, DR, 19 August 1975, pp. A14–17.

114. Chanda, *Brother Enemy*, p. 17.

115. *China Quarterly*, no. 64, December 1975, p. 797, quoting *Le Monde* of 13 September 1975.

116. Twining, in Jackson, ed. *Cambodia 1975–1978*, p. 137.

117. Author's interview with Sok Sam, Kompong Som, 1980.

118. Author's interview with Ung Pech, who worked in Kompong Som from September 1975 until his arrest in April 1977. Phnom Penh, 7 September 1980.

119. Author's interview with Muk Chot, who worked on the Phnom Penh-Kompong Som railway line from 1975 to 1979. Toul, 28 October 1979.

istry of commerce (which appear to have survived intact). They list twenty-one Chinese ships that brought aid to Kompong Som in 1975. The *Honqi 153* returned to Cambodia on 15 May, bringing 3,000 tons of rice, 61 tons of cloth, 522 kilograms of antimalarial chloroquin, and three tons of other medicines (all tonnage figures are metric). Seven other ships followed in July 1975, the first two bringing nearly 4,000 tons of railway equipment and 4,000 tons of fuel. The first shipment of rice, over 10,000 tons, arrived on 12 July, along with 21 tons of medicine and 200 sewing machines. Four more Chinese ships arrived before the end of July, carrying 8,600 tons of rice, 3,000 tons of fuel, 300 jeeps, and 3,000 tons of "military equipment of all kinds."[120] The archives, however, record no further arms shipments that year. Ieng Sary requested a deferment, pending a military aid agreement with China.[121] The level of other aid also fell off. Two more Chinese ships arrived in August, four in September, and four in October, but only three in November-December 1975.[122]

In all, China's aid to Cambodia during 1975 included 61,000 tons of rice, 30,000 tons of fuel, 3,000 tons of kerosene, 200 tons of machine oil, 250 tons of pesticides, 3,300 tons of cloth, 60 tons of medicines, 1.8 million hoes, 200,000 shovels, 5,000 pesticide sprays, and 20,000 bicycles.[123] But acknowledgement of all this in the political record is rare. A confidential Center report noted on 19 September that "the Chinese and Koreans have given us a number of tractors,"[124] though the Chinese ones did not arrive that year! Democratic Kampuchea's public pronouncements and internal propaganda both stressed its "self-reliance." Officials of the Northwest Zone told trusted workers in 1975 that North Korea had offered many tractors and other aid,

120. Also aboard the last four Chinese ships in July 1975 were 200 tons of machine oil, 2,600 tons of plowshares, 237,000 shovels, 148,000 hoes, 9,000 railway sleepers, 1,000 cases of railway equipment, 3 diesel engines, 2,200 tons of cloth, 200 tons of cotton, 1,400 tons of jute, 19 tons of jute seed, and 34 tons of medicine.

121. Speech by Wang Shangrong, Phnom Penh, 6 February 1976, *People's Revolutionary Tribunal* Document no. 2.5.05, p. 6.

122. Cambodian National Archives (CNA), "Sarop sompearea chumnui krup phnaek taam kpal nimuoi nimuoi" ("List of aid materials of all kinds on each ship"), March 1976 (?), archives of the Ministry of Commerce of Democratic Kampuchea, Box 7, Dossier 32. See also Box 1, Dossier 5, "Report on the materials on the first ship," Phnom Penh, 2 October 1975; the report on the "sixth ship," which arrived on 20 July, lists "guns and bullets," but there is an empty space in the weight column.

123. CNA, records of the Ministry of Commerce of Democratic Kampuchea (henceforth CNA, MC-DK), Box 7, Dossier 32, "Benchhi touteak sompearea robos mitt chen dael baan totuol pi khae 6–75 dol 21-4-76" ("Complete list of materials from our Chinese friends received from the month of June 1975 to 21-4-76"). The figure given here for diesel alone delivered in 1975 is 30,000 tons, but Box 7, Dossier 35, "Touteak phaenkar chumnui chen phnaek preng ontoneak khnong chhnam 1975 dol thngai 30 khae 9 chhnam 76" ("Complete Chinese fuel aid plan in the year 1975 up to 30–9-76"), says 20,000 tons.

124. "Examine the Control," 19 September 1975, p. 11.

but that Khieu Samphan had refused it, saying "Cambodia is its own master, growing rice." During Samphan's August visit to China, the officials added, "Mao had expected to receive requests for aid, but instead Khieu Samphan signed a contract to sell rice to China!"[125] In the first six months Cambodia exported to China 2,400 tons of rubber, 2,200 tons of logs, 200 tons of black pepper, 113 tons of coconuts, and 39 tons of *sleng* (*Nux vomica*) seeds (for the extraction of strychnine).[126]

The North Korean Connection

The first non-Chinese aid to Democratic Kampuchea was probably a North Korean shipment of cloth and medicine that reached Kompong Som in mid-1975.[127] Twenty tractors, as well as hydroelectric power generators, followed.[128] In early 1976, two-thousand-ton Korean ships brought more tractors and agricultural machinery, and Korean technicians built a small fish processing plant near Kompong Som, staffed by ten advisers.[129] Four ships sailed for Korea in 1976, with 5,000 tons of Cambodian crepe fiber and other rubber products, 132 tons of white sesame, and 7 tons of soya.[130] North Koreans trained pilots and airport workers and provided electrical generating plants and large pumps and other equipment for ambitious irrigation projects in the countryside. A Cambodian interpreter reports: "The Koreans ate well, five or six times more than the people of Kampuchea. . . . They would secretly ask what rations the people got, or observe for themselves, but sometimes it was hidden from them. However they did not get involved in [Cambodia's] internal affairs."[131]

A CPK defector added, "These North Koreans look like Chinese. They are light-skinned and small. They usually wear white-rimmed spectacles, black pajamas and a white short-sleeved shirt, and white canvas shoes. . . . Traveling from one place to another, they close all the car windows for fear of contracting malaria. They require great cleanliness in the preparation of their meals. They use a clean white napkin under their plates of rice and other

125. Author's interview with San, who worked as a statistician for the CPK Region 5 Committee in 1975–76, Paris, 29 May 1980.
126. CNA, MC-DK, Box 1, Dossier 5, report on material exported from Kompong Som to China in 1975, dated Phnom Penh, 2 October 1975.
127. CNA, MC-DK, Box 1, Dossier 5, "Sekkedey reaykar ompi sompearea kpal korei" ("Report on the materials on the Korean ship"), 2 October 1975.
128. CNA, MC-DK, Box 1, Dossier 2, "Sarop sompearea noam coul pi borotes pi khae 5 dol khae 12 chhnam 75" ("Total materials imported from abroad from May to December 1975"), p. 3; "Examine the Control," 19 September 1975, p. 14.
129. Ung Pech interview, 1980.
130. CNA, MC-DK, Box 7, Dossier 33, report dated 21 December 1976.
131. Author's interview with Kun and his wife Bopha, Montbard, 1 February 1980.

dishes. If a single fly lands on the food during a meal, they stop eating. They are in the habit of washing their own clothes. They love to drink coconut milk."[132]

Cambodia imported North Korean products. Commerce ministry warehouses on 30 September 1976 contained 200,000 meters of "Korean and Yugoslav cloth," 110 Korean drills and 56,000 drill bits, 2,000 padlocks, and an assortment of tools, lathes, and steel parts, as well as 6,000 cans of Romanian canned fish.[133] Pyongyang also provided less prosaic assistance. In what Democratic Kampuchea described as "the first visit of an art delegation," a North Korean song and dance troupe—led by the director of the propaganda department of the Korean People's Army—toured Cambodia in November 1976. Phnom Penh Radio asserted that the visitors were "warmly greeted by city dwellers." They performed for Khieu Samphan, Nuon Chea, and Ieng Sary and visited Angkor and the nearby countryside. Information Minister Hu Nim proclaimed that Cambodians were "greatly impressed by the ideological and artistic value of the Democratic People's Republic of Korea's sound and progressive new arts."[134]

China and Cambodia in 1976

On 12 October 1975, a second Chinese military delegation to Cambodia "submitted a draft aid plan to Phnom Penh for its approval."[135] Cambodia appears to have taken its time, but in the meantime, China supplied four new coastal patrol vessels for the DK naval base at Ream, near Kompong Som.[136] Then Cambodia suddenly told China it needed the outstanding ten thousand tons of promised military aid, as soon as February or March 1976. The deputy chief of the Chinese general staff, Wang Shangrong, quickly visited Democratic Kampuchea for talks with Son Sen. China pledged delivery of four thousand tons of weaponry and thirteen hundred vehicles by the end of March and, soon after, a hundred 120-millimeter artillery pieces and shells.[137] Then, on 10 Feb-

132. Lim Mean, a former crk member who defected to Thailand on 2 November 1978, was interviewed by Thai officials on 15 December 1978. A 29-page French translation of the Thai debriefing report was kindly provided to the author by Roland-Pierre Paringaux in 1979; this story appears on p. 18.

133. cna, mc-dk, Box 4, Dossier 16, "Benchhi khleang pholitphol borotes kit trim thngai 30-9-76" ("Warehouse list: foreign products as at 30-9-76").

134. U.S. CIA, FBIS, Asia-Pacific, 17 November 1976, p. H1, Phnom Penh Radio of 16 November 1976; and 2 December 1976, p. H1-5, Phnom Penh Radio of 1 December 1976.

135. Chanda, Brother Enemy, p. 17.

136. Twining, in Jackson, ed., Cambodia 1975-1978, p. 138; Bangkok Post, 1 May 1979, has the number of patrol boats China provided.

137. Speech by Wang Shangrong, Phnom Penh, 6 February 1976, People's Revolutionary Tribunal Document no. 2.5.05 (translation), p. 6.

ruary, the two sides signed a new military aid treaty. During 1976, China was to supply "the necessary weapons and equipment for on-the-spot training of core officers" for a new military airport and parts of antiaircraft and radar regiments, plus four navy escort ships and four torpedo boats, parts of army tank and signals regiments and of three artillery regiments, and a fully equipped pontoon regiment. Five hundred Chinese military personnel would come to Cambodia in 1976 to carry out this training.[138] Four hundred seventy-one Cambodian air force and 157 navy personnel would leave for training in China.

China promised to deliver 130-millimeter artillery and tanks in early 1977 and, in the same year, four more navy escort ships and four torpedo boats, antiaircraft batteries for the air force, and radar equipment. On completion of the military airport in central Cambodia, China would also hand over six jet fighter-aircraft and two bombers and begin constructing more airfields. The aircraft would be disassembled, Wang Shangrong told Son Sen, packed for shipment to Cambodia, and reassembled there. He added, "Submarines and tankers may go straight to Kampuchea." In 1978, there would be more tanks and radar equipment, two more navy escort ships, and four more torpedo boats.[139]

China was not well prepared for such a large program. Shangrong confessed to Son Sen, "In 1976 we need over 100 interpreters. . . . However, now we have only 10 interpreters. We hope that you will try to settle part of the problem."[140] The demands on Cambodia were also high. Five thousand workers and three thousand CPK soldiers toiled in the port to service external aid and trade.[141] Chinese technicians and officials in Kompong Som numbered over two hundred men and a few women interpreters.[142]

Continuing the late 1975 trend, Chinese economic aid fell away in 1976. The DK commerce ministry records only seven ships arriving in Kompong Som between 1 January and the anniversary of the CPK victory on 17 April. Yet Ung Pech reports Chinese ships arriving in Kompong Som "every day," bringing trucks[143] and presumably the massive amounts of military equipment ordered

138. These included 320 air force, 120 naval, and 50 tank and artillery experts.
139. Speech by Wang Shangrong, pp. 2–4. The actual military equipment China delivered by 1979 included 2 fast gunships each over 800 tons, 4 patrol boats, 200 tanks, 300 armored cars, 300 artillery pieces, six jet fighters, two bombers, and 30,000 tons of assorted ammunition. See "'Squandered Chinese aid' spelt Pol Pot's ruin," *Bangkok Post*, 1 May 1979.
140. Speech by Wang Shangrong, p. 5.
141. Author's interview with Ung Pech, 1980. Pech's figures of 6,000 workers, including over three thousand former Khmer Rouge soldiers, and 3,000 troops, are slightly qualified by Sok Sam, also interviewed in 1980, who says there were 7–8,000 workers in Kompong Som in 1976.
142. Sok Sam interview, 1980.
143. Ung Pech interview, 1980. Sok Sam (1980) says that on average in the DK period 6–8 ships came each month, with a maximum of fourteen, except in mid-1978, when perhaps 28 ships arrived in a single month.

in February. The railway worker on the line to Phnom Penh reports that in 1976 the trainloads of Chinese rice were replaced by weapons, steel, machinery, and cloth.[144] Fuel shipments continued: sixteen thousand tons in the first four months of 1976. But no rice or medicine arrived after October 1975. From January to April, Democratic Kampuchea imported only 1,600 tons of kerosene, 230 tons of pesticide, and 326 tons of cloth. No nonmilitary shipments arrived in March, and only two arrived in April.[145] There was still no sign of the tractors China had promised. After a year of Chinese aid to Cambodia, the DK ministry of commerce drew up a list of materials that had not arrived according to plan: 300 tractors, 20 bulldozers, 7 graders, 3 steamrollers, 3 cranes, 20 forklifts, 50 power saws, 14,000 assorted tools, 10 transplanting machines, 3 tugboats, and 1,000 thermometers, plus 10 movie cameras, film, and 5 projectors.[146]

In May 1976, Cambodian pilot Pech Lim Kuon defected and flew his helicopter out to Thailand. Kuon had been one of five pilots training ten Cambodians to fly UH1H helicopters; the other four teachers were Chinese.[147] He reported that "large shipments of Chinese rice had been arriving at Phnom Penh by air." Pochentong airport became the base for four hundred Chinese workers and officials, as well as DK trainee pilots and technicians.[148] There were "well over a thousand Chinese in Phnom Penh and cities around the country," serving as technical advisers.[149] They furnished textile, bottle, glass, cement, and rubber factories. A few Chinese medical teams taught simple surgical techniques to Cambodian doctors; more flew in during 1976 when "serious epidemics" flared.[150] The wife of a Chinese embassy official, Fu Xuezhang, broadcast regularly for the Chinese-language service of the Voice of Democratic Kampuchea. China had replaced the United States as the paramount external power in Cambodia. As Gareth Porter has written, "In the first postwar year, [China] emerged as the one foreign state with a significant role in Kampuchea, . . . and the only military assistance programme."[151] The only

144. Author's interview with Muk Chot, 1979.

145. CNA, MC-DK, Box 7, Dossier 32, "Benchhi touteak sompearea robos mitt chen dael baan totuol pi khae 6–75 dol 21-4-76" and "Sarop sompearea chumnui krup phnaek taam kpal nimuoi nimuoi."

146. CNA, MC-DK, Box 7, Dossier 32, "Benchhi touteak sompearea robos mitt chen dael baan totuol haoy pi khae 5–75 dol khae 4–76" ("Complete list of Chinese aid materials already received from May '75 to April '76"), 29 April 1976. The year's plan for medical aid was 241 tons; "59.307 tonnes and 666 cases" arrived.

147. Bruce Palling's interview with Pech Lim Kuon, Bangkok, 3 May 1976.

148. New York Times, 26 May 1976; Twining, in Jackson, ed., Cambodia 1975–1978, p. 137.

149. Washington Post, 4 May 1976, quoted by Porter in Elliott, ed., Third Indochina Conflict, p. 118 n. 40.

150. Elizabeth Becker, When the War Was Over, New York: Simon and Schuster, 1986, p. 286.

151. G. Porter, in Elliott, ed., The Third Indochina Conflict, p. 78.

other embassies in Phnom Penh were those of Vietnam, North Korea, Laos, Cuba, Albania, and Yugoslavia.

An elderly Chinese diplomat posted to Phnom Penh has revealed that by 1976 his government believed massacres were occurring. "We heard about violence. Not exact stories but rumors. We did guess many were dying in the countryside at the hands of local functionaries." In the capital, China's diplomats were living better than anyone in Cambodia. "The embassy was cool in the hot season. There was a swimming pool large enough for exercise and ample space for the staff. The mission had its own Chinese chef, and food was flown in weekly from Peking." The isolation took a toll, though. "We were all nervous and bored . . . The Cambodian government asked us not to go on walks but we went anyway. One or two soldiers followed us always, usually walking fifty yards behind . . . we saw quite a few small factories where young girls were sewing. But we couldn't visit them. We could only see the factories funded directly by our assistance projects. . . . We were kept apart just as other foreigners. . . . In one and a half years I never saw a Cambodian taking a promenade."[152]

China's premier, Zhou En-lai, died in January 1976. The news provoked suspicion in the Cambodian foreign ministry: "We must beware of China. It is true that we owe her a good deal, and it is a great country. But she wants to make us her satellite."[153] Zhou's demise spelled political trouble not only for his Chinese protégé, Deng Xiaoping, but also for his Cambodian one, Sihanouk, who resigned as Democratic Kampuchea's head of state on 4 April. During March, an anti-Deng campaign built up in Beijing, and Deng was forced to resign on 7 April. The Cultural Revolution radicals, "the Gang of Four," reached the peak of their influence. A month later, four Chinese ships cut through Vietnamese waters flying the DK flag "as big as anything," Nuon Chea told the Standing Commiteee.[154] This was China's apparent response to the opening of frontier talks between Democratic Kampuchea and Vietnam. Only three Chinese civilian supply ships had arrived in March and April, and the four May arrivals were probably carrying arms. But little was known of this in the outside world. The *Far Eastern Economic Review* concluded that "Hanoi has snatched away Peking's trump card in Indochina. . . . The hardliners and the pro-Hanoi faction have won the struggle."[155]

152. Becker, *When the War Was Over*, pp. 285–87.
153. Laurence Picq, *Au-delà du ciel: Cinq ans chez les Khmers Rouges*, Paris: Bernard Barrault, 1984, p. 52.
154. "Examining Vietnamese Reactions," 14 May 1976, p. 4. This was unusual; Kompong Som pilot Sok Sam says that Chinese ships coming to Cambodia would normally fly the Chinese flag, except when in the port of Kompong Som, when they would fly the DK flag. (1980 interview.)
155. Edith Lénart, "Phnom Penh's New Hardliners," *FEER*, 7 May 1976, p. 22.

The CPK kept up its requests for more Chinese military aid. On 15 May, Son Sen reported to the CPK Standing Committee that he had "met with Chinese diplomats and technicians to announce the opinion of the Standing Committee concerning the construction of a weapons factory. They agree with the plan." The Chinese offered technical advice and suggested a factory labor force of two thousand would be required. The Standing Committee decided to build the factory near Phnom Penh, but to keep it "extremely secret."[156]

To pay for all this, Cambodia exported rubber on the Chinese ships. The railway worker on the Phnom Penh-Kompong Som line reports Cambodian rubber and rice heading for the port from 1976.[157] Ung Pech recalls that "Kompong Som was full of it. All ships took away rubber or rice."[158] By mid-1976 Cambodia had exported thirteen thousand tons of rubber to China and North Korea.[159] In October the S.S. Le Du departed for Beijing with another seven thousand tons, along with four hundred tons of kapok, pepper, and sleng seeds. Prum Nhiem signed the invoices for the Le Du's cargo.

On the same ship, Nhiem dispatched a very different line of products: much rarer, more expensive, low bulk items. The new Cambodian exports to China comprised one hundred tons of lotus seeds, eighty-seven tons of coffee, seventeen tons of frangipani flowers, five tons of chaulmoogra seeds, five tons of malva nuts, and four tons of cardamom. With this cargo went some animal parts valued for their medicinal, even aphrodisiacal properties: two cases of tiger bones and two cases containing 3,003 gecko heads.[160]

The gecko, a large tropical lizard, is prized in China. And appropriately for an aphrodisiac, in Democratic Kampuchea the gecko was intimately connected with rubber production. Lim Mean, a former CPK member who later defected to Thailand, says the story began among a group of Chinese advisers stationed in the rubber plantations of Mimot, a remote part of the Eastern Zone. These thirty Chinese men worked in denim jeans and jackets, sometimes short-sleeved, and wore canvas shoes, Mean recounted. "When the Chinese went out to work, a Khmer Rouge bodyguard unit always followed them everywhere. If they heard the cry of 'Tek-khé' [the gecko's characteristic

156. "Minutes of the Meeting of the Standing Committee, 15 May 1976," 2 pp.

157. Author's interview with Muk Chot, 1979.

158. Twining, in Jackson, ed., Cambodia 1975–1978, p. 135; Ung Pech interview, 1980. The first record of this for 1976 is of a 3,000-ton shipment of crepe rubber to Canton on 21 May. CNA, MC-DK, Box 7, Dossier 33.

159. N. Chanda, "Phnom Penh's Undercover Men," FEER, 10 December 1976, p. 50.

160. CNA, MC-DK, Box 7, Dossier 33, invoices dated 30 September. The tiger bones from at least ten animals, weighed 108 kg. See New York Times, 15 March 1994, p. C12, 6 June 1993 (which notes that "the real animal parts are so expensive that often the medicines may have only trace elements"), and 7 September 1993; FEER, 19 August 1993, pp. 22–28.

sound] they went after it themselves." Dropping their tools, the Chinese would take off into the forest. The sight of black-clad Khmer Rouge soldiers tracking Chinese technicians in denim suits after lizards between rubber trees must have been worth seeing. The Chinese would keep the animals alive until they had enough to send a shipment home, when there would be a mass slaughter. At any rate, the wild gecko chases disrupted installation of the latex treatment machinery the Chinese were supervising. In the end, says Lim Mean, "Pol Pot had to intervene. He approached the Chinese embassy in Phnom Penh. He said that when the Chinese went off like that to catch the geckoes on their own, it created many problems for their guards. If they should suffer a mortal accident it would cause trouble for Cambodia and China. If the Chinese need geckoes, the Pol Pot government would arrange to get them some. Let them indicate how many they wanted." The Chinese also wanted certain species of fruits and plants that "have the qualities for healing many illnesses."[161]

The first evidence of animal products' being collected for export is a list of such materials stored in ministry of commerce warehouses in May 1976: twenty "No. 1" snakeskins, two bearskins, a tigerskin, 140 kg of musk deer antlers, 40 kg of tortoiseshell, 20 kg of buffalo horn, 20 kg of tiger bones, and 70 kg of monkey bones.[162] In July, the ministry listed natural medicinal products that China had requested. These included tiger bones, panther bones, dried geckoes, and pangolin (scaly anteater) scales, as well as cardamom, *sleng* seeds, frangipani, and other plant products.[163] A new trade agreement between Democratic Kampuchea and China was signed on 26 August.[164]

The S.S. *Le Du* left Cambodia on 2 October, the first in a series of ships that carried to China a vast wealth of Cambodian forest products. In one sense it represented nothing new. These were the type of exotic items long treasured in China that had formed the basis of the tribute gifts Cambodian monarchs sent to the Middle Kingdom for centuries.[165] But the scale of these exports grew quickly. The cargo of the S.S. *Le Du* was only the start of an unprece-

161. Account of Lim Mean (see note 132, above); the story above appears on pp. 14–15, where Mean claims to have seen this group of Chinese experts in 1977. He said that China also wanted a small species of fruit, *tbal kai*, and the plant *makleua*. Part of Mean's account appeared in *Le Point*, 328, 1 January 1979, pp. 34–35.

162. CNA, MC-DK, Box 7, Dossier 31, *Benchhi pholitphol bontaop bonsom bonthaem* ("List of additional miscellaneous products"), dated Phnom Penh, 24 May 1976.

163. CNA, MC-DK, Box 7, Dossier 35, "Voathotheat daem somrap phsom thnam taam somnom por rebos mitt chen" ("Medicinal raw materials requested by our Chinese friends"), 17 July 1976, 7pp. Pangolin scales are also used for aphrodisiacal purposes.

164. BBC SWB, FE/W893/A/16, 1 September 1976, citing Phnom Penh Radio of 27 August 1976. The agreement was signed by Vorn Vet.

165. See for instance F. Hirsh and W. W. Rockhill, *Chau Ju Kua: His Work on the Chinese and Arab Trade in the 12th and 13th Centuries*, New York: Paragon Reprints, 1966, pp. 52–53, 55–56,

dented plunder of Cambodia's ecology. It was unequaled in scope since at least the seventeenth century, when in a single month (July 1639) Dutch agents in Phnom Penh bought no fewer than 125,000 deerskins for export to Japan.[166] In that period the deer population of southern Cambodia virtually disappeared.

There are no prices on the invoices Prum Nhiem sent to China on 30 September. But since 1 May, China had delivered over 50,000 tons of fuel.[167] Chinese products in D.K. warehouses also included 4 million yards of cloth, 10 million cigarette lighter flints, 25 tons of sugar, 74,000 hoes, 15,000 cases of DDT, 200 sewing machines, 2,300 bicycles, and 1,700 shovels.[168] But the *Le Du*'s valuable cargo was only part of Cambodia's payment for the massive amounts of weapons and fuel delivered since April 1975. And there was more on the way. Until now, Ung Pech had noticed only small boxes of ammunition being moved from the docks in trucks. From August 1976, he began to see "artillery, tanks, guns, two or three convoys a month." At the same time, "huge amounts of rice were exported in late 1976." Pech, an engineer responsible for the conveyor belt that loaded the sacks onto the ships, says that nearly every day a ship departed with a load of Cambodian rice.[169] The U.S. government also got reports of rubber being exported *via* Kompong Som.[170]

In late December 1976, a Chinese delegation visited Cambodia to sign an economic and scientific protocol. In his welcoming speech, Vorn Vet hinted at the military aid program when he praised "the all-out support accorded us" by Beijing, assuring the visitors that Cambodians "highly value economic cooperation with China."[171] In fact, Democratic Kampuchea was paying dearly for a massive arms buildup, while refusing "so-called humanitarian aid" in the

---

221–22. (Eric Tagliacozzo provided this reference.) In the nineteenth century, when much of Cambodia was under Thai rule, forest products such as ivory, cardamom, gambodge, rhinoceros horns, hides, skins, peacock feathers, elephants, etc., constituted a major part of the Siamese junk trade with China. Puangthong Rungswasdisab, "War and Trade: Siamese Interventions in Cambodia, 1767–1851," Ph.D. Diss., University of Wollongong, 1995, p. 55 citing Thai sources.

166. See W. J. M. Buch, "La Compagnie des Indes Néerlandaises et l'Indochine," *Bulletin de l'école française d'extrême-orient*, 37 (1937), p. 207.

167. CNA, MC-DK, Box 7, Dossier 35, "Touteak phaenkar chumnui chen phnaek preng ontoneak khnong chhnam 1975 dol thngai 30 khae 9 chhnam 76" ("Complete Chinese fuel aid plan in the year 1975 up to 30-9-76"), dated 15 October 1976.

168. CNA, MC-DK, Box 4, Dossier 16, "Benchhi khleang pholitphol borotes kit trim thngai 30-9-76" ("Warehouse list: foreign products as of 30-9-76").

169. Ung Pech interview, 1980. I have yet to find D.K. records for exports to China over this period in late 1976.

170. Twining, in Jackson, ed., *Cambodia 1975–1978*, p. 135.

171. U.S. CIA, FBIS, Asia Pacific, 27 December 1976, pp. H2, 5, Phnom Penh Radio of 26 December 1976.

name of self-reliance.[172] A Chinese press delegation also toured Cambodia for two weeks. On its departure, the delegation's leader promised to "take with us the excellent impressions we have gained." He added, "A radiant democratic Cambodia is emerging in the east like a glowing red sun rising."[173]

Trade with Thailand

The town of Poipet, on Cambodia's western border, is linked with the Thai town of Aranyaprathet by road and a long-unused railway bridge. Otherwise "still untouched by the war" a week before it ended in April 1975, Poipet was swollen by refugees to a population of fifty thousand.[174] As the CPK approached victory, the road from Battambang was closed, then reopened, and on 17 April, trading stopped in Poipet market, then restarted in the morning.[175] On 19 April, the five-hundred-strong CPK 17th Battalion, including many young women, led by six officers, occupied the town. They proclaimed themselves "soldiers of Sihanouk," led by the "National Liberation Movement."[176] A few days later, a senior CPK official in Poipet told a Thai journalist that the border would be opened to Thai visitors in ten days' time.[177] This never occurred. On 24 April, the Khmer Rouge evacuated the town for fear that "Thai troops might invade Cambodia."[178] But the following day, they sent a delegation of twenty for talks with Thai officials.[179]

Confusion reigned throughout the Northwest Zone in the aftermath of victory. Like the other towns in the Zone, Poipet was not evacuated immediately, and the victors' initial policies favored the continued operation of markets. The causes of the confusion seemed to be the distance from Phnom Penh and apparent political differences among Northwest Zone cadres and perhaps between the Zone leadership and the Center (see page 50). Factions emerged early in Poipet. The talks with Thai officials on 25 April were led by a commander codenamed Khanawong, who promised to reveal his real identity "at our victory celebration to be held very soon."[180] He never did, and soon

---

172. "So-called humanitarian aid" is the term used in the DK constitution, which recognizes no real "humanitarian aid." D. P. Chandler, "The Constitution of Democratic Kampuchea (Cambodia): The Semantics of Revolutionary Change," *Pacific Affairs*, Fall 1976, p. 513.

173. FBIS, Asia Pacific, 27 December 1976, p. H7.

174. *Bangkok Post*, 12 April 1975; Bangkok *Nation*, 28 April 1975. Poipet's own population was given as ten thousand. For more on Poipet at the end of the war, see *FEER*, 28 November 1975, and the letter and reply of 9 January and 13 February 1976.

175. *Bangkok Post*, 13 and 19 April 1975.

176. *Bangkok Post*, 19, 20, and 28 April 1975.

177. Bangkok *Nation*, 23 April 1975.

178. *Bangkok World*, 26 April 1975; *Bangkok Post*, 25 and 28 April 1975.

179. *Bangkok Post*, 26 April 1975.

180. *Bangkok Post*, 27 April 1975.

disappeared from the border. The next CPK leader to appear was Khek Penn, alias Sou, using the code name Colonel Vichai. He announced that Poipet's victory celebration would be held on 7–9 May and promised to invite Thai police officers, "if they trust us." He said, "We are afraid of Thailand and will not do anything harmful to her and her people."[181] Penn, a former schoolteacher, was a member of the Zone Committee who had brought many "new people" into the administration.[182] He favored reestablishing towns, schools, and currency.[183] But by the end of May, Khek Penn had left Poipet in the charge of another official, known to Thais as Major Suwan.[184] In July, however, Suwan was accused of embezzlement, Poipet market burned to the ground, and he was replaced.[185] Two new faces appeared at the border. One was Hak Sreng, representing a "trade mission appointed by the Military Committee in Phnom Penh."[186] The other, "Friend Nguan," offered Thai smugglers 15 percent less than his predecessor had. He was stabbed by Thai traders and robbed in mid-September.[187]

The stakes were high and rising. In June, ten thousand liters of gasoline were smuggled daily from Thailand by motorcycle.[188] By late August the figure rose to twenty thousand liters. In early September, DK officials bought U.S.$29,000 worth of Thai rice.[189] By late September they were reportedly buying ten times that amount *daily*, paying more than double the normal Thai prices for both rice and diesel. Errol de Silva, the first Western journalist to enter Cambodia since April, traveled from Poipet to Battambang in September. He met Pouvong, one of the three top Khmer Rouge leaders in Battambang, and saw him carrying "about $20,000" in hundred-dollar bills.

Pouvong complained to de Silva, "Who is there to give us food? Supplies from China and Russia are not coming in due to the confusion as to who was the real power in Cambodia."[190] This ill-informed statement illustrates the distance between the CPK Center and Cambodia's regional administrations. The

181. *Bangkok Post*, 2 May 1975.

182. See Vickery, *Cambodia 1975–1982*, pp. 111, 167; see also author's inteview with San, who worked for the CPK Region 5 Committee in 1975–6: "It was in Regions 4 and 5, under Khek Penn (Sou) and Hing, that the most intellectuals were recruited to work with the Khmer Rouge" (Paris, 29 May 1980).

183. See Chapter 3, p. 96.

184. Bangkok *Nation*, 31 May 1975; *Bangkok World*, 24 June 1975; *Bangkok Post*, 23 July 1975.

185. *Bangkok Post*, 23 July 1975.

186. *Bangkok Post*, 25 July 1975.

187. *Bangkok Post*, 13 August and 19 September 1975.

188. *Bangkok Post*, 1 July 1975.

189. Bangkok *Nation*, 2 September 1975.

190. Errol de Silva, "Where They Burn Money to Cook the Food," *Bangkok Post*, 24 September 1975; see also Bangkok *Nation*, 2 September 1975.

Center wanted no Soviet aid, and supplies of Chinese aid were indeed arriving. Obviously the Center was not sending much of it to Battambang. San, a former teacher who worked in Sisophon for the Region 5 CPK committee and was involved in the purchases from Thailand, said he never heard of any rice arriving in Battambang from China. And the rice supplies left behind by the Lon Nol regime from international aid and the late 1974 harvest were running out. So, trade with Thailand was booming. San and other teachers worked with Khek Penn to buy rice, medicine, salt, and clothing from Thailand, often paying in gold.[191]

Pouvong's description of Russia as a potential ally along with China is suggestive of the Vietnamese position in international affairs, which was even-handed compared to that of the CPK Center. So is his willingness to admit a foreign journalist to Battambang and grant an interview. But Pouvong did not seem hostile to the Center, explaining the lack of aid from Phnom Penh by asserting its impossibility: "There is no central government for another six months."[192] His rationale for Cambodia's situation was a relatively moderate response to what he saw as an emergency: "We all have to work to make the country strong. Otherwise, there won't be any food. . . . Soldiers as well have to work in the fields. We feed everybody—even our former enemies. But they must work in the fields like everyone else."[193]

Another leading official in the Northwest Zone at this time was said to be responsible for the city and province of Battambang. This was Phan Treung, who was described as a Khmer national of Vietnamese descent, the former owner of the "Tokyo" beauty salon.[194] The U.S. embassy in Bangkok reported in August 1975 that "one Cambodian observer argues that Phan Treung is not linked so much to the center-oriented KC [Khmer Communists] as to those under strong Hanoi influence. . . . Refugees from Battambang province say that, since Phan Treung's arrival (perhaps in June) the military presence has changed from Khmer to a number of . . . native-born Cambodians of Vietnamese stock. . . . Furthermore, several said they were certain the Vietnamese were formerly workers on the rubber plantations in eastern Cambodia. (Perhaps this explains a recent AP story that Vietnamese advisers have been seen among KC troop units in the province.)"[195]

San, the former teacher from Sisophon. was sent for political education in mid-1975. None of the Northwest Zone leaders there referred to Hanoi as an

191. San, interview with the author, 29 May 1980.
192. Bangkok *Nation,* 2 September 1975.
193. *Bangkok Post,* 24 September 1975.
194. *Bangkok Post,* 23 July 1975.
195. See "The New Cambodia: Life in the Provinces," Extracts from an Airgram Report by an Officer of the American Embassy at Bangkok, 26 August 1975 (declassified in 1978), p. 9.

"enemy" or even a "revisionist" regime. San asked about this: "But the Vietnamese have a notion to create an Indochina Federation, to take over our country," as the Lon Nol regime had alleged in its wartime anticommunist propaganda. The zone division's political commissar replied, "That is not true." He blamed the allegation on "the U.S. imperialists, who had created it to divide us from each other." The commissar commented that "some" Vietnamese were "devious" (kil) and "nasty" (kouc) and had some hypocritical ideas, but insisted that "the Khmer and the Vietnamese were friends, brothers and sisters" and that contacts continued.[196] At the village level, in 1975–76 local Khmer Rouge also described the Vietnamese communists as "brothers."[197] This line may have represented the remnants of what were once described as "old line Khmer Rouge," a faction reported active in western Battambang in the early 1970s.[198] A moderate, or pro-Vietnamese, tendency did exist in the Northwest. Though not dominant, it had a continuing influence, epitomized by Khek Penn and some of the other ex-teachers and older veterans in the Zone leadership.

Cambodians continued to stream across the border into Thailand. Twenty-four hundred fled into Aranyaprathet in four days in July 1975. Further south, another nineteen hundred crossed the border in late August.[199] In mid-September, Thai officers crossed the border into Cambodia's Oddar Meanchey province. The Center reported that the Thais wished "to discuss the Khmers who have escaped to Thailand and about the border. It seems that it was urgent. It does not seem that they come as spies. Importantly, they want to meet and discuss with us." The Center decided to allow the refugees to return.[200]

196. San, interview with the author, Paris, 29 May 1980. San recalled the commissar's criticism of Vietnamese who "had come to help fight Lon Nol but had exploited and robbed the people, so that in 1973 they had sent all the Vietnamese back" and the "Vietnamese brothers and sisters had left." The Vietnamese, he claimed, had not wanted the Khmer "to do much fighting [but] wanted to help and take the victory over Lon Nol, but the Khmer Rouge wanted to be independent." San reiterated that the commissar did not see this as a problem between the two regimes, and that he explicitly rejected the allegations that Vietnam was "revisionist" or wanted to bring Cambodia into an "Indochina Federation."

197. Author's interview with another former teacher, Chik, Strasbourg, 1 November 1979. Chik had lived in a base village of Region 5 of the Northwest Zone. At least until November 1976, people in neighboring Oddar Meanchey Province were also allowed by the local Khmer Rouge to bring their radios "out into the open and tune into the Cambodian services" of Vietnam as well as China and Phnom Penh. See "Life in Cambodia: Extracts from an Airgram Report by an Officer of the American Embassy at Bangkok," 31 March 1977, report declassified by the U.S. Department of State, 6 July 1978, p. 7.

198. J. J. Zasloff and A. E. Goodman, eds., *Indochina in Conflict: A Political Assessment*, Lexington, Mass.: D.C. Heath, 1972, frontispiece map.

199. *Bangkok Post*, 14 July, 27 August 1975.

200. "On the Control and Implementation of the Political Line of Gathering Forces for the Party's National Democratic Front," "Document No. 6," 22 September 1975, pp. 7–8. Translation by C. Boua.

So in late October 1975, Foreign Minister Ieng Sary made an official visit to Bangkok, in a chartered Chinese Boeing 707. He told the Thai prime minister, Kukrit Pramoj, that Cambodia declined international aid and would rather help itself without Thai assistance. Sary did, however, begin official trade with Thailand, claiming that Cambodia needed rice, sugar, refined oil, and salt, and that it could supply timber and smoked fish.[201] Regularization undercut much of the border trade and soon left Thai businessmen in Aranyaprathet complaining that the Khmer Rouge owed them twenty million *baht* in credit.[202] A new Cambodian border liaison office was established, this time a committee of three, headed by Khek Penn, with Hak Sreng, who represented Phnom Penh, and an unknown, Oum Choeun. They announced their plan to buy ten thousand tons of salt per month for Cambodia's preserved fish industry, and said they expected the demand to double by early 1976.[203] Thai-Cambodian border liaison meetings were to be held each Thursday.

Trade was not the only border issue. Frontier demarcation was another. The two sides were using different maps, with small but clearly overlapping claims. Although Cambodia, using the original treaty maps of 1904, had legality on its side, the cpк Center proved more malleable with Thailand than with Vietnam. "While nuts-and-bolts negotiator Chan Yourann insisted on the treaty maps as the sole basis of frontiers, Foreign Minister Ieng Sary over-ruled Yourann and indicated the matter was still open to negotiation." Sary came to Poipet on 17 November to meet the Thai foreign minister and inaugurate the liaison committee.[204] On 14 December, Khek Penn came to Poipet for further negotiations. He agreed to repay Cambodian debts to Thai merchants and "presented the Thai delegate with a terrified Thai farmer who had been kidnapped by cpк forces."[205] The Thais proposed a joint border-marking team and the creation of extra local markers. Penn took these proposals to Battambang, then to Phnom Penh. But he returned to Poipet without instructions, and as the year ended there was still no word from the Center.[206] The idea was apparently dropped. As in the case of Vietnam, border negotiations were suspended, and Democratic Kampuchea's prickly insistence on unilateral concessions by the other side played a part. A foreign visitor to Cambodia in February 1976 reported that "sometimes the Thai officials would demand meetings with the

201. Bangkok *Nation*, 31 October 1975; *Bangkok Post*, 13 November 1975.

202. *Bangkok Post*, 3 December 1975.

203. *Bangkok Post*, 18 November 1975; Bangkok *Nation*, 18 November 1975.

204. S. Heder, "Thailand's Relations with Kampuchea: Negotiation and Confrontation along the Prachinburi-Battambang Border," unpublished paper, Cornell University, December 1977, pp. 2–4, 75, n. 163, citing an "interview with a U.S. State Department official, 7 December 1977," and 23.

205. Chandler, *The Tragedy of Cambodian History*, p. 376 n. 48.

206. *Bangkok Post*, 13, 15, 17, 20, 22, 19 December 1975.

Kampuchean cadres. But when the appointment was decided, the Thais would claim that it was upon Kampuchea's request. The Kampuchean leaders consider such claims an insult to their dignity." Ieng Sary even "cancelled an appointment on February 25, 1976, as the result of Thai claims that it was Kampuchea who had demanded the meeting."[207]

Meanwhile, Pouvong and Phan Treung dropped from sight. In March-April 1976, a "courteous and well-educated" cadre in the Northwest Zone expounded a new foreign policy: "China helped Kampuchea without preconditions. She was a sister-nation." Vietnam, by contrast, was now seen as a "constant danger."[208]

Another problem on the Thai border was continued Cambodian factional strife. Former Cambodian prime minister In Tam, attempting to organize resistance to the CPK from Thailand, was blamed for a border clash between Thais and Cambodians in mid-December. But In Tam asserted that there had been "a conflict between two revolutionary groups among the Khmer Rouge. He said one group of twenty-four Khmer Rouge were pursued across the border by seventy others who had been confronted by Thai border patrol police. 'I had nothing to do with it,' he said."[209] But he was forced to leave Thailand three days later, and there followed "a lull in violent incidents in the area from February 1976 to January 1977."[210] But the flow of refugees continued. By February 1976, there were nearly ten thousand Cambodians in Thailand, and in November the total reached twenty-three thousand, plus the five thousand ethnic Thais from Koh Kong.[211]

The U.S. government's Cambodia watcher at this time reported that "Cambodian rubber began appearing in Aranyaprather in 1976, generally a dirty, inferior product. No one knew from what part of Cambodia it came or whether it had been produced years earlier or was newly produced. The consensus was that it was old."[212] Other exports included "small quantities of teak, gemstones, hides, and dried fish."[213] A second Thai-Cambodian border summit in June 1976 produced an agreement to "strengthen and expand" contacts.[214] Thai products began pouring by the truckload and the trainload into Phnom Penh warehouses. On 18 June, for instance, Cambodia purchased 660 rain-

207. Hamad Abdul Aziz al Aiya, "Modern Kampuchea," translated 1976 manuscript in the possession of the author, p. 36. Al Aiya was the PLO representative in Beijing at the time.
208. Le Figaro (Paris), 11 February 1977.
209. Bangkok Nation, 20 December 1975.
210. Heder, "Thailand's Relations with Kampuchea," pp. 25 (citing Bangkok Post, 23 December 1975), 13–14.
211. Heder, "Thailand's Relations," pp. 12, 26; Bangkok Post, 27 August 1975.
212. Twining, in Jackson, ed., Cambodia 1975–1978, p. 135.
213. Chanda, "Phnom Penh's Undercover Men," FEER, 10 December 1976, p. 50.
214. Heder, "Thailand's Relations," p. 31.

coats, a ton of sugar, 100 knives, 100 axes, 100 sickles, 100 ploughtips, 15 kgs. of cabbage seed, and 5 kgs. of lettuce seed.[215] Now these might have been for general distribution, like some of the Thai products imported the next month (eight tons of sugar, two tons of salt, one and a half tons of soya bean and other vegetable seeds, 24,000 nylon sacks, 35,000 bottles of penicillin, machine oil and machine parts, sulfuric acid, a ton of red, green, purple, blue, and yellow paints, and black cloth), but new items in the July consignments suggest a rather specific consumer: 40 sacks of charcoal, 60 kg of potatoes, 110 sacks of rice, 44 sacks of flour, 45 kg of quinine, 125 kg of vitamin C, and 125 kg of vitamin B-1.[216] It is likely that the Center was now stocking its larder with Thai products. A ministry of commerce stocklist of materials from Thailand dated 30 September reveals that much remained in stock after more than three months. The axes, knives, sickles, ploughtips, and sugar imported in June had gone nowhere. Supplies of vitamins C and B-1 were down to 100 kg each; of the two tons of salt, 1.9 tons remained, as did half a ton of cabbages, 31 kg of lettuce, 16 kg of radishes, 17 kg of carrots, and 10 kg of peanuts. The CPK Standing Committee did its shopping in Aranyaprathet.[217]

Records for the rest of 1976 suggest a reduction in trade with Thailand, though Phnom Penh continued to import small quantities of machine oil and parts, nylon, flour, and dyes. Two hundred thousand bottles of Thai penicillin and ten thousand cotton scarves (*kroma*) were counted in the stocktaking of 30 September 1976, but the only "recent" import from Poipet was another twenty thousand bottles of penicillin.[218] Within a week, a brutal military coup in Bangkok overturned Thailand's democracy. The same period saw important ructions in Phnom Penh, and soon a new organ, the Khmer Company for Foreign Trade, was exploring another market: Hong Kong.[219] A new step in the centralization of Democratic Kampuchea's economy began.

Purchases from Hong Kong recorded in the September stocktaking were few, all recent: forty-one cases of potatoes, six thousand packs of pickled meat, twenty buckets of liquid chloride, and some movie equipment and film. All but the latter quickly left the warehouses.[220] Demand in Phnom Penh for products

215. CNA, MC-DK, Box 7, Dossier 34, list of materials that left Poipet for Phnom Penh on 18 June 1976.
216. Ibid., "Office 72" lists of materials that left Poipet for Phnom Penh on 5, 9, 11, 15, and 22 July 1976.
217. CNA, MC-DK, Box 4, Dossier 16, "Benchhi khleang pholitphol borotes kit trim thngai 30–9-76" ("Warehouse list: foreign products as of 30-9-76").
218. Ibid.
219. CNA, MC-DK, Box 7, Dossier 34, "Office 72" list of materials that left Poipet on 7 November and arrived in Phnom Penh on 9 November 1976, is headed "Time No.: 1", and is the first to be signed by "the Khmer Company for Foreign Trade." The first such list for materials arriving from Hong Kong is dated 27 December 1976.
220. CNA, MC-DK, Box 4, Dossier 16, *Benchhi khleang*, 30 Sept. 1976.

from Hong Kong was high, and supply was to follow. In mid-1976 three DK officials arrived secretly in Hong Kong via Beijing. In October they set up the Ren Fung trading company "in a communist-Chinese bank." Though the company secretary, Miss Ho Hat, denied any connection with Democratic Kampuchea, all four of Ren Fung's directors, including managing director Van Rit, were Cambodian. "We don't have anything to sell now," Ho Hat told journalist Nayan Chanda. An anonymous Hong Kong Chinese intermediary did most of Ren Fung's purchasing, and the Peking-controlled China Resources Company paid for it. An exception was four hundred tons of DDT, purchased for US$450,000 from the Montrose Chemical Corporation, "the first-ever commercial deal since the imposition of the US embargo and for which the American company received US Government clearance on humanitarian grounds."[221]

The first shipment from Hong Kong arrived in Kompong Som in late December. Aboard were 840 tons of DDT and 1,250 sprayers, 800 tons of gunny bags and twine, 600 tons of flour, 200 tons of fuel and oil, 29 tons of sulfuric acid, 50 tons of batteries, 9 tons of penicillin, 4 tons of nivaquin, quinine, and chloroquin, a ton of vitamins, 7 tons of film and equipment, and supplies of chemicals, machinery, tools, and spare parts.[222] It was an expensive new venture. Chinese patronage continued to marginalize Cambodia's relations with its neighbors, drawing the country into a different orbit.

Further new openings included DK trade missions to Yugoslavia, Albania, Romania, China, and North Korea in September and October.[223] The European communist countries they visited were those most independent of the USSR and closest to China. In mid-October Ieng Sary also visited Yugoslavia, which promised Cambodia U.S.$2 billion in aid. Within two months, a Yugoslav freighter left for Cambodia with a US$3 million load of 1,300 tons of tractors and other equipment.[224] In the second half of 1976 Cambodia also sold rubber and fruit to Singapore and made an unprecedented agreement to accept a gift of antimalarial drugs worth U.S.$12,000 sent by the American Friends Service Committee, again with Washington's approval, via China.[225]

Japan, however, was another story. On 19 September, Phnom Penh

221. Chanda, FEER, 10 December 1976, pp. 49–50.

222. CNA, MC-DK, Box 7, Dossier 34, "Benchhi totuol tumninh pi khleang kompong som taam kpal hong kong . . . thngai ti 27 khae 12 chhnam 1976" ("List of Goods Received from Kompong Som Warehouses by Ship from Hong Kong . . . 27 December 1976.") Two appendices detail losses from the 3,000-ton cargo. 900 sacks of flour (4 percent) were ripped open or missing, 4 motorcycle crates "fell open" on the boat, and three crates of batteries fell into the sea, only two of which were recovered, while others disappeared aboard ship.

223. U.S. CIA, FBIS, Asia Pacific, 1 November 1976, p. H1, Phnom Penh Radio 29 October 1976.

224. "Intelligence," FEER, 14 January 1977, p. 5.

225. Chanda, FEER, 10 December 1976, p. 50; FEER, 28 January 1977, p. 5.

announced that Democratic Kampuchea and Japan had decided to establish diplomatic relations at ambassador level.[226] This never happened, but the announcement signaled a momentary change of heart. Soon after their victory of April 1975, CPK leaders had informed Tokyo that Cambodia would not need diplomatic relations with Japan "for the next 200 years."[227]

Intellectual Suspects:
Cambodians Return from Abroad

Meanwhile, over one thousand Cambodians living abroad were returning home.[228] The Center approved their admission in September 1975. Noting that they were "all intellectuals," the Center decided "to gather them all in . . . in the sense that they don't remain outside, which would lead to our political loss." But there was a problem: "If they come, what do we give them to do?" And an answer: "Laboring work." The arrivals from overseas faced "even more laboring" than intellectuals who had defected from Lon Nol's regime in 1972–73 and had been put to work in the fields. The newcomers had to "be trained and educated in the new society."[229]

An important feature of the new society, now definitive, was the abolition of money. The Center reached this decision on 19 September. Charting this course, it argued from Chinese experience: "The Chinese now pay wages to state workers, etc. Wages lead to private ownership because when you have money you save to buy this or that. . . . Mao Zedong said China must continue to have the Great Cultural Revolution four to ten more times. Zhou Enlai said the possibility of the capitalist system returning to control of state power in China is still a problem."[230] An unresolved question was the extent to which Cambodia would follow a Chinese model. On arrival in Phnom Penh, nearly all the returnees were first put through twenty-day political education courses, which revealed CPK thinking and views of the outside world.

The first home were officials and associates of the CPK. Thiounn Mumm, one of four sons of an elite palace family long linked with Pol Pot, returned from France in September.[231] Laurence Picq, a young French teacher,

---

226. "The Week," *FEER*, 1 October 1976, p. 5.

227. D. P. Chandler, personal communication from the Saigon ambassador to Tokyo at the time.

228. Y Phandara, *Retour à Phnom Penh*, Paris: Métailié, 1982, p. 147, gives a figure of "over 1,700."

229. "On the Control and Implementation of the Political Line of Gathering Forces for the Party's National Democratic Front," 22 September 1975, pp. 7–8. *Khosang* has been translated here as "educate."

230. "Examine the Control," 19 September 1975, p. 25.

231. Phandara, *Retour à Phnom Penh*, p. 205.

had married Suong Sikoeun, a Cambodian student in Paris, in 1967. Sikoeun had since joined Ieng Sary's foreign ministry staff. On 10 October 1975, after six years in Beijing, Picq and their two daughters arrived in Phnom Penh to join him. The flight carried seventy other Cambodians. Picq was the only Westerner to live through the DK regime. At the airport, Sirin, a Cambodian she had known in Paris, failed to recognize her, warned that talking was "forbidden," and ordered her into a car. Her first impression was of "an empty planet." "Not a soul, not a dog, not a bird, not even a flower."

That evening, Sirin explained to Picq "the superiority of the Khmer revolution over all past revolutions, in particular because of the abolition of money and the evacuation of the cities." Meals were eaten in common. On the fourth day, Khieu Samphan came to address the returnees at a formal meeting. Rising to the podium, he noticed Picq, the only Westerner in the audience. Samphan had her excluded from the meeting. Sirin advised her: "For the next few days, you will look after your children. If you wish, you may also look after other children, and later, the Organization will look after you."[232]

Husband and wife Peh Bun Tong and Kim Heang had arrived on the same flight from Beijing. They report that Khieu Samphan lectured on "building socialist revolution." He did not mention foreign policy, suggesting that official decisions had yet to be made. The couple were then sent to a cooperative in the North for thirteen months of "ploughing and harvesting the land with the people" in Stung Trang district, run by Ke Pauk's brother-in-law Oeun.[233] This earliest group, from Beijing, were separated from later returnees.[234]

Slogans repeated in political sessions in Phnom Penh included "The Organization excels Lenin and is outstripping Mao." Picq's husband reminded her that "for a hundred years, the French colonists, your ancestors, pillaged us. That is why living conditions here are difficult today. You are the only French woman here. You have the incomparable opportunity to be able to give value to your life. But French pride smothers you. You must learn revolutionary modesty."[235]

Kun, trained as an industrial engineer in North Korea since 1971, left Pyongyang with his wife Bopha in October 1975. They stayed a month in Beijing, then returned to Phnom Penh in November. They were met by a foreign ministry official named Sân and given a week to rest at the former Czech embassy. They then heard a series of lectures from Sân on the history of the anticolonial and anti-imperialist struggles. In December, Kun began working

232. Picq, Au-delà du ciel, pp. 1, 16–19, 23–24.
233. Author's interview with Peh Bun Tong and Kim Heang, Paris, 18 November 1979.
234. Author's interview with Tri Meng Huot, Paris, 15 February 1980. Huot had returned to Paris in 1979. He and his wife were murdered there several years later.
235. Picq, Au-delà du ciel, pp. 37, 43.

as an interpreter for North Korean irrigation technicians in various parts of Cambodia. Bopha stayed in Phnom Penh to work in the foreign ministry.[236] Chem Snguon was an experienced Sihanouk regime diplomat who had continued to serve the exiled prince as his ambassador in Cairo. He returned home on 19 December. He was immediately sent to Chup, in the East, with half a dozen others. They worked in the fields and were allowed no contact with ordinary people. In August 1976 they were brought back, to another work camp at Chrang Chamres on the outskirts of Phnom Penh, while more recent returnees were being sent out into the countryside.[237]

Cambodian physicist Tri Meng Huot left Paris in December 1975 with over fifty others from France and "all over Europe." In Beijing the group swelled to nearly two hundred. On arrival at Pochentong airport, he recalled, "no government officials met us, just two worker-peasants, one driving. . . . They did not say anything from Pochentong to Phnom Penh. We had thought a lot about the changes but had not seen the new situation, the new system. When we got there we woke up. But some knew it would be quiet like that. Most of us Khmers who wanted to go back had only one thought, wanting to go back to help the nation. So we went, whatever the system. We all knew it would be hard work." The returnees were taken to the former Khmero-Soviet Technical Institute, where Khieu Samphan lectured to the group for three days. This time he covered both domestic and foreign policy. He claimed that "if people had stayed in Phnom Penh they would have died because there was no rice."[238] Huot added: "He wanted us to see that now we were actually eating gruel, but in the future we will eat rice and it will be easy, there will be dessert. . . . the future of the country was good." To this end, Samphan said: "It is like we have climbed a sugar palm tree. Now we are making leaf boxes up in the sugar palm tree."[239] Next would come sugar palm juice, and palm sugar cakes.

Samphan's analogy was extraordinary. A Khmer folktale tells of Chau Cak Smok, who made palm leaf boxes for a living, which Cambodians regard as a joke. But as he worked, he dreamed of making money, buying chickens, pigs, and goats, getting rich, and then taking a wife, and having servants, whom he dreamed of kicking around. Launching a kick in midair, Smok fell out of the tree. A series of hilarious events follows as five people try to help him, but all-around stupidity leads to the death of all six. Samphan's choice of this allusion

236. Author's interview with Kun and his wife Bopha, Montbard, 1 February 1980.

237. Author's interview with Chem Snguon, Phnom Penh, 2 January 1986.

238. Huot commented, "But I saw that the important reason was different. They wanted to dissolve the society into a society of equality. In Phnom Penh there were capitalists, intellectuals, people who did this and that, at all levels even down to pedicab drivers. . . . All those people had to transform themselves into a peasant class, and leave." Author's interview with Tri Meng Huot, 1980.

239. Ibid.

to illustrate plans of the DK leaders reveals more than his lack of a sense of humor.

Turning to international affairs, Samphan described the United States as "a real rich person's country" with many "internal problems and big conflicts." Vietnam was more of a preoccupation. Although the cpk "had not requested" the 1970 Vietnamese intervention, "the Vietnamese friends" had "participated" (*ruom chomnaek*) in the struggle against the common American enemy. "Problems came to light which could be resolved," and the Vietnamese had agreed to leave in 1973. Samphan claimed that "so far we can resolve the problems with neighbouring countries," but hinted at "complex problems in the future."

Samphan also pointed out that China and Cambodia were dissimilar, since "some of their problems were different." This theme was developed by another lecturer, Mau Khem Nuon, known to the students as Phom. A former student at the Khmero-Soviet Institute, Phom had taken to the jungle in the mid-1960s. His older brother Keo Chenda, a former anti-French fighter, had been in Hanoi since 1954. Phom told the returnees that Democratic Kampuchea had no money or markets, unlike China, where "they buy and sell" and "raise various animals privately." "In Cambodia," Phom explained, "nothing is private, everything is communal: property, eating, work, everything." Phom pointed out that Chinese working abroad would "buy a television for their home in Beijing." But in Cambodia, "there is one communal radio at everyone's disposal, for all to listen to." Phom stressed that Democratic Kampuchea "can't rely on China" and "must take the stand of independence-mastery."[240] The same applied to relations with Vietnam. Phom made a good impression on many returnees.[241]

Chang Sieng, who had gone to France to study medicine in early 1975, returned home in February 1976. With one thousand francs in his pocket (which he kept for the next three years), Sieng arrived back in Phnom Penh with forty-seven Cambodians, the fourth such group of returnees from France. They immediately joined the others for a twenty-day political course at the Khmero-Soviet Institute. Khieu Samphan lectured for the first two days. He distributed documents entitled "Build and Defend the Country" and "Produc-

240. In January 1976 DK foreign ministry officials remarked that "we must beware of China . . . she wants to make us her satellite." Picq, p. 52. The same view was expressed the following year (p. 106).

241. Tri Meng Huot said "In general Phom was a good man. I never saw any of his faults. I used to talk with him, sometimes he called us to talk. . . . He seemed a kind person. . . . I don't know what he was a traitor to. . . . Some told me he was cia, some kgb. His death had to be the result of one or the other!" Another returnee described Phom as "a good person" who had welcomed the returnees warmly and conceded that in 1976 life was difficult but promised that 1977 would be much better. In October 1976, Phom again paid the returnees a visit and inquired how they were getting on.

tion: Internal and External Plans." He told his audience of several hundred educated Khmers about economic reconstruction and life in revolutionary society, pointing out some of the differences from previous regimes, such as communal eating. Samphan also stressed that Democratic Kampuchea was neutral and formed no alliances. He rarely mentioned Vietnam, but he did describe it as still a "friend," though the Vietnamese had been "a little sly" (*kil bontec*) in 1971 and 1972, when they "had not respected equality, love and loyalty." Samphan stressed Democratic Kampuchea's friendship with China and told how it exchanged goods for Chinese machinery. He told the students that normally the Chinese just provided aid and asked for no repayment, but "we did not agree to accept gifts, and would pay." Sieng recalls: "One coconut for one hoe, the Chinese said. But the Khmer said, Take two coconuts."[242]

In March 1976, on the final day of the political study course, Phom "represented Khieu Samphan." He passed out a document entitled "Private Property" and said they needed to learn "to work in the rain and wind" like the people, and to give up "private" possessions. He would say things like "Don't miss your wife and children, don't love equipment and material goods so much, learn to abandon them. Just be content with two sets of clothes, and a toothbrush. Get rid of that second watch, and the necklace." Sieng says Phom threatened no coercion; "it was just up to us to follow this advice." He also told the returnees about policy on money. At first, Phom said, the regime had intended to use money, "but the people had considered that would not be equality," because salaries would always be unequal, so a "provisional" decision had been made against it. "Our cadres have a slightly higher ration than the people, but not much higher." He predicted that the people's living conditions would rise every year and catch up with those of cadres "when we get three tons per hectare." China, on the other hand, "still uses money." Democratic Kampuchea was ten years ahead of China at its liberation, a model country for the world, Phom said.[243]

The next month, Phom took a small group aside to study the history of the CPK since its foundation in 1951.[244] He was apparently becoming more selective about his audience, perhaps considering the later arrivals less trustworthy. A young woman who had returned from the USSR expressed her disappointment, saying that the Soviet Union was communist but unlike Democratic Kampuchea, "there was food to eat and people worked to a limited schedule." Some former Lon Nol military personnel returned from training in the United States and disappeared, never to be seen again. Another forty Cambodians

242. Author's interview with Chang Sieng, Creteil, 18 October 1979.
243. Ibid.
244. S. Heder's interview with Ong Thong Hoeung, Khao I Dang, 28 February 1980.

arrived from Paris in early May. One, electrician Khuon Thlai Chamnan, spent the next six months at the former Khmero-Soviet Institute, but in that time Phom gave only one lecture to the two hundred to three hundred returnees living there. They spent their time demolishing makeshift huts and planting vegetables.[245]

In small-group discussions in June 1976, Phom made important criticisms of China, "especially Zhou Enlai's line," recalls Ong Thong Hoeung, who had studied political economy at the University of Paris. Phom accused Zhou of having encouraged the CPK to negotiate with the United States. "He said Zhou En-lai was half-baked, not truly revolutionary.... He praised Albania saying it has a more correct line. He criticized the use of currency, the existence of markets, [and] private property rights."[246] Meanwhile, Ieng Sary was giving political lectures to cadres of his foreign ministry. In mid-1976 Bopha, who had lived in North Korea with her husband, attended a course that "Ieng Sary taught from documents for five days." He lectured on foreign and domestic policy, including economic self-reliance. In contrast to Phom, Ieng Sary was critical not of Zhou En-lai but of his opponents. Bopha says that Sary and his deputy Hong, and a woman lecturer, all "criticized the Gang of Four" in China. "They weren't happy with them," she recalls, adding that, in further contrast to Phom, Sary made no mention of Albania. "They attacked Vietnam and the United States most strongly. As friends they liked China, then Korea, then Romania, and the nonaligned nations."[247]

Hoeung continues, "Phom also said the political consciousness of Chinese experts who came to Cambodia was not high. For example, they have a regular salary and come to our country where they can't spend money, he said. The Chinese say they can save money and would buy a sewing machine after going back to China. Phom said he was not sure which way the Chinese revolution would go." This was because of political differences within the leadership there. As if to emphasize his point, he did not include these comments in the written documents he distributed. As for Hanoi, "Phom said the Vietnamese have a big-brother attitude. Even though the Vietnamese are friends, we have to be alert against the danger of Vietnamese expansionism. But he made no criticism of the internal line of Vietnam," though he said "the Russians were 100 percent revisionists."[248]

245. Author's interview with Khuon Thlai Chamnan, Chatenay-Malabry, 9 August 1979.

246. Heder's interview with Ong Thong Hoeung, Khao I Dang, 28 February 1980.

247. Author's interview with Kun and his wife Bopha, Montbard, 1 February 1980. Bopha's account contradicts that of of Sauv Kim Hong, who arrived later and says Sary "did not make any criticism of the Chinese" (see below). Hong arrived later than Bopha, possibly after the lectures she refers to. Moreover, the regime's leaders trusted returnees from North Korea like Bopha more than those from France like Hong. See Vickery, *Cambodia*, p. 163.

248. Heder's interview with Ong Thong Hoeung, 1980.

Another returnee, Sauv Kim Hong, recalls hearing claims that "our system was superior to the Chinese system" and that "the Chinese experts in Cambodia had come to study with us." Hong was told of Chinese advisers asking "how much money it costs to build this dam" and Cambodians responding that "the dams were built by the people, we don't spend money in our country." Hong adds, "I remember another cadre who said that the Chinese made a Cultural Revolution for a certain period and then stopped. But we are making a Cultural Revolution every day." He recalls Phom saying this, and also remembers Thiounn Prasith, DK ambassador to the U.N., revealing that the Chinese "were perplexed and waiting to see whether it would be possible not to use currency in Kampuchea."[249] But Prasith's superior, Ieng Sary, was far more critical of Hanoi than of Beijing. First, Sary blamed Vietnam for "betraying" the Khmer communists under the 1954 Geneva Convention, though China had been responsible.[250] Unlike Phom, Sary did not describe the Vietnamese as "friends," but claimed to have tried "to make people aware of the Vietnamese danger" as early as 1964. While Phom described limited "problems" with Vietnam in 1971–72, Sary was more expansive: "During the five-year war [1970–75], the Kampuchean Party had to fight not only against the USA but also against Vietnamese occupation forces. The Vietnamese mistreated the population."[251]

In June 1976, six Cambodian students returned home from Yugoslavia. One of them had already met Sary at a 1972 closed meeting in Tirana, Albania. He remembers Sary's claim at that early stage to have mounted a "strong defence" against Vietnamese in northeast Cambodia before 1970 and to have "attacked them and driven them back into their country." Phom warmly welcomed this new group from Yugoslavia, but now, after the ending of border negotiations with Vietnam, he took a new line. The student from Yugoslavia says, "He was saying what he had been told by the Party in his own study sessions. He said the Vietnamese were enemies, because Vietnam had attacked Tang and Wai Islands after liberation."[252] Phom thus elided the 1975 U.S. attack on Tang, launched in retaliation for Cambodia's seizure of the *Mayaguez*, with the Vietnamese attack on Wai, retaliating for DK raids on Phu Quoc and Tho Chu. Forgotten were Pol Pot's apology for "ignorance of geography" and Mok's outright attempt to conquer Vietnamese territory.

In late September 1976, thirty returnees were sent to work in factories. Chamnan and five others went to a metal factory in the capital's southern suburbs. He took charge of the electricity network. Most of the more than five

249. Heder's interview with Sauv Kim Hong, 29 February 1980.
250. See Kiernan, *How Pol Pot*, ch. 5.
251. Heder's interviews with Sauv Kim Hong, Khao I Dang, 28 and 29 February, 1980.
252. Author's interview, Tuol, 28 October 1979. The interviewee requested anonymity.

hundred factory workers were peasant boys and girls, some as young as fourteen. They came from every province, including the East and Northeast. The factory produced agricultural machinery such as rice threshing and milling machines. It had previously belonged to Chinese entrepreneurs, but was now run by a former CPK officer and his deputy, a Cambodian Chinese who had worked in the factory in the past. They were assisted by other soldiers and by four ethnic Chinese engineers educated in Hong Kong who knew the factory well. But the factory received no foreign aid, and no Chinese or other foreign advisers were to be seen.

The workers met twice a day in groups of ten for work meetings and self-criticism sessions. Chamnan's group of six "new people" did not attend, but had separate "lifestyle" meetings every three days. Under the headings of politics, consciousness, and work, they discussed questions such as "Are you in step with the revolution yet?" and "Are you still thinking about private property?" and "Do you still miss your wife and children, have you given them up completely yet?" The last question would be asked at every meeting. Chamnan recalls that he would say "I miss my wife and children." Another worker would reply, "We must learn from the people, the workers, the peasants, the army, who are the heroes, who helped liberate our nation. Some have not yet seen their wife and parents. Even now, after the war is over, they are building the country." At special work meetings, they would be instructed on the necessity of obedience and asked "Are you happy in your work? Or do you work just because you must?" Discussion also included the results of each person's labor. After six weeks' factory work, Chamnan and the other returnees moved to Phnom Penh's western suburbs to grow vegetables to "support themselves."[253]

In late October, Hing Sopanya, her husband Yim Nolla, and their two young daughters came back from France with two other Khmer families. They joined more than one hundred returnees at a reception center in the suburb of Boeng Trabek. A committee had been appointed to lead the newcomers; it was headed by Hao, a veterinary science graduate just back from the United States, and his deputy, Tri Meng Huot. Hao and Huot were supervised by a portly ethnic minority cadre from the northeast named Sin. In his late twenties, Sin visited the center often and gave weekly political lectures. He was barely literate, and he ordered the burning of two engineering books Nolla had brought from France. Sopanya recalls, "We found some other books that someone had left behind at Boeng Trabek, and some of us were reading them when we were told that this was 'wrong.'" Sin's deputy, an ethnic Khmer named Morn, had recently learned to read.

Sin's lectures began early in the morning and lasted until nearly midnight.

---

253. Author's interview with Khuon Thlai Chamnan, 1979.

He told the returnees that they belonged to a social class that had enjoyed privileges and had exploited other classes that possessed no capital. He stressed that the country was now developing and progressing, and exhorted returnees to work hard and put up with their rations of rice gruel. Sin explained that "imperialism and the CIA want to destroy us, and we must struggle against them by working hard." He did not mention Vietnam, China, Albania, or the USSR.

Now Ieng Sary's critique not only of Hanoi, but also of China's Gang of Four, may seem surprising. But it is confirmed by a CPK Central Committee member, who recalled, "After Mao's death there was apprehension inside Kampuchea . . . people were afraid that chaos and confusion in China might affect our solidarity with China. It was said that if the Gang of Four stayed [in power] it would be problematic because their attitude towards Kampuchea was not good."[254] It is true that in October 1976, on hearing of the arrest of the Gang of Four, Sary is said to have whispered, "No, it can't be true! They are good people."[255] Without evidence of Sary's private view, this suggests a preference for China's radicals, but given what we know it just as likely betrays unwillingness to voice criticism of China—by asserting that its winning faction would not arrest "good people." This recalls Pol Pot's pragmatic view, expressed in 1967, that "China is a great country."

One who had expressed interest in the Cultural Revolution was Phom. In mid-December, Phom reappeared to address a large meeting. He told the returnees that 1976 had seen two rice harvests and gave figures for amounts consumed and sold abroad and for the increase in land under cultivation. The Khmer people were "the strongest in the world, and motivated by great anger." Phom announced that a new national target of three tons per hectare had been set for 1977.[256] But he also remarked to a group of returnees "that Deng Xiaoping was a revisionist and only Albania was a true friend of Kampuchea."[257] Phom's admiration for Tirana was not new; he had been praising its policies since March 1976.[258] But with the demise of the Gang of Four in

254. Heder's interview with Chap Lonh, Chantaburi, 12 March 1980; and p. 152, above.
255. Chanda, *Brother Enemy,* p. 74. The witness says Ieng Sary's remark was "barely audible."
256. Author's interview with Hing Sopanya and Yim Nolla, Creteil, 14 November 1979.
257. Author's interview, Tuol, 28 October 1979. The interviewee, who requested anonymity, stated that Phom made this statement at the time of the arrest of Chhouk Meng Mao [8 December 1976] and Phung Ton [29 April 1977]. Since Phom himself was arrested on 8 April 1977, the correct date is the December one. Phom's reasoning, the interviewee said, was that in 1972 only Albania (unlike China) had advised the Khmer Rouge to eschew peace negotiations.
258. Chang Sieng (1979) says that in March 1976 Phom also described Albania as "good" and "friendly."

October, the return of Deng was imminent, and both China and Cambodia were heading for a break with Albania. Phom's views were now controversial. Denunciation of Deng and praise for Albania were tantamount to support for the Gang of Four.[259] A crisis was looming.

On 14 December Sopanya, Nolla, and their daughters left Phnom Penh with two hundred other returnees. They boarded boats that headed up the Mekong to Kompong Cham, then walked thirty kilometers inland to Stung Trang.[260] Chamnan followed in a smaller group.[261] Meanwhile, Bun Tong and his wife left Stung Trang after thirteen months' work in the fields. "We had been tempered; as intellectuals, we [now] knew about the people's living conditions." They returned to Phnom Penh and joined about four hundred others who had spent varying periods in different places. After a month, two hundred of these people went to Stung Trang to join Sopanya's group.[262] Four hundred of Cambodia's most highly educated professionals and intellectuals were now growing vegetables in forest clearings, with three hundred more in work camps in Phnom Penh. Their foreign connections had ended their careers.

259. He was not to last much longer than they did. The Center was about to purge all Cambodian communists who had expressed support for them. Ben Kiernan, "Pol Pot and the Kampuchean Communist Movement," in Kiernan and Boua, eds., *Peasants and Politics in Kampuchea*, pp. 228, 239–41, 300.

260. Author's interview with Hing Sopanya and Yim Nolla, 1979. They report that the first group left on 10 December and a third group followed in February 1977.

261. Author's interview with Khuon Thlai Chamnan, 1979. He reports that an earlier group consisted of 60 people, his group, 50 to 60.

262. Author's interview with Peh Buntong and Kim Heang, 1979.

II

Writing on the Slate, 1975–77: The CPK Project

CHAPTER FIVE

An Indentured Agrarian State, 1975–77: The Base Areas The Southwest and the East

A Tour of Democratic Kampuchea

Leng Sei and the other Cambodian women who traveled to Vietnam in September 1976 brought an invitation for Ha Thi Que to make a return visit in November. They followed up with a second letter, inviting Que to lead a Women's Union delegation. The one-week visit began on 7 February 1977. Ha Thi Que and her companions, a Catholic Vietnamese, a textile worker, a doctor, and a Khmer speaker, drove from Ho Chi Minh City to the border. Leng Sei met them there with about 50 Cambodian women and a male interpreter. The women wore their hair short, in what Que calls "Chinese style," and wore blue or black skirts with white blouses. A dozen DK soldiers in two jeeps provided an escort.[1]

Ha Thi Que remembers that "we shook hands and got in the cars, and soon arrived in Svay Rieng. It was completely deserted but for a sentry box with two soldiers, who raised the barrier. There was no one in the city. Almost all the shutters had been removed and the windows broken. We went to the guest house. There was no one there but maids. We rested, then ate a meal. There was no electricity or running water, and water had to be brought upstairs for us to wash our hands. After an hour we headed for Phnom Penh. We crossed the Mekong on the Neak Leung ferry. Leng Sei told us of some of the battles that had taken place there, and about the coordination between Vietnamese and Cambodians in the fight for Neak Leung. I knew about the battle, and we agreed on the details of the events. When I said something happened at such and such a place at such and such a time, they said, 'Yes, that's right.'" Things seemed off to a good start.

Between the border and Phnom Penh, the guests saw only three oxcarts and two bicycles. People dressed in black were working in the fields one or two

1. Author's interview with Ha Thi Que, Hanoi, 4 November 1980. Other details of the Vietnamese women's delegation are also taken from this interview.

kilometers from the roadside. The Cambodians said these were "people's communes," recalls Ha Thi Que, possibly on the lookout for things Chinese. By the road were occasional old women supervising infants and naked children catching fish or crabs and husking rice. Que remembers stopping for a drink: "Children gathered around, but they were all driven away. I asked two old women through the Vietnamese interpreter what they were doing. They said they were taking care of the children, who have to become 'self-sufficient.' But we were pushed away by the Cambodian Women's Association officials. That is the only contact I had with the Cambodian people on the whole visit." Close to the capital, the visitors saw new, one-room houses on stilts, set several hundred meters back from the road. The Cambodians told them that they were trying to build a house for everyone, so there would be "neither rich nor poor." They had demolished urban and rural homes to build these new, smaller ones.

Coming into Phnom Penh, the Vietnamese found an empty city. According to Que, "lots of coconuts had fallen to the ground, but there was no one to eat them. There were only birds and geckoes." (And not for long.) In the guest house near the Vietnamese embassy that afternoon, Ieng Thirith and about one hundred people presented the visitors with flowers. Thirith, wife of Ieng Sary, explained that she was "representing the Women's Association of Democratic Kampuchea" and would be taking care of them.[2] Her sister, Khieu Ponnary, wife of Pol Pot and president of the Women's Association of Democratic Kampuchea, did not appear. The Vietnamese met no one else in the capital. They requested interviews with workers and peasants, and these were promised.

The next morning they set off on a three-day round trip to Angkor, escorted by the two jeeps and a car carrying the food. Thirith wore all-black pajamas and sandals. They saw many people along the way, also dressed in black, working on what their hosts called irrigation works. But there were no interviews. The exchange was limited to the Vietnamese asking the contents of the bamboo cylinders they saw people carrying and their hosts replying "rice and gruel to bring back to their family to eat." Those who cooked for the Vietnamese along the way would not even respond to questions about the food, which was mostly Vietnamese. Que suspected they were from the military. Thirith, who Que says speaks good Vietnamese, having lived in Hanoi during the early 1970s and given birth to children there, nevertheless declined to use the language of her guests. Que, for her part, claims to have been consummately diplomatic. "We did not ask about Sihanouk, or about China. We just wanted them to understand Vietnam, that's all. We did not want to irritate

---

2. For the DK account of the meeting and Ha Thi Que's speech, see Phnom Penh Radio, 8 February 1977, in United States Central Intelligence Agency, Foreign Broadcast Information Service (FBIS), Asia Pacific, 9 February 1977, p. H5, and 10 February 1977, pp. H1–2.

them. We never once mentioned the word 'Indochina,' but just praised their independence and freedom while promising to maintain solidarity and support each other when necessary. They said very little."

The party stopped three times along the way. The junction town of Skoun was empty. The hosts spread a plastic sheet on the ground and put out some snacks. Thirith told Que of the battles at Skoun in 1971, when, she said, many young Vietnamese communist soldiers had sacrificed themselves for the common cause. The midday meal was eaten in Kompong Thom, in what the Cambodians said was a newly constructed guest house, surrounded only by rice fields. Siemreap was also deserted, "quiet but for birds singing" and more geckoes. Que and the other women were "a little afraid at nighttime." They were welcomed by dozens of well-wishers, including two regional leaders, but no women. On inquiry the Cambodians explained that their local counterpart was ill. "The next day they brought a young woman who said she was a representative of the women of Siemreap. She had light skin and we guessed she was a Chinese resident, but we didn't say so."

In the morning the guests saw the temples of Angkor Wat and Angkor Thom and the crocodile farm in Siemreap. Que says she insisted on visiting an irrigation worksite. The Cambodians agreed, but instead took the Vietnamese to "a small dam, where they said the peasants no longer work." At dinner that evening, Que pressed the point, and the Cambodians agreed again. "But in the morning they told us that Phnom Penh did not approve, and that we must head straight back that day." At a Phnom Penh textile factory the next morning, the visitors were told how the former workers had all been sent for "reeducation." The factory was now operated mostly by newly recruited peasants. The Cambodian hosts claimed that some could now operate seven textile machines simultaneously, after only three months. The Vietnamese textile worker, who had twelve years' experience, could operate eight machines. She asked to see one such Cambodian worker in action. She was told the operator was ill. That afternoon's visit to a pharmaceutical factory was no more convincing. Its director, a seventeen-year-old woman, said the factory produced tetracycline, aspirin, and antidiarrheal tablets. There was no machinery; mixing was done by hand. The workers were mostly illiterate, twelve-to-fourteen years old, all wearing black. The director needed no engineers or technicians: "the people can master the plant." Que recalls "a long argument" over technical expertise, especially in pharmacy. The director insisted Cambodia did not need it. Then Ieng Thirith intervened. She said the lack of technicians and pharmacists was overcome by a Cambodian "formula" developed in the struggle against the French and the Americans. "It was not a happy visit. They hated us and thought we were inquisitive," confesses Que.

A second exchange occurred in discussions with the DK Women's Association. Thirith, who had earlier explained that Cambodian married women now lived together in groups apart from their husbands, was outlining the new pregnancy leave policy. It involved, she said, two months' rest from labor; pregnant women and new mothers were given lighter duties, and milk was provided if necessary. The Vietnamese doctor pointedly asked how women got pregnant with spouses separated. This angered Thirith, who retorted, "You do not understand the problem of women at all." Que claims the Vietnamese saw no pregnant women in Cambodia, nor anyone smiling or even chatting.

Que was puzzled by the role of the Women's Association. She asked about its leader, Khieu Ponnary, and was told she was sick. She was not mentioned at all in Phnom Penh Radio's coverage of the visit. Nor did the Cambodians privately describe Ponnary as the president of the association, though no one else seemed to occupy the position. Her sister Thirith "made speeches and expounded on Women's Association policy. But when we met, Ieng Thirith told me she was charged with taking care of me, and said nothing about the Association. I got the impression there was no real Women's Association, or if there was, they were trying to do away with it." Ponnary is said to have been ill since 1975, and later to have suffered insanity. At any rate, the only other member of the association's Standing Committee ever identified was the mysterious "Ren" who had traveled to Vietnam in a junior capacity the previous year. Late in 1976 Ponnary and Thirith's mother arrived from France, but "her daughters failed to visit her for two months."[3] It seems that Thirith directed Que's tour on her husband Sary's behalf, for the foreign ministry rather than the Women's Association.

On the morning of their last day in Cambodia, the Vietnamese women were received by Khieu Samphan, Sary, and Thirith. "It was a courtesy visit, lacking sincerity. Khieu Samphan expressed thanks to the Vietnamese party, government and people for their support in the struggles against the French and Americans." Professing to be "deeply touched" by the sacrifices of the Vietnamese on Cambodian battlefields, Samphan mentioned Skoun in particular, saying that their defeat of Lon Nol's 1971 offensive there had enabled the Vietnamese to withdraw and the Cambodians to fight the United States.[4] Thirith now told Que that Pol Pot would receive her that afternoon. Some hours later, however, Thirith returned to explain that the party secretary had a cold, but had sent a message for Que to convey to Hanoi. This was that "misunderstandings should not be allowed to lead to harmful relations." Thirith added that Cambodia took "full responsibility" for border attacks on Vietnam's

3. D. P. Chandler, *Brother Number One: A Political Biography of Pol Pot*, Boulder, Westview, 1992, pp. 139, 173.

4. This message did not appear in Phnom Penh Radio's brief account of the meeting that day. See FBIS, Asia Pacific, 14 February 1977, p. H1.

Dac Lac province in November 1976. They had been the work, she said, of DK frontier guards. The CPK Central Committee had been unaware of the incidents and regretted them. Before their departure, the Vietnamese were taken to see Cambodia's Independence Monument, which their hosts explained had been "built by Sihanouk," but the message was clear.[5] On their last evening, the guests attended a performance of Cambodian songs by soloists and a choir. There was no dance. The hall was empty but for the guests, ten members of the Vietnamese embassy, and as many Cambodian hosts. "And that was our visit," Que concludes. "We had had no contact with the Cambodian people; they had prevented us from asking questions of ordinary people."[6]

What *was* happening to the people of Cambodia?

A Peasant Revolution?

The Center's quest for total domestic and substantial regional power by massive military buildup had indentured Cambodia's economy to China's indefinitely. Domestically, Democratic Kampuchea's population was also a bonded workforce, unpaid and lacking even a guarantee of subsistence rations.

Before 1970, Cambodians ate on average about 600 grams of rice per person per day, compared to 440 grams in other rice-producing countries. Poor peasants in Cambodia consumed about 400 grams, compared to 110 grams in Java.[7] During the latter stages of the 1970–1975 war, a daily ration of 150 grams of U.S. aid rice was provided to half of the one million rural refugees in Phnom Penh. Many of the rest were eating even less. In April 1975, USAID reported that from 1970, Cambodia had "slipped in less than five years from a significant exporter of rice to large-scale imports, and when these ended in April 1975, to the brink of starvation." The agency predicted that "to avert a major food disaster," Cambodia would need "from 175,000 to 250,000 metric tons of milled rice" to take its population through to February 1976. China had sent 61,000 tons of rice by October 1975, when supplies stopped coming. This was about half the level of U.S. rice deliveries to Cambodia up to April 1975.[8] The Chinese aid then ended, and postwar consumption patterns varied by

5. This message to Vietnam contradicted the CPK line that the Sihanouk regime had *not* been an independent one. Ben Kiernan, *How Pol Pot Came to Power*, London: Verso, 1985, ch. 6, esp. pp. 224–26.

6. Author's 1980 interview with Ha Thi Que.

7. Jean Delvert, *Le paysan cambodgien*, Paris: Mouton, 1961, pp. 154–5, 532; and *Susenas*, "National Social and Economic Survey of Indonesia, 1963–1970," carried out in cooperation with the U.N., Jakarta.

8. From December 1974 to April 1975, the U.S. PL 480 program had delivered 123,128 metric tons of rice to Cambodia. See U.S. Agency for International Development, draft Termination Report for Cambodia, April 1975, Part 6, "Cambodia's Food and Fibre Needs: The PL 480 Assistance Program to Cambodia for Rice and Other Commodities," p. 5.

region and season. The used Nestlés condensed-milk can, which held about two hundred fifty grams of milled rice, soon became the standard DK rationing measure. With a major shortfall, famine loomed whatever the CPK did. But its decision to evacuate the cities, for political not humanitarian reasons, compounded the problem, as did the second, even more disastrous deportation of the former city dwellers.

Socially, the population was divided into two groups. The evacuated city dwellers and peasants living in areas under Lon Nol control until April 1975 were now called the "new people" (*neak thmey*), or "depositees" (*neak phñoe*). They made up 30 percent of Democratic Kampuchea's population.[9] The peasant majority, who had lived for several years in insurgent areas called "the bases," were the "base people" (*neak moultanh*), or the "old people" (*neak chas*).

Economically, the country had become one, "a gigantic workshop"[10] of indentured agrarian labor. Cambodians of all races and classes worked long hours, without wages or leisure, on projects in which they had no say. Subjected to military discipline, most lived in thatch huts or barrack-style houses, with couples usually separated from other family members and, as Ieng Thirith explained, often even apart from spouses. Work teams took meals in separate shifts in mess halls.

What kind of society was this? In *Cambodia 1975–1982*, Michael Vickery proposed one interpretation: "It was . . . a complete peasant revolution, with the victorious revolutionaries doing what peasant rebels have always wanted to do to their urban enemies." Thus, Vickery says, "the violence of DK . . . did not spring forth from the brains of Pol Pot or Khieu Samphan."[11] Rather, "nationalism, populism and peasantism really won out over communism." Democratic Kampuchea, then, was no Stalinist or communist regime, but "a victorious peasant revolution, perhaps the first real one in modern times." The Center was "pulled along" by "the peasant element," who as a mass dominated the revolution and took it in a direction the leadership could not have

9. "On the Control and Implementation of the Political Line of Gathering Forces for the Party's National Democratic Front," CPK Center "Document No. 6," dated 22 September 1975, states that the population consisted of "70 percent old and 30 percent new workers and peasants" (p. 7). Other evidence of the size of the population living in Lon Nol areas in April 1975 confirms this ratio. See Kiernan, "The Cambodian Genocide: Issues and Responses," in George Andreopoulos, ed., *Genocide: Conceptual and Historical Dimensions*, Philadelphia: University of Pennsylvania Press, 1994, pp. 218–19 and n. 5.

10. Phnom Penh Radio, quoted in W. Shawcross, "Cambodia under Its New Rulers," *New York Review of Books*, 4 March 1976, p. 25.

11. M. Vickery, *Cambodia 1975–1982*, Boston: South End, 1984, p. 286, and Vickery, "Violence in Democratic Kampuchea: Some Problems of Explanation," paper distributed at a conference on State-Organized Terror: The Case of Violent Internal Repression, Michigan State University, November 1988, p. 17.

"either planned or expected."[12] Thus Vickery considers Democratic Kampuchea an illustration of what happens when a peasantry assumes power: "It now appears fortunate that those who predicted a predominance of agrarian nationalism over Marxism in China and Vietnam were mistaken."[13] The Center comprised "middle-class intellectuals with such a romantic, idealized sympathy for the poor that they did not imagine rapid, radical restructuring of society in their favour would lead to such intolerable violence."[14] And "they did not foresee, let alone plan, the unsavoury developments of 1975–79. They were petty bourgeois radicals overcome by peasantist romanticism."[15]

Documentary evidence undercuts this view that Cambodia was undergoing a "peasant revolution." The Center had decreed in September 1975 that "our new peasants," the former city dwellers, had no means of production, "so they are workers"—not peasants at all. The same applied to the base people: "We can't push forward modern agriculture by remaining peasants."[16] Vickery provides corroboration, already noted, of an initial order from Phnom Penh to "kill urban evacuees indiscriminately." This order, which went out to both the Southwest and the Northwest Zones,[17] came from the Center—if not the very "brains of Pol Pot and Khieu Samphan." This was no spontaneous populism.

Another problem with Vickery's analysis is his lack of evidence from peasant sources. Among the ninety-plus interviewees he presents in his survey of Democratic Kampuchea,[18] only one is a peasant. This single interviewee hardly supports the notion of a peasant revolution, reporting that "they were fed well, but overworked and subject to 'fierce' discipline."[19] A family Vickery describes as "half peasant-half urban" (though most "had long since ceased doing field work") said "that their many cousins, aunts, uncles, etc., . . . had perished, mainly of hunger and illness, although they were peasants . . . In the opinion of the survivors, DK mismanagement had simply been so serious that

12. Vickery, *Cambodia*, pp. 289–90, 66; "Violence in Democratic Kampuchea," p. 17.
13. Vickery, *Cambodia*, p. 290.
14. Vickery, "Violence in Democratic Kampuchea," p. 14.
15. Vickery, *Cambodia*, p. 287.
16. "On the Control and Implementation," p. 5, and "Examine the Control and Implementation of the Political Line to Save the Economy and Prepare to Build the Country in Every Field," "Document no. 3," 19 September 1975, p. 6. (Translations by Chanthou Boua.)
17. Vickery, *Cambodia*, pp. 98, 112.
18. Vickery states: "I have made no attempt to count the number of people with whom I talked. . . . Interested readers can do that for themselves." (*Cambodia*, p. xi.) I counted 92 interviewees, including 17 teachers, 13 former students, 6 former Khmer Rouge, 4 people described as "bourgeois," "intellectual," or "elite," 3 "businessmen," 3 engineers and a doctor, 7 former Lon Nol officers and 3 soldiers, 6 carpenters, a radio mechanic, a truck driver, and 12 others of backgrounds identified as urban. The remainder are unidentifiable by background. Vickery says (p. 85) that "bourgeois refugees . . . have provided most of the information used here."
19. Vickery, *Cambodia*, p. 112.

not even peasants could survive."[20] Nearly all Vickery's oral testimony comes from male urban evacuees, interviewed in refugee camps in Thailand in 1980.[21] A more representative sample of the population of the Southwest Zone will be presented below.

A counterpoint to Vickery's thesis is the work of Kate Frieson, *The Impact of Revolution on Cambodian Peasants, 1970–1975.* Frieson "takes issue with the view that the Red Khmers enjoyed widespread peasant support" before 1975.[22] In her view, "Cambodian peasants were unwitting participants in a revolution whose leaders were faceless, whose goals were hidden, whose tactics were terrifying, and whose strategies seemed to offer little or nothing of benefit to peasants. . . . Peasant support for the Red Khmers was not given out of commitment to the movement but out of a basic human desire to survive the exigencies created by the war."[23] Using the work of James C. Scott, particularly *Weapons of the Weak: Everyday Forms of Peasant Resistance,* Frieson characterizes "peasant survival strategies" in Cambodia as "digging in, bending low, and cursing inwardly."[24]

While there is much truth to this view of the Cambodian revolution, it also is too extreme. A similar problem of sources is involved. Frieson interviewed over a hundred Cambodian women and men, "mostly of rural, semi-literate backgrounds." However, many of the 111 names she lists are known intellectuals; sixteen are identified as peasants or farmers. Ninety or so were interviewed abroad—in Thailand, the United States, Australia, and Canada. The exceptions are twenty "villagers"[25] interviewed in Cambodia; of sixteen named, at least five are not peasants.[26] Moreover, Frieson's interviews were conducted from 1988 to 1990, fifteen years after the events, and thus are subject to memory loss and error. Her case is persuasive for the vast majority of peasant new people, who either had no contact with the CPK or did what they could to avoid the war and the revolution until 1975. But Frieson uses the tes-

20. Ibid., p. 106.

21. Nine of Vickery's 90-plus informants are identified as female. See note 18, above.

22. Kate G. Frieson, *The Impact of Revolution on Cambodian Peasants, 1970–1975,* Ph.D. Diss., Department of Politics, Monash University, Australia, 1991, p. iii. Frieson initially picks an easier target: "Did the majority of Cambodian peasants support the Red Khmer revolutionary movement?," and is careful to state: "It would be wrong to argue that there was no rural support for the Red Khmers" (p. 14). But she also exaggerates her case by concluding that, "in peasant perceptions, there is *nothing* to be gained by making sacrifices for the good of the state" and that "Khmer peasant political loyalties to the Red Khmers *never* went very far" (pp. 12, 18, emphases added). Frieson is now preparing her work for publication.

23. Ibid., pp. 9, 16.

24. Ibid., p. 11. See James C. Scott, *Weapons of the Weak: Everyday Forms of Peasant Resistance,* New Haven: Yale University Press, 1985.

25. Frieson, *The Impact of Revolution,* p. 4.

26. They are In Tam, Ly Sorsane, and Chea Soth, Loth Suong, and Chea Samy.

timony of only two base people. This is not a representative sampling of seventy percent of Cambodia's population.[27]

I will show that widespread peasant support for the Khmer Rouge did exist in 1975. This conclusion is based on about five hundred interviews, about half of them with peasants, mostly in 1979 and 1980, close to the events at issue. Over one hundred were conducted with refugees in France, and nearly all the rest in Cambodia. Though I do not argue that the cpk enjoyed *majority* peasant support, that question is not easily resolved. Further, far from all being passive victims, low-moving targets, or terrified onlookers, many peasants did take initiatives of their own—for *and* against the revolution, and on separate issues. On the other hand, I will show the theory of a cpk-led peasant revolution to be untenable. Just as effectively as it had already devastated the lives of Cambodians of other races, the course the cpk took eventually alienated nearly all ethnic Khmer peasants as well, though even as late as 1976 such an outcome was by no means obvious to them.

Up to April 1975 most of the population was organized into "mutual aid teams" (*krom provas dai*), small farming groups of ten to fifteen families. In the words of an Eastern Zone peasant, this form of social organization had brought "real prosperity."[28] Effective control (not ownership) of land, stock, and equipment remained in peasant hands, usury and rental payments were abolished, and taxation was relatively light. However, beginning in May 1973, and especially after victory in 1975, most *krom* were merged into larger, "low-level cooperatives" (*sahakor kumrit teap*), which grouped together several hundred people or a village, in a small version of Chinese communes. These sahakor were less popular, as state taxation and regimentation of working life increased. In some areas, however, private family life, and even religious life in many villages, continued as before. Then another stage began, that of "high-level cooperatives" (*sahakor kumrit khpuos*). This final reorganization was accompanied or soon followed by enforced communal eating and severe restrictions on family life.

DK policies deprived peasants of three of the most cherished features of their lifestyle: land, family, and religion. Cambodia's population became unpaid indentured laborers. They were organized into massive labor gangs, but were increasingly assigned individual rather than collective daily targets. While proclaiming a communal ideal, the cfk atomized its citizens to assure maximum social control. It succeeded. Their work transformed the countryside, flattening age-old earth bunds; replacing tiny dikes and irrigation channels; throwing up walls of earth to make long, straight canals; effacing small irreg-

---

27. "On the Control and Implementation," p. 7.
28. Author's interview with Sang, a base peasant, O Reang Au, 6 October 1980.

ular paddies and creating hectare squares of rice land. Between 1975 and 1977,
Cambodia became "a huge checkerboard." But some of the squares were blacker
than others.

The Southwest Zone

Vickery's explanation of the evacuation of Phnom Penh is that the
Center saw that "it would have been impossible to hold the support of their
peasant army," unless enemies were punished and a departure made from the
1917 Bolshevik model of maintaining a normal administration and urban privilege.[29] So when the urban populations were deported to the countryside, the
base people participated "with some glee" in the persecution of "their class
enemies."[30] We shall test this thesis against the testimony of forty-seven
people who lived in the Southwest, half of peasant background, including
twenty base people.

The Southwest Zone comprised Regions 13, 33, 35 and 25. Its low-grade
but densely populated rice lands were broken by the Elephant Mountains,
whose ranges straddled the borders between the provinces of Kompong Speu,
Takeo, and Kampot. Takeo, one of Cambodia's top three rice-producing
provinces, was the most important lowland area. But its western district, Tram
Kak, abutted the uplands, including neighboring Chhouk district of Kampot.
Further south, in Kirivong district, Takeo's flood plain broached the Vietnamese border. Coastal Kampot (Region 35) was Cambodia's only major
source of salt, giving the Southwest an advantage over other Zones.

In early 1976, the Southwest had a population of 1.5 million.[31] Though
most were peasants, Vickery's account of the Zone is based on the accounts of
twelve non-peasants only. They include Stephen Heder's interviews with two
CPK cadres and Vickery's own with four former students, a French teacher, a
Lon Nol soldier, and a medic, an agricultural engineer, "a girl from the 'new'
people," and "an attractive, well-educated woman of the former urban bourgeoisie." None of Vickery's interviewees were base people. Such accounts are
unconvincing documentation of a "peasant revolution." Vickery further concludes from them that in the Southwest "there was no policy to exterminate
intellectuals, or professionals, or even Lon Nol officers, in general" and that
"starvation was not generally a problem," which "indicates some success in
the DK agricultural reorganisation." We shall test these conclusions too. They

29. Vickery, "Violence in Democratic Kampuchea," pp. 20, 5.

30. Vickery, "Cambodia (Kampuchea): History, Tragedy, and Uncertain Future," *Bulletin
of Concerned Asian Scholars [BCAS]* 21, 2–4, 1989, p. 47.

31. *Kumrung phankar buon chhnam khosang sangkumniyum krup phnaek rebos pak, 1977–80*,
translation in *Pol Pot Plans the Future*, p. 52.

broach key issues, for Vickery rightly calls the Southwest "the zone of 'Pol Potism' *par excellence*, the power base of the Pol Pot central government," whose influence spread "over the entire country."[32]

By 1975 the Zone administration was dominated by Mok, a member of the CPK Standing Committee, and his thirteen brothers-in-law, daughters, sons, and sons-in-law. As Mok's power grew, his relatives rose through the ranks. In 1976, his daughter Khom was promoted from CPK secretary of Tram Kak district to deputy secretary of Region 13, before dying of illness the next year. Mok's brother-in-law, San, a former schoolteacher, followed her as Tram Kak's secretary in 1977–78. Her widower, Khe Muth, was secretary of Kompong Som and commander of the DK navy. A second son-in-law, Boran, would follow in Mok's footsteps as Zone secretary in late 1978. A second brother-in-law, Tith, was chief of District 109. In 1977 a third son-in-law, Soeun, was promoted from division commander to secretary of District 107, and a fourth, brigade commander Ren, was promoted to division commander. In the same year Mok's son Chong was promoted from secretary of District 55 to secretary of Region 33.[33]

Region 33 (Kompong Speu-North Takeo)

According to one account, during the 1970–75 war, Chong's district was "the toughest sanctuary of the Khmer Rouge movement."[34] It was probably Chong's forces who kidnapped twelve men of Heng Samrin's 126th Eastern Zone regiment in the district in 1973. The CPK secretary of Region 33 at that time was Saing Rin.[35] A carpenter at the Region headquarters recalls Rin as someone who was "good to the people, [who] did not kill people, and liked making love to women a lot." Rin was "not cruel like Mok." But Region 33 was still one of the harshest in the country, and it became harsher, especially for the base people, when Mok's son Chong took over from Rin in 1977.

As secretary of one of Region 33's five districts, from 1975 Chong would

32. Vickery, *Cambodia*, pp. 86–100, 98–9, 86.

33. Information on Mok, his family, and their positions comes from the author's interviews with a CPK member from 1973 and DK subdistrict chief, Kirivong, 25 August 1980; a CPK member from 1973 and DK subdistrict committee member, Kong Pisei, 17 September 1980; an anonymous source in Takeo, 16 July 1980; and Ouch Sruy (who met Chong in Prey Krabas in mid-1975), Stains, 11 August 1979; and from S. Heder's interview with a Region 13 cadre, Sakeo, 8 March 1980. Savann, interview with the author, 26 August 1980, says San was Mok's son-in-law, not his brother-in-law. On Soeun, see also Kiernan, *How Pol Pot*, p. 415, and "Orphans of Genocide: The Cham Muslims of Kampuchea under Pol Pot," *BCAS*, 20, 4, 1988, p. 26.

34. Pin Yathay, *L'Utopie Meurtrière*, 1980, p. 91.

35. Ith Sarin, "Nine Months with the Maquis," in T. Carney, *Communist Party Power in Kampuchea*, p. 34.

tour Prey Krabas (District 55) in his Japanese car, wearing a white short-sleeved shirt that distinguished him from his black-clad subjects.[36] After the evacuation of Phnom Penh, Seng Horl, a teacher whom we met in Chapter 2, brought his family of nine safely to his native village in Prey Krabas. "No one ran to welcome us," Horl recalls. "My mother watched us arrive from a distance. . . . Mother did not dare come and ask me anything." The village chief quickly confiscated Horl's goods and burnt his Khmer and French books and his diploma, saying they were "imperialist" items and warning of "U.S.-CIA enemies" among the people. "My mother had never seen my children, but she did not dare approach us until the village chief and militia had left. She said to survive, you had to do three things: . . . know nothing, hear nothing, see nothing." Horl was not allowed to stay in his mother's house that evening. The militia camped near his family, "listening to us talk." In the first few days, Horl's nephew, an army officer, and a former police inspector disappeared. "Police, officers, military policemen, and pilots were killed immediately."

The hamlet consisted of forty families of base people and twenty people from Phnom Penh. After a week, Horl and his family were sent to join a group of two hundred teachers' families in a *wat*. A separate group included three hundred factory workers and doctors. Over three thousand ex-soldiers from the district were also grouped together, in another wat (Buddhist monastery). Six professors disappeared, but teachers, workers, and doctors were "spared" and could "live normally." They received at least 250 grams of rice per day, measured in used cans. "The hardest lot was that of the soldiers"; many were killed. The rest received one half can of rice per day until June, when they were again deported, to Battambang. The base people remained in their villages; parents of evacuees could not visit their children "even if we were sick." Phnom Penh people were called "enemies." But at night the base people, who had enough to eat, would secretly bring rice to the wat to exchange with new people for clothes or gold. The teachers' group worked in *krom* (groups) of ten families. Each krom was provided two pairs of draft animals, two plows, and one cart. Their work, however, was often interrupted arbitrarily; they were ordered around "to make things hard for us." In October 1975, the teachers' village was dispersed and Horl sent to a village near his home.

Long Van, thirty-five, an airplane mechanic, went to his native village in the same district, with an extended family of seventeen.[37] The village population of six hundred was evenly divided between base and new people. Van recalls, "My parents were base people, so the Khmer Rouge dared not bother me for fear of alienating the base people." First they created eleven *krom*, each

---

36. Author's 1979 interview with Ouch Sruy. See also Chapter 3.
37. Author's interview with Van, Strasbourg, 1 November 1979.

of five new families supervised by five families of base people, given an equitable amount of land for their own needs. Each family received equal rations, though the base people had additional stores. "This system was productive. There was a good rice crop, and we planted potatoes," says Van. But most base people thirty or older hated the CPK, silently resenting the loss of their right "to eat their fill and have freedom to do what they liked." Only younger base people, and those in authority, seemed enthusiastic.

In the first seven months, six elderly people died in the village from starvation and disease. People ate gruel but could also fish and forage. Three people were arrested, including a student from Phnom Penh whose father had died, leaving him alone. "He was sad and depressed, and broke the regulations. He was taken away and killed." Two generals in a nearby village were executed. Van insists, however, that the Khmer Rouge "were not yet barbaric," at first attempting to reassure the population. Van put it this way: "In order to kill people they did very good things. They did not lose our trust then; we were still feeling our way with them. Their tactics were good, so that we would believe them until they arrested and killed us."

One group of locals, former poor peasants, had been put in an "empty-handed krom" of their own. Van asserts that "they were lazy and remained lazy, and got no good results. So the system was changed." Now the village chief introduced a rice-growing regime Van describes as "contrary in every way." The krom were formed into larger *kong ha* (groups of fifty) and *kong roi* (one hundred) and sent to build dams during the rainy season instead of preparing the fields. "They planted the rice too late, and it drowned. They were more interested in building irrigation works than in growing rice." Every night the workers attended meetings in which speakers criticized the Lon Nol regime. Shortages loomed.

In September 1975, "those who did not work actively" were dispatched to the Northwest Zone. Two months later, the remaining new people followed. A meeting of the subdistrict was held to inform them that their arrival had allegedly increased the local population by a factor of ten,[38] and that Prey Krabas could not support them. Van's extended family of seventeen walked through deserted fields for twenty-four hours to a railway station, where they waited eleven days with a large crowd. They slept in the rain, on the road, beside dikes, and in rice fields. Two neighbors of Van's died of pneumonia before the train arrived. That night the evacuees began their second deportation. In December 1975, Horl's family followed, along with "all the Phnom Penh people in Takeo, rich or poor."

38. This seems unlikely. The actual figures given were 2,000 base people and 20,000 new people, which are both far too low. I suspect the numbers were propaganda on Chong's part. Author's interview with Van, Strasbourg, 1 November 1979.

We last saw medic Kem Hong Hav running a CPK checkpoint on his motorcycle. He took his family of ten to his father's house in Kong Pisei (District 54). The more than four hundred evacuees outnumbered the base people in the village. "My father was a base person, so we could live with them. He was loyal, the Khmer Rouge trusted him." But Hav did not get on with his father. He even feared execution, knowing base people who were afraid of the victors. However, here the latter were "still kind," concentrating on "attracting us to them, educating us"; they "did not yet worry us for what we had done in Phnom Penh."

New and base people received equal rations. "If a cow was killed, everyone would get a kilogram of beef. When you came back home from work you would find it waiting for you." Also, "new and base people worked equally hard," the latter supervising. "They did not yet send us off to dig earth or raise dams." Workers were formed into krom, and into kong of thirty to forty. At weekly meetings they were urged to "obey the rules of Angkar," and not to resist the revolution. "The real poor people liked the Khmer Rouge. They were not so intelligent, and happy to eat equally with the educated and rich people with whom they were angry. They liked the system and really hated the Phnom Penh people, because we had not struggled for the revolution and equality alongside the Khmer Rouge." No CPK forces were stationed nearby. "It was the base people and the village chief who were the Khmer Rouge; there was no need for troops."

With "spies watching all the time," Hav dared not ask his father too many questions. But by June his father considered Hav's presence too risky, and pleaded, "Do you want to let me live longer or not? You must go to another place. . . . One day there will be danger for me." His father dared not identify the threat, but Hav sympathized: "He had to follow the revolution, which we both knew was wrong." Before leaving, Hav protected his father by asking a cadre for permission to move elsewhere. His mother used their oxcart to take Hav and his pregnant wife to the village of his in-laws in Takeo.

On arrival in Prey Krabas district, Hav described himself as a civil nurse, hiding his military background. This village was more prosperous, and life was easier. His wife's father was a landed middle peasant, who had once employed a servant to mind his cattle and clear undergrowth. The servant was now the village chief. The subdistrict operated a hospital, and though Hav was not allowed to work there, he visited it when ill. "They really looked after you. . . . There was still good medicine from Phnom Penh, and I got better. The nurses were . . . not well-educated but obeyed the rules; they were good for the revolution, and served the people for its benefit. They demonstrated equality, without classes." Exceptions were CPK soldiers and supporters, who received better treatment. Schooling continued for all children under eleven, though "the teachers were ignorant."

Hav and his wife set up house next to her parents and worked in their krom. Other new and base people also worked together. "Just as before, the base people worked hard, in front of us, as models for the new people. They did not stop for wind or rain. They worked harder than us, on behalf of Angkar. For us, who were not yet tempered, it was hard. We were angry but dared not say so." The most committed few, "the ignorant ones" as Hav calls them, "had abandoned all their property and worked for Angkar; they had really forgotten the past, and were enthusiastic."

Rations were regular, one can of rice per day. People were only allowed to forage for food on completion of individual work targets. "One day they would say we could forage after digging two cubic meters each, but the next day they would give us three cubic meters. Targets were always changing. If we did not complete the target, it was not a problem, but they would take note of it. They would say your thinking was not good. But nothing would happen." After a time, Hav was considered to have served Angkar loyally, and earned a "good name." Individual daily targets, more rigidly enforced in other parts of the Southwest, would become an important weapon of CPK control.

Terror remained another. Soldiers and "rich people" were taken away for execution. Many of Hav's in-laws disappeared: former officials, pilots, soldiers, professors. In September 1975, prominent families and families of dead Lon Nol soldiers were rounded up and sent to Battambang. In November, Hav was ordered to follow, along with all other new people and those base people considered disloyal. First he went to see his parents again in Kompong Speu. He found that eating had been communalized, consumption had fallen, and "all property was gone." Hav's father was "having a bad time," though some base people still liked the revolution. The new people, who were "very unhappy," were about to be evacuated to the northwest. Thousands of new evacuees from Prey Krabas walked to Takeo city to board the train. Khmer Rouge provided an oxcart for Hav's wife, who had given birth three days before; her father insisted on coming too, "even if it meant death." The crowd waited ten days in the open, with "shit everywhere." Medicine ran out, and death struck. "Hardship, persecution, and hunger began."

Yun, a mathematics teacher who became a Lon Nol officer, had driven his sedan south out of Phnom Penh and spent a month in Region 25. Then he again loaded his family of eight and their belongings into the car and pushed it in the rain for five days to his native village in Prey Krabas. He found ten families of new people living among seventy families of base people. Twenty Phnom Penh families lived in two neighboring villages. The locals, much more numerous, were evenly divided between those who had lived there during the war and those like his wife's wealthy aunt and uncle, who had fled to Takeo city and returned after April 1975. They told Yun that "many soldiers had been killed" when the crk took Takeo. "There was more killing there than in Phnom Penh, because the population was smaller and the victims easier to identify." A military police officer from Phnom Penh had been killed three days after arriving in the village. Despite threats, there were no more executions or disappearances there in 1975. Food rations were high: up to three cans of rice per day for adults, nearly one for children.

Some base people had benefited from the revolution, but most newcomers and many others were unhappy. "Goods had been collectivized during the war, and there was no freedom to speak or write or move." The villagers worked in krom of ten to twenty families. Sick people could rest. Production was high, with both dry and wet season crops. Ten thousand people from every village in Prey Krabas were sent to work in ten-day shifts on a new dam, thirty meters wide by seven high. Each subdistrict had to move five hundred cubic meters of earth. Each person had to dig and carry 2.5 cubic meters per day. On completion, they had to help other members of their krom, then of their kong, village, subdistrict, other subdistricts, and so on. Over two months later the dam was completed. In late December, all thirty Phnom Penh families in Yun's village and the two neighboring ones, and five families of base people not sufficiently trusted, were sent to Battambang.[39]

Hong Var, a teacher of Khmer language and literature in Phnom Penh, took her two daughters to her native Takeo province. They settled with sixty-seven other evacuee families in a village of 120 base families. The peasants sheltered the city people, sometimes four families to a house. This led to quarrels, so the Khmer Rouge built small thatch huts, four meters square, for the families unable to live harmoniously with others. The huts were called the "New Village." Var and her daughters remained with a base family. Workdays were usually long. Sometimes Var worked over fourteen hours. Waking at 1 A.M., she worked until 7, and then from 7:30 until 11:30, and from about 1 till 5 P.M. She had never planted rice before and was unhappy. The locals taught her well enough but usually mocked her. Khmer Rouge cadres would say, "Look at your hands, they are used to holding a pen, not to hard work." The peasants, when uprooting rice seedlings, would tap them against their feet to shake off the soil. They would make sure the soil went all over Var, from meters away. She vainly tried to reciprocate. Everybody worked equally hard, but the base people got more attention and more food. When the peasants received rice, Var got gruel. If they got meat, she might get rice with salt. "If a pig was killed only the peasants could eat pork." But there was no starvation in the village in 1975. Var says most of the peasants "really liked" the Khmer Rouge, who worked with them in the fields. But about one in four base people were hos-

39. Author's interview with Yun, Creteil, 12 November 1979.

tile, mostly older peasants who supported Sihanouk and were disappointed that he had not been reinstated. Some kept the prince's portrait in their homes. In December 1975, all seventy new families were moved out of the village and taken by train to Battambang. Var and her daughters went too.[40]

Srey Pich Chnay, twenty, a fine arts student at Phnom Penh University, went to a village of two hundred base people that was swamped by five hundred families of newcomers. Here the peasants were more hostile. Supporters of the Khmer Rouge, they had been through the war with them and learnt to hate city dwellers as "oppressive." The cpk favored base people with more food and easier work. Peasants, as well as Khmer Rouge, told newcomers, "You used to be happy and prosperous. Now it's our turn." But the peasants were divided. Chnay says about half the base people were rich and the others poor peasants. They sometimes quarrelled. The poor regarded the rich as "bloodsuckers" who had "taken from the poor" their large plots of land, oxen, or buffaloes. The cpk resolved disputes by confiscating excess wealth of rich peasants or by sending them away. New people were systematically deprived of possessions. A Mercedes 220, along with most other city cars that had arrived in the village, was cut in two across the middle. The metal from the rear was used to make plowshares, the motor was adapted to drive a water pump, and the wheels were attached to oxcarts. Everyone, including children, worked very hard, usually twelve- or thirteen-hour days, plus about six nights each month on particular tasks and occasional compulsory evening political meetings. On 29 December, all five hundred families of Phnom Penh people walked to Takeo to board the train for Battambang.[41]

Until 1975, Sruy, thirty-four, had run the truck pool at the ministry of agriculture. Evacuated from the capital, he first went south to Region 25, but four months later he was told to go to Battambang. So one night with his brother, a Lon Nol military officer, Sruy escaped by boat to his native village in Prey Krabas. Within days his brother had been executed. The village chief, a relative, showed Sruy the grave, a pit containing seven or eight bodies. Later Chong, the district chief, came by in his car. "We Phnom Penh people were scared of him." More frightening, however, was the subdistrict chief's authority to kill people without asking Chong's permission. Sruy was sent to work in the forest. Phnom Penh evacuees were not allowed to live with base people, who had large houses of their own. The new people slept in huts, subsisting on a can

---

40. See Var's story in Kiernan and Boua, eds., *Peasants and Politics in Kampuchea*, pp. 338–344; Var Hong Ashe, *From Phnom Penh to Paradise: Escape from Cambodia*, London: Hodder and Staughton, 1988.

41. Author's interviews with Srey Pich Chnay, Lumphouk refugee camp, Surin, Thailand, on 5 March 1979, and in a neighboring village on 15 March and 19 April 1979. For Chnay's full story see Kiernan and Boua, eds., *Peasants and Politics in Kampuchea*, pp. 344–52.

of rice per day, plus salt. They had only leaves to add to their gruel, and no kerosene to light the nights. Children, who received half a can of rice, fought over food at mealtimes. Though base people were better off, only the younger ones liked the revolution. "Most of the rest were unhappy, but dared not say so. We were meant to be their enemies but were not in fact. The base people were loyal out of fear."[42]

Chheng Leang went to yet another village in Prey Krabas, with one hundred base families and over two hundred new. They worked together, though base people had lighter tasks and more food. The newcomers' meagre rice ration was supplemented each week by a kilogram of fish per krom or some salt. The village chief, "a pure peasant" according to Leang, "just told us what to do, and did not work." He described the new people as "enemies" who had worked for "American imperialists." They had been "deposited in the care" of the "revolutionary strugglers" for education. But in October and November 1975, after the planting was done, the CPK evacuated Sruy, Leang and "all new people" to Battambang.[43]

This second deportation occurred throughout the Southwest with the 1975 crop, which the deportees had helped plant, still standing. It left the harvest to be shared by many fewer mouths. This could have greatly improved the living conditions of those remaining. The Southwest now comprised only base people. We have heard new people describe views of the base people. Base people have also spoken for themselves. Hen, member of a CPK subdistrict committee in Kong Pisei (District 54), Region 33, admits that "the people had been afraid of me since 1973," when he had joined the party. But the next year, when CPK executioners killed his younger brother and two relatives, all base people, he feared for his own sake. "I had lost faith since 1974, but I worked on to survive."

Three thousand Phnom Penh evacuees arrived in Hen's subdistrict in April and May 1975. They joined the four thousand base people, but were housed separately, in the "New Village." In July the population was again divided, now into three groups. The "full rights people" (*neak peñ sith*) were those base people with "good politics," no relatives among the new people or the executed, and a commitment to hard work. Base people with "bad biographies" were demoted to "depositee" (*neak phñoe*) status along with most new people, and the rest comprised the intermediate group, "candidates" (*neak triem*). In 1975 and 1976, the workday in the fields was sometimes extended by two or three hours of night labor. People were raised or demoted in the hierarchy according to whether their work was "vigorous, medium, or weak." The sys-

---

42. Author's interview with Ouch Sruy, Stains, 11 August 1979.
43. Author's interview with Chheng Leang, Stains, 11 August 1979.

tem's demands on its subjects were so great as to divide and redivide them, which also added to the administrator's burden. Hen remarks, "I could not control all this. It was difficult to administer."

Up to 1975, Hen says, base people had "believed in the revolution," but they were disillusioned by the enforced separation from relatives now returned from Phnom Penh. "Belief was replaced by anger and fear," Hen recalls. He was demoted to candidate party status because he had relatives among the cpk's victims. Retaining his administrative position, Hen followed instructions to give base people, who already had their own stores and poultry, more food than the new. "The Phnom Penh people did not know how to grow rice. They were traders and market gardeners. . . . Production was low, consumption was low." About two hundred new people (7 percent) died of disease or starvation in 1975. Many Lon Nol officers were killed, while infantrymen were spared "unless they resisted or did something against the rules, such as stealing."

The 1975 harvest was reasonable, and rice rations were provided in the communal kitchens until early 1976. From then on people ate rice gruel, and another two hundred died, mostly new people, some from eating poisonous plants out of hunger. Poor natural conditions made the 1976 harvest worse. Lon Nol soldiers now seemed to be singled out for execution even if they had not broken any rules. In 1977, Hen was transferred to an even "tougher" sub-district. People labored "night and day," some nights with a four-hour shift for sleeping at the worksite. Production was higher, but two hundred to three hundred people still died each year, "because of bad health due to the harder work, while rations were middling." Sixty to 70 percent of the rice they produced went to the state. Base people suspected of crimes were regularly "sent up to higher levels"—which meant death. In 1977–78, deportations of peasants peaked, and "the base people lost faith one hundred percent."[44]

Samuoeun, a Kong Pisei peasant who joined the revolution in 1974 at age 23, did not see her parents again until 1979. Her worksite comprised a "division" of mostly female workers, commanded by a male former cpk officer. Samuoeun was in the 11th Battalion, which was divided into companies (*kong roi*) of one hundred women, and in turn into three platoons (*kong ha*), each with three squads (*krom*). Pheap, the women's leader from Kampot, was "a very kind person, who joked with us a lot." No Women's Association existed. At first the regimen was reasonable, and the atmosphere was one of resignation. "When we chatted amongst ourselves in our krom, we talked about when we lived at home with our parents, in the old society, about growing rice and making a living." In 1976–77 Samuoeun's squad dug canals, moving five to ten cubic meters of earth per day.

44. Author's interview with Hen, Kong Pisei, 17 September 1980.

Rations consisted of gruel in the second half of 1975, rice throughout 1976. Samuoeun saw no killings before late 1976 and says the women "liked the revolution in 1976." But in 1977 several women in her squad were executed, and others were threatened with imprisonment. "They did not force us to work hard by supervising us with guns. They just told us to work hard. . . . We feared prison so we tried hard." The squad returned to planting rice, with a target of a hectare per day. If they failed to achieve that, they would be accused of not trying. The most productive years were 1977 and 1978, but much of the rice the women produced was removed after milling. They now ate rice for three to four months each year, gruel and *trokuon* (water morning glory) soup the rest of the time; there was no starvation, however.

In 1978 Pheap was transferred to the Northern Zone, and Run, a "crueler" leader, arrived from Kampot. "Sometimes she chatted and joked with us, and sometimes she was angry with us. . . . She did not work in the fields with us much. . . . We had to work much harder than before. . . . I just went to work for long hours and did not rest till evening," Samuoeun recalls. Sometimes the women labored until 8 or 9 P.M.[45]

Hap, sixty, a base peasant from Kong Pisei, recalls that the Khmer Rouge "persecuted us from 1973," when two of his sons disappeared. He never knew why. Probably because of his loss, after 1975 he was classified as a "candidate." At first people worked in krom of fifteen to twenty, but these were disbanded in favor of "village cooperatives" of forty to fifty families. "We had to do whatever they said. There was not enough to eat. Production was not very high." In his village of forty families, ten people died of starvation from 1975 to 1978. Those who could not work got no food. Hap's recollections of the DK regime included meetings in which "some of us listened, and some didn't"; schools in some of the villages, where children "were mostly taught to work"; and hospitals, which he avoided, where "the doctors were youngsters."[46]

Yem, who had once been a CPK militiaman in Bati (District 56) of Region 33, had fled the area in 1973 when the CPK relocated peasants north to Kompong Speu. He escaped to Phnom Penh. Now evacuated from the capital, Yem headed for his home village, but was ordered to move on. With over seven hundred new families, he joined a hamlet of fifty base people. The locals "gave us cakes, meat and rice" and slaughtered cattle. "These base people were good. One told me they didn't like the Khmer Rouge but had not been able to escape. . . . Region 33 had been communalized during the war. . . . Region 33 base people were even unhappier than the new people. All were equal in Region 33." After a month, however, the Khmer Rouge ordered the new people sepa-

45. Author's interview with Samuoeun, Kong Pisei, 13 September 1980.
46. Author's interview with Hap, Kong Pisei, 13 September 1980.

rated from the old, and established communal eating halls for each group. A meeting was called, and several thousand people assembled at a wat, surrounded by troops. People were ordered to sit on the ground in separate groups for males and females, young and old. Yem was surprised to see two men seated in the crowd behind him get up to address the meeting. They were members of the Region 33 CPK committee. "They asked us what all we new people had been doing, who were teachers, soldiers, bosses." Two hundred families headed by Lon Nol officers and soldiers were sifted out, along with seventeen families headed by teachers, from the other five hundred new families. In the next months four people disappeared, including an officer, a soldier, and a man who complained to his wife of insufficient food. Yem claims the orders from *Angkar Leu* (the High Organization) were to feed everyone equally, but that local cadres secretly gave the base people more. This is unlikely given Hen's report, but the effect was the same: one hundred new people starved in three months.

Over five hundred survivors were enlisted in a mobile work unit (*kong chalat*), a large labor gang that was to become a hallmark of CPK workforce organization. They went to dig dams and canals two days' walk away, joining tens of thousands of workers from the region. Soldiers' and teachers' groups labored separately. The work was hard, sickness no excuse. As elsewhere, daily targets were individually set. Each worker had to dig five cubic meters of earth per day; krom of ten people helped one another reach the target. Troops patrolled the area, but did not come close to the laborers or supervise their work. The fifty base people did that. "But they worked hard like us, even harder. Our group leaders (*mekrom*) were very loyal Khmer Rouge base people."

In July 1975, while Yem was working at an irrigation site, a cadre asked where his birthplace was. Yem said he was a peasant from Kandal province, and was told, "Angkar will let you go there." A new exodus began. Two hundred families walked sixty kilometers on a can of rice (250 grams) per person. Some died on the trek. The rest arrived at their destination to be told that there were no trucks to take them on, and they would all have to go back! More died. Back in Bati they found crowds of new people "from all over Region 33." There was no food for them, and many more died waiting a week in the rain. Fifty trucks, each with two armed drivers, took the deportees to Pursat, where they boarded trains to Battambang.[47]

Mek, thirty-two, had been production manager in a Phnom Penh cigarette factory for eight years. With his extended family of twenty, he was also evacuated to Bati in 1975. In Chambak subdistrict, ten thousand new people joined four thousand base people in seven villages. For three months Mek labored on

47. Author's interview with Yem, Strasbourg, 31 October 1979.

roads and irrigation works, on rations of 1.5 cans per day. In July he began planting rice. Fifteen people worked each hectare; on dam projects, targets were individual—three cubic meters each per day. Rations fell to one can per day, but remained sufficient for nutrition. There was no starvation in 1975. But at year's end, one hundred new people in the subdistrict were executed at Wat Koh, a former monastery, for "moral offenses." These included, Mek says, "the use of old, happy words." Young village militia members were eavesdropping on conversations.

The base people received their rations in sacks, not cans, of rice. The new people had no contact with them. "The Khmer Rouge trusted all base people," Mek claims. But after the harvest at the end of 1975, trucks came to collect the paddy. More than ten truckloads from each village were taken to Phnom Penh, Mek says. In April 1976, communal eating began. There was "lots" of rice for three months, then only gruel from July 1976 to April 1977, a few months of rice again, then more gruel. The last few months of each year, before harvest time, were always the worst. Private foraging or other work was forbidden. "You could not even catch fish in the rice fields." In 1976, even more new people were killed, and in 1977 the CPK began killing base people. Mek saw victims arrested, bound, and taken away on pony carts toward Wat Koh.[48]

Samath, the carpenter in the Region headquarters who had joined the revolution in 1970, agrees that conditions got much worse in 1977, after Saing Rin's arrest and replacement as region secretary by Mok's son Chong. "In 1977–78, every few days they arrested people in our group of fifty to sixty workers." One of the disappeared was Samath's younger brother, a peasant accused of being a "Vietnamese agent."[49]

Region 13 (Southern Takeo)

Immediately to the south was Region 13, and Tram Kak District (*District 105*). Tram Kak was Mok's birthplace, run by his daughter Khom from 1973 to 1976, when she was replaced by her uncle-in-law San and promoted to CPK deputy region secretary in place of her husband Muth after his 1975 transfer to Kompong Som.[50] Democratic Kampuchea proclaimed Tram Kak one of three "model districts" (*srok kumruu*) in the country.[51] Mok's brother-in-law Tith was CPK secretary of Kirivong (District 109), and in 1977, his son-in-law Soeun became CPK secretary of Treang (District 107). Region 13 was the heartland of "the Pol Pot zone."

48. Author's interview with Mek, Phnom Penh, 5 July 1980.
49. Author's interview with Samath, Kong Pisei, 17 September 1980.
50. The region secretary from 1970 to 1976 was Saom. Heder interview, Region 13 cadre, Sakeo, 8 March 1980.
51. Author's 1980 interview with Savann, who lived in Tram Kak district in 1977–78. He

It is also controversial. A Region 13 cadre who fled to Thailand in 1979 with the remnants of the DK regime recalls that "on May 20, 1973, there were meetings everywhere to proclaim the cooperativization movement." Teams of twenty families were formed, and "all land and draft animals were collectivized." The cadre claims that "we were successfully able to get everybody into the cooperatives without bloodshed. The rich and middle peasants were dissatisfied but there was nothing they could do," partly because the majority of the population were "poor and lower-middle peasants" who previously had had only eight months' or less supply of rice each year. But production did not increase. In 1974, "the results were not better than the previous year, just better distribution, equal distribution." Any surplus was taken to "special, separate storehouses for the Organization."[52]

Compare this account with that of a former CPK soldier who stayed in Cambodia after Democratic Kampuchea's fall: "Persecution began in 1973–74, when everything was collectivized. Communal eating was introduced in May 1973, in groups of twelve families. [Soon] people were eating banana leaves, sugar-palm roots, coconuts, and finally weeds. Then there was nothing left at all. In the end the people rebelled, killing cadres in all villages. . . . So the Khmer Rouge had to give in, and in 1974 private eating was once again allowed."[53]

The same conflict of evidence characterizes the post–1975 period. According to another Region 13 CPK Cadre who fled to Thailand, "In 1975 the standard of living in Takeo was okay. In 1976 there was enough to get by."[54] More evidence is required to resolve the controversy over Region 13.

Sum, a former Phnom Penh official, took his family of seven to Tram Kak. Over fifty new families settled in a village with fifteen families of base people. They worked together in two shifts per day, from 6 to 11 A.M. and 2 to 6 P.M. During the planting season, women worked hardest, from 3 A.M. to 1 P.M. and then from 3 to 8 P.M. The base people, who "liked the Khmer Rouge" and supervised the new people, worked as hard as the new people generally but got better rations. The new people's rice rations depended on how hard they worked: Sum's family received three and a half cans of rice per day. There was no starvation in the village in 1975 and no killings. Hourly personal work targets were set from late 1975. The village chief, a base person, was a former monk, which Sum says explains "why he was not a killer." The new people

---

named Democratic Kampuchea's other "model districts" as Prasaut Thmey (in Svay Rieng) and Kompong Tralach Leu (Kompong Chhnang). Phnom Penh Radio on 28 February 1978 recalled that Prasaut district had received "the 1976 red flag of praise handed down for their achievements by the Party and Government of Democratic Kampuchea" because "they had planted so much rice." *FBIS,* Asia Pacific, 2 March 1978, p. H2.

52. Heder's interview with a Region 13 cadre, Sakeo, 8 March 1980.
53. Author's interview with a former CPK soldier, Tram Kak, 16 July 1980.
54. Heder's interview with a person from Region 13, Mai Rut, 16 March 1980.

included no Lon Nol officers, only rank-and-file soldiers who "were put to work like everyone else." No one from the village was evacuated to Battambang in the second deportation of late 1975.

The introduction of communal eating around April 1976 improved consumption for Sum's family, who were not skilled at fishing or fending for themselves in the countryside. But for the base people, used to living off the land, the new prohibition on foraging made their lives worse, while new people who still had gold could buy extra rice from cadres. Also in mid-1976, children were separated from their parents. Sum's four children aged eight to fifteen were enlisted into mobile work brigades (*kong chalat*). Sum could only see them every couple of months. They were given lessons one or two hours per day, but "they did not dare tell us whether they had enough to eat." The base people lost the company of their children too, and they now became disillusioned with the regime.

A peasant woman from Tram Kak confirms this picture. She says "persecution of the people began in 1975," before any killings, starvation, or communal eating. Festivals and religion were banned. The new people who arrived in her village were given rations of up to one can per day, while the base people "had our own rice in the house." But not for long. "Three months after the new people arrived, I was sent with all my family and twenty other families to District 109 [Kirivong], to work in the fields. They said if we did not go, we would be sent to another province." As elsewhere, the CPK treated these base peasants as unpaid indentured laborers, uprooting them almost at will, on the basis of a grand plan alien to the traditional aspirations of a peasantry.

Tam Eng, the ethnic Chinese Phnom Penh tailor, left her shop with the nine children in her care. After six weeks they safely reached Tram Kak district, where four of the children found their father. She spent a month in a village where rations were better than adequate and people could forage for more. Those over fifty were given light work. There were no killings. The cadres even "spoke softly to us, to make us brave in our hearts and try hard." People were asked to work to their capacity, and the sick were able to rest.

But then the CPK assigned ethnic Chinese to separate hamlets, and Eng had to move fifteen kilometers away to a village of one hundred Chinese families. They were supervised by thirty families of krom chiefs, "red base people who had rice in their homes, ducks, chickens, and pigs." It took Eng and her five children a month to build their own hut. Her children cut bamboo in nearby hills, while she sewed palm thatch. Six cans of rice per day, and up to a can of salt per month, was the family's ration. They and the other Chinese new people were forbidden to forage, even outside working hours. "If we raised chickens, we had to tell Angkar how many eggs [they laid] per day, how many were hens, etc. We were not allowed to eat our own eggs. If my children were caught fishing or foraging at lunchtime, they were given planting to do before being allowed home again. And if they came back late for work [in the afternoon], the krom chief would complain, and they would disappear." Eng says all 130 families, even the base people, were confined to a one-square-kilometer range, and though they still ate meals privately, they could add only leaves to their rations. "Fishing and foraging were said to be attempts to survive individually" when others could not, Eng recalls. The restrictions were enforced by the militia, who used spies.

The rice growing system was successful. There were three annual crops, and irrigation networks were extended. People over sixty were given light work. The rest rose early, attended work meetings at 6 A.M., and began work at 6:30, returning home in the afternoons. The evacuees were simply told what to do, their targets set on an individual basis. Twenty people would plant fields in a line, working forward until each completed a row, moving on until thirty fields were completed each day. Rations depended on fulfilling one's target. Sick people got half rations, which discouraged even the genuinely ill from resting. "We bled like chickens whose throats had been cut," Eng says.

A school continued to function, with over thirty students, including Eng's daughter. But Eng considered the makeshift hospitals unhygienic. The staff kept medicine in beer bottles, offered a herbal mixture with flour for headaches, and administered injections of coconut milk (which Eng refused). There were no deaths from starvation in 1975, because many of the Phnom Penh Chinese had brought clothes and gold, which they could exchange for extra rice. But much of each harvest was secretly trucked away by night. People ate gruel every day, and the margin of survival was slim. Bodies swelled from malnutrition. Eng divided most of her ration among the children. "I became just skin and bones, and thought I would die."

One family came to blows over food. Returning from two weeks' carting of earth in the hills, a son discovered that his father had been setting aside some of their rations in case he fell ill. The son quickly seized the rice and began to cook it. The father abused him, saying, "That's my rice. Angkar does not give me enough." The father then struck his wife, and the son attacked him. Tam Eng rushed up and saw him standing on his father's throat. The father screamed for the krom chief, who tied the boy to a tree overnight. The next day the son had to lift twenty-five cubic meters of earth, and the father fifteen. Had the boy not completed his punishment, the next day's would have been thirty-five cubic meters. But he did, returning home that night to assault his father again. He was then taken "to study," disappearing for a week, but contrary to everyone's expectation, came back alive, the cadres explaining that he was a good worker who had tripled his quota.

Another boy was not so lucky. Caught planting potatoes, he was killed on the spot. In addition, during 1975 over thirty doctors, soldiers, and other Chinese new people were identified and taken away from the village at night. "We did not see them killed, but locals told us they would die." Then the Khmer Rouge called a meeting and asserted that the thirty men had all escaped to Thailand. "Don't worry about what they are doing," they announced. At this several of the abandoned wives stood up and remarked that their husbands were "happy now, sleeping in wooden mosquito nets." The cadres did not challenge them. In December 1975, Eng managed to pass herself off as Vietnamese and got her family across the border. The other four children she had brought from Phnom Penh were all murdered in 1977, along with their father, a postal worker.

A female base person describes the Tram Kak district prison, established in her village, Kraing Ta Chan, in 1973. One of the first victims was a Khmer returned from Hanoi. In 1975, "many new people died here." The victims, she claims, were not interrogated, but stripped to their shirts and then murdered. The killers kept regular hours, 6 to 11 A.M., 2 to 6 P.M., and 7 to 9 P.M. Growing rice and performing craft work in the village, she saw them at work "every day and night." "The Khmer Rouge knew I was aware of this. They warned me up to twice a day: Don't tell outsiders." In 1976, she was classified as a "candidate" because two uncles who lived in Phnom Penh had been killed, and was deported to Kirivong.

A Model Village

Tram Kak had a "model cooperative" (*sahakor kumruu*). This was Leay Bo village, where foreign delegations would be taken in 1978. Three peasants from the village explain the organization of this embryonic CPK utopia. Lei was born there but left for Phnom Penh at age seventeen. She returned in 1975 with seven others. In 1975 and 1976 most former officials were executed; "we could only hide a few." Lei lost two uncles. Communal eating began in early 1976. Having lived in Phnom Penh, Lei was a "deportee." Those with deportee relatives became "candidates." Those with none were "full rights people." This was the same population classification as in Kong Pisei. It soon was used nationwide. Its categories derived from the Leninist *party*'s "full rights" and "candidate" members. The first important difference was that the rigors of party admission were applied in Democratic Kampuchea to most of the *population*, not to a vanguard political elite. In other words, a new, demanding definition of citizenship was applied, though the "rights" of full citizenship were few. The second key difference was that a third of the population, the deportees, were not even considered eligible "candidates" for such citizenship.

In 1977, new cadres took over Leay Bo and called separate meetings for each category. They instructed the deportees to "temper" themselves: "Don't be like you were in Phnom Penh." Then they formed the three categories into separate cooperatives. The full rights people stayed in Leay Bo and were called "kong No. 1." They wore only black. Deportees and candidates were assigned to different cooperatives, called kong Nos. 6, 7, and 8. They were moved to another area within Leay Bo subdistrict. Nineteen seventy-seven and 1978 were the worst years. "We worked incessantly," Lei recalls. Sometimes they rose at 3 or 4 A.M., or even 1 A.M. "It all depended on them. There was no rest time. Only 'attack' [*veay samrok*] time." On the tenth and twentieth of each month, meetings provided some respite. Pigs and cattle were slaughtered for food, and rice served. On other days, rations comprised soup made of trokuon, a nutritious but not very tasty plant. Trucks came to take the rice away. Several people died of starvation, and three times Lei fell ill and went to "hospital." Mild illness was diagnosed as "disease of the consciousness," or laziness, and rest denied. Various illnesses were treated with the same herbal medicine. Most serious ones proved fatal. Three members of Lei's family of seven were killed in 1977, and many villagers starved to death in 1978. "Only full rights people liked Pol Pot," she concluded.

Sok, forty-seven, was a "full rights" peasant in Leay Bo. Recalling Khmer Rouge arriving in the village in 1970, Sok says, "Until 1975, they were good. Then, . . . we were under their control. . . . From 1975 noone liked the Khmer Rouge, they were different from their original politics. They had said they were going to raise the living standards of the poor, so they won. But when they took over they collectivized everything: cattle, buffalo, plates, everything. . . . they put it all in one place. You could only eat what you were given. . . . And anyone they suspected of not being happy with them, they killed." There were "one or two" killings in 1975, but more in 1976, when a relative of Sok, another base person, was executed on suspicion of hiding rice in his house. The CPK attempted to distract people's attention from their situation by informing the peasants that life in Cambodia was superior to that in Vietnam, where people were reduced to eating chaff, while Chairman Mao's socialism was bringing progress to China. When the villagers were separated by category in 1977, the full rights people remained in Leay Bo, but were now joined by other poor peasants from the hills to the west, Mok's native area. The newcomers were described as the "support base" of the revolution. Though some were illiterate, they took over the village and subdistrict administration, and killed many people in 1977 and 1978, Sok says.

The full rights people were now subdivided again. A new subcategory, "No. 1 full rights," comprised those who had had no relatives on the Lon Nol side *and* had "many children who served Angkar." This privileged the newcomers from the hills. "No. 2 full rights people" had relatives both on the Lon Nol side and in the revolution. For his own kinship with people from the Lon Nol areas, Sok was was now demoted to "No. 3 full rights," equivalent to candidate status in the previous classification.[55] Now, candidates were also redivided into three subcategories. Sok explains, "No. 1 candidates had four or five relatives who served Lon Nol, and, say, one who served Angkar." No. 2 and No. 3 candidates had no relatives in the CPK network. And the deportees from the conquered Lon Nol areas were in turn divided into subcategories 1, 2, and 3, depending on their "consciousness and hard work."

Here in the heart of Democratic Kampuchea—a model cooperative in a model district, in the Pol Pot zone *"par excellence"*—clan politics was solidifying into a baroque hierarchy of caste. This is not surprising. Pol Pot and his in-laws dominated at the national level, as did the Mok family dynasty at the Southwest Zone and Region levels. Just as racialist ideology had determined CPK policy toward minorities and foreigners, other blood ties among the majority Khmer determined one's place in the DK social system.[56] The racial template with which the Center viewed the outside world was also applied to Cambodian society. The result was the official construction of rival kin networks, competing in a zero-sum game and reflecting the role ascribed abroad to historic racial antagonisms. These emerging kinship structures were a departure from traditional peasant society, which had "no larger organized kin groups beyond the family or household."[57] The deliberate social classification resembled a census, a process characteristic of modernity, not of peasant community. Multilayered, carefully calibrated, rigidly institutionalized, the new DK caste system had as little to do with peasant class politics as the new centralized labor management system had to do with peasant farming.

"Full rights" in Democratic Kampuchea was a relative term. Sok's citizenship, if even half-full, was near-fancy. On the second anniversary of victory, Phnom Penh Radio conceded that "our people" had only "sufficient rights." These were defined: "They enjoy the right to be the masters of the land, fields, and gardens, and to be the masters of all work performed. They have adequate

55. A new person who lived in Tram Kak in 1977 and 1978 says that the "full rights people" there were subdivided into "party people" (*pakachun*), "core" (*snoul*) group members (candidate party members ?), and "ordinary [base] people." Author's interview, Preah Bat Chuon Chum, Kirivong, 26 August 1980.

56. For structural similarities between kinship and nationality, see David M. Schneider, "Kinship, Nationality, and Religion in American Culture: Towards a Definition of Kinship," in Robert F. Spencer, ed., *Forms of Symbolic Action*, AES Monographs, dist. University of Washington Press, Seattle, 1969, pp. 116–25; and Schneider, "What Is Kinship All About?," in Priscilla Reining, ed., *Kinship Studies in the Morgan Centennial Year*, Anthropological Society of Washington, 1972, pp. 32–63. May Ebihara kindly provided these references.

57. May Ebihara, *A Khmer Village in Cambodia*, Ph.D. Diss., Columbia University, 1968, p. 148.

living quarters and in particular they have a sufficient, even abundant, food supply."[58] What, then, about the "full rights" of relocated base people like the poor peasants from the hills of western Tram Kak? Chet, a peasant woman from Leay Bo, had lived there since the 1950s. In 1973, when she was fifty-five, the Khmer Rouge had forcibly evacuated her family and others west toward the mountains. "There we lived normally for a year, then they moved us to another place to grow rice privately once again. After a year or two, we were driven up there again." Chet got back to Leay Bo only in 1975, but she was now considered a "tempered" graduate: "I was called 'full rights' because I had been evacuated high up" into Tram Kak, a privilege. In her words, "only people from up there were allowed to live here." Despite her status, Chet was still barred from Leay Bo; she was sent to another village a kilometer away.

With the introduction of communal eating in 1976, "we full rights people ate the same as the rest. The food was not good." At first rations comprised a spoon of rice each, but in 1977–78 gruel and trokuon soup became the norm. In the same period several people in Chet's village were executed, full rights and educated new people, "anyone who said anything wrong." The women worked as hard as the men, "and were killed just like the men if they did anything wrong." Chet's husband died of illness, leaving her alone. Cadres had her mind infants and toddlers. She sums up her experience: "I just tried to live. . . . I'm just one of the people, I don't know. . . . I'm ignorant. I was not allowed to learn anything." Chet's case underlines the challenge of *learning*—or even sacrificing—enough to acquire full rights in Democratic Kampuchea. The "model" was a double misnomer.

Chai, twenty-three, a peasant from Treang (District 107), became a new person when the CPK overran his village near Takeo in 1975. For the rest of that year the cadres he met were "soft," using persuasion rather than force. Rations consisted of gruel from the beginning, but he encountered no starvation in 1975 or 1976. "Things gradually got worse and worse." Chai was tainted by an uncle's service as a Lon Nol soldier. The uncle and his son, Chai's cousin, were killed within two years.

Phnom Penh evacuees mixed with the villagers. In early 1976, communal eating was introduced. Children were assigned to different worksites according to their ages. Small children and those in their early teens labored separately. Chai and all adolescents were conscripted into the 2nd Mobile Division, one of two ten-thousand-strong labor units in the Southwest Zone. Its leader was Mok's son-in-law Ren, who was also a military commander. Chai was a member of a mobile regiment of fifteen hundred who worked at several irrigation

---

58. Phnom Penh Radio, 12 April 1977, *FBIS*, Asia Pacific, 14 April 1977, p. H2.

sites in Koh Andeth (District 108), commanded by a thirty-year-old named Seng. Targets were compulsory, and production high—four harvests a year. Trucks came to take the rice away. Seng claimed it was exported in exchange for machinery, but none came. Seng would often call meetings that lasted until 1 A.M. Then the workers had to be up early, laboring from 4 A.M. until noon and from 1 to 6 P.M., then tending vegetables from 7 to 10 P.M. Those who complained were killed, especially in 1977 and 1978, amid mass starvation and death from exhaustion. Chai estimates that fewer than one thousand of the 2nd Division's ten thousand young workers survived in 1979.

Chea, sixty, was another "new" peasant from Treang. In 1971 she had fled the Khmer Rouge (who then burnt down her large house along with dozens of others in the village), and returned home in April 1975. Not daring to lie, Chea admitted she had lived in Phnom Penh with a relative who was a policeman. They asked if her son had fought in the Lon Nol army. Chea insisted he had been conscripted. He was taken away for two years' hard labor on rations of gruel. "He was afraid of saying anything for fear of execution." Ten wealthy, prominent people disappeared in 1975.

The CPK subdistrict chief and five of the village leaders were all from Tram Kak. Locals from Treang were trusted only as kong chiefs, and in krom committees of three base people in charge of ten new families. "But they were our base people. . . . They did not kill people; we just worked to support them. They had all the power, and more to eat." But the food was controlled by higher-ranking cadres from Tram Kak. "They were the ones who decided whether we went hungry or not." Daily rations consisted of two cans of paddy (about three hundred grams of milled rice) for ten people, one-third of a bare minimum diet. The new people could exchange their belongings for more, but they soon ran out of resources. In early 1976, formation of a "village cooperative," and the construction of a long canteen for communal meals eaten in shifts, probably made things worse. The able-bodied worked until 10 P.M. on irrigation works, and there were good annual harvests, but trucks came to remove the rice. There was large-scale starvation that year, especially among ethnic Chinese. Chea's grandson disappeared. Chea says "there were not many killings in 1976," though "people who stole food out of hunger were taken away by the police, and starved to death in jail."

The appointment of Mok's son-in-law Soeun as CPK secretary of Treang district in 1977 brought significant changes. The food situation improved. But the local base people fell from favor, becoming "ordinary citizens" like the new people. They were replaced by more outsiders, who came from Tram Kak with Soeun. Large-scale killings also began. Chea's son, the former soldier, was called to a meeting, after which all the male new people were taken away "to study," never to return. Three other sons were also killed in 1977. Their crime was climbing sugar palms during the harvesting season. In 1978, Chea says, the situation eased, for "everyone had already been killed."

Bich, a sometime employee of the U.S. embassy in Phnom Penh, had moved back to his wife's native village in Kirivong (District 109) in April 1972. Six months later CPK troops took the village and asked everyone there "to go higher up for a while." The villagers were evacuated fifty kilometers into the hills of Kampot. Living conditions there were "very tough," with forced labor but no killings "unless you did something wrong." Two months later, the villagers were again relocated, to Tani in Kampot. They had to grow and find their own food. As in the similar evacuations in Tram Kak in this period, former officials were taken away "to study."

Returning in 1975 to Kirivong, people settled down to growing and eating rice once again. But other evacuees, new people from the cities, outnumbered the base people like Bich. The district CPK secretary, according to a local sub-district chief, "protected a lot of new people, so he was taken away and replaced by Tith, Mok's younger brother-in-law."[59] By the time communal eating began in mid-1976, Bich says, gruel was the normal ration. Work requirements increased. In late 1976, a new categorization divided people into separate hamlets. The largest group were the urban deportees, followed by Bich and others classed as "candidates." "Full rights people" were the fewest, but at any rate, in Bich's view, "no one ever liked the Khmer Rouge, because of the hard work and little food." Children of all three categories were taken from their parents, though "full rights children were superior to others," according to Bich. But the highest caste had other origins. Most cadres who ran this village, as in other parts of Region 13, were outsiders "from higher up in the hills, for instance above Tram Kak, in District 105." Under Tith's leadership, they killed many deportees, including Bich's elder brother, who was murdered in 1977, and some of the "candidates" who had been Lon Nol officials. Bich also lost another brother, whereas his wife and five children survived.

One couple arriving from Phnom Penh was assigned to a village in Kirivong of 900 base people and 260 new people. The husband, who had worked in the information ministry in the capital, was soon taken away "to study." He was allowed to see his wife for one day a month in 1975, twice a month in 1976. However, in April 1977 his wife was told he had been taken to "cut timber in the mountains." She never saw him again, and believes he was executed. In those first two years, she says, fifty-four people of the village were executed, including wives of those previously executed. In 1977 she and five other local women were sent to work in Kompong Speu.

Ngaol, a subdistrict chief in Kirivong, was a poor peasant, illiterate and

59. Author's interview with a CPK subdistrict chief, Kirivong, 25 August 1980.

innumerate. His small plot of land was usually flooded, and in the Sihanouk period, like his parents, he had worked as a laborer. He joined the CPK militia in 1970 and the party in 1973, becoming chief of his native Ream Andaeuk sub-district. But starvation struck the area in 1973–74. "At first I was happy that the poor people were raised up, but later we could not resolve the people's living conditions, and we fell into the Pol Pot period." So did the band of White Scarves whose story begins this book. Ngaol was the first DK official they met, he who hosted and disarmed the victims.[60] With the arrival of the new people in 1975, Ngaol recalled five years later, the subdistrict's population doubled to eight thousand. Half were deportees. One-third, base people with relatives from Phnom Penh, became "candidates," and the remaining base people, one-sixth of the total, were classified as "full rights" like Ngaol himself (who had relatives among both base and new people). In each village, six or seven of them joined the CPK.

From 1975 Ngaol received orders "to watch soldiers, teachers, and their networks," if they had many relatives on the revolutionary side. Deportees with few relatives among the base people, he says, "were to be smashed (komtech)." Sarun, one of the new people, offers a different interpretation of the population categories: "To spy on the new people, they fed one or two of them well and got them to do it. The candidates were those base people related to the new people. The third group were Party members with no connections or relatives outside the base people." As in Tram Kak, kinship—rather than geography, class, or politics—was the critical factor.

Ngaol was ordered to kill two hundred people. These directives always came from district chief Tith, who instructed Ngaol to arrest people and hand them over to district security forces. Those executed in 1975 included teachers, students, and intellectuals. More were killed in 1976, including a Hanoi-trained CPK cadre who had tried to implement orders "not badly." Ngaol says most of the killings were the work of Kirivong district security forces. "We could only kill people in the subdistrict if the district [level] approved." But he denies any unauthorized murders, and adds that no orders ever came to stop any killings.

Sarun accused Ngaol of killing fifty people in the subdistrict. Sarun recalled, for instance, that he arrested thirteen teachers in early 1976 in Svay Sor village—site of the massacre of the White Scarves soon after. The victims had expressed the view that "socialism was never like this system" they now lived under, and were accused of taking advantage of the proximity of the Viet-namese border to organize resistance. Sarun says Ngaol led the teachers away. But Ngaol denied his involvement in such killings. He pointed out that he was

60. Author's interviews, Preah Bat Chuon Chum, Kirivong, 26 August 1980.

demoted to deputy subdistrict chief in 1977 because of his relatives among the new people. But he agreed that two hundred people were indeed killed, mostly in 1978, presumably after he had handed them over to the security forces. He also admitted executing two people who planned to flee to Vietnam. Tith considered this "treason," and told Ngaol to "kill them off" (*komtech caol*). "The district chief came to make sure I did it." Ngaol also asserts that he was instructed to collect most rice from the villages. He was told it would be exchanged for pumps, sewing machines, "things that the people liked." These did not arrive, but people worked long hours on half rations. Ngaol says that from 1975 to 1978, fifty people in the subdistrict starved to death.

Most victims of killings and starvation were new people. The new and base people lived side by side, but enjoyed different levels of food consumption, for the new people had no house gardens. The two groups had conflicts, but there were further divisions among the base people. Ngaol says that at first, "the full rights people liked the system." But around 1977, they became disillusioned, because "they had to work very hard, for fear of being demoted to candidate or deportee status," while candidates could be promoted. A Tram Kak woman, deported to Kirivong in February 1976 and classified as a "candidate" there, has a different view. She was unable to complain, for fear of jail or death. "If we said anything they would say we were obstructing the wheel of history. We would lose our arms and legs. . . . We never knew when we would ever see the light of happiness and dignity. The revolution of Pol Pot's Khmer Rouge was the darkest black."

Meanwhile the Phnom Penh evacuees in Kirivong were again deported, in the reverse direction. Sarun recalls that "in early 1977 all Kirivong new people were sent to be tempered in Tram Kak district, thousands of them. They were afraid we would go to Vietnam." Sarun and his wife and fifty other families went from Svay Sor. In Tram Kak, Sarun was sent to join 3 Company of the district kong chalat. They worked 2 A.M. to 3 P.M., nine days in ten. Sarun met his wife every tenth day. Rations were lower than in Kirivong. We have seen how in Tram Kak the three population categories were subdivided into nine after the arrival of the "support base" upland people. Now, when Sarun and the other new people came from Kirivong around the same time, a *tenth* population subcategory was created. This was a category "even lower" than that of the local new people. The newcomers from Kirivong were called "bandits" (*chao prei*), presumably because of alleged plans to flee to Vietnam. Sarun recalls: "We lived in different villages from the local [new people], who ate better than we did."

Around the end of 1977, a group of Europeans and Chinese came to visit the model cooperative in Tram Kak. Sarun's mobile unit was laboring nearby. He recalls that the night before, the workers were informed they would stop next day at 10 A.M., get a new set of clothes each, and then proceed to the communal mess hall. "Anyone who fought over the food would be withdrawn [*doh ceñ*, usually meaning execution], because the foreigners were coming to photograph." At 10 A.M. they all left the worksite, washed their oxen and plows, and then bathed. "Anyone who wasn't washed clean would be withdrawn." They each received a box of tobacco. Sarun has two vivid memories of this visit. For the first time in years, he saw European faces: three bearded, two with long hair, the other bald. Also "one of us ate so much he fell over backwards, was taken to hospital, and never came back."

Region 35 (Kampot)

Veasna, the former sports teacher, trekked south out of Phnom Penh for six weeks through Regions 33 and 13. Base people in one Takeo village complained to him that life was "really tough," because of the collective work, the lack of food and material goods, and executions of base people as alleged "CIA spies." Veasna pushed on in the hope of joining his wife, who in early April had taken a boat from Kompong Som to Vietnam. By June, Veasna was in Kampot, only fifteen kilometers from the border. He had reached the Southwest's Region 35, run by Kang Chap and a "military assistant for security affairs."[61]

Veasna got no further. With two hundred families of evacuees from Phnom Penh and Kampot city, he was sent to a large village of base people in Kompong Trach (District 77). He was confined to a hamlet with other new people: former teachers, officials, and soldiers. Having many relatives among the base people worked to his advantage. During the next seven months the CPK arrested twenty teachers, officials, wealthy city people, and soldiers and led them off, hands tied behind them. He later saw the rank-and-file soldiers laboring on the Phnom Penh-Kampot railway, but the others all disappeared. Veasna and those remaining worked the fields, rising at 4 A.M. The system was inefficient because of their supervisors' ignorance of rice cultivation. A "model" work team of thirty men labored for three months and harvested only 75 percent of the amount they had sown as seed! The village chief, a thirty-year-old from Chhouk district, was illiterate and unable to ride a bicycle.

The daily ration for new people was only 150 grams of milled rice. Veasna saw several people die of starvation, and a friend saw twenty more deaths. A Khmer-Chinese family who had lived in the center of the village before the war were barred from their house and had to build another. Meanwhile the children died of exposure. As elsewhere, base people had food stores, draft animals, oxcarts, and other property, none of which was communalized in 1975.

---

61. "Life in Southern Cambodia," Extracts from an Airgram Report by an Officer of the American Embassy at Bangkok, 25 January 1977 (declassified in 1978), pp. 3–4.

However, Veasna's base people relatives told him, "nobody liked the Khmer Rouge but they did not know where to run." Unlike new people, the base people did not consider escape to Vietnam. Veasna fled across the border in December. He was lucky. A year later the U.S. embassy's Cambodia watcher in Bangkok made a study of Kampot and neighboring areas. On the basis of refugee testimony, he reported that the CPK had "executed more people in 1975 than in 1976." However, "death from disease and malnutrition—most likely in combination—was greater in 1976 than in 1975."[62] A DK official who fled Cambodia in October 1976 reported that by August "the whole of western Cambodia, as well as the southwest region, was suffering from famine," and there was "widespread starvation in Kampot."[63] Worse was to come.

A Railway Worker's Life

While Veasna fled to Vietnam, another former teacher, Muk Chot, thirty, was laboring a few miles north along the train line. With his family and his uncle, a former railway worker, Chot had responded to the CPK's April appeal for skilled workers and was sent back to Phnom Penh. Sixty railway workers, led by a former colleague who had joined the revolution, were told to repair the track to Kampot. Chot's family was housed in Phnom Penh, where communal eating began in 1975. His team worked their way down the line.

In June 1975, the team was joined by fifty former students and fifty demobilized CPK soldiers, mostly from the Northern Zone, some of whom had been wounded and had recovered enough to assume nonmilitary duties. In late 1975, with the railway functioning again, the workers were separated into krom. Thirty young women, including some medical students, went south to Kampot. Chot was assigned to a krom of eleven Khmer Rouge and nine new people, to maintain ten miles of track in the Tuk Meas subdistrict of Kampot. They replaced old sleepers with new Chinese ones. It was heavy work, every day and five nights per week, under lights operated by Chot. But food was adequate in 1975. A Khmer Rouge doctor cared for the workers with stocks of foreign medicine. Rations provided by the communications ministry in Phnom Penh were reduced in 1976 to less than a can per person, and from mid-1976 meals consisted of gruel. The workers grew their own vegetables, and foraging was allowed. Three wives did the cooking, and everyone ate together. The soldiers were young peasant bachelors with up to four years' military service. None had attended high school and some were illiterate. At first they considered new people inferior, "but we grew to like one another."[64]

62. Ibid., p. 6.
63. FEER, 12 November 1976, p. 5.
64. Author's interview with Muk Chot, Toul, 28 October 1979.

In the Villages of Kampot Province

"None of us ever got to visit our families," says Chot. Leaving the subdistrict was forbidden, and contact with villagers required permission. But over the next three years, Chot discovered that his life was privileged compared to that of people in the cooperatives. Nobody in his krom was executed. Most victims were new people: in 1975–76, Lon Nol soldiers, in 1977–78, former Lon Nol officials and teachers. In 1977, Chot says, "People who just came from Phnom Penh, and were not even officials, were also killed. I saw this, and the Khmer Rouge told us they were doing it, 'cleaning up' the 'CIA group,' and later the 'KGB' and 'servants of the Vietnamese.'" Base people also suffered. "When I first arrived . . . the base people liked the Khmer Rouge. They had fought Lon Nol together, and life was not yet communal. They were happy." But when communal eating began in 1977, they became disillusioned by the low rations and the ban on foraging.

Uch, thirty-four, was a porter in Kampot city until 1975. Evacuated to Kompong Trach, he found new people like himself and "candidate" base people were soon separated from the "full rights" peasants, who got fancier clothes. In 1975 workers labored in krom. But the next year cooperatives were established, "making us suffer a lot." People subsisted on gruel and potatoes. Some, accused of "little things," went to prison and starved to death. The U.S. embassy in Bangkok reported: "In June, 1976, near Kompong Trach, a Cambodian watched seven ordinary people killed before everyone's eyes by being beaten on the backs of their necks in the rice field. Their 'mistake' had been to complain about the food ration. The same source claimed that, in his village, if one did anything considered to be illegal, he was killed. . . . An 'error,' if discovered, means death in the south, refugees claimed."[65]

Moch, thirty-one, a peasant, had fled Kompong Trach for Kampot city in 1974 and was sent back there in April 1975. With eighty-five families of new people, Moch arrived home to find that the nine hundred families of base people there all "really believed in the Khmer Rouge." The two groups ate separately. The full rights people made up 70 percent of the village population, with the remainder equally divided between candidates and deportees. For the first months, new people got a can of rice daily, but rations soon fell. Communal eating began in January 1976, and by August gruel was the norm. Moch's wife and parents died of starvation that year. However, there were no killings in 1975–76. Alleged malingerers did hard labor at a new worksite called the "lazy village."

Even Moch's devastating personal losses seem to have been overshadowed

65. "Life in Southern Cambodia," 25 January 1977, p. 5.

in his mind by what followed. "Everything began," he says, in early 1977. Food rations deteriorated badly, and Moch calls that year "the time of starvation." New and base people began to eat together in the communal mess halls, with a base person "watching" each table of six new people. Worse, in early 1977, the CPK began murdering people. In April and May, "seventeen families of new people were completely wiped out," and the best of their clothes distributed to base people. But the latter were not spared the new repression. The district chief, Suos, executed the parents of some of his own soldiers. Also in early 1977, children aged three and over were taken from their homes to a children's center. Parents could visit them or bring them home only for short stays. Those aged ten and over were sent to worksites. This appears to have undercut the previously high level of peasant support for the revolution. In 1977 and 1978, Moch says, "only half of the base people believed in the Khmer Rouge." Divisions appeared in CPK ranks too. In the second half of 1977, a local military commander, an educated man in his forties called Rin, who Moch says "had not harmed the people," mutinied and took his unit over the border into Vietnam.[66]

In 1979, Uch returned to his native Kampot district. Locals told him of a massacre that had occurred there on 21–22 April 1975. According to their account, Khmer Rouge drove "one hundred truckloads" of Lon Nol officials and soldiers from Kampot and Kompong Som to a cliff overlooking the sea at Bokor, bound the victims, and threw them over the edge. Two survivors were later captured and executed. District chief Chet Chhaom, a former distillery worker from Kompong Som, was often seen holding a bottle of rice alcohol or threatening people with an automatic pistol. Up until 1977, most victims were new people. But that year Chhaom was himself executed by a new, illiterate district chief, Mon, who was "even tougher." Mon came from Koh Sla in Chhouk district, the upland area to the north, and brought new village and subdistrict cadres with him. They "killed the full rights, candidates and new people." In August and September 1977, Mon's squads massacred four truckloads, over two hundred men and women, of a "rebellious" chalat unit. Loudspeakers blared music to drown their dying screams. Mon's crackdown in Kampot resembles that of cadres from the same range of hills west of Tram Kak, who were taking over districts in Region 13.

Pheap, twenty-four, and her husband were peasants who had fled the Khmer Rouge in 1974 "because they were so tough" and "oppressive." "I was poor, and had nothing to eat," she recalls, and they tried fishing in Kampot and Kompong Som. In 1975, the couple were sent back to their village. The new subdistrict chief, like Mon, was from Koh Sla in the hills to the north. He hated

66. Author's interview with Moch, Kompong Trach, 29 August 1980.

and starved new people, and he killed Pheap's husband in 1976. According to Uch, 70 percent of the population of Koh Touc subdistrict perished. His own family survived but his younger brother and "over twenty cousins" were killed. His assertion is supported by Pheap, who says that three villages on the outskirts of Kampot were evacuated to Koh Touc, as well as a local peasant couple, who say that Koh Touc subdistrict became home to one thousand new people in 1975, all of whom perished in Democratic Kampuchea.[67]

The peasant couple, Mai and Leng, were base people in a village of eight hundred ruled by the CPK since 1972. The husband, Leng, then fifty-six, recalls that the revolutionaries had not harmed people at first. They had created a Peasants' Association, but he didn't know what it did. "I did what I was told. I worked in the fields and on irrigation." After 1975, only ten of the eight hundred base families were accorded "full rights" status. Leng says, "We had no idea how we were classified. They would ask us questions, then they would put us on a list somewhere." He was classified not as "full rights" but as a "No. 1 base person," a "middle" group of three subcategories of base people. "I heard there were meetings, but they did not let us know what they were doing." As elsewhere, this probably reflected the fact that the couple's children were new people. Some new people were executed in 1975 and 1976, but rations were distributed to all, and no rice was taken from the village. Communal eating began on 1 January 1977, and as usual consumption fell. Leng says, "They created complete collectivization, and we had to do what we were told, out of fear." Mai, then fifty-six, recalls that children were put in separate centers for boys and girls: "If they told us to look after children for them, we did it. If they told us to look after chickens, we just looked after chickens. We were not allowed to know anything. . . . I could rest only one day in ten. If you did not do it, you got no food." The couple also report "many killings in 1977."

Mam, a forty-two-year-old woman evacuated from Kampot city to Chhouk district, provides insight into life in the CPK heartland of Region 35. With her teacher husband, she joined forty-eight families of new people in a village of 220 base families who "liked us at first." Rations were more than adequate in 1975, one and a half cans per day. New and base people ate together. In 1975, the Khmer Rouge "only killed Lon Nol military officers, and in 1976 ordinary soldiers." But in early 1976 "persecution began," and in 1977, "teachers, customs officers, doctors, and intelligence agents" were taken off and murdered. Mam continues, "In 1977–78, we new people were not allowed to do anything, not even allowed into the kitchens. The base people stopped liking us. They hated us so much we had to leave as soon as we had eaten." While the base people "ate their fill" of rice, fifty to sixty new people existed on only seven cans per day. But the number executed was triple the number of those who starved, Mam says.

This village in Chhouk district is an exceptional if not unique case of residual peasant support for the CPK. As Mam puts it, "The base people and the Khmer Rouge liked one another. The base people liked the Khmer Rouge right up until the fraternal Vietnamese liberated us" (early 1979). These base people were clearly favored. "Not one of them died," Mam asserts to demonstrate their privileged status. They had "good clothes" confiscated from the urban evacuees, who "wore rags," an annual ration of "one shirt, and one pair of trousers." New people were not allowed to wear *kromar*, Khmer scarves.[68]

But even in this village of most dedicated CPK loyalists, base people had no instinctive hatred for city dwellers. The hill peasants' initial reaction to the latter's arrival was not hostile but hospitable. Only after a couple of years of CPK persecution of new people did the base people participate in the oppression. This was not a case of the CPK's being "pulled along by the peasant element," but the reverse. The significance of Chhouk, and probably Mok's nearby homeland, upland Tram Kak in the same hills over the Region 13 border, is that the CPK was able to pull most of the local peasantry along with them for the duration. For the same reason, these districts were unique even in the Southwest.

Region 25 (Sa'ang-Koh Thom)

The fertile watered area between the rivers south of Phnom Penh was known in Democratic Kampuchea as Region 25. It had a controversial history. Initially part of the East, it was transferred to the Special Zone in 1971. When the Special Zone was abolished in mid-1975, the Center displayed its favoritism by not returning Region 25 to the East but instead giving it to the Southwest. Its first CPK secretary, So Pum, a Hanoi-trained former Khmer Issarak, had returned to the Eastern Zone after having been ousted in 1971.[69] Vorn Vet replaced Pum with Non Suon, who had been Issarak chief of the Southwest in the early 1950s[70] and was a leader of the old, pro-Vietnamese generation of Khmer communists. In his 1978 confession, Vorn Vet recalled that in 1970 Non Suon had been prepared "to fight Ta Mok."[71] With Suon's departure for Phnom

68. Author's interview with Mam, Kampot, 29 August 1980.
69. For the 1970–75 history of Region 25, see Kiernan, *How Pol Pot*, pp. 320–21, 331–34, 343–44, 380–84. A local peasant recalled, "Before 1973 Vietnamese came through here. The Thieu-Ky troops looted and shelled villages. The communists were all right." Author's interview, Koh Thom, 1 August 1980.
70. *Chamlaiy dop pir* ("Reply of No. XII"), confession by Non Suon in Tuol Sleng prison, 29 November 1976, p. 3. On the pre-1975 demotion of Non Suon, see Kiernan, *How Pol Pot*, pp. 88, 190, 201, 314.
71. Vorn Vet, untitled confession, December 1978, 54 pp., at p. 31.

Penh after victory, Mok appointed Som Chea, a former courier for the CPK Center, as Region secretary. But many cadres appointed and trained by Pum and Suon remained in place.

Yem, the Lon Nol soldier who had defected from the CPK militia in Region 33, describes wartime Region 25 as "soft." He was stationed near the boundary between the two Regions. "In Region 25 they had gold, clothes, rice and vegetables, and the Region 25 organization came to exchange them with us in Region 33. But in Region 33 anyone caught involved in such exchanges would be shot, the cadres told us. Region 25 had plenty of exchange, it was not yet communalized. Base people could get radios for rice." After 1975, base and new people from Region 25 tell the same story as elsewhere in the Southwest. Life failed to improve for the locals with the second deportation of urban evacuees, who had helped with the 1975 planting but were not around to share the 1976 harvest. In fact, despite the rich natural environment in the region, conditions deteriorated from a harsh but often tolerable local regime supported by many peasants in 1975 and 1976 to nightmarish conditions and generalized killings by 1977.[72]

Ney, fifty-five, a base peasant from Koh Thom district, says communalization had begun in 1973.[73] Peasants were organized into groups of fifteen, then thirty families, but production stagnated for lack of available land. "Then in 1975 everything was collectivized. . . . [the years from] 1975–76 were not happy times. We worked too hard with too little to eat. . . . In 1976, we did everything we were told." Meals were now eaten communally. One reason for the hardship was that over one hundred Phnom Penh families arrived in 1975. New people "were everywhere," doubling the population of the land-scarce village. Ney asserts that "the Khmer Rouge did not call the city people 'enemies,' but told us to prepare food to welcome them, to help them and find them suitable houses."[74] The two groups ate equal rations of corn, which were adequate though city people complained about the uselessness of their cash savings. There was no starvation since "people helped one another," though family life remained private. In late 1975 several Phnom Penh people were killed on suspicion of being former Lon Nol officers and officials. There were more executions in 1976, and "many" in 1977; in that year and the next, the victims' families were also murdered. In all, the CPK killed over two hundred Phnom Penh people and about half the base people of the village, most in 1977 and

72. Author's interview with Yem, Strasbourg, 31 October 1979.
73. Interview with the author in village of Prek Thmei, Koh Thom, 1 August 1980.
74. This is confirmed by a former courier for Non Suon, who told S. Heder that his instructions in April 1975 were "to prepare food, water, and lodging for the evacuees," and that only Lon Nol "ministers" and soldiers "responsible for lots of killing" were considered "enemies." Heder interview, Sakeo, 7 March 1980.

1978. No one died of starvation. In 1978, children were separated from their parents and housed in special centers.

Phnom Penh people evacuated to Region 25, who lived there in the second half of 1975 before relocation to the northwest, confirm the picture of relative prosperity in the immediate aftermath of the war.[75] But they also noticed some ominous signs. Tan Peng Sen, a twenty-three-year-old medical student who reached his native district of Sa'ang in Region 25 in late April 1975, knew of no killings before his departure in January 1976. Sen heard only that "high-ranking officers in Sa'ang had been rounded up for study." The Sa'ang district chief was a former school inspector from Chhouk in Kampot, Region 35, whom Mok had switched with his predecessor. However, the base people in Sa'ang, Sen says, "treated us as relatives" even though the CPK here "told them not to trust us 'enemies.'" Base and new people worked together in krom. The base people's status was so much higher than newcomers' that "we were their prisoners," though the two groups secretly exchanged goods. Rations fell from one and a half cans of rice in May and June, to corn thereafter, supplemented by whatever rice people could grow and by other plants cultivated secretly. New people who had brought enough goods, such as jewelry, could manage. "Those without had a hard time." Meals remained private in 1975.

In June 1975, a relative in the CPK army who had participated in the seizure of the capital came to meet Sen. Secretly, this man explained the base people's new dislike for the CPK. "They had wanted Sihanouk back, and had not thought that the country would be changed as it was." In December, Sen was assigned to a labor krom like the chalat.[76] He was sent to a worksite and not allowed to visit his parents on pain of "jail, low rations, and possible death." Sen's krom of thirty-two, including its leaders, worked and ate together.

Yun, the mathematics teacher who had left Sa'ang for Prey Krabas, had stayed only a month for lack of food for his two children. In a village of over fifty families of base people and four hundred of new people, rations had consisted of only a bushel (tau) of corn beads per person per month, half a bushel for small children. No one starved, but two people were taken away to "study." First to disappear was Yun's cousin, a former official at the Phnom Penh city hall; second was the renowned Cambodian singer Sinn Sisamuth. Their families were left alone, but Yun became "too afraid to stay there." Yun alone recounted peasant awe of the newcomers: "From what I saw, the base people

---

75. See also Vickery, *Cambodia*, pp. 89–92, for additional similar accounts.
76. Tan Peng Sen (interview with the author, Alençon, 3 October 1979) says the term *chalat* was not used, and he did not hear it until he reached Battambang in 1976. Pin Yathay mentions another term, *komrong*, in use in Region 25 in mid-1975, denoting 60-person work groups of new people. Vickery, *Cambodia*, p. 90.

did not like the Khmer Rouge either. They could not understand why the Khmer Rouge won the war against us."

At the age of ten, Ang Ngeck Teang was evacuated from Phnom Penh with her mother, four brothers and sisters, and five other relatives. They walked south and settled briefly in the Koh Thom district of Region 25. The locals were "very happy," and "nice to us too, and gave us enough to eat." Teang's memory of a month-long stay is tranquil: "We gathered thatch and dug dams. . . . We boys and girls worked separately from the adults. After gathering thatch we had time to catch crabs and mussels to eat. . . . It was a happy time. . . . we had no idea [what would happen later]. We had enough to eat; the base people gave us food so we could all eat together. There was no food problem. . . . I saw no killings, nor heard of any."[77]

Savon, a medical student, also went with his family to Koh Thom. New-comers, who doubled the village's population, were billeted in the homes of base people and given food if they needed it. Their first task was to dig a canal. They were told to work with the peasants and follow their instructions. Savon says the work was "not so hard" and the instructions "easy." The locals were "hospitable," expecting hard but not excessive work. The sick were not expected to work, and new people did not complain even secretly, Savon says. There was plenty of food, including rice, beans, and fish. People could fish in their spare time, so long as work schedules were maintained. Cadres "did not cause any trouble," and Savon found them "humane," knowing "right from wrong." Many of these local cadres were part-Vietnamese. They appealed to city dwellers to emulate them. The base people, for their part, "liked the Khmer Rouge." They had helped the revolution during the war, and often talked about war-time struggles and the U.S. bombardment. The new people received equal treatment. "We had freedom," says Savon. "If we needed something, we just let the Khmer Rouge know." But discipline was strict. "If people were told not to do something they just did not do it. If they were told to go to bed at night and not to talk, they obeyed." Savon believes anyone who talked favorably of Sihanouk would have been executed, though no killings occurred in the three months he spent in the village.[78]

Before escaping to Takeo, Sruy, former manager of the agriculture min-

77. Author's interview with Ang Ngeck Teang, Toulouse, 9 December 1979.

78. Author's interview with Savon, Chatenay-Malabry, 9 August 1979. Tam Eng spent four nights in Koh Thom in April 1975. She says that "the base people there did not like the Khmer Rouge, and were afraid of them." The society had become polarized into rich and poor peasants, though the richness of the area meant that even the poor had never been threat-ened by starvation. "The poor who had nothing supported the Khmer Rouge in order to live. . . . The poor liked the Khmer Rouge, the rich did not. Those who had land, houses and rice, did not like the Khmer Rouge because it was all taken from them. Those who liked us told us so." Author's interview, Paris, 24 January 1980.

istry's truck pool, spent four months in Koh Thom. He lived in a village of 150 base families, 340 new. He agrees that in 1975, the peasants were divided. "Some were secretly unhappy," but "most base people liked the Khmer Rouge." Their rice ration was three cans daily, triple that of the new people. "They worked less than us and gave us orders. They called us 'capitalists' if we just laughed casually." Male new people each had to dig four cubic meters of earth per day, females half that amount. They could go fishing on completion of their targets. Sick workers had their rice rations reduced to half a can. Fifty new people in the subdistrict—Lon Nol soldiers, police, and intelligence and customs agents—had to do hard labor twelve hours per day. "In 1975 it was still all right," Sruy says.

Bu, a schoolteacher from the outskirts of Phnom Penh, arrived in Koh Thom with his family of eleven. They spent over three months in a village where evacuees outnumbered base people, but there was no food problem and no killings. Some high-ranking Lon Nol officers disappeared "to study." The base people described the local Khmer Rouge as "kind," and were not afraid of them. "They simply liked them," he says. The village chief was married to a part-Vietnamese.[79]

Lanny, twenty-two, and her family went to her mother's village in Sa'ang district and spent three months there. The CPK quickly registered everyone, taking the ages and numbers of people in each family, and put them to work. The village comprised one hundred families, two-thirds of them new people, most with relatives among the base people. "The base people generally liked the Khmer Rouge, although some hated them secretly but did not dare say so. . . . Some were nice to us, some cruel." The base people were mostly poor, and considered the Phnom Penh population as "all rich." The rations of corn were barely adequate, but the newcomers could get more by exchanging goods with the base people. There was no starvation during the three months. Six to eight people, including a schoolteacher and Lon Nol officers, disappeared from the village to "study."[80]

A group of peasant base people interviewed in their village were hazy about when they first began to suffer CPK persecution. After the Khmer Rouge arrived in 1972, the peasants said, "they didn't persecute us much." People ate their fill and "there were not many killings; we worked together." But in 1975 the CPK "really did it." Confiscation of property, inadequate food, and collective work "day and night" characterized 1975, though the peasants did not seem to consider this as "persecution." In 1976, "heavy treatment began," including killings, which reached a peak in 1977. The peasants had few doubts about the

79. Author's interview with Bu, Creteil, 18 October 1979.
80. Author's interview with Lanny, Creteil, 18 October 1979.

personalities responsible. Post-1975 Region Secretary Som Chea, they said, was "good to us like Non Suon . . . not the same as Pol Pot." They denounced Chea's superiors and his successor in 1977–78, Prak. Other base people offer similar accounts.

Sok, also born in Region 25, was a teacher there. In 1971, at age thirty-one, he joined the revolution with a dozen other local teachers. They worked for So Pum and then Non Suon until 1975. After two years in the Regional Culture Department, Sok was sent to tend rice land belonging to its performing troupe; a *petit bourgeois*, he had to be "tempered." Non Suon may have purged some of So Pum's staff. Also in 1973, peasants were organized into krom. But there were no killings before 1975, under either leader. "People were happy, and considered the revolutionary line to be good. Everyone followed it, and there were many volunteer recruits." Though closer to Pum, Sok defends Suon too: "Suon was not interested in killing. He said clearly during the war that rations must be limited, but after victory there would be happiness and better living conditions. . . . Non Suon was not responsible for any killings. They began in the bases after he had gone."

Suon's 1975 replacement by Som Chea, then a district chief, brought other changes as well. Non Suon's prediction proved inaccurate. Som Chea moved the region headquarters into Takhmau city, on the outskirts of Phnom Penh, and had little contact with the people. Sok was transferred to a worksite on the Vietnamese border. But rations were adequate for all, and when communal eating began in 1976, new and base people ate together, though cadres ate separately. "Things were reasonably all right in 1975–76." The CPK executed "high-ranking officers, one by one," and a few teachers among the new people, including Sok's brother in 1976. Landless base peasants were given local authority, and other peasants were spared the repression: "If any middle or upper peasants were taken away in our Region in 1976, they were very few."

But in 1977 the tide turned. "Many" middle and upper peasants and "most teachers among the new people" were executed. "They started to clean up everyone, even the base people. At that time they began what they called 'the class struggle,' and took away 'upper classes' to be tempered. They were killed for small offences." Sok was brought back from the Vietnamese border. Conditions deteriorated in 1977, though it was a lush rice-growing district. "If they wanted to temper people they would give us four ears of boiled corn each per meal, and we each had to move six cubic meters of earth per day. Sometimes you did not get four full ears, you might just get corn cobs." After a few days, normal rice rations would resume. There was no starvation. All deaths were from killings.[81]

81. Author's interview with Sok, Prek Ambel, 1 August 1980.

Seng was another local schoolteacher who remained in Region 25 as a base person after the Khmer Rouge takeover of his area. Like Sok, he joined the administration (but not the CPK) in 1971, when he was thirty-two, working for So Pum and then Non Suon. Peasants labored in krom; conditions were deteriorating by 1974, though still "reasonable." Seng recalls: "The problems began in 1975. It was tight from then on." Soon after victory, all property was communalized and stored under the control of ten-family "cooperatives" and eventually of entire villages and subdistricts. From early 1976, individual work targets were set: five cubic meters of earth per person per day. "The work was demanding, and food inadequate. In some places it ran out, and people starved or swelled up." But no one starved in this rich riverbank environment. Though they risked execution, people could steal enough fruit to survive. "From early 1976, if you said the food was not tasty, or if you stole corn, you would be killed."

Seng worked for Non Suon until Suon's arrest in late 1976. "I was sent back home to raise earth. Some intellectuals who made mistakes were killed, others who had made no mistakes were sent home to be watched for mistakes. Some were killed then, even for saying something minor." Several relatives disappeared in late 1976. Conditions steadily worsened: "In 1975–76 they were mainly concerned with gathering people together and working," but the years 1977 and 1978 were "much tighter." Children were taken from their parents and placed in separate barracks. In 1978, two more relatives of Seng's both teachers, disappeared. In Seng's village, all the male new people were sent to "break rocks," and they never came back either. The 1977 deterioration seems related to yet another purge: the arrest of the Region 25 secretary, So n Chea, by Center security units on 15 March 1977.[82] Chea was replaced by Prak, who Sok says had first appeared in 1975, when he was appointed to the Region Committee. His leadership in 1977–78 was another Southwest Zone disaster.[83]

Bopha Sinan, who came to Region 25 from Phnom Penh in 1975, recalls that, "until April 1977, the Khmer Rouge were all right." She does not hold them responsible for the starvation that struck the village where she lived from 1975 to 1976. Its population was about two thousand, mostly from Phnom Penh. While the base people experienced no shortages, the new people who "had arrived with nothing" received just a spoonful of rice per day, and died in the "hundreds" in the first two years. In addition, about ten former Lon Nol officers and soldiers in the village were executed. The CPK did not

82. People's Republic of Kampuchea, *People's Revolutionary Tribunal Held in Phnom Penh for the Trial of the Genocide Crime of the Pol Pot-Ieng Sary Clique*, August 1979, Document no. 2.5.24, DK S-21 document, "Important Culprits (Arrested from 1976 to April 9, 1978)," English translation, p. 4.
83. Author's interview with Seng, Prek Ambel, 1 August 1980.

harm the base people in 1975 and 1976, appointing the poorest to the militia and the village administration. "At first the base people liked the Khmer Rouge," she says. But in 1978, most turned against them. Communal meals, which began in late 1976, offered only gruel and soup, and in 1977 all children over five were taken from their parents. In 1977–78, the rate of killings more than doubled. Over twenty new people were killed in the village, and hundreds in the subdistrict. Base people were spared execution, but this did not prevent their alienation from the DK regime.[84]

The Center's 1975 export target, to "sell 2 million tons of rice" in 1977, was not achieved. But there was "a most satisfactory rice harvest" in late 1976. Phnom Penh Radio announced in January 1977: "Today . . . there is a surplus of some 150,000 tons of rice." This was to be exported, to earn capital "for national defense and construction efforts."[85] That explains the lowering of rations in most places in 1977 and 1978.

As the CPK entered its third year of power, conditions were seriously deteriorating throughout the Southwest. On the second anniversary of victory, Khieu Samphan addressed a mass meeting in Phnom Penh. In the first three months of 1977, he said, "our people have become more enthusiastic and seething in their struggle to build the country. First, our workers and peasants are increasingly content with their new administration. The poor and lower middle peasants are content. So are the middle peasants. Besides this, those of the other classes from Phnom Penh who are also patriotic now see more clearly that this administration is correct, highly patriotic and independent. They have become increasingly aware that following the line of independence is not easy. They know that this road is certainly not strewn with roses, and shortcomings are not unknown, but it is an honorable, noble road. Therefore, they have become more determined." There were "profound changes" in the countryside. "In many places," Samphan said, "water is flowing freely, and with water, the scenery is fresh, the plants are fresh, life is fresh and people are smiling." The audience broke into applause.[86] Two weeks later, Phnom Penh Radio repeated that Cambodians "are proud of and content with this administration and value it *more than their own lives*."[87] In Democratic Kampuchea's heartland, the Southwest Zone, the regime was now on a genocidal track.

84. Author's interview with Bopha Sinan, Washington, D.C., 26 March 1980.
85. Phnom Penh Radio, 27 January and 12 April 1977, FBIS, Asia Pacific, 1 February 1977, p. H3, and 14 April 1977, p. H1.
86. Phnom Penh Radio, 15 April 1977, FBIS, Asia Pacific, 18 April 1977, p. H4.
87. Phnom Penh Radio, 28 April 1977, FBIS, Asia Pacific, 5 May 1977, p. H2. Emphasis added.

The Eastern Zone

Just as Region 25 was the most habitable part of the southwest, the Eastern Zone, just across the Mekong, was the least bad area of Democratic Kampuchea. The CPK Center reported in December 1976 that "so far this year, the strength of the labor force is rather feeble. Only in the East is the labor force not feeble."[88] The Zone's population in mid-1976 was 1.7 million.[89] This figure included probably three hundred thousand new people. In a second deportation, parallel to that from the Southwest to the Northwest, one hundred thousand new people were again evacuated, to the Northern Zone, late in 1975.[90] The Zone's base people numbered about 1.4 million.

The first account of the East to reach the outside world was that of a refugee who said that in Region 20, "the Khmer Rouge are less brutal than elsewhere."[91] The next testimony came from two refugees interviewed in 1976 by U.S. personnel in Thailand: "One person who came from eastern Cambodia claimed that executions are much fewer because the more sympathetic Khmer Rumdos are in control there. He noted that they have generally required only that former [Lon Nol] officers from the rank of second lieutenant upward shave their heads and do forced labour." The second account revealed that the Eastern Zone communists "continue to allow Buddhism to flourish, execute people rarely, make people work only a normal working day, and let them eat and dress better" than in other Zones.[92] In late 1977, *Asiaweek* concurred: "By most accounts, life in the eastern region" was "a good deal easier," and the regime there "less harsh."[93] The point is a comparative one.

On the basis of eleven refugee accounts from the East, collected in Thailand in 1980, Michael Vickery concluded that before 1978, "the entire East had been a relatively good zone, both for base peasants and new people. It had many good agricultural districts, and the administration there was in the hands of disciplined communists with long revolutionary experience. The zonal authorities did not deprive the population by sending excess rice to Phnom Penh, and

---

88. "Report of Activities of the Party Center According to the General Political Tasks of 1976," 58 pp., translation in *Pol Pot Plans the Future*, p. 197.

89. "Kumrung phankar buon chhnam khosang sangkumniyum krup phnaek rebos pak, 1977–80" ("The Party's Four-Year Plan to Build Socialism in All Fields, 1977–80"), dated July-August 1976, p. 13, table 1. For a translation, see Boua, Chander, and Kiernan, eds., *Pol Pot Plans the Future*, pp. 45–119. Table 1 appears on p. 52.

90. Kong Samrach, testimony at the "Cambodia Hearing," Oslo, April 1978, typescript, 8 pp. In December 1975 Samrach was sent to the Northern Zone with 100,000 other "new people" in the East.

91. *Straits Echo* (Penang), 5 June 1976. For details see Vickery, *Cambodia*, p. 134.

92. "Cambodia Today: Life Inside Cambodia," U.S. Embassy report from Thailand, 21 September 1976, pp., at 4, 13.

93. *Asiaweek*, 2 December 1977, p. 42.

urban intellectuals, as such, were not usually mistreated."[94] Vickery is on solid ground here. Timothy Carney has also concluded that before 1978, "life in general" in the Eastern Zone was "better than many other areas," although he stresses the relative nature of this judgment.[95] Katuiti Honda, who conducted surveys in 1980 on deaths in four eastern communities, found that there had been "few victims till early 1978."[96] The major critic of the Eastern Zone, Stephen Heder,[97] after interviewing 250 refugees, wrote that conditions for deportees "in the East had sometimes been marginally better or, even considerably better" than elsewhere.[98] Zone secretary So Phim was in the Center's view "suspect for keeping the Eastern Zone relatively prosperous."[99] Communal eating spread slowly in the Zone and, David Chandler writes, Phim "still enjoyed widespread, threatening popularity" as late as the end of 1977. A refugee recalls that Phim "wore ordinary clothes and loved the people."[100]

There is much more research to confirm this picture, with specific exceptions.[101] In 1979 and 1980 I interviewed eighty-seven people, including thirty-three peasants and twenty-three women, who lived in the five regions of the Eastern Zone between 1975 and 1979. They included forty base people, twenty-seven new people, and twenty CPK cadres. Of the sixty-seven civilians, ten mentioned specific victims of killings by Eastern Zone cadres in the years

94. Vickery, *Cambodia*, p. 136.

95. T. Carney, "The Organisation of Power in Democratic Kampuchea," in K. Jackson, ed., *Cambodia, 1975–1978: Rendezvous with Death*, p. 86.

96. Katuiti Honda, *Journey to Cambodia*, Tokyo, 1981, chs. 3 and 5.

97. Heder first suggested that the Eastern Zone anti-Pol Pot rebel Heng Samrin was "a kind of Kim Philby character" who had "been passing all the secret documents of the Cambodian Communist Party to the Vietnamese all along." According to Heder, in 1959 Samrin was "infiltrated into the ranks of the Cambodian revolution by the Vietnamese . . . and he rose as high as he could, and when it became impossible for him to continue to operate, he fled to Vietnam, just as Kim Philby fled to the USSR." (Heder, in *The Call*, organ of the Communist Party of the USA (Marxist-Leninist), 5 March 1979, p. 11.) In 1980 Heder changed his mind, writing that Samrin had been an "anti-Vietnamese" nationalist and was now "in at least temporary political eclipse" under Vietnamese military occupation and the pro-Hanoi "Pen Sovan regime" ("From Pol Pot to Pen Sovan to the Villages," Institute of Asian Studies, Chulalongkorn University, Bangkok, May 1980, pp. 16–17, 7.) In 1981 the "eclipse" did prove temporary. Samrin became secretary-general of Cambodia's ruling party, replacing Pen Sovan, who was detained for ten years. Vietnamese troops withdrew from Cambodia in 1989, but only with the Paris Peace Agreement in October 1991 did Heng Samrin's political career finally seem over. Heder now accused Samrin of having committed "war crimes" against Vietnam in late 1977 (pers. comm., April 1992). For Heder's evidence, see *Southeast Asia Research*, 5, 2, July 1997, pp. 138–42. See also p. 373, below.

98. S. Heder, *Kampuchean Occupation and Resistance*, Institute of Asian Studies, Chulalongkorn University, Monograph No. 27, January 1980, p.7.

99. Heder quoted in Chanda, *Brother Enemy*, p. 252.

100. D. P. Chandler, *The Tragedy of Cambodian History: Politics, War, and Revolution Since 1945*, New Haven: Yale University Press, 1991, pp. 296, 377.

101. See Kiernan, "Wild Chickens, Farm Chickens, and Cormorants: Kampuchea's East-

1975 and 1976; they listed around two hundred victims in all. At least five of the ten were not eyewitnesses, so there is no certainty about all these killings. Six interviewees mentioned general categories of people liable to execution in that period: "intellectuals and Lon Nol officers"; "most military, officials, and rich people"; "many Lon Nol officers"; "only well-educated people"; "one or two who refused orders or were lazy"; and "not many like in 1977." Thirteen interviewees reported people disappearing "to study"; and from the testimony of five such people, some apprehended in this way were executed. However, most were released, and despite some exceptions large-scale deaths in detention do not appear to have occurred before late 1976.

Of the two hundred killings, thirty were in a single district (Chantrea, Svay Rieng, Region 23), which, alone among the Zone's thirty-two districts—perhaps because of its strategic location, at the tip of the "Parrot's Beak" and surrounded on three sides by Vietnamese territory—appears to have been taken over by Southwest Zone cadres in 1975–76.[102] Another eight to ten deaths occurred during an abortive uprising led by former Lon Nol regime figures in Region 22 in November 1975. About 130 of the executions reported in these first two years were dated at mid- to late 1976. For the sixteen months after April 1975, then, specific executions reported by the sixty-seven non-CPK interviewees outside of Chantrea district numbered about twenty. An executioner I interviewed confessed to seven more killings. There were, obviously, more executions in the many Eastern villages not covered by this sample, and in 1975 and 1976 these probably numbered in the thousands (but under ten thousand). Twenty-nine of the non-CPK interviewees asserted that no one from their villages was killed in 1975 and 1976; another ten mentioned no killings; ten described uncertain circumstances that may have led to executions; and two others mentioned executions of CPK cadres. Starvation took a heavy toll in two of the interviewees' villages in the year 1975: twenty deaths were reported in one Chantrea village, fifty in a village in Memut district (Region 21). These cases aside, accounts agree that the rations and other food available were adequate for basic nutrition in 1975 and 1976.

Large numbers of people were imprisoned in 1975, but the information available—from three of the five Eastern Regions—suggests the vast majority were released after a brief detention. This distinguishes the East from the other

ern Zone under Pol Pot," in D. Chandler and Ben Kiernan, eds., *Revolution and Its Aftermath in Kampuchea*, Yale University, Southeast Asia Studies Monograph No. 25, 1983, pp. 136–211; Kiernan, *Cambodia: The Eastern Zone Massacres*, Columbia University, Center for the Study of Human Rights, 1986.

102. Kiernan, "Wild Chickens," p. 201 n. 6. Some of the information that follows first appeared there.

Zones of Democratic Kampuchea. In *Region 22*, for instance, one thousand new people were arrested in May 1975 in Koh Sautin district. Twenty civil servants and merchants were released almost immediately; four hundred former Lon Nol regime officials were "given permission to rejoin their families" in July; and of the other 580 Lon Nol army personnel, "junior officers and soldiers returned in great numbers" to the villages in September 1975. Senior officers did not return by December. One of those released called the prison regime harsh but said "nobody had any intention of escaping."[103] Another new person, Thun, twenty-two, who lived in Srey Santhor district from April 1975 to December 1976, reported that the revolutionaries there "did not persecute the people, and there were no killings." She added, "They genuinely reeducated a lot of new people. There were schools, and the teachers were well-qualified."[104] Vickery describes another Region 22 prison camp in mid-1975, in O Reang Au district: "Some executions of Republican officers occurred, but food was adequate, and prisoners, all urban new people, were *gradually* trained to do hard work. At first they were allowed to set their own pace to get used to the work and eventually brought to the condition of real peasants. They then had one month of political education, and in July 1975, 67 of them were sent to the base village of Toul Sralau, where they were mixed directly in with the old peasants . . . and when they had been there for three months they were considered equal to the base people, although not yet quite in the Candidate or middle category."[105]

In *Region 23* in 1975, over six hundred people, including three hundred teachers, were imprisoned in Svay Rieng district and then released, apparently in 1976.[106] In Meanchey Thmey district prison, after three hundred inmates died in five months from lack of medicine and overwork, the remaining sixty-four prisoners were released on 30 September 1975.[107] In Svay Teap district, 193 prisoners were returned to their villages in March 1976.[108] A Lon Nol soldier, arrested in Kompong Rou district and jailed for eight months, was released in early 1976 with three hundred others.[109] At Svay Prohout, "more than a hundred Republican soldiers and a handful of high-ranking civilians"

103. Kong Samrach, testimony at the "Cambodia Hearing," Oslo, Norway, April 1978, typescript, 8 pp. In December 1975 Samrach was sent to the Northern Zone.

104. Author's interview with Thun, Kompong Thom, 16 October 1980.

105. Vickery, *Cambodia*, p. 134.

106. Author's interview, Svay Thom, 29 August 1981. The interviewee was imprisoned and then released.

107. Author's interview with Muk Sim, one of the released prisoners, Svay Rieng, 16 January 1986.

108. Honda, *Journey to Cambodia*, p. 90. Toward the end of 1976, however, presumably in connection with the Southwest Zone's purge of Region 23 cadres at that time, the prisoners began to be recalled, and most were subsequently executed.

109. Author's interview with Khuon Ken, Svay Rieng, 15 January 1986.

were imprisoned for ten months. "Conditions were harsh and so was daily work, but rations were sufficient, and there were few deaths." The prison was closed in April 1976, and the prisoners released.[110]

In *Region 24*, an imprisoned base peasant from Peam Ro district was released in April 1975 along with 170 others. He estimates that 70 percent of all prisoners in the seven jails in Region 24 were also released. A former chauffeur for the French embassy in Phnom Penh was imprisoned for three months' "reeducation" along with one hundred other new people who arrived in Kompong Trabek district in mid-1975. Then they were released and assigned "normal" work in the fields.[111]

Most interviewees who reported executions or starvation in their villages in 1975–76 described the revolution and their life at that time as "no good." Of the other fifty-five non-cpk interviewees, forty-four expressed opinions on the subject, in a complex and nuanced range. Seven described the regime and living conditions in 1975–76 as "no good" primarily because of hard work and low rations, but reported no executions or starvation. Another seven placed the revolution between "no good" and "tolerable" (*kuo som*) or "all right" (*kron bao*). Twenty-one described it in terms such as "tolerable" or "all right," and nine used terms like "good" (*la'o*) or "not a problem" (*ot ey te*). Further, ten of the new people reported that in 1975–76 the base people in their villages supported the revolution, though they themselves did not.[112]

In general, the situation in the Eastern Zone was notably better than that in the Southwest.[113] This changed from late 1976, when Southwest forces began to move into the East in strength. Continuing the trend begun in 1971, when Region 25 was transferred from the East, and pursued with the arrest of its cpk secretary, Som Chea, in March 1977, Southwest cadres also purged the cpk secretaries of the neighboring Regions 24 (August 1976) and 23 (March 1977). Under Southwest and Center military occupation, these now became known as the "Twin Regions." They remained only nominally part of So Phim's Eastern Zone cpk branch, which was effectively reduced to three Regions in the Zone's north.[114] There, evidence of massacres is much rarer (and

110. Chandler, *The Tragedy of Cambodian History*, p. 282.

111. Interviews with author, Peam Ro, 7 October 1980, and Phnom Penh, 11 September 1981.

112. For an attempted explanation, see Chandler and Kiernan, *Revolution and Its Aftermath in Kampuchea*, p. 141.

113. Further evidence in Kiernan, "Wild Chickens," *Revolution and Its Aftermath*, pp. 136–38.

114. Ibid., p. 185. The confession of Touch Chem, alias Soth, cpk secretary of Region 21, says, "In September 1976 Brother Chan went to be the Secretary of Region 24." This confirms Chan's collaboration with the Center against the East, detailed below. "Responses of Touch Chem, called Soth, Secretary, [Region] 21, Eastern [Zone]," 18 May 1978, p. 13. Translation by S. Heder.

none inculpates surviving Eastern Zone cadres such as Heng Samrin, Hun Sen, or Chea Sim[115]).

But as in the Southwest, conditions deteriorated throughout the Eastern Zone in 1977. Several interviewees described that year and early 1978 positively. But in contrast to 1975–76, no one else used terms like "good" or even "tolerable." All reported many executions in 1977–78, and most described performing heavier work and receiving less food. Around the end of 1976, rations were reduced, and in a number of places, foraging prohibited, even outside the long working hours. Malnutrition spread and starvation struck some villages.

Peasants and Party in the Base Areas

Our examination of the two major Zones of Democratic Kampuchea, with 3.2 million of the 7.7 million Cambodians alive in 1976, allows us to draw some conclusions about the nature of the revolution. Was this a class-based "peasant revolution"? Do identifiable peasant initiatives come into the category of gleeful persecution of evacuees? According to a participant in the evacuation of the capital, "Many base people went into Phnom Penh dressed in black as usual. We thought there were so many Khmer Rouge. But they went to the New Market and other places to get goods, after their new people

115. In response to allegations by William Shawcross in the *New York Review of Books*, I noted that "after five years this has yet to be demonstrated" (10 May and 27 September 1984). A decade later no evidence had surfaced. In an account of the murder of his family at the hands of Khmer Rouge in 1975–1979, Saren Thach (*Washington Post*, 30 October 1989) confused Heng Samrin with So Phim, crx Zone secretary. Samrin was not the Zone's top political official, but its third-ranking military officer; in Prey Veng from 1975 until his 1978 mutiny, Samrin is unlikely to have been responsible for the deaths of Thach's family in Svay Rieng. Similarly, Hun Sen, an Eastern Zone deputy regimental commander until his defection in mid-1977, would not have participated in the 1973 attack on Kompong Cham city in the Northern Zone, as Thach alleges. (The battalions involved were probably Ke Pauk's Northern troops, allied to Pol Pot.) Likewise, the "cross-border massacre of Vietnamese civilians" on 24 September 1977 was carried out under the orders not of Hun Sen, who had defected in June, but of Son Sen. Thach's article was reprinted as "Who Wants Cambodia Ruled by Hun Sen?," in *International Herald Tribune*, 2 November 1989. See the reply by Elizabeth Becker, "The Khmer Rouge Killers Should be Prosecuted," *IHT*, 6 November 1989. Ironically, in 1983 it was Becker who had launched the rumor of the bloody past of unnamed leaders of the post-DK regime, partly relying on musings by S. Heder. Eight years later Heder conceded that "after a careful examination of all the available evidence, I can so far find no evidence that any of the ex-Khmer Rouge in positions of high political authority in today's Cambodia were involved in large-scale or systematic killing of Cambodian civilians. . . . I would hasten to add that this conclusion is based on a wide variety of different types of evidence, including evidence from sources extremely hostile to the State of Cambodia [Hun Sen] regime" (*Reflections on Cambodian Political History*, Strategic and Defence Studies Center, Australian National University, Working Paper No. 239, 1991, pp. 11–12). For Heder's bias against rebel Eastern Zone cadres, see n. 97 above.

relatives had arrived from Phnom Penh."[116] The city people had given their rural cousins the directions. This was peasant ransacking of the city, but it also underlines kinship and collaboration between new and base people.

Class-based "mugging" of city people *was* often the result when new people had to exchange jewelry for peasants' rice or corn. In one Takeo village, when the new people were being sent to the Northwest, poorer peasants took advantage of their plight. They "advised" the city people to leave behind goods like bicycles. The peasants asserted that "Angkar" needed these things, but it was they who had their eyes on them. Takeo also produced the vivid image of peasant women adeptly aiming sprays of soil, shaken loose from rice seedlings, at the nearest green city dweller. Hong Var reveals the mudslinging dénouement of this class skirmish: "One day, one of the women who had come from Phnom Penh, but who had grown up in the countryside, could not bear this cruelty any longer and retaliated by lobbing lumps of mud in a similar fashion at some of the 'old' people. The poor woman was immediately attacked by all the others. We were powerless to help since they were more numerous than us and we were afraid that they would turn on us next."[117]

In Battambang, in particular, there was a more serious settling of scores, sometimes by local peasants. CPK soldiers tore apart Lon Nol's bombers at Battambang airport after the victory. A week later, in the village of Svay Kong, outside Battambang, three Khmer Rouge accosted and shot down a former Lon Nol soldier. Having recognized him, they were now settling a grudge from the war. A young woman from Battambang city, avoiding a political meeting, was asleep on an oxcart behind her house. The shot woke her with a start. The woman watched in horror as the men sliced open the soldier's stomach while he was still alive. They removed his liver, proceeded to fry it over an open fire, and ate it. This was a traditional Khmer ritual for drawing strength from enemies. But the CPK cracked down. The witness recalls, "A big leader called Sam'un came and took the three killers away for execution. He called us to a meeting and said that otherwise, they would do it again, and that they were terrorizing the people. That was 'corrupt politics,' he said. Sam'un told us not to be afraid."[118]

Fine arts student Chnay was arrested in Battambang in early April 1976. A former classmate had nominated the two of them, after educated people had been asked to come forward and help the regime by returning to their former occupations. Those who had registered were taken in four trucks to a rice mill in Sisophon. They were roped together in groups of ten. Some were beaten,

116. Author's interview with Yem, Strasbourg, 31 October 1979.
117. Var Hong Ashe, *From Phnom Penh to Paradise*, p. 77. See also p. 53.
118. Author's interview with Thuy Bounsovanny, Creteil, 14 October 1979.

and all interrogated. The Khmer Rouge demanded: "What section of the Lon Nol army did you work in?" Some "confessed" falsely out of fear. One hundred fifty men disappeared. Seventy-eight remained, including thirty-two chained in a room with Chnay. After three months, Chnay and others managed secretly to remove their chains. They decided to run for it, but Chnay changed his mind because of his bleeding feet. Four men got out. Chnay heard gunshots outside. The next morning, Chnay and the other twenty-seven were taken out, blindfolded, and separated into three groups. Twenty men were shot dead. Just as Chnay's group of eight stepped forward to be shot, a large car pulled up. A high-ranking cadre with a Phnom Penh accent got out and ordered that the shootings cease since the prisoners had done no wrong. Chnay was released. He suspected that the cadre was an ex-teacher and that the jail attendants had planned the killings.[119]

Many other accounts describe Khmer Rouge killing Lon Nol officers and soldiers in 1975, in circumstances that could have been spontaneous, like some executions of civilian officials. In Battambang, peasants also wreaked postwar vengeance on former landgrabbers. Battambang was the only province of major landlordism in Cambodia. In the Thmar Kaul area, hundreds of hectares had belonged to a Khmer-Thai family since the nineteenth century. Five hundred hectares had also been appropriated by a French company. With independence in 1954, the French company returned all the confiscated land to only three or four families, and about a hundred peasants were deprived of their livelihood. According to a former Sihanouk official, "inquiry after inquiry" produced no action. In the rebellions of 1967–68, the peasants fought for the land and in 1975 demanded revenge. They urged the CPK to kill their former oppressors.[120]

But by 1977, the DK system was so tightly organized and controlled that little spontaneous peasant activity was possible. Even in 1975–76, such incidents were the exception rather than the rule—perhaps even in Battambang. Vickery's "peasant revolution" is a myth. He is closer to the truth in the Eastern Zone, and in the remote hills of Tram Kak and Chhouk districts, than in the Southwest Zone as a whole. There is no sign of the Center or Zone leaderships being "pulled along by the peasant element." This does not mean the CPK lacked widespread peasant support, however, at least in 1975–76. Base people in most villages identified with the victors. Frieson's analysis is also inadequate. We must return to the "peasant survival strategies" framing her conclusions.

119. Author's interviews with Srey Pich Chnay, March-April 1979.
120. This happened in April-May 1975 in the Thmar Kaul area. Author's interview with Thuy Bounso, who knew the area very well in the late 1960s and heard the story from refugees after 1975; Paris, 6 June 1980. For further information see Kiernan, "The Samlaut Rebellion, 1967–68," in Kiernan and Boua, Peasants and Politics in Kampuchea, esp. p. 192.

In *Weapons of the Weak*, James C. Scott identifies a range of historical Southeast Asian peasant responses to domination: "The account of resistance in the precolonial era would perhaps be dominated by flight and avoidance of corvée labor and a host of tolls and taxes." Frieson's interviews with peasant new people who fled the CPK before 1975 illustrate this time-honored theme. Her and my own interviews also show another survival strategy: "digging in, bending low, and cursing inwardly."[121] But the arsenal of weapons of the weak is well-stocked. Ammunition from modern Southeast Asia includes not just reluctant compliance or even deliberate foot-dragging, but also "wilful and massive *non*-compliance." Scott's armory supplies "small arms-fire in the class war" in the form of "stubborn and sporadic acts of petty resistance." Having broken out its contents, peasants pass along and load up blunderbusses of "dissimulation, poaching, theft, tax evasion, avoidance of conscription." They can even deploy artillery: "boycotts, quiet strikes," and "malicious gossip." Pertinently, Scott illustrates these strategies with examples from communist Vietnam: the "surreptitious expansion of private plots, the withdrawal of labor from state enterprises for household production, the failure to deliver grain and livestock to the state, the 'appropriation' of state credits and resources by households and work teams, and the steady growth of the black market."[122]

There is evidence of similar phenomena in Democratic Kampuchea, but not as much as in Vietnam. There are several reasons. First, the DK state was much more omnipotent. Cambodian peasants had much less room to maneuver than their Vietnamese counterparts, who maintained access to markets, currency, wage labor, schools, cities, travel, and communications. Vietnamese peasant willingness to resort to survival strategies does not necessarily signal political rejection of a regime allowing those options. Nor, second, were Cambodian peasants in 1975–76 united in a belief that the DK regime threatened their survival or even their interests. Many undoubtedly made the most of opportunities to hide food, favor their kin, fleece new people, fish at night, pick fruit "belonging to Angkar," and underreport village productivity to higher authorities. The risks were much greater in Democratic Kampuchea than in Vietnam. Even so, peasant support for the regime enforcing the sanctions remained surprisingly high until 1977. *Support* for an established order, perhaps especially a new revolutionary one, is another option for peasants, one that many base people chose.

In my view, ideological as well as economic issues were at stake. In 1975–76 nationalism was pervasive, victory sweet, hope millennial. The regime

121. Frieson, *The Impact of Revolution*, p. 11.
122. James C. Scott, *Weapons of the Weak: Everyday Forms of Peasant Resistance*, New Haven: Yale University Press, 1985, pp. 298–304, emphasis added. See also Scott's *Domination and the Arts of Resistance: Hidden Transcripts*, New Haven: Yale University Press, 1990.

talked incessantly about empowering peasants and raising living conditions. Many were prepared to give it time. And to sacrifice much. The regime also kept its darker secrets, like plans for communal eating and campaigns against family life. When it unveiled and enforced them, peasants felt betrayed. In another of Scott's works, *The Moral Economy of the Peasant: Rebellion and Subsistence in Southeast Asia*, he argued that peasants maintained a moral right to their subsistence. Peasant families were units of consumption, and rebellions "the revolts of consumers rather than producers." Exploitation was not the issue so much as the material conditions required for a peasant livelihood. These were often achieved by class reciprocity: part of the crop in exchange for "protection."[123] Rural relations can be a compromise involving peasant sacrifice, in kind or in labor, in return for peasant reward—*being left alone with an adequate subsistence*.

Some peasants charged Democratic Kampuchea with betrayal of precisely such a deal. In July 1975, two hundred Battambang families fled to Thailand. Deported from their homes, each group of thirty families had been given a cow and three pairs of oxen and ordered to work from 6 A.M. to late afternoon. "The land was theirs," they were told. All they had to do was "make it produce." Although they saw "no mass killings," they fled *en masse*. One explained, "We could take working hard, but not without enough to eat."[124] Frieson notes this phenomenon in 1970–75: "As long as people's livelihoods were untouched and their food source was secure, they could put up with the Red Khmers, and even support their cause. Once food became scarce, the support, whether feigned or real, began to be taken away."[125]

The same result was writ large in the late 1970s. The CPK made it increasingly clear that subsistence was not its priority, and people could expect no material return for their sacrifices. On 16 February 1978, DK Radio asserted: "Our masses of collective workers, peasants, and army have struggled to serve the nation and the people according to their respective tasks without receiving *any* personal benefits such as salaries, rank, prestige, or title. In fact, they have always been interested *only* in freedom, unity, their cooperatives and national society as a whole as distinct from private property."[126] The commentary made no mention of material living standards, private or collective, which fell under the discarded rubric of "private property."

In some cases, peasants may prefer a judicious, even an unfair compro-

---

123. James C. Scott, *The Moral Economy of the Peasant: Rebellion and Subsistence in Southeast Asia*, New Haven: Yale University Press, 1976, p. 11, 13, 161–62.

124. *Bangkok Post*, 26 July 1975.

125. Frieson, *The Impact of Revolution*, p. 202.

126. Phnom Penh Radio, 16 February 1978, FBIS, 17 February 1978, p. H1. Emphasis added.

mise—if it guarantees subsistence—to all-or-nothing strategies like open resistance or flight. The looming starvation that prompted the two hundred Battambang families to flee was not yet a prospect in the Southwest and Eastern Zones by mid-1975. Alternatively, peasants may resort to collective action, not individual coping by "cursing inwardly." This can mean acting as an entire village, like the Battambang exodus; or reifying a kinship network, like those mapping the Southwest Zone; or even acting on the basis that peasants possess common class interests, as the CPK claimed. But the collapse of living standards below subsistence levels had to provoke resistance or flight.

Worse, peasants were *not* left alone after trucks carried off their harvest. Besides confiscating their subsistence, the D.K. state raided other hoards of peasant treasure. Its transformation of the country in 1975–77 was also a massive, three-pronged incursion into the most guarded private realms. The Center spearheaded its systematic assaults on peasant ties to land, family, and religion with punishing search-and-destroy missions into the economic, personal, and spiritual provinces of peasant life. But these areas were heavily contested, and required aggressive, indefinite state patrolling. Of the three, one peasant world seems to have been the most cherished and least pacified. The loss of land ownership and of religious freedom, our social history of Democratic Kampuchea suggests, was less important to peasants than the devastating blows administered by the ending of home meals and the enforced separation of children from parents. Along with massacres that threatened peasant life itself, it was the CPK's attack on the family that alienated peasant supporters. By now many peasants—not all—could only "curse inwardly." But their families remained uppermost in their minds. Surviving family units, physically separated, were emotionally preserved.

CHAPTER SIX

An Indentured Agrarian State, 1975–77 (II): Peasants and Deportees in the Northwest

The Southwest and Eastern Zones were long-held CPK base areas with overwhelmingly peasant populations. In the Northwest, on the other hand, most of Battambang had remained under Lon Nol's control until 1975. Its peasants were mostly "new people," and its urban areas swollen with refugees. In late 1975 many more urban evacuees arrived. The Northwest offers an interesting contrast to CPK rule in other Zones.

Following the evacuation of Phnom Penh, there were two population movements from the Southwest (and also the new Western Zone) to the Northwest. From mid-1975, the Southwest was cleared of almost all new people, as well as "unclean" base people.[1] Heng Teav, a member of the Northwest Zone CPK Committee, claims that "Pol Pot's group did this" from Phnom Penh, in collaboration with the Southwest leaders. The Northwest leadership of Moul Sambath (alias Nhim), Teav says, "resisted" the deportations. "We resisted sending a lot of people. . . . There were already one million [in the Northwest] and they were bringing hundreds of thousands more. But they had already rounded them up and closed the trap . . . when Ta Nhim found out that they were transporting the people of Phnom Penh once again. . . . While they were transporting them, we struggled, saying: 'Don't transport them here.' They were throwing them away."[2] Battambang *was* underpopulated, and it is possible that the Zone might even have agreed with the Center in September 1975 that "the Northwest needs 500,000 additional forces."[3] But its

---

1. Former mathematics teacher Yun says his group of new people was deported along with five families of Takeo base people whom the Khmer Rouge considered "not yet clean" (*chres sralah*). Former medic Hav agrees that suspect or disloyal base people were removed from the Southwest: "Only the hardcore people remained." Author's interviews, Creteil and Stains, 1979. (See Chapter 5.)

2. Author's interview with Heng Teav, Phnom Penh, 14 January 1986.

3. "Examine the Control and Implementation of the Political Line to Save the Economy

leadership could not have been expected to feed the eight hundred thousand dumped there after the planting season.[4]

A third major population movement began in early 1977. The Center dispatched Southwest Zone cadres and loyal base people to take over the Northwest. They purged the politically suspect cadres of the CPK's Northwest Zone branch. The new people expelled from the Southwest in 1975 now found themselves under Southwestern rule once again.

The Second Deportation

Ten-year-old Ang Ngeck Teang, her family of eleven, and six other new families from her village in Region 25 were loaded onto a boat on the Mekong in mid-1975.[5] They were ferried upriver to Kompong Chhnang, then placed in trucks that headed north of the Tonle Sap lake, taking Highway 6 to Siemreap city. From there they traveled by oxcart to Battambang. Yem, the soldier who had fought on both sides, was in one of the first groups to leave Takeo, in July 1975. Fifty Chinese-made trucks from Phnom Penh picked up two hundred families in Prey Krabas. Each vehicle had a driver and guard, both armed. They drove through Phnom Penh and then northwest along Highway 5 on the south shore of the Tonle Sap. In Pursat they disembarked and were told to wait for a train to Battambang. People already there had been waiting a month, though Yem managed to leave within a day. Food ran out, and more people died.

At the end of September, as the first corn, manioc, and sweet potatoes were ripening, Dr. Oum Nal, former deputy head of a Phnom Penh hospital, was deported again, from the Western Zone. Seven thousand, five hundred sixty other deportees formed the seventh train convoy to Sisophon, in the Northwest. Dr. Nal rode on the roof of a carriage. "Like in the film of Doctor Zhivago . . . I relived his adventures."[6] Airplane mechanic Van traveled by rail with another large group from Prey Krabas in November. Two people died on the train.[7] The passengers were given bread. They slept at Pursat, then continued to Sisophon.

---

and Prepare to Build the Country in Every Field," CPK Center "Document no. 3," dated 19 September 1975, p. 31. Translation by Chanthou Boua. (See Chapter 3.)

4. For the eight hundred thousand figure, see p. 97, above. Northwest Zone Committee member Heng Teav confirms this, estimating "over half a million new arrivals, but not a full million." Author's interview, 1986.

5. References to interviews cited in this chapter may be found in Chapter 5.

6. *Le Figaro* (Paris), 11 February 1977. English translation in "Human Rights in Cambodia," Hearing Before the Subcommittee on International Organizations of the Committee on International Relations, House of Representatives, 3 May 1977, pp. 59–62.

7. The trains would stop to bury the dead, as Hav, who also left Takeo in November 1975, confirms.

Van, his wife and week-old baby, and their group of seventeen who had left Phnom Penh together in April, all arrived safely. With the five hundred new families from his village, Chnay, the former fine arts student, reached Takeo city on foot on 1 January 1976. The wait at the railway station, and the train journey to Sisophon, took about a month. The train was packed. Several people sitting on top of the carriages fell off and were killed. Others died in the cramped conditions. Several perished in Chnay's group of twenty families, and many fell ill.[8]

Savy, twenty-six, working at the Sisophon railway station, watched them arrive. Over seven thousand "skinny, unhappy people" came on each train, every two days. Four or five died on each train. The deportees were immediately investigated, and soldiers separated from the rest. Some soldiers and even teachers were killed. After a night in Sisophon, evacuees were sent north to Phnom Srok or Preah Net Preah districts, several hundred to a village. The trains returned to Phnom Penh with salt from Thailand.

A two-part revolutionary song was taught to children in Region 4. A soloist playing the role of a new person would begin by singing to a base person:

New Person:
My story ends here now, with regrets for not joining in the liberation to
   protect friends and family,
To stop the enemy from oppressing them further,
To drive out Sek Sam Iet [Lon Nol's governor of Battambang], to
   obliterate and destroy him.
Your story, friend, is of much mourning and misery.
As for me I give myself to Angkar
I give my heart and soul,
And undertake to serve Angkar and the people.

To this the base person replies:

Base Person:
I have liberated Phnom Penh and Siemreap.
There is no more news from Veal Baek Chan [a Lon Nol military base].
We strove to struggle, chase, hit and strike
To liberate Battambang for the people.
Our troops have won; now friends do not fear.
The enemy will lose both night and day.
Only ten are left of twenty who joined.
We have surrounded the defeated enemy.[9]

8. For Chnay's full story see Ben Kiernan and Chanthou Boua, *Peasants and Politics in Kampuchea*, pp. 344–52.

9. Author's recording of songs learnt in Democratic Kampuchea by the Pel family, Toul, 4 November 1979.

Region 5: 1975–76

Somehow, Teang, Yem, Van, Chnay, and the other new people we met in the Southwest all made the journey safely from Takeo and Region 25. They came in different convoys, but many ended up in close proximity. Though not acquainted, their lives intertwined. Cross-checking their accounts, and drawing on local base people as witnesses, provides a picture of the next three years in the Northwest.

Of the Zone's seven regions, Region 5 received easily the largest number of new settlers. In 1975 its four districts had a population of one hundred seventy thousand, to whom were soon added two hundred thousand to two hundred ten thousand urban deportees from the Southwest and West. Most went to just two districts: Preah Net Preah and Phnom Srok.[10] This overburdening of the Region helps explain why, as Vickery notes in a comprehensive survey of the Northwest Zone, conditions in Region 5 became "probably the worst" of the four regions that made up the old province of Battambang. But Region 5 was not the nightmare that survivors from the much poorer Regions 2, 6 and 7, where evacuees were abandoned to die by the thousands in the barren hills and forests of Pursat province, have described.[11]

So, Region 5 makes an important and medium-case study of the Northwest. Four themes emerge. One is the food shortages, first in late 1975 and again in mid-1976, before each end-of-year harvest. These resulted from the massive influx of people without adequate food stores. The Center sent no rice to the Northwest to help it through these lean periods.[12] Nor could the new laborers assist with the Northwest's first harvest, in December 1975-January 1976, for the existing population had planted only land it could manage.

A second theme is the Zone's apparent attempt to cope with the labor surplus and its unfortunate timing by emphasizing the long term. Massive irri-

10. Author's interview with San, a Region 5 statistician in 1975–76 (Paris, 29 May 1980.) San added that the Center had planned to deport 230,000 people to Region 5, but that the number of people who actually arrived was between 200,000 and 210,000. The other two districts in Region 5 are Sisophon and Thmar Puok.

11. Michael Vickery, *Cambodia 1975–1982*, pp. 102, 114–18. Many of my own informants from the seven Regions of the Northwest Zone corroborate Vickery's conclusions. In the Krakor district of Pursat (Region 7), one of the worst-hit areas, the district's 1975 population of 12,750 reportedly fell to about 6,000 by December 1976. (Letter from Anthony M. Paul, 28 March 1977, reprinted in "Human Rights in Cambodia," 3 May 1977, pp. 8–9.)

12. In an interview with S. Heder on 9 March 1980 in Sakeo camp, a boat pilot who was in the DK water transport unit from 1975 to 1978 said, "In 1975 there was no transportation of rice either from Phnom Penh to the [Zones] or vice-versa. . . . There was no transportation of rice to the Northwest or to the North." Stocks of "thousands of tons" of rice found in the capital after victory were "used to feed factory workers and ministry workers in Phnom Penh" and the armed forces. In 1976, rice from the Northwest went to Phnom Penh "by truck and train."

gation projects were initiated, with Region-wide labor management. This centralized employment strategy failed, and over time the huge Regional workforce had to be broken into smaller units at each of various levels. Food supplies ran out anyway.

A third theme is the reduced importance of the peasantry. Though the Northwest CPK enjoyed some rural support, most peasants there were new people. The Northwest was the Zone with the smallest peasant base, and this was soon swamped by more new people, doubling its population. Northwest peasants suffered more than others as their smaller numbers gave them lower priority, though this only marginally relieved the pressure on the new people.

The final theme is the intermittent use of terror for social control and labor discipline. The postwar massacres of April–May 1975 entered a second round with the arrival of a new wave of "class enemies" at the end of the year. Both purges were limited in scope and duration. But then a third wave of killings took a new toll as the newly emerging political structure struggled to both dominate and feed a population it could not support. The task demanded deft administration. It was handled more brutally in some areas than in others. The CPK in the Northwest Zone predominantly comprised former schoolteachers, and some were admired by the urban evacuees for attempts to reduce suffering that was probably beyond solution. As Vickery has recounted, people from Region 4 "mention in particular" Khek Penn, "who often toured around the villages with his wife and a theatrical group, keeping an eye on local conditions and providing a bit of entertainment."[13] A man from District 42, near Maung, typically calls Penn "a good man, not a killer," who presided over reasonable living conditions in 1975–76.[14]

Others resorted to terror. This showed signs of abating in 1976, but the conditions favored the emergence of a harsh, deceptive, dictatorial regime. While the Southwest Zone reaped the harvest that the former city population had planted there, the Northwest had to try to feed them. It often failed. It confronted much larger challenges than the Southwest Zone did, problems not of its creation but the Center's. The death toll in the Northwest in 1975–76 was concomitantly much higher, though the murder toll may not have been.

Yem did not go straight to Region 5. From Pursat he took the train to Region 3. He was assigned to a krom of fifty houses in a village of three hundred families of new people, some of whom were put in charge. Yem's krom was headed by a Lon Nol soldier. Cooperativization had not begun in Region 3, and the CPK administration was unable to absorb the newcomers. For the three

13. See Vickery, *Cambodia 1975–1982*, pp. 105–6.
14. Author's interview, Phnom Penh, 2 January 1986. This man said Khek Penn's dismissal and murder by the Center in 1977 were followed by much killing and inadequate food rations in a very productive area.

months Yem was there, neither rations nor communal meals were provided. Base people only visited to inspect the village every few weeks. The desperate deportees had authority to exchange whatever they had with them. Radios were swapped for rice. "The base people were good to us. They helped us, as in Takeo. . . . We came with nothing," he recalls, "and at least ten people died every day in my krom." Nevertheless, according to Yem, "Region 3 was lax," reflecting factional differences and confusion. Geographical conditions varied, and daily rice rations ranged widely from 110 grams per person to 250, 320 and even 700 grams ("too much," according to one informant).[15] Vickery asserts that for urban evacuees, Region 3 "was probably the best area of the entire country."[16] Yem says new people there were given minor posts, even recruited into the army,[17] and exchange and travel were allowed. He comments, on the basis of experience on both sides of the Cambodian revolution, "In Battambang, the revolution was young. . . . I stayed with the Reds one night, at O Sralau. . . . The revolutionary troops played old society songs. . . . The Khmer Rouge there did not yet know about the rules that applied in Takeo, in Region 33." Yem could exchange or beg oranges or bananas from the Khmer Rouge. "I joined the chalat with a lot of other new people, and the troops gave us food when they saw us." Rations for chalat workers were adequate.

In late 1975, Yem walked to Battambang through Region 4 and received permission to take the train north to Sisophon. He comments, "I could never have done that in Region 33," back in the Southwest. cpk soldiers, seeing his poor condition, gave him Vitamin B-1 and B-12 tablets. He reached the Phnom Srok district of Region 5 to find it "even softer": "The Khmer Rouge there also gave us enough food, to persuade us to stay. I decided there was no need to flee. I could fish and do other things. . . . Then in the dry season there was enough to eat. I was harvesting, and got two cans [of rice per day], more if I worked hard. And we could store some under the house, they didn't mind." Few starved in the first half of 1976. New people far outnumbered the locals. A defector from Lon Nol's 12th Brigade, a friend of Yem called Yon, was appointed krom chief. The base people in Region 5, Yem says, were divided over the cpk. The district and village chiefs who had promoted Yon belonged to the majority faction. But a purge in mid-1976 removed them from power. The

15. *Christian Science Monitor,* 4 February 1976; *Washington Post,* 12 February 1976; François Ponchaud, *Cambodia Year Zero* (Paris: Julliard, 1977), p. 83; and David Chandler, Ben Kiernan, and Muy Hong Lim, *The Early Phases of Liberation in Northwest Cambodia: Conversations with Peang Sophi,* Monash University Center of Southeast Asian Studies, Working Paper No. 10, 1976, p. 7.

16. M. Vickery, "Democratic Kampuchea: Themes and Variations," in David Chandler and Ben Kiernan, eds., *Revolution and Its Aftermath in Kampuchea,* p. 116; and Vickery, *Cambodia 1975–1982,* pp. 102, 110–14.

17. Yem claims that "most of the Khmer Rouge troops in Battambang were new people." Author's interview.

village chief was executed. The purge coincided with a tightening of CPK control and confiscation of private rice stocks. Yon, Yem, and the district chief all fled to Thailand in June 1976. Mid-1976 was something of a turning point. Locals from Region 5 corroborate Yem's account. Some have positive attitudes about the first years. Chik became a village teacher in Thmar Puok in 1970, at age twenty-two. During the war, Khmer Rouge came to help with the harvest, and they nominated future subdistrict and district chiefs. They promised to "raise up the poor, destroy the rich and the corrupt, and drive out the American imperialists." Just before the war ended, Chik recalls, "all the villagers joined the Khmer Rouge." During a clash with Lon Nol troops, they helped transport ammunition, provided rice, and helped remove and hide the wounded. "They wanted the Khmer Rouge to win, because a minority of the Lon Nol troops stole their money and animals, whereas none of the Khmer Rouge persecuted people. . . . The locals liked the Khmer Rouge, gave them money, and even went to Sisophon to buy them medicine. . . . At night the villagers passed food and guns to the Khmer Rouge. They tried to hide this from me, but I didn't mind. The Khmer Rouge didn't persecute me either." Just before the war ended, Chik and ten families left the village for the safety of Sisophon. They all returned after the CPK victory.

Chik says the village's 1975 population was 1,224, comprising two hundred peasant families. At first the victors selected a local rich man as the new village chief. But three weeks later he was dismissed, though not harmed, and replaced by a committee of three poor people, with a new militia of a dozen peasants. A cattle rustler, a landlord, and another man were executed. After two months, the villagers were organized into ten-family krom. In August 1975, these were enlarged to fifty families. One krom was sent to a new area to grow cotton. Then, in October, the whole village became a single work unit. Young men, women, and children were assigned to three separate kong for plowing, while the middle-aged did the planting. This did not work well, and the Khmer Rouge settled on thirty-family krom. Targets were collective: a krom with eight plows was assigned a hectare of land; then twelve women had to plant it. Chik would leave home at 4 A.M., plow until 11, and then from 2:30 to 4:30 P.M. "Then we would raise dikes, help with the planting, and then eat. There were no free nights." Meals remained private for two years, and there was no starvation. Each household had rice reserves, chickens, and ducks. There were "normal deaths from disease."

The fifty families who had gone off to grow cotton came back in early 1976. Around the same time, Chik was assigned to the chalat. He spent seven months building dams and laboring at various sites before returning home. Meetings were held every few nights. The CPK told the villagers they had defeated the imperialists "empty-handed" and were now building a new society, predicting a high standard of living within several years. They would transform backward ways into modern agriculture. Cattle, which would be replaced by tractors, could then be killed for food. The whole countryside would be electrified. The villagers, Chik says, "really liked" the CPK. But by mid-1976 labor requirements were becoming harsh. Chik worked "hard all year round, even when there was no point, . . . even in the rain." It was only at this stage that the locals began to lose faith in the Khmer Rouge. Even though travel was restricted, word of killings spread. Refugees trying to get to Thailand were constantly being intercepted and executed by Region and Zone troops stationed near the border. Still, Chik looks back on 1975 and 1976 as years of "no problems."

Sovanny, a peasant from Thmar Puok, was seventeen when Khmer Rouge entered her forest village of one hundred families in April 1975. They told the peasants, "Please work hard in the fields for progress." "They chatted with us. It was happy. They taught us to sing songs every night, and helped us with planting and transplanting. The people were not concerned. The Khmer Rouge were kind and lax." After three months came the question "Who wants to serve the revolution?" Sovanny recalls, "I did not know what was happening and I raised my hand, with two girls and some boys. They took our names."

Sovanny spent a year in the Region 5 *chalat kong pises* ("special mobile workforce") west of Sisophon. A thousand city and country men and women worked together, building high dams across creeks and rivers. "They told us to work hard, even when tired, in order to make socialist revolution," Sovanny giggled as she recalled. "This was the message at first, we just believed them. They were good to us at first. Some of us liked them. I didn't." The workers labored "day and night, without rest," on collective tasks. But Sovanny says they did so "happily, chatting and laughing together." They also ate together; rations were adequate in 1975–76, though each worker received only one set of clothes. Male and female cadres "helped us in whatever we did, and worked alongside us."

Sovanny returned home in late 1976. She avers that there were no killings until 1978: "At first they did not kill. . . . They were good, for three years." On reflection, however, she recalled that Northwest Zone forces had "only killed teachers, intellectuals, big people—six or eight people in my village."

Other locals are much more negative about Region 5. Savy, a rice farmer, says, "The Khmer Rouge treated us well for the first three months or so, but it gradually worsened after that. . . . They took our personal possessions: carts, pots, pans, etc. The people just did whatever they were told." Savy spent six months in the Region carpentry unit in Sisophon, comprising fifty new people. "There were no problems. . . . We worked quietly and cheerfully." One or two people were arrested every two months, purportedly to be "sent back to their homes." But there was plenty to eat, and Savy describes life as normal. Then, after his wife's uncle fled to Thailand, Savy was sent to Preah Net Preah with his father-in-law. But kinship cut both ways. Savy had a younger brother in the D.K. army. The soldier got Savy transferred back to Sisophon in August 1976, where he participated in a cotton-growing cooperative of two thousand base people. He was given a cart and two cattle and told to plow a hectare a day. There was no night work. Rations were mainly gruel, but "it was easy. . . . Things were lax in the units. You just did what you were told." The base people were all, like Savy, relatives of Khmer Rouge who had brought their families from the hills north of Siemreap in 1975. "They were all pro-Khmer Rouge, loyal, real peasants. They had never seen cars or money. They did not know a car when they saw one."

Hong, whose family was massacred near Sisophon two weeks after the CPK victory, says the three hundred other families in his village were organized into ten-family krom, and put to work on rice cultivation and irrigation construction. "In 1975 we still had food, and could forage." Meals remained private, though the hundred new families had most of their belongings confiscated within two weeks of arrival. In 1976, rations were reduced to gruel; in July communal eating began, in hundred-family groups. "We ate banana stalks, like pigs. It was hard." Hong fled, reaching Thailand on 30 August 1976.

Sarun, twenty-one, son of a poor peasant in Preah Net Preah, lived in a village of twenty-five hundred. It was not a base village, and many of the men had been drafted into the Lon Nol army. When the CPK took over in 1975 they listed everyone's names and created three categories: the wealthy and government officials, rich or middle peasants, and poor peasants and workers. Four families of "rich" people, who had owned two oxcarts or two plows, were massacred. All land, tools, and livestock were communalized. Rations were adequate. In August 1975, male and female youths were drafted into the chalat, and Sarun's young sister was sent to a children's group. His parents cried "like rain" as the children departed. Sarun began a three-year career in the Region 5 chalat. In the next month or so, seven thousand families of townspeople arrived in the village, now organized into four cooperatives. All unmarried youths followed the peasants into the Region 5 chalat, which mustered five thousand workers. Each kong of one hundred had its own communal kitchen. Rations of a can per day made a bowl of gruel for each person, sometimes with salt and *prahoc* (preserved fish paste), and fish every two weeks.

The chalat's first major task was to build a reservoir. They raised a 7-km retaining wall, 10 m wide at the base and 6 at the top. The CPK "never explained why." Sarun doubts that water could have entered the reservoir and that it was "built to help the farmers." It took less than six weeks, but overwork and lack of food killed many of the workers "like animals," Sarun says. On the chalat's next assignment, a four-month stint clearing forest, many more perished. By late 1975, four hundred of the five thousand chalat workers were dead. Sarun had begun coughing blood, and was allowed a month in a Sisophon hospital. Rations there comprised gruel and salt. Starving patients cut human flesh from corpses beside them and barbecued and ate it. Sarun returned to his unit at the end of the year. Youths worked in the rain, supervised by unarmed Khmer Rouge who did not work. Workers complained bitterly, and malingerers were executed.

In January 1976, the Region 5 chalat was divided into two. Some remained to tend crops on the land they had cleared. The rest of the five thousand were sent to a new dam site in Preah Net Preah district. There they were joined by district-level chalat from Region Five's four districts, as well as newly arrived urban youths. Twelve thousand workers labored at the site for two months. Rice rations were provided. Then in late March, ten thousand workers were sent to another site in the district to build a third dam. Rations were reduced to simple gruel. Sarun worked there for twenty days. In late April, the district chalat were sent back to their districts and the Region chalat was broken up again. Some workers were sent back to work the land they had cleared the previous year. Sarun and others went with the Preah Net Preah district chalat and were assigned to maintain the second new dam, build more irrigation works, and grow dry season rice with the water now available.

Sarun spent the next two years there. He would rise at 3 or 4 A.M., work until 11 or 12, eat some gruel, and resume work until 5 or 6 P.M. Meetings were held for an hour or more as often as one night in three. Sometimes the theme was the workers' livelihood, but it was usually "struggle in work." Five instructions were always stressed. The first was "solidarity and independence." The other four invoked obedience, to "the political line," "the authority," "the rules and regulations," and the "plans set by Angkar."

Into this turbulent scene came the new people from the Southwest. Youngster Ang Ngeck Teang, with seven families from Region 25 in oxcarts, reached Region 5 in mid-1975. They settled in a village of five hundred, mostly base families, in Preah Net Preah district. "The base people were very keen on the Khmer Rouge," Teang recalled, explaining their enthusiasm: "They did whatever they were told because they were afraid of death." The newcomers had to reveal their former occupations to the local CPK. Former Lon Nol soldiers were then executed, while "workers" were spared. Teang says they were instructed, "Do what you are told. Don't resist the line, or you won't be spared." Communal eating began immediately, and gruel was served throughout the year except for two months after the annual harvest, when dry rice was plentiful. However, in 1975–76, meals included salted fish and prahoc paste every two days. There was little starvation.

Dr. Oum Nal was able to get an overall picture after his arrival in Sisophon at the end of September 1975. His former orderly from Phnom Penh was running the Region 5 medical service,[18] and his wife ran the Sisophon maternity hospital. By November, Nal learnt the disastrous consequences of the sudden influx of tens of thousands of deportees: "Ninety percent of the women did not undergo menstruation. . . . The causes of this nearly general irregularity were evident: nutritional deficiency, forced labor, psychic traumas, etc. But to enumerate them in this way would mean to criticize the infallibility of the Angkar, a crime punishable by the death penalty. . . . In the 'new villages,' the mortality rate then reached more than 50 percent, and the survivors did not fare any better. Production, the main worry of the Angkar, went down to zero." In the maternity hospital, "most of the newly born died by accident from puerperal fever." The orderly had Nal secretly translate a French obstetrics handbook for him.[19]

The late 1975 harvest was "one of the best in years,"[20] and conditions improved temporarily. But deportees kept arriving. Hong Var and her two daughters, Somaly, seven, and Panita, three, were sent from Takeo to Region 5's Phnom Srok district in December. They lived there four months, until rice supplies ran low. The Region administration then moved them, with two thousand other Phnom Penh families, to Thmar Puok district. Var found herself in a village of over one thousand people. A "small number" were executed in 1976, when, she says, "the killings began." There was no food shortage, but conditions steadily deteriorated. Movement was restricted to within five kilometers. In 1976, children were taken from their parents and assigned communal tasks. Somaly and Panita made natural fertilizer. In late 1976, family meals were ended and communal eating became compulsory.

Military medic Hav, who had arrived in Sisophon from Takeo in November 1975, went on to a village in Preah Net Preah district. Conditions in the six subdistricts varied: "Some were easy and some hard. Some of the cadres were light, others were heavy." Hav was sent to a "harsh" subdistrict, Rohal, with a population of five thousand new and base people. The latter had their own homes and "a better life." Here the new people were called *neak chileas* (evacuees). Hav joined a krom of ninety-three families, with over four hundred people. They each received a can of rice per day, and much more for several months after the annual harvest. Midday meals in the field were served communally; family life remained private. But by mid-1976 rice rations ran low.

18. Nal says this man was a brother of the crk Region 5 Secretary, Hing. San, who says he knew Hing well and worked with him closely, says that Hing had a younger brother named Chhou who had completed three or four years toward a medical degree and was now working as a doctor or medical aide in the Sisophon hospital. (Interview with the author, 29 May 1980.) For further information on Hing's family, see below.

19. *Le Figaro*, 11 February 1977.

20. *New York Times*, 21 January 1976; and "Life Inside Cambodia," Extracts from an Air-

There had never been much salt or meat. People ate banana stalks and leaves. Production was low, and many people starved in 1976. Discipline was fierce. "You could be taken away if you quarrelled over food with your wife, or complained ever so slightly at work. We were afraid each night of what task would be given to us the next day."

Interrogated on arrival in Sisophon, Van had confessed that he had been an airplane mechanic. With thirty-two new families, including doctors, engineers, and six other former air force personnel, he was sent to Preah Net Preah. On 7 January 1976, the heads of the thirty-two families, and nearly three hundred hundred former students and teachers, assembled in the grounds of the monastery known as Wat Chup. Dr. Oum Nal was another of the "397 probationers," who were nearly all from Phnom Penh. Nal recalled that the wat was "surrounded by barbed wire, teeming with sentries." Breakfast was served at 7 A.M.: "rice soup as much as one liked and fried fish, served by revolutionary girls with revolutionary songs and music." Then the Region 5 CPK secretary, Men Chun (alias Hing), a thirty-five-year-old former professor, arrived with an escort of armed jeeps.

Hing addressed the crowd: "The *Angkar* is happy to receive you here. The *Angkar* needs you. . . . Today we begin a new era of happiness. Our country has overcome difficulties, the heritage of the imperialist super-traitors. The regime has become stable. Kampuchea has been given a democratic constitution, which will be read to you. . . . *Angkar* asks you only to be loyal, sincere and straightforward." A lavish lunch was followed by an order for the probationers to write their autobiographies and to "frankly" express their "desires and longings." Some people requested the reunification of families, others freedom of worship or the reopening of universities.[21]

Van recalls hearing Hing tell the crowd that Khmer Rouge soldiers "could do everything, and did not need foreign training like in the Lon Nol period." Other speakers added that "no other revolution in the world did what they were doing, even China, which had long been making revolution." There would be no more classes or capitalists. "But now, Hing said, *Angkar* was still short of some things. *Angkar* had no capital. So they asked all the Khmer people to go and grow rice. The ricefields was their capital. They relied only on agriculture to build from a backward to a progressive agriculture, and even industry. To grow rice required irrigation works. So all of us intellectuals had to work in the fields." Van says that the CPK was executing former soldiers, but not targeting intellectuals. At 4 P.M. that day, they were asked if they had any

---

gram Report by an Officer of the American Embassy at Bangkok, 31 March 1976 (declassified 1978), p. 10: "We must admit to being surprised that the rice harvest was as bountiful as refugees generally claim."

21. *Le Figaro*, 11 February 1977.

questions. "Some got up and asked *Angkar* to provide medicine, and to open schools again." Others with limited strength asked for light work. Another doctor criticized corruption among the cadres. Another asked Hing: "*Angkar* has eliminated all internal and external enemies, such as the United States. There are none left. Would *Angkar* eliminate all skilled people as well, or not?" Van says Hing was so angry he closed the meeting. But Oum Nal recalls "a joyful, artistic and revolutionary party for the probationers" that evening. Troops guarded them overnight. Nal recalls that at dawn, "the imprudent young people, who had expressed their sincere longing, were herded in the courtyard." Soldiers tied their hands behind their backs and put them on a truck. Van says fifty-two doctors and engineers were arrested. They were shut up in a house in Battambang city for fifteen days, "all in the same room, their feet attached to a central log, without being able to move, wallowing in their excrements."[22]

Over the next six days, the remaining newcomers at Wat Chup were tested. On the second day they had to rewrite their autobiographies. Nal carefully reproduced the same version, adding in the section for requests: "I wish to pass my life producing rice and to devote my strength to the *Angkar*." Once, Van recalls, the group was denied food. Another day, they were given burnt rice "to see if we could be tempered." On the morning of 10 January 1976, a list of forty-five names was read out. Nal's was on it. "They asked us to get out, take our belongings and to stand, two by two. Armed soldiers surrounded us. . . . After an agonizing wait, a truck, escorted by an armed jeep, stopped in the courtyard." Late that afternoon the group arrived in Battambang. Twelve were told they would "return to Phnom Penh" and ordered to disembark. The other thirty-three were taken to the abandoned central jail and put to work restoring it. Their work regime was the same as elsewhere: ten hours of daily work and the regulation ration of 70 grams [about two ounces] of rice with a sprinkle of salt. On 20 January, some members of the original group of fifty-two were brought to the jail, "emaciated, filthy, and covered with rags . . . the ropes cutting into their flesh." Three more times the prisoners had to write their autobiographies. "Each time one of us got caught. One of my friends, a physician from Phnom Penh, admitted in the end that he had been mobilized for some months as a medical officer. He disappeared the following morning." Thirty of Nal's group remained in the jail.

Back at the wat, Van says, more groups were taken away. Nal reports others coming to the jail, then being taken away, bound. In the end forty families and eighty-three youths remained at Wat Chup. Van was finally sent to the nearby Region 5 Worksite to bring in the harvest, then dig irrigation works. This was

22. Ibid.

"Chup State Worksite." A productive site shown to Chinese and Korean visitors, Chup boasted tractors and other machinery and extended over the area occupied by four abandoned villages. Its two thousand workers were base people from other parts of Region 5 and neighboring Siemreap province (Region 106). Relatives of crk soldiers, Van says they were loyal to the Khmer Rouge, who respected them as "high-level" citizens. The thirty-two families with whom Van had left Sisophon were among the few from Phnom Penh. An exception was Hav, who had arrived in the same village a month earlier. In February, five of the other air force personnel were taken away. Their families followed a few days later. Van later heard the men had been killed.

For the first three months, the new people were given rations but kept out of the worksite's communal canteen. But when they were considered to have graduated to an appropriate level, they could eat in the canteen. There was no shortage of food. Van's village of one hundred people included the thirty-two new families and ten base families. During 1976, six children died from disease and two elderly people passed away. In mid-year, Van and his family got permission to transfer to a nearby village of five hundred. One person disappeared there in 1976, and few died. This was better than elsewhere in Battambang. "I was lucky to have been sent to the state worksite. . . . Even before I went there, homeless people were dying under trees in the market square. Some from nearby villages came to beg food from us."

Meanwhile, in March 1976 Nal's group of thirty prisoners was taken from Battambang jail to another pagoda, Wat Kandal. This was "a kind of detention and reeducation camp," offering three substantial daily meals daily. A "courteous and well-educated" cadre took charge of "completing our education." On 4 April, the thirty were "given a new pack: pants, a black jacket with a red-white checkered *krama*." They were transported west to Region 3. They were assigned to a village of 560 families, "with 1,000 organized into 4 regiments, that is, 12 battalions divided into three working teams according to age and physical stamina." In the communal kitchen, workers could "eat as much rice as you wanted," but take none away. Nal found this "life of a beast of burden" intolerable. On 16 April, he set out on a 22-day journey to escape through the jungle to Thailand.[23]

Yun, who left Takeo at the end of December 1975, went to another village in Preah Net Preah district. It was newly established and contained eighty evacuee families and forty local peasant families, all new people. Since April 1975 the peasants had faced food shortages, at times existing on rations of chaff, but they remained strong. "They had been sent out on to the plains for a week, and then allowed back." This made them deportees like the city dwellers. Yun was appointed clerk, and after taking down each family's statis-

23. Ibid.

tics, was made chief of his krom of ten families. Rations consisted of a daily can of rice. Toward the end of the year, they fell to half a can plus salt, but people could secretly fish. From October to December, fever killed many children. But Yun says there was neither starvation nor killing in 1976, with the exception of the disappearance of a Lon Nol intelligence agent. Chheng Leang, who had arrived in November 1975, was sent to a village in the same district, and found life "even harder than in Takeo," but there were few killings.[24]

Seng Horl also arrived in Preah Net Preah from Takeo in January 1976. Assigned to a village of eleven hundred, he spent three months harvesting rice along a river. One day he came upon twenty skulls in a pond and thirty in another spot. "In every pond there were skulls." He was told they were the results of "killings after victory." He knew a Lon Nol general and a Phnom Penh couple who were killed by Northwest Zone cadres in 1976.

The Region Leadership

Schoolteacher San had friends in the Khmer Rouge, with whom he had been in contact since 1973. At the end of April 1975, they called him back to Sisophon. San attended a three-day political education program with thirty students, peasants, and Lon Nol regime officials. The lecturers were Sa Rum (alias San), thirty-four, another ex-teacher who was political commissar of the Northwest Zone Division, and Hing, Secretary of Region 5. These two leaders, San says, "liked and trusted intellectuals and wanted to employ them." He says that Regions 4 and 5, headed by Khek Penn and Hing, "recruited the most intellectuals."[25]

After a week's productive work to "learn from the people," and further political education, Hing made San a statistician for the Region 5 Committee. San traveled the Region for five months compiling information on its population, production, and resources. He concluded that the base peasants had a good relationship with the local CPK: "Angkar trusted the base people, who were loyal to Angkar. They had been educated and understood the politics and theory." Hing also trusted San, employed him in Sisophon on economic and political matters, and confided in San on sensitive intra-party issues.[26] Other

---

24. Author's interviews with Nou Yun and Chheng Leang, 12 November and 11 August 1979.

25. A resident of District 42 in Region 4 agrees. Author's interview, Phnom Penh, 2 January 1986.

26. For instance, Hing secretly told San in June 1975, before Yuon's murder, that Hou Yuon had "departed from the line and had been sent by *Angkar* to a cooperative for reeducation and would come back and be a leader again after living with the people for a period." This may have been a semi-official version of the story before the murder. San later heard, again probably from Hing, that "Hou Yuon wanted to circulate money [and allow] Buddhism, and opposed the evac-

cadres, however, opposed giving such "new people" administrative tasks.[27] A member of the Region Committee named Or Vuth "hated Sihanouk" in particular. Vuth bitterly recalled the Sihanouk regime's bombing of Khmer Rouge in the Samlaut area and its poisoning of local wells to flush them out. "Nearly everyone died," Vuth told San. Political commissar Sa Rum, on the other hand, emphasized to new people that since 1970, Sihanouk had "helped Angkar." So the CPK "left him in the president's chair." The prince was a propaganda asset in the international arena, "an exception among royalty, so they don't forget him." However, Rum added, Sihanouk now "couldn't do whatever he likes" and "had to obey Angkar's line, like everyone else." The commissar described a new Cambodia that would be egalitarian, independent, and self-reliant. In the future, Sa Rum said, the people would "sell" rice to the state, which San found curious because "there was no money then." But like Khek Penn, Sa Rum seems to have anticipated the reintroduction of currency, for he said that from rice sales to the state the people "would get money to buy clothes" and other goods. It was not until 19 September 1975 that the Center was able to impose the final decision to abolish money.[28]

Dr. Oum Nal's former Phnom Penh neighbor was not only chief of the Region 5 medical service, he was also Hing's brother. He immediately introduced Dr. Nal to Hing's Region 5 Committee "as a civilian physician, honest and devoted to the people." For two months (October and November 1975), Nal was adopted by the Region Committee "as a permanent guest or rather like a boarding servant."[29] Hing, whose father was a Phnom Penh jeweller,[30] had been a member of the first class to graduate from the prestigious Yukanthor High School in the capital. He became a teacher in Phnom Penh's private, leftist-run Kambuboth high school, then joined the underground against Sihanouk in 1965–66. San says Hing had married a "pure peasant." After victory they lived with their child in Sisophon. A second child was born in mid-1976. Besides the medical chief and his wife, two more of Hing's brothers played a role in Region 5. One was an official in the Region commerce department, another a village cadre.[31]

In early December 1975, however, Dr. Nal's presence in the Region Com-

uation of the towns. The extremists regarded this as revisionism. Hou Yuon could not be spared." Hing later also told San that Vice Minister of Information Tiv Ol had been sent to a cooperative to be "tempered" before returning to his post. Author's interview with San, Paris, 29 May 1980.

27. San explained, "There were the Khmers from Hanoi, and those from Paris, and they did not get on. Even the ones from Paris were divided, between the extremists and the ultra-nationalists led by Pol Pot, and the moderates like Hou Yuon." Ibid.

28. See p. 98, above, and "Examine the Control," 19 September 1975, pp. 24–25.

29. Le Figaro, 11 February 1977.

30. Ibid.

31. Author's interview with San, Paris, 29 May 1980.

mittee headquarters was ruled "against the directives of the Angkar." Nal was transferred to Preah Net Preah with forty-four other former doctors, architects, lawyers, and technicians. San, too, was dismissed as Region statistician. "There was a political change. They no longer trusted us." San attributes this to the "illiterate veterans" who "were jealous of our capacities." That tendency had previously been overruled by the Region Committee. Why did it now predominate? Like the evacuation of the cities, and the new hostility towards Vietnam, this seems to be another case of initial Northwest Zone instincts being overruled by the CPK hierarchy. It may have accompanied the late 1975 disappearance from their positions in Battambang of Pouvong and Phan Treung. Their fate is unknown. All the intellectuals working with the Region 5 Committee were to be killed, San says. "Most of us were killed in early 1976." But like Dr. Nal, San was spared, and sent to a state worksite in Preah Net Preah, "a model worksite" where cadres were "reeducated." San found that most of the one thousand inmates were base people, wives of CPK soldiers, and local "new" peasants allowed to remain in their homes. The regime at this state worksite was one of hard, forced labor under the supervision of illiterate base people. During 1976 food rations were reasonable, ranging from one to three cans of rice. By year's end, San was allowed to transfer to a nearby cooperative, and was reunited with his wife and children.

On the basis of his inside experience, San is able to describe with some precision the execution policy in the Northwest Zone in 1975–76. The CPK hierarchy sent written instructions. "Their documents said they had to kill Lon Nol officers and agents, and those officials who resisted them. . . . They told us that they would kill the officers and agents." The CPK military performed the task. "The books I read in 1975," San continues, referring again to instructions from the Center, "talked about killing wives and children of officers as well. . . . But in Battambang, in practice, it varied from place to place. . . . Many teachers who resisted were killed in 1975. I was not, because I didn't resist." San, who saw soldiers execute a man in late 1975, concludes that killings were deliberate: "In 1975–76, they would arrest people and interrogate them in prison and then if they found nothing serious they would release them. So there were a few humanitarians in the revolution."[32] The official in charge of economics on the Region 5 Committee was Loch Chhot, a former middle school teacher. Horl had taught with him in the 1960s. On hearing that Horl had arrived in Preah Net Preah, Chhot came to ask after him. Horl, afraid of contact with Chhot, tersely replied that he could survive as a worker. Chhot left him alone. Horl agrees that "civilians, teachers, rank-and-file Lon Nol soldiers, had no problems" under the Northwest administration.

32. Ibid.

The record is mixed. In 1976, Yun worked for four months in the Region 5 carpentry unit. Ta Val, a former Phnom Penh teacher in his forties, was the Region cadre responsible for irrigation works. The size of the Region 5 chalat had tripled in a year to fifteen thousand male and female youths. Val wanted new houses for the district headquarters. Yun helped put up "nice wooden houses, with three big rooms, including a guest room." He says Val was a cruel man, who wore a pistol and "acted like a cowboy in a film." He had masses of workers build bridges, laboring "in the sun without shirts." Chheang Leang accuses Val of starving his workers on gruel and salt and forcing them to labor in the rain. If they caused him trouble, "Val would throw them off the top of the dam." Horl adds: "When he took out his gun, people died." Sam Ath, another member of the Region 5 CPK Committee, was responsible for the CPK soldiers' own worksite.[33] Leang worked under Ath for four months. "He would summon pretty girls and make love to them, and when they got pregnant, he would say that they were "children of capitalists" and "generals," former members of oppressive classes, who had been sleeping with other such people. And he would have them killed."

Chnay's group of twenty families from Takeo arrived in Sisophon in late January 1976. Loudspeakers greeted them with instructions for single people over fifteen years of age, of both sexes, to assemble and join the chalat (mobile work groups). After ten days they were taken to a worksite of two thousand four hundred men and three thousand women, nearly all from Phnom Penh, and organized into kong of one hundred and krom of 10, each led by three local villagers. This was Chup State Worksite, one of nine sites in Region 5 where Chnay would work over the next three years. Many locals who had served in the Lon Nol army worked there, along with military evacuees like Van who was already there. It was two hundred yards from Yun's village. At first the work was hard but the food adequate, and the youths talked, laughed, and sang songs while they worked. Pairs of them operated an earth-moving bucket. But after a few weeks, their supervisors began to frown upon singing and laughing. One youth was told: "Finishing your job is the only task to think about." Each person now had to carry two buckets, using a shoulder pole, to move three cubic meters of earth per day—or do without food. Rations fell, and working hours lengthened, but there was no starvation. Val supervised Chnay's kong and four others. He told them anyone attempting escape to Thailand would be shot. Val always carried his pistol, and often disregarded CPK injunctions about use of polite language. A team of ten prepared food for Val and four peasant subordinates.

In April 1976, Horl also went to work at Val's dam site. The first six weeks, he

33. Author's interviews with Srey Pich Chnay, Surin, Thailand, 5 and 15 March and 19 April 1979.

agrees with Chnay, were "not really forced labor." People worked in rows of twenty to thirty, passing along small baskets of earth. Then individuals each had to carry two baskets on a shoulder pole. However, in late May difficult individual targets were introduced: two cubic meters per day, then three, then four. Children aged twelve and up also worked at the site. Pairs of fifteen-year-olds, or three under-fifteens, had to move a cubic meter. "Some youngsters missed their parents and ran back to the village. They were arrested, tied up, and brought back to work."[34] Sruy, who went to a different village, also in Preah Net Preah, says that his village chief beat ten people to death in 1976. These included a former Lon Nol officer and his wife and child; a mentally deranged youth, killed in the forest near Sruy's house; four teachers; and an engineer. Then the executions ended, and as people adapted to the new diet, fewer died of disease.

The U.S. embassy's Cambodia watcher in Bangkok had already noted that "executions are declining in number." He reiterated this in another confidential report in September 1976: "We continue to believe that our statement remains generally accurate," though not for all Regions. (I independently and unwittingly shared this view at the time.[35]) Some refugees, the State Department expert added, reported "a new wave" of killings, but other recent escapees from the Northwest "said they knew of no executions in their villages in the past few months," and "others claim there are no executions" in their areas. "Iron discipline is still maintained," often by keeping a "little list" of "those who committed errors"—not by immediate execution as in the Southwest.[36] A few months later, the officer again cabled Washington: "Most refugee accounts continue to support the conclusion that the number of executions is now lower than during the first ten months or so after the takeover."[37]

In late October 1976, twenty-four former Lon Nol soldiers and two other "thin Cambodian males" escaped to Thailand from Sisophon district. They had left their families behind, and when asked about their fate, one remarked that he "assumed the Khmer Communists would be true to form as in the past and not harm them." The group had fled after their ten local "cooperatives" had

---

34. For Horl's account of a "July 1976" massacre by Val, which Chheng Leang places in early 1977, after the arrival of the Southwest Zone cadres in Region 5, see below, p. 238.

35. Ben Kiernan, "Social Cohesion in Revolutionary Cambodia," *Australian Outlook*, 30, 3, December 1976, pp. 371–86. For a later view and a recantation, see Kiernan, "Why's Kampuchea Gone to Pot?," *Nation Review* (Melbourne), 17 November 1978, and "Vietnam and the Governments and People of Kampuchea," *BCAS*, 11, 4, 1979, pp. 19–25; 12, 2, 1980, p. 72.

36. "Cambodia Today: Life Inside Cambodia," Extracts from an Airgram Report by an Officer of the American Embassy at Bangkok, 21 September 1976 (declassified in 1978), p. 3; "Life in Southern Cambodia," Extracts from an Airgram Report by an Officer of the American Embassy at Bangkok, 25 January 1977 (declassified in 1978), p. 5.

37. "Life in Cambodia," Extracts from an Airgram Report by an Officer of the American Embassy at Bangkok, 31 March 1977 (declassified in 1978), p.8, citing the accounts of refugees who had fled to Thailand by early January 1977.

been combined into two, each comprising seven hundred families, in mid-August. They reported that below-average rainfall, combined with "the general weakness of the population owing to malnutrition," now "particularly severe," meant that the amount of land under cultivation in 1976 was as much as 50 percent lower than in 1975.[38] Disaster loomed.

After his five-month spell in jail and in labor camps, Chnay had rejoined the chalat in August 1976, to find rations again cut by half. The work was harder, and rests very rare; only occasionally were workers allowed to go fishing after work. Some female workers stopped menstruating. Women and ethnic Chinese began to die of starvation and diseases like dysentery. In the villages, elderly people perished, but conditions were better than in the chalat. Cows, chickens, bananas, and coconuts added to the diet of the villagers. Local officials attempted to count all these assets and prevent people from eating them, but not always successfully. Children would watch out for approaching Khmer Rouge while their parents killed a chicken. Discovery would bring a reprimand.

For his part, Horl says that in 1976 many people in his area died of disease, though there was no starvation. By September the situation was still "middling." Meals remained private. "We could move around, and forage for trokuon, and easily find mussels and crabs in that season. We planted potatoes and watermelons near our houses. So there were not many deaths." However, food ran out before the harvest, and famine struck late in the year. Four hundred of the eleven hundred people in the village died in November and December 1976. He says, "There was not enough ground to bury people. Bodies piled up." Neighboring Prasath subdistrict was hit even harder. Four cooperatives of four thousand Phnom Penh families had been set up on unoccupied low-lying land. It flooded in the rainy season, leaving no land on which to grow vegetables. Horl says three thousand families were wiped out in November and December 1976. The population of one cooperative in Preah Net Preah district fell from 5,017 to only 2,982 in November.[39]

One reason for the 1976 starvation was the Center's demand for rice for its own staff and for export to China. Every day in each harvesting season, a hundred workers loaded twelve hundred to sixteen hundred tons of grain onto trains of thirty to forty wagons that headed "downriver towards Phnom

38. "Life in Sisophon District of Northwestern Cambodia," Extracts from an Airgram Report by an Officer of the American Embassy at Bangkok, 1 November 1976 (declassified in 1978), 2 pp. The refugee questioned about their families said the "usual practice, which he expected to see carried out this time, as well," was for the Khmer Rouge "to move the remaining family members out of the village to another area."

39. Author's interview with Seng Horl, 1979; François Ponchaud, "Situation interne du Kampuchéa Démocratique en 1977," report to "Cambodia Hearing," Oslo, 23 April 1978, p. 13. Reproduced in part in *Bulletin d'Information sur le Cambodge* (BISC), No. 2, May 1978, p. 8.

Penh,"[40] taking about forty thousand tons of rice per season. By late 1976, Chnay and the chalat youths were sure "everything was going wrong." But they had no idea what to expect next.

Déjà Vécu: The Second Coming of the Southwest, 1977

The Center's direct influence in the Northwest gradually increased, along with its involvement in the Thai border trade (see Chapter 4). In August 1975 the U.S. embassy in Bangkok had reported that since May, the Pailin sector (Region 1) had been the only source of "reports of the willful killing of former government officials and soldiers."[41] A second embassy report described the two hundred CPK soldiers there in early 1976: "They are the only people in the town of Pailin, except for the sector chief who has a reputation for defiling local womanhood. The KC [Khmer Communists] wear either green or black clothing, but some 50–60 percent of them reportedly have red patches either on their shoulders or breast pockets. One refugee source has heard the latter called Ieng Sary troops, and he linked them to the central government. They are said to carry out all executions, whereas the former just guard the people and are rather harmless and sympathetic."[42]

The next step was a tour of the Northwest by Ieng Sary's wife, Ieng Thirith, minister of social action, in mid-1976. Thirith claims to have gone there at "the request of Pol Pot to investigate charges of shortcomings in the health, diet, and housing of the workers." She later told a journalist what she found in the Northwest: "Conditions there were very queer. In Battambang I saw they made all the people go to the rice fields. . . . The people had no homes and they were all very ill. . . . I saw everybody in the open rice fields, in the open air and very hot sun, and many were ill with diarrhea and malaria." Could this have resulted from the Center's deportation of eight hundred thousand people to that Zone? Not at all, Thirith concluded. "Agents had got into our ranks,"

---

40. R.-P. Paringaux, "Cambodia under the Khmer Rouge," *Guardian Weekly* (London), 14 January 1979, p. 13. (This information may refer only to 1977 and 1978, since the informant also "said he worked in a rice paddy in 1976.") In a 9 March 1980 interview with S. Heder, a boat pilot who worked in the DK water transport unit from 1975 to 1978 conceded that in 1976, rice from the Northwest went to Phnom Penh "by truck and train," though the amount was "very little," and that some of it was exported to China. According to Center statistics, DK exported 50,000 tons of Northwest Zone rice in 1976. "Point de vue sur le plan quadriennal (1977–1980)," French translation of a DK document dated 22 December 1976, *People's Revolutionary Tribunal*, Phnom Penh, August 1979, Doc. No. 2.5.07.

41. "The New Cambodia: Life in the Provinces," Extracts from an Airgram Report by an Officer of the American Embassy at Bangkok, 26 August 1975 (declassified in 1978), p. 3.

42. "Life Inside Cambodia," Extracts from an Airgram Report by an Officer of the American Embassy at Bangkok, 31 March 1976 (declassified in 1978), p. 18.

namely, the Northwest Zone cpk branch. "We were not yet in full control in 1976. . . . All the power was in the hands of the [Zone and Region] governors, they were very powerful. They controlled millions of people and we, the government, *we controlled nothing* but factories."[43] This extraordinary statement recalls the Center's 1975 fear that its monopoly of political and military power failed to prevent it from becoming a "satellite" of traders.[44] So once again the Center sought more power. It turned to its loyalist base.

Savy, working near Sisophon at the end of 1976, saw the first contingent arrive. Trains brought in over two thousand Southwest Zone people to Region 5 alone. They came in "whole families," even bringing their parents. Their black uniforms indicated that they were *kasekor kumruu* (model peasants). According to Savy, "They claimed they could get twenty tons per hectare [*sic*], so they had brought their model to apply in our area." The newcomers split up into four or five families per subdistrict and spread "to every subdistrict in Region 5." In Savy's cotton-growing cooperative, the Southwesterners made a good initial impression as "real peasants." However, their arrival meant the immediate introduction of communal eating, in early 1977. They soon "quarreled with the local Region 5 officials," who began to "disappear daily, from krom and kong chiefs up." Whereas the Northwest cadres Savy knew had announced no clear policy toward Vietnam, the newcomers were very anti-Vietnamese.[45] Savy concludes, "Under the Southwest life was tougher and tighter than before. We worked day and night. Rations fell." This view is shared by most informants from Region 5 and elsewhere in the Northwest Zone.

A group of female Southwesterners, many of them aged only seventeen or eighteen, arrived in Preah Net Preah district in early 1977. They were led by *Me* ("mother") Chaem, who was about forty and who assumed a district administrative position. Chnay heard that her husband was a drunkard. In Chnay's chalat, the women were led by a local, *Neary* ("Miss") Kom, a former teacher in her thirties. She was very "sweet" to the people, unlike her followers from

43. Becker, *When the War Was Over*, pp. 246–47. Emphasis added. See also S. Heder's interview with Ta Liev, "one of the top Khmer Rouge leaders in Sa Keo," 9 March 1980. Leav claimed, "In the Northwest, Vietnamese agents like Ros Nhim [Muol Sambath] were taking rice from the cooperatives at the expense of the people and keeping it for themselves. They put it in storehouses in the towns and also hid it away to use it in the future struggle against the Center. They kept the rice away from both the Center and the people thus betraying both the people and the Center. . . . The people were starving. The people had no faith in the collective regime." But we know (n. 40, above) that the Northwest had provided rice to the Center in 1976 (though not as much as the Southwest extracted from the Northwest in 1977–78).

44. See Chapter 2, p. 62 above.

45. This is corroborated by Chheng Leang, who says his group first heard the term *khmang yuon* (Vietnamese enemy) only in 1977.

Takeo. But they were all very active, asking people about their problems and distributing medicine and clothes. Food was the biggest problem. The new women distributed much-improved rations for one month, but then gruel rations resumed and hunger set in again. The women also enquired about people's personal histories.

Meanwhile, another group of new officials arrived in helicopters from Phnom Penh. These high-ranking newcomers, in league with the Southwesterners, struck terror into the hearts of the local Khmer Rouge. The result was a vain attempt to prove their political loyalty. One visitor from Phnom Penh was Pol Pot himself. A soldier recalls hearing him telling a cpk meeting in the northwest in April 1977 of the need to "purify" the zone.[46]

Early in 1977, Chheng Leang says, Ta Val called a meeting of his dam workers. He announced they could return to their former occupations if they revealed their backgrounds. Otherwise, "you'll be in trouble, still working in the fields, as prisoners." So, Leang says, "the officials and students all fell for it." Those who said they had been workers or pedicab drivers went back to laboring on the dam. But two hundred former students of law, medicine and pedagogy were loaded onto trucks—for a year of breaking rocks, during which some died from overwork and hunger. Leang and another two hundred former Lon Nol officials, intelligence agents, soldiers, customs agents, police, doctors, and teachers were taken off in trucks to the security office.[47] In an extraordinary break, eighty of the officials staged a mass escape. They scattered. Leang fled back to his village. The political convulsions wracking the Zone kept the authorities off his track for a year. The Southwesterners had more urgent targets.

One day in April, Southwest forces ambushed and killed Ta Val as he was returning from the reservoir. They said he "collaborated with reactionaries." Horl's former friend, Region economics chief Loch Chhot, was killed in May. In June, Sam Ath, Val's former superior, was arrested and executed along with all his cadres. Their crime was said to be their oppressive and lazy behavior. The Preah Net Preah district chief, Maong, was also arrested, along with the subdistrict chief and the cooperative chiefs, militia chiefs, and kong

46. Chandler, *The Tragedy of Cambodian History*, p. 376 n. 47.
47. Seng Horl dates this incident in July 1976, rather than early 1977. Horl's account is that Val called over four hundred former teachers, students, and Phnom Penh people to a meeting, announcing that they had the freedom to speak their minds. They should bring up any criticisms, and *Angkar* would help resolve them. "Some believed him, and asked for schools to be opened, for money to be used, to help the people's livelihood, for freedom. Those who asked for these things were sent to one side. Others like me, who knew what was going on in the communist system, got up and said: "I follow Angkar's rules. I obey Angkar." We were put in another place. The first group disappeared for good. They were killed, over 200 of them."

chiefs—about ten people from each cooperative. All were replaced by South-westerners.

The Northwest Zone Division's political commissar, Sa Rum, was arrested on 20 June 1977 and taken to Tuol Sleng prison in Phnom Penh. Meanwhile, the Region 5 Secretary, Hing, "took his forces to a dam site called Kamping Puoy in Battambang and armed them to fight against the forces of the Center. But the Center found out about this plot, and the cadre from the Southwest was sent to replace him."[48] When the purge team came for him, Hing was living near Van's village. He attempted to escape and hide. But he was caught and taken to Tuol Sleng on 20 August. Another member of the Region 5 Committee and a former member both followed on 2 September.[49] None survived.

During 1977 many ordinary people were also led away by soldiers.[50] According to Chnay, former city dwellers among them were undoubtedly killed, whereas peasants were relocated. Leang also says that in 1977, four hundred people, including doctors, engineers, and a number of formerly prominent Cambodians, were taken to Sisophon; "all disappeared." In 1976–77, daily rations fell as low as a half-can of rice, less for children, and sometimes nothing for three days. Other villages went hungry as well, after being told that their rice was needed in Leang's village. But it never arrived there. "People ate lizards and geckoes." In one village, forty died of disease in a single day. "Even some of the gravediggers died on the job," Leang says. By the end of 1977, of the Region 5 chalat workforce of fifteen thousand, fewer than seven thousand remained. Women no longer menstruated.

Four cadres from Takeo and Kampot arrived in former mathematics teacher Yun's village in Preah Net Preah subdistrict in February and March 1977. They immediately demoted local the cadres, executed the district chief and a number of local troops, and instituted communal eating. Two big mess halls were built, one for each kong of one hundred families. "We were allowed to eat our fill and had strength for three or four months. Then it became tough again." A daily meal of rice and one of gruel soon became just spoonfuls of gruel. The new leaders told the villagers that nearby Rohal subdistrict was short of food and that the rice was being shipped there. But, Yun says, the people of Rohal were told the reverse. Hav, who lived there, confirms this. Like Leang, he thinks the Northwest's rice was now being shipped to China. So does San: "They said they were taking it to other villages that needed it more,

48. S. Heder's interview with Sauv Kim Hong, Khao I Dang, 28 February 1980. For further evidence of rebellion by Northwest Zone cadres, see Pin Yathay, L'Utopie Meurtrière (Paris: Laffont, 1979), pp. 317–22.

49. People's Revolutionary Tribunal, Document no. 2.5.24, "Important Culprits (Arrested from 1976 to April 9, 1978)," English translation, p. 6.

50. An exception: Sruy reports no murders in his village in 1977, after the ten in 1976.

but as far as I could see this did not happen, and those villages remained badly off."[51] Yun did not claim to know where the rice went, but he found the new work regime harder. He had to walk four kilometers to work at 5 A.M., and did not return till after dark. Whereas labor targets under the Northwest cadres had been "totally collective," a kong of twenty to twenty-five people now had to plant a hectare before they could go home each day. Three months after the Southwesterners came, they murdered a friend of Yun's and other former officials.

The Southwesterners arrived in former medic Hav's village in late 1976. In that year his krom mustered ninety-three families. The next two years were the hardest. By late 1977, a daily can of rice was shared among five people. People dropped like flies. From mid-1977, the Southwesterners began attacking Vietnam in speeches. Hav comments, "When they announced this 'struggle to the death,' we were really happy, and hoped that the Vietnamese would arrive quickly. The killings became more and more numerous, since they did not trust us. They knew we would rather go to Vietnam. . . . I saw the killings myself."

Eight women from Takeo and two from Kampot arrived in mechanic Van's village in early 1977. They also took over the nearby Chup State Worksite, dispersing the two thousand workers, mostly base people privileged by the Northwest cadres, to the cooperatives. Ten Southwest women also went to each cooperative. "At first they were very good. . . . They planted rice with the local women. They asked them all why they were skinny, and heard all that the village chiefs and militia had done wrong. . . . The people trusted them and thought they had come to help." But then food rations were cut, and there was much starvation in 1977. Late in the year, a few ex-Lon Nol soldiers in Van's village were secretly arrested, and three or four other people were taken away "to study."

Former teacher Seng Horl had a friend named Kimsean who had been jailed with Oum Nal in early 1976. Kimsean reappeared later that year at a worksite in Prasath subdistrict, joining his wife, a pharmacist, and their three children. In April 1977, Southwest forces arrived. Horl knew some of them from his time in Takeo. They purged the Northwest cadres, whom they labeled "agents of Hu Nim," Democratic Kampuchea's information minister, who had been arrested on 10 April. Horl hesitated: "The Southwest might be lax. Let's see." But the newcomers arrested Kimsean, this time with his wife and children, murdering them all as well as a female former Phnom Penh politician. Horl suspects their task had been to investigate everyone's background and report on them. They also introduced communal eating, but maintained individual work targets.

In young Teang's village in Preah Net Preah, a new cadre came from Takeo in 1977. That was also the worst year for killings. A family of urban evacuees was massacred, another person shot for stealing food. Rations fell with production. It was a low-lying area, where locals planted "floating rice." The CPK disregarded their warnings and tried to plant another variety and to build a dam. The dam burst. The crop was flooded and lost. The villagers, Teang recalls, all became "very skinny," and wandered into Regions 3 and 4 begging for food. In 1977 and 1978, many died of starvation, including all ten members of Teang's family, leaving her alone at the age of thirteen.

San's cooperative was taken over by a woman from the Southwest in mid-1977. At first conditions improved slightly, because the Southwest cadres redesigned the week, declaring every tenth day a rest day. But "we had to spend it at meetings." Other survivors make the same points. As elsewhere, the number of killings increased. San reports that the Southwest executed the local cadres, then killed their wives and children; they said this practice "avoids vengeance." Phnom Penh people were also murdered, and "even base people." The Northwest cadres had usually released prisoners who had done nothing "serious," but the Southwest cadres killed them. "No one was released" in 1977–78, San says. The late 1976 harvest had been poor, and most of it had been collected by the new authorities anyway. The food situation became very bad from early 1977, and at mid-year, "people began dying in large numbers from starvation and disease." In San's cooperative, "one to three people died every day." The CPK "had to set up a committee of four or five people to take care of the burials in our cooperative." Local palm sugar prevented the massive tolls suffered in places where "thirty people died every day." Most who died of starvation were men.

In late 1977, the new rulers dismantled San's former worksite. In the cooperative where he now worked, eating was communalized. At first there were three meal shifts for men, women, and children, then one for children and one for adults of both sexes. The Southwest cadres attempted to equalize new and base people by giving the former positions formerly reserved for base people, such as kitchen work. The day began at 5 A.M. A fifteen-minute break in mid-morning would be followed by the children's meal shift at 10 A.M., and that for adults at 11 A.M. There would be an hour's rest after lunch, then more work until 5 P.M.

In Thmar Puok district, the influence of the Southwesterners preceded their arrival. Hong Var says communal eating began there in late 1976. From June to August 1977, the local leadership was purged several times. Rations became tight. In Var's village of one thousand people, about one hundred died as a result of executions, starvation, and disease in 1977.[52] Chik, a base person

---

52. Hong Var does not specifically mention the Southwesterners. See her accounts, "Your Hands Are Not Used to Hard Work," in Ben Kiernan and Chanthou Boua, eds., *Peasants and*

in Thmar Puok, concurs: communal eating began in his village in early 1977. Poultry and draft animals were collectivized, after which "nothing progressed." In 1977–78 one or two villagers died every month. Also in 1977, the three members of the district committee were arrested and killed. The new leadership called the Vietnamese "enemies" rather than "brothers" as before. A Lon Nol officer wounded during the war, who had retired in the village, was now arrested with his family. They all disappeared. But no Southwest cadres had yet come to the village. Sixty former Lon Nol soldiers and four former teachers survived there.

They were luckier than the new people of another Thmar Puok village. According to a refugee, "They deported the new people to go and work far away: on the way, they ambushed them, then came back to tell their wives and children who had remained in the village that the ones who had departed were enemies who had infiltrated, and hidden arms and grenades. Angkar had uncovered and killed them. The wives and children were deported elsewhere." François Ponchaud adds, "All the former officials and military who had managed to survive for two years were actively sought out and executed; there are several reported cases where the wives and orphaned children were executed. 'At Phum Prasath Andèt, 118 women and children were executed.'" In July 1977, newcomers arrested the local cadres and "many base people," later explaining that they "had killed them all." Elsewhere in Thmar Puok, a refugee reported, the newcomers told the people that *Angkar Loeu* was sending the local cadres "to the Southwest Zone." They were loaded onto trucks, hands behind their backs. Some "were even put into sacks." Chhuoeun, a member of the district committee, told a crowd, "The cadres who worked like me have all been killed. I am now alone, and I do not know what will happen to me. My life is in your hands, those of the people." In September, young workers in the village of Rohal Saung "rebelled against the subdistrict chief." The district chief "came with a group of soldiers" and killed eighteen youths, a girl, and eight others. A villager recalls the population there being accused of "treason, for having wanted to restablish a regime of freedom."[53]

In Preah Net Preah, the base people also suffered from the Southwest's domination. Horl says that they had been on good terms with the Northwest Zone cadres, "who were their children and relatives." But the Southwesterners killed these local cadres, alienating the peasantry—and producing a new solidarity between new and base people. Local peasants concur. Sarun, working in the district chalat, recalls the arrival of male and female cadres from the Southwest in early 1977. "They were very tough, and began a largescale series

Politics in Kampuchea, 1942–1981, London: Zed Books, 1982, pp. 338–44; and Var Hong Ashe, *From Phnom Penh to Paradise: Escape from Cambodia,* London: Hodder and Stoughton, 1988.

53. Ponchaud, "Situation interne," pp. 6–7.

of arrests and executions." Anyone in any way connected with the Lon Nol government disappeared, including former village chiefs and schoolteachers, and people "who had been Lon Nol soldiers even just for one day." Sarun's boyhood friend from his village was arrested and killed.

The newcomers also established a strict regime of food and work. Rations were reduced further. Ten people subsisted on eight cans of rice per day. People too sick to work were not always fed. When earthworks were being raised, each worker was assigned three cubic meters to shift each day, and was only fed when this task was completed. Sometimes workers kept going until midnight, and friends came to help them.

After three years in the chalat laboring at various sites around Region 5, Sarun says, he came across no villages whose people were not mistreated. The CPK claim to help the peasant classes was just "propaganda," he says, noting that he never saw any sign of assistance for the rural people. Although he says former city people suffered a lot more and died in much greater numbers than peasants, food rations were the same for both groups who lived and worked side by side in the cooperatives, as well as those in the chalat.

In her unit of the Regional chalat, Sovanny saw no Southwest Zone cadres before early 1978, but she reports "starvation on a large scale" in 1977–78. Back in her home village, too, "in 1977 food began to be taken away" and six people died of starvation there in 1977–78. This was also because rations became more tightly controlled. Larger, "company"-sized mess halls for one hundred people replaced the ten-family krom kitchens. On the other hand, "happy" collective work also came to an end in 1977: individual daily harvesting targets now had to be completed in order to receive food. The practices of increasing collective cooking and reducing collective work were only superficially inconsistent. Both gave the authorities greater control over the population.

When the Southwest cadres arrived, "mass killings started." Before 1978, "only big people" had been killed. The new rulers executed not only the local Northwest leaders, but also "the little people, anyone," including former Lon Nol soldiers. "They killed my brother and father and mother who had been soldiers. . . . My mother's throat was cut." Sovanny's uncle, a former village clerk, and his three children were also killed. In all, thirty of the village's one hundred families were slaughtered. They were buried nearby. "After the Southwest came, . . . the villages were quiet." Unlike their predecessors, the new rulers refused to work alongside the peasants; they "just used us." Sovanny says the Southwest cadres offered the people "only their theory."[54] A refugee account from Phnom Srok district confirms "a change in *Angkar*" there too, in

54. Author's interview with Sovanny, Limoges, 8 December 1979.

August 1977. "This *Angkar* arrested the old cadres and killed them. It kills the people without discrimination, for the smallest fault."[55]
There was one continuity despite the 1977 purge of Region 5. The Northwest Zone had already found the large work units it established in 1975–76 unmanageable, and had begun to dismantle them, breaking down the cooperatives in Chik's village as well as dispersing the Regional chalat into smaller units. The new Southwestern rulers continued this trend with their abolition of the Chup State Worksite and the Preah Net Preah reeducation camp. But they also moved rapidly toward imposing the individual daily targets that had long characterized the Southwest Zone. This placed much more pressure on all workers.[56] So did their enforcement of communal cooking, reduction of rations, and proliferation of violence, trends already evident in the Southwest as well.

The Center's involvement in all this is clear from the roles of Ieng Sary, Ieng Thirith, and Pol Pot. The reports that cadres arrived by helicopter from Phnom Penh, and that the newcomers arriving from August 1977 were generally "better educated" and "better trained" than their predecessors,[57] suggest high-level preparation for the purges. There is also the Center's own documentary record. The Center *Santebal* (Special Branch) record of 242 "important culprits arrested from 1976 to 9 April 1978" shows only two Southwest Zone officials among them, and none after mid-March 1977.[58] By contrast, in the next ten months, no fewer than forty Northwest Zone officials were imprisoned in Tuol Sleng. The list excludes many other less "important" cadres and those killed or jailed in the Zone itself.

On the second anniversary of the CPK's victory, 17 April 1977, Mok addressed a meeting at Prey Nop, in Kampot province. "We must drive all the pro-Vietnamese from the revolutionary ranks," he proclaimed.[59] Northwest Zone victims of Mok's purge teams by year's end included the Zone Party branch chief of staff and a member of the staff; the political commissar of the Zone's 1st Army Division and a division command staff member; the deputy political commissar of its 2nd Division and a Division command staff member; the CPK secretaries of Regions 1, 2, 4, and 5, and consecutive secretaries of Region 7; the deputy secretary of Region 3 and consecutive deputy secre-

55. Ponchaud, "Situation interne," p. 7.
56. A partial exception was Chnay's experience in late 1977, when he was sent to clear forest for three months' training. Each worker there had to clear one-sixth of a hectare per day; if they achieved this, their rations would be increased.
57. Ponchaud, "Situation interne," p. 9. See *BISC,* No. 2, May 1978, p. 7.
58. These two were Som Chea (alias Chea Sdong), secretary of Region 25 (arrested 15 March 1977), and "Koong," "Chief of Staff of the Zone Office" (1 October 1976). *People's Revolutionary Tribunal,* Document no. 2.5.24, "Important Culprits," p. 4.
59. Ponchaud, "Situation interne," p. 10.

taries of Region 4; and five other members and two former members of Region executive committees.[60] In mid-1977, Khek Penn addressed a public meeting in the Maung district of Region 4. According to a refugee, "he told the base people that they should not abuse the city evacuees or seek revenge for old wrongs. If the new people did not know how to work, the villagers should help them learn, rather than punish them for their ignorance."[61] Word soon reached the Northwest Zone office that Penn was to be appointed a DK ambassador abroad. He was delighted. A car came from Phnom Penh to take him, his wife, and their children to the capital. On arrival there, he was delivered to Tuol Sleng. Penn's family perished with him.[62]

Consistent with the Center's continuing push for total control, its takeover was still deemed insufficient. A Center cadre involved in the purges put it this way: "In 1977 a few Southwest cadres came in to try to improve the situation but the situation was very bad. . . . And our purge of the Northwest cadres was incomplete." Some locals retained Region and district posts, whereas "others had taken to the hills . . . and attempted to gather forces to counter-attack. All this made it impossible for us to correct the situation."[63] The Center demanded nothing less than absolute power.

Rice production and distribution were the services most severely disrupted by the purges. Consecutive chiefs of the Zone Rice Hulling Service were incarcerated in June and August 1977, along with the head and deputy head of the Zone Food Store (both on 16 July) and *three* consecutive chiefs of the Zone Agriculture Committee in the second half of the year.[64] When Democratic Kampuchea's 1977–1980 Four Year Economic Plan was drawn up in July 1976, the Northwest was the only Zone for which the Center made no specific pro-

60. A list of "Northwestern Region Leadership Purges, 1977–1978" is reproduced in Jackson, *Cambodia*, p. 105–6.

61. Vickery, *Cambodia 1975–1982*, p. 106.

62. Author's interview with Heng Teav, Phnom Penh, 14 January 1986. As noted, a man who lived in Region 4 says Penn refrained from arbitrary killings and presided over reasonable living conditions in 1975–76. Penn's dismissal and murder, he says, were followed by much killing and inadequate food rations in a very productive area (author's interview, Phnom Penh, 2 January 1986). One S-21 document dates Penn's arrest at 21 June 1977, another at 22 July.

63. Ta Liev, "one of the top Khmer Rouge leaders in Sa Keo," interview with S. Heder, 9 March 1980. In 1975, Leav "escorted foreign diplomats to the Thai border" and returned to the Northwest in 1977–78. His overall view was, "In the post-1975 period, politically the best Regions were the Southwest and the West. There work was carried out relatively well, and there were relatively few traitors."

64. *People's Revolutionary Tribunal*, Document no. 2.5.24, "Important Culprits," pp. 5–8. The chief of the Northwest Zone Construction Committee was arrested on 10 August. The other nine Zone officials arrested in 1977 held positions related to production and distribution of crops and goods for export or transport out of the Zone.

vision for rations for the population. The Southwest Zone was allocated 470,000 tons "for consumption by 1.5m people" out of its anticipated 1977 production of 1.14 million tons. Other Zones were allowed different amounts for consumption. The only exception was the Northwest, which was expected to produce 1.62 million tons of rice in 1977, but which was allotted no consumption item in the Center's calculations.[65]

Even in the Southwest, as we saw in Chapter 5, the 1977 death toll was high. In the Northwest, it probably reached the tens of thousands in Region 5 alone. Looking back at 1975-76, the checkered performance of the Northwest Zone administration now seemed relatively benign, despite the massive, pressing problems it had faced. Perhaps forty thousand people had perished throughout the Zone in 1976, mostly from starvation, while violence seemed to be abating.[66] But in 1977, the toll probably exceeded one hundred thousand, as massacres escalated to the highest levels ever.

In October 1977, Phnom Penh Radio suggested this was a national phenomenon. It recommended "constantly nursing the seething hatred and blood rancor against national and class enemies" as well as "smashing and stamping out old views."[67] The survivors had another year to go.

Official Repertoires and Hidden Transcripts

In December 1976, Pol Pot complained, "Sometimes there is no active opposition; there is only silence."[68] The Center strained its ears for noisy acquiescence. It usually got sullen subservience. Angkar's antennae were omnipresent, but sometimes too far out of range to pick up the surreptitious smirks of its subjects.[69] It instead attempted to jam the cultural airwaves by broadcasting and inculcating, especially in the young, an entire new repertoire of revolutionary songs. One of the earliest in the Northwest was "Raise Dams,

---

65. See Boua, Chandler, and Kiernan, eds., *Pol Pot Plans the Future*, pp. 59–60. Table 8, "Plan for Rice Production and Capital Accumulation" for the Northwest, omits this item, though it is included in the equivalent tables for the Southwest (Table 14, p. 65); the East (Table 11, p. 62); the North (Table 17, p. 68); the West (Table 20, p. 71); and the Northeast (Table 29, p. 80); as well as "Autonomous Regions" 106 and 103, and even for the Center and Zone armed forces (pp. 74, 77, 83, 86). Also unlike the other Zones and Regions, no amount was specified for "gift to the state" from the Northwest Zone, though evidence in this chapter (n. 40) shows that under Southwest control, northwestern rice *was* sent to Phnom Penh.

66. Reports of U.S. embassy in Bangkok, p. 234, above. Nayan Chanda, "Cambodia: When the Killing Had to Stop," added, "Most observers agree that the worst excesses of the reign of terror are over. . . . Largescale executions have apparently stopped" (*FEER*, 29 October 1976, p. 20).

67. Phnom Penh Radio, 31 October 1977, FBIS, 3 November 1977, p. H2.

68. Boua, Chandler, and Kiernan, eds., *Pol Pot Plans the Future*, p. 184.

69. See James C. Scott, *Domination and the Arts of Resistance: Hidden Transcripts*, New Haven: Yale University Press, 1990.

Dig Canals," whose lyrics stated: "With water we grow rice, with rice we make war."[70]

Peasants, soldiers, and intellectuals all had their quiet ways of mocking their conditions and CPK responsibility for them. In 1978, a Siemreap peasant ditty reversed Democratic Kampuchea's claim of improving living conditions by storing water for dry season cultivation:

> Before, we cultivated the fields with the heavens and the stars, and ate rice.
> Now, we cultivate the fields with dams and canals, and eat gruel.

A shorter couplet based on this was common throughout Democratic Kampuchea.[71] During their 1977 takeover of the Northwest Zone, Southwest cadres brought new songs. For instance, "We Children Love *Angkar* Boundlessly" went as follows:

> Because of Angkar, we have a long life ahead,
> A life of great glory.
> Before the revolution, children were poor and lived lives of misery.
> Living like animals, suffering as orphans.
> The enemy abandoned all thought of us.
> We were just skin and bones, our bodies emaciated,
> We lived in anxiety.
> We slept on the ground and woke up in anxiety.
> Picking through scraps, wandering and begging for food.
> Now the glorious revolution supports us all
> Secure in health, full of strength to develop collective lives.
> With clothes to wear, not cold at night.[72]

The possibilities for irony were many. In Region 5, a base person recalls, "from late 1976 we were forbidden to sing." The reason was the villagers' tendency to make subversive readings of the lyrics of CPK songs. One song had encouraged peasants to work hard year-round, relying on their own meager resources. The peasants found this too close to the truth to refrain from ironic comment. They punned on the word "drought" to suggest that in the dry

---

70. Author's recording of songs learnt in Democratic Kampuchea by the Pel family, Toul, 4 November 1979. This particular song was taught to the Pel children in Region 4, Battambang, in 1975. For further discussion of DK songs, see John Marston, "Metaphors of the Khmer Rouge," in May Ebihara, et al., eds., *Cambodian Culture Since 1975: Homeland and Exile*, Ithaca: Cornell University Press, 1994, pp. 105–18.

71. Author's interview with Tev Savanna, Strasbourg, 31 October 1979. The shorter version goes: *tveu srae ning meek, si bae; tveu srae ning pralay, si babaur* ("cultivate the ricefields with the heavens, eat rice; cultivate the ricefields with canals, eat gruel").

72. Songs learnt by the Pel family. This song was taught to the Pel children in mid-1977 in Region 4. See also Marston, "Metaphors of the Khmer Rouge," pp. 110–11.

season, rain was replaced by sweat and tears, highlighting the small clothing ration for an inefficient new routine:

> With one pair of trousers and one scarf, never drought [or "dry"]
> Fight hard to cultivate the fields till both dry and rainy season are over.

"After that," Chik says, "we were taught songs from Phnom Penh; we were allowed to sing only those."[73] Most dealt with the themes of poverty and violence, such as these verses taught in Region 1 in 1977:

> We peasants were once very poor and miserable,
> Living in hardship, pain and suffering,
> teetering at the edge of the forests and hills

> With nothing to eat or wear in the heat and shivering cold,
> A life of tremendous suffering.
> With no medicine or anything that we need.
> At mealtimes we served our food on jungle leaves
> The hated enemy exploited us, we had no rights or freedom
> We lived in twilight under the imperialist yoke.
> The vile Lon Nol treated us barbarously for a long time.

> We resolved to follow the line of the bright revolution
> To scatter the Americans and exterminate their lackeys.
> All Kampuchea will be prosperous and glorious.[74]

A song introduced in Battambang in 1978, "The Children of the Southwest Regions," went: "We children welcome and greet the armed forces, who have been vigilant, friends, vigilant in smashing the enemy." Another, "The Motherland of Kampuchea," was more explicit:

> The American imperialists and their lackeys
> Their lackeys owe us blood as hot as fire.
> The hot and angry war ensured that Kampuchea will never forget the enmity
> Will not forget the severe oppression.
> Seize hold of guns to kill the enemy quickly.[75]

Most peasants had other concerns. A complaint in Region 5 went "Where do people work ceaselessly and not have enough to eat?"[76] An Eastern Zone

---

73. Author's interview with Chik, Strasbourg, 1 November 1979.

74. Songs written down by Ms. Thouch Phonsopheary, in an interview with the author, Nanterre, 25 November 1979. This song was taught in Region 1 of the northwest in 1977.

75. Songs learnt by the Pel family. These two songs were taught in Battambang in early 1978.

76. Author's interview with Chik, Strasbourg, 1 November 1979.

peasant remarked that food served in the communal messes consisted of *pi muk*, a pun meaning both "two courses" and "two faces." The first face, he said, was one's own, and the second was its reflection in the bottom of the aluminum bowl, so thin was the watery gruel that comprised the single course.[77]

Insiders' criticisms were naturally more political. Soldiers of the 203rd Battalion, jailed in the Western Zone in 1977, communicated their thoughts on the system to other inmates in a typical subversive couplet:

Abolish the monarchy, establish Angkar.
Abolish taxation, establish "donations."[78]

The barracks humor of new people, on the other hand, tended to be more intellectual. The very term *Angkar* (the Organization) was a subject of mockery to foreign-educated graduates returning home. In 1976, one of them recalled, "We were told Angkar was coming, and we were to go to a study session [to meet Angkar]. . . . We had never met Angkar, and we jokingly asked one another: "Is the Organization really coming, or a *representative* of the Organization?"[79]

Silence often reigned even in the ranks, among people who were happy to serve the revolution. The dead hand of authority was felt everywhere. In Phnom Penh itself, for instance, "the young combatants, ordinarily so gay when doing manual work, dared not chat in the presence of the office personnel, and the latter were careful not to engage them in conversation. The ambience was rather sad." Addressing a seminar in the capital in July 1978, Ieng Sary remarked, "We have noticed that the principal interested parties, our fraternal peasants, often dare not take the platform when a chance is offered them to speak. However, they have something to say. It is with them in mind that I have designed a new method of applying democracy." Then Ieng Sary paused. A witness says that everyone held their breath. Then Sary went on: "For a true application of democracy, I will designate those who will have to speak their minds. If they refuse to exercise this right, they will be immediately expelled."[80] Silence joined the list of prohibited acts (just as the DK Constitution's "abolition" of unemployment made unpaid labor compulsory).[81]

The Center's ears keened, of course, because of the rarity of eye contact between rulers and ruled. Survivors often explain their survival by their refusal to look their superiors in the face. Face-to-face meetings were avoided

---

77. Author's interview with a peasant in Prek Chrey, Prey Veng, 7 October 1980.
78. Author's interview with former jail inmate Moeung Sonn, Sarcelles, 25 October 1979.
79. Author's interview in Tuol, 28 October 1979. The interviewee requested anonymity.
80. Laurence Picq, *Au-delà du ciel: cinq ans chez les Khmers Rouges*, Paris: Barrault, 1984, pp. 74, 128–29.
81. See D. Chandler, "The Constitution of Democratic Kampuchea: The Semantics of Revolutionary Change," *Pacific Affairs*, Fall 1976.

by a downcast eye. People tried to remain anonymous, unchallenging subjects: The Center's policy of atomizing the population, and thus minimizing lateral social communication, drove its remnants underground or into cramped social spaces Angkar had yet to penetrate. Regrets were muttered on an oxcart, lovers arranged nighttime forest assignations, ex-monks were greeted unobtrusively in a communal mess, parents or spouses were mourned behind trees. On the other hand the CPK's success in making people labor and eat *en masse*, wear the same clothes and hairstyles, and spend nearly all leisure hours in the same supervized ways, reduced the interest in and the opportunites for privacy and personal communication. In the eyes of the rulers, the collective developed a familiar presence, but each family and individual became inscrutable. Meanwhile the terror minimized meaningful vertical communication. Angkar lost eye contact with its subjects while continuously spying on them.

On the other hand, Angkar's overweening presence seems to have denied some peasants any experience of personal space or time, to which they could withdraw and consider their verdict on Democratic Kampuchea. They thus drew no distinction between their own private and Democratic Kampuchea's official views. Asked if they had personally liked the CPK, some peasants have replied, "Of course, we had to like them, we had no choice!" Youngster Teang expressed this when she said that "the base people were very keen on the Khmer Rouge, and did whatever they were told because they were afraid of death." Material danger and threat of physical harm could impress a vulnerable psyche.

-   A Cham villager describes his experience this way: "They could beat us if they felt like it, even if we had obeyed their laws. There were no laws. If they wanted us to walk, we walked; to sit, we sat; to eat, we ate. And still they killed us. It was just that if they wanted to kill us, they would take us off and kill us."[82] An ethnic Chinese made a similar comment: "We were just like ducks, not told anything, just fed when they felt like feeding us. When told to walk, we walked; to stop, we stopped; to sit, we sat."[83] We shall now see how this culture of domination affected ethnic groups such as the Chams and the Chinese.

82. Author's interview in Kompong Trabek, Prey Veng, 16 December 1986, referring to the northwest.
83. Author's interview in Toui, France, 4 November 1979, referring to life in a Phnom Penh factory.

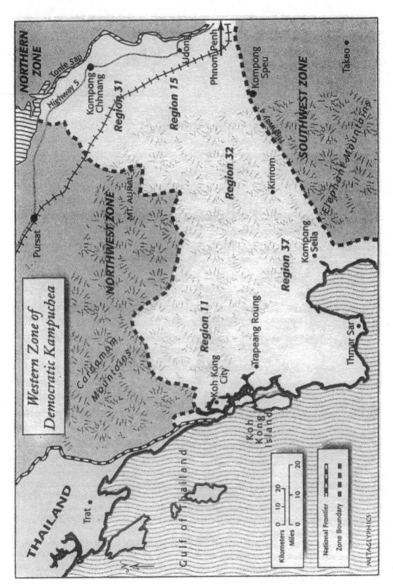

Western Zone of
Democratic Kampuchea

NORTHERN ZONE

Tonle Sap

Highway 5

Kompong
Chhnang

Region 31

Region 15

Udong

Phnom Penh

Kompong
Speu

SOUTHWEST ZONE

Takeo

Pursat

NORTHWEST ZONE

MT. AURAL

Region 32

Kirirom

Highway 4

Elephant Mountains

Cardamom
Mountains

Region 11

Region 37

Kompong
Seila

Trapeang Roung

Koh Kong
City

Thmar Sar

THAILAND

Trat

Koh Kong Island

Gulf of Thailand

Kilometers 0 10 20
Miles   0 10 20

National Frontier

Zone Boundary

METAGLYPHICS

Map 2

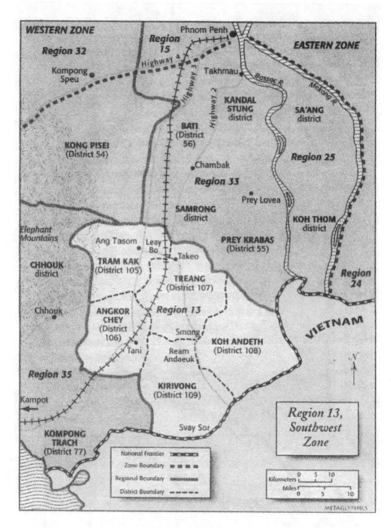

Map 3

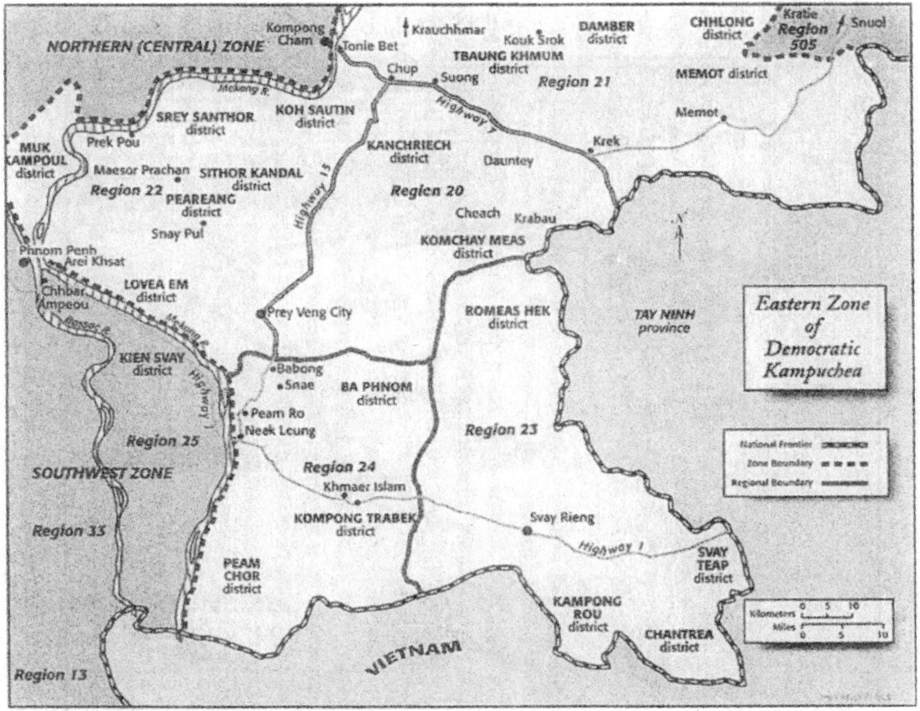

NORTHERN (CENTRAL) ZONE

MUK
KAMPOUL
district

Prek Pou

Maesor Prachan SITHOR KANDAL
district

Region 22 PEAREANG
district

SREY SANTHOR
district

Snay Pul

Mekong R.

Kampong
Cham

KOH SAUTIN
district

Tonle Bet
Chup

Krauchhmar

Highway 13

Highway 7

Suong

KANCHRIECH
district

Region 20

Daumtey

Kauk Srok

TBAUNG KHIMUM
district

Region 21

Krek

Cheach Krabau

KOMCHAY MEAS
district

CHHLONG
district

Krabie
Region
505

Snuol

MEMOT district

Memot

DAMBER
district

TAY NINH
province

ROMEAS HEK
district

Region 23

Sway Rieng

Highway 1

SWAY
TEAP
district

CHANTREA
district

KAMPONG
ROU
district

VIETNAM

Eastern Zone
of
Democratic Kampuchea

National Frontier
Zone Boundary
Regional Boundary

Kilometers 0   5   10
Miles 0   5

Prey Veng City

Babong
Snae
Peam Ro
Neak Loung

BA PHNOM
district

Khmaer Islam

KOMPONG TRABEK
district

Region 24

PEAM
CHOR
district

Phnom Penh

Chbar
Ampeou

Arei Khsat

LOVEA EM
district

KIEN SVAY
district

Mekong R.

Highway 1

Region 25

SOUTHWEST ZONE

Region 33

Region 13

Map 4

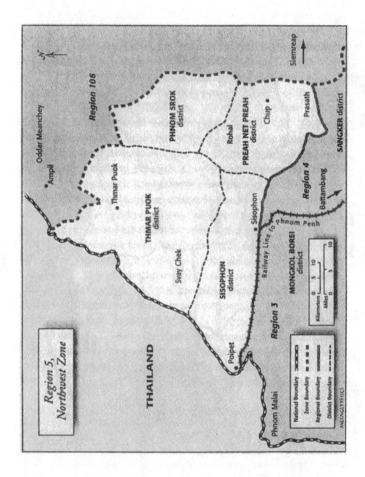

Map 5

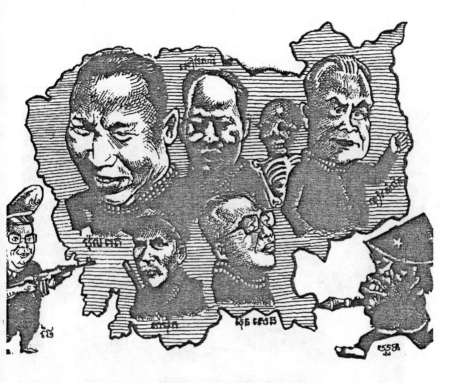

1. The CPK Center. Clockwise from top left: Pol Pot, Ieng Sary, Khieu Samphan, Son
Sen, Mok. Thais and Vietnamese patrol Cambodia's western and eastern frontiers.
Courtesy *Samleng Poirott Khmaer* newspaper, Phnom Penh, 1994.

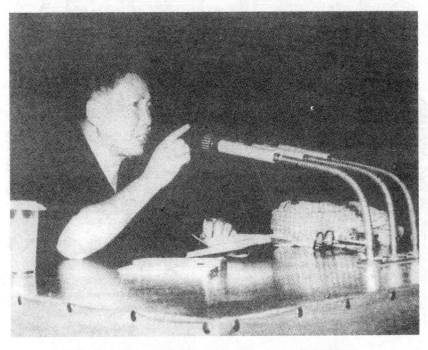

2. CPK general secretary Saloth Sar, alias Pol Pot, addressing a closed meeting in Phnom Penh after the 1975 Khmer Rouge victory. Photo courtesy Ung Pech.

3. Pol Pot (left) and CPK deputy secretary Nuon Chea (third from left) on the march after their overthrow, in western Cambodia in early 1979. Ieng Sary is eleventh from left. Photo courtesy *Far Eastern Economic Review.*

4. From left: Hou Yuon (executed 1975), Norodom Sihanouk, Son Sen. Angkor Wat, March 1973.

5. Cambodia's National Bank, dynamited by the Khmer Rouge after 1975. Author's photo, Phnom Penh, 1980.

6. A MiG fighter plane, part of China's aid to DK. Author's photo, Phnom Penh, 1994.

7. Headquarters of Mok, cpk secretary of the Southwest Zone. Author's photo, Takeo, 1980.

8. Headquarters of Chou Chet, cpk secretary of the Western Zone (executed 1978). Author's photo, Chbal Monn, Kompong Speu, 1980.

CHAPTER SEVEN

Ethnic Cleansing:
The cpk and Cambodia's Minorities,
1975–77

During the colonial period, French ethnologists churned out studies of Cambodia's small exotic tribal communities. They practically ignored the majority Khmer. Independence reversed this problem: now the minority cultures were neglected. The hill tribes officially became "Upper Khmers" (*Khmer Loeu*), while Muslim Chams became "Islamic Khmers." Like the Thai and Lao minorities, these groups were not counted separately in the 1962 census, the only one conducted in postwar Cambodia, sparking controversy over their numbers.[1] Cambodia's Chinese are better known.[2] But the Vietnamese community has yet to be seriously studied. The fate of all minorities in Democratic Kampuchea has been particularly neglected. The official Democratic Kampuchea view, published in 1977, was that they totaled only 1 percent of the population. "Ninety-nine percent" were allegedly Khmers.[3] Chams, Chinese, Vietnamese, Thais, Lao and twenty other groups, who comprised close to 20 percent of the population,[4] were virtually erased from history by the cpk.

Historian David Chandler overlooks the minorities too. His *Tragedy of Cambodian History* offers no descriptions or estimates of the DK death toll among ethnic groups. Chandler states that the cpk "seems to have . . . discriminated

1. Michael Vickery, "Comments on Cham Population Figures," *BCAS*, 22, 1, 1990, pp. 31–33, and Ben Kiernan, "The Genocide in Cambodia, 1975–1979," *BCAS*, 22, 2, 1990, 35–40.
2. William E. Willmott, *The Chinese in Cambodia*, Vancouver: University of British Columbia, 1967, and *The Political Structure of the Chinese in Cambodia*, London: Athlone Press, 1970.
3. *Democratic Kampuchea Is Moving Forward*, Phnom Penh, August 1977, p. 6. Contrast the more nearly correct figure, broadcast by New China News Agency in English on 28 September 1977: "There are over 20 nationalities in the country; the Khmer account for 80 percent of the population" (bbc *swb*, FE/W951/A/8, 19 October 1977). Three months later, a Chinese cabinet minister visiting Phnom Penh pointedly referred to the "people of all nationalities in our country." FBIS, Asia Pacific, 27 December 1976, p. H4.
4. Peter Kunstadter, *Southeast Asian Tribes, Minorities, and Nations*, explains that the figure for minorities, at 14 percent of Cambodia's population, is an underestimation (p. 4, n. c).

against the Chams," who were "unsympathetic to the revolution," treated Chinese "poorly," though China may have helped protect them, and "ordered the execution of ethnic Vietnamese." Yet he concludes: "By and large, the regime *discriminated against* enemies of the revolution rather than against specific ethnic or religious groups." He reveals no basis other than DK's for regarding the victims as "enemies of the revolution,"[5] and does not specify what "discrimination" meant in Democratic Kampuchea. In his biography of Pol Pot, Chandler discusses the minorities in a few sentences.[6] He rejects terms such as chauvinism and genocide, which, he says, invite "egregious" parallels with Hitler.[7] Michael Vickery does see Democratic Kampuchea as a "chauvinist" regime, at least in its final years, but largely because of its anti-Vietnam foreign policy. He considers the Cham in the context of the ban on religion, also rejecting the charge of genocide, even against the Vietnamese minority.[8] And in his writings on Democratic Kampuchea, Stephen Heder ignores the race issue, pointing out merely that "foreign influences and impingements were minimized."[9] We shall see how inadequate such descriptions are.

The Muslim Chams

Paul Mus called the Chams "the lost children of Indian culture."[10] Their original home, Champa, one of Southeast Asia's early Hindu-Buddhist states, was defeated by Vietnam in 1471. Five centuries later, sixty thousand Chams remained in central Vietnam.[11] But more lived in Cambodia, where

5. D. P. Chandler, *The Tragedy of Cambodian History*, pp. 263–65, 285, emphasis added. On the ethnic Vietnamese, Chandler mentions the 1975 "repatriation" of "nearly all," relegating to a later endnote a 1977 Center order for "the execution of ethnic Vietnamese residents in Cambodia" (pp. 285, 375 n. 36). Chandler's anti-Vietnamese bias appears in a 1984 analysis of Cambodia: "*Unfortunately,* the imposition of foreign control, however humiliating it is . . . does not seem to arouse emotions as intense as the possibility that 'Pol Pot' might at some stage return to power" ("Cambodia in 1984: Historical Patterns Re-asserted?," in *Southeast Asian Affairs 1985*, Singapore, 1985, p. 182, emphasis added).

6. D. P. Chandler, *Brother Number One: A Political Biography of Pol Pot*, Boulder: Westview, 1992, pp. 141 and 18, which mentions "the Cham (Vietnamese and Chinese minorities)."

7. Chandler, *Tragedy*, p. 3; *Brother Number One*, p. 4.

8. Vickery, *Cambodia 1975–1982*, pp. 255, 258, 264–65, 181–82. In a letter of 15 March 1990, Vickery wrongly suggested that "virtually all Vietnamese were expelled in 1975." Chandler agreed; see note 5, above, cf. pp. 296–98, below.

9. Stephen R. Heder, *From Pol Pot to Pen Sovan to the Villages*, Bangkok: Chulalongkorn University Center of Asian Studies, May 1980, p. 1.

10. Paul Mus, "Cultes indiens et indigènes au Champa," *Bulletin de l'Ecole Française d'Extrême-Orient (BEFEO)*, 33, 1933, pp. 367–410. English translation by I. W. Mabbett in I. W. Mabbett and D. P. Chandler, eds., *India Seen from the East: Indian and Indigenous Cults in Champa*, Monash Papers on Southeast Asia, No. 3, Melbourne, 1975 (see p. 53).

11. G. Moussay, "Coup d'oeil sur les Cam aujourd'hui," *Bulletin de la société des études Indochinoises de Saigon*, 46, 1971, p. 10. Cham literature was still "abundant" in Vietnam.

their ancestors had migrated. They had adopted Islam and intermarried with "Malays," becoming the largest "indigenous" minority in Cambodia.[12] Their fate in 1975–79 was determined largely by CPK Center perceptions of a shared premodern history of Champa and Cambodia.

The Chams were among the first in Southeast Asia to undergo Indian cultural influence.[13] A sixth-century Cham temple is the region's oldest such monument.[14] When the Chinese overran Champa in A.D. 605, they seized 1,350 works on Buddhism.[15] Cham architecture betrays Indian, Vietnamese, Chinese, Indonesian, Malay, and Khmer influences; a ninth-century Cham complex has been called "possibly the most astonishing aesthetic experience produced by Buddhism."[16] The Chams "naturalized" Indian gods, while local earth deities were Hinduized. The goddess of Nha-trang, Po Ino Nagar, slowly became identified with Uma, wife of the Hindu god Siva.[17]

Cham fleets sacked Angkor in 1178 and Hanoi in 1371. But a century later, the Vietnamese turned the tables. The Cham king was executed along with fifty thousand subjects.[18] The victors divided Champa into three principalities, and Vietnamese peasants colonized it. But Cham religion persisted, as Po Ino Nagar "reverted to her primordial condition."[19] Siva was replaced by Po Klaun Garai, a deified Cham king, and Indra survived as the god In.[20] By 1700, Islam had replaced Buddhism, as it had in much of Southeast Asia.[21]

Meanwhile, Muslim traders established themselves in Cambodia. By 1600 its capital, Lovek, had a Malay quarter. In 1642 a Khmer prince seized the throne with Malay help.[22] Muslim influence peaked when the new king converted, taking the name Ibrahim. He plunged into a holy war against the Dutch East India Company. In battles on the Mekong in 1643–44, Dutch forces lost 156 men. A thousand Khmers were killed. Ibrahim's forces captured

12. Vickery, *Cambodia 1975–1982*, p. 11.

13. Mus, *India Seen from the East*.

14. Georges Maspéro, *Le royaume du Champa*, Paris, 1928. Translation of ch. 1, Yale University, Southeast Asia Studies, 1949, p. 49.

15. Ian W. Mabbett, "Buddhism in Champa," in D. G. Marr and A. C. Milner, eds., *Southeast Asia in the Ninth to Fourteenth Centuries*, Canberra: Australian National University, 1986, p. 294.

16. Mabbett, p. 299, quoting Boisselier.

17. Mus, *India*, p. 4.

18. C. Bain, *Vietnam: Roots of Conflict*, Englewood Cliffs: Prentice-Hall, 1967, p. 66; Jean Chesneaux, *The Vietnamese Nation: Contribution to a History*, trans. Malcolm Salmon, Sydney: Current Books, 1966, p. 29.

19. Mus, *India*, pp. 36, 38.

20. Ibid., p. 51. On Po Klaung Garai, see G. E. Marrison, "The Chams of Malacca," *Journal of the Malayan Branch of the Royal Asiatic Society*, 24, 1, 1951, p. 95.

21. Pierrre-Yves Manguin, in a persuasive study, "L'Introduction de l'Islam au Champa," *BEFEO* 64, 1979, pp. 255–87, dates the Islamization of Champa at some time between 1644 and 1676.

22. Mak Phoeun, ed., *Chroniques royaux du Cambodge (de 1594 à 1677)*, Paris, EFEO, 1981, pp. 185, 342.

Dutch ships, which his Malay allies sailed into battle.[23] Ibrahim's Khmer enemies eventually overthrew him, with Vietnamese assistance. He was captured and died in Hue in 1650. But Cham influence at the Khmer court lasted until the French Protectorate began in 1863.[24] In Champa itself, nearly all the population was said to be Muslim by 1675.[25] In 1940, six thousand of the fifteen thousand Chams still in south-central Vietnam were Muslim. Po Ino Nagar was now identified as Po Havah, or Eve, wife of the prophet Adam.[26]

The "disappearance" of Champa after 1471 is a myth. In 1594 the Chams were still strong enough to help the Malay state of Johor resist Portuguese attack. Cham merchants were active in Southeast Asia until 1697, when Vietnam took over the last Cham port, but a distinct Cham territory was not directly absorbed until 1835.[27] The Vietnamese conquest of Phan Rang in 1693 sent five thousand Cham refugees (including much of Cham royalty) into Cambodia. They settled north of Phnom Penh,[28] and their descendants today form a distinct community of Chams, who still use their Indic alphabet and practice a Hinduized form of Islam.[29] But perhaps the largest Cham migration to Cambodia occurred in the late 1790s.[30] The country's oldest mosque was built north of the capital in 1813. In 1874, the first French census counted twenty-six thousand Chams, 3 percent of the Cambodian population.[31] In 1936 it was estimated there were eighty-eight thousand Chams in Cambodia, and by 1975, two hundred fifty thousand. By 1979 their numbers would under normal circumstances have reached at least two hundred sixty thousand.[32]

23. W. Buch, "La Compagnie des Indes Néerlandaises et l'Indochine," *BEFEO* 1937, pp. 219–21.

24. Marcel Ner, "Les Musulmans de l'Indochine Française," *BEFEO*, 41, 2, 1941, pp. 169, 196.

25. Manguin, p. 271.

26. Ner, p. 154; A. Cabaton, "Indochina," *Encyclopaedia of Islam*, Leiden: Brill, 1971, Vol. 3, p. 1210.

27. Manguin, p. 276–78; Po Dharma, "A Propos de l'exil d'un roi cam au Cambodge," *BEFEO*, 62, 1983, p. 254, n. 5; or, by one account, as late as 1883 during the French conquest (M. A. Jaspan, "Recent Developments among the Cham of Indochina: the Revival of Champa," *Asian Affairs* (London), vol. 1, 1970, p. 171.

28. D. G. E. Hall, *A History of Southeast Asia*, London, Macmillan, 1985, p. 462.

29. Juliette Baccot (Françoise Corrèze), *On G'nur et Cay à O Russey: syncrétisme réligieux dans un village cham du Cambodge*, Paris: Faculté des Lettres et Sciences Humaines, 1968.

30. Jean Delvert, *Le paysan cambodgien*, Paris: Mouton, 1960, p. 22. See also Po Dharma, pp. 253–266.

31. Delvert, p. 426. For the official census figure, see G. Porée and E. Maspéro, *Moeurs et coutumes des Khmers*, Paris: Payot, 1938, trans. Keith Botsford, Human Relations Area Files, 1952, p. 12.

32. The last two estimates are based on the 1936 census figure of 73,000, adjusted for error to 88,000 (Ner, pp. 179–180), and the 1955 count of adult male Chams, pointing to a growth rate of at least 2.7 percent since 1936 ("Les Khmers Islam . . . ," *Angkor*, 30 June 1956, p. 4; J. Corfield provided the reference). The minimum figure it gives for Cham adult males (females did not vote until 1958) on the 1955 Cambodian electoral roll is 29,786. This must be doubled to include Cham females over twenty-one, and then projected to include Chams

They are concentrated in about seventy villages near the banks of the Mekong and Tonle Sap in Kompong Cham province in the east and Kompong Chhnang and Pursat in the west.[33] Most practice small-scale family fishing on the rivers. But others live in thirty villages in Takeo and Kampot near the south coast. The Chams are the only substantial Muslim minority in Southeast Asia that is not regional, but rather is spread more or less throughout the host society. Muslims form a near-majority in only one district—Krauchhmar, in northern Kompong Cham. They live together in big villages, their houses clustered side by side. In the 1950s, the Chams there numbered well over twenty thousand, in "very big communities" of garden farmers, fisherfolk, butchers, foresters, and weavers.[34] Other Chams monopolized the livestock trade in the Phnom Penh area. Since Buddhism prohibits the slaughter of stock for food, Khmers often prefer to sell stock to the Chams.[35]

Cambodia's Muslims, all Sunnis, are considered "fervent." By 1940 Kompong Cham province boasted forty mosques for its thirty-three thousand Muslims, and over five hundred, or one in fifty Cham men, had made the pilgrimage to Mecca.[36] There were probably over one thousand *hajis* (pilgrims) in Cambodia in 1975.[37] Twenty-five Chams had graduated from centers of Islamic

---

of both sexes under 21. (I use the national proportion: the number on the 1958 national electoral roll was 39.16 percent of the then Cambodian population, noted in J. Delvert, *Le paysan cambodgien*, p. 305.) Thus the Cham population in Cambodia *as early as 1955* numbered around 150,000. There are no accurate subsequent estimates since Chams were not counted separately in the 1962 census. (J. Migozzi, *Cambodge: faits et problèmes de population* [Paris: CNRS, 1973] gives a figure of 150,000 for 1968, but offers no source.) Migozzi's accepted national growth rates from 1955 to 1970 (2.65 percent for 1955–60, 2.83 percent for 1960–65, and 2.95 percent for 1965–70), and a 1970–75 national growth rate of 2.46 percent (Kiernan, "The Genocide in Cambodia, 1975–1979," *BCAS*, 22, 2, 1990, p. 38), suggest a 1975 Cham population of over 248,000. Alternatively, an average 1936–75 population growth rate of 2.7 percent p.a. (Migozzi, pp. 207–12, 226, modified for the early period by Ner's contemporary research [Ner, pp. 179–80]), but of only 1 percent in 1975–78, would indicate a population of 260,000 Chams in 1979. Vickery, unaware of the 1955 Cham count, and mis-stating Migozzi's national growth rates for that period, claims that "there had never been 250,000 to begin with," but only about 191,000 in 1975. On this false statistical basis, Vickery denies that the Chams suffered genocide, asserting that the toll was closer to 20,000 than 100,000. See his "Comments on Cham Population Figures," *BCAS*, 22, 1, 1990, pp. 31–33, and my response, "The Genocide in Cambodia," *BCAS*, 22, 2, 1990.

33. Delvert, pp. 22–23. By 1975 there were 118 Muslim villages (each with a mosque) in the country, including 36 "Malay" villages in Kampot. (Author's interviews with Cham leaders Tep Ibrahim, Chrang Chamres, 10 January 1986, and Mat Ly, Phnom Penh, 29 January 1986.)

34. Delvert, pp. 605, 610–11.

35. R. Jauffret, "Possibilités de l'élevage bovin et bubalin dans les provinces du 1er secteur vétérinaire du Cambodge (Kandal-Kompong Speu-Kompong Chhnang)," *Bulletin économique de l'Indochine*, November 1939, p. 1016.

36. Delvert, p. 23; Loubet, pp. 61, 208.

37. By the 1970s, about 80 Chams went to Mecca annually. Author's interviews at Chrang Chamres, 15 September 1980.

learning; nine had completed six years of study at Al-Azhar University in Cairo. However, as Vickery notes, "Many Chams claimed before the war that they were held in contempt by the Khmer and were objects of discrimination, and ill-feeling between these two sections of Cambodian society certainly existed *in some localities*. Many Khmer regarded Chams with a mixture of awe and fear. They were believed to be accomplished in the black arts; and Phnom Penh ladies used to cross over to Chrui Changvar, a Cham community on a peninsula where the Mekong and Tonle Sap rivers meet, to get predictions about the future, love potions for husbands and lovers, and noxious prescriptions for rivals."[38]

In many localities, the relationship was closer. In one of two Cham villages near Oudong, the everyday language is Khmer. In both villages, Marcel Ner recorded in 1940, mixed marriages of Chams to Khmers, Vietnamese, or Chinese were "extremely numerous (about 10 percent)," and led to the partner's conversion to Islam. In Kampot, half the Muslims had given up their original language for Khmer, and the rest could speak Khmer fluently. Chams and Khmers there were linked by "language, lifestyle, a long shared existence and a good mutual understanding," and "only separated by religion." Ner considered Khmer-Cham relations in general "a happy symbiosis": "The Khmers get on well with them. They feel that they have brought an element of activity that the country needs, and I have never heard expression of the fears or irritation that they often display about other groups."[39]

Ner also rejected the accepted view that the Chams were "an ethnic remnant in the process of disappearance," of interest only to scholars. Ner showed how the Chams "are rapidly increasing in numbers" and would multiply faster if their high infant mortality rate was reduced. Official figures undercounted them by 20 percent. They were "very prolific."[40]

But the historiography of the Chams sighs with sympathy for their supposed extinction. A British scholar wrote in 1950, "The Chams are now but a declining remnant . . . a disappearing race," who "were once a great nation."[41] A French writer claimed they had been "one of the great powers of Indochina," but "only a few miserable relics of the race" remain. He lamented "the sad degeneracy of this fallen race."[42] Another incorrectly stated that only in Phan Rang do Chams still use their Indic script, "the only treasure that the Chams have retained from their glorious past."[43] This past, as archaeology res-

38. M. Vickery, *Cambodia 1975–1982*, p. 181. Emphasis in original.
39. Ner, pp. 169, 175, 192, 194–95.
40. Ner, pp. 179–81.
41. Marrison, pp. 90, 98.
42. Antoine Cabaton, "Chams," *Encyclopedia of Religion and Ethics*, 3, 1910, pp. 341–42.
43. Moussay, p. 10. A similar mistaken reading of Cambodian history by the Pol Pot

cued it from the clay, served merely to highlight a doomed future. In the twentieth century, Chams have suffered from two myths: the glory of their "empire" has been exaggerated, and so has their present plight. A romanticized view of Cham doom helped deprive them of rights in 1975–79. They were called "Malays" by the French,[44] and after Cambodia's independence, received a new, equally inaccurate label: "Islamic Khmers." Again their ethnic origin was denied. In the perverse sense, Chams became victims of History.

On the one hand, they were an old enemy of Vietnam, and a reminder of the Khmers' glorious kindred past. On the other, they were living omens of a looming Cambodian future, one the CPK Center set out to erase from History's agenda. Cambodia would never "disappear" the way Champa allegedly did. The reason why, in the Center's view, Chams comprised less than 1 percent of the Cambodian population was simple: "The Cham race was exterminated by the Vietnamese"![45] This appears to be Democratic Kampuchea's *only* official statement about them. It was convenient for the Center that "no" Chams should have survived the events of 1471–1697. Those who did, and in 1975 there were probably more Chams in Cambodia alone *than there had ever been in Champa*, were simply not to be recognized, even as victims. They were to "disappear" as a people.

Essentially rural, Chams rose to political prominence only in the armed forces. No Muslims were members of Cambodia's National Assembly in the 1960s. But the postwar era of liberation movements had an impact on Chams. In February and March 1965, as U.S. ground troops stormed South Vietnam, Sihanouk hosted a "Conference of the Indochinese Peoples." Communist and neutralist groups from Vietnam were invited, but so were a dozen or so shadowy committees of Chams and various other minorities. Most were sponsored by Lon Nol and "his deputy for these mysterious affairs, the colonel Les Kasem, of Cham origin." Charles Meyer continues, "Here we touch upon one of the "great political ideas," which was the unification by Cambodia of all the so-called Mon-Khmer peoples *against* the Vietnamese. The batty Lon Nol thus drew upon scientific research into the common cultural background of the Austro-Asiatic peoples, whom he of his own accord baptised 'Austrians' [*sic*], to find justification for his dream. . . . His dispatch of emissaries to the Mons in Burma and to the several thousand Chams on the coast of Annam was a fruitless fantasy."[46]

---

regime is discussed in Kiernan, "William Shawcross, Declining Cambodia," *BCAS*, 18, 1, 1986, pp. 56–63. See also Chandler, "Seeing Red: Perceptions of Cambodian History in Democratic Kampuchea," in Chandler and Kiernan, *Revolution and Its Aftermath in Kampuchea*, pp. 34–56.

44. Ner, p. 197.

45. *Livre Noir: Faits et preuves des actes d'agression et d'annexion du Vietnam contre le Kampuchéa*, Phnom Penh, September 1978, p. 6.

46. Charles Meyer, *Derrière le sourire khmer*, Paris: Plon, 1971, pp. 269–70; Jaspan, "Recent."

When Lon Nol overthrew Sihanouk in 1970, he pursued his "Mon-Khmer" cause with such publicity as to cause embarrassment to his U.S. allies. As the war spread, his armed forces grew rapidly, and Les Kasem was given command of a separate Cham battalion. In 1970–72, "it was reported to have systematically destroyed and exterminated 'Khmer Rouge' villages which they occupied. Their notoriety was such that finally the government realized they were counter-productive and the battalion was split up."[47]

Meanwhile many Chams had joined the communists. As early as 1950, a Cham elder named Sos Man had been one of the first Cambodians to join the Indochina Communist Party. For three years, Man was deputy chief of the anti-French underground "Workers Committee" of Kompong Cham. In 1953–54 he studied at the Tay Nguyen guerrilla warfare school in Vietnam's central highlands, graduating with the rank of major.[48] After the French defeat, he traveled to Hanoi and commenced political studies that took him to Moscow and, for two years, to Beijing. Sos Man returned home in 1970 and joined the Eastern Zone CPK committee. He also established the "Eastern Zone Islamic Movement," which he ran with his son Mat Ly. Man traveled the Zone encouraging Chams to "carry out the revolution."[49]

Sos Man was prestigious,[50] but unique. In other Zones, no Islamic political organizations were tolerated by the CPK leadership dominating those areas during the 1970–75 war. In fact, the Southwest Zone saw the earliest attacks on Cham culture. At first, Cham women were forced to cut their hair short in the Khmer style, rather than wear it long as was their custom; then the traditional Cham sarong was banned (along with other colorful clothing favored by Khmers). Peasants were increasingly forced to wear only black pajamas; restrictions were also placed upon religious activity. These prohibitions all began as early as mid-1972 in the Southwest,[51] on Mok's orders.

Ten Cham villages in Treang district (Region 13) were taken over by CPK forces in 1972–3. The new rulers led all the inhabitants to the mountains of Angkor Chey district, where they spent a year. Nao Gha, a Cham peasant woman from Smong village, then thirty-eight years old, went with one hundred dred village families. "They did not persecute us there. . . . Our leaders were from among us Chams. . . . They still treated us well, let us work and fend for

47. Vickery, *Cambodia 1975–1982*, p. 11.

48. See Kiernan, *How Pol Pot*, pp. 90, 125.

49. Gaffar Peang-Meth, "Islam, Another Casualty of Cambodian War," in Douc Rasy, *Khmer Representation at the United Nations*, London, 1974, p. 253; author's interviews with Mat Ly, son of Sos Man, in Phnom Penh, 13 August 1980 and 29 January 1986.

50. Peang-Meth, p. 253.

51. Kenneth Quinn, "The Khmer Krahom Program to Create a Communist Society in Southern Cambodia," airgram from U.S. Consul, Can Tho, to Department of State, 20 February 1974, pp. 23–26.

ourselves. They said good things. . . . In 1974 they sent us back home." Other Cham villagers added that the Khmer Rouge made a good initial impression. They fetched water and gathered manure. "They helped us a lot . . . like fathers and sons," one claimed.

What is significant about 1970–75 is the relocation of all the Southwest Zone Chams and of Cham populations in the Northern Zone in 1973–74 (but apparently not in the Eastern Zone). In Angkor Chey, the Southwest Zone Chams were officially called *moultanh phñoe* (depositee base people). This is the earliest known use of that term for deportees. It predates the 1975 evacuation of Phnom Penh, whose population became the archetypal deportees.[52] The Chams seem to have been the prototype. Most significant, the Southwest Zone Chams were *still* called deportees even after they had returned to their home villages in 1974. This suggests the classification was originally intended for Chams, for racial reasons rather than geographical ones. Their original classi- fication as deportee base people is another elaboration of the baroque social hierarchy that emerged in the Southwest Zone, a construction of clan and family networks. It highlights the parallel "blood" concepts of race and kin- ship in CPK ideology and practice.

In Kompong Chhnang province, of the Southwest, Khmer Rouge forces took over Chhouk Sor subdistrict in 1970. Ka Chu, a local Cham blacksmith then aged forty-five, recalls: "From 1970 to 1972 they used politics, not killing. It was good. . . . The people really believed them. They wanted freedom, hap- piness, and food. . . . The Khmer Rouge said that if we don't struggle, our reli- gion and nation will all disappear. . . . The U.S. imperialists would take our country and abolish our religion and race, turning us into American nationals. They said that if we don't struggle hard, 'be careful or you'll end up like Champa. . . . Now that you have come to live in Kampuchea, you must struggle hard. . . . Do not follow the example of Champa, which did not struggle. That is why you have no country.'"

Meanwhile, B-52s were bombing the subdistrict. In Chhouk Sor, twenty Chams were killed, and others were killed and wounded in smaller-scale air raids. It was at the height of the U.S. bombing, in June 1973, that the CPK cracked down. The local cadres were replaced, the villages evacuated. Ka Chu's group was sent thirty kilometers into the forest, where their possessions and labor were collectivized. Starvation struck, continuing in 1974 when com- munal eating began. Also in June 1973, religion was prohibited, and Cham girls had to cut their hair "like boys." At the same time came the proclamation that "all enemies" in the subdistrict had to be "smashed." The CPK called them

52. And the 1976 evacuations of Cham villages in the North and the East, whose inhab- itants were then labeled deportees (see below).

"internal enemies." As Ka Chu recalls it, "If they asked you something and you said something bad or in protest, you would disappear that day for ever."[53]

Pol Pot was based in the Northern Zone, where Ke Pauk was military commander. In April 1973, they distributed a CPK document entitled *Class Analysis and the Class Struggle*. It discussed the ruling classes and the oppressed proletariat, and went on: "All nationalities have labourers, like our Kampuchean nationality, except for Islamic Khmers, whose lives are not so difficult."[54] Such "class" analysis is really racialist. Proportionally, more Chams than Khmers were independent fisherfolk and small traders, but plenty of Chams were peasants and many were rubber plantation workers.[55] Probably, there were proportionally more Cham laborers than Khmer. But an image of the archetypal Cham, the small independent fisherman, dominated the Center's view of this entire racial group. Worse, the Chams were also, potentially, a weak link in the CPK state. With their distinct language and culture, large villages, and independent national organizational networks, the Chams probably seemed a threat to the atomized, closely supervized society that the Center planned. In Pauk's native Baray district, Os El, a local Cham peasant, reports that in August 1973 ten families were chosen for deportation from each of three Cham villages. Another local peasant, Ya El, recalls that when his pregnant daughter became ill, she was accused of malingering and killed along with her husband and four children.[56] The Chams were considered an obstacle to the establishment of cooperatives. Another CPK Northern Zone document, dated February 1974, records *Decisions Concerning the Line on Cooperatives of the Party in Region 31:* "Concerning fraternal Islamic Khmers, delay having them join [cooperatives]; . . . organize them into mutual aid teams. . . . *However, it is necessary to break up this group* to some extent; do not allow too many of them to concentrate in one area."[57]

This is the earliest record of the Center decision to disperse the Chams. Their first rebellion against the CPK, provoked by the new cooperatives, was in Region 31. Abdul-Gaffar Peang-Meth wrote in mid-1974, "The Khmer Moslem fishermen were forced to register their catch with the Communist local cooperative and sell their catch to the cooperative at a low price. Later, the fishermen were required to buy back their fish from the cooperative at a much higher price. When on February 23, 1974, the fishermen expressed their resentment in a demonstration, the Communists tried to disperse them through

---

53. Author's interview with Ka Chu, Kompong Tralach, 5 September 1980.
54. CPK document translated into English by S. R. Heder.
55. "In 1955, of 15,000 workers in all the plantations in Cambodia, 4,247 were Cambodians and 4,021 were Islamic Khmers." Delvert, pp. 590–91.
56. Author's interviews with Os El and Ya El, Trapeang Chhouk, Baray, 15 October 1980.
57. CPK document translated by S.R. Heder. Emphasis added.

talking. When this failed, the Communists began shooting into the demonstration, killing and wounding more than 100."

These events took place on the west bank of the Mekong. Across the river in Region 21 of the Eastern Zone, the cpk line also hardened:

> Sos Man continued to practise his Moslem faith. . . . By 1973, however, Sos Man and his Communist colleagues began to preach openly about Communism, and to open political training schools and organize cooperatives. Most significantly, they began to tell the people that the Moslems devoted too much time to religious matters and not enough time to revolution. . . .
> From October 1973, the Khmer Moslems carried out demonstrations against the Communist suppression of their religious belief, through the beating of ceremonial drums in their village mosques as a sign of protest. When the Communists stressed that they would not allow prayers five times a day as the Khmer Moslems required, the invaders who had abducted only selected villagers, began to arrest the Khmer Moslems in earnest, beginning November 1973. . . . [By mid-1974] at least 300 Khmer Moslems have been arrested, a large majority of whom are from Krauchhmar district, Kompong Cham province. Most of the arrested persons were prominent Moslem villagers and religious leaders, especially Koranic teachers.[58]

The Region 21 secretary at this time was Seng Hong (alias Chan), whom Pol Pot promoted the next year to deputy Zone secretary. Sos Man's attitude toward this repression is unknown. He could have done little to oppose it. He was seventy-two years old. In September 1974, Pol Pot personally visited the East for a Zone party congress, and the Eastern Zone Islamic Movement was disbanded. Sos Man was expelled from political life and confined to a village. His dismissal coincided with the arrest, in August 1974, of seventy-one other Eastern Zone Khmer communists trained in Hanoi. Ten of them disappeared shortly thereafter.[59]

By December 1974, arrests of Cham leaders in Trea village of Krauchhmar district provoked a rebellion.[60] Casualty figures are unknown, but a Cham-dominated insurgency known emerged in Region 21, in association with local Sihanoukists and Vietnamese.[61] Nevertheless, Sos Man's son Mat Ly retained his post as a member of Tbaung Khmum district committee; he was probably

---

58. Peang-Meth, p. 253–54.
59. Mat Ly interviews; see also Kiernan, *How Pol Pot*, pp. 386–87.
60. Mat Ly interviews.
61. See Chapter 3, p. 68, above. James Fenton, *Washington Post*, 24 November 1974, and Donald Kirk, "The Khmer Rouge: Revolutionaries or Terrorists?," unpublished paper, 1974, copy provided by its author.

the country's highest-ranking Cham by 1975. Severe restrictions on travel, trade, and the slaughter of livestock all affected the Chams, but these were often seen as merely wartime measures, and in the East as yet there was no sign of a CPK policy to disperse the Chams—that is, to destroy them as a community. Many Chams continued to support the revolution, even acting as cadres. A graduate of Al-Azhar University who lived in Tbaung Khmum after 1970 recalls that "from 1970 to 1975 life was normal. There was no persecution yet. People believed in the Khmer Rouge then. U.S. bombs fell on my village in 1971, burning it to the ground and killing several people. Some Cham villagers joined the Khmer Rouge as soldiers. . . . In 1974 suffering was imposed in some places, like Trea village. But it was not severe until Buddhism and Islam were abolished at the end of 1975."[62]

Cambodia's smallest Cham community is in Takeo village, on the Vietnamese border north of Svay Rieng (Region 23). Before 1970, thirty-two Cham families lived here with one hundred Khmer families, fishing, market gardening, and growing rice. Sen Osman, who was born in the village, studied under the *hakkem*, or community leader, Ta Los. Soon after the 1970 coup, insurgents came to the village and set up an administration. For five years, "there was no persecution, no communal economy, and no killing," Osman says. But there was war. Saigon troops, landing in helicopters, carried off women: "They kidnapped people alive from here. . . . Tanks fired on people. Many troops came through here. Some of the population fled, and as many died. . . . Most of the persecution was by the U.S. and Thieu-Ky forces."

Osman estimates that thirty Khmer villagers died in U.S. bombings, but no Chams died or disappeared in the war. By 1975 only fifty families remained in the village, over half of them Cham. The revolution appealed to them partly as a result of their ordeal. They joined *krom provas dai* (mutual aid teams) in 1973. Osman claims that until 1975, the CPK "were easy on us, not a problem." Religious and social life continued. Sos Man visited the village and met the hakkem. Osman recalls, "The Chams here believed in him."

The Eastern Zone

The 1975 Rebellions in Krauchhmar. Cambodia's largest Cham community is in Region 21, part of Kompong Cham province, east of the Mekong and north of Highway 7. Region 21 included the fertile riverbank land of Krauchhmar district, the Chup rubber plantations, and the rice lands of Suong in Tbaung Khmum district. Krauchhmar was home to perhaps thirty thousand Chams by the 1970s. Four "very big communities" hugged the east bank of the

---

62. Author's interview with Toun Ibrahim, Phnom Penh, 19 September 1980.

Mekong—at Trea, Svay Khleang, Chumnik, and Poes.[63] They came under insurgent control in 1970, when Lon Nol's regime lost control of the upriver areas, and thus their inhabitants became "base people." The Chams of this region were some of the strongest supporters of the revolution—until 1975. In *Cambodia Year Zero*, François Ponchaud reported the account of a forty-year-old Cham from Krauchhmar. Two Cham brothers in the CPK army returned home after the 1975 victory:

> One night the sons came home to visit their father and told him all their exploits—how they had killed Khmers, eaten pork, and liberated the country. "Come with us," they told him, "and follow the revolution." The old man didn't say a word but went out of the house; he came back armed with a cleaver and killed both his sons. He covered their bodies with a big cloth and then went to tell his neighbours: "Come and see the two enemies I've killed!"
>
> When he pulled back the cover his friends said, "But those are your sons!" "No, they're not," he retorted, "they are enemies to our people and our religion and so I killed them." He told his story and everybody said he had done right, and they decided to kill all the Khmer Rouge in the village. They did it that night.

The next morning, troops surrounded the village and massacred "everybody in it, with mortars, machine-guns and bayonets."[64]

In 1977, a Malaysian newspaper published accounts by three Cham refugees naming thirteen Islamic dignitaries killed in a Krauchhmar village in mid-June 1975. Three were said to have been executed for leading prayers instead of attending a CPK meeting, the other ten for presenting a petition for marriage ceremonies.[65] The first inside information came in 1978 from Vietnam, where a former Democratic Kampuchea soldier from Tbaung Khmum District claimed five hundred people had been "exterminated" in a riverbank village.[66] Mat Ly, from the Tbaung Khmum CPK committee, identified the place as Koh Phol (Productive Island), a Mekong Cham community of 350 families, in Rokar Khnaor subdistrict. In June or July 1975, Ly asserts, the Krauchhmar authorities attempted to collect all copies of the Koran there, and obliged Cham girls to cut their hair. When villagers staged a protest, troops fired into the crowd. Chams slaughtered half a dozen soldiers with swords and

63. Delvert, p. 605.
64. François Ponchaud, *Cambodia Year Zero*, London: Allen Lane, 1978, pp. 153–54.
65. *Islamic Herald* (Malaysia), vol. 3, no. 6-7, Oct.-Nov. 1977, pp. 8–14, cited in *Bulletin d'information sur le Cambodge* (Paris), no. 5, Oct.-Nov. 1978, p. 8. The village where they were killed was "Deras" (Trea?).
66. Xat Xon, age 23, interview published in *Kampuchea Dossier*, I, Hanoi, 1978, p. 33.

knives, but reinforcements came, massacred many Chams, and pillaged their homes. A few villagers escaped by swimming the Mekong, and some got safely to Vietnam. But troops evacuated the island, razed the village, and changed its name to Koh Phes (Island of Ashes), Mat Ly says. A week later, in nearby Svay Khleang, villagers with machetes killed a CPK officer and two soldiers. Troops then massacred 70 percent of the villagers.[67]

Deportees taken south to Tbaung Khmum told Sop Khatidjah, a forty-nine-year-old Cham evacuee from Phnom Penh, what happened. She says, "They resisted because they were angry." These Chams were "Khmer Rouge," who had fought for the CPK anticipating "positions of power after victory." When they won, however, "they were disarmed, their religion was abolished [, and] they now had to eat collectively." Party squads arrested "the learned religious people, and took them to be killed." One night Chams killed twenty-eight Khmer Rouge with knives and stakes. In the ensuing repression, Cham casualties were much higher. "Early in the morning, the Khmer Rouge tied people up and took them away to die in the middle of the river. Maybe hundreds died, 2 or 3 boatloads were taken every day. Even the sick in their homes were put on boats and tipped into the water."[68] Kob Math, a twenty-year-old Cham base person who lived upriver, agrees that the Muslims rebelled after they learnt of the Democratic Kampuchea plans to ban their religion and language, make them eat pork, and break up Cham communities. He says about twenty Khmer Rouge and fifty Chams died in the uprising, and many other Chams were killed in reprisals.[69] Ponchaud adds that in November 1975, Chams in Trea village of Krauchhmar also rebelled: "Then the Khmer Rouge tore the village apart with B-40s and smashed the heads of any survivors with pick-handles. The corpses were thrown aside and left.

67. Author's interviews with Mat Ly, 1980. This section is mainly based on the author's twenty-nine further interviews with Chams who lived through the DK period. All were tape-recorded in Cambodian villages, mostly in 1980. Several dozen others were not taped. An additional fifty interviews were later conducted with Cham refugees by Nate Thayer (in Thailand) and Dan Dickason (in the United States). Dickason interviewed Yasya Asmath, who studied at the "basic school for Islamic scholars," in Chumnik village of Krauchhmar, until the end of 1973, when he fled to Vietnam. In 1979, Asmath returned and visited Koh Phol, which was abandoned. He heard this account from local Chams: "In 1975, the Khmer Rouge asked the Cham religious leader in that village to close the mosque and the Islamic school within one week. The people in that village were a very strong community, very strong believers, and they did not close the mosque or the school. So after a week, when the Khmer Rouge came again, there was fighting. . . . The people killed five of them. . . . The Khmer Rouge sent thousands and thousands of troops to that village, and took away all Cham Muslim families. . . . They destroyed the village completely with artillery."

68. Nate Thayer's interview with Sop Khatidjah, fifty-eight, Nong Samet, September 1984.

69. Nate Thayer's interview with Kob Math, 30, Khao-I-Dang, 5 June 1985.

They even stuck heads on pikes and exposed them along the banks of the Mekong."[70]

No eyewitness to these rebellions can be found, and the troops involved in the repression have not been identified. They were Eastern troops, but whether they were Zone-, Region-, or district-level forces is unclear. Hem Samin, a Hanoi-trained communist then a political prisoner in the Zone, blames the Zone CPK secretary, So Phim, for the first repression of local Chams: "It was he who signed the orders for Phuong to kill the Chams in Trea in 1974. He was nasty."[71] A different view, at least of the 1975 events, is offered by military commander Heng Samrin, who arrived in Prey Veng from the capital in mid-July 1975 and began to muster a 4th Eastern Zone division. He says his Zone troops did not go to Krauchhmar during the repression. "It was the Security (*santesok*) forces," he said, of the local administration: "district, subdistrict, and village."[72] Stephen Heder concurs with this: "I can as yet find no evidence for the involvement of Centre troops, of Zone-level troops of the East. . . . or of the East Zone Security Service. . . . in these incidents. It looks to me like the suppression of the Cham was handled more locally, e.g. by [Region] 21 and district-level troops and security committees."[73]

Region 21 was then headed by Seng Hong (alias Chan), who was soon promoted to Deputy Zone secretary, apparently by Pol Pot, over So Phim's candidate, in a revamp of the Zone CPK Committee. Chan was the only Eastern Zone leader to survive the Democratic Kampuchea period without rebelling.[74] After Chan's late 1975 promotion, Ouch Bun Chhoeun joined the Region 21 Party Committee. Chhoeun's 1980 account avoided mention of the 1975 violence, but admitted the "very inadequate living conditions" of the people of Krauchhmar, "the toughest area of all." Asked about the Chams, Chhoeun replied:

There was no policy of [allowing] minority nationalities. Everyone was mixed together. There was only one race—the Khmer . . . from liberation in 1975. Pol Pot was very close to the Jarai and other minorities but he scattered the Islamic race.

70. Ponchaud, p. 153.
71. Author's interview with Hem Samin, Takhmau, 28 September 1980. Samin later added, "The affair of the Cham nationals, the Moslems in the areas along the riverbank around Trea and other places, was a matter of orders from So Phim. He was a real savage." S. Heder's interview with Hem Samin, Phnom Penh, 8 July 1981. Typescript provided by Heder. Samin had been arrested in August 1974, and the killings at Trea occurred in December 1974; Samin could not have been a witness to Phim's role.
72. Author's interview with Heng Samrin, Phnom Penh, 2 December 1991.
73. Stephen Heder, personal communication, 15 April 1991.
74. See Kiernan, "Wild Chickens, Farm Chickens, and Cormorants: Kampuchea's Eastern Zone under Pol Pot," in David Chandler and Ben Kiernan, eds., *Revolution and Its Aftermath in Kampuchea*, pp. 136–211, esp. pp. 153ff.

The reason was that the Muslims had an organisation called "FULRO Champa," to defend the interests of the Muslims, led by Les Kasem, a colonel in Phnom Penh during the Lon Nol period. So Pol Pot did not trust the Muslims. After 1975, in the eyes of the state organisation there were no Muslims at all.[75]

Hun Sen, an officer of the 55th Company of Region 21's Special Forces regiment, had lost an eye on 16 April in the battle for Phnom Penh. He was still recuperating in the hospital in September 1975 when he was appointed regimental chief of staff. He immediately returned to his base in Memut district, near Vietnam. Within two days, the Region 21 chief of staff, Kun Deth, sent the regiment an early-morning order to muster and proceed to join in the repression of the Cham revolt, which had broken out the previous month. All unit commanders were ordered to report for duty in Krauchhmar, bringing their troops with 60-, 80-, and 120-mm mortars and DK-75 artillery. Hun Sen declined to leave his base on the grounds that, as regimental chief of staff, he was not a member of the regimental command. He reported back that "60 percent of my men suffered from malaria" and that, still suffering from his wounds, "I had to go back to the hospital the next day." He spent the next two months in the hospital, and his regiment did not move. As a result, he says, the repression was carried out by Krauchhmar district units, led by the CPK district secretary, a man named Pha, on orders from Region 21 secretary Chan, and his subordinates, Chhoeun and Kun Deth.[76]

A local Khmer who had worked for the revolution in Krauchhmar since 1970 confirms the 1975 repression, but claims that a "moderate" Cham cadre remained on the Krauchhmar CPK committee, like Mat Ly in Tbaung Khmum. He also describes So Phim as "a good man," but blames "some district chiefs," possibly including Pha, for "following Pol Pot's orders." The Cham district committee member, he asserts, "loved the nation and people."[77]

Whoever was responsible, the upheaval along the Mekong in 1975 was the Cham people's response, in the area where they were strongest, to the DK campaign against their religion, including the assassination of their leadership. Heng Samrin, for his part, is in no doubt as to ultimate responsibility. He had heard Pol Pot proclaim the abolition of religion in May 1975. And, he added, it was Pol Pot who gave instructions "to force the Cham people" to

75. Author's interview with Ouch Bun Chhoeun, Phnom Penh, 30 September 1980.

76. Author's interviews with Hun Sen, Phnom Penh, 21 October 1980, and New York, 23 September 1991; and Hun Sen, "All the Cambodian People Became Hostages of War," *Wall Street Journal*, 31 March 1992.

77. Author's interview with Ieng, Koh Thom, 1 August 1980. Ieng also praises Iem, a third district committee member until 1978. "Everyone liked (Iem) in Krauchhmar, there was never any quarrel with him." Iem and the Cham were "all right, moderate."

carry out orders "just like normal Khmers." "So they forced them to eat pork, to stop believing in religion . . . [and] had them raise pigs. . . . Anyone who resisted was killed, as on the island. . . . Pol Pot said this."[78] The CIA station at the U.S. embassy in Bangkok claimed to have intercepted radio transmissions from Phnom Penh ordering the execution of Cham leaders in a village in "central Cambodia."[79] Whether or not this explains any of the violence in Krauchhmar, it suggests that the Center was directly involved in the repressions, even at the village level. The claim by Phnom Penh Radio at the height of the violence that "Islamic Khmers" were now "considered equals" and "are free for their religious duties" can be discounted.[80] In lectures to foreign ministry staff in 1976–77, Ieng Sary and his aides sometimes touched on the nationalities issue. According to a witness, "They just talked about one nationality—the Khmer. They did not mention the Chams. . . . They did talk about 'minorities,' but did not specify. . . . The Chams they did not like, because they had killed revolutionary cadres. . . . The Chams and Chinese were capitalists. They had been saying this for years."[81]

The other Region 21 district with many Chams was Tbaung Khmum. When the Center disbanded the Eastern Zone Islamic Movement in 1974, its president, Sos Man, had been confined to a house on Highway 7 there. According to Mat Ly, from 1970 to 1974 his father had enjoyed So Phim's support, but "later Phim obeyed Pol Pot and withdrew his confidence, but built a house in which Sos Man would live quietly." Man was told he was "too old" to work for the revolution. In September 1975, his son says, two strangers arrived on a motorcycle at Man's house and offered him "medicine." He took it, and died that night, at age seventy-three.[82] Like the Cham cadre in Krauchhmar, Mat Ly remained on the Tbaung Khmum committee for two years, but Ouch Bun Chhoeun, from the Region Committee, says Ly was "like a phantom—he had no freedom."[83]

In October and November 1975, religious practice was abolished in Tbaung Khmum, communal eating introduced, and Cham villages dispersed. Toun Ibrahim, a local Cham educated in Cairo in the 1960s, says the deportation of

78. Author's interview with Heng Samrin, Phnom Penh, 2 December 1991: "I had not received direct orders from Pol Pot on this since before liberation, but the people whom he ordered directly said: 'Angkar khang loeu [the high Organization] said this.'"
79. Michael Vickery, "Democratic Kampuchea : CIA to the Rescue," BCAS, 14, 4, 1982, p. 47.
80. 30 July 1975, broadcast at 6 A.M., monitored by Associated Press, Bangkok. Translation by Kuor Peng Kry. I am grateful to Denis Gray for allowing me to peruse the AP bureau files.
81. Author's interview with a woman employee of the DK foreign ministry, Montbard, 1 February 1980.
82. Mat Ly interviews, 1980, 1986.
83. Ouch Bun Chhoeun interview, 1980.

Chams from all twelve villages in Kor subdistrict showed that "Pol Pot wanted to wipe out the Cham race," though no killings had yet occurred. Twenty Cham families were moved out of Kor village, which had been entirely Cham. Five were sent to Thnong, three kilometers away, which was entirely Khmer. Ibrahim comments, "It was like a foreign country. There was no contact with people back home at all, except when we were ordered to go back for meetings." Some Khmer families from Thnong were sent to Kor and mixed with the Chams remaining there, who included two hajis, both of whom survived Democratic Kampuchea. However, most Chams from Kor village were sent across the Mekong to the Central Zone. These included nine hajis, one a former teacher of Ibrahim's, Haji Sa'e, who was killed in the Central Zone with his family. All eight other hajis evacuated from Kor also perished there, as did a relative of Ibrahim's. Chams from a neighboring subdistrict in Tbaung Khmum were sent even further away. On 1 February 1976, a local official called a meeting and invited Muslims who wished to leave Cambodia to declare themselves. Two weeks later they were loaded onto twenty-five trucks and taken to the Northwest Zone. Seven truckloads of Chams went to the hills of Pursat, the rest to Battambang.[84]

Meanwhile, in Kor subdistrict, Chams who had become village chiefs, village committee members, or team heads were all dismissed during 1976. In the middle of the year, killings began, although no particular ethnic or occupational group was singled out. At the end of 1976, Ibrahim's brother was taken away from Thnong for execution. "In late 1976 people were taken away in horse-carts. In late 1977 they were taking them away by the truckload. 1977 was the most fearful year. . . . Killings were general."

In June 1975, Sop Khatidiah had arrived in the neighboring subdistrict of Damber-Kauk Srok with her husband, two sons, two daughters, son-in-law, and grandson. Her mother and a son age sixteen had died on the fifty-day walk from Phnom Penh. As the family passed through two Cham villages in the east of Tbaung Khmum, Boeng Pruol and Chirou, locals told Khatidjah that the two mosques had been dismantled by Khmer Rouge who took over the area in 1973–74. Chirou was her mother's village: all 120 Cham families there had been dispersed, like the 280 families of Chams of a third village, Tham Tou. The hakkem from Boeng Pruol, Haji Ismael, and his wife were sent east to Damber along with Khatidjah's family and other Chams. Later they were joined by the Chams from Koh Phol, the rebellious Mekong island.

They went to a "pure Khmer" village, but at first Chams could at least practice Islam. Local officials told Khatidjah that Chams could pray privately so long as their work performance was not affected. She was put to work

84. *Bulletin d'information sur le Cambodge* (Paris), no. 5, October/November 1978, p. 8.

tending rice seedlings, in return for rations of rice. Haji Ismael was even exempted from work; because of his religious devotion he was considered "crazy" by the Khmer Rouge, who also asked his wife to stay at home to care for him. It was still possible for them to speak Cham privately, at the risk only of a "lecture" (*kosang*) if overheard; and they could wear traditional Cham clothing.

In August 1975, Khatidjah's husband and son-in-law were killed. They were arrested on the same day and taken "to study" in a nearby village. They never returned. Khatidjah says the CPK assumed they had been Lon Nol soldiers or police, because of their khaki clothing; in fact, they had left Phnom Penh wearing the khaki uniforms of the garage where they had worked as attendants. After they were taken away, Khatidjah asked her neighbors what would happen. They replied, "Don't hope, auntie. . . . They went to a stake and a hoe." Khatidjah and her daughter were widowed. They had to care for a grandson, four, a daughter of Khatidjah's age eleven, and her two sons, eight and four.

Things got worse by mid-1976. A meeting was called of all ethnic groups in the area. Party officials announced, "Now we are in 1976, we have to go by a different plan. . . . There are to be no Chams or Chinese or Vietnamese. Everyone is to join the same, single, Khmer nationality." There was to be "only one religion—Khmer religion," though Khatidjah notes the Buddhist wats were emptied and "no religion at all" was permitted. Movement between villages was banned. Speaking Cham was forbidden: "We were not allowed to use the (Cham) words *yas* ("mother") or *chik* ("father") to address our parents. We had to use the (Khmer) words *me* and *puk*." Communal eating was introduced, and the Chams had to eat the same food, "equal" to everyone else, and to help raise pigs. Cham teams rotated weekly at one piggery, Khmer teams at another. However, older Chams could refuse pork, if they did not use their reduced nutrition as a reason to work less hard. Khatidjah too could avoid pork, because her nephew was chief of her work team. But it was forbidden to teach young Chams to refuse pork. Cham women had to cut their hair. Traditional Cham clothing and funerals were banned. Khatidjah explained these policy changes as a reaction to the Koh Phol rebellion.

Khatidjah's single daughter, who was enlisted in a girls' work team, was away for months at a time. The young children she saw every few weeks. Khatidjah harvested and planted rice and tended vegetables. Food rations were lowest in 1977. At fifty-one, she had to work very hard, "carrying water thirty times each morning and thirty times each afternoon." A fellow worker, a sixty-two-year-old woman, died of exhaustion digging the ground. Khatidjah's widowed daughter was sent to cut timber in the forest. In late 1977, she was hit by a falling tree. After coughing blood for nine months, she died. The family was not even allowed to claim her body from the hospital. No executions of villagers followed the two in 1975. But once soldiers discovered

Khatidjah at prayer. "They watched me and said: 'Grandma, do you like guns or do you like praying?'" Only Haji Ismael was allowed his daily prayer.

Despite the general suppression of their culture, Chams could not attend the same meetings as Khmers, who were in turn divided into "base" and "new" people. (The deported Koh Phol Chams were no longer considered base people.) At their meetings, Khmers were told, "Don't trust Chams. They are like enemies whom we have defeated. . . . It is normal that defeated enemies will not lie still. . . . In their hearts they are still traitors to us."

Khatidjah's twenty-four-year-old son was killed in the Central Zone in 1977, along with all his in-laws. Her brother died of starvation there in the same year, and she lost several nieces and nephews in Siemreap province.

In December 1978, the Australian journalist Wilfred Burchett visited a Cambodian refugee camp in Vietnam's Tay Ninh province, in the shadow of the "Black Virgin Mountain." He found six hundred Chams there. Burchett asked Sen Mat, thirty-five, "a big, well-built Cham" who had fled in March 1978, why he had left. Mat replied that "Chams were to be exterminated" in Democratic Kampuchea. He cited the Koh Phol events, claiming "1,108" Chams had been gunned down with artillery and heavy machine guns. Eight people survived and escaped that night, after being left for dead on the spot, he said. Mat added that the Democratic Kampuchea authorities had "forced us to eat pork on rare occasions when meat was available," and also "accused us of wearing our hair long like Vietnamese, and being under Vietnamese influence." Ironically, the Democratic Kampuchea regime's preoccupation with the historical relationship between Chams and Vietnamese was provoking a new one. "Right at the frontier," Mat said, "the Vietnamese gave us everything we needed, even money to buy a forge." Burchett watched the Chams smelt shell casings and beat them into axe-heads and sickles. "Really swords into plough-shares," he commented. Towering over them was the mountain of the "Black Virgin," the Vietnamese name for the ancient Cham earth goddess, Po Ino Nagar.[85]

Regions 22, 23, and 24. In 1975 El Yusof, then forty-five, was evacuated from Phnom Penh. He made his way to Maesor Prachan in the Peareang district of Prey Veng (Region 22). Two prominent Chams also arrived in the vicinity: Imam Haji Res Los, the Grand Mufti of Cambodian Islam, and Toun Haji Srong Yusof, hakkem of the Noor Alihsan mosque north of Phnom Penh. Both dignitaries were killed in a nationwide campaign, waged from August to October

85. Wilfred Burchett kindly provided the author with the typewritten record of his interviews at Tan Chau, Tay Ninh, on 7 December 1978. On the "Black Virgin," see Thai Van Kiem, "Thien-Y-A-Na, or the Legend of Poh Nagar," *Asia*, vol. 4, 1954, p. 408, and Nguyen The Anh, "The Vietnamization of the Cham goddess Po Nagar," *Vietnam Review*, 3, 1997, pp. 193–207.

Table 1. Death Toll of Islamic Leaders in Democratic Kampuchea

Group	No. in 1975	No. of Survivors in 1979[a]
Hakkem (community leaders):	113	20
Hakkem rong (deputies):	226	25
Haji (Mecca pilgrims):	over 1,000	c. 30
Teachers at Koranic schools:	c. 300	38
Graduates of foreign Islamic institutions:	25	2
Members of the Islamic Central Organisation of Kampuchea:	(?)	1

[a]Source for Table 1: author's interviews with Cham officials in the People's Republic of Kampuchea. They gave these details for the most prominent Cham victims: Imam Haji Res Los, Cambodia's Grand Mufti, was thrown into boiling water and then struck on the head with an iron bar, at Konhom, Peam Chisor, Prey Veng, on 8 October 1975; Haji Suleiman Shoukri, the 1st Mufti, was beaten to death and thrown into a ditch, at Kahe, Prek Angchanh, Kandal, in August 1975; Haji Mat Sles Suleiman, the 2nd Mufti, was tortured and disembowelled in Battambang, on 10 August 1975; Haji Mat Ly Harun, Chairman of Cambodia's Islamic Association, died of starvation in prison at Anlong Sen, Kandal, on 25 September 1975; Haji Srong Yusof, Lecturer in Islamic Studies, was killed at Peamchor, Kandal, on 19 October 1975; Man Set, President of the Islamic Youth Association, disappeared in the DK period.

1975, to exterminate the country's Islamic leadership. In 1980 Frances Starner of *Asiaweek* interviewed Srong Yusof's widow, Soss Sar Pitah, at Noor Alihsan mosque. Starner reported, "When their father was taken away, her three eldest children—all in their twenties—and their 12 year-old brother tried to escape. But Khmer Rouge soldiers, she said, pursued and slaughtered them. Subsequently, when she saw friends taken away 'with hands tied for execution,' she fled with her remaining children into another district."[86] (See Table 1).

El Yusof had arrived in Maesor Prachan village with thirty other "new people" from Phnom Penh to join three hundred families of base people. The subdistrict chief, a part-Chinese Khmer named Eak, proclaimed, "Now we are making revolution. Everyone becomes a Khmer." This unusual definition of revolution was ominous for Chams. Nevertheless, Eak is recalled by another new arrival, Bunheang Ung, as "strict" but "sympathetic to the plight of the evacuees."[87] Yusof adds that in 1975 the CPK "used persuasion to some extent," although there were occasional killings from 1975 to 1977, mostly of new people who did something "wrong." In 1976, pressure on ordinary Chams began. Religion was banned, as was the Cham language. "They said to us: 'Chams who eat pork, and are prepared to raise and slaughter pigs, will be spared,'" implying that others would not be. Yusof dates this in early 1976, but

86. Frances Starner, "The Chams: Muslims the World Forgot," *Asiaweek*, 21 November 1980, pp. 24–25.

87. Martin Stuart-Fox and Bunheang Ung, *The Murderous Revolution : Life and Death in Pol Pot's Kampuchea*, Sydney: APCOL, 1985, p. 42.

it appears to have coincided with the introduction of communal eating. According to Ung's account, communal eating began in Maesor Prachan sub-district on 6 September 1976. Ung recounts the impact on the Chams living there. "When communal eating was introduced they were forced to eat the same as everyone else, including rice gruel sometimes containing a few morsels of pork fat. Two old [Cham] men in Maesor Prachan refused to eat with the rest of the hamlet. After a week of boycotting communal dining, the two were arrested and shot. . . . Later a Cham youth caught cooking a chicken in his home was arrested and sent to the gaol of Snaypol. Like others sent for re-education he was never seen again."

Martin Stuart-Fox writes that in this area, "repression of the Cham steadily increased during the next two years" (1977–78), as it did for other ethnic minorities. "Anyone could be arrested for using a language other than Khmer, a rule which applied even in private and which affected mostly Chinese and Chams."[88]

Four hours upstream from the Vietnamese border and the Plain of Reeds, past shores lined with groves of mango, banana, coconut, bamboo, water tamarind and sugar palm, a small village of thatch huts is strung out alongside the Trabek River, serene in the quiet, golden late afternoon sun. The mud-brown waters are almost undisturbed by the woman standing at the stern of her long narrow wooden boat and punting slowly upriver hugging the western bank. In front of each hut she passes are bamboo fish cages and timber contraptions of various kinds and sizes, pulled clear of the water or half-submerged and camouflaged with twigs. This is Khmaer Islam Village, in the Kompong Trabek district of Prey Veng, the *Khmer Rumdos* stronghold of Region 24. In 1970, over one hundred Cham families lived in this village, making a living by fishing the Trabek River. Haji Ismael, seventy, a fisherman with a wife and four children, was born in the village. He became hakkem in 1968.

Haji Ismael says Khmer Rouge first came to the village in 1971, but did not persecute or kill people before 1975. Meanwhile, the village was attacked by U.S. and Lon Nol aircraft. An August 1972 bombing raid killed seven villagers, damaged the mosque, and destroyed a hundred houses. "Then the people all ran away," Haji Ismael says. Some of their sons joined the Khmer Rouge, and many took refuge in Phnom Penh. When the cpk conquered it and won the war, the people of Khmaer Islam village returned home. Four years of deprivation and death awaited them. Haji Ismael says Chams "were persecuted even more than the majority population" in Democratic Kampuchea.[89]

88. Stuart-Fox, pp. 87, 128.
89. Author's interview with Haji Ismael, Kompong Trabek, 16 January 1986. By then there were still only 74 families in Khmaer Islam village, living in 49 households.

A December 1986 survey of thirty-three of the forty-nine Cham households in the village revealed that those surviving households, which had comprised 223 persons in 1975, lost fifty-four family members by 1979. The death toll was 24 percent; most deaths were attributed to murder by the Khmer Rouge. The thirty-three families had thirty-six of their members murdered. Further, Ismael pointed out, thirty other families left no survivors at all. An old woman, Ai Sah, seventy-three, who said she was now mentally disturbed, claimed to have lost "eighty grandchildren" in Democratic Kampuchea, including three entire families of twelve, ten, and nine members. The Democratic Kampuchea death toll in Khmaer Islam seems to have been 40 to 50 percent of its population, or about 300 out of 650. Females in 1986 made up 56 percent of the village population (207 out of 371), and over 60 percent of adults. Many were widows.

Haji Ismael notes three major features of the first several years of CPK rule: the destruction of religion, the introduction of communal eating, and the harsh work requirements. He identifies the commencement of the persecution of his people with the destruction of the partly damaged mosque and the prohibition of religious practice, in 1974–75. In 1974, dispersal of the Cham population also began. When the war ended in 1975 and the refugees from the bombing returned, a strict dispersal was immediately enforced. As Ismael tells it: "In the Pol Pot period, we Chams were not allowed to live together. We were dispersed into every village. 4 or 5 families were sent here, 4 or 5 there. . . . 10 families were sent to some villages, 3 families to others."

Nineteen seventy-five also saw the first Khmer Rouge killings of villagers. Several were executed as *s'tec sompoan* (recalcitrants) in that first year. Ismael recalls, "Once they banned religion, people gave it up. . . . There was no resistance here as in Krauchhmar and Peareang. . . . We did not dare to continue religious activity because they came and watched us, and would take us away and kill us, if we did."

Killings increased with the introduction of compulsory communal eating in 1976. Family cooking was prohibited. Several more Muslims were executed in 1976 or 1977 for stating that they would not eat pork, as many more in 1978. In all, five men and three women from the village were executed for their opposition to eating pork. Though rarely if ever served in the communal mess halls anyway, pork was opposed by Muslims on principle: "In fact we never saw pork, but it was an excuse for the Khmer Rouge to kill people who said they would not eat it." Meanwhile, everyone was required to work hard in the fields, "on only two spoons of rice per day."

From mid-1976 to mid-1977, the Center purged Region 24. The Region secretary, Suas Nau (alias Chhouk), was arrested and executed. Region 24 came under the firm control of Mok's Southwest Zone forces,[90] whom Ismael con-

90. See Ben Kiernan, "Wild Chickens," pp. 175–86.

trasts with So Phim: "In the Eastern Zone forces there were Chams, sons (of ours) who had joined after 1970, and some Chams were cadres. The Eastern Zone forces were led by So Phim. They abolished religion and established communal eating in 1976; that was harsh. But (otherwise) they were not much of a problem. . . . So Phim was not responsible for much persecution or killing. Pol Pot and the Southwest Zone were killers."[91]

An ethnic Chinese in Region 24 recalls Chams living near his village until the Southwest takeover: "They were killed in 1977, a family of eight people. I saw it. The Khmer Rouge said the Chams were not of Khmer nationality: they were an enemy nationality, because they had rebelled in 1975."[92]

April 1975 brought a smooth transition to peace in Takeo village of Region 23, Sen Osman says. However, in early 1976, the CPK banned Buddhism, closed the village Islamic school, and prohibited prayer. "They said religion is treachery, treason against the revolution, against the Leninist line, a feudal system. So it was no good, and had to be abolished." Communal eating "cooperatives" demanded hard work "day and night like torture. . . . without enough food or clothes or sleep or medicine." In the mess halls, Chams "had to eat and drink what they were not supposed to eat and drink, according to their religion." These new impositions were enforced after Region 23 also fell under the control of Southwest Zone cadres. From early 1977, Chams were "really forced" to eat pork. Res San, a local elder, takes up the story: "Pork was served to both Khmers and Chams, in the gruel. The food was poor; we couldn't eat the pork but could not find it [to remove it]. . . . Chams were 'put aside' if they did not eat it, meaning they were to be killed. . . . We were called 'protestors' and 'enemies' if we did not eat the pork. Hakkem Los was killed for refusing to eat pork."

Sen Osman describes this period as "a search for internal enemies and agents—enemies in words, enemies at work, inactive (people)": "So if you said something a little wrong like 'We are all tired,' they would take you away and kill you. Ta Los, Ta Mit, the teacher El, and all their families were taken away—nearly 30 people, one after another."

The Cham village community was quickly dispersed. From January or February 1977, "everyone" was evacuated, scattered to about six villages in the district, "say, two or three families to each village, but even they were separated from each other in those Khmer villages." The Khmer families of Takeo village were also dispersed, and people from nearby were brought in. Osman comments sadly, "So that was the end of living side by side, . . . caring for one another. It was broken off completely. There was no more trust. We were to think only of the Pol Pot line." Osman was sent to a village where "torture of

91. Author's interview with Haji Ismael, Kompong Trabek, 16 January 1986.
92. Author's interview with Ngoy Taing Heng, Caen, 6 October 1979, on Chams in Peam Chor village.

the Islamic people just kept on increasing": "They had never eaten pork. . . . Anyone who refused to eat it was called an enemy, 'a class enemy' is what they said. 'You are not shedding the customs and habits of the feudal system. This means you are resisting the revolution.'"

Res San went to a different village. In late 1977, he says, "I was accused of waiting for the Vietnamese to come, to kill cattle for them to feast on. I did not say anything." He was arrested with two Khmers and jailed for two weeks. There were no killings where San was. But sixty deported Takeo villagers disappeared in 1977–78.

Savee bin Kasim was fifteen years old when the Khmer Rouge evacuated him from Phnom Penh to the Eastern Zone, where he spent a year before being again evacuated to the Northwest Zone. In 1984, in the Nong Samet camp on the Thai border, Kasim told Nate Thayer in an interview that Cham "base people" in Democratic Kampuchea had been treated better than "new people" such as himself, "especially in the Eastern Zone."[93]

As we have seen, many Chams from Koh Phol were evacuated to the Northern Zone, or to other parts of the East. In both cases they were deprived of their status as *penh sith* (full rights) base people. In other Cham areas, such as Kompong Trabek, the population had fled to Phnom Penh during the 1970–75 war, and in Democratic Kampuchea this fact deprived them of "full rights." However, one Cham peasant woman claimed to have had "full rights" status in Region 24, and others confirmed that some Chams had. In other Zones I was unable to find Cham base people who had "full rights" status. Only from the East is there evidence that the *whole Cham group* was not deprived of such status as a matter of racial policy.

Kratie, upriver from the Eastern Zone, was known as Autonomous Region 505 and was supposedly administered directly by the Center. Two accounts suggest consistent persecution of Chams there as well. In Sambor district, the prohibition on speaking the Cham language was imposed in 1977. First and second offenses were punished with reeducation sessions, but a third meant death. The same applied to religious practice, including the rejection of pork. A Khmer who lived there comments that the CPK "wanted the Chams and Chinese to become Khmers." In 1977, Chams in Sambor openly rejected pork, knowing that this would mean eventual execution.[94] Their fate is unknown, but in Snuol district, where Chams were also forced to eat pork, a family of eight who refused to do so were all executed in 1977.[95]

93. This corresponded, Kasim said, with CPK favoritism towards peasant base people in general. Nate Thayer's interview with Savee bin Kasim, 24, Nong Samet, September 1984.
94. Author's interview with Sopheara, Phnom Penh, 23 September 1980.
95. Author's interview with Mon, Phnom Penh, 5 July 1980.

The Northern (Central) Zone

Across the Mekong from the Eastern Zone is the less densely populated North, re-named the Central Zone in 1976. It comprised northern Kompong Cham, Kompong Thom, and Preah Vihear. A relatively small number of Chams lived there, concentrated in three major areas: on the bank of the Mekong opposite the Eastern Zone, in the "red soil" plantation area of Chamcar Loeu district, and further north in the Baray district of Kompong Thom.

One Muslim leader says, "Chams died in the largest numbers in six or seven subdistricts along the Mekong's north bank in Kompong Cham. . . . Not a family survived, only one or two people."[96] In 1940, the 380 Cham households in three riverside villages of Kang Meas district had supported two Muslim schools with fifty students each.[97] Normal population growth would have brought these communities to a total of about twelve hundred families by 1975. The three villages increased to five, all in DK Region 41.[98] Most of their inhabitants were dispersed in 1975–77. From Antung Sor village, only one Cham survived, living alone under a Khmer name. Another survivor, physician Tin Yousos Abdulcoyaume, claims to have witnessed a Khmer Rouge burning five Cham children to death in Kang Meas.[99]

The neighboring riverbank district of Kompong Siem was also in Region 41. In 1940, three thousand eight hundred Chams lived in the district.[100] By 1975, the Cham population had reached two thousand families, in seven villages. "All have perished," the new PRK government claimed in 1983.[101] It has not been possible to confirm this assertion, but the one independent account available from Kompong Siem district is suggestive. In Chronieng village, twelve Khmers were killed in 1975–78, of whom eight were "new people." But in 1977 alone, thirteen families of Chams were murdered, over eighty people in all. They too were new people, and had been associated with the Lon Nol armed forces.[102]

Samah Ni, a Cham fisherman and farmer from Chrang Chamres in the northern suburbs of Phnom Penh, was evacuated from the capital in April 1975. Three of his children were killed by Khmer Rouge during the evacuation. With three brothers and sisters and his eldest son and daughter-in-law, Ni

96. Author's interview with Tep Ibrahim, 1986.
97. Ner, pp. 175–76.
98. These five villages were Antung Sor, Angkor Ban, Khsach Sor, Svay Tahen Krau, and Svay Tahen Khnong. See *The Destruction of Islam in Former Democratic Kampuchea*, Phnom Penh, 1983, p. 13.
99. *The Destruction of Islam*, pp. 13,19; Tep Ibrahim, 1986 interview.
100. Ner, p. 176.
101. *The Destruction of Islam*, p. 13. The seven villages are named there.
102. Author's interview with Nop Sophon, who lived in Chronieng village, Trean subdistrict, in the D.K. period. Phnom Penh, 18 January 1987.

made his way to Batheay in the Choeung Prey district of Region 41. He says the CPK district chief, known as "friend Sao," was a tolerant man who "never killed." Sao provided adequate rations and permitted freedom of movement in the district. Ni adds, "My father was a holy man; when he first arrived he kept praying and would not give it up. The lower-level team and section chiefs informed friend Sao that there was an old man who was still religious, a Muslim Khmer who was still praying to Allah. 'What should be done? Don't let him.' But Sao said: 'Let him do what he wants, according to his religion and custom. Don't forbid him.'" Ni claims that there had been no killings under Sao's authority in 1976, but that in January 1977 "the killings began." Sao was executed, and Ni's fourth son and three brothers and sisters were all killed in 1977.

Tes Osman, thirty-two, was born into a Cham family of Chamcar Andong village, in Chamcar Loeu district (Region 42). Khmer Rouge had taken over the village in 1970, and the five hundred Chams there had become base people. In 1975 they were dispersed. Only twenty Cham families were allowed to remain, "section leaders, militia, etc., the ignorant ones," Osman claims. These remained "base people," while the vast majority were classified as "new people," like the population of Phnom Penh, because they had now been evacuated from their homes. "Only twenty families survived to 1979."

Tep Ibrahim worked for a state import company when Phnom Penh fell in 1975. He was then thirty-four, with a wife and two children. They walked to Chamcar Loeu, and, with one hundred fifty other families of Cham evacuees, went to the large village of Speu, home of five thousand Cham base families. After two weeks, all but seventy of the families in Speu were dispersed. The mosques were closed and religion was banned. Ibrahim's family was placed in the nearby hamlet of Speu Kor. In early 1976, many Chams and Khmers from Krauchhmar district and the Eastern Zone were brought in trucks to the Chamcar Andong rubber plantations. Ibrahim saw "ready-made pits," where he believes "hundreds and hundreds" of Chams were massacred. In March and April 1976, small cooperatives were formed, which enforced collective eating: "We were no longer allowed to go looking for food (they said there was 'no time'), so we had less to eat. For the first two months there was plenty of gruel. Some people ate seven dishes in a sitting. But later there was only a couple of watery spoonfuls each. . . . We were forced to eat pork; some could not, and vomited it up."

By mid-1976, base people who had supported the revolution became disillusioned, partly because of the hard labor regime. The day began at 4:30 A.M. (or 3:30 A.M. for the strongest workers) with a ten-kilometer walk to a worksite. Working hours were from 8 A.M. to 4 P.M., and work continued at night in harvest season. The 1976 crop was good, but it was loaded onto trucks and carted away, causing much starvation in 1976–77. People subsisted on bananas and sweet potatoes. Ibrahim's two children, and his brother's two children, all died in 1977. Worse, his aunt was arrested, and her son, Ibrahim's cousin, was told by Khmer Rouge to visit his mother in the hospital. There, "they slashed his stomach and dumped him in a well"; Ibrahim says he witnessed this himself. Later the man's children were taken away too. So were half a dozen Cham cadres, including some from Speu Kor.

In early 1977, Ibrahim was working in a mobile fishing detail in Stung Trang on the Mekong, opposite Krauchhmar. A second roundup of Chams from both sides of the river began when officials "spread the rumour that Malaysia was exchanging gasoline for Chams. When we heard that, we all got together and wanted to go. . . . Trucks came and stopped by the water every day. . . . But we didn't get to the truck on time. . . . I even tried to run after the truck." Many Chams were waiting to board the trucks. Luckily, Ibrahim did not. Those who did were taken to the Chamcar Andong plantation, with local Chams: "They were told they could go to Battambang province. . . . Some were told they were being taken to Malaya in exchange for gasoline. They were taken away one night. There are none left of those who went from Speu village. . . . Two days after they had left, their scarves and shirts were brought back and distributed to children. . . . They were taken and thrown [into pits], killed off. . . . I [later] lived near Chamcar Andong. I went to cut bananas there one day. The whole district was smelling." Of the 150 Cham families who arrived in Speu in 1975, 43 decimated families survived in 1979.[103]

A political purge occurred around the end of 1976. Its leaders were Ke Pauk, the Central Zone secretary, and his younger brother-in-law Oeun, Region 42 CPK secretary. Ibrahim saw Pauk in September 1976, accompanying visitors from Beijing. He describes him as "big, fat and dark."[104] Not long after the purge began in earnest. Chea Much, a laborer in Kompong Cham City, observed the repression. He says that in late 1976, "they disbanded all the old troops and sent them home. . . . These were replaced by new troops, all very young, from the Southwest Zone. The old cadres and military leaders were

103. Peh Bun Tong, brother of the DK ambassador to China, spent 1975–78 in a neighboring cooperative of 8,000, with 100 Cham families. He offers the CPK view: At first the Chams lived in their villages, "but their big leaders were not happy with the revolution," and shot some Cham cadres. The "big property-owning Chams" resisted the revolution. "Then Angkar had to take the Cham and not allow them to live together as Chams in one place. It took them to live with us Khmer, mixed with the Khmer. . . . Angkar did not arrest them, but just separated them." He denies that Chams were forced to eat pork, asserting that at a festival in his cooperative, they refused, and so the authorities had cows slaughtered for them. Author's interview, Paris, 18 November 1979. Bun Tong lived in Sopheas, Stung Trang district, Region 42.

104. Ibrahim describes Pauk's brother-in-law Oeun as "short and fat."

accused of being traitors, 'Khmer bodies with Vietnamese minds.' These accusations began in early 1977. . . . Before 1977, the Reds only persecuted Lon Nol soldiers to a small extent; some were killed, others spared. Then after a time they took away all the soldiers, till none were left. Then the Southwest cadres came and persecuted the Chams, who only know how to be Chams, and the Khmers as well. Both groups began to disappear."[105]

There is an association between persecution of Chams and that of Khmers accused of having "Vietnamese minds." The racism is explicit in one case, introverted in the other.

Boeng subdistrict, in the Baray district of Kompong Thom (Region 43), includes three Cham villages, home to 450 Cham families. According to Os El, a local Cham peasant, thirty of them had already been sent north to Kravar subdistrict. Ya Mat, who went to work as an artisan for the CPK in Chaeung Daeung subdistrict, claims that "in 1975 there was a phrase that they used to instruct us": "There was a document saying that now, if we did not eat [pork], they would not let us 'live in the revolution.' They would abolish us (*romleay caol*). There was no Cham race or Cham country. . . . In Vietnam they had all been abolished. In Champa they had all been abolished too. We had come to live in Kampuchea, but there were (to be) no Chams, no Chinese, no nothing. People who obey . . . survive."

In October 1976, according to Os El, the three villages were evacuated thirty kilometers to the north and dispersed over four subdistricts, ten to fifteen Cham families to each village. They were mixed with base people there, but they were no longer recognized as base people themselves. They were now placed in the same category as the "new people" or "depositees" (*neak phñoe*) and called "depositee peasants" (*kasekor phñoe*) or, an intermediary category, "candidate peasants" (*kasekor triem*). No Chams were placed in the third, most-favored category, "full rights." Like urban evacuees, the Chams were explicitly denied rights. Khmers were brought to live in their evacuated villages.

Ya Los, a Cham mehanic, was deported to Bak Sna subdistrict. He says that from late 1976 on, "many people were taken away, many were beaten (to death) and there was little food." One Cham family, told they were going to "find new land" for growing rubber in Chamcar Andong, were taken by truck to the security office in Kompong Thmar, where they disappeared. Ya Los says that from 1976, Chams were obliged to eat pork: "Villagers higher up didn't have to eat pork and crab meat. . . . We ate it, and vomited it up again. They would not give us salt, or anything else, even gruel, in its place. But next morning they would use us to work again."

Ya Los recalls how things came to a head: "The district Security chief, Von,

105. Author's interview with Chea Much, Prey Totoeng, 4 August 1980.

called a meeting in 1977. . . . He said that the Chams were not to be spared. . . . In three days we were to be rounded up and got rid of, he said. I was not there, but our team chief *(protean kong)* told me about it." Another local Cham claims that the team chief even told him the reason why Chams "were not to be spared," which was to be found "in the history of the country Vietnam." Los believes the Chams were saved when, the next morning, a messenger came to take Von away and Von was executed by his superiors. Like the execution of Sao in nearby Choeung Prey, this event appears to have marked the arrival of Southwest Zone cadres. But they were no more lenient with the Chams.

In July 1977 in Kravar subdistrict, twenty families of Chams were loaded onto security trucks from Kompong Thmar and Svay Tong and driven off, never to return. Ya Mat, who had relatives among this group, pointed out that they had "eaten pork and so on, and still they were killed." Mat explained this by reference to a "1978 document" from the Center, "about the Constitution of 1975–76." He recalled that it discussed "subversion," and went on:

> It was Document No. 163, page 163 [?]. . . . It said we will not spare the Chams, because if spared they will resist, [and produce] revisionism. . . . It said that the Cham race is not to be spared because it has a history of resisting the socialist revolution, and also in the Champa period. . . . "So we undertake a policy of discarding them *(leah bong)* now." They were hand in hand with the Vietnamese, so they must all be killed off. It said that the Chams had already rebelled once, in the Eastern Zone. . . . It said we had fled persecution in our Vietnamese country, and could not be trusted. . . . The document said that "now, they must be smashed to pieces *(komtech caol)*. Whatever department they are in, they must be smashed to pieces."

Mat's account was corroborated by Os El, who claimed to have seen "Document 163" in June 1978. It belonged to Yong, El's supervisor of public works, who was based in nearby Chan Lehong (which, significantly, is Pauk's native village). El said he secretly read the document there.[106]

In 1979, 364 Cham families survived in the three villages in Boeng. One hundred and twenty Cham families had perished, villagers told me in 1980. Yasya Asmath, thirty-two, is a native of one of the three villages, Trapeang Chhouk. His father, Imam Yasya, was religious leader there in the 1960s. Asmath lived under the Khmer Rouge from 1970 to 1973, then went to Vietnam. He revisited his native village in March 1979, soon after the overthrow of Democratic Kampuchea. He found that his parents and two brothers had survived, but two other brothers had been killed (one beheaded, the other

---

106. It has not been possible to obtain a copy of this document or confirm its authenticity. But El named Yong's direct superiors as Oeun and Bin—Pauk's brother-in-law and nephew—and Poch, a Southwest Zone cadre who had arrived in early 1977.

disemboweled) by the CPK. Asmath also lost many relatives and friends. Two of the three village mosques had been destroyed, the third used as a pigsty, then a warehouse. According to the PRK report, a village dignitary, Haji Yousos Aony, had been "condemned to live and eat with pigs in a pig-sty until his death in July 1975."[107] Further north, in the Santuk district of Region 43, Vickery reports, Chams were "particular targets of execution," especially after 1976.[108]

The most remote part of the Northern Zone was Preah Vihear province (Region 103), a vast forested area on the Thai border. It had no Cham base people, but new people came in large numbers. In July 1975, 710 families were evacuated from Region 25 by boat across the country from south to north, to Samrong in Preah Vihear. They included one hundred families of Chams and sixty Chinese families. Sim Sakriya, forty-three, was one of the Chams. By 1978, only seventy-one people remained alive, including forty-five survivors of the one hundred families. Just three families of Chinese survived, but Sakriya's figures suggest that the greatest proportional toll was among Khmers. Chams were not singled out here, yet two-thirds of them perished after deportation to an inhospitable area.[109] Deportees received the most oppressive treatment irrespective of their race. Most Chams in base areas however, were, as we have seen, singled out for classification as deportees by fiat— for reasons of race, rather than geography as for other races.

Yusof, a sixty-seven-year-old trader from Takeo, was evacuated by boat to Preah Vihear in September 1975. He arrived with fifteen hundred other Cham and Khmer new people, several months after Sakriya's group, and was sent to a different district. They were split up; only four families of Chams went with Yusof, along with three hundred Khmer and Chinese. They joined about one hundred base people, supporters of the revolution. There was no ban on speaking Cham, and the local Khmer Rouge cadres were "good to us to some extent." "They were not so tough; they didn't insult us." The first year, 1976, was "still soft enough, all right"; fairly adequate rations were distributed and meals were eaten freely at home. What Yusof called "normal killings" involved "small numbers of people taken away."

In 1977, killings increased, children were taken from their parents, the rice crop was removed, and collective eating introduced. Cooking utensils were all confiscated, and people had to eat rations of "bamboo in soup, boiled with a little rice and banana" or soup made from salt, banana stalks, and tiny fish. They ate with the one spoon each person was allowed to keep. From late 1977,

107. *The Destruction of Islam*, p.10.
108. Vickery, *Cambodia 1975–1982*, p. 125, contradicting his claim that "Chams from the Northwest and North assert that they were not the object of any special attention by the authorities" (p. 182).
109. Author's interview with Sim Sakriya, Chrang Chamres, 2 January 1987.

the base people no longer favored the revolution because everyone was under-nourished, and both base and new people were being arrested. Yusof and his family survived, partly because Chams were not singled out for persecution; as in Samrong, the deplorable living conditions were shared by all races.[110]

The Southwest Zone

Four major communities of Chams in the DK stronghold, the Southwest Zone, are to be found in Takeo, in the rice lands of Treang district; in coastal Kampot; in Kandal province, on the lower Bassac River in Koh Thom district; and in the Phnom Penh area.

Takeo, Mok's home, saw the first known use of the term "depositee." The term was originally used there to distinguish Cham villagers from Khmer villagers. "Persecution began" in Takeo after April 1975, according to Nao Gha, a local Cham peasant woman. Chams and Khmers from Phnom Penh came to live in a Cham village there. Villagers were now obliged to work "night and day" on irrigation projects. Killings began; Khmers were executed for minor infractions at least every couple of months. Religion was banned. Kung Mun, then fifty-nine, recalls a CPK decree that "only production" was allowed, no "useless" festivals.

In 1976, communal eating was instituted and private gardening and for-aging forbidden in the Cham villages. Pork was served in some dishes, but the elderly people were unable to swallow it. The Cham village chief of Smong, a man named Sim, "allowed us not to eat pork," a peasant recalls. Kung Mun adds that local Cham cadres also "looked after the people." Later the same year, however, Sim was dismissed as village chief, accused of encouraging the Chams "not to eat pork." It became compulsory to eat pork. Those who refused were served only water. Several people who feared starvation attempted to flee to Vietnam. They were captured and executed. "The Khmer Rouge accused the Vietnamese of killing people whom they themselves had killed," says a peas-ant relative of the victims. The sacked Cham village chief, Sim, did manage to escape to Vietnam in 1977. (He returned home after the overthrow of Democ-ratic Kampuchea.) Other Cham cadres disappeared in 1976–77 after transfer from their posts.

In 1977, the Cham language was banned. Nao Gha recalls CPK cadres saying that now only Khmer was allowed: "There are no Vietnamese, Chinese, Javanese—only the Khmer race. Everyone is the same." Nao Gha claims that the Khmer Rouge "hated" Chams. She quotes the Treang district chief, Mok's

110. Author's interview with Yusof, Chrang Chamres, 15 September 1980. Vickery, *Cambodia 1975–1982*, p. 129, gives another example of this exceptional pattern in Preah Vihear (Region 103).

son-in-law Soeun, who told several large meetings in 1977 and 1978 that the Chams were "hopeless." Soeun went on: "They abandoned their country to others. They just shouldered their fishing nets and walked off, letting the Vietnamese take over their country." These racialist pronouncements, based on a reading of fifteenth-century events, left Nao Gha cold. She volunteered, "I don't know about that, it happened long ago. I don't know which generation it was."

Soon the CPK announced that the Chams had "to mix flesh and blood with the Khmer." They were evacuated from their homes for a second time. This time the ten Cham communities were dispersed over three subdistricts. The CPK burnt Nao Gha's village of Smong; its inhabitants were scattered among eight villages in Tralach subdistrict. Four or five families were sent to some villages, six or eight to others. Nao Gha went to Kantuot village with five Cham families. "The Pol Pot regime did not trust us. They did not let us do anything; they did not let us into their kitchens. . . . They were afraid we would poison the food or something." Popular prejudices against Chams were alive in the CPK, fueled by the more educated prejudices and policies of the Center.

All Chams were called "depositees," Nao Gha says, "even the base people." This was because they were a "minority" nationality. The Khmers were "full rights" and "candidates," she adds, presumably excepting the new people, or deportees. But Chams were classified in that group out of racial discrimination. 1977–78 was the period of greatest persecution, according to Nao Gha. Kung Mun says "all the hajis died in 1977." Five educated hajis, natives of Smong, were taken to the hills near Tani in Kampot and presumably killed there. Mun lost four relatives in 1977–78; some starved to death rather than eat pork. Nao Gha lost three brothers to starvation. In her group of five Cham families in Kantuot village, there was one death from illness, and in other villages, at least four Chams were killed for refusing to eat pork. "They were accused of being holy men in the old society," she says.

Deportations of Chams also occurred in Kampot, further south. A former peasant reports being evacuated from Kompong Som to a Cham base village called Prek Toal in 1975. "They were in charge of us, observing what we did or said wrong. . . . I couldn't say anything, we were dependent on them. . . . We were too afraid to do or say anything wrong. . . . We didn't eat what they did. When we got two cans [of rice], they got four. They were still masters of the land. . . . The Cham base people liked the Khmer Rouge." At the end of 1975, however, these Chams were deported, as in other areas after the Koh Phol uprising. "The base village officials had been hiding rice and sugar; that is why it was so hard," this man asserts. So the authorities proclaimed that the seventy families of Chams would all be "transferred" seventy-five kilometers east, across Kampot province. "They did not want to go, they were crying. They missed their land, and were not able to collect all their chickens and ducks to take with them. But they still seemed loyal. . . . The Khmer Rouge told us not to miss them." They were replaced by two hundred Khmer families, including many new people evacuated from Kampot. The fate of the 350 Chams from Prek Toal is unknown. "We were all on the same road, if we did not go along it, we would be killed."[111]

Two riverbank settlements in Koh Thom district, known as "Cham" and "Upper Cham" villages, were the homes of about five hundred Cham base families in the early 1970s. After the 1975 victory, private property was confiscated and money abolished. People worked day and night on small rations. Disaster descended around April 1976. The CPK closed the mosques, banned Islam, and prohibited Cham as a "foreign language." The two Cham communities were dispersed; some were sent to neighboring villages in the district, others to the Northwest Zone. In local mess halls, Chams were forced to eat pork. Killings for infractions of regulations reached a peak in 1977, when Khmer Rouge searched homes for gold. Half a dozen Cham families escaped to Vietnam; their relatives were persecuted.

One hundred Chams died in the district between 1976 and 1979. Over one hundred more died after being sent to the Northwest. According to a 1982 PRK study, eighty-three Koh Thom Muslim families perished in Pursat alone; the only survivor was Haji Ahmad. The father, mother, and three brothers of Math Toloh all died in Battambang. Toloh, now deputy village chief, claims that the nearby village of Po Tonle was turned into a vast torture and execution center where thirty-five thousand people were murdered, including about twenty thousand Chams.[112] These figures are probably exaggerated, but the claims of mass murder at Po Tonle are supported by Chams from Koh Thom interviewed in Thailand.[113] Local Chams also claimed that "we were persecuted much more than Khmers." In 1980, 222 families survived where there had once been 500.[114]

The former village of Prek Tapeu (Prek Pra) south of Phnom Penh near the suburb of Takhmau was the home of over three thousand Cham Muslims in 1975. In 1979, only six hundred survived, according to Hakkem Toluos Math. (The 1940 population was eight hundred.) "More than four-fifths of our fellow

111. Author's interview with Ong Nha, Kampot, 29 August 1980. For another massacre of Cham families in Kampot, see Henri Locard and Moeung Sonn, *Prisonnier de l'Angkar*, Paris: Fayard, 1993, pp. 159–60.

112. *La Communauté Islamique au Kampuchéa*, Phnom Penh, 1983, pp. 29–31. In this book the two Cham villages are called Anlong Sor Loeu and Anlong Sor Krom.

113. Nate Thayer's interviews with Mat Sman, 20, and Saleh, 21, at Nong Samet, September 10, 1984.

114. *La Communauté Islamique au Kampuchea*, p. 29. By late 1982, the population had increased from 1,060 to 1,131 people, in 234 family groups.

villagers had been cut down by the Khmer Rouge," Math said in 1983. He cited population dispersal, forced labor, exhaustion, hunger, disease, and mistreatment, including the obligation to eat pork, "as a simple method of persecution." 1978 saw the worst massacres, including that of Hakkem Haji Idris, who Math said was hung by the feet from the branch of a tree and smothered with buckets of boiling water.

The largest Cham community in Phnom Penh was established at Chrang Chamres, in the northern suburbs of the capital. One hundred fifty Cham families from this area were evacuated to the North in 1975; only forty-three incomplete families survived. Others went to the Southwest and West. A survey of twelve surviving Cham family groups in Chrang Chamres's Second Subdistrict in 1986 yielded the following results: There were 111 people in the twelve families in early 1975. At least seven of these died in the first year, including two who were murdered; four died in 1976; thirteen in 1977, including five murdered; two died in 1978; and thirteen others died at some point between 1975 and 1979, making a total of thirty-nine deaths in four years, or 35 percent of the 111 family members. The sample includes one family of nine who fled to Vietnam in 1975, all of whom survived. Of the other eleven families, only one had lost none of its members in Democratic Kampuchea.[115]

The other large Cham community in the capital was Chrui Changvar, across the Sap river east of Phnom Penh. In 1940, Ner reported three hundred Cham households there.[116] By 1975, when the village was evacuated, they may have numbered about nine hundred families. In 1979–80, only seventy families returned there. By 1985, eighty Cham families had returned.[117]

In 1981 the Japanese journalist Katuichi Honda reported death tolls for two Cham communities. *Imam* Him Mathot told him that he had been evacuated from Phnom Penh to Kompong Speu with five hundred Cham families, totaling about three thousand people. Fewer than seven hundred survived in 1979, according to the Imam: "Half the deaths were due to starvation, and the other half by execution." Mathot lost eight of the fourteen members of his family. Across the river from Phnom Penh, he added, a Cham community of

---

115. Survey conducted by the author with Gregory Stanton (see also p. 273, above). In 1940, Marcel Ner reported 340 Cham families in Chrang Chamres (Ner, p. 166). By 1975 there were over 1,000. In 1986, only 280 local families remained there. (But they had been joined by sixteen hundred Cham families from other parts of the country. These people, having concentrated in what was now the center of Cham life, would presumably account for up to ten thousand Chams missing from other villages.)

116. Ner, p. 165.

117. M. Vickery, *Kampuchea: Politics, Economics and Society*, London, 1986, p. 164. Vickery's informant put the 1975 population at only 150 families, which is unlikely. There were at least four hundred Cham households there. See Vu Can, "The Community of Surviving Muslims," *Vietnam Courier*, 4, 1982, p. 31.

450 families in 1975 had been reduced to 50 families, "and almost every family had lost members."[118]

The Northwest and West

In Battambang, as Vickery asserts, the Chams may not have suffered more than Khmer, particularly in Khek Penn's Region 4.[119] But in most of the Northwest, as elsewhere, they still faced the execution of their leaders and the bans on their language and dietary customs. To Hosan recalls that in early 1976, his cooperative chief in Battambang announced that only the Khmer language was permitted. "Not only Cham but any language, e.g., Chinese or Lao, was forbidden. You could not speak Cham secretly at home. . . . At night the militia would come by the houses and listen. . . . Some Chams were killed for speaking Cham." An old man was shot for refusing to eat pork.[120] Their status was clearly inferior.[121]

Chams from both the Southwest and the East, both new and base people, were deported to the Northwest along with a million former city dwellers.[122] These Cham families were forcibly dispersed among the Khmer population, prevented from reassembling or practicing their religion, and forced to eat pork when it was served; the youths were separated from their parents. The usual CPK Center racial/historical preoccupations emerged with the Southwest takeover of the Zone. A peasant woman reports that two families of Chams in Region 3 were all murdered in 1977, accused of being "Vietnamese."[123] Late in 1977, Region 3 authorities brought in some skilled Cham workers from Region 1. Five months later, after one of the Cham blacksmiths had an illicit love

118. Honda, pp. 132–39.
119. Vickery, p. 182. Four accounts I obtained, all from Region 4, agreed: author's interviews in Strasbourg, 31 October 1979; Limoges, 1 December 1979; and Toulouse, 9 December 1979 (2). I have discussed elsewhere the fate of Chams in the Northwest and Western Zones. Kiernan, "Genocidal Targeting: Two Groups of Victims in Pol Pot's Cambodia," in P. Timothy Bushnell, et al., eds., *State Organized Terror: The Case of Violent Internal Repression*, Boulder: Westview, 1991, esp. pp. 218–23. Also Kiernan, "Orphans of Genocide," BCAS, 20, 4, 1988, pp. 27–30.
120. Author's interview with To Hosan, Prey Veng, 17 January 1986.
121. Pin Yatay describes the Chams in Pursat as "the favourite targets of the sadism of the Khmer Rouge." Their fishing community on the Great Lake had been "uprooted" and dispersed. But the discrimination only brought them closer to their Khmer fellow-sufferers. "The persecuted were from all backgrounds. There were Chams or Islamic Khmers, Chinese, even Vietnamese who had not gone back to their country. We no longer had any concept of difference. We were the new people lined up against the old. We shared the misery. . . . We did not denounce one another." Pin Yatay, *L'Utopie Meurtrière*, Paris: Laffont, 1979, pp. 231–32, 253.
122. *Bulletin d'information sur le Cambodge* (Paris), no. 5, October-November 1978, p. 8.
123. Author's interview with Tan Kong Sy, Toulouse, 11 December 1979.

affair, the couple was executed, along with five Cham men who had worked with the man. According to a witness, this did not seem a racial pogrom, "but just that the Khmer Rouge wanted total control of our activities"—including people's private lives. But they imposed a racial form of collective responsibility.[124] Power and race were intertwined.

The one large Cham community in the Western Zone comprises three villages of Kompong Tralach district in Kompong Chhnang, which had about five thousand Chams in 1940. Marcel Ner described them as "the most faithful in Cambodia to the Cham traditions," having absorbed little Malay influence and practiced little intermarriage. "In their mosques and Koranic schools the teaching and sermons are in Cham, and knowledge of Arabic is restricted to the alphabet and some formulae. They jealously preserve some Cham manuscripts which tell of their history; several people can read them, and even appear to know long passages by heart. The women maintain the authority that Cham customs accord them."[125]

These Cham base people were targeted by the cpk. By 1975, all Chams holding positions such as cooperative chief or work team leader were dismissed from their posts. Local blacksmith Ka Chu says, "They lost their rights. Even those Chams who had fought for the Khmer Rouge were withdrawn [from the armed forces] and put on fishing detail. No Chams had freedom or rights then." By 1976, the Chams were being forced to eat meals that included pork, on pain of withdrawal of the salt ration or even death. Around the same time, the Cham communities were scattered over eight or nine subdistricts in Kompong Tralach, in groups of "two, five or up to twenty families per village," according to Sos Men, another local Cham peasant. "No large groups were allowed," Ka Chu concurs; only twenty to thirty people were left in each Cham village. Killings of Muslim leaders began in 1974. Ka Chu says that his hakkem and another dignitary were both killed in 1975 after being interrogated about their religion. In 1975, about five hundred new people, both Chams and Khmers, arrived from Phnom Penh and Battambang, and over the next four years about ten hajis were executed. Ka Chu claims to have compiled a list of 150 learned men from Chhouk Sor subdistrict who were killed in the 1970s.[126]

Hamat was born in Kompong Tralach in 1943. He became a fisherman at Chrang Chamres. When Phnom Penh fell, "the whole village of Chrang Chamres" was evacuated to Kompong Tralach. Locals were not allowed to return to their villages; they were dispersed with other Cham new people. Hamat, separated from his family, was sent to a cooperative called Stung

124. Author's interview with an anonymous ethnic Chinese Cambodian, Limoges, 7 December 1979.
125. Ner, p. 170.
126. Author's interview with Ka Chu, Kompong Tralach, 5 September 1980.

Snguot, where there were forty Cham families; the Khmers included about ten base families. In August 1976, "all the Chams were executed in Stung Sngout. ... Not one family remained. ... I saw people taken away, whole files of them." Hamat, felicitously transferred to a fishing detail at Longvek, only returned to Stung Snguot in 1978. The Cham children there had followed their parents to their deaths. Hamat remembered the CPK slogan: "Dig up the grass, dig up the roots." He was the only survivor of the forty Cham families.[127] Sok Sokhun, a Khmer evacuee from Phnom Penh, lived in Stung Snguot throughout the DK period. He claims that between September and November 1976, ten thousand Cham and Chinese new people were executed in the Ampil Tik subdistrict of Kompong Tralach.[128]

The Ethnic Chinese

In the 1960s, Cambodia's four hundred thousand Chinese lived in rural areas in "a substantially highter proportion than in most other Southeast Asian countries."[129] Most rural Chinese were involved in trade or usury, however, and when revolution swept the countryside after 1970, the vast majority fled to Phnom Penh. One refugee, a Chinese woman then forty-six years old, fled the fighting. At first she was "afraid of Phnom Penh," but her husband managed to get an official post, and she opened a tailor shop. By early 1975 the Chinese population had become basically an urban one.

When they were driven into the countryside in April 1975, many Chinese, like urban Khmers, went back to their villages of origin, mostly in the East and the Southwest. In the second forced evacuation later that year, however, most Chinese, like most urban Khmers, were transferred to the Northwest Zone. Many Khmer refugees report that ethnic Chinese suffered the most, as they were unused to laboring in the fields even if they had rural origins. In this case they were not targeted for execution *because of their race*, but like other deportees they were made to work harder and under much worse conditions than rural dwellers. The penalty for infraction of minor regulations was often death.

127. Author's interview with Hamat, Chrang Chamres, 10 July 1980.
128. Author's interview with Sok Sokhun, Phnom Penh, 10 July 1980.
129. W. E. Willmott, *The Political Structure of the Chinese in Cambodia*, p. 6. This does not mean that the majority of Chinese in Kampuchea were ever rural dwellers, or that many of them were peasant farmers. Of thirteen ethnic Chinese refugees I interviewed, five were born in small townships, two of them in very remote villages. Only six were born in Phnom Penh. The thirteen ethnic Chinese (at least half were literate in Chinese) survived the DK period in Cambodia, and were interviewed in France in 1979. They lived in four Zones of Democratic Kampuchea (the Northwest, the Southwest, the East, and the West), and three of them lived and worked in Phnom Penh from 1975 to 1979. The largest number lived in the Northwest. Of the thirteen, seven were female. Only one of the thirteen interviewees was a base person.

Probably around one hundred fifty thousand Chinese died in the Northwest alone between 1976 and 1978. Stephen Heder, who subsequently surveyed fifteen hundred refugees about the fate of their family members in these years, suggests that equal numbers of Chinese died from each of the three main causes: execution, starvation, and disease. (Heder estimated the same breakdown for deaths among urban Khmers, although they died at half the rate of the Chinese.) This assertion is supported by my own interviews with survivors from the Northwest.

The Chinese who stayed behind in the Southwest or Eastern Zones were far fewer in number, but they fared much better, especially in the East until 1978. Life was still hard, however, as the "best" account from the Southwest makes clear. It was worse, even for base people, in the rugged, inhospitable Western Zone. In Phnom Penh in the same period, life was quite different. Starvation was never a problem for DK factory workers (or Chinese interpreters for the advisers from Beijing). However, there was an ever-present fear of arrest, and many Chinese in the capital disappeared or were executed.[130]

Ang Ngeck Teang, aged ten, was evacuated from the city with her mother, four brothers and sisters, and five other relatives. By mid-1975 they were all settled in a village in Northwest Region 5 inhabited mainly by five hundred base families. In 1977, Teang says, both new and base children were separated from their parents. The children were taught revolutionary songs and a little of the Khmer alphabet by a young woman from Takeo. "She was not nice. Whatever was not tasty, we got to eat. She hated Phnom Penh people; only children of base people got shirts. . . . The base people were used to farm work and did what they were told, so the Khmer Rouge liked them. The Phnom Penh people had never done it before and they were called lazy."

This is the only axis of discrimination Teang mentions. It was an important one for the Chinese, of course. But in the final analysis, everyone else in Teang's village seems to have suffered almost as much, including the base people. Teang noted that in Siemreap, by 1979, former Vietnamese civilian residents "had all been killed by the Khmer Rouge. Only Khmers and Chinese were left."[131] Nor did other ethnic Chinese, who survived Democratic Kam-

130. See Table 3, Chapter 10, p. 432, below.
131. Author's interview with Ang Ngeck Teang, Toulouse, 9 December 1979. Teang described the 1979 change of regime: "When the Vietnamese came, the Khmer Rouge ran away. . . . The Vietnamese were good . . . very honest. If we had a chicken we could exchange it for some soap from them. If we asked them for food, they gave it. If we were sick, they gave us medicine. My hand was infected . . . they cured it. . . . I asked them for a lift to Phnom Penh, where my elder brother found me. . . . My house had been destroyed by the Khmer Rouge, demolished, the television destroyed, etc." Teang's long-lost brother took her across the Thai bc⁻ᵈ⁻⁻ and eventually to France, where she appeared encouragingly optimistic about her future.

puchea in Regions 3 and 4, mention racial discrimination or persecution, though they all suffered terribly. One woman lost her brother, father, and her grandfather, as well as her brother-in-law and another relative (a technician trained in China in the 1960s but accused of being a CIA agent), both executed in 1977. Another ethnic Chinese reported that in his village of four thousand six hundred people, over one thousand died of starvation and disease and at least ten people were executed in 1977.[132]

Hun, an ethnic Chinese woman from Pailin, reveals some interesting details concerning the policy toward the Chinese in Region 3. On 17th April 1975, she recalls, "the representatives of the Chinese population got together in the Pailin market and took gifts of sugar out to welcome the incoming Khmer Rouge." Twelve days later, however, the town was forcibly evacuated. Hun left Pailin for the countryside with eleven members of her family. They were resettled with eighty other evacuated Chinese families, in what the CPK called "the Chinese village." Nearby were "the Khmer village" for ethnic Khmer evacuees and "the old village," where the base people of the area continued to live. The chief of Hun's village was a Chinese new person.[133]

This quasi-segregationist policy was a remnant of the 1970–75 period. It resembles the case of Koh Kong (Region 11), where another ethnic Chinese woman, whose village came under Khmer Rouge control in 1970, recalls that the local Vietnamese, Chinese, and Khmer populations were administered through separate organizations. This was a region of such liberal rule that she called the local administration *khmaer krohom serei* (the free Khmer Rouge). As we saw in Chapter 3, the latter were executed in 1974 by hard-line Center forces; the ethnic organizations were then abolished, and "hard times began."[134]

Likewise, in Region 3 in late 1975, Hun reports, the three separate groups were dispersed. Hun's and four other Chinese families were sent to live with forty Khmer families. This move came with severe new restrictions on freedom of movement and freedom to barter. As a result, Hun says, it was "better to be with Khmers," as Chinese had few other ways of obtaining food on their own. Vietnamese residents "were told to go to Vietnam": "At that time all the Chinese who could speak Vietnamese went [disguised] as Vietnamese. In some groups of ten families only two or three families stayed. Only four or five families were left in my group of ten. . . . Many went because Angkar gave them nothing and made them work, and their resources would run out within months. . . . They abandoned all their goods."

132. Author's interviews with Ung Soutine, 9 December 1979, and an anonymous informant, Limoges, 7 December 1979.
133. Author's interview with Be Kheng Hun, Toulouse, 9 December 1979.
134. For details see Kiernan and Boua, *Peasants and Politics in Kampuchea*, London 1982, p. 275. (Tan Hao interview.)

Hun reports no starvation for the next three years, although killings took place in 1977 and 1978. "A Chinese in my group, in his fifties, with glasses, was talking one night with the husband of my young sister-in-law. He was taken away by troops. I don't know why. . . . Then the husband was taken away. . . . We didn't dare ask what had happened to him; we had been warned that the whole family would be taken away." Partly because of such discretion, other members of Hun's family survived.

Two more women who lived in the Northwest make it clear that it was dangerous to be a Chinese there, but both suggest that the reasons were other than racial, though ethnic minority rights were completely suppressed. Hong Var, who lived in Region 5, never admitted having been a schoolteacher in Phnom Penh. Var says she would certainly have been executed. So she pretended she could write only in a very clumsy style. Sometimes she would claim, when asked her former profession, that she had sold fried bananas in Phnom Penh. Khmer Rouge would usually express surprise at this, noting that her skin was not as dark as that of Khmer workers and peasants, more like a Chinese. She would then reply glibly that she had sold fried bananas in a stall in the shade. Sometimes she was believed; if not, she feared being suspected as a Chinese, therefore a "capitalist trader," and would then add that she had been a maidservant to a Chinese family. One way or another, she managed to survive, almost miraculously. Tae Hui Lang, an ethnic Chinese woman who lived in Region 4, offers a compatible comment. "We were not even allowed to speak Chinese; we were accused of being capitalists. . . . We were killed off."[135]

In the Northern Zone, the 1975–76 dispersal of Chams was not always accompanied by a similar policy towards the Chinese. Near a hamlet in Region 42 where Chams had to live among Khmers was an entire village of ethnic Chinese.[136] But as in the Northwest, the segregation phase gave way to forcible assimilation, or worse. In January 1978, a former student escaped to Thailand from Siemreap (Region 106). He reported executions of Lon Nol soldiers ever since 1975, and added: "In 1977, they started killing capitalists, students, monks, and even Chinese and Vietnamese, even if they could speak Cambodian. These classes were killed by being beaten to death with poles."[137] A former Lon Nol soldier escaped from the same province in May 1978. He reported continuing massacres of Lon Nol soldiers and Chinese. "In 1977, there were still ethnic Chinese in Cambodia. . . . In June or July, two Chinese stole manioc

135. Author's interviews with Hong Var, Aranyaprathet, 2 and 3 April 1979, and Tae Hui Lang, Chatenay-Malabry, 10 August 1979. See Kiernan and Boua, *Peasants and Politics in Kampuchea*, pp 338–44, 358–62.

136. Author's interview with Tep Ibrahim, 1986.

137. "Account of Sam Damawong," Interview with Cambodian Refugee in Buriram, Thailand, conducted by American embassy officer in June 1978. Report No. 10, declassified 1978.

planted by the collective. They were caught and hauled to a field about five hundred meters from the village. They were clubbed to death and fell into holes prepared in the field. In the two districts in which I lived, many Chinese were taken away in late 1977 and 1978. None was left." Militia members informed him that they had been executed.[138]

In Region 37 of the Western Zone, Chinese leaving the city of Kompong Som in April 1975 were initially segregated.[139] But later, a Phnom Penh evacuee reports, they were forcibly dispersed and treated "the same as all new people, the same as Vietnamese and Chams." In 1977, base people whom the DK authorities favored accused the Chinese of being "traitors to China." Overall, he says, "Chinese were treated more harshly than the Khmers," receiving shorter rations and suffering more disappearances and more overt killings. Chinese, Vietnamese, and Chams were all "killed to the same extent" in Region 37.[140]

Tan Hao, a young ethnic Chinese woman, was recruited into the Region 37 chalat in December 1975, along with ten thousand male and female youths age thirteen and over. They began building a dam. Hao says that over two thousand of these workers died in 1976, mainly from starvation and disease. But the authorities also began "to kill ordinary people, without explaining what they had done wrong." The victims were simply summoned "to work in the forest." In November 1976 the chalat was transferred to rice cultivation, and Hao joined a sewing team of forty-eight workers. After three months her team was sent to join two hundred other women working at a new clothing factory. A new, even tougher cpk local leadership arrived and purged its predecessors. During 1977, ten of the workers were taken away and killed. Hao also saw a group of Khmer Rouge seize people too weak to work effectively in the fields and beat them to death. The villages of Region 37 were haunted by starvation. By late 1977, ten people were sharing one can of rice per day. Hao's four brothers and sisters and her mother all died of starvation during that year. She says ethnic Chinese and especially Vietnamese "were all killed towards the end of 1977." Others were asked if they "liked the Vietnamese," so they too could be "sent back to Vietnam." Hao continues, "Some Khmers said they were Vietnamese, so they could get to Vietnam, which they said was a happy country." She saw more than twenty truckloads of people drive off from Sre Umbel and Prey Nup. Their bodies were later found dumped nearby. Hao herself saw executions of "many people" considered "Vietnamese spies." Their families were also slaughtered.[141]

138. "Account of Thu Hat," Interview with Cambodian Refugee in Surin, Thailand, conducted by American embassy officer in June 1978. Report No. 17, declassified 1978.

139. Moeung Sonn, interview with the author, Sarcelles, 25 October 1979. He said the Chinese were taken to Tané or Sre Ambel. (See Locard and Sonn, *Prisonnier de l'Angkar.*)

140. Author's interview in Kampot, 29 August 1980.

141. Author's interview with Tan Hao, Alençon, 4 October 1979.

A Chinese from the Northwest Zone, who posed as a Vietnamese but failed to reach Vietnam in the expulsions of late 1975, spent the next three years in Prey Veng, Region 24, of the Eastern Zone. Heng says that the Khmer Rouge were "no good."

> They immediately killed any 17 April people ("new people") whom they suspected of being enemies. . . . They spared only dark-skinned people. . . . [One cadre] hated the ethnic Chinese. . . . In 1976. . . . they began looking for "capitalists," rich people, meaning people who had cars, brick houses, or owned factories—who were mostly Chinese where I was. I know of only one Khmer who was killed. They persecuted the new people a lot in 1975–76. . . . The old people [base people] got rice, we got gruel. . . . The base people like and trusted the leaders in 1975–76. . . . In 1977 they searched for the middle class, to execute them . . . I was suspected; they questioned me three times a month.

Heng says hundreds had died by 1978 in his village of five thousand. But he noted only one racial massacre, of Chams in 1977.

A second picture of the East is provided by Ly Chhiv Ha, an ethnic Chinese woman who spent eight months in Prey Veng in 1975 (before being evacuated to the Northwest, in the opposite direction to Heng in the same period). Ha settled with half a dozen other Phnom Penh families in an eastern village of about seventy families of base people, who "were quite loyal to the Khmer Rouge" and who considered themselves participants in the revolution. While she was there, Ha found food rations adequate and the work regime lenient; "I never heard of any killings (there)." However, new people were still officially described as "enemies," and two of her four children died for lack of medicine. After the new people were sent to Battambang in early 1976, Ha's two remaining children died before the year was out. Another relative was executed in the Northwest; of her original family group of eleven who set out from Phnom Penh in April 1975, only three were alive in 1979.

Region 25 in the Southwest was the native area of much of the capital's Chinese population. When evacuees headed there in large numbers in April 1975,[142] local authorities initially segregated the races. Tan Peng Sen, a Sino-Khmer youth, reports that Chinese families who declared themselves had "had the right to our own krom." He was assigned to a krom comprising over ninety Chinese families. Khmers were prohibited from joining it. But after two months, the Chinese krom was dissolved and its members assigned to Khmer and mixed kroms.[143] Tam Eng, the ethnic Chinese tailor from Takeo, reports a

---

142. Author's interview with Savon, Chatenay-Malabry, 9 August 1979.
143. Author's interview with Tan Peng Sen, Alençon, 3 October 1979.

segregation policy in Region 13, arguably the most hard-line area in the country.[144] "The Khmer Rouge said Chinese had to go live in a Chinese village." Khmers from Phnom Penh, Chinese, and base people were all segregated, as in Region 3. Then in late 1975, the policy change in Regions 3 and 25 was again paralleled in Region 13. As Eng put it: "The Khmer Rouge said: 'Chinese are to go to China, Vietnamese to Vietnam, Khmers to [stay in] Kampuchea.' I did not want to go to China, because it was red too, so I said I was Vietnamese. . . . Vietnamese residents were exchanged for salt from the Vietnamese government." Although Eng revealed no racially targeted persecution, the "repatriations" signaled a DK policy decision that ethnic minorities would no longer be recognized. Thus, while ethnic segregation was, curiously, associated with policy moderation, the new nationwide policy to disperse ethnic groups represented a suppression of minority rights: a choice between expulsion and forced assimilation.

An example is the case of Muk Chot, a Chinese Protestant from Phnom Penh, who was driven out of the capital in 1975 with his wife and six other family members. They also went to Region 13, and spent the entire DK period there. Chot recalled no killings or starvation, but his four children were taken away in mid-1976. The youngest, eight and ten years old, were put to work moving earth with other village youths aged over seven. Chot and his wife barely saw their children every two months. "They didn't dare tell us whether they were getting enough to eat." Also in mid-1976, enforced communal eating was imposed. But Chot found this system "less trouble for us, who did not know how to fend for ourselves, catch fish, etc. But for those who knew how, it was worse." (In most of the country, such foraging was now banned. As Tam Eng put it: "Fishing and foraging was said to be an attempt to survive individually while others did not have these products.") This was the point at which the ten to twenty families of base people in Chot's village became opposed to the revolution. Until then, they had been "followers of the Khmer Rouge—one and the same group." Now they were disillusioned by the ban on private eating and by enforced separation from their children. In this case the effect of CPK policy was politically ironic: to alienate the revolution's peasant base, its alleged beneficiaries, while satisfying the food needs of a non-Khmer, former Phnom Penh official—so long as he was prepared to abandon his culture.

In early 1977 the CPK increased the work demands on the population as part of what they called a "great leap forward." Chot comments: "They treated us like dogs; we dared not protest." The only hint of racial discrimination con-

144. Author's interview with Tam Eng, Paris, 24 January 1980 (see Chapter 5); on Region 13, see Kiernan, *How Pol Pot*, esp. pp. 334, 337, 354, 362–3. Ethnic segregation was also the initial policy in Prey Krabas, Region 33. Author's interview with Seng Horl, Cretell, 3 December 1979.

cerned the ethnic Vietnamese: "In 1977 they said ethnic Vietnamese could go home to Vietnam. Some were taken from a nearby village. I don't know where to." We may find out in the next section.

What emerges from most accounts is that there was no noticeable racialist vendetta against people of Chinese origin, particularly in the Northwest, where most of the Chinese perished. However, some exceptions to this, and important nuances, emerge from interviews with survivors. The Chinese were seen as the archetypal city dwellers, and therefore as ineligible for "full rights," and rarely even "candidate" status. They were nearly all "deportees," generally assumed to be "capitalists." But they were usually seen as "foreign" in the same sense that city people generally were. This is social or geographic rather than racial discrimination. It might be countered that (unlike the majority of Khmer) rural Chinese were placed in inferior social categories because of their race, and that Chinese of unknown origin were automatically assumed to be urbanites, whereas Khmers could at least attempt to persuade the DK authorities that they were peasants. In general, though, the tragedy of Cambodia's Chinese was not that they were singled out for special persecution by an anti-Chinese regime, but rather that a pro-Chinese regime subjected them to the same brutal treatment as the rest of the country's population.

It may be true as a general statement that despite prohibition of their language and cultural autonomy, ethnic Chinese would have been safe enough in DK if they could satisfy their rulers that they were of poor social origins. But the CPK presumption, for racial reasons, was always that they were not, and more than two hundred thousand people died as a result of this and a general prejudice against city dwellers. It is difficult to choose between their fate and that of tens of thousands of Chams and Vietnamese, and hundreds of thousands of Khmers, targeted for execution even though undoubtedly of poor social origins.

For Cambodia's ethnic Chinese, Democratic Kampuchea was the worst disaster ever to befall any ethnic Chinese community in Southeast Asia. Of a 1975 population of 430,000, only about 215,000 Chinese survived the next four years.[145] The Chinese succumbed in particularly large numbers to hunger and diseases like malaria. The 50 percent of them who perished is a higher proportion than that estimated for city dwellers in general (about one-third). Fur-

145. The pre-D.K. population figure of 430,000 is from W. Willmott, *The Chinese in Cambodia* (Vancouver: University of British Columbia Publications Centre, 1967), p. 16. S. Heder's survey of Cambodian refugees indicated that 50 percent of the Chinese died in D.K. The survey was carried out on the Thai-Cambodian border in 1980 and 1981. Fifteen hundred people provided data on 15,000 individuals (members of their immediate families). For details, see *Hearings before the Subcommittee on Human Rights and International Organizations of the Committee on Foreign Affairs*, House of Representatives, Ninety-Eighth Congress, November 16 and 17, 1983, statement by D. Hawk, esp. pp. 124–25; Kiernan, "Kampuchea's Ethnic Chinese under Pol Pot: A Case of Systematic Social Discrimination." *Journal of Contemporary Asia*, 16, 1, 1986.

ther, the Chinese language, like all foreign and minority languages, was banned, and so was any tolerance of a culturally and ethnically distinguishable Chinese community. The Chinese community was to be destroyed "as such." This CPK policy, like that toward the Chams, could be construed as genocide.

The Ethnic Vietnamese

The CPK had expelled perhaps 150,000 ethnic Vietnamese civilians from Cambodia by September 1975, about the same time as the dispersal of the Cham and ethnic Chinese communities within the country. Some of those expelled were massacred on their way to Vietnam. Three members of the DK navy who later escaped to Thailand reported the slaughter in Kampot of sixty-five Vietnamese trying to leave Cambodia in June 1975.[146] However, perhaps ten thousand more, mostly with Khmer spouses, stayed in Cambodia.[147]

By mid-1976, Vietnamese were forbidden to leave Cambodia.[148] Heng Samrin says the first massacres began in that year, but did not yet constitute a specific national campaign. "It was not Pol Pot and Nuon Chea. . . . It was at the level of implementation." There were anti-Vietnamese directives, he said, but officials responsible for carrying them out used excessive violence. "They even ordered husbands to kill their own wives who were Vietnamese. . . . And they even went so far as to kill those of us who were attached to their wives and children. This is what they commanded."[149] The Center gave a lead in 1976 by arresting twenty-five alleged "Vietnamese spies," two other unspecified Vietnamese, and a "Vietnamese bar girl" (with a Khmer name). All were killed.[150]

146. "The New Cambodia: Life in the Provinces," Extracts from an Airgram Report by an officer of the American embassy at Bangkok, 26 August 1975 (declassified 1978), p. 5. Chams attempting to flee to Vietnam were also massacred (Locard and Sonn, *Prisonnier de l'Angkar,* pp. 159–60).

147. The estimated ethnic Vietnamese population in Cambodia in early 1970 was 450,000; 310,000 are thought to have fled to Vietnam by August that year, leaving 140,000 (Migozzi, *Cambodge: Faits et problèmes de population,* p. 44). Assuming 2.46 percent population growth from 1970 to 1975, ethnic Vietnamese in Cambodia in April 1975 would have numbered around 160,000. The 1970 emigration was also "partly offset by some net Vietnamese immigration" by 1975 (economist-statistician W. J. Sampson, letter to the *Economist,* 26 March 1977, p. 4). If, as Chanda's research suggests, 150,000 Vietnamese left from April to September 1975 (*Brother Enemy,* p. 16), the number remaining could have been well over 10,000. A Kampot villager reports, "Where I was, all the Vietnamese went back to Vietnam. In some other villages, some stayed." Author's interview, Kompong Trach, 29 August 1980. See below for more evidence of Vietnamese who remained in DK.

148. Author's interview, Kompong Trach, 29 August 1980.

149. Author's interview with Heng Samrin, Phnom Penh, 2 December 1991.

150. "Benhchi chhmou neak tous dael coul khnong chhnam 1976" ("List of the Names of Prisoners Who Entered in the Year 1976"), S-21 (Tuol Sleng), dated 26 May 1977. The "bar-girl" is on p. 16, at no. 497.

Then, on 1 April 1977, the Center did send out a specific order.[151] Left alone for a few minutes while waiting in the office of the district chief of Oudong (Region 15 in the Western Zone), a mechanic named Ros Saroeun surreptitiously read the order. This "Directive from 870" (the CPK Center) instructed local officials to arrest all ethnic Vietnamese, and all Khmers who spoke Vietnamese or had Vietnamese friends, and hand them over to state security forces. Saroeun's wife was Vietnamese, and he rushed home to warn her. But as Nayan Chandra reports, she already knew. "A Vietnamese woman in the village had been bludgeoned to death by the Khmer Rouge and buried just outside the village after they had sent her Khmer husband to cut wood in the jungle." The husband later found his wife's corpse.[152] Saroeun and his wife managed to disguise her identity.

The largest massacre appears to have occurred in Kompong Chhnang province, where "about 420 Vietnamese adults and children were executed" in mid-May 1977.[153] Further north, in Pursat, a Khmer named Heng Chor later recounted that "in March 1977 Khmer Rouge cadre killed his former wife, who was of Vietnamese descent, along with five of his sons, three daughters, three grandchildren, his mother-in-law, eight from his sister-in-law's family, [and] seven from his brother-in-law's family."[154]

On the coast of Region 37, officials again called on "Vietnamese" to volunteer for repatriation. Two groups of volunteers assembled in 1977, including Chinese "and even some Khmers who did not want to stay," hoping to pass themselves off as Vietnamese. Both groups were allegedly massacred in turn.[155] In the Northwest Zone, a Khmer woman recalled that in mid-1977, after the arrival of the Southwest Zone cadres, the authorities "started killing people with any Vietnamese blood."[156] A man from the Northwest adds that after Southwest cadres came in May 1977, six ethnic Vietnamese were murdered in his village in August.[157] In the North in 1977, officials began arresting ethnic Vietnamese, "even if they could speak Cambodian," beating them "to death with poles."[158]

151. Carney, "Organization of Power," in Jackson, ed., *Cambodia 1975–1978*, p. 83 n.3, refers to a *1978* "nationwide campaign against the few remaining Vietnamese, their spouses, or ethnic Khmer born in Vietnam." See below and the following section for evidence of these campaigns, which began *before* 1978.

152. Chanda, *Brother Enemy* pp. 86–87.

153. *FBIS*, IV, 2 September 1977, p. H1, *Bangkok Post*, 1 September 1977.

154. Interview with Heng Chor, 52, of "Turakur," Pursat. Hawk collection, Cornell Univ. Archives, box 1.

155. Author's interview, Kampot, 29 August 1980.

156. Becker, *When the War Was Over*, p. 252, describes this as the result of "a new directive, in the middle of 1977, to kill off a new category of enemy—people of Vietnamese ancestry."

157. Author's interview with Sing Y, Alençon, 3 October 1979.

158. United States Departement of State, "Interview with Cambodian Refugee in

Mau Met was an Eastern Zone cadre whose wife was part Vietnamese. In 1975 she had been allowed to remain because her husband was Khmer. Met was in charge of the agriculture department in Memut district on Region 21's border with Vietnam. In 1977, all ethnic Vietnamese were rounded up and killed. More than two hundred women were executed, and in some cases their Khmer husbands as well. In all other cases, the husbands were jailed. Met was the only exception, he says, because of his needed agricultural skills.[159] In one Region 24 village, in 1977 the CPK killed ten Vietnamese women married to Khmers.[160]

In Kratie province in the northeast, officials in 1977 described Vietnamese as the *setrew prowatisas* (historic enemy) and began a hunt for people of part-Vietnamese origin.[161] These were executed, along with ethnic Chinese and former Lon Nol soldiers.[162] In Region 23 (now under Mok's control), a Chinese woman was suspected by the authorities of being Vietnamese. She was arrested in December 1977 and executed along with four of her five children. The woman's Khmer husband escaped with their youngest daughter, age nine, and made it across the border to Vietnam, where they were jailed for six months on suspicion of being Khmer Rouge infiltrators.[163] Then they were allowed to stay in Vietnam another year, which got them through 1978.

The Khmer Krom

Vietnam's seven hundred thousand ethnic Khmers are known in Cambodia as Khmer Krom, or Lower Khmers. They speak Cambodian with a detectable Vietnamese accent. A small but steady migration to Cambodia since the nineteenth century established sizable Khmer Krom communities in Phnom Penh and in the northwest. Before 1975, several prominent Phnom Penh politicians were Khmer Krom, as were CPK leaders such as Ieng Sary and Son Sen, both of whom were born in Vietnam's Mekong Delta.

In 1973, Southwest Zone CPK secretary Mok told a group of cadres that

---

Buriram, Thailand, Conducted by American Embassy Officer in June, 1978," Report No. 10, declassified 1978, p. 1.

159. Author's interview with Mau Met, Kompong Cham, 5 October 1980. Preap Pichey, another former Memut district cadre, concurs: "Vietnamese civilians in Memut were killed in 1977, not in 1975 or 1976. They began to kill them without mercy in 1977, even Khmers with Vietnamese wives were not spared." Interview with the author, Kompong Cham, 8 October 1980.

160. Author's interview with Prak Voa, Kompong Trabek, 9 October 1980.

161. *Asiaweek*, 2 December 1977, p. 43, and Ponchaud, "Situation interne," p. 10.

162. Author's interview with Mon, who spent the DK period in Snuol district of Kratie. Phnom Penh, 5 July 1980.

163. Author's interview with the former pedicab driver for journalist Neil Davis, 5 December 1992.

Vietnam was an aggressor on Cambodian land, and that he felt "very sorry for the people of Kampuchea Krom."[164] This is poignant, but doubtful. All accounts of massacres of Khmer Krom in the 1975–77 period attribute them to Mok's own Southwest Zone forces. The first were the killings of two thousand former members of the U.S.-trained Mike Force who tried to cross from Vietnam into Region 13 in the first year after the war ended. (See Introduction.) But local Khmer Krom were targeted at the same time. In Region 33 of the Southwest, two evacuees from Phnom Penh were executed in Prey Krabas district in 1975 "when they were identified as Khmer Krom." In the same Region in early 1976, three entire Khmer Krom families were massacred in a wat in Bati district. The authorities claimed that "they could speak Vietnamese.[165]

In late 1975, Bounchan Samedh had been sent to the Bakan district of Region 2, in the Northwest Zone. She found that "the base people there were all Khmer Krom who had been living there for twenty to thirty years. . . . All the officials there were Khmer Krom." These officials persecuted the new arrivals, for instance, by making them work even when ill. Samedh's daughter, who had just given birth, was given only three month's rest before having to return to hard labor. New vegetable crops were planted, but yielded nothing for the first year. In that time, Samedh's entire family of twelve died of starvation, disease, and overwork. Political malice played a part in this, but as in Region 5 and other parts of the Northwest, it is not clear that the land could have supported so many new people without substantial aid from outside. The Center sent only mouths to feed. Samedh notes philosophically, "The Khmer Krom were bad people, but we didn't see them take anyone away for execution."

Then, in early 1977, Mok's Southwest Zone cadres arrived. The province chief of Pursat was accused of treason. "Anyone they suspected was killed: former government officials, they did not even spare teachers. Then they collected all the Khmer Krom in Bakan district, new and base people, and put them in a cooperative called Thnal Totung. Later in 1977 they killed all the Khmer Krom as 'traitors.' . . . They were told they were being taken to a new 'front,' seventy to eighty at a time. I saw the bodies later in big pits." Five hundred to seven hundred Khmer Krom were murdered in Bakan district in 1977, Samedh says. The new Southwest officials had to replace even the militia. "They dismissed the old militia, and selected new ones from the children of 'pure people,' not those base people with relatives who had lived in 'enemy territory,' the towns. The Khmer Krom base people were of course all dead. Only pure Khmer base people remained." The Southwest Zone cadres, young

164. Author's interview with Ngaol, a cpk member since 1973 and a D.K. subdistrict chief in Region 13. Kirivong, 25 August 1980.

165. Author's interviews in Strasbourg, 1 November 1979, and Phnom Penh, 5 July 1980.

women in their twenties, characteristically divided up this surviving population along kinship lines.[166]

For the period 1975–1977, those responsible for massacres of Khmer Krom appear to have been limited to Southwest Zone forces. But in the Western Zone, authorities announced in 1977 that any Khmer Krom who arrived there would be executed, while Cambodia would retake the territory of Kampuchea Krom.[167] For this purpose, the next year Democratic Kampuchea issued ironic charges that Khmer Krom "are victims of the worst cruelties" in Vietnam. "It is forbidden for them to speak, dress, eat or learn according to [their] traditions on pain of death and the male babies are strangled at their birth."[168] But it was the *territory*, not its population, for which Mok had felt "very sorry."

The Thais and the Lao

By August 1975, over five thousand of Cambodia's ethnic Thais had fled across the border into Thailand.[169] Most of the remaining thirty-five thousand or so had been evacuated east from Koh Kong province during the repression of 1974–75. Little is known about their fate. In January 1977, the Cambodia watcher in the U.S. embassy in Bangkok reported, "Two men from Koh Kong claimed that much of the province has been kept purposely empty." Only two of its four districts had CPK administrations.[170] Thirty-two Thais were arrested in Kompong Som on 7 May 1976. In Phnom Penh, the *Santebal* listed at least fourteen of them as "Thai spies." All thirty-two were executed on 24 May. Another Thai, picked up two years later as far away as the Eastern Zone, was killed on 8 April 1978.[171]

A community of two thousand Shans, originally from Burma but ethnically related to the Thais, lived in the border town of Pailin, where they mined gemstones. They were known to Cambodians as the "Kola" minority. The ethnic Khmer, Chinese, and Vietnamese populations in Pailin were evacuated on 26 April 1975, but the Kola remained behind another week. Then they were

166. Author's interview with Bounchan Samedh, Melun, 17 November 1979.

167. Author's interview with a former CPK soldier and youth organization *(Yuvakok)* member, Kompong Chhnang, 1 September 1980.

168. *Voice of Democratic Kampuchea (VODK)*, 18 October 1978, translation by D.K. embassy in Beijing, p. 2. Six days later, Democratic Kampuchea repeated that Vietnam "kills all the male babies at birth." *VODK*, 24 October 1978, translation, p. 1.

169. *Bangkok Post*, 27 August 1975.

170. "Life in Southern Cambodia," Extracts from an Airgram Report by an Officer of the American Embassy at Bangkok, 25 January 1977, declassified 1978, p. 4.

171. "Les Etrangers," list of Tuol Sleng prisoners compiled by Ung Pech from S-21 records; "List of the Names of Prisoners Who Entered in the Year 1976," S-21, dated 26 May 1977.

evacuated on 1 May.[172] Their fate is uncertain. In 1979, "no traces" of them could be found.[173] A Kola woman living abroad found that of forty relatives, thirty-nine had been killed or died in Democratic Kampuchea; one survived and fled to Thailand.[174]

The Sa'och were another small community in western Cambodia. They lived on the peninsula north and east of Kompong Som, where many worked in coastal coconut plantations around Prey Nop. Their area straddled the Southwest and Western Zones. A new person who arrived on the Southwest side in 1975 found only Khmers. The Sa'och, he said, had been "withdrawn at liberation" and moved "into the high forest where few dare enter." Another new person, who lived on the Western Zone side, says the Sa'och "lived apart from the base and the new people, in their own place. . . . They had their own cadres in charge of them." A third says the Sa'och "had struggled alongside the Khmer Rouge during the war," and were now working with them "in charge of the people."[175] If so this tiny ethnic group was an exceptional case, but not the only one, as we shall see.

Cambodia's ethnic Lao minority is concentrated in the northeastern provinces of Stung Treng and Rattanakiri, bordering Laos. But there were also at least six isolated Lao-majority villages on the Thai border near Sisophon (in Region 3), totaling about 1,800 families.[176] Phi, an ethnic Lao rice farmer from Kaup Thom village, says that twenty-five Khmer and twenty-five Lao families had long lived together there without racial antagonism. The Lao residents were bilingual, and few of the peasants were landless. Fearful of the unknown, Phi fled to Thailand just before the CPK victory, but returned home after six days when he heard peace had been established. Five nights later, the village's fifty families were forcibly evacuated. As new people, they were moved twice more to different worksites in the next two years. Among Phi's wife's family of twelve, six died in 1975. Phi also witnessed the execution of a fellow Lao villager who had secretly exchanged gold for rice, which he was caught hiding. From the start, speaking the Lao language was prohibited, though in other ways Lao and Khmer were treated equally. Only twenty of the original fifty families from Kaup Thom village remained together in 1979. A few others had been scattered, but half the village's population had perished

172. *Bangkok Post*, 27 August 1975, referring to the Kola as "Thai Yai."
173. People's Revolutionary Tribunal Held in Phnom Penh, August 1979, Document 2.4.02, "Report on Some Typical Cases of the Genocidal Crime Committed by the Pol Pot-Ieng Sary Clique against National Minorities," p. 8.
174. Thant Myint U, personal communication, New Haven, 21 September 1993.
175. Author's interviews in Kampot, 29 August 1980, and with Moeung Sonn, 1979.
176. People's Revolutionary Tribunal, Document 2.4.02, p. 8. An ethnic Lao interviewee named six of the villages. Author's interview with Phi, Toulouse, 11 December 1979.

from hunger. Two of Phi's three children were among them.[177] Of the eighteen hundred Lao families in the Sisophon area, according to a 1979 report, "only 800 families have survived but all of these surviving families have lost some of their family members. On the whole more than fifty percent of the local population have been killed."[178]

In the Southwest Zone in April 1976, cpk security units in Region 33 picked up two Lao mechanics, the wife of one, and another Lao woman. The fate of these four Lao is unknown, but they are unlikely to have survived custody.[179]

The Tribal Minorities

In the Ministry of Foreign Affairs

Pol Pot and Ieng Sary's first followers in the Northeast Zone in 1967 were their Jarai bodyguards, Chan and Thin. After victory in 1975, Kea, another of Pol Pot's ethnic minority bodyguards, slipped out of Phnom Penh and fled back to his village in Mondolkiri.[180] But twelve others, young men adorned with large earrings, remained behind to accompany Pol Pot on a trip south of Phnom Penh on Christmas Day 1975.[181] In 1976, Pot's personal bodyguards were still tribal people from the northeast, who spoke Khmer with difficulty. Two were Jarai from Rattanakiri, and two others were Tampuon. In lectures to foreign ministry officials in 1976–78, Ieng Sary praised such tribal people, who "dared to sacrifice their lives to save their chiefs."[182] Sary and his aides even claimed that "the revolution had begun in the Northeast." As Bopha, a woman who attended these lectures pointed out, "the cradle of the revolution was actually in the west," but the Northeast was "where Ieng Sary and Pol Pot had lived" from 1967 to 1970.[183] Pol Pot gave the tribal northeasterners the same credit: "We relied on the people and to crown it all these people were *only* the poverty-stricken local people of the remote rural areas.

177. Author's interview with Phi, 1979.

178. People's Revolutionary Tribunal, Document 2.4.02, p. 8. This is consistent with Phi's independent account.

179. "Les Etrangers" (see n. 171, above).

180. See Chapter 3, above, pp. 80–86.

181. Heng Samnang, personal communication, 17 December 1993. Samnang met Pol Pot on that occasion.

182. Kate G. Frieson, "The Impact of Revolution on Cambodia Peasants, 1970–1975," Ph.D. Diss., Department of Politics, Monash University, 1991, p. 88; Chandler, *Tragedy*, p. 348, n. 52, and *Brother Number One*, pp. 218 n. 47, 209, nn. 17, 18.

183. Author's interview with Bopha, a former DK foreign ministry cadre, France, 1 February 1980.

This was because our revolution came out of the jungle."[184] He did not mention ethnicity. But these small minority groups were the only ones whose languages the Center did not ban.

Sary and his cadres referred to "minorities" in the abstract, by the official term *bang p'oun chun cheat* (fraternal nationality people). In practice this meant only the northeastern tribal groups—the Jarai, the Kouy, and the Phnong, with occasional references to the Stieng, the Brao, and the Tampuon. Bopha recalls, "They said the hill-tribes were faithful to the revolution, were not traders, and they had class hatred." Such Khmer Loeu cadres in the CPK apparatus were concentrated in Sary's foreign ministry.[185] But a few had military commands. An illiterate tribal northeasterner in his twenties commanded a battalion in Battambang in 1975. The 502nd Division, which was responsible for constructing a new military airport in Kompong Chhnang in 1978, was under the command of Lovei, the only Khmer Loeu in his division, which comprised mostly former Eastern troops.[186]

In the foreign ministry (code named "B-1"), whose staff of 150 included only 12 officials,[187] minority cadres were deliberately given higher status than the Khmer intellectuals and diplomats who had returned from abroad. Laurence Picq, a French woman working in the ministry, has provided information about their role. Young men and women from Preah Vihear province, probably Kouys, made up the nucleus of the ministry staff. In late 1976, a northeastern tribesman named Houn took over the ministry's transportation section. According to Picq, "his sudden promotion left him astounded. Having only ever seen trucks from afar, he categorically refused to climb into the cabin or onto the tray. Lightly clambering on the roof, he sat there cross-legged, arms folded, staring straight ahead, as if on elephant back." The fourth-ranking cadre in the foreign ministry was a northeasterner named Cheam. In 1978 Ieng Sary brought in another named Voeun, from the office of the Central Committee, to train the ministry's interpreters.[188]

---

184. Pol Pot, "Long Live the Great Revolutionary Army of the CPK!," *Tung Padevat*, 8, August 1975, p. 43. Emphasis added. A contemporary journalistic account is T. D. Allman, "Cambodia 1970: Rock and Rebellion in Remote Ratanakiri," *Bangkok Post*, 1 February 1970, pp. 13–14.

185. Author's interview with Bopha, France, 1980. Educated returnees rarely knew which particular ethnic group Khmer Loeu came from. They usually divided them into "Khmer Phnong" or "Lao Phnong" (those who preferred Lao-style "sticky" rice).

186. Author's interviews with San, Paris, 29 May 1980; Chhin Phoeun, Kong Pisei, 17 September 1980.

187. Laurence Picq, *Au-delà du ciel: cinq ans chez les Khmers Rouges*, Paris: Barrault, 1984, p. 76. Picq notes other foreign ministry offices code named B-2, B-4, and B-6 (p. 42). See below.

188. Y Phandara, *Retour à Phnom Penh*, Paris: Métailié, 1982, p. 132, and Picq, *Au-delà du ciel*, pp. 31, 95, 209, 124. Besides Cheam, Kun mentions another leading minority cadre in the ministry, named Tuon.

Tri Meng Huot, a returnee from France recalled, "It was hard for us to get to know them. . . . Angkar liked them, and regarded them as the most loyal of all. This was not said openly but it could be observed. We could see that they were the bodyguards of the big people. [The minority groups] were all there, even Lao. Some spoke Lao in front of us. . . . Some told us they had only learnt Khmer in the period of the revolution, meaning since 1970. They [now] considered themselves Khmer, but there were Jarai, Lao, even Kouy. . . ."[189] A Lao cadre from Stung Treng province, a man named Savon, had charge of three foreign ministry "offices" in the capital in 1977 and 1978. These were the camps known as B-32, for more than sixty returned former diplomats; B-30, for returned students; and B-31, for their children.[190]

About four hundred more returned students had been sent to the Chamcar Loeu district of the North in December 1976. For nearly two years, they lived in neighboring camps, called B-17 and B-18. Over this period, most were arrested and executed, but survivors recall how the place was run. In charge of both camps was Kan, a cadre from Rattanakiri in his mid-twenties who had once led a bodyguard unit for Pol Pot and Ieng Sary. Kan was not well educated, but had "a very strong revolutionary standpoint." He commanded a platoon of Center troops, mostly tribesmen from Rattanakiri and Mondolkiri, and some from Kompong Thom.[191] Kan was assisted by one Khmer and four tribal cadres named Thea, Meang, Mat and Hom, all under thirty. Kan, Thea, and Mat all carried guns. Thea, a twenty-four-year-old, had been Pol Pot's personal bodyguard, and had entered Phnom Penh with him on 24 April 1975. A returnee from France, Hing Sopanya, says that "Pol Pot and Ieng Sary had brought him up since he was very young," including teaching him to read and write. She found Thea more literate and politically knowledgeable than Sin, another minority cadre who had lectured the returnees on politics in Phnom Penh the previous year. "He had seen more and was more able to discuss things. He knew about politics from reading the party's magazines and didn't say the same things over and over again." In their houses, Thea and Meang displayed photographs of themselves, taken years before, in their scant jungle garb. Now they wore black cotton uniforms like everyone else, but they continued to speak their own tribal languages among themselves. Another northeastern minority cadre was Khon, a twenty-five-year-old who had been Hou Yuon's bodyguard from 1967 to 1975.

189. Author's interview with Tri Meng Huot, Paris, 15 February 1980.

190. Author's interview with Peh Bun Tong and Kim Heang, Paris, 18 November 1979. Tong said Savon reported to the office of the CPK Center, headed by Chhim Samauk (alias Pâng). See also Y Phandara, *Retour à Phnom Penh*, pp. 97, 145, 151, 189.

191. Author's interview with returnee Khuon Thlai Chamnan, Chatenay-Malabry, 9 August 1979.

Probably because of Hou Yuon's demise, Khon was not part of the camp leadership, and his movement was restricted, though he could give orders to returnees. However, all these cadres were supervised by yet another "office," known as B-20. Kan was concurrently deputy chief of B-20. His superior was Soeun, an ethnic Khmer in his late forties, the highest ranking cadre the returnees saw. He was from a rural background and had been educated in a Buddhist wat. Soeun gave political lectures to the returnees comprising production figures for the cooperatives, praise of Democratic Kampuchea, and, from 1977, condemnation of Vietnam. In one speech that year, Soeun mixed very strong criticism of Vietnam with another statement: "We can't trust any foreign countries, including China." They were all enemies of Cambodia, he said. Sopanya recalls the alarm this provoked, as people whispered, "In that case, where do we overseas returnees fit in? Are we 'enemies' also? What is happening? The Khmer alone are now in dispute with everybody."[192]

Consistent with this chauvinist turn, as time went on, minority cadres were increasingly swept up in the purges. In late 1977, Khon was taken away by an armed CPK squad, never to be seen again. His wife disappeared soon afterwards. In early 1978, over one hundred purged cadres, some with their wives and children, arrived in Chamcar Loeu for "re-education from zero again." Many were of hill-tribe origin, some from Rattanakiri and Mondolkiri, and some Kouy from Kompong Thom. Later came more minority women whose husbands were now considered traitors. Over the ensuing months, many, perhaps all, of these people disappeared. Groups of five to ten, sometimes whole families, were taken away.[193] Back in Phnom Penh, the foreign ministry's ethnic Lao cadre, Savon, disappeared in May 1978.[194]

In the Northeast Zone

In September 1975, the CPK Center surveyed the arable land throughout Cambodia. In the Northeast Zone, it assessed the land as "reasonable," but added, "The only shortcoming is that the people are not used to working the

192. Author's interviews with returnees Hing Sopanya and Yim Nolla, Creteil, 14 November 1979, and with an anonymous returnee educated in Yugoslavia, Tuol, 28 October 1979. (Ith Sarin, *Sronos Prolung Khmaer* ("Regrets of the Khmer Soul"), Phnom Penh, 1974, says that in 1972–73 Hou Yuon had two Khmer Loeu bodyguards.)

193. Author's interviews with Hing Sopanya, 1979, and Chang Sieng, Creteil, 18 October 1979.

194. Author's interview with Peh Bun Tong, 1979; Y Phandara, *Retour à Phnom Penh*, p. 118. Savon's superior, Pâng, was purged on 22 April 1978. Tri Meng Huot (1980 interview) said the Khmer Loeu initially "had many high positions. Later there were problems, but at the beginning Angkar liked them."

land."[195] Phnom Penh Radio was more optimistic: "The hill people of Rattanakiri province have grouped themselves into small villages on the plains to
devote themselves to the cultivation of rice." In each subdistrict, the radio
continued, "the population has begun to dig small canals and dams." The CPK
was pursuing its policy to resettle the hill people in the valleys, as sedentary
agriculturalists.[196] Then, in August 1977, the radio broadcast a lengthy commentary on Mondolkiri province without even referring to its various nationalities. The hill tribes had now become "patriotic people" and "cooperative
peasants."[197]

The U.K. Minority Rights Group, after sending a fact-finding mission to
Cambodia's northeast in 1992, charged Democratic Kampuchea with forced
assimilation of the hill people. "Some were brought down from the hills to
work on irrigation projects" for the purpose of wet land cultivation. Other
highlanders "felt that their identity was being eradicated by the Khmer
Rouge. Many examples bear this out. First, the Khmer Rouge confiscated the
ceremonial jars which were used to ferment rice for rice wine. Second, under
the pretext of making ammunition, the Khmer Rouge also took away their
ceremonial gongs."[198] According to State of Cambodia officials, 12,231 rice
wine jars and 12,245 gongs were confiscated. There was resistance. In one
incident, local tribespeople shot a CPK cadre dead with a bow and arrow. They
then approached a "new person" and asked him to write the higher authorities a letter, informing them that the cadre had been killed by a bear.[199]

In his "confession," Koy Thuon revealed that in January 1976, Pol Pot
addressed a meeting in Phnom Penh about "the problem in Rattanakiri." Pot
accused Zone deputy secretary Um Neng of incorrectly implementing the CPK
line on "solidarity of the nationalities." Neng had accused both lower-level
cadres and villagers of being "traitors," and had sent troops to apprehend

195. "Examine the Control and Implementation of the Political Line to Save the
Economy and Prepare to Build the Country in Every Field," CPK Center "Document no. 3," 19
September 1975, p. 16.

196. Phnom Penh Radio, 13 June 1975, 7 P.M. Translation by Kuor Peng Kry, AP, Bangkok.

197. *FBIS*, Asia Pacific, 10 August 1977, pp. H1–2, Phnom Penh Radio, 6 August 1977.
I found only one case of Democratic Kampuchea's officially recognizing a minority group
by name. It asserted that a member of the "Monong national minority" in *Vietnam* had
accused Hanoi of being "the cruelest exterminators of the national minorities." "Voice of
Democratic Kampuchea," 17 November 1978, translation by DK embassy in Beijing.

198. *Minorities in Cambodia*, London: Minority Rights Group, 1995, which adds: "Moreover, the highlanders were forbidden to speak their own languages and had to learn
Khmer . . . husbands and wives were often separated" (pp. 12–13). If so, this distinguished the tribal people living in the Northeast Zone from those working for the regime
in Phnom Penh and other Zones, where at least they were allowed to converse in their
tribal languages.

199. Jim Taylor, personal communication, 9 January 1986.

9. The director of Tuol Sleng Prison ("S-21"), Khaing Khek Iev, alias Deuch, at a work meeting at Tuol Sleng. Photo courtesy Ung Pech (undated).

10. The Tuol Sleng leadership and their families. In the back row, Deuch is second from right, his chief interrogator Mam Nay (alias Chan) at left. Photo courtesy Ung Pech (undated).

11. Mam Nay with a file of S-21 cadres. Photo courtesy Department of Manuscripts and University Archives, Cornell University (undated).

12. Mug shots of Tuol Sleng prisoners. Author's photo, 1980.

13. Tuol Sleng. Author's photo, 1980.

14. Part of the Tuol Sleng archives. Author's photo, 1980.

15. Khmer Rouge soldiers at the Thai border, 1975. Photo courtesy *Bangkok Post*.

16. CPK Northwest Zone official Khek Penn, alias Sou (executed 1977), on the Thai border, 1975. Photo courtesy *Bangkok Post*.

17. Cambodian government soldiers and police officers hold back a crowd of demonstrators protesting outside the house of returning DK leader, Khieu Samphan. Author's photo, Phnom Penh, 27 November 1991.

18. Chinese advisers and Tuol Sleng prison staff pose at Angkor Wat, Cambodia. DK photograph, courtesy of Tuol Sleng Museum, Phnom Penh.

19. Pol Pot (left) and his deputy Nuon Chea (second-from-left) pose for an undated order-of-rank photograph of the cpk Center in a Cambodian railway carriage. Photo courtesy Ung Pech.

them. According to Koy Thuon, "A number of very good cadres were arrested and taken off to be killed. And others took their families and relatives and all fled to Vietnamese and Lao territory. And this movement was increasing."[200] But by the end of 1976 Um Neng had been promoted, replacing Ney Sarann as Zone secretary. Neng held that position for the next two years, as the flight of the hill people continued. By 1979, twenty thousand refugees from northeastern Cambodia had arrived in Laos alone.[201]

According to official State of Cambodia statistics, 3,913 people were murdered in Rattanakiri province during the DK period. These killings took place at six specific sites in the province. The majority of the victims (2,253) were of ethnic minority origin,[202] though these figures suggest that smaller ethnic groups in the province—Khmer, Lao and Chinese, perhaps mostly urban evacuees—also suffered a high toll. However, sociologist Patrick Hughes, who worked in Rattanakiri in 1992 and 1993, believes the total DK toll in the province was much higher. Hughes interviewed local people who told of many summary executions in the forests that were unrecorded in DK or soc statistics. One plausible estimate was a death toll of around 50 percent of Rattanakiri's highland population.[203]

Downriver in Kratie province (Region 505), in mid-1975 a thousand deportees from Svay Rieng arrived by boat. They were sent to live in "malaria-infested jungle" east of the Mekong. This was Sambor district, inhabited by the Phnong ethnic group. The newcomers noticed that elderly Phnong went "almost naked," wearing simple lap-laps, or sometimes shorts "brought from Phnom Penh by Angkar."[204] Phnong cadres had been appointed, some quite recently. Phnong would adopt Khmer names on joining the revolution or the chalat work brigades (in the case of youths). Sopheara, one of the new people, describes the Phnong cadres: "They understood nothing, and knew nothing about progress—only about their traditional system. They did what-

200. Koy Thuon, "Soum courup angkar ciati snaeha . . ." ("To Angkar with Respect and Love"), S-21, confession dated 4 March 1977, pp. 5–6.

201. UNHCR figures, provided to the author in Phnom Penh in 1980. See also Kimmo Kiljunen, ed., Kampuchea: Decade of the Genocide, London: Zed, 1984, table 5, p. 47.

202. Statistics provided to Jae Ku by soc officials in Rattanakiri in 1993. See Minority Rights Group, Minorities in Cambodia. Twenty Buddhist monks were also among the victims.

203. Patrick Hughes, personal communication, 17 December 1993. See also Hughes' article in the Phnom Penh Post, 9 April 1993; Hughes warns that the toll estimate of "75 percent" is a misprint for "50 percent." Hughes was human rights officer in Rattanakiri for the UN Transitional Authority in Cambodia for fifteen months.

204. Kratie was known as "Autononous" Region (damban svayat) 505. This status, like that of Region 106 (Siemreap-Oddar Meanchey), conferred autonomy only from the Zones, for Region 505 "policy came directly from the Center." But its fate was linked with that of the neighboring Eastern Zone.

ever *Angkar* told them. They were faithful to us, too, as long as we were to them, and if they had food they gave it to us to eat. Some of them helped us. Others just read the Party documents and struck at us. They spoke Khmer well, along with their own language, which they spoke at home. They were allowed to do this, although speaking Vietnamese, Chinese, French and English were prohibited. Their class was the lowest, raised to the highest. They could do whatever they liked. At first they liked the revolution and worked better than us." In 1975–76 the Sambor district chief, a former teacher named Ni, treated new and base people equally. Sopheara says that Ni "did not see us as different classes" and "did not strike at the enemy, such as new people." There were no killings from 1975 to 1977, though about twenty people in Sopheara's village died from malaria and malnutrition in 1976.[205]

Along with the Eastern Zone, Kratie is widely regarded by Cambodians as the best place to have lived during the DK period.[206] In 1976, when the Region 505 CPK secretary, Kân, died, he was replaced by Yi and his military assistant, Kuon, whom new people described as tolerant leaders. But in 1977, following the purge of Northeast Zone secretary Ney Sarann, Yi and Kuon were arrested.[207] In Sambor district, Ni was also purged in 1977 as "a traitor to the Party." The tribal Phnong, according to Sopheara, now became discontented because of low food supplies. "Privateness was not allowed in the revolutionary period, so they were not allowed to hunt or shoot animals as they had always done." Collectivization and collection of the rice crop from late 1976 also reduced food rations for both base people and new people. The work regime intensified and, as elsewhere, individual targets were introduced. Each person had to dig five cubic meters of earth per day; completion sometimes required working until 10 p.m. In early 1977, Sopheara was sent further into the forest, to a cooperative of two hundred people, including fifty newlywed couples and half a dozen Phnong families. The cooperative's president was an illiterate Phnong named Ta Blout, who had joined the revolution only a year or so before. According to Sopheara, Blout knew "the most" about CPK ideology, but that involved only terminology, not theory. "At meetings he said the same things over and over again, while we slept."

Kratie is also the home of the ethnic Stieng people. A woman who spent most of the DK period in a Stieng village claims that "most of them were ignorant, and wanted power," and at first they "liked the revolution." The

205. Author's interview with Sopheara, Phnom Penh, 23 September 1980.

206. *Asiaweek*, 2 December 1977, p. 42: "By most accounts, life in the eastern region—particularly around Kratie—was a good deal easier"; Vickery, *Cambodia 1975–1982*, pp. 130–31.

207. Information from Timothy Carney, "Camp 007" [sic], 24 March 1980, provided by Stephen Heder; and author's interview with Mme. Thun Saray, Phnom Penh, 23 September 1980 (she and her husband spent the DK period in the Sambor district of Kratie).

base people were all awarded "full rights," while the subdistrict's seventy families of Phnom Penh evacuees became "candidates." The third category, deportees, was not used. Until 1978, this woman says, "Kratie region was the best of all. Many people survived, and there were not many killings." However, by 1977 the base people, including the Stiengs, "hated the Khmer Rouge." In that year, children over seven were taken from their parents. The woman reports that separation of spouses, long working hours, the ban on religion, and the CPK's refusal to give Sihanouk power also provoked disillusionment.[208]

The Kouy minority live in the forests of the Northern Zone. The CPK dispersed some of them, but they were frequently favored. A base village of one hundred families in Preah Vihear included four or five Kouy families. Yusof, a Cham deported there, says Kouy cadres also held middle-ranking posts in the province. But the Kouy "were living like Khmers, with no separate culture." "They spoke Khmer with us, but only Kouy among themselves."[209] The case of the Kouy probably resembles that of the Sa'och in the Southwest. The tinier the ethnic group, the more favorably the CPK treated it. Even where they were allowed to speak their own languages, however, the minorities were culturally assimilated and suffered the restrictions imposed on the rest of the population.

In early 1978, a Chinese film crew arrived at Chamcar Loeu, in the north, to make a movie about the history of the Cambodian revolution. They visited B-18 and enlisted the labor of some of the educated returnees to reconstruct "Revolutionary Base No. 24," where Pol Pot had lived during the 1970–75 war. A set was built: the house he had lived in, a guerrilla hospital, and thatch cottages deep in jungle, "where an aeroplane flying overhead could not see anything." The purged tribals in B-17 were not allowed near the set. Later that year, the completed film was shown in Phnom Penh, where Hing Sopanya saw it. It portrayed the early stages of the revolution, when Pol Pot lived in the Northeast, showing tribespeople in their traditional garb. "We saw the house Pol Pot used to live in, with pictures of Marx and Lenin in his room. We had put those things there. It was staged."[210]

208. Author's interview with Mon, Phnom Penh, 5 July 1980.
209. Vickery records the assertion of a former naval captain: "Although the Kuys were the favored base peasants, when one of their villages revolted, the entire population of 700 people was killed" (p. 126). Some reports suggest, however, that the CPK retained support among Kouys as late as 1994, when Khmer Rouge forces including Kouy troops recaptured their Anlong Veng base. *Indochina Digest*, 11 March 1994, p. 2.
210. Hing Sopanya, 1979 interview.

III

The Slate Crumbles, 1977–79:
Convulsion and Destruction

CHAPTER EIGHT

Power Politics, 1976–77

The internal political life of the CPK regime appears to outsiders even more impenetrable than it did to ordinary citizens of Democratic Kampuchea, few of whom knew anything about it. The Center regarded "secrecy as the basis" of its revolution.[1] But the accounts of occasional witnesses, and surviving internal documents, allow us to trace the Center's gradual assertion of control over the fourteen thousand-strong party apparatus.[2] This casts light on the renewed repression and the squeeze on rural living conditions in 1977, detailed in Part 2. In 1976 and 1977 the Center murdered or jailed most leading CPK officials, in both the capital and the countryside, whom it saw as moderate or troublesome.

The two most important were Koy Thuon, in Phnom Penh, and So Phim, head of the Eastern Zone. The Center's main victims in this period were members of putative "networks" headed by these two, both originally from Kompong Cham province. Most were either intellectuals associated with Koy Thuon from his days as leader of the Northern Zone or, more recently, the commerce ministry; or cadres and commanders in the Eastern Zone or of Eastern origin.

As early as the Sihanouk period, U.S. intelligence agents had noticed that Phim's Eastern Zone was "in close liaison with the Viet Cong" and more "ideologically communist-oriented" than all other Khmer Rouge groups, who in 1975 and 1976 still engaged in "frequent conflict" with Eastern forces. The easterners were distinguishable by their green uniforms and more moderate behavior during the evacuation of Phnom Penh and in the subsequent

---

1. Chanthou Boua, David Chandler, and Ben Kiernan, *Pol Pot Plans the Future*, New Haven: Yale Council on Southeast Asia Studies, 1988, pp. 220–21, 173; Laurence Picq, *Au-delà du ciel: Cinq ans chez les Khmers Rouges*, Paris: Barrault, 1984, p. 26.

2. Pol Pot told the Vietnamese ambassador to Democratic Kampuchea, Pham Van Ba, in September 1977 that the CPK had fourteen thousand members. Author's interview with Pham Van Ba, Ho Chi Minh City, 28 October 1980.

administration of their Zone.[3] Speculation that So Phim shared the Center's political worldview, a honeypot tasty to DK sympathizers, has yet to attract any fluttering evidence.[4] Though Phim formally ranked fourth in the CPK hierarchy, I have found no sign of his participation in Center decisions in Democratic Kampuchea's first two years. For the crucial year from September 1975 to August 1976, the evidence shows Phim to be well out of the loop.[5]

Koy Thuon was popular in parts of his Northern Zone and among CPK intellectuals. Sihanouk, who met Thuon at Angkor Wat in 1973 and again in 1975, found him "a very nice man."[6] When Thuon told a Vietnamese official in September 1975 that Hou Yuon was suffering from "heart disease," he was not dissembling.[7] At the victory congress in May, both men had attempted to relieve some of the harshest policies of the CPK leadership. After Yuon's murder in August, Thuon lost the struggle against the abolition of money. In October, Thuon still occupied the fifth position in the CPK Standing Committee hierarchy, with responsibility for domestic and foreign trade. But he apparently fell to the sixth position the next month.[8] A purge was in the works.

Tuol Sleng

The nerve center of the purge apparatus was the *Santebal,* or Special Branch. The CPK official most directly responsible for it was Kaing Khek Iev, a short, spindly schoolteacher. In the 1960s, Iev had been deputy principal

3. See Chapters 1 to 3, and 5, pp. 205ff.; and "Cambodia Today: Life Inside Cambodia," 21 September 1976, Extracts from an Airgram Report by an Officer of the American Embassy at Bangkok, declassified 1978, p. 13, recording the account of a refugee, apparently a former CPK soldier, who reached Thailand in July 1976, noted that the Eastern Zone forces were much more lenient than their counterparts west of the Mekong, and "reported frequent conflict between the two forces where their jurisdictions meet."

4. For presentation of this view without supporting evidence, even from confessions extracted under torture, see S. Heder, "Khmer Rouge Opposition to Pol Pot: 'Pro-Vietnamese' or 'Pro-Chinese'?," in *Reflections on Cambodian Political History,* Canberra: Australian National University, Strategic and Defence Studies Centre, Working Paper No. 239, 1991, p. 3. Heder displays idiosyncratic anti-Eastern Zone bias. See p. 206, n. 97, above.

5. Though the Vietnamese were told in July 1975 that Phim ranked fourth in the CPK hierarchy, two reports from 1975 and 1976 place him fifth, after Son Sen, whom the Vietnamese were told was not on the Standing Committee. Associated Press, Bangkok, 18 April 1975, and Bruce Palling's interview with defecting helicopter pilot Pech Lim Kuon, Bangkok, 3 May 1976. See further below.

6. Norodom Sihanouk, interview with J. Pringle, A. Paul, N. Chanda and others, Beijing, January 1979. Tape kindly provided by Anthony Malcolm.

7. Author's interview with Kieu Minh, Phnom Penh, 22 October 1980.

8. "Meeting of the Standing [Committee], 9–10–1975," p. 1; "Standing [Committee] Meeting, 2–11–75 at 7 p.m.," p. 1.

of Balaing College, in Pol Pot's home province of Kompong Thom.[9] A leader of a riot in which a bus was burnt outside a police station, he was jailed by Sihanouk from 1967 to 1970.[10] French scholar François Bizot, captured by the CPK in Kompong Chhnang in late 1970, was briefly interrogated by Iev, who used the revolutionary name Deuch. In his few months' captivity, Bizot "discovered that Deuch believed all Cambodians of differing viewpoints to be traitors and liars, and that he personally beat prisoners who would not tell the 'truth,' a matter which drove him into a rage."[11] After the Special Zone was established in 1971, Vorn Vet and Son Sen appointed Deuch to run its security services. A CPK defector who met Deuch in either 1972 or 1973 recalled him as "ill-tempered, impatient, and doctrinaire."[12]

The Santebal came to be dominated by a Kompong Thom cabal. One of Deuch's lieutenants was Mam Nay, a tall, thin, pock-faced former natural science teacher. Nay had been taught by Son Sen at the National Pedagogy School, from which he graduated in 1956. Two years later he became principal of Balaing College in Kompong Thom. In 1967, he was jailed by Sihanouk along with Deuch, then his deputy principal. Another leading Santebal official was Nath, a former mechanic in the Kompong Thom electrical works. The only leading Santebal official not from Kompong Thom was Hor, who was recruited from the Special Zone, also a Center bastion. Hor joined the revolution in 1966 at age sixteen and became a full CPK member in 1973.[13] He was to sign many execution lists.

Deuch moved his operation to the capital with the rest of the Special Zone after the 1975 victory. Some of the prisoners Deuch brought along, who had been arrested as early as January 1975, were to be held in the capital for nearly two years.[14] Deuch's headquarters was now renamed "S-21." He continued to report to Son Sen, who was formally given national CPK authority over party security matters in October 1975. Deuch employed fifty-seven new prison guards between June and December 1975. During that year, 154 prisoners were incarcerated, mostly in Phnom Penh's former Bethlehem chapel.[15] At

9. According to Ung Pech (1980 interview with the author), a former inmate who in 1979 became the first director of Tuol Sleng Museum of Genocide in 1979, Deuch's father was Chinese and his mother Kaing Siew part Chinese. He was born in Choyaot, Kompong Chen subdistrict, Staung district, Kompong Thom.

10. Kiernan, *How Pol Pot Came to Power*, pp. 261, 265; Stephen Heder, personal communication.

11. Vickery, *Cambodia 1975–1982*, p. 152.

12. Chandler, *Tragedy*, p. 359 n. 77.

13. I am grateful to Ung Pech for these details.

14. "Benhchi neak tous (coh pum toan os te pruos cam baan tae ponning)" ["List of Prisoners (incomplete because we have only this many)"], undated (January 1977?), 14 folio pp.

15. M. Vickery, personal communication; *Cambodia 1975–1982*, p. 151; D. Chandler, personal communication.

least one fortunate man, Hem Sambath, was released after interrogation.[16] S-21 may have had a space problem.

In January 1976, S-21 moved to Takhmau, on the southern outskirts of Phnom Penh.[17] By March, Deuch had employed another twenty warders. In June, the prison moved again to new premises: the former high school, now known as Tuol Sleng. This site could hold up to fifteen hundred prisoners at a time.[18] The Santebal quickly began to flourish. By early 1977, Tuol Sleng employed at least 111 warders. Most, like Hor, came from Region 25, the rest from elsewhere in the Special Zone, Kompong Chhnang, or Kompong Thom. These people were beholden to the Center, not only because of their geographical origins, but also because of their very young age. Eighty-two of the one hundred and eleven warders were aged seventeen to twenty-one. Only a half-dozen had joined the revolution before 1973, and only two had worked for the Santebal before April 1975.[19] These people were to imprison and kill the vast majority of veteran CPK cadres.

The Bombing of Siemreap City

On 25 February 1976, one of Koy Thuon's former charges exploded. Siemreap city, capital of Autonomous Region 106, where Thuon had been active during the war, was rocked by two waves of five-hundred-pound bombs, six hours apart. Democratic Kampuchea announced that fifteen people had been killed and thirty injured, but a defector later claimed there were "about 100 deaths, including 30 soldiers."[20] No fewer than four possible culprits have been identified. Democratic Kampuchea radio quickly blamed U.S. F-111 bombers, which it said had flown off towards Thailand. Stephen Heder suspected Thai Air Force F-5 jets.[21] And John McBeth suggested Vietnamese

16. Chandler, *Tragedy,* p. 373 n. 24.

17. For this reason prisoners were recorded as having been "sent to Takhmau" in this period.

18. Vickery, personal communication; Anthony Barnett, "Inside S-21," *New Statesman,* 2 May 1980, p. 671.

19. David P. Chandler, personal communication, based on 111 Tuol Sleng warder biographical forms filled out in February 1977.

20. *Asiaweek,* 26 January 1979, p. 15.

21. See Stephen Heder, "Thailand's Relations with Kampuchea: Negotiation and Confrontation along the Prachinburi-Battambang Border," Cornell University, December 1977, pp. 27–28, 77–79. Democratic Kampuchea continued to insist on U.S. responsibility, even after its open break with Hanoi. See U.S. Central Intelligence Agency, *Foreign Broadcast Information Service (FBIS),* 2 December 1976, p. H1, 9 November 1977, p. H3, and 17 March 1978, p. H2. As late as December 1978, Democratic Kampuchea officials in Siemreap told Western visitors: "We have evidence that it was not Vietnam but was done by the CIA, by agents in Thailand." Malcolm Caldwell diary typescript, p. 67.

MiG's, later conceding that Chinese-built MiGs from Phnom Penh were another possibility.[22]

DK aircraft may have been involved—the cpk secretary of Region 106, Pa Thol (alias Soth), had called a clandestine meeting in Siem Reap city the previous day. Soth brought in "at least 30 communist leaders" from Region 106, Kompong Thom, and possibly as far south as Kompong Cham, according to a local company commander who defected to Thailand in 1977. At the meeting, this officer claimed, "All the soldiers in [Region] 106 wanted to create a rebellion that would allow people to go back and work as they did before the capture of Phnom Penh. . . . The thought was to start a revolt and to bring back some acceptable practices of the old regime."[23] Could the Center have discovered the plot and attempted to bombard the conspirators? The injured included "three Khmer Rouge leaders who had stayed behind after the previous day's meeting."[24]

Questions about the affair still outnumber answers. What motive could Vietnamese, Thai, or U.S. authorities have had? What knowledge of the conspiracy? What aim? Why would Hanoi, Bangkok, or Washington target an anti-DK movement? On the other hand, the cpk Center had not used such tactics of repression before, why would it do so in this case ?

McBeth rules out a U.S. role, quoting American diplomats to the effect that all U.S. warplanes had left Thai bases in December 1975. But Heder points out that F-111s could have carried out the raid from the Philippines or Taiwan. McBeth describes the raid as "Vietnam's first major strike at the Pol Pot regime." But the bombs struck Democratic Kampuchea's *enemies*. Did Hanoi attack some other target, accidentally injuring the conspirators? McBeth's sources say that at 3 P.M., "at least three bombs hit an arms depot a short distance from a hotel [and] set off secondary explosions in the ammunition dump that lasted nearly two hours. The hotel was destroyed and the blasts blew out the windows of the villa behind the hotel." (The three wounded conspirators were staying in the villa.) Such a coincidence would be less far-fetched if the theory of a MiG-19 jet did not rest upon unnamed, "well-placed sources," presumably American intelligence agents, who in 1979 had other reasons to suddenly implicate Hanoi. The only eyewitness testimony suggesting a MiG is an interviewee who said the plane "was silver with swept-back wings." McBeth's sources further assert that the raid occurred "in the afternoon, not in the

22. John McBeth, "That Was No F-111; That Was a MiG," *Asiaweek*, 26 January 1979. When I questioned McBeth about his story, he agreed there was no reason to suspect Vietnamese more than Chinese MiGs. See also Vickery, *Cambodia*, pp. 127–28, 322 n. 229, where Vickery wrongly says I "accepted as fact" the involvement of a Vietnamese MiG.

23. *Asiaweek*, 2 December 1977, pp. 36–37.

24. Ibid., 26 January 1979, p. 15.

morning," though another eyewitness confirms a morning explosion.[25] Yet another on-the-spot account insists there were two raids, "once in the morning, and then at about 2 P.M.," as Democratic Kampuchea's 1976 protest note charged. This person continues, "I talked to a former Lon Nol pilot who was with me at the time, and he said they were F-111s or F-105s, or both."[26]

McBeth's U.S. sources claimed the Vietnamese attacked "in response to a clash between Khmer Rouge forces and Vietnamese regulars on a Lao-Cambodian frontier a day before." I found no evidence of such a clash.[27] But there is evidence of a Thai-Cambodian clash two days before the raid. A PLO official in Cambodia at the time, who immediately visited the bomb site with Swedish and other diplomats from Beijing, reported that on February 23, "Thai fishing boats, protected by armored vessels, intruded into Kampuchea's territorial waters. . . . Some Thai boats were sunk and a Kampuchean vessel damaged." Ieng Sary, the Palestinian said, had cancelled an appointment with Thai officials scheduled for the day of the raid.[28] But this report, too, lacks corroboration.

On the available evidence none of the four theories seems convincing. But the raid calls for explanation. Extraordinary coincidences must be considered. A morning ground explosion, then an unrelated air raid; an unprecedented, rogue decision by U.S., Thai, or Vietnamese air commands; a foreign raid merely coinciding with the Cambodian conspiracy; or one launched with full knowledge and timed to destroy it? Two possibilities require the least complicated assumptions. First, because of geographical proximity, Thailand could have gained knowledge of the conspiracy more easily than the United States or Vietnam. Indeed, the CPK defector says that on the previous day, the conspirators had "mapped out an escape route to Thailand in case their rebel forces became encircled."[29] There may have been some prior arrangement with the Thai military. But why would Thailand turn on its co-conspirators?[30]

Second, the rebels' fear of detection by the Center seems justified. A radio communication from a Siemreap loyalist could have quickly alerted the Center

25. Vickery, *Cambodia*, p. 128.

26. Author's interview with Sovannareth, Rouen, 10 October 1979.

27. N. Chanda reported from the Cambodian–Lao border that "the situation on the border has been deteriorating since the end of 1976"—not before. *Far Eastern Economic Review (FEER)*, 12 December 1978.

28. Hamad Abdul Aziz al Aiya, "Modern Kampuchea," a 37-page translated 1976 manuscript in the possession of the author, p. 36. Al Aiya was the PLO representative in Beijing at the time.

29. *Asiaweek*, 2 December 1977, p. 36.

30. Indirect evidence only hints at a Thai role. When CPK defector Lim Mean (alias Peam) arrived in Thailand in November 1978, Thai intelligence debriefers recorded that "Peam says that in 1977, in the town of Kompong Cham, there was a large explosion. This was an arms and ammunition depot. There were sizeable losses and damage. The Khmer Rouge said that this was the plan of comrade Seuy (or Sey?), chief of the army. Among those arrested and killed were Seuy, Chak Krey, Soth . . . " This could place the explosion in early 1976, a clear reference to the Siemreap bombing, not to Kompong Cham. A mistake by Peam, or his Thai

to the conspiracy and given the physical location of its leaders. This is as likely as any other possibility, despite the weakness of the case for a MiG and the Center's slow followup on the ground in Siemreap. Soth and his co-conspirators continued to run Region 106 for a year after the raid. But Koy Thuon vanished within a month. The bombing and the mystery of Koy Thuon's disappearance may be linked to another series of explosions, in Phnom Penh itself in April 1976.

Trouble in Phnom Penh

By mid-March, Thuon was demoted to the seventh position in the CPK hierarchy, though he was still running foreign trade.[31] He fails to appear in subsequent Standing Committee records, however. He was not named to the new cabinet in April.[32]

The last time Thuon's name appears in the minutes of party meetings is on 17 March. He chaired a meeting of four members of the CPK's Purchasing Committee to review lists of foreign orders. Their first decision, concerning railway and textile factory machinery, attests to the political atmosphere: "The Committee dares not decide on some of the lists of equipment, and leaves them to the Standing [Committee] to examine first." However, the Committee daringly amended other lists, adding and removing various items "according to need." It noted, almost casually: "*Angkar* has already decided correctly on some lists of equipment, which the Committee does not alter." But the Purchasing Committee did not consider *Angkar* omniscient. It decided that "some other lists, such as those concerning the people's livelihood, agricultural and factory instruments, electricity, etc.," required changes. It made twenty amendments. The price of tetron fabric was too high; Cambodia should buy only cotton. The order for large electric generators should also be canceled. Tractors of twelve horsepower were "too small, with only two wheels," and should not be bought. Instead the committee "request[ed] purchase of 55 and 35 h.p. tractors."[33]

---

interrogators, is unlikely. Thais could have altered his testimony to avoid discussion of the Siemreap bombing. French translation of the Thai transcript, p. 6.

31. "Minutes of the Standing Meeting, 11 March 1976," p. 1; "Komnot haet ong prochum kana kammathikar riep cam tumninh dael trew tinh, thngai 17 mina 1976" ("Minutes of the Meeting of the Purchasing Committee, 17 March 1976"), p. 1.

32. Moreover, Thuon's name was omitted from a list of members of the CPK's Commerce Committee. "Summary of Decisions Made by the Standing Committee on 19–20–21 April 1976," pp. 1, 5–6. (See also "Minutes of the Standing Committee Meeting on 7–5–76," p. 1.) Translation by Chanthou Boua.

33. "Minutes of the Meeting of the Purchasing Committee, 17 March 1976." Present were Koy Thuon, Vorn Vet, Sua Vasi (Doeun), and Phouk Chhay; none survived Democratic Kampuchea.

Here the committee stumbled onto a minefield. Tractors were tainted items in Democratic Kampuchea. The next year, for instance, Khieu Samphan would boast that "we have no machines." Instead, Cambodians "do everything by mainly relying on the strength of our people."[34] China had in fact sent two hundred small tractors, but, according to a Chinese embassy official, they were left to rust. Pol Pot described them as useless "iron buffaloes."[35] So the Purchasing Committee was broaching an important issue. And apart from its dangerous preference for large tractors, the committee's forthright tone may also have irked Angkar.

In his "confession" the next year, Phouk Chhay reported that at the end of March 1976, he was quietly approached by Doeun, a member of the Purchasing Committee. Doeun whispered, "Wait and see, brother Thuch [Koy Thuon] might be in trouble. Angkar no longer trusts him. And maybe he will be removed from office. Therefore be careful. Especially, act as if you know and hear nothing. Act as if you have never known him at all."[36]

On 30 March, the party Center adopted "a framework of procedures for implementing our revolutionary authority." The decision was entitled "The Authority to Smash [people] Inside and Outside the Ranks." In the villages, the Zone and Autonomous Region Standing Committees "must decide" on whom to "smash" (komtech). This Center order temporarily decentralized political control, leaving Soth in command in Autonomous Region 106. But it also legitimized political murder. For its part, the Center claimed the authority to "smash" its personnel "around the Center's offices." This gave it the capacity to deal with Koy Thuon without interference from his Northern Zone network. The general staff was given the same unchecked power over the Center armed forces.[37] The target here was probably Chan Chakrey, army deputy chief of staff[38] and former commander of Heng Samrin's 1st Eastern Zone division. Chakrey had come under Center suspicion the previous year.[39]

The first indication of what followed emerged only the next year. A CPK

34. FBIS, 18 April 1977, p. H5, Phnom Penh Radio, 15 April 1977.
35. "Squandered Chinese Aid Spelt Pol Pot's Ruin," *Bangkok Post,* 1 May 1979, pp. 1, 3. See also *Pol Pot Plans the Future,* p. 314, where Pol Pot is quoted by Hu Nim as favoring a Region "which does not use machinery at all, only the labor force."
36. Phouk Chhay confession, "Ompi sakammapheap rebos khnyom niw knong muntir angkar" ("On My Activities in the Organisation's Office"), S-21, 5 April 1977, p. 3.
37. "Decisions of the Central Committee on a Variety of Questions," *Pol Pot Plans the Future,* p. 3. Unlike other CPK leadership documents, this lacks a precise description of the meeting's status and quorum.
38. *Kampuchea Dossier,* II, Hanoi, 1978, p. 65; Heder interview with Um Samang, Sa Keo, 10 March 1980.
39. "Kar prochum ajentraiy thngai 9–10–75" ("Meeting of the Standing [Committee] on 9–10–1975"); see Ch. 3, p. 101, above.

defector told U.S. officials in Thailand that Chakrey had "attempted to poison Pol Pot." The defector said Chakrey was motivated by the 'hardships' the people had to endure. A cook related to a Chakrey accomplice added poison to the CPK secretary's food. The plot was foiled, however, "when one of the guards at Pol Pot's headquarters inadvertently sampled the food in the kitchen and died immediately."[40] It seems the conspiracy went undiscovered. But this was not all.

"Around April 1976," recalls a former Eastern Zone soldier stationed in Phnom Penh, "artillery was set up at Chbar Ampeou," Chakrey's base just across the river east of Phnom Penh.[41] The aim was "to bombard Pol Pot's headquarters." The soldier continued, "I knew some of the troops who were involved in this plan. . . . They did not know where the orders came from. Anyway, the Center found out about the plan and suppressed it before it could be carried out."[42]

Information Minister Hu Nim was later to describe Chakrey as "sizzling, impetuous, proud, and swaggering." At a meeting with Nim around this time, Chakrey allegedly revealed, "I do not hang around, waiting for this and that, like Khuon [Koy Thuon]. . . . Whenever an opportunity arises, I will attack."[43] At 4:35 A.M. on 2 April, grenades went off behind the royal palace. After sunrise a leaflet was found there, proclaiming, "The Master Sergeant Is About to Come out and Fight." Two days later, Santebal officers arrested a soldier named Yim Sombat, who confessed to having thrown the grenades. He named seven others involved, but said they had not wanted to kill anyone, only intending a disruption. They had acted on instructions from two officers, one of whom had left the leaflet. These officers commanded a company of Chakrey's 170th Division, stationed behind the palace. According to a Santebal report, their battalion commander immediately fled, "almost to the border." This hints at possible Vietnamese involvement. But the commander probably fled to the Eastern Zone. He returned to Phnom Penh on 25 April, and the division reassigned him to bridge construction detail.[44] On 5 May, the Santebal hauled in Yim Sombat's father, a garage attendant.[45]

Meanwhile, the two company commanders were arrested on 12 April. Presumably under torture, they implicated both Chakrey and Chhouk, CPK secre-

40. Kenneth Quinn, "The Pattern and Scope of Violence," in Jackson, ed., *Cambodia 1975–1978*, p. 195–97.
41. Boua, Chandler, and Kiernan, eds., *Pol Pot Plans the Future*, p. 298.
42. Stephen Heder's interview with Um Samang, who came from Region 21 and who was stationed in Phnom Penh from May 1975. Sa Keo, 10 March 1980. Samang added, "There was no fighting."
43. Boua, Chandler, and Kiernan, eds., *Pol Pot Plans the Future*, p. 299.
44. This and information in subsequent paragraphs come from Kaing Khek Iev (Deuch), "Sekkedei sorop domnaer ruang pi mun" ("Summary Report on Previous Events"), S-21, 6 August 1976, 6 pp.
45. "List of the Names of Prisoners Who Entered in the Year 1976," S-21, dated 26 May 1977, no. 1377.

tary of Eastern Region 24. The Santebal concluded that their aim was "to strike at the influence of the Kampuchean revolutionary party both among the people and abroad." The machinery of state repression ground slowly. As the two officers were being worked over, at an April 19 meeting the Standing Committee dropped Koy Thuon's name from the Commerce Committee. It also demoted Chakrey. The deputy chief of staff was deprived of his command, demoted to the rank of a "mere cadre with the division general staff, helping the general staff in attack operations, not in direct charge of forces."[46]

On 12 May, the Santebal arrested Chok Yun, the battalion commander from the 73rd Regiment who had initially fled. Yun "confessed" that Chakrey had ordered him to try to kill Sihanouk at the palace,[47] and his superiors, commanders of the 73rd Regiment and the 170th Division, to "kill the Organisation" (that is, Pol Pot) at a meeting celebrating the first anniversary of victory in the olympic stadium on 15 April. As Pol Pot addressed the crowd that morning, however, "the plan went wrong and it failed."[48] Someone may have been arrested on the spot. That evening, only Khieu Samphan's afternoon speech was broadcast over the radio.[49]

Chakrey was arrested on 19 May, the commanders of the 73rd and the 170th the next day.[50] The latter's chief of logistics fled east to Region 24.[51] Santebal chief Deuch reported to Pol Pot that he had uncovered a larger "espionage" organization, which he called "the rubber plantation network." This accusation was another strike at the Eastern Zone. "They fired guns and shells at Wat Saravann and Wat Unnalom, and fired volleys at the School of Fine Arts, and one shell opposite the Palace. The distribution of leaflets was done by this group directly, in combination with the network in the 170th."[52]

46. "Summary of Decisions Made by the Standing Committee on 19–20–21 April 1976," p. 4.
47. Later Ieng Thirith claimed, "The Vietnamese agents tried to kill Sihanouk. One of them threw a hand grenade on him in the Royal Palace in 1976. We got the culprit red-handed." Mukundan C. Menon, "Interview with Madam Ieng Thirith," November 1979, *Third World Unity* (New Delhi), p. 9.
48. Deuch, "Summary Report," p. 3.
49. Bruce Palling's interview with defecting helicopter pilot Pech Lim Kuon, Bangkok, 3 May 1976.
50. "Important Culprits," p. 2.
51. Author's interview with Sin Song, Phnom Penh, 12 August 1980.
52. Deuch, "Summary Report," p. 4. It is unlikely that in a report to Pol Pot Deuch would have invented such incidents in the capital itself: presumably Pot was already aware of them. In 1978, S-21 repeated, "The Chakrey group exploded grenades behind the Royal Palace, [and] fired on the National Museum" ("The Last Joint Plan," in Jackson, ed., *Cambodia 1975–1982*, p. 299). In a 1978 publication, Democratic Kampuchea downgraded Chakrey to "the chief of the units stationed in the south of Prey Veng province," betraying sensitivity to the seriousness of these events (*Livre Noir: Faits et preuves des actes d'aggression et d'annexion du Vietnam contre le Kampuchéa*, Phnom Penh, Ministry of Foreign Affairs, September 1978, p. 98).

A 1977 defector reported that six hundred of Chakrey's troops had joined the mutiny.[53] The cpk's internal magazine, *Tung Padevat*, proclaimed in its June 1976 issue, "We have destroyed the enemies within our country and scattered many of them. They have no strong forces."[54] David Chandler has argued, on the other hand, that all this involved more smoke than fire: "The soldiers, it seems, wanted to be demobilized and allowed to return home," and possibly "mutinied for better living conditions and the right to get married."[55] Such issues may have been a factor. But Chandler overlooks the testimony of a string of defectors—three in 1977 and 1978, and another cpk source in 1980— all suggesting much more was afoot.[56] The coup plot charge seems corroborated. But the targeting of an alleged "rubber plantation network" quickly broadened the scope of the Center's crackdown.

Targeting the East

In this period, February to May 1976, Democratic Kampuchea was undertaking a massive military buildup (see Chapter 4). The Center may have considered Phnom Penh vulnerable. In April, ten regiments were stationed in the capital—a soldier for nearly every member of its civilian population of twenty thousand.[57] In early June, Pol Pot warned not of foreign incursions, but of possible internal unrest: "The Party suggests that the majority of the armed forces must stay with the people. Only a sufficient number are along the borders."[58] But Chakrey's arrest had occurred on the very day that Ieng Sary broke off Democratic Kampuchea's border negotiations with Vietnam. During over two months of torture in Tuol Sleng prison, Chakrey was forced to confess that he belonged to an espionage network directed by the Vietnamese, the cia, and the Soviets.[59] Newly threatened by internal dissension, the cpk leadership also needed scapegoats for its foreign policy.

53. François Ponchaud, "Situation interne du Kampuchéa Démocratique en 1977," paper presented at the "Cambodia Hearing," Oslo, February 1978, p. 4.

54. *Tung Padevat*, no. 6, June 1976, p. 20.

55. Chandler, *Brother Number One*, pp. 133, 223 n. 23. He offers no evidence; the only possible evidence I found is in Hu Nim's confession (*Pol Pot Plans the Future*, p. 298), where Chakrey allegedly said, "The soldiers don't have enough, and they are hungry."

56. Chandler, *Tragedy*, wrongly states that "nearly all the evidence against Chakrei's plot comes from S-21" (p. 374 n. 28), but concedes that "a genuine antigovernment plot at this time cannot be ruled out" (n. 29). See also pp. 318 n. 30, 321, above.

57. Pech Lim Kuon, interview with Bruce Palling, 3 May 1976, pp. 6, 19.

58. *Tung Padevat*, No. 6, June 1976. See *Pol Pot Plans the Future*, p. 10. For public consumption this emphasis was reversed in 1978; see *Livre Noir*, p. 98.

59. See Chandler, *Brother Number One*, p. 134, and *The Tragedy of Cambodian History*, p. 288.

Chakrey may have hoped for support from his former commander, Eastern Zone leader So Phim. But Phim, officially a member of the CPK Standing Committee, had attended none of the fourteen meetings since September 1975 for which records are extant.[60] And in early May 1976, Phim went to China for medical treatment. He did not return until August.[61] During his absence, the Center first removed the military foundation of Eastern Zone influence in Phnom Penh: the 170th Division. The Chakrey arrests were followed on 9 July by that of a fourth member of the division's staff. Chakrey's wife, Moeung Heng, was jailed on 19 September. By November, 241 serving and former members of the 170th had been imprisoned in Tuol Sleng. Immediately after the Santebal had moved there in June, the number of arrests increased to fill the new spaces available. In the July-September quarter, 570 incoming prisoners were registered, half as many again as in the previous six months.[62] None survived.

Meanwhile the Center moved on the East itself. July and August saw the arrests not only of Chhouk, secretary of Region 24, but also of Ly Phen, political commissar of the Eastern Zone armed forces, and Bun Sani, director of the Zone Rubber Plantations.[63] In August, Deuch claimed that Ly Phen was a CIA agent "hidden inside the CPK according to the slogan 'learn from the revolution to strike back at the revolution.'"[64] Bun Sani was presumably held responsible for the "rubber plantation network." The implications for So Phim were ominous. The Center was now concentrating on undermining him. These seven Eastern Zone figures were the *only* leading cadres arrested from May to August 1976.[65] The Santebal claimed that from July to September 1976, the dissidents distributed "tracts and propaganda and posters"

60. The CPK Standing Committee meetings for which minutes, including lists of those present, survive, took place on 9 October and 2 November 1975, and 9 January, 22 February (two), 28 February, 11 and 13 March, and 3, 7, 14, 15, 17 and 30 May 1976. I am grateful to a Cambodian source and to David Chandler for providing me with copies.

61. S. Heder, *Reflections on Cambodian Political History,* p. 7.

62. "Benhchi chhmou neak tous dael coul khnong chhnam 1976" ("List of the Names of Prisoners Who Entered in the Year 1976"), S-21, dated 26 May 1977.

63. "Important Culprits," pp. 12–13. This translation mistakenly dates Ly Phen's arrest at 8 July 1977; it was mid-1976. See Deuch, "Summary Report," pp. 4, 6. Ly Phen's S-21 code number, "IV," reveals he was arrested before Ruos Phuon (9 July 1976, code no. "VII"). Chakrey was "I," Chhouk (28 August 1976) "VIII."

64. Deuch, "Summary Report," p. 4.

65. In the S-21 list of 242 "important culprits" arrested in the two years from 1976 to 1978, the only people apprehended from May to August 1976 were from the Eastern Zone or the former Eastern 170th Division. "Important Culprits," esp. pp. 1–2, 12; and Kiernan, "Wild Chickens, Farm Chickens, and Cormorants," in Chandler and Kiernan, *Revolution and Its Aftermath in Kampuchea,* pp. 175–86, esp. p. 183. Of two other important prisoners arrested in this period, at least one, Chu Bun Liet (code no. "VI"), was also connected to Chakrey's former Eastern group. Deuch, "Summary Report," p. 6.

that Chhouk had allegedly brought in "from the east," but "no largescale activity was possible."[66] Perhaps discouraged, Chhouk seems to have antici- pated his fate. A woman from Region 24 reports that before his arrest, Chhouk organized the release from prison of several truckloads of educated new people, whom he advised to flee to Vietnam, saying, "You are many and I am alone. You will survive and I will die."[67]

Koy Thuon, for his part, disappears from view at this time. Democratic Kampuchea later announced that he had been arrested some time in 1976.[68] Another source says he was placed "under house arrest near the Independence Monument."[69] In light of later events it is possible that he briefly evaded cus- tody.[70] A 1976 Santebal manual records that during a meeting, "an internal enemy escaped . . . from the interrogation place." The document adds, "There's only been this one occasion on which a spy has escaped," but it was "the most bitter defeat that our Special Branch Ministry has ever had."[71] Democratic Kampuchea was in crisis.

Setting up a Government

Apart from the military buildup and the tensions with Vietnam, two domestic policy problems confronted the Center in this period. The first was setting up a public political structure: a presidency, a cabinet, and a legis- lature. Following proclamation of the constitution in January, elections were scheduled for 20 March. Two weeks beforehand, Sihanouk voluntarily resigned as head of state. Even this private gesture angered Pol Pot, who told the

66. "List of Statistics of the Santebal S-21," p. 58. See note 71, below.
67. Author's interview, Phnom Penh, 2 October 1980. This woman described Chhouk as "a good man," and said that in Region 24, 1975 was "okay" (*kron bao*), 1976 was "a bit tougher," but 1977 was "very tough," because the CPK began arresting and "killing all sorts of people." And "the end of 1978 was even worse."
68. *Livre Noir*, p. 73. That Thuon was first arrested in 1976 is also indicated in Vorn Vet's 1978 confession: "After the Chakrei affair broke, . . . the Party decided to arrest the con- temptible Thuch [Koy Thuon] and the network of intellectuals" (undated, p. 43).
69. Author's interview with Hun Sen, Phnom Penh, 21 October 1980.
70. A member of the Vietnamese embassy in Cambodia in 1975-78 insisted that he saw Thuon personally in Phnom Penh in "late 1976" (author's interview with Kieu Minh, Phnom Penh, 22 October 1980). In 1978 François Ponchaud reported the account of a CPK military defector who claimed that Koy Thuon had attended a rebel meeting in Oddar Meanchey province in September 1976. (See below.) If so, Thuon was recaptured. He was taken to Tuol Sleng on 25 January 1977 and executed on 17 March. *People's Revolutionary Tribunal*, Phnom Penh, August 1979, Document no. 2.5.24, DK S-21 document, "Important Culprits (Arrested from 1976 to April 9, 1978)," English translation, p. 13; and "The Last Joint Plan," 1978 S-21 document, English translation, p. 10 (in Jackson, *Cambodia 1975-1982*, p. 304).
71. "List of Statistics of the Santebal S-21." This Tuol Sleng interrogation manual con- sists of handwritten notes on pages numbered 51-115 of a workbook. The quotation is trans- lated by Stephen Heder.

Standing Committee that the prince had no right to resign until told to do so. Described six months earlier as "a scab that drops off by itself,"[72] Sihanouk now had to await his instructions. Khieu Samphan reported that the prince had "crawled and begged" to step down.[73] But the Center insisted on deciding even the timing of its subjects' powerlessness.

In the elections, only approved candidates stood, and there was no campaigning and little voting. The Center chose the 250 successful candidates, according to one of them, Mat Ly, who says that peasants in cooperatives could not participate: "only workers at worksites voted."[74] Pol Pot secured a seat in the new Cambodian People's Representative Assembly (CPRA) as a representative of "rubber plantation workers." On 30 March, before the assembly could meet, the Center resolved the "question of setting up the government, [which] we have repeatedly discussed back and forth among ourselves ever since May [1975]." Pol Pot would head the new cabinet, with three deputy prime ministers: Ieng Sary for foreign affairs, Vorn Vet for the economy, and Son Sen for defense. The Center also made another decision: "Sihanouk is ripe now. He has run out of wind. He cannot go any further forward. Therefore we have decided to retire him, according to the wishes of others."[75] Three days later, only hours after grenades had exploded behind his palace, the prince submitted his "request for retirement," explaining that the CPRA would "elect the patriots who are to be members of the Government."[76]

The CPRA assembled for the first time on 10 April for a one-hour evening meeting at the old sports stadium. It chose a CPRA Standing Committee of ten. Nuon Chea became its president; Mok, its first vice president; and Khek Penn, its second vice president. Though the Center had resolved the previous month that So Phim would become first vice president,[77] Mok was now promoted over him. Chakrey's coup attempt, and his eastern connection, were the probable reasons. The CPRA Standing Committee seemed designed as a kind of party "senate," representing the Zones rather than the Center. Phim's removal was compensated for by inclusion of three Eastern representatives, Mat Ly among them.

The next morning everyone re-convened at the Chatomuk Auditorium in Phnom Penh. On the way in the door at 7 A.M., all 250 representatives were given clean white shirts. After everyone had changed into them, Phouk Chhay opened the program. Then Nuon Chea and Khieu Samphan spoke, for

72. See Chapter 3, p. 100, above.
73. Chandler, *Brother Number One*, pp. 114–15.
74. Author's interview with Mat Ly, Phnom Penh, 13 August 1980.
75. Boua, Chandler, and Kiernan, eds., *Pol Pot Plans*, pp. 6–7.
76. FBIS, Asia Pacific, 5 April 1976, p. H1, Phnom Penh Radio, 4 April 1976.
77. Boua, Chandler, and Kiernan, eds., *Pol Pot Plans*, p. 7.

nearly two hours. Samphan assured the representatives that "our Assembly has not stemmed from any election trick."[78] Mat Ly noticed Hu Nim in the audience, "looking upset." At 9 A.M. the proceedings were closed. Everyone filed out again, handing back their white shirts as they left the building.[79] They never reconvened. It was quickly announced over the radio, however, that at 2:30 P.M., "the CPRA resumed its work, debating around the clock all the topics of the agenda for three consecutive days."[80] Khieu Samphan asserted that "our people's genuine representatives have come into the Assembly as if it were their own home, to debate freely to solve the problems of our nation."[81]

Thus on 14 April, it was announced that the CPRA had chosen "Pol Pot" as Democratic Kampuchea's new prime minister. It was the first time Saloth Sar had used this name. Previously, he had been known only as "Pol," "comrade Secretary," or "the Organization."[82] Likewise, Nuon Chea, until then known as Nuon, now assumed his official name. Sok Thuok (alias Vorn) was proclaimed deputy prime minister for the economy under his new name, Vorn Vet.[83] He presided over six economic committees: agriculture, industry, rubber plantations, communications, energy, and commerce. The heads of each committee were not named, because of Koy Thuon's disappearance from the Commerce Committee.[84] But it was announced that they would hold cabinet rank, making Vorn Vet a super-minister. At the same level, Ieng Sary and Son Sen were reappointed deputy prime ministers for foreign affairs and national defense. Thiounn Thioeunn became minister of health, and his brother Thiounn Mum, minister of energy.[85] A third brother, Thiounn Prasith, headed the Asia department at the foreign ministry. A fourth, ex-businessman Thiounn Chum, would take charge of Democratic Kampuchea's finances in

78. FBIS, Asia Pacific, 16 April 1976, p. H12, Phnom Penh Radio 13 April 1976.

79. Mat Ly, interviews with the author, Phnom Penh, 13 August 1980, and with S. Thion and M. Vickery, 27 August 1981.

80. Phnom Penh Radio on 13 April also said the 11 April session had closed at 11.30 A.M. but gave no starting time. FBIS, Asia Pacific, 16 April 1976, p. H14.

81. Ibid., p. H4, Phnom Penh Radio, 15 April 1976.

82. For the use of the term "the Organization" to describe Pol Pot personally, see Boua, Chandler, and Kiernan, Pol Pot Plans, p. 232, and Chandler, Brother Number One, p. 114.

83. Chandler incorrectly states that apart from Saloth Sar, "none of the other members of the government would take new names at this time" (Brother Number One, p. 117). Vorn Vet had been known as Vorn since 1965 and as "Vet" from 1959 to 1965 (Vorn Vet, typed confession, undated [December 1978?], p. 1), but never before as "Vorn Vet." The names "Pol," "Nuon," and "Vorn" were still used on 30 March 1976; Pol Pot Plans, p. 7.

84. At a meeting on 19–21 April, the CPK Standing Committee still could find no head for the Commerce Committee, and on 7 May it decided to appoint Non Suon, transferring him from the Agriculture Committee and grooming Sua Vasi (Doeun) to take up the job several months later.

85. Y Phandara, Retour à Phnom Penh, Paris: Métaillé, 1982, pp. 106, 127.

1978, completing the transition from court to communism of a prominent palace family, much as Pol Pot himself did.[86]

For his part, Khieu Samphan replaced Sihanouk as head of state, becoming president of the new state presidium. So Phim became his first vice president, a nominal position previously proposed for Sihanouk's aged, loyal aide, Penn Nouth.[87] There is no evidence that the state presidium ever met. This fiction only highlighted the mysteries of a new government run by unknown names and composed of unnamed ministers. The new, formal face of Democratic Kampuchea was no more open than the old one.

Confusion abounded within and without the country. The pilot who flew out to Thailand on 30 April knew that Saloth Sar was Democratic Kampuchea's top leader, but added that "Pol Pot" was "not an important man," and even said he knew *both* men were "fat," as he had flown each of them in his helicopter![88] The head of the Asia department of the DK foreign ministry, Thiounn Prasith, told Cambodian officials in Paris that Pol Pot had fought in the anti-Japanese resistance in the 1940s and that he had been born in a village on the Vietnamese border, where he had worked in a rubber plantation.[89] (As late as February 1978, the DK ambassador to China denied that Pol Pot was Saloth Sar, who he said had "died during the war."[90]) None of this information was correct.

On 22 April, the new cabinet convened in Phnom Penh. Pol Pot began by pointing out that the "old government in the framework of the United Front" had been replaced by "a revolutionary government purely for the worker-peasants of the pure Communist Party of Kampuchea." He added, "So we start to show our face. . . . Our government is not a coalition like before. We take full responsibility for the rights and wrongs, the good and bad, the gains and losses, inside and outside the country, for friends and enemies. No one else besides us." One of the new government's tasks was "to push the people to be happy."

Pol Pot then pointed out that "the American imperialists and their lackeys . . . hoped that Sihanouk and his lackeys would still have a lot of influence [and] possibilities to again gather forces in order to stir up trouble and give us difficulties in all fields. . . . So we would have to divide state power, [and give] some to Sihanouk, that is, there would be red and blue together, not pure red."

86. See Kiernan, *How Pol Pot*, pp. 29–32, for details of the Thiounn brothers' pedigree and careers.

87. Boua, Chandler, and Kiernan, eds., *Pol Pot Plans*, p. 7. Ros Nhim of the Northwest was named second vice president of the State Presidium.

88. Bruce Palling, interview with Pech Lim Kuon, Bangkok, 3 May 1976.

89. *Far Eastern Economic Review,* 25 June 1976.

90. Y Phandara, *Retour à Phnom Penh*, p. 56.

Such power-sharing was out of the question. "This is the plan of the American imperialists. . . . The same for Russia. If we work with Sihanouk, we could not speed up. They would look for occasions to attack us from both west and east. They hoped that Sihanouk and his lackies would raise the nationalist flag against the revolution. But Sihanouk could not raise the flag, he pulled it down instead. Nobody [else] pulled it down, he did it himself. When Sihanouk resigned there was no reaction from the world. . . . That is what angered them the most."[91]

The second domestic policy problem facing the cpk was the adoption of an economic strategy for the future. A stopgap 1976 plan had been developed, but a new Four-Year Plan was required for the period from 1977 to 1980. Pol Pot hinted at its significance in a speech to Western Zone officials in June 1976. From 1977, he said, the state would "take rice from the Zone to make purchases," and therefore production targets for 1977 "will be higher, much more than three tons per hectare," even up to eleven tons by 1980.[92]

The cpk Standing Committee adopted a 1977-1980 Economic Plan along these lines at an extended meeting from 21 July to 2 August.[93] It is not known who attended, but the Eastern and Western Zone leaders, So Phim and Chou Chet, were both absent in China.[94] Another Center meeting was held from 21 to 23 August, which Phim and Chet, who returned to Phnom Penh on the same plane, might have attended. Exactly when they returned from China is unknown, and the minutes of the meeting do not survive. But we do have Pol Pot's speech explaining the plan. He pushed for rapid decision, because "enemies attack and torment us." He added, "From the east and from the west, they persist in pounding us and worrying us. If we are slow and weak, they will mistreat us."[95]

Sin Song, a former commissar in Chakrey's division who had become a Region 24 economics cadre under Chhouk, asserts that the Center now used Chakrey's "confession" to implicate Chhouk. "Whether he had in fact said it or not, they showed what it said about Chhouk to So Phim. Therefore [Phim] had to pass on the order to arrest Chhouk, because of this document."[96] Chhouk was detained on 28 August. Three days later, on his first day in Tuol Sleng, he wrote a short note protesting his innocence and revealing that he

91. "Speech of the Comrade Secretary at the First Ministerial Committee Meeting, 22 April 1976," pp. 2-3.
92. See Boua, Chandler, and Kiernan, eds., *Pol Pot Plans*, p. 12 and Document 2.
93. See Ibid., p. 37 and Document 3; Chandler, *Brother Number One*, pp. 120ff.
94. Heder, *Reflections*, p. 7. Chou Chet had gone to China on 26 June, after Pol Pot's visit to his Zone.
95. See Boua, Chandler, and Kiernan, eds., *Pol Pot Plans* , pp. 120-21 and Document 4.
96. Author's interview with Sin Song, Phnom Penh, 12 August 1980.

knew immediately what was in store for him: "I die under the red revolutionary flag!"[97] He was soon confessing to "shortcomings" in his adminstration of Region 24: "My standpoint on the offensive to interrogate traitors in order to clean up [the enemy] was not fierce. I left them time to enable them to escape. Prisoners were continually getting away." Worse, enemies got in: "In establishing the armed forces I did not [just] bring in base people. People such as outcasts. . . . were buried [within the forces]. I am not sure of their background. In establishing the administration I liked theorists who could talk and write."[98] Chhouk begged the party to "forgive" him and to "spare my life." The next day Deuch sent a copy of the confession to "the Organization." The charges were disseminated to other CPK leaders.

The accusations against Chhouk seem to have worried So Phim. A carpenter in Phim's district recalls his mood after his return from China: "So Phim denounced [Chhouk] as a traitor in accordance with the information he had received from above, from the Center."[99] In September, Phim's Center-appointed deputy, Seng Hong (alias Chan), was appointed to run Region 24.[100] The proclaimed danger from "internal enemies" may have led Phim to approve this and at least major sections of the Four-Year Plan, for the reasons Pol Pot advanced. The stage was now set for a much larger CPK conference to adopt the plan officially. It was scheduled for the next month,[101] probably to coincide with the party's twenty-fifth anniversary: 28–30 September 1976. But in the meantime, events took a new turn. Mao Zedong died in China on 9 September. Democratic Kampuchea declared a period of mourning from the twelfth to the seventeenth. Ieng Sary returned from an overseas trip on the eighteenth, and on that day Pol Pot made a public speech praising "Marxism-Leninism-Mao Zedong Thought," indicating for the first time the CPK's ideological debt to China.

On 20 September, former Northeast Zone secretary Ney Sarann was arrested, perhaps at that day's cabinet meeting, which proposed "to allow Comrade Pol Pot . . . to take temporary leave."[102] Two days later, the CPRA

97. See Kiernan, "Wild Chickens, Farm Chickens, and Cormorants," p. 184.

98. "Chamlaiy Suas Nau leuk ti muoy" ["The First Response of Suas Nau"], S-21, 1 September 1976, 16 pp.

99. See Kiernan, "Wild Chickens," p. 186.

100. "Responses of Touch Chem, called Soth, Secretary, Sector 21, Eastern Region," "Record of the History of the Traitorous Activities of Soth Himself," S-21 confession, 18 May 1978, p. 13, translation kindly provided by S. Heder.

101. See Boua, Chandler, and Kiernan, eds., Pol Pot Plans, p. 124.

102. BBC SWB, 28 September 1976, FE/5323/B/1. Six days later, Ney Sarann was asked by interrogators, "What had the Organization proclaimed about the question of the meeting on 20 September 1976?" "Khmer Rouge Prison Documents from the S-21 (Tuol Sleng) Extermination Center in Phnom Penh," David Hawk (ed.), document 5, "Measures in the Interrogation of IX [Ney Sarann]," note to Deuch, 26 September 1976 (my translation).

Standing Committee met. Mat Ly did not attend. No more is known of either of these brief gatherings. But they do not appear to have resolved all issues in the Four-Year Plan. They may even have presented unwelcome challenges to the Party leaders. On 23 September, the Santebal "received instructions from the Organization to use torture" on prisoners. The next morning they gave Ney Sarann "about 20 whippings with fine rattan," and in the afternoon, "20–30 whippings with electrical wire."[103] Keo Meas, "a very senior and widely respected veteran"[104] who had once ranked sixth in the CPK hierarchy, was arrested on 25 September. The next evening, according to Meas' interrogator in Tuol Sleng, "after threatening him a couple of times, I told him to pull off his shirt and put the arm shackles on him. . . . Prevented him from sleep and put him with the mosquitoes."[105] Meanwhile, Deuch told interrogators to "remind" Ney Sarann of "the welfare of his wife and children; does he know that his wife and children have been detained; now that he's here does he know what's to become of his wife?" The interrogators reported to Deuch that "the threat was made: there's no avoiding torture if you don't confess." Deuch then authorized the use of "both hot and cold techniques" on Sarann. His interrogators reported, "We went to intimidate him, telling him to prepare himself for the torture to be continued." That evening, as they approached Sarann "to carry out torture with our bare hands," he "started to confess by asking us to clarify what he was to report."[106]

That same day saw the public announcement that Pol Pot was temporarily stepping down as DK prime minister "in order to take care of his health which has been bad for several months."[107] The next day, Nuon Chea was appointed "acting prime minister." And the *next* day, 28 September, was to have been the first of three days of celebration of the party's twenty-fifth anniversary. The "1976 Study Session" began instead, chaired by Pol Pot, now even deeper in the shadows than before.[108]

Pol Pot's opening address was a skilful performance in a crisis, skimming the surface of the issues facing the party. The strong undercurrent of the purges that had preempted the CPK's historic meeting could have provoked

103. "Khmer Rouge Prison Documents," document 5, reproduced in Jackson, ed., *Cambodia 1975–1982*, photo 13, mistakenly labeled as pertaining to Hu Nim, instead of Ney Sarann.

104. Heder, *Reflections*, p. 7.

105. "Khmer Rouge Prison Documents," document 7, Pon to Deuch, 27 September 1976. Thus, Keo Meas ("X") was tortured at least from his second day of incarceration. Heder, *Reflections*, p. 7, fails to note this.

106. "Khmer Rouge Prison Documents," document 5, 26 September 1976; see also Jackson, photo 13.

107. BBC SWB, 28 September 1976, FE/5323/B/1.

108. See Boua, Chandler, and Kiernan, eds., *Pol Pot Plans*, p. 165.

unpredictable countercurrents and destabilized CPK rule. The CPK was perceptibly changing course. A show of hysteria by the captain at that point might have overturned the ship of state. Instead, Pol Pot assumed a *fait accompli*, and carefully fostered a steady-as-she-goes approach. He stressed the need for "democratic centralism," by which he meant to emphasize that the Center's leadership was correct and required only party discipline. "Good leadership must nourish, strengthen and extend solidarity and internal unity for ever," he said, adding: "This is an old problem. If we have solidarity and internal unity, we can resolve any problem. On the other hand, if the solidarity and internal unity are not good, a comfortable situation is still fraught, and a difficult situation becomes even more confused." This was only the slightest hint of a threat, fading into a vague prospect of "confusion." But the onus was placed squarely on the audience. "We must encourage the spirit of responsibility for solidarity and internal unity, and the capacity for endurance and struggle; we must struggle in whatever way necessary for unity." He denied the Center's role in the purges: "In this spirit, we do nothing to violate solidarity and unity." He needed his listeners to do nothing as well. The appeal for support was phrased in terms of not rocking the boat: "Therefore, wherever we live, whatever work we do, whomever we lead, whatever we say, we must carefully consider solidarity and internal unity." Moreover, just in case anyone *was* tempted to think the Center had made mistakes, he promised to correct them: "Whenever we forgetfully overlook something and violate our solidarity and internal unity, then we quickly wake up and start to make immediate changes."[109] The CPK's helm was in good hands. Nothing drastic would happen on Pol Pot's watch.

It is not certain that his appeal was successful. On 30 September, the Santebal reported, unspecified dissidents "carried out disruptive activities with troops."[110] Another source mentions "a small battle in the streets of Phnom Penh between soldiers of the Eastern Zone and the . . . Northern Zone."[111] But both Pol Pot and the Santebal had every reason to invent military threats, though armed resistance existed in outlying regions.[112] Pot needed to rally the

109. "Bongring ning bongrik kar duk noam rebos pak knong royea kal thmei nei padevat sangkumniyum ning kar kosang sangkumniyum" ("Strengthen and Expand the Party's Leadership in the New Period of Socialist Revolution and Building Socialism"), 28 September 1976, pp. 2ff., 20–21.

110. "List of Statistics of the Santebal S-21," p. 58.

111. Elizabeth Becker, *When the War Was Over*, New York: Simon and Schuster, 1986, p. 273, citing no source or specific date.

112. See Chapter 3. In 1976, five people were arrested and sent to Tuol Sleng for having "escaped to the jungle" in Region 37, possibly hoping to join ethnic Thai-led insurgents. Other prisoners were described as a "Cham bandit" and a "Khmer Sor bandit," and another as having "lived with bandits" in Pursat. "Benhchi chhmou neak tous dael coul khnong chhnam 1976" ("List of the Names of Prisoners Who Entered in the Year 1976"), pp. 38, 42, 18.

party around him as he dealt mercilessly with respected, popular rivals. And the Santebal, recently equipped with spacious new premises, was having difficulty filling them. "New people," for instance, had been arriving since November 1975, but in steadily declining numbers. Quarterly figures for 1976 show the trend: 157 from January to March, 80 from April to June, and 31 from July to September.[113] Of all 570 incoming prisoners in the July–September quarter, one-third were from the 170th Division alone.[114] Future Tuol Sleng prisoners would need to come from other groups.

The Center's "Summary of the Results of the 1976 Study Session" was triumphant: "As for the Party's 1977 Plan, we have now reached complete agreement with one another." First, it said, "we have been scrubbed clean and nurtured in political standpoint, consciousness, and organisation," but second, the party had thrown itself into "a fierce and uncompromising fight to the death with the class enemy . . . *especially in our revolutionary ranks.*" The summary ended with a warning that used another metaphor of physical purity: "let there be no holes at all for the enemy to worm his way into the insides of our Party."[115] This was a turning point in the revolution. On 7 October, Keo Meas wrote from his prison cell, "I am just lying here waiting to die."[116]

Meanwhile another veteran communist, Agriculture Minister Non Suon, was supervising returned students laboring at his state worksite at Angkor Chey, thirty kilometers southeast of Phnom Penh. Suon planned a model agricultural station there. Ninety-eight returnees arrived on 10 September. A longtime aide says that Suon warned the three hundred base people there "not to mistreat the friends who had returned from abroad." In a public welcome on 13 September, Suon asked them to join with "our brothers and sisters here." He praised them for their "national soul." The fact that they had been living abroad and had wanted to return, Suon said, meant that they cherished their country. The returnees report that the base people at the worksite, who got on well with the local population and Angkor Chey cadres, were scornful of the returnees and made them work hard. But returnees say none of their number disappeared at Angkor Chey—in contrast to the periods before and after their three-month stint there. Unlike lecturers in Phnom Penh, Non Suon said nothing to the returnees about Vietnam. Moreover, a group of about thirty "White Khmer" *(Khmer Sor)* rebels remained active in the Angkor Chey area. They were involved in shooting incidents in 1976. Suon's aide says he "knew

113. List of 745 new people sent to Tuol Sleng, compiled by Ung Pech in 1979–80, giving name, place of origin, profession, and dates of arrest and execution.

114. "List of the Names of Prisoners Who Entered in the Year 1976," 26 May 1977.

115. See Boua, Chandler, and Kiernan, eds., *Pol Pot Plans*, Document 5, undated, pp. 168ff., emphasis added.

116. Heder, *Reflections*, p. 9.

they were there but didn't do anything about them, although I never knew clearly that he had contact with them."[117]

By October 1976, So Phim apparently began to realize what had happened during his absence in China. About a month after Chhouk's arrest, the local carpenter reports Phim as remarking, "It seems that Chhouk and all those people are not traitors." According to the carpenter, "Phim complained a lot at the end of 1976 and early 1977." But complaints could not save Chhouk, who wrote his thirty-second and last confession on 13 November. It was "A list of Names of Traitors in the Network of IX [Ney Sarann]." There is no record of Chhouk's date of execution.

Before 1975, Hang, an ethnic Chinese, had worked in his father's Phnom Penh textile plant by the Tonle Sap. Hang's family of nine were sent to work in the T-7 weaving factory, alongside three hundred young female "new workers," peasant soldiers from the East and Southwest Zones. The factory director was Chaem, a former officer from Chakrey's 1st Eastern Division. In November 1976, Chaem was accused of sleeping with a worker in a grove. The couple were arrested, and two days later it was announced that both had been executed. Within weeks the deputy director and the member of the T-7 committee, both Easterners, were also arrested. Chaem was replaced by a Southwestern cadre. Hang says workers asked angrily, "Why do they keep taking people away to disappear like that?" Forty-one eastern workers, led by Chaem's former messenger, Veng, "all got together to stage a strike, refusing to work or do anything." At midnight that night, "they cut down banana trees to make a raft, to swim across the river" to the Eastern Zone. Hang was on sentry duty that evening, patrolling the grounds with two other workers. He saw a crowd down by the river and asked who they were. "They did not dare reply. We called to one another, and went down and saw the 41 people, and another person who was showing off and wanted to fight them all. . . . Then a woman said, "Don't fight, we are making revolution. We only talk, that is enough." A guard ran to summon the troops defending the city. They called in more soldiers by radio. By now three or four people had crossed the river and disappeared. Others, out in mid-stream, were captured by Khmer Rouge marines. All 41 were caught." Security units took them away. Veng was assigned to breaking rocks in the Southwest. The other strikers were "tempered" for months, then dispersed to different factories.[118]

Meanwhile the net spread wider, to Koy Thuon's former foreign trade officials. The deputy director of Kompong Som port was arrested on 19 October.

117. Author's interviews with a former agriculture ministry staff member, Prek Ambel, 21 July 1980, and with two returnees who worked at Angkor Chey, Creteil, 18 October 1979, and Tuol, 28 October 1979.

118. Author's interview with Hang, Hagenau, 2 November 1979.

Non Suon, who had briefly replaced Thuon as commerce minister earlier in the year, returned from a trade mission abroad on 1 November. He was arrested at the airport. Prum Nhiem, who had effectively snared the leadership of the Lon Nol regime in April 1975, and then taken charge of Democratic Kampuchea's foreign trade, was apprehended on 25 November.[119]

Non Suon's arrest was followed by that of two hundred associates: CPK members close to him in the agriculture ministry, CPK youth league members, ministry technicians, Suon's wife, children, and bodyguards, and the wives of his cadres. One technician was arrested on 1 January 1977, after being invited to Phnom Penh "to meet the Agriculture Minister." There was none. The technician was sent to Prey Sor jail outside the capital, with fifty technicians and more spouses of cadres. A car arrived daily to take people away. After three months, Non Suon's wife and two children disappeared.[120]

The rate of arrests skyrocketed in late 1976. Of 1,622 prisoners who entered Tuol Sleng in 1976, 1,200 were arrested in the second half of the year (including 150 members of the Center's S-21 apparat itself). Six hundred thirty people entered the prison in the October–December quarter.[121] This figure represented an expansion in at least four categories of perceived enemies. It included 185 "new people," reversing the decline in arrests of such people (sextupling the previous quarter's figures). Nine foreign-educated returnees had been arrested by the end of September 1976; fifty-six were apprehended in October, and seventeen more went to Tuol Sleng in November-December. Twenty had been executed by year's end.[122] Similarly, eighteen "important" CPK leaders were incarcerated in the October–December quarter, compared to twelve for the first three quarters of 1976.[123] The number of innocent victims at the other end of the political hierarchy also increased dramatically. From January to September, the Santebal had arrested thirteen wives and five children of its prisoners. But from October to December 1976, as many as sixty-five wives, twenty children, and five

119. "Important Culprits," pp. 13, 16, 17.
120. Author's interview with a former technical aide to Non Suon, Prek Ambel, 21 July 1980.
121. "List of the Names of Prisoners Who Entered in the Year 1976," which has 1,622 names, omitting 29 included in "Important Culprits." Chandler, following his source (Anthony Barnett, "Inside S-21," New Statesman, 2 May 1980, p. 671), asserts that Tuol Sleng prisoners arrested in 1976 numbered 2,250 (Brother Number One, p. 130; Becker gives similar figures, When the War Was Over, p. 276, also without a source. This now seems an exaggeration. Those imprisoned in 1976 were listed by number, in six ledgers, up to 2,250, but nos. 1481-1940 (between the fifth and sixth ledgers) are missing and may not have been used. If so, the 1976 total would have been 1,790, closer to the 1,622 figure on the 1976 List, plus 29 "Important Culprits."
122. "Etudiants et fonctionnaires provenant des pays étrangers," S-21 list compiled by Ung Pech, 1979.
123. "Important Culprits"; Ung Pech's 1979 list of 745 "new people" sent to Tuol Sleng (see n. 113).

mothers of prisoners were incarcerated in Tuol Sleng.[124] In Phnom Penh, as in the Southwest and Northwest Zones, a genocidal process was in motion.

Differences in political perspective fueled the process. On 30 November, Hu Nim described "the enemy" in traditional terms, as "imperialism, old and new colonialism and all stripes of exploiting classes."[125] He had not kept up with the Center's running list. On 20 December, the Center convened a meeting at the party school in the former French embassy.[126] Pol Pot proclaimed to the audience: "In 1976, we expelled three major spy networks, which had been concealed for several years." But, he warned, the danger was not over, for "treacherous, secret elements . . . have been entering the Party continuously . . . they're not gone at all." He had identified "a sickness inside the party," adding, "We cannot locate it precisely. The illness must emerge to be examined. . . . We search for the microbes within the Party without success. They are buried. As our socialist revolution advances, however, seeping more strongly into every corner of the Party, the army and among the people, we can locate the ugly microbes. They will be pushed out by the true nature of the socialist revolution. . . . If we wait any longer, the microbes can do real damage. . . . They will rot society, rot the Party, and rot the army." Therefore, Pol Pot advised, "Don't be afraid to lose one or two people of bad background. . . . Driving out the treacherous forces will be a great victory. . . . Everyone must be verified. . . ." As before, the danger was internal. "The big problem is in the interior. . . . We must resist spies along the frontier, but the important thing is to guard against them in the interior of the country."[127]

A major target was the party's Eastern Zone branch. At the December meeting, the East was instructed to send the center fifty thousand tons of rice in 1977.[128] Another CPK cadre recalls "a Central Committee plan to sweep out all the Eastern Zone cadres." Southwest Zone cadres were to implement it: "Starting in December 1976 wave after wave of the Eastern Zone cadres were arrested. . . . The explanation of this was that there were many traitors in the East, while the Southwest had fewer."[129]

---

124. "List of the Names of Prisoners Who Entered in the Year 1976."

125. *FBIS,* 2 December 1976, p. H5, Phnom Penh Radio, 30 November 1976. Hu Nim did not mention "revisionism," for instance.

126. S. Heder's interview with a member of the DK water transport Unit. Sa Keo, 9 March 1980.

127. Boua, Chandler, and Kiernan, eds., *Pol Pot Plans,* Document 6, pp. 210, 183–86, 191.

128. A member of the audience recalls a burden placed on the East alone: "There was no mention of the capabilities of the other Zones" (Heder interview, 9 March 1980). The report of the conference does give the East's export target as 50,000 tons, but with the same figure for the Northwest, whereas the Southwest is given a much lower target, 30,000 tons. Chandler notes the burden on the East ("A Revolution in Full Spate," in David Ablin and Marlowe Hood, eds., *The Cambodian Agony,* p. 170).

129. S. Heder's interview with Um Samang, Sa Keo, 10 March 1980.

The next month, Chhouk's former economics cadre Sin Song was arrested in Region 24. He was not sent to Tuol Sleng, but was detained with ten others in a house in a large compound that soon held five hundred prisoners. Those arrested with Song included the Region battalion commander, the chief of the regional information and culture department, the chief of the regional hospital, and two subdistrict chiefs. Following Chhouk's arrest, Southwest Zone officials were in the process of taking over the East's "twin" Regions 23 and 24. "They interrogated me," Song recalled three years later. "They showed me Chhouk's account and asked me about it." This handwritten "confession" was not in Chhouk's hand, nor was it signed by him; it bore an unidentified thumbprint. "It said Chhouk had made me a general in the traitor resistance network in Region 24. It also said Chhouk had revealed that I had buried five hundred rifles in order to prepare to attack the party, and that I had radios. . . . But this was not true. It was just a trick to wipe out cadres."

In early July 1977, Sin Song and two other prisoners escaped. Evading a manhunt, they made it to Vietnam seven nights later. Perhaps in retaliation, on 9 July, the five cadres who had been arrested with Song were all executed.[130] Three days later, Chhouk's former deputy, who had replaced him in August, was also arrested and sent to Tuol Sleng.[131] The Center's first takeover of an Eastern Region was complete. But it had planted the seeds of its own successor. Sin Song would return to Cambodia as part of a new government in 1979.[132]

The Northern Zone

At the same time as Mok's Center-sponsored Southwest forces were purging the Northwest and the "twin Regions" of the East, a third political convulsion was ravaging the North. During the 1970–75 war, the Northern Zone had been deeply divided between the followers of Zone secretary Koy Thuon and those of military commander Ke Pauk.[133] When Thuon was transferred to Phnom Penh after victory, part of his network remained in place north of Kompong Thom city. And from the south, Eastern Zone influence from across the Mekong River also served to moderate Pauk's policy. According to a 1975 U.S. embassy report, Region 22, on the south bank of the

130. Author's interview with Sin Song, Phnom Penh, 12 August 1980.
131. "Important Culprits," p. 11.
132. Sin Song became the new deputy minister of the interior and, later, minister of the interior, a post he held until 1993. Jacques Bekaert reports, "Sin Song has carefully maintained a balance between the various party factions, and is usually respected by other party members." *Bangkok Post,* 25 April 1992, p. 5. He was later charged with involvement in political repression in 1992–93 and a bloodless coup attempt in 1994.
133. See Kiernan, *How Pol Pot Came to Power,* pp. 355–57.

Mekong, "had a surprising influence" in the North. The Zone leaderships of So Phim and Ke Pauk "kept aloof from each other." But at the next level down, Region 22 personnel worked in Northern Regions 43, 42, and 41. This was most apparent in Region 41, on the north bank of the Mekong. (One district of Region 22 was also on the north bank.) Region 41, headed by Sreng, was also the home of both Hou Yuon and Hu Nim, with whom Sreng had long been associated. Monks reported Hou Yuon's visit to a local wat just before the victory, and local cadres had orders to protect Hu Nim's uncle, who was also a monk.[134]

But after Koy Thuon's 1975 departure, Pauk set out to consolidate his grip on the Zone. In early 1976, Pauk appointed his brother-in-law Oeun to the Region 42 cPK committee.[135] In late 1976, Pauk's wife Soeun became secretary of Chamcar Loeu district and then deputy chief of Region 42 under her younger brother Oeun. Oeun's wife Heang ran the district hospital in Chamcar Loeu. Soeun and Oeun's father, Saet, became chief of the Region 42 youth league, and his wife, Thou, Pauk's mother-in-law, became chief of the Region Women's Association. Pauk's nephew on his father's side, an orphan named Moeun, took over the Region 42 security forces. His cousin Bin, another nephew of Pauk's, had been chief of security in Baray district since 1975. He is described by locals as "a big killer" and "very cruel." Two other nephews, Hul and Huon, were commander and deputy commander of the 2nd Zone Division.[136]

With the final arrest of Koy Thuon on 25 January 1977, the Center moved to bolster Pauk's dominance in the North even as it struck at the former Northern divisions quartered in the capital.[137] The deputy director of the Northern Zone rubber plantation was taken to Tuol Sleng on the same day as Thuon. Sreng, the Zone deputy cPK secretary, followed on 18 February. With Sreng came the directors of the Zone transport service and hospital and a member of its industry committee. The next day, it was the turn of the deputy political commissar of the Zone's 117th Division. Five days later, a member of the staff of the director of the Zone rubber plantation followed. The plantation's director saw the writing on the wall after he was called to a "meeting." He escaped with a truckload of troops heading east for Vietnam.[138] He was

134. "Khmer Refugee Walks out from Phnom Penh," Extracts from a Cabled Report from the American Embassy in Bangkok, 5 June 1975 (declassified in 1978), p. 3.

135. Tep Ibrahim describes Pauk as "big, fat, and dark" and Oeun as "short and fat." Author's interview, Chrang Chamres, 10 January 1986.

136. Information in this paragraph came from the author's interviews in Pauk's native area of Chhouk Khsach, Baray district, Kompong Thom, 15 October 1980.

137. The following details are from *People's Revolutionary Tribunal*, Document no. 2.5.24, "Important Culprits," pp. 8–10.

138. Author's interview with Uk Prathna, Phnom Penh, 21 January 1987. Prathna became a rubber plantation worker in Stung Trang in late 1976.

captured the next month. Koy Thuon's network had probably been strongest in the Zone commercial service. Its chief and deputy chief were both incarcerated in Tuol Sleng on 19 March. Two days later another member of their executive committee joined them, two more on 10 May, and a sixth in June. The deputy chief of the Zone industry committee was arrested in early May, his chief two weeks later.[139] Between mid-February and late April, 112 civilian officials from the Northern Zone were imprisoned in Tuol Sleng.[140]

Meanwhile the Center targeted Oeun and Suong, the commanders of two former Northern divisions. Their divisions, the 310th and 450th, were based in Phnom Penh, but elements of them had been stationed in the East since 1975.[141] Vorn Vet later confessed, "The Party had me take them both to Battambang, in order to remove them from their units. I did whatever I could to make them believe that the Party sent them there to fulfill real tasks. I was afraid that they would realize the situation and flee back to Phnom Penh or go to the Northern Zone, making the Party lose trust in me, saying that I had released them. At that time we stayed in Battambang so many days without *Angkar* making the decision, that I sent a telegram to *Angkar* to make a quick decision. Then *Angkar* decided to arrest them . . . I dared not stand up for them, and helped arrest them and take them to Phnom Penh."[142] Oeun and Suong entered Tuol Sleng on 19 February. A third former Northern division commander was jailed a month later. By late April, nearly four hundred subordinates had joined them in Tuol Sleng. On 4 April, Santebal officers massacred 110 troops of Oeun's 310th Division in one day.[143]

In mid-1977, the Northern Zone was revamped and renamed the Central Zone. Pauk became its CPK secretary, his brother-in-law Oeun deputy.[144] The purges continued. In August and September, the secretary of the Zone's 174th Division, the commissar of its 901st Regiment, several more leading Zone officials, and the secretaries of Regions 41, 42, and 43 were all taken off to Tuol Sleng. In all, thirty-five "important culprits" from the Northern Zone CPK branch were killed there in 1977.[145] Chhueun, husband of Pauk's half-sister,

139. *People's Revolutionary Tribunal*, Doc. 2.5.24, pp. 8–10.

140. "Benhchi chhmou neak tous dael coul cap pi thngai 17.2.77 dol 17.4.77." ("List of Names of Prisoners Entering from 17.2.77 to 17.4.77"), S-21, 29 April 1977.

141. Heder interview, Sakeo, 9 March 1980. These three formerly Northern divisions were the 310th, the 450th, and the 920th, commanded by Oeun, Suong, and Chhin. The 310th and the 450th Divisions were "forces that I formed myself," Koy Thuon had told Hu Nim in 1975. See Boua, Chandler, and Kiernan, eds., *Pol Pot Plans the Future*, p. 281, 316.

142. Vorn Vet confession, 54 pp., at p. 43.

143. "List of Names of Prisoners Entering from 17.2.77 to 17.4.77."

144. Author's interviews in Chhouk Khsach, Baray district, 15 October 1980.

145. The recently appointed heads of the Northern Zone transport, industry and commercial services, the new deputy director of the Zone rubber plantation, and the head of the Zone security office were all purged in September and October 1977. "People's Revolutionary

became the new Region 42 secretary.[146] Pauk's dominance of the Zone was now complete. His power could only expand.

Region 106: Rebellion

Meanwhile, in neighboring Region 106, scene of the 1976 bombardment of Siemreap, another conflagration had broken out. A CPK military defector who reached Thailand at the end of 1977 claimed that the previous year Koy Thuon had plotted a coup in conjunction with Soth, secretary of Region 106. This account of Soth's second attempt at rebellion suggests that Thuon had indeed briefly escaped the capital. At a September 1976 meeting in Oddar Meanchey province, north of Siemreap, Thuon and Soth had planned a coup in Phnom Penh for 1 January 1977. A radio station was set up in Oddar Meanchey to broadcast the appeal for a general uprising.[147] Another report says the mutiny had been planned for 17 April 1977.[148] But it never took place. After his second arrest on 25 January, according to the defector, Koy Thuon revealed under torture the names of his co-conspirators. Soth was arrested on 21 February. His deputy and the commander of Region 106's 335th Division were taken into custody five days later. Eleven other Region 106 officials followed within a week.[149] The roundup also included ten colonels and senior military officers, all four district chiefs and two district officials in Oddar Meanchey, and six subdistrict chiefs from Ampil district on the Thai border.[150]

An uprising occurred anyway. In Chikreng district, southeast of Siemreap on the road to Phnom Penh, a local woman named Channa, evacuated from Kompong Kdei market in 1973, offers a base person's view of the changes. The victory of 1975, she says, had brought executions of Lon Nol soldiers, confinement of former teachers in labor camps under starvation conditions, wide-

---

Tribunal," Document no. 2.5.24, DK S-21 document, "Important Culprits (Arrested from 1976 to April 9, 1978)," English translation, pp. 8–10.

146. On 9 March 1980, in an interview with S. Heder, a former Northern Zone official claimed that "Chhueun, who is the brother-in-law of Ta Pauk" and "was married to the younger sister of Ta Pauk" became secretary of Region 42 in 1977. Pauk had no sisters, but Chhueun could have been the husband of a half-sister. Local sources describe Oeun initially as Region 42 chief and later as deputy Zone secretary.

147. F. Ponchaud, "Situation interne du Kampuchéa Démocratique en 1977," p. 3. On the basis of the CPK military defector's testimony, in this 1978 paper (pp. 3–4), Ponchaud correctly named many of the officials arrested for involvement in the plot ("Important Culprits," p. 10). See B. Kramer, "Cambodia's Communist Regime Begins to Purge Its Own Ranks," Wall Street Journal, 17 October 1977: "Military intelligence officials in Thailand believe the purge followed an attempted coup d'état in Phnom Penh."

148. Asiaweek, 2 December 1977, p. 36.

149. "Important Culprits," pp. 10–11.

150. Ponchaud gives their names and posts in "Situation interne," p. 4. These officers and officials were sufficiently low-ranking to be excluded from S-21's "Important Culprits" list.

spread hunger for the new people generally, and bans on religion, money, and barter, which affected base people like Channa. And after 1975, occasionally somebody would disappear at night. But otherwise life for base people "continued as before," and Channa even asserts that in 1975–76 the former Region 106 cadres "didn't kill many people." A refugee agreed, telling State Department interviewers in Thailand that Region Secretary Soth was "not too strict."[151] But another, new person Thach Keo Dara, charged that the Region 106 cadres had made people "live like animals, killed them for a yes or a no," and "made them work for a meager pittance without the right to complain." From 2 February 1977, Dara asserted, Region 106 authorities had conscripted seven hundred workers from each village in Siemreap province to build a dam on the Tonle Sap, which "provoked a great wave of anger throughout the region."[152]

A contingent of khaki-clad troops in Chinese army trucks arrived in Chikreng from Phnom Penh on 8 February. Reorganizing local units, they arrested the district chief and replaced him.[153] Around the same time, according to Hui Pan, then a DK village chief, "all fifty or so Siemreap province officials were suddenly ordered to report to Phnom Penh." Two weeks later, word came back that these people were "CIA agents" who had "killed many people so that the people wouldn't like Angkar."[154] On 11 March, four planes landed at Siemreap airport. Sovannareth, a fifteen-year-old working in Sautnikom district, to the east, saw two Dakotas fly in from Phnom Penh. That same day, three "leaders" in Chikreng encouraged the population to revolt. Eyewitness Thach Keo Dara said the rebellion began in Pring village when "200 to 300 inhabitants armed themselves with machetes, spears, pitchforks and knives and headed, on foot or on horseback," for the new dam site. En route, they killed a prison commandant. The worksite supervisors, surprised on the spot, fled into the forest and were hunted down. Two men they had persecuted were awarded the privilege of hacking them to death. Rebel leaders Boy and Rip then sent the workers back to their villages. The next day a crowd of eight hundred tracked down two more CPK officials. Their livers were cut out and their bodies "chopped into a thousand pieces." The next day two village chiefs were massacred, and the wife of one disemboweled. For six days, "the villagers rejoiced."[155]

151. Jackson, ed., *Cambodia 1975–1978*, p. 202.
152. Thach Keo Dara, "Une révolte de la population," *Sereika*, no. 24, October 1978, pp. 7–8 (mis-cited in Chandler, *Tragedy*, p. 375 n. 40, and *Brother Number One*, p. 224 n. 30).
153. Ponchaud, "Situation interne," p. 5.
154. Kramer, "Cambodia's Communist Regime."
155. Ponchaud "Situation interne," p. 5, which names the three rebel leaders as Pây ("Boy"), Reup ("Rip"), and Chham; author's interview with Sovannareth, Rouen, 10 October 1979; and Thach Keo Dara, "Une révolte de la population," which dates the rebellion at "11 April."

Channa recalls people in Chikreng massing in "very big demonstrations." But she also draws attention to the role of new district officials, "mostly from Takeo," who claimed their predecessors were traitors to the party and executed them. These new arrivals from the Southwest, says Channa, "used cold politics, and the people were hopeful, thinking that the Khmer Rouge were gone for good and even that the new group represented Sihanouk's Party." The new district chief proclaimed that "a change was coming and that things might get better, that those who had destroyed the temples were traitors." Prisoners, including Channa's younger brother, were freed from the jails. She recalls, "We were happy, and attended the demonstration." Large meetings of new and base people assembled to support the new leaders. "But the new cadres were red just the same. It was a lie, to see who was resisting the party. . . . These cadres were the cruellest of all." The demonstrators were soon arrested. "There were killings throughout 1977. . . . They started arresting and executing people, one after another. . . . People were put on trucks and taken away, night and day. . . . There was no prison. People were just killed." [156]

Like the previous year's explosions, the Region 106 rebellion remains partly a mystery. The Center may have incited or manipulated it. Much depends on the different dates given for the start of the uprising: either 11 March, when the aircraft arrived from Phnom Penh, or 11 April, a few days before the planned mutiny by CPK dissidents. One date is probably a mistake for the other. The February arrival of Phnom Penh troops to launch a purge (including Soth's arrest) suggests that a spontaneous popular uprising, if the most likely explanation, may not be the only one. The Center's repression was massive. One source, suggesting a toll of eight to ten thousand deaths, claims that Eastern Zone troops were brought in to conduct the slaughter. [157] But the ear-

156. Ung Channa, interview with the author, Paris, 30 November 1979.

157. Vickery, *Cambodia 1975–1982*, p. 127. Ponchaud, "Situation interne," 1978, p. 5, reports that the troops arriving in February wore khaki uniforms, which might suggest they were Eastern Zone troops. But by this point the distinction between khaki-clad Eastern units and black-clothed troops of the Center and other Zones was blurred. At the end of 1975, for instance, a Northwest Zone-level battalion wore "green uniforms" ("Cambodia Today: Life Inside Cambodia," Extracts from an Airgram Report by an Officer of the American Embassy at Bangkok, 21 September 1976 (declassified 1978), p. 12). In 1977, the U.S. embassy in Bangkok's Cambodia watcher wrote, "There is dispute over whether the wearer of green fatigues is different from the wearer of black pajamas; this writer believes there is no difference between the two" ("Life in Cambodia," Extracts from an Airgram Report by an Officer of the American Embassy at Bangkok, 31 March 1977 (declassified 1978), p. 7). Ponchaud says the Region 106 repression was carried out by newly arrived troops "from Phnom Penh" ("Situation interne," p. 5). A refugee who did think the troops were easterners specified that their leader was "Ta Sae," that is, Kang Chap, former Southwest Zone Region 35 secretary, now head of the D.K. Judiciary Committee. The refugee says Sae "talked with a Kompong Cham accent" (author's interview with Sovannareth, Rouen, 10 October 1979). Becker, *When the War Was Over*, pp. 250, 274, claims Eastern Zone involvement in the repression, but cites no

of arrests and executions." Anyone in any way connected with the Lon Nol government disappeared, including former village chiefs and schoolteachers, and people "who had been Lon Nol soldiers even just for one day." Sarun's boyhood friend from his village was arrested and killed.

The newcomers also established a strict regime of food and work. Rations were reduced further. Ten people subsisted on eight cans of rice per day. People too sick to work were not always fed. When earthworks were being raised, each worker was assigned three cubic meters to shift each day, and was only fed when this task was completed. Sometimes workers kept going until midnight, and friends came to help them.

After three years in the chalat laboring at various sites around Region 5, Sarun says, he came across no villages whose people were not mistreated. The CPK claim to help the peasant classes was just "propaganda," he says, noting that he never saw any sign of assistance for the rural people. Although he says former city people suffered a lot more and died in much greater numbers than peasants, food rations were the same for both groups who lived and worked side by side in the cooperatives, as well as those in the chalat.

In her unit of the Regional chalat, Sovanny saw no Southwest Zone cadres before early 1978, but she reports "starvation on a large scale" in 1977–78. Back in her home village, too, "in 1977 food began to be taken away" and six people died of starvation there in 1977–78. This was also because rations became more tightly controlled. Larger, "company"-sized mess halls for one hundred people replaced the ten-family krom kitchens. On the other hand, "happy" collective work also came to an end in 1977: individual daily harvesting targets now had to be completed in order to receive food. The practices of increasing collective cooking and reducing collective work were only superficially inconsistent. Both gave the authorities greater control over the population.

When the Southwest cadres arrived, "mass killings started." Before 1978, "only big people" had been killed. The new rulers executed not only the local Northwest leaders, but also "the little people, anyone," including former Lon Nol soldiers. "They killed my brother and father and mother who had been soldiers. . . . My mother's throat was cut." Sovanny's uncle, a former village clerk, and his three children were also killed. In all, thirty of the village's one hundred families were slaughtered. They were buried nearby. "After the Southwest came, . . . the villages were quiet." Unlike their predecessors, the new rulers refused to work alongside the peasants; they "just used us." Sovanny says the Southwest cadres offered the people "only their theory."[54] A refugee account from Phnom Srok district confirms "a change in *Angkar*" there too, in

54. Author's interview with Sovanny, Limoges, 8 December 1979.

were thrown into open ricefields." She claims half the population of Upper Kouk Thlok perished in 1977 alone.

According to François Ponchaud, the revolt quickly extended south, "into all of Staung district," in neighboring Kompong Thom province.[162] In April, Sovannareth watched it spread north towards Siemreap. "The rebels arrived in Sautnikom and began stealing rice and clothes. The old soldiers were disarmed." They at first tried to hide by mingling with the people, but were identified and driven away. "Then a new group of troops arrived two or three days later, and arrested all the old cadres and soldiers and some of the people, and took them in trucks to Siemreap to be killed, saying they were going 'to study.' Then the new forces began arresting the people and killing them, for the first time since the 1975 wave [of killings]. Of my group of fifty new youths, twenty were taken away at this time. So were all the teachers. . . . I ran home, pretending to be sick."[163]

According to Hui Pan, the new province officials now began telling each village leader, "The chief wants to see you." They never returned. "In this way, all the old village chiefs were betrayed." Pan himself, led away with his hands tied behind his back, managed to cut himself loose; he reached Thailand in June. Another refugee reported five hundred village chiefs and one thousand soldiers "taken away" in Region 106 in mid-April 1977.[164] In July, the commander of a CPK artillery unit in Oddar Meanchey escaped with news of the arrest since April of eight hundred officers and men in that province. "Simple soldiers were led away with their hands tied behind their backs. Officers weren't tied up until they reached Siemreap."[165] By 17 April, eighty-four Region 106 cadres had reached Tuol Sleng.[166]

Kang Chap replaced Soth as secretary of Region 106, which was renamed Region 46 and included in a new Northern Zone, along with Preah Vihear province. (Pauk's old Northern Zone became the Central Zone.) Thach Keo Dara agrees with Channa that Kang Chap's "new team" proved "even harsher and crueller than the old. . . . Even the base people were affected. The conditions thus became more and more difficult."[167] Channa recounts how new cadres from Takeo introduced the three social categories long familiar in the Southwest. "They called meetings, only of base people, and they told us that [only] the lower peasants were [now] the base people, the workers of the Party." These

162. Ponchaud, "Situation interne," p. 5.
163. Author's interview with Sovannareth, 1979.
164. *Asiaweek*, 2 December 1977, p. 36.
165. Kramer, "Cambodia's Communist Regime."
166. "List of Names of Prisoners Who Entered from 17.2.77 to 17.4. 77," S-21, 29 April 1977.
167. Thach Keo Dara, "Une révolte."

became "the full rights people." Other base people, such as Channa's group of 1973 evacuees from Kompong Kdei, now "a different class" of once-prosperous townspeople, were reclassified "candidates." And new people, the 1975 evacuees, were now called "depositees." They "could be sent anywhere." The work regimen intensified. People were organized into krom of twelve members. In the planting season, they worked sixteen hours per day, with daily targets that sometimes kept workers going until midnight. In the harvest season, each krom had to reap one hectare of land per day, and thresh the rice as well, an impossible task, Channa says. The new district chief would summon people for execution from their workplace. "People who ran home briefly at lunchtime to grab something to eat would be called away if they were caught." People were warned of hidden enemies "within each of us," meaning private sentiments. "If we kept our own plates, we were considered enemies," Channa recalls.[168]

Dissension in the Western Zone

During two prison terms in Western Zone jails, new person Moeung Sonn obtained a rare view of political unrest there. In November 1975, Sonn was arrested and interrogated in a fairly relaxed manner by three cadres running the Region 37 prison. Khon, Kheng, and Yon, all former teachers who had joined the cpk, did not torture Sonn, and when he pleaded for mercy, promising "to work hard for the revolutionary organization for the rest of my life," the triumvirate decided to spare him. He was given odd jobs to do around the prison. "They looked after me very well, because they were educated and had some empathy for me." One night, Khon sent a soldier over to explain that unless Sonn worked hard and broke no rules, "he would not be able to help me." Sonn considered this a friendly warning, suggesting that others in the cpk had no interest in protecting him. In June 1976, Sonn and eighty other prisoners were released.[169]

The prison was soon abandoned. About a month later, Sonn discovered a possible reason. Khon himself had been arrested and executed, along with an

168. Author's interview with Ung Channa, 1979.
169. Author's interview with Moeung Sonn, Sarcelles, France, 25 October 1979. Sonn was ambivalent about the record of cruelty of these prison officials. He said they "only killed about half or less of their prisoners" and "spared the rest," without discriminating between new and base people. "They showed much understanding and their interrogations were not brutal. They would believe you if you refused to respond to moderate beatings, so they would spare you." Yon, for instance, "didn't kill many people, a few." Most executions in Region 37 in 1975–76 did not occur in this prison, Sonn said, specifying the mass killings of Lon Nol officers and later soldiers by the 203rd Region battalion. He added that the treatment he received from the prison triumvirate was "different from the second time I was in jail," in 1977, under a harsher faction closely aligned with the Party Center. (See below.)

aide. Meanwhile Yon had also been dismissed from the Zone prison and sent to run a cooperative in Prey Nop, where Sonn was now living. Yon had decided to fight back. In April 1977, he plotted an uprising with other Prey Nop district officials. He may have had little choice. In this period, a squad from the Region 37 office stormed the house of his former comrade Kheng. Forewarned, Kheng had opened fire on his attackers, but the troops overwhelmed him and shot him to death.

After this, Sonn went to see Yon. "He was all right. He liked me and recognized me. He had the idea of liberating all of Prey Nop district from the yoke of Pol Pot's group. . . . He was a former Khmer Rouge soldier, but he had different ideas from them. He saw that the leadership was barbaric. . . . By that time, he had drawn up a plan. He had so many people building dams, so many in cooperatives, and he was going to bring them all together to a festival in Prey Nop." The rebel network extended beyond the district, to Region 37's security unit, the 202nd battalion. "They would all go: soldiers, chiefs of the kong chalat. They had discussed it and reached agreement to declare the liberation of Prey Nop." However, the plot was discovered by the Region 37 secretary, Sary, a former officer of the 1st Western Division, whose elderly commander, Paet Soeung, was Zone military chief and third on Chou Chet's Western Zone Committee. Sary arrested Yon the day before the 17 April 1977 anniversary celebration.[170]

Sonn attended the meeting, expecting calls for rebellion against the Center. Instead he heard of Yon's arrest. "I lost all hope. The speakers told us not to worry if cooperative leaders or members of the district commitee disappeared. 'Don't worry, they are traitors. . . . We must go after their hidden agents who have not yet been apprehended. We must unite to search for them so that they can all be exterminated.'" Sary disbanded the 202nd, replacing it with his other Region battalion, the 203rd, which in 1975 had carried out mass executions of defeated Lon Nol soldiers. "From that day on, three to five people disappeared from every cooperative each night." Within a month, the 203rd battalion was in turn disarmed by Paet Soeung's 1st Division, which quickly occupied Region 37, taking control of every cooperative.[171]

Rearrested in May 1977, Sonn was taken to the Zone prison in Kampot province, run by the 1st Division. It consisted of two large buildings and two small ones, then housing over a hundred prisoners, mostly soldiers and cadres from the 202nd battalion. During the next forty days, Sonn says he "saw everything—cadres from regiments and battallions coming in all the time."

---

170. Author's interview with Moeung Sonn, 1979; S. Heder's interviews with Chap Lonh, former Region 37 deputy secretary, Chantaburi, 12 March 1980, and with Phak Lim, Sa Keo, 9 March 1980.

171. Moeung Sonn, 1979 interview.

The 202nd battalion's commander, Raeun, was alleged to have made contact with Vietnam, while the 203rd's commander, In, was accused of being an agent of the Thai- and U.S.-based anticommunist In Tam. The next morning the chief interrogator arrived, a man from Takeo with one year of high-school education. At 7 A.M. he began to work over the prisoners. Four soldiers assisted him in administering physical punishment. Three of Raeun's troops died under torture that first morning. Sonn, fifth on the list to be interrogated, saw the three bloodied bodies as he entered the interrogation room. The man from Takeo immediately asked, "How many years have you been in the CIA?" Sonn refused to answer, and was beaten six times with a stick, then sent back to his cell.

In July 1977, CPK deputy secretary Nuon Chea visited the Western Zone for a conference of party cadres. He complained to them that "enemies and various classes" controlled a "fair number" of cooperatives in the Zone. Nuon Chea singled out Region 32, where Chou Chet was based. In one district, he claimed, former Lon Nol soldiers were running cooperatives. Nuon Chea also mentioned Region 37, charging that ethnic Chinese "employers" were running krom and kong of up to thirty families. This, he stressed, was "no way to build socialism."[172] Chea went on to note that local traitors and dangerous party members had been wiped out in the previous six months. These included members of CPK committees of Regions 15, 31, and 37. Nevertheless, Chea warned, the backgrounds of all party officials had to be reviewed, now including those at the Zone level. Four days later, the security chief of Region 32 was taken to Tuol Sleng. The Region 32 military commander followed in August. The Region 37 secretary, Sary, was spared, probably because of his personal link with Soeung and his role in the 1977 repression; he died of a liver ailment later in the year.[173]

Languishing for nine months in the Zone prison, Sonn learned that his fellow inmates included his former village chief from 1975, a woman promoted to subdistrict chief before being arrested in early 1977. Her replacement as village chief was another prisoner. Both were executed. Another inmate was the cooperative chief who had sent Sonn off to his first prison term; already in jail for a year, he had suffered several beatings, and was very thin. They

172. Carney, "Organization of Power," in Jackson, ed., *Cambodia 1975–1978*, pp. 86, 322, dating the speech at 25 July 1977; Heder, *Pol Pot and Khieu Samphan*, p. 16, identifies the Center's representative as Nuon Chea but dates his visit to the West at June 1977, citing Chou Chet's confession. If that is correct, Chea would have been personally involved in the repression described by Moeung Sonn in Region 37, whose CPK secretary was arrested on 19 July 1977 ("Important Culprits," p. 4). Chea's speech on the purge to the Western Zone conference followed six days later (Carney, p. 322).

173. "Important Culprits," pp. 4–5; Carney, "Organization of Power," citing *Tung Padevat*, 8, August 1977, pp. 20, 24, 31; S. Heder's interview with Chap Lonh, Chantaburi, 12 March 1980.

were all interrogated and forced to write confessions, like S-21 prisoners in Phnom Penh. Each day twenty to thirty people were tortured. More arrived daily in trucks. Lists of the top prisoners were sent with reports to Paet Soeung, who personally signed their death warrants. "People were taken away every night, and their clothes brought back." Boys who brought in the prisoners' food told Sonn that those taken away would become "fertiliser for coconut and banana trees."[174]

The 1st Western Zone Division's military base was at Longvek, on the Tonle Sap River. There Yusof, a Cham blacksmith attached to the division for nearly two years, was publicly questioned by Paet Soeung around this time. Soeung called him in front of a large meeting, and asked whether Cham Muslims were secretly "turning to Buddhism." The extraordinary question unsettled Yusof, a former Islamic scholar. He only knew that he had to keep his background secret, for fear of being killed. "I replied that I didn't know, but just did what I was told. ... I said I was not concerned about religion. I had been wrong once, and now I was on the correct path. After I had said this, they applauded me."[175]

Escalating Repression in Phnom Penh

Meanwhile, back in the capital, as we have seen, "the Party decided to arrest the contemptible Thuch [Koy Thuon] and the network of intellectuals."[176] Thuon was accused of sexual misconduct. His arrest in late January was followed the next day by the arrests of Touch Phoeun, minister of public works, and of the deputy secretary of the energy ministry. In Tuol Sleng on 5 February, Koy Thuon wrote in a confessional autobiography that soon after joining the party in 1960, he had accepted 500,000 riels from a man named "Furkly, a CIA chief wearing five stripes," to whom Thuon had reported on party affairs at their meeting in a Phnom Penh suburb.[177]

Doeun (Sua Vasi), the ex-Northerner serving as both commerce minister and head of the office of the CPK Central Committee, was a former associate of Thuon's. But when Thuon had first run into trouble the previous year, Doeun had advised Phouk Chhay to "act as if you have never known him." Doeun now received similar treatment from Vorn Vet: "Even with Doeun who lived

---

174. Author's interview with Moeung Sonn, 1979. See also Henri Locard and Moeung Sonn, *Prisonnier de d'Angkar*, Paris: Fayard, 1993. For an evasive account by the former deputy CPK secretary of Region 37 who became a regimental political commissar of the 1st Western Division (Carney, "Organization," p. 104), see S. Heder's interviews with Chap Lonh, Chantaburi, 11–12 March 1980.

175. Author's interview with Yusof, Chhouk Sor, Kompong Tralach, 5 September 1980.

176. Vorn Vet, untitled confession, undated (December 1978?), p. 43.

177. "Sakammapheap kbot padevat rebos khnyom (Koy Thuon)" ("The Activities of Me (Koy Thuon) in Betrayal of the Revolution"), S-21, 5 February 1977.

with me, I made out as if we were in conflict, giving him unfriendly looks, and not saying much."[178] Doeun was apprehended on 12 February.[179] Three hundred sixty-five other prisoners entered Tuol Sleng that month. For March, the intake soared to 1,059.[180]

The head of Pol Pot's personal office (known as K-1), Ket Chau, was arrested in February 1977.[181] Under interrogation, he named three ethnic minority members of an alleged dissident "network" in the office. Chau said they had been associates of Ney Sarann in the Northeast. The three were Khami, an ethnic Tampuon "in charge of protecting *Angkar* on the outside," and Kuon and Sami, two Jarai who were "head of the outside bodyguard section" and "head of the K-3 office."[182] All three quickly disappeared.

Six weeks after Koy Thuon's arrest, prison chief Deuch wrote him a polite letter. It began with understatement, noting from Thuon's latest confession that the prison "environment" had "helped to educate you a lot."[183] Deuch went on:

> From what I personally observed from all your reports so far, I see that you yourself, like Vasi [Doeun] and Men San alias Ya [Ney Sarann], carry out strenuous activities because of your strongly-held beliefs.

> I observe that this accords with the truth. I would like to express my thanks and appreciation.

> But please make a further report, clearly and correctly, as follows: Why is your belief so wholehearted—if the CIA is discredited, Vietnam is discredited, and the Free Khmer movement is discredited, and their physical forces have suffered disintegration, defeat and dissolution more than is thought?

> This is the issue that you have not yet accurately reported. This is the issue that you are avoiding.

---

178. Vorn Vet, 1978 confession, p. 43.

179. "Important Culprits," pp. 13–14.

180. "Benhchi chhmou neak tous dael coul niw khae kompeak 1977" ("List of Names of Prisoners who Entered in February 1977"), S-21, 2 March 1977; "Benhchi chhmou neak tous dael coul niw khae minaa 1977" ("List of Names of Prisoners Who Entered in March 1977"), S-21, undated.

181. "Important Culprits," p. 18.

182. "Chamlaiy rebos Ket Chau—Sem, protean muntir angkar, Ompi chhmou pak puok Sem niw muntir angkar ("The Response of Ket Chau alias Sem, head of the Organization's office, Concerning the Names of Sem's Clique in the Organization's Office"), Part 2, "21 March 1977" (signed 19 March 1977), p. 3. David Chandler kindly provided a copy of this document.

183. Deuch, untitled letter to [*"bang"*] Koy Thuon, dated 3 March 1977. Copied by the author from Koy Thuon's file, Tuol Sleng Museum archives, 1981.

In the hope that you will report frankly.

Deuch.

This letter encapsulates the process and mentality of S-21. First, Deuch's acknowledgement that dissidents such as Koy Thuon, Doeun, and Ney Sarann had acted from political conviction is important. It was a rare and private concession. Prisoners were routinely forced to confess that they were not Cambodian political actors, but mere agents of foreign powers, motivated by greed or cowardice rather than conviction or dedication. Deuch consciously required such statements for propaganda purposes. He saw the danger in revealing the fact that leading Cambodian communists could honestly dissent from party Center policies. The account of "General Furkly" handing Thuon 500,000 riels was thus a requirement of political dogma. Deuch was not so paranoid as to believe it. However, he still considered CPK dissenters to be *objectively* working in concert with foreign powers. Thus, he queried their hope for success without the ability to rely on foreign material aid.

The next day, Thuon wrote two more confessions, totaling twenty-three pages, naming nineteen members of his alleged rebel network. Thuon may have tried to protect associates who still had a chance: by luck or by design, twelve of those named had already been incarcerated. The others included Information Minister Hu Nim, Western Zone secretary Chou Chet, and Northeast Zone Secretary Um Neng.[184] There the paper trail ends. Koy Thuon disappears from history as mysteriously as he had from the cabinet a year earlier.

To celebrate the second anniversary of victory over Lon Nol, S-21 staff compiled a list of the names of all prisoners arrested in the two months prior to 17 April 1977. The 1,566 names on the list roughly equal the number arrested in the whole of 1976. Among these victims were 240 officials of Koy Thuon's former commerce ministry, 218 more suspect members of S-21, 155 public works officials, 80 from the general staff, 50 from the industry and agriculture ministries, and 37 from foreign affairs.[185] Those arrested in this period also included the commander of the battalion responsible for the security of the Center's office (26 February); Phouk Chhay, from that office (14 March); the CPK political instructor for Cambodian returnees from abroad, Phom (8 April); and Information Minister Hu Nim, who "gave himself" to the party on 10 April, after "two work meetings with Brother No. 2 [Nuon Chea]."[186]

According to one report, an early 1977 meeting of the CPK Standing Committee in Phnom Penh discussed the recent poor harvest. Hu Nim reportedly

184. "*Ompi phaenkar riepcom pak thmei muoi . . .* " ("On the plan to establish a new party . . . "), Koy Thuon confession, S-21, dated 4 March 1977, p. 6.

185. "List of Names of Prisoners Who Entered from 17.2.77 to 17.4. 77."

186. "Important Culprits," pp. 15, 18; Boua, Chandler, and Kiernan, eds., *Pol Pot Plans*, p. 316.

suggested that the population needed some material incentive to produce more, and when asked what this would mean in practice, he replied that money would have to be reintroduced.[187] Another source, a CPK regimental commander who defected to Thailand in 1978, claims that "several members of the Party such as Hu Nim and [Ros] Nhim asked the Party to have mercy on the people." It was their view, the defector claimed, "that the Party must act to carry out democratic actions according to a democratic system. They said that the working people must not be persecuted, and foreign aid must be accepted so that the Cambodian people do not suffer too much. Such opinions were regarded by the Party as opposition."[188]

Early in January 1977, Hu Nim recorded in his confessions, he had been "disturbed and tormented" by theoretical documents about collectivism distributed at a CPK branch study session. He relates the suicide of Prom Sam Ar, a comrade whose feelings of despair and straightforward political complaints Hu Nim hints he shared, but suppressed: "If I had not done so I would have had my face smashed in like Prom Sam Ar."[189] In late February, the entire Phnom Penh Radio broadcasting team was arrested.[190] For each of the more than fifteen hundred prisoners apprehended in the two months to 17 April, S-21 carefully recorded the name, alias, gender, position, organizational unit, date of entry to Tuol Sleng, and "miscellaneous" details. In the last column, 633 names are followed by an abbreviation of *komtech* (smashed). One hundred seven prisoners were "smashed" on 17 and 18 March.[191]

The CPK Standing Committee convened again on 11 April, the day after Hu Nim's arrest. Those present were Pol Pot, Nuon Chea, "Phin" [*sic*, So Phim?], Mok, Vorn Vet, Ieng Sary, Moul Sambath, Ke Pauk, and Son Sen. The meeting resolved in part that "each unit, each group, each Ministry must retain the initiative within its services to continue the purge, pursue the enemy and carry out normal tasks."[192] This is the only CPK Standing Committee meeting of the

187. Author's interview with Thun Saray, Phnom Penh, 10 September 1980. Saray said he was told of this meeting by a base person in his village in Sambor district, Kratie, in 1977 or 1978.

188. Account of Lim Mean, a CPK regimental commander who defected to Thailand on 2 November 1978, interviewed by Thai officials on 15 December 1978. French translation of Thai transcript, p. 8.

189. Boua, Chandler, and Kiernan, eds., *Pol Pot Plans the Future*, pp. 311–13.

190. Picq, *Au-delà du ciel*, p. 97.

191. "List of Names of Prisoners Who Entered from 17.2.77 to 17.4.77." Over six hundred were noted as having been killed during this period, up to thirty more between 17 and 29 April 1977, when the list was completed. The other nine hundred were presumably killed in the succeeding months.

192. *People's Revolutionary Tribunal*, Document no. 2.5.23 (French version). Only this part of the document has been released by Phnom Penh or Hanoi. It is difficult to speculate on its remaining contents.

DK period for which there is evidence of So Phim's possible attendance.[193] We have no indication of how he might have intervened or voted. But it is possible that Phim's presence on this occasion propelled an attempt to stem the power of the Santebal. The resolution basically reaffirms the March 1976 policy of decentralized social control. If that was Phim's intention, he failed, and his Eastern Zone was one of the most prominent casualties.

On 14 April, under its new management, Phnom Penh Radio proclaimed, "Respected brothers and comrades-in-arms: Your blood, red and fresh, flows swiftly like streams and rivers wetting the hallowed soil of our beloved Cambodian motherland."[194] Eleven days later, Tuol Sleng was holding 1,132 prisoners. There were more or less equal numbers of military, regional, and central officials. The largest single categories were from the ex-Northern divisions (311 prisoners) and civilian officials of the Northern (127) and Eastern Zones (81).[195] By 7 May, the total had risen to 1,273. But only three Eastern prisoners remained; at least seventy-eight of their colleagues had perished. Also missing were at least 107 ex-Northern troops. Most of the disappeared were executed. But on 25 April and 7 May, two prisoners were also recorded as having "died under torture."[196] This reveals mistakes by the staff, who were supposed to make victims talk. Four days after his arrest, Hu Nim submitted the first of seven written "confessions" to his interrogator, who appended a note to Deuch, saying: "We whipped him four or five times to break his stand, before taking him to be stuffed with water." On 22 April, the interrogator reported, "I have tortured him to write it again." Five weeks later, Hu Nim was abject: "I am not a human being, I am an animal." He was "smashed" on 6 July, the same day as Phouk Chhay and 125 others.[197] Hu Nim's removal signaled the destruction of all the CPK officials known to have identified themselves with China's Cultural Revolution.[198] Phom was probably the most influential, but the others included Phouk Chhay and Deputy Information Minister Tiv Ol, who was arrested on 6 June.[199] But the demise of the leftist

193. Vorn Vet's confession notes Phim's presence at a "Party Center meeting" in "mid-1977," possibly a different gathering (pp. 44–45).

194. *FBIS*, 15 April 1977, p. H1, Phnom Penh Radio, 14 April 1977.

195. The general staff (73 prisoners), as well as the ministries of commerce (74), industry (56), public works (54), and foreign affairs (47) and Kompong Som port (47) were also well represented. Hawk, "Khmer Rouge Prison Documents," document 10, Daily Report on Prisoners, 25 April 1977.

196. "Khmer Rouge Prison Documents," document 11, Daily Report on Prisoners, 7 May 1977. The figures for the other categories sampled in note 195 above were General Staff 81, Commerce 70, Industry 55, Public Works 75, Foreign Affairs 54, Kompong Som 71.

197. *Pol Pot Plans*, p. 227. The S-21 execution record and a translation are reproduced in Anthony Barnett, Chanthou Boua, and Ben Kiernan, "Bureaucracy of Death," *New Statesman*, 2 May 1980, p. 699.

198. See also Heder, *Reflections*, "Khmer Rouge Opposition to Pol Pot."

199. "Important Culprits," p. 15.

tendency within the CPK did not not slow the purges, because their origin lay elsewhere.

Nhek Chamroeun, a disabled CPK soldier recruited by Tiv Ol in the East in 1971, had two brothers working with the deputy information minister in Phnom Penh. According to Chamroeun's account, "In 1976, Tiv Ol became very critical of the Pol Pot regime and was driven almost to despair. When the Pol Pot regime saw his attitude, . . . Tiv Ol was arrested, and all his followers were arrested wholesale." Chamroeun's eldest brother and parents were all executed. Another brother escaped to the East and told Chamroeun what had happened, warning him to be careful. Disregarding his own advice, Chamroeun's brother returned to Phnom Penh, and was quickly arrested and killed.[200] The most senior Easterner in the capital, Siet Chhe, a former secretary of Region 22 who had replaced Chakrey on the general staff, was incarcerated on 29 April 1977.[201]

But as the genocide gathered speed, more and more of the victims, even at the nerve center of the repression, were nonpolitical. On 1 July, 114 women were killed in Tuol Sleng, including 90 whose "function" was listed as "wives" of prisoners previously executed. Eight more were simply listed as widows, and two more as married to "unknown husbands." Two others were a mother and a sister-in-law of executed prisoners. The next day, thirty-one sons and forty-three daughters of prisoners, fifteen of them taken from "children's centers," and a nurse described as an orphan, were slaughtered.[202]

Instability persisted even as mistrust spread. In April and May, troops in the Phnom Penh area were forbidden to have any contact with the population. The new regulation was announced to both soldiers and civilians.[203] A Bangkok Cambodia-watcher asserts that "according to reliable sources," in August 1977 the Center summoned Mok to Phnom Penh to repress a coup attempt there.[204] At a meeting of Zone and Region secretaries in the capital later in the year, Pol Pot announced that of Democratic Kampuchea's fifteen military divisions, only four were "loyal," and they were all on the border. The other eleven had already resisted the central authorities, and their commanders had been arrested. Pot also revealed that there had been another attempt to poison him during 1977. It had been foiled only by his missing a meal.[205]

200. Katuiti Honda, *Journey to Cambodia*, Tokyo, 1981, pp. 120–121.

201. "Important Culprits," p. 3; Kiernan, *How Pol Pot*, p. 340.

202. Hawk, "Khmer Rouge Prison Documents from the S-21 (Tuol Sleng) Extermination Center in Phnom Penh," documents 4 and 14, Execution Schedules for 1 and 2 July 1977.

203. Author's interview with former 502nd Division soldier Chhin Phoeun, Kong Pisei, 17 September 1980.

204. Jacques Bekaert, "Story of Commander X," *Bangkok Post*, 4 March 1988. Ponchaud, "Situation interne," p. 6, notes that "In August, the arrests continued, and it even seems there was a coup attempt, with massacres in Phnom Penh and Battambang."

205. Author's interview with Thun Saray, Phnom Penh, 18 January 1986. Saray's source

Pol Pot visited China in late September and publicly announced the existence of the CPK. His return saw an acceleration of the massacres. On October 15 alone, a record 418 Tuol Sleng prisoners were executed by the Santebal. Three days later, another 179 perished, followed by 88 more victims on October 20 and 148 on the 23rd.[206] The Center kept a close eye on all this. On 5 October, Son Sen had written to "Beloved Comrade Deuch," explaining, "It is necessary to conserve paper." He warned against accepting all statements from those being interrogated. "Some of their responses also attack us. Some of them attack purposefully. Some of them are afraid and just talk and talk." There was no discussion of the killings.[207]

Meanwhile the Center was showing redoubled interest in So Phim and the Eastern Zone. A cadre from Ponhea Krek who knew Phim well says he saw Pol Pot visit Phim at his headquarters there twice during 1977, at least once with Ieng Sary. (Pol Pot had not come there in 1975 or 1976.)[208] The results of the visit would soon emerge. Early in December 1977, Cambodia received a visit from China's model commune leader, Chen Yonggui. The inspiration for the Maoist "Learn from Tachai" movement, Chen was now deputy prime minister of China. On 4 December, accompanied by Pol Pot and Vorn Vet, Chen left Phnom Penh for the Eastern Zone. They were welcomed by local leaders So Phim and Phuong (DK minister of rubber plantations), Phim's deputy Chan, Lin, and two thousand cadres. Phnom Penh Radio's coverage of the event is instructive. Phim was described as "Vice-President of the State Presidium, Secretary of the Eastern Zone CPK Committee, and Chairman of the Eastern Zone Committee to Serve the People." This listed his posts in the state, the party, and the administration. The first and third posts, however, were honorific and derivative. Power was vested in the party hierarchy, especially since the official declaration of the CPK's existence two months earlier. Thus Phuong, listed next, had his posts named in the appropriate order: announcement of his membership on the CPK Central Committee preceded that of his state post in charge of the rubber plantations. The interesting point here is that the announcer had omitted to describe So Phim even as a member of the party Central Committee, *let alone as a member*

was an unnamed "one-legged man who was the division commander in the Northeast Zone." Not to be outdone, Pot's sister-in-law Ieng Thirith later asserted, "The Vietnamese also tried to poison me thrice in 1977. Fortunately I ate very little of the poisoned food all the time." M. C. Menon, "Interview with Madam Ieng Thirith," *Third World Unity* (New Delhi), November 1979, p. 9.

206. Barnett, "Inside S-21," p. 671.

207. Hawk, "Khmer Rouge Prison Documents," no. 21, letter from Khieu to Deuch, 5 October 1977. Heder's translation.

208. Interview with the author, Krek, 7 August 1980.

of its Standing Committee.[209] His party status had dropped lower than Phuong's. He was replaced on the Standing Committee by Son Sen, with Vorn Vet moving up to Phim's No. 4 position.[210] As deputy prime minister, defense minister, and the CPK leader responsible for the Santebal, Sen's star had been rising since mid-year.[211] Had Phim noticed, this was the writing on the wall.

The next month, Phnom Penh Radio specifically appealed to people in Phim's home subdistrict, Dauntei, to "prepare themselves to wipe out the enemy aggressors *and their clique of supporters.*"[212] So Phim was in the Center's sights.

And Phnom Penh Radio, of course, was in new hands. Though the disappearance of Hu Nim eight months before remained unacknowledged, his replacement was revealed in December. The new minister of information was Yun Yat, wife of Son Sen.[213] Yat took office just after the arrest of Leng Sei, who had led the women's delegation to Vietnam the year before. Since May 1975, Leng Sei had run Phnom Penh's 17 April Hospital. When her husband, Deputy Information Minister Tiv Ol, was taken to Tuol Sleng in June, "*Angkar* removed her and held her secretly for a period." On 17 December, Sei was arrested. After five weeks' interrogation by Pon, she completed a fifty-five-page "confession." Pon commented: "The important thing is that she was with her husband throughout."[214] Sei was executed.

Six thousand, three hundred thirty prisoners were "smashed" in Tuol

209. BBC, SWB, 7 December 1977, Fe/5686/A3/2, Phnom Penh Radio, 6 December 1977. This was no mistake. A similar New China News Agency account (ibid.) apparently omitted even Phim's *Zone* party position, while giving Phuong's and that of "Pem Rine" (a member of the Eastern Zone CPK committee's Standing Committee). The DK embassy in Beijing published a French translation that again omitted Phim's membership on the CPK's Central Committee or its Standing Committee (*Bulletin quotidien de "La Voix du Kampuchéa Democratique": Résumé*, "Emission du mardi 6 décembre 1977," p. 1).

210. This is S. Thion's analysis of diplomatic reports at the time (Thion and Kiernan, *Khmers Rouges! Matériaux pour l'histoire du communisme au Cambodge*, Paris: Albin Michel, 1981, p. 291). The exclusion of So Phim from the Standing Committee in this period is corroborated by the account of Chap Lonh, then a member of the CPK Central Committee; see *Revolution and Its Aftermath in Kampuchea*, p. 208, n. 60.

211. Trooper Chhin Phoeun of the 502nd Division recalls that Son Sen's name appeared in June and July 1977 on defense orders posted on buildings in Phnom Penh. Author's interview, Kong Pisei, 17 September 1980.

212. *FBIS*, 30 January 1978, pp. H12–13, Phnom Penh Radio, 27 January 1978 (employing the translation "supporting clique"), emphasis added. (Dauntei was also the base of Heng Samrin. BBC SWB, 27 February 1979, FE/6053/A3/11–12.) "Clique of supporters" or "supporting clique" referred to *internal* Cambodian opponents, not the USSR or other Vietnamese allies: in *FBIS*, 2 February 1978, pp. H1–2, Phnom Penh Radio distinguished this term from "big imperialist powers" supporting Hanoi (31 January 1978).

213. See *FEER*, 30 December 1977, p. 5. No announcement for foreign consumption was made until February or March 1978, when Yun Yat was named minister of information and education. *FBIS*, 13 March 1978, p. H2, Phnom Penh Radio, 10 March 1978.

214. "Ateita lekha muntir paet P-17" ("The Former Secretary of Hospital P-17"), S-21, p. 1.

Sleng during 1977,[215] almost quadruple the 1976 total. Two years of Center purges had targeted two major categories: soldiers and intellectuals (like Hu Nim and Tiv Ol) from the Northern Zone formerly associated with Koy Thuon, and So Phim's network of cadres and former Eastern Zone troops. These particular *Santebal* tasks were now approaching completion.

The next year, Khieu Samphan told Sihanouk that the Center had had to punish Koy Thuon because he was "an agent of the Vietnamese and the CIA." Sihanouk pressed his host: "Are you sure?" Samphan confessed: "No."[216]

215. Barnett, "Inside S-21."
216. Norodom Sihanouk, taped interview with James Pringle and others, Beijing, January 1979.

CHAPTER NINE

Foreign Relations, 1977–78: Warfare, Weapons, and Wildlife

1977: War Begins

The end of 1976 had seen relative peace on Cambodia's borders. But in December, Pol Pot ordered the CPK to "make long-term preparations for a guerrilla war and for a war using conventional forces."[1] In January 1977, DK officials began withdrawing from all bilateral frontier liaison committees.[2] In Phnom Penh in the same month, a soldier of the Center's 11th Division recalls hearing for the first time that Vietnam was an "aggressor" and an "enemy" of Democratic Kampuchea. The deputy division commander, a northeastern tribal cadre named Lovei, announced this at a battalion study session.[3] On 27 January, on the border with Thailand, a raid by Democratic Kampuchea troops killed over thirty Thai villagers.[4] At almost the same time, Cambodia began to clash with Laos.[5]

But the Vietnamese border saw the most serious violence, launched from Democratic Kampuchea's Southwest Zone. Summarizing many press reports, *Keesing's Contemporary Archives* concluded: "The situation gravely deteriorated from March 1977 onwards. According to an official Vietnamese document published on 6th January 1978, the Cambodian forces made raids into the Vietnamese provinces of Kien Giang and An Giang on March 15–18 and 25–28 1977, along a sector nearly 100 kilometres long from Ha Tien (Kien

---

1. Chanthou Boua, David Chandler, and Ben Kiernan, eds., *Pol Pot Plans the Future*, pp. 190–91.

2. *Kampuchea Dossier*, I, Hanoi, 1978, p. 132. Phnom Penh Radio announced on 14 February 1977 that the road between the capital and Ho Chi Minh City had been reopened. *Far Eastern Economic Review (FEER)*, 25 February 1977, p. 5. This announcement had little effect, however.

3. Author's interview with Chhin Phoeun, Kong Pisei, 17 September 1980.

4. N. Peagam, "Questions after the massacre," *FEER*, 11 February 1977, pp. 9–10; *FEER*, 25 February 1977, p. 5.

5. After a visit to southern Laos, Nayan Chanda reported in 1978 that "the situation on the [Lao-Cambodian] border has been deteriorating since the end of 1976." *FEER*, 12 December 1978.

Giang) to Tinh Bien (An Giang). Strong Cambodian forces launched concerted attacks on Vietnamese army posts and border villages in An Giang between April 30 and May 19, killing 222 civilians, and shelled Chau Doc, the provincial capital, on May 17. *These reports were corroborated by Vietnamese refugees reaching other Asian countries,* who stated that the civilian population had been evacuated from Ha Tien on May 16 and from Chau Doc on the following day after the two towns had been shelled."[6]

The Democratic Kampuchea side at this time gave no hint of being threatened. *Tung Padevat's* June 1976 assurance that "the enemy is hesitant towards us. . . . It is impossible for the enemy to attack us"[7] had been reaffirmed by Pol Pot in December: "Our enemies are no stronger than we are. They cannot attack us openly, so they attack us slyly along the frontier, and try to eat us from within; they steal border markers along the frontier indiscriminately. The big problem is in the interior. . . . We must resist spies along the frontier, but the important thing is to guard against them in the interior of the country."[8] Pol Pot saw Democratic Kampuchea's main enemies as internal. Khieu Samphan, too, announced on 17 April 1977: "Our national defense situation is improving yearly. In particular, in 1977 the situation is far better than that in 1976."[9] The April 1977 issue of *Tung Padevat* explained, "Our enemies no longer possess a fifth column in the bosom of our party and people to use as a nucleus from which to foment counter-revolutionary activities with the aim of overthrowing our regime. . . . From another point of view, *they are no longer able to attack us militarily from the outside.*"[10]

6. *Keesing's Contemporary Archives,* 27 October 1978, 29269 (my emphasis). Quoted in Anthony Barnett's draft reply to Laura Summers' article in *Bulletin of Concerned Asian Scholars (BCAS),* 11, 4 (1979). See also *FEER,* 31 March 1978, p. 12, for corroborative details of these early 1977 Democratic Kampuchea attacks on Vietnam. In a 1980 interview with the author, Ha Thi Que, leader of the February 1977 Vietnamese women's delegation to Democratic Kampuchea, claimed the Vietnamese were then still inclined to optimism: "We parted on good terms. The Vietnamese embassy [in Phnom Penh] told us that we were received better than any previous delegations from Vietnam, and that the Cambodians were really sorry about the [November 1976] Dac Lac incidents." (See Chapter 5.) But Que found this "impossible to understand," given what happened later.

7. *Tung Padevat (Revolutionary Flags),* No. 6, June 1976, translation by Chanthou Boua. This document was deposited at Cornell University's Olin Library by T. Carney. Although many independent sources concur that the fighting began in March 1977, *Livre Noir,* the official DK history of the conflict, in its discussion of "Vietnamese aggression" in 1977, mentions only the Vietnamese incursion in December (pp. 98ff.).

8. *Pol Pot Plans the Future,* p. 191.

9. U.S. Central Intelligence Agency, Foreign Broadcast Information Service (FBIS), Asia Pacific, 18 April 1977, p. H3, Phnom Penh Radio, 15 April 1977.

10. *Tung Padevat* No. 4, April 1977 (emphasis added). I am grateful to Gareth Porter for a partial translation.

Who, then, had started the fighting in March? *Tung Padevat* continued:

Faced with this encouraging situation, what position could we adopt? Should we attack our enemies more fiercely, or should we be content with the results obtained: . . . We should attack them without respite on every terrain by taking our own initiatives and by scrupulously following the directions of our party, both in the internal political field and in the field of foreign relations. . . . We must fight the enemy coming from the outside in all theatres of operations and in every form.[11]

Two Cambodian refugees in France have provided eyewitness accounts of the 1977 border fighting. Heng had escaped to Vietnam from Svay Rieng province in October 1975. He was given permission to live and work as he chose, and he settled down in the mixed Khmer-Vietnamese village of Ke Mea, in Tay Ninh province. He found that the Vietnamese authorities referred to the Khmer Rouge as "brothers," and he heard of no border fighting during 1976. Then, in May or June 1977, the Khmer Rouge shelled Ke Mea, killing "hundreds of people," ethnic Khmers as well as Vietnamese. The Vietnamese authorities still insisted that the Khmer Rouge were their "friends." Not until early 1978 did they mount loudspeakers in the villages "telling their people what the Khmer had done."[12]

Veasna had fled to Vietnam from Kampot in December 1975. He too was allowed to live normally. Settling very close to the border, in the village of Ap Sase (Ha Tien, Kien Giang), he "could see the Khmer Rouge working every day." He also saw no fighting between Cambodia and Vietnam during 1976. Then, Veasna asserts, "the Khmer Rouge started the fighting." Just before the middle of 1977, DK troops attacked across the border and massacred two hundred civilians in nearby Prey Tameang village, including ethnic Khmers as well as Vietnamese. Soon after, in mid-1977, came another Democratic Kampuchea attack. Veasna says: "I saw this in actual fact with my own eyes, since my house was 500 meters from the border. When the Khmer Rouge crossed the border everybody ran and grabbed their children and all ran into their houses. But the Khmer Rouge came into our village and burnt down houses and burnt goods, and killed about twenty people who were not able to run away."

Veasna continues, "The population asked the Vietnamese military to fight back against the Khmer Rouge, but they replied that they didn't have orders from above to do so. In 1977, the Vietnamese did not go into Cambodian territory."[13] Again, this is confirmed by Western sources. Bernard Edinger reported

11. *Tung Padevat*, No. 4, April 1977.
12. Author's interview with Heng, Flers, 8 October 1979.
13. Author's interview with Veasna, Caen, 7 October 1979.

that "during the summer" of 1977, "hundreds of people were killed when Cambodian troops stormed close to 40 villages set up within Vietnam's 'new economic areas' programme." Edinger noted that "reliable sources said there was no doubt that the fighting was started by Cambodian central authorities."[14]

Inside Democratic Kampuchea, a base person from Region 25 recalls how the 1975–76 policy theme of "gathering people and working" changed in 1977 to "talk about offensives and victory over Vietnam." Another adds that "in 1977 the Khmer began attacking hard," and says he witnessed Democratic Kampuchea forces "shelling markets on Vietnamese territory."[15] Also in the Southwest, a woman then living in Kirivong (Region 13) reports witnessing a major Cambodian attack on Vietnam on 30 April 1977: "We were growing dry season rice. . . . They attacked at 2 o'clock all along the border, within fifteen minutes of each other. . . . I could see fires burning all along the frontier, houses burning." Two weeks later, the D.K. subdistrict chief, addressing a public meeting, boasted of the incursion, claiming "20,000 Vietnamese soldiers and civilians killed in one night." He and other cadres alleged that "the Vietnamese had built their houses on Khmer land, beside the [Vinh Te] canal." He claimed this "Khmer land" had now been "liberated." But the woman was sure the Democratic Kampuchea army had invaded Vietnamese territory.[16]

Conquering Kampuchea Krom (the Mekong Delta)

She was right. In June 1977, the DK foreign ministry drafted a secret "History of the Kampuchea-Vietnam Border," which conceded among other things that the Vinh Te canal was twelve hundred meters beyond Cambodia's border.[17] This document set out to demonstrate that past "royal and feudal authorities," along with French colonialists, had "caused the loss of the territory in Kampuchea Krom" to "Vietnamese swallowers of Kampuchean land." The report concluded that "because the border between Kampuchea and Vietnam was determined in violation of justice towards Kampuchea, the government of Democratic Kampuchea demands changes at some points in the

14. See, for instance, "Cambodians Behead Vietnam Villagers," by Bernard Edinger, AAP-Reuter, *The Asian* (Melbourne), November 1977, p. 11.
15. Author's interviews with Seng and Sok, Prek Ambel, 1 July 1980.
16. Author's interview at Kraing Ta Chan, Tram Kak district, 16 July 1980. This woman identifies the main speaker as Nuoeun, chief of Som Subdistrict, in Kirivong District, Region 13 of the Southwest Zone.
17. "Prowatt prumdaen Kampuchea-Vietnam" ("History of the Cambodia-Vietnam Border"), DK foreign ministry "internal document," 15 June 1977. It concedes that in 1873, "French colonialists gave the Vinh Te canal to [Vietnam and] drew the border 1,200 metres inside Kampuchean territory." (pp. 6, 13).

present border line." It added that the DK army "resolves to defend its territorial integrity." A contradictory principle was applied to the sea border. The foreign ministry conceded that the French-drawn Brevié Line had been a mere "administrative" maritime demarcation, "but Democratic Kampuchea considers it a state border between Kampuchea and Vietnam which has been left by history."[18] In August 1977, the regime published *Democratic Kampuchea Is Moving Forward,* a magazine packed with glossy photographs of people working determinedly at national construction. The frontispiece was a map of Democratic Kampuchea showing the Brevié Line as the national sea border between Cambodia and Vietnam, though no agreement on it had ever been reached.[19] This was the signal for further Cambodian incursions.

The sharp escalation in DK raids from September 1977 is corroborated by Western sources. *Keesings* continues: "The Vietnamese document of 6 January 1978, *which was supported by reports from U.S. intelligence sources,* stated that from September 24 onwards Cambodian forces totaling about four divisions had launched continuous attacks along the entire border of Tay Ninh province, and that over 1,000 civilians had been killed or wounded in this area between September 24 and late November."[20] *Asiaweek* concurred: "Most intelligence analysts in Bangkok agree that Cambodian raids and land grabs escalated the ill-will . . . until peace was irretrievable."[21]

Prisoners in Tuol Sleng had to obey ten regulations. Number eight was: "Don't make pretexts about Kampuchea Krom in order to hide your jaw of a traitor."[22] It seems that prisoners, to disguise their alleged "treason" and save their lives, felt tempted to falsely declare that they believed Kampuchea Krom should be taken back from Vietnam. The prison regulation makes little sense unless it was well known in Democratic Kampuchea that the Center favored retaking Kampuchea Krom as a policy of patriotism.

By 1977 this was already a dominant theme in the Southwest Zone, especially in its heartland, Region 13. A soldier of the 2nd Zone regiment, captured by Hanoi the following year, claimed that in March 1977, Mok himself had

18. Ibid., pp. i, 16. Emphasis added.

19. See Chapter 4. In 1976, "Phumisas Kampuchea pracheathipathaiy" ("Geography of Democratic Kampuchea"), published by the DK education ministry, had featured a map of Cambodia without a sea border. The revised DK map is in *Democratic Kampuchea Is Moving Forward,* Phnom Penh, August 1977. It is presumably the source for an unsubstantiated *Far Eastern Economic Review* report of "the recent publication in Phnom Penh of a map locating the Vietnamese island of Phu Quoc inside Khmer territory" (*FEER,* 16 December 1977, p. 17).

20. *Keesing's Contemporary Archives,* 27 October 1978, 29269 (emphasis added).

21. *Asiaweek,* 22 September 1978.

22. A translation of this list of Tuol Sleng regulations appeared on the cover of the *Sunday Times Magazine* (London), 11 May 1980. In 1980 I photographed the Khmer original, which was written on a blackboard.

predicted a May 1977 incursion into Vietnam "as far as the first sugar-palm tree, Saigon."[23] A Takeo woman deported during the DK period to Kirivong district recalls local cadres talking of conquering Kampuchea Krom at meetings around May 1977. Within a year the rhetoric had escalated: "The Vietnamese and the Khmer are life-and-death enemies. Even though our frontiers are close, we have to attack and seize Vietnam."[24] A Khmer Krom peasant, kidnapped in a 1978 DK raid into Vietnam, says that at a meeting of three thousand people in Kirivong in June of that year, cpk speakers announced that "Vietnamese territory is Cambodian territory." A Kirivong peasant deported to Mok's home subdistrict in Tram Kak in 1978 recalls cadres there saying, "Kampuchea Krom is our territory. Either the Vietnamese will get it all or the Khmer will. . . . We have to unite our forces in order to get the territory of Kampuchea Krom back."[25] A former student laboring in the same district recalls hearing Mok's son-in-law, San, address a mass meeting of four subdistricts in February 1978. San proclaimed: "The acute aim of the revolution is to fight and take the territory of Kampuchea Krom. So therefore, we have to temper our standpoint and consciousness, and work hard in the rear to produce, to support the Revolutionary Army to get the territory back." In June 1978, the security chief of Tram Kak district repeated this message: "All we Khmers must join together in all possible ways to fight to get back the territory of Kampuchea Krom."[26]

This would not be an easy task, and the population had to be carefully prepared for it. The political line was kept secret at first. A "full rights" peasant in the cpk's model village in Tram Kak recalls that from 1975, cadres described Vietnam in political education sessions as vulnerable and "poor," with "only chaff to eat." Then later, "from 1977 Vietnam was described as an enemy." At the separate meetings for deportees, the line was disseminated more slowly. For instance, a local woman deported to a neighboring village in 1975 says that "at every meeting from 1977 on," Vietnam was said to have "no strength" because its people had "only chaff to eat."[27]

Elsewhere in the Southwest, a cpk member from Region 33 confirms the

23. *Kampuchea Dossier,* II, Hanoi, 1978, p. 72 and photograph 5, reproducing the Khmer text.

24. Author's interview at Kraing Ta Chan, Tram Kak district, 16 July 1980: "From early 1977 they started talking at meetings about taking back Kampuchea Krom." This corroborates the soldier's confession.

25. Author's interviews with Chan and Chip, Phnom Den, 26 August 1980. Chip attributes the latter statements to his village chief and the chief of Trapeang Thom subdistrict, where Mok was born.

26. Author's interview at Preah Bat Chuon Chum, 26 August 1980. The first meeting involved people from Tram Kak, Nheng Nhang, Kus, and Samrong subdistricts. San added, "Sihanouk is a feudalist." The Tram Kak security chief's name was Phen.

27. Author's interviews in Leay Bo, Ang Tasom district, 15 July 1980.

1977 proclamation: "We must fight to get back Kampuchea Krom." A base person in Region 25 says that in 1976 and 1977 lower-ranking cadres "began talking about getting back Kampuchea Krom." A Phnom Penh woman sent to the same Region reports that in 1978, cadres told villagers including herself that Democratic Kampuchea wanted "to get back Kampuchea Krom."[28]

On the other side of the country, the policy was initially unclear. In Region 4 of the Northwest Zone, a local cadre boasted in 1975 or 1976, "We defeated the American imperialists. Now we can also defeat Thailand and Vietnam and regain the territory from them that historically belonged to Cambodia." Six months later, however, Khek Penn came to the same village. He announced at a meeting that Cambodia simply wanted to defend what was now its own territory and to live in peace, and that there should be no talk of fighting Thailand or Vietnam to win back lost territory.[29] After Penn's arrest, the line changed again. Lang Sim, a Khmer refugee now in France, was in Battambang in mid-1977 when new cadres arrived from the Southwest. At a meeting in her village at the end of that year, the cadres announced that Democratic Kampuchea "aimed to fight to recover Kampuchea Krom from Vietnam, as well as Surin and other provinces from Thailand."[30] Southwesterners arriving in Region 3 in late 1977 claimed progress on this front: "Some of our land in Kampuchea Krom is in their [Vietnamese] hands, and some is in ours."[31]

Southwest Zone cadres from Kampot arrived in the Saut Nikom district of Siemreap (Region 106) in March 1978. At that time, Sovannareth, nineteen, was working in a bean-growing unit in the district. He recalls that the southwest cadres "arrested the previous local leaders, and made us suffer more." Then, in June 1978, at a meeting of one thousand people in Kong village:

> The big leader spoke. His name was Ta Meng; he was about fifty years old, and killed people like anything, right in front of others. He talked about . . . the war between the Revolutionary Army and the Vietnamese. He said they had killed 30,000 Vietnamese in Svay Rieng province, destroyed 50 tanks, and shot down four Russian-made planes. In order not to waste anything, he said, the bodies of the tanks had been used to make plates for the people to eat on . . .
>
> Their plan was to take back Kampuchea Krom. He said that the Vietnamese were swallowers of Khmer land and that "the Khmer people

28. Author's interviews with Hen, Kong Pisei, 17 September 1980; Sok, Prek Ambel, 1 August 1980; Bopha Sinan, Washington, D.C., 26 March 1980. The cadres Bopha quoted included district, subdistrict, and village officials in Sa'ang, Region 25.
29. Author's interview with Tae Hui Lang, Chatenay-Malabry, 10 August 1979. She referred to Khek Penn (alias Sou) as "chief of Region 4," or "the district chief, Sou."
30. Author's interview with Lang Sim, Limoges, 7 December 1979.
31. Author's interview with Tan Kong Sy, Toulouse, 11 December 1979.

resolve to again liberate the Khmer land in Kampuchea Krom." He talked all about "Moat Chrouk" [the Khmer name for Vietnam's Chaudoc province] and "Prey Nokor" [Ho Chi Minh City] and so on. He called for the recruitment of ten youths from each village to join the army . . . [32]

Such proclamations were not the preserve of Southwest Zone cadres. Similar statements were made by Center officials. The director of Kompong Som port, Thuch Rin, told dock workers around the end of 1977, "Kampuchea Krom is Cambodian territory."[33] Kun, a Khmer interpreter for North Korean advisers who traveled widely in Democratic Kampuchea, said that the policy of retaking Kampuchea Krom from Vietnam was "not official," in the sense that it was not mentioned in official statements and publications. "Perhaps it was the party line, but for propaganda they said they did not want to do it." Nevertheless, Kun went on, "right though 1978, from the beginning of the year until the end, everybody I met in the army was talking in those terms." The aim of retaking Kampuchea Krom was announced "secretly by cadres at the executive level."[34] Nguon Son, a worker in a large Phnom Penh factory, recalls that around November 1978, Ta Khon, the director of the factory, said in a meeting that "we aim to liberate the people of Kampuchea Krom and have already liberated ten to twenty thousand of them."[35]

Prince Sihanouk later revealed what DK leaders had told him: "In the past, they said, our leaders sold out Kampuchea Krom, sold out South Vietnam to the Vietnamese. Our armies can't accept the status quo. We must make war against Vietnam to get back Kampuchea Krom. As the first step, if there are [sugar] palm trees, the soil is Khmer. In Chaudoc and Ha Tien, there are still palm trees. We must occupy."[36] Sihanouk adds:

32. Author's interview with Sovannareth, Rouen, 10 October 1979. He adds, "The Southwestern cadres put up banners denouncing the 'Vietnamese aggressors of our land who are trying to form an Indochina Federation.' Another banner asked the Vietnamese a question: 'You want us to join a Federation: do you know how to manufacture guns?' Another said: 'I am a Cambodian, and I resolve to fight the Vietnamese, and others, 'Long live the great and strong Kampuchean revolution.' There were many other banners as well. We sat on the ground during the meeting, which lasted from 6 p.m. to 10 p.m. The village chief talked about how the people resolved to work hard so that guns and ammunition could be brought to defend the country. Fifteen village chiefs from the district also talked for about ten minutes each, telling us to 'destroy all bad habits and oppressive acts.'"

33. Author's interview with pilot Sok Sam, Kompong Som, 18 July 1980. He says that Thuch Rin made this statement in 1977 or before September 1978. Kompong Som is in the Western Zone; Moeung Sonn reports that while in jail with 1st Division troops in the Western Zone in 1977, he heard much about a "special plan" to "take Vietnamese territory such as Koh Tral [Phu Quoc island]." Interview with the author, Sarcelles, 25 October 1979.

34. Author's interview with Kun, Montbard, 1 February 1980.

35. Author's interview with Nguon Son, Strasbourg, 31 October 1979.

36. N. Sihanouk, Speech to the Asia Society, New York, 22 February 1980. Sihanouk adds in his book that after their 1975 victory, the Khmer Rouge had "tried to conquer a part of

The Pol Pot government rejected all the proposals for a peaceful solution presented on several occasions (in particular 5 February 1978) by the Hanoi government.... In 1978 .`. . Khieu Samphan confided to me . . . that his (Khmer Rouge) soldiers were "unstoppable": whenever they saw sugar palms in the territory of Kampuchea Krom [South Vietnam], these patriotic soldiers could not prevent themselves from crossing the frontier and advancing "until they came to the last Khmer sugar palm" . . . According to Son Sen . . . his glorious "Revolutionary Army of Kampuchea" thought itself capable of dealing very easily with Giap's army, and the much more puny one of Kukrit Pramoj and Kriangsak Chamanond (Thailand)![37]

Democratic Kampuchea was also attempting to promote an armed uprising by Khmer Krom against the Vietnamese government. Pol Pot sent agents across the border to foment a revolt.[38] In 1978, frontier troops in Region 24 told Kun that Democratic Kampuchea was "secretly sending guns to Kampuchea Krom . . . to the Khmer Krom to help them fight the Vietnamese." DK foreign ministry officials told Tri Meng Huot in the second half of 1978 that "Kampuchea Krom is struggling hard. . . . It wants to be reunited with us Khmer." They added that "preparations were being made" within Vietnam and that Khmer Kampuchea Krom (KKK) rebels had obtained a radio. The officials told Kun that Democratic Kampuchea "would do what it could to liberate" Kampuchea Krom.[39]

A mid-1976 CPK journal had described what it called "the continuous non-stop struggle between revolution and counter-revolution" in the following terms: "We must have the standpoint that the enemy will continue to exist for 10, 20 or 30 years. The national struggle is the same as the class struggle; in a word, the struggle between revolution and counter-revolution will be contin-

---

Kampuchea Krom and committed horrible atrocities on a large number of Vietnamese male and female civilians (including old people, women and children)." *Chroniques de guerre . . . et d'espoir*, Paris: Hachette-Stock, 1979, p. 114.

37. *Chroniques de guerre*, pp. 114, 81, 79. In December 1978, the chief of the DK foreign ministry's Asia department, Thiounn Prasith, told a visitor that the existence of sugar palm trees "shows you are in Kampuchea and not Vietnam." He added, "When the Vietnamese come they get rid of palms as the border is clearly marked." Quoted in Malcolm Caldwell's diary of his visit, typescript, p. 17.

38. Chandler, *Brother Number One*, p. 148; *A History of Cambodia* (2nd ed., 1992), p. 220.

39. Author's interviews with Kun, 1 February 1980, and Tri Meng Huot, Paris, 15 February 1980. Huot concluded that what DK called Kampuchea Krom's "independence" meant reintegration into Cambodia. DK aid on its behalf included ironic charges that Khmer Krom "are victim of the worst cruelties" in Vietnam. "It is forbidden for them to speak, dress, eat or learn according to [their] traditions on pain of death and the male babies are strangled at their birth." *Voice of Democratic Kampuchea*, 18 October 1978, translation by the DK embassy in Beijing, at p. 2.

uous. . . . When we are strong they are weak, when they are weak we are strong . . ."[40] Note that "we" are always "strong"! The conception of a zero-sum game between Cambodia and Vietnam was echoed at the local level. Cadres in Kirivong (Region 13 of the Southwest) explained in the same period that Cambodia and Vietnam were enemies who "could not look at each other or speak to one another."[41] In Region 31 in 1977, a subdistrict cadre proclaimed that Democratic Kampuchea "could not co-exist with Vietnam." "Either Vietnam or us had to go."[42] In the Tram Kak district of Region 13, local officials proclaimed in late 1978: "If the Vietnamese are all gone, the Khmer remain; if the Khmer are all gone, the Vietnamese remain."[43] In Region 25 by 1978, a slogan had it that "each Khmer can kill thirty Vietnamese."[44]

Phnom Penh Radio charged that entire "generations of Vietnamese" had "devised" cruel strategies "to kill the Cambodian people" and "exterminate" them. Vietnamese were alternately called the "historic enemy" and Cambodia's "hereditary enemy."[45]

DK Irredentism across the Thai Border

Serious incidents along the border between Cambodia and northeast Thailand also started in early 1977.[46] These attacks by CPK or joint CPK-Thai communist forces were characterized by a brutal militarism, unlike what is known of the operating methods of the communists in other parts of Thailand at that time, where the tendency was to use more political persuasion to win the support of the population.

Around December 1977, according to the Bangkok journal *Thai Nikorn*, a secret agreement was reached between a representative of the Communist

40. *Tung Padevat*, No. 6, June 1976, p. 21.

41. Author's interview with a woman deported to Kirivong district in early 1976. Tram Kak, 16 July 1980.

42. Author's interview with Men, Kompong Tralach, 5 September 1980. The cadre was named Phan.

43. Author's interview with a Khmer Krom kidnapped by a CPK raiding force in March 1978 and deported to Tram Kak district. Phnom Den, 26 August 1980.

44. Author's interview with Seng, a former teacher and Region 25 base person. Prek Ambel, 1 July 1980.

45. Phnom Penh Radio, 10 November 1978; *Asiaweek*, 2 December 1977, p. 43; Statement of the Government of Democratic Kampuchea, Phnom Penh, 2 January 1979, p. 11.

46. *Sydney Morning Herald*, 8 August 1977, reports the Thai prime minister's claim that "Khmer Rouge troops from Cambodia had made 400 incursions into Thai territory since January." Moeung Sonn reports that in the Western Zone prison in 1977–78, troops of the 1st Western Division (commanded by Paet Soeung) told him that DK forces had attacked Khlong Yai town in Thailand "around 1976." "It was their plan to take Thai territory." Interview with the author, Sarcelles, 25 October 1979.

Party of Thailand (CPT) Northeastern Committee and the CPK secretary of Oddar Meanchey province (adjacent to Surin), representing the CPK. The negotiators agreed

> to set up a mixed force of CPT and CPK in order to act in the southern part of Northeast Thailand . . .
>
> It was agreed that the Cambodians would send one unit of forces to join the CPT movement, in order that the mixed force should use Pol Pot's lessons on how to seize power, i.e. wherever the conditions are ripe for striking against the stable underpinnings of Thai civil servants, an effort should be made to strike, and every day and every night in order to terrorize Thai officials. Wherever conditions are not ripe, a report should be made to the central unit of the Cambodian side. If it should be thought appropriate, *the Cambodian base unit will enter Thailand and strike against the base without the mixed force having to become involved*.[47]

The Thai communist guerrillas in this southern part of northeastern Thailand (mostly Surin, Buriram, and Sisaket provinces) were nearly all ethnic Khmers of local origin. Their movement, which enjoyed the use of about a dozen base camps inside northern Cambodia (formalized in the December 1977 agreement), was internally known as *Angkar Siem,* or "the Thai Angkar."[48] It is curious that a Thai group would describe itself as virtually the Thai branch, as the word *Siem* implies, of a characteristically named Cambodian movement. Unless, of course, certain "Thai military strategists" were correct in thinking that "Phnom Penh increased its support for the Thai communist insurgency along the northern Cambodian border to back irredentist claims on a wide swathe of Thai provinces settled by a mixed Khmer-descended population."[49] A similar evaluation of Pol Pot's designs by the CPT leadership, as well as a realization of the political disaster created by the use of brutality against the Thai border population and Chinese pressure on Pol Pot to stabilize the Thai front in order to concentrate his forces against Vietnam, may have been one reason for the CPT's cracking down on the activities of Angkar Siem around mid-1978.

This did not stop the CPK. Sovannareth recalls that the irredentist rhetoric in Ta Meng's speech in Siemreap in June 1978 was not limited to Kampuchea Krom:

47. *Thai Nikorn,* 14 May 1979 (emphasis added). I am grateful to Walter Irvine for the translation.

48. *Angkar,* the Khmer term meaning "the Organization," was the word used by the CPK to describe itself. *Angkar Siem* also used the code name "Kang no. 18." *Bulletin d'information sur le Cambodge (BISC),* Paris, no. 1, April 1978, p. 4.

49. *FEER,* 5 August 1977.

He also said that Thai planes had attacked Cambodia's Oddar Meanchey province, and that "we are preparing to attack the Thai in order to take back the Khmer land in Thailand." Later he said: "We will have to fight Thailand in 1979, and we will certainly win. The Thais do not know how to fight because they have never fought before. For example, we went into their villages and killed them and burned their houses, and there was nothing they could do." He said they aimed to get back the provinces of Surin and Sisaket and so on from Thailand.[50]

In this connection one may legitimately ask the purpose of a long road through the forest of northern Cambodia parallel with the Thai frontier. Work began on this road in early 1977, according to a participant in work-teams of teenage Khmer peasant boys.[51]

Meanwhile, Thailand's reception of Cambodian refugees entered a very harsh phase. Fifteen thousand Cambodians were already in Thailand. During the second half of 1977, Thai troops murdered a thousand more refugees soon after they had crossed the border.[52]

DK Irredentism across the Lao Border

After a visit to southern Laos in 1978, Nayan Chanda reported that "the situation on the [Lao-Cambodian] border has been deteriorating since the end of 1976."[53] This has now been confirmed by a former Lao foreign ministry official with experience in the border area. This person, who wishes to remain anonymous, says that DK troops stationed at the frontier often "fired indiscriminately" at Lao citizens and "did not hesitate to fire on Lao bathers or anything living near the Mekong River." Significantly, he adds that the Democratic Kampuchea regime actually laid claim to southern Laos: "The Lao ambassador to Phnom Penh, a former monk who spent many years studying Buddhism in Phnom Penh in the 1950s, told us that Democratic Kampuchea revendicated all territory in Laos where there are stone inscriptions with "Khom" [old Khmer] script. . . . This stretched of course far to the north of Vientiane!"[54]

50. Author's interview with Sovannareth, Rouen, 10 October 1979.
51. Author's interview with Sat, Surin province, 12 March 1979. See Kiernan and Boua, *Peasants and Politics in Kampuchea*, p. 336.
52. See F. Ponchaud, "Thaïlande: Refugiés utiles—Refugiés inutiles," *BISC*, no. 1, April 1978, pp. 3–4, for details. *Wall Street Journal*, 17 October 1977, reports fifteen thousand Cambodian refugees then in Thailand.
53. *FEER*, 12 December 1978.
54. "The problem of territorial revendications was mentioned too by the director of Department no. 1 of the Lao Foreign Ministry, that is the political department dealing with the socialist countries." Personal communication to the author from a former Lao foreign ministry official, November 1993. The source adds that Lao policy favored correct or even

This recalls Khieu Samphan's and Son Sen's claims on all Vietnamese territory where sugar palms grew.[55] Democratic Kampuchea's historical irredentism targeted all three of Cambodia's neighbors. But its aggression against Vietnam was the most serious, and it provoked the strongest reaction on both sides of the border.

Dissidence in the East

The 1977 Eastern Zone Purges

In early 1977, the CPK Center established a new command structure in the East. The Zone's southern "Twin Regions" had been occupied by Southwest forces and were now administered by Seng Hong (alias Chan). The Center established a new "Highway 1 Front" where the highway runs through Regions 23 and 24 to Ho Chi Minh City. Direct military command was assumed by Son Sen, chief of the Center's general staff. On Highway 7, from Kompong Cham city in the Central Zone through Eastern Regions 22, 21, and 20 to the Vietnamese frontier province of Tay Ninh, a second new Front Committee was set up, headed by So Phim with Ke Pauk as his deputy.

These new military structures marginalized Heng Samrin and other officers of the Eastern Zone general staff. Further, DK economy minister Vorn Vet moved to Kompong Cham to assume control of supply and logistics along Highway 7, while Pauk brought a division of Central Zone troops and set up his headquarters near Kandol Chrum in Region 21.[56] All these units reinforced troops of the 310th, 450th, and 920th Center Divisions, stationed in the East since 1975—though these former Northern Zone Divisions were now being thoroughly purged.[57] The East, like all other Zones except the Southwest, was now substantially occupied by outside forces, to a much greater extent than the North. Pressure on So Phim was heightening.[58]

---

close relations with Democratic Kampuchea. A secret DK foreign ministry report complained that Cambodian land "lost" in the 1890s included "Attopeu, which is in Lao territory nowadays." *Prowatt prumdaen Kampuchea-Vietnam*, 15 June 1977, pp. 5, 7.

55. *Chroniques de guerre*, pp. 79, 81.

56. Author's interview with Region 21 deputy secretary Ouch Bun Chhoeun, Phnom Penh, 30 September 1980.

57. Heder interview, Sakeo, 9 March 1980. On the purge of these divisions, see Chapter 8, above.

58. The ideological pressure was also apparent in neighboring Kratie, Region 505 (see Chapter 7, on the 1977 purges there). In Sambor district, Vietnam was described as an enemy from 1977 (author's interview with Sopheara, Phnom Penh, 23 September 1980). In Prek Prasap district, Vietnam became the "historic enemy" in 1977 (*Asiaweek*, 2 December 1977, p. 43).

In December 1976, Pol Pot had complained of the flow of refugees to Vietnam and Thailand: "New people keep running off. We must arrange to put old ["base"] people in their place."[59] But base people also fled. Six Eastern Zone military defectors reached the Vietnamese border near Memut in early July 1977, around the same time as Sin Song and his two fellow escapees further south. This group included a twenty-five-year-old officer named Hun Sen, who had joined the CPK in 1971. Since late 1975, Sen had been chief of staff of the Region 21 Special Regiment. Promoted to deputy commander in early 1977, he became responsible for a fifty-kilometer stretch of the border. In March, Hun Sen says, the Special Regiment received instructions to attack the Vietnamese village of Or Lu, in Loc Ninh province. The order apparently came through Seng Hong, deputy Zone secretary, and Kev Samnang, zone military commander. At a meeting in Region 20 around this time, Seng Hong publicly advocated a war for "Kampuchea Krom" and even "Prey Nokor" (Ho Chi Minh City).[60] Hong is the only Eastern Zone leader ever known to have spoken in such terms.[61]

The Special Regiment's political commissar, Sok Sat, and his deputy Chum Sei both opposed the order to attack. The purge began in April 1977 with the disarming of the Regiment's 75th Battalion. Within two weeks, CPK security officials arrested one hundred of its officers and men. Then the 35th, 55th, and 59th Battalions were disarmed. By June, Hun Sen asserts, two hundred Region 21 military cadres had been killed, including the Special Regiment's commissars, Sok Sat and Chum Sei. Sen was put in command of the offensive. But he discovered that "twenty of my fellow soldiers were being purged." He decided against the offensive and also against killing the commander responsible for the purge (perhaps Region 21 chief of staff Kun Deth), for fear of provoking "a larger purge for the rest of us." Hun Sen continues, "If I killed that commander I [would have had] to order the rest of the troops to rebel." He claims he could have mobilized twenty-eight hundred troops of the Special Regiment and the one thousand-strong Memut district force. But most had been disarmed. "I realized that if we started to fight back I might be able to capture one or two districts only. What would happen if we were under counter-attack? That was

59. *Pol Pot Plans the Future*, p. 191.

60. Author's interview with Im Lei, CPK youth organization (Yuvakok) member since 1973, who heard Chan say this in Mesang district of Region 20 in early 1977. Ba Phnom, 29 July 1980. Hun Sen said that Seng Hong and Kev Samnang both followed Pol Pot's instructions on seizing Vietnamese territory. Interview with the author, 21 October 1980.

61. Unidentified cadres did so: "In 1978 they said the territory of Kampuchea Krom is Kampuchean territory so we have to attack and liberate it again in combination with our brothers and sisters who are now struggling there." These statements were first made in the East in 1977, and openly in 1978—concomitant with Seng Hong's rise. Author's interview with former Eastern Zone cadre, Kandol Chrum, 28 July 1980.

why I decided to withdraw some of my forces. Then we went into Vietnam. I took only five officers with me." One was the Special Regiment's commander, Chum Horl. The six took to the jungle on 20 June. Hun Sen claims to have left about four hundred men near the border. "When we crossed into Vietnam we were given enough rice to eat—although the Vietnamese pointed their guns all the time at us. . . . Later on the Vietnamese put me into jail for twenty-two days. The Vietnamese refused to believe what I told them—that the Khmer Rouge were going to attack."[62]

The purge also struck Region 21 political cadres. At least three of eight district CPK secretaries, including one member of the Region Committee, were arrested in the year to early 1978, along with possibly two more district secretaries named as "traitors" in their comrades' Tuol Sleng confessions.[63] One of the first soldier defectors, from Tbaung Khmum district, reported three hundred cadres arrested in March 1977 in his district alone, including "those in charge of economic, social, and military affairs." Another victim was Chang Samat, commander of a Region 21 battalion. The same soldier reports the massacre of "200 officers and men" of the Region 23 armed forces "on the night of March 31."[64] The head of the Zone agriculture committee asserts that Region 21 security chief Yin Sophi, aided by Deputy Zone Secretary Seng Hong, himself arrested "five hundred to one thousand" Eastern cadres in 1976 and 1977.[65]

Meanwhile, the commander and the political commissar of the Eastern Zone's 3rd Division were taken to Tuol Sleng. Two hundred of the Division's officers were executed, "including the platoon commanders," a former 3rd Division soldier reports. He adds: "The rank and file were dispersed, and replaced mostly by Central Zone troops in a newly constituted 3rd Division."[66] Troops from other Zones also replaced soldiers of the 4th Eastern Division. Its political commissar, Phan, was arrested, but its commander, Heng Samrin, and most of his officers survived. In 1977 one of his deputies, Heng Kim, was appointed to head the new 5th Zone Division.[67]

62. This account is based on the author's interviews with Hun Sen, Phnom Penh, 21 October 1980, and New York, 23 September 1991; S. Heder's interview with Sen dated July 1981; Hun Sen, "All the Cambodian People Became Hostages of War," *Wall Street Journal*, 31 March 1992; and what is apparently Sen's anonymous account in *Kampuchea Dossier*, I, Hanoi 1978, p. 34.
63. Kiernan, "Wild Chickens," in *Revolution and Its Aftermath in Kampuchea*, pp. 167–68.
64. Former D.K. soldier Sat Son, *Kampuchea Dossier*, I, Hanoi 1978, p. 33–34.
65. Author's interview with Men Chhan, Phnom Penh, 25 September 1980; Kiernan, "Wild Chickens," p. 167.
66. The Third Division's commander was Poeu Hak; its political commissar, Pen Cheap, entered Tuol Sleng on 29 March 1977 ("Important Culprits," p. 12).
67. Author's interview with Heng Samrin, Phnom Penh, 7 December 1992. Samrin said the 5th Division was created in early 1977 with five thousand eastern troops. Hun Sen put it at late 1977 (1991 interview).

An "Eastern Zone Conference" was held on 17 July. It is not known who convened the meeting, but an official report of it was sent to the deputy chief of the Zone military staff, Heng Samrin. The report predicted a large-scale border conflict, in which Vietnam would have to "strain to stop us." It went on: "We must also be prepared to go into enemy territory to collect intelligence . . . in order to prepare for victorious attacks." However, whereas Southwest Zone forces had already begun such attacks in March, the Eastern Zone would only do so "if the enemy commits aggression." Agreement on an offensive was lacking: "We must first generalize our unity." One problem was "the cowardly position of a group of traitors who kneel down and work as lackeys of the Vietnamese."[68]

The violence spread. The administrations of the "Twin Regions" 23 and 24 had already been thoroughly purged. In Region 20, too, the secretaries of Prey Veng, Mesang, and Kanchriech districts were executed in 1975, 1976, and 1977, and the remaining two district chiefs, Chea Sim of Ponhea Krek and the secretary of Komchay Meas, were named in Hu Nim's confession of 28 May as members of Chhouk's "traitorous" network. In Region 22, five of the eight district CPK secretaries were arrested between early 1977 and early 1978. So were two of the four members of the Region 22 committee, including the region deputy secretary.

Meanwhile, half a dozen ethnic Thai rebels from Koh Kong province, led by Sae Phuthang, sailed from Thailand to southern Vietnam in July 1977. They brought the first of ten appeals from the anti-DK Koh Kong rebels, still holding out on the Thai-Cambodian border, asking Vietnam for help. After a two-week visit, including a meeting with Vietnamese officials in Ho Chi Minh City, Phuthang and his comrades returned to Thailand empty-handed. The Vietnamese, still attempting to patch up their relations with Democratic Kampuchea, had declined to help the rebels.[69] But in the same month, the small groups of Eastern Zone dissidents led by Hun Sen and Sin Song also arrived in Vietnam. In Kampot province around the same time, Ta Rin, an educated officer in his mid-forties, assembled a unit of his troops and led them over the border into Vietnam.[70] In the fall of 1977, these people joined up with defectors from the 1973–75 period like the northeastern minority cadres Bun Mi, Bou Thang, and Seuy Keo, and with other Hanoi-trained Cambodian communists like Yos Por, who had fled to Vietnam from the Southwest Zone in 1974, and

68. *Kampuchea Dossier*, II, Hanoi 1978, photograph 1, reproduces part of the text of this document, which has been translated in part by Stephen Heder, who regards it as authentic (*The Call*, Chicago, 5 March 1979). I am also grateful to Gareth Porter for a translation of part of the document.

69. Author's interview with Sae Phuthang, Phnom Penh, 8 December 1992.

70. Author's interview in Kompong Trach, 29 August 1980.

Hem Samin, one of two Hanoi-trained Cambodians who had escaped deten-tion in Democratic Kampuchea in August 1976.[71]

Many others were fleeing across the border as well. By October 1977, there were sixty thousand Cambodian refugees in Vietnam, quadruple the number in Thailand.[72] The previous month, Yos Por says, "so many Khmer refugees had crossed into Vietnam, [that] the Vietnamese called me away from farm-ing to look after these refugees."[73] And perhaps to begin organizing them for resistance. Soon the Vietnamese would decide to hit back.

On the night of 24 September, elements of the reconstituted 3rd Eastern Zone Division, under the general command of Son Sen, crossed into Tay Ninh province and massacred nearly three hundred civilians in five villages of Tan Bien and Ben Cau districts. Many of the victims were local ethnic Khmers and ethnic Vietnamese former residents of Cambodia. Taken by surprise, Vietnamese units only reoccupied the area a week later, by which time they were also confronting the 5th Eastern and 18th Central Zone Divisions.[74] Several days after the 24 September attack, a Central Zone company com-mander returned from the scene of the massacre. He remarked with sadness, a witness related, that "he had never expected the revolution to come to what he had just seen and done." After composing a brief suicide note, he shot himself.

The Tay Ninh massacre coincided with Pol Pot's triumphant visit to China and his public declaration of the cPK's existence and of his own leadership of the Party. On 5 October the Chinese ministry of defense signed a protocol for the delivery of arms to Cambodia. These involved "a complete set of equip-ment—from walkie-talkies to jet fighters—needed to build all three branches of the Cambodian armed forces."[75]

71. Author's interviews with Yos Por, Phnom Penh, 11 September 1980; and Hem Samin, Takhmau, 28 September 1980. Chanda, *Brother Enemy*, p. 198.

72. *Wall Street Journal*, 17 October 1977. S. Heder wrote that "the reception of these refugees in Vietnam was friendly (indeed in many ways friendlier than that in Thailand)," and that "Kampuchean refugees in Vietnam, although immersed in the rigors of that country's post-war economic problems, seem to be freer from harassment and have more freedom of movement (again, as long as they stay out of politics) than those in Thailand." Heder, "Thai-land's Relations with Kampuchea: Negotiation and Confrontation along the Prachinburi-Bat-tambang Border," ms., Cornell University, December 1977, pp. 14, 70. (For an earlier concur-ring report, see W. Shawcross, *FEER*, 2 January 1976, p. 9, quoted in Chapter 4.)

73. Author's interview with Yos Por, 1980.

74. Author's interviews at the raid site, 27 October 1980. Locals said the attack was "mainly" by the 3rd Eastern Division. Attackers apparently included the Center 221st Division (*sic*, Regiment?), stationed in the East. (Heder interview with cPK Central Committee member Chap Lonh, Naval Camp 62, Chanthaburi, 12 March 1980.) Chanda, *Brother Enemy*, p. 195, says Heder believes the 4th Division was involved. For Heder's description of events, and different prior dates, see *Southeast Asia Research*, 5, 2, July 1997, pp. 138–42.

75. Chanda, *Brother Enemy*, p. 200.

Nayan Chanda reports that the first significant Vietnamese military retaliation came that month.[76] "After driving armored columns up to fifteen miles into the bordering Cambodian province of Svay Rieng, the Vietnamese feigned retreat. As a battalion of Khmer Rouge infantry entered Vietnamese territory in hot pursuit, another waiting Vietnamese column swung from the side and caught several hundred of them in a mousetrap." By November, "an anti-Pol Pot resistance was in the making," led by ten to fifteen cadres, most of them veteran communists and former members of the old Indochina Communist Party. A Vietnamese source adds that in Cambodia, "starting in November 1977, secret food reserves were set up in the jungle. However, no date was set as yet for the uprising."[77]

As fighting continued over the next several months, Hanoi prepared for a major incursion in December that would involve thirty to sixty thousand troops with air, armor, and artillery support.[78] Nil Sa'unn, who was working in

76. Ibid., p. 196. Chandler (*Brother Number One*, p. 147), citing Chanda, dates the Vietnamese retaliation to "late September"; Chanda specifies October. Sources suggesting earlier Vietnamese military incursions into Cambodia suffer from anti-Vietnam bias. *Bangkok Post* (1 September 1977, see also Chanda, p. 198) alleged that on May 2–9, Vietnamese aircraft bombed ammunition dumps 15 miles inside Cambodia, but ignored the serious earlier Cambodian attacks on Vietnam such as that of 30 April. Vickery says that "from July to September 1977 the Vietnamese apparently really did violate Cambodian territory," and in September DK "retaliated"; his source is S. Heder ("The Kampuchean-Vietnamese Conflict," *Southeast Asian Affairs 1979*, Singapore, 1979, pp. 166, 172–73). Heder claims that "in late July and early August, the Vietnamese . . . struck into Kampuchean territory." Heder's sources are "Reuters, Kuala Lumpur, 6 August 1977," and *Ban Muang*, Bangkok, 24 July 1977. A search for the former uncovered only a London *Sunday Times* Reuters report citing the Thai prime minister as saying that "serious border clashes" between Vietnam and Cambodia involved "both sides engaged in bomb attacks" (7 August 1977). A *Sydney Morning Herald* report from Kuala Lumpur described "both sides making bombing raids along their common border" (8 August 1977). This does not support Heder's bare assertion of Vietnamese cross-border attacks. (The *Ban Muang* report could not be located.) Heder anyway concedes that Democratic Kampuchea had begun "to initiate military activities" as early as April or May, but he considers these "part of a negotiating strategy," and like the *Bangkok Post* he ignores the earlier, major DK attacks on Vietnam, acknowledging only "artillery barrages and occasional small-scale forays" (p. 165). Evans and Rowley consider Heder's argument "convoluted, apologetic nonsense" (*Red Brotherhood at War*, London: Verso, 1990, pp. 104–5). DK Radio conceded on 14 January 1978 that "the Vietnamese expansionist and annexationist enemy began launching assaults and violating our territory in November 1977" (*FBIS*, 16 January 1978, p. H4). In his May 1978 confession, the Region 21 CPK secretary wrote, "In September, the Vietnamese had not yet attacked. By 30 October 1977, the Vietnamese had already invaded" ("Responses of Touch Chem, called Soth, Secretary, Sector 21, Eastern Region," "Record of the History of the Traitorous Activities of Soth Himself," S-21 confession, 18 May 1978, p. 13, trans. S. Heder, who provided a copy).

77. Chanda, *Brother Enemy*, p. 198; *Kampuchea Dossier*, II, Hanoi, 1978, pp. 63–64. Interestingly, November 1977 is the date given by Democratic Kampuchea for the defection of Heng Samrin to Vietnam. I accepted this in "Wild Chickens," p. 172, but it appears incorrect.

78. Heder, "The Kampuchean-Vietnamese Conflict," p. 166, citing the *Washington Post*, 5 January 1978.

the fields near Pauk's headquarters at Kandol Chrum, recalls how the offensive began: "On 22 December two Vietnamese tanks drove into Kandol Chrum township in an attempt to contact So Phim. Then they turned back towards the border." Inside the tanks, it appears, were several Khmer revolutionaries who had previously fled to Vietnam. Hun Sen, Hem Samin, and eight others accompanied the Vietnamese forces on missions across different sections of the border. Samin managed to penetrate into Svay Rieng province dressed in black with a squad of ten bodyguards. He heard the people's grievances, but leading cadres were nowhere to be seen. "We tried to make contact, . . . but no way; we couldn't."[79]

Sa'unn continues: "On 31 December, Vietnamese tanks and infantry appeared again and we all ran away." A district cadre in Ponhea Krek agrees that both the Central and Eastern Zone troops on the border quickly retreated west, in disarray. "No one knew who was in command of what or who was where." Widespread looting and destruction were alternately blamed on the Vietnamese, the Eastern Zone forces, and the Central Zone troops.[80]

In this atmosphere, a critical incident occurred on 29 December. Region 21 security chief Yin Sophi and twelve of his troops were traveling in a truck along a forest road in Damber district, fifteen kilometers north of Highway 7. Coming in the opposite direction was Sareth, military commander of Heng Samrin's 4th Eastern Zone Division, on a motorcycle, accompanied by two bodyguards. The two leaders recognized each other. Both vehicles stopped. Sophi got out and shook hands with Sareth, then drew a gun and shot him dead. Sareth's bodyguards immediately opened fire, killing Sophi and all twelve of his men.[81] This incident may have finally convinced Pol Pot and the Center that, unlike the other Zones of the country, the East could not be brought under control without a conventional military suppression campaign.

On 6 January, the invading troops returned to Vietnamese territory. Over one hundred thousand Khmers from all sections of the border took the opportunity to escape with them.[82] One of them was Heng Samrin's brother Heng Samkai, chairman of the Eastern Zone couriers, who had made his own assessment. "We had come to realize that it was impossible to overthrow Pol Pot on our own. We had to seek Vietnamese help." Samkai reached the border in January 1978 and was flown to Ho Chi Minh City in a Vietnamese heli-

79. Author's interview with Hem Samin, 1980.

80. The district cadre continues: "When the Vietnamese withdrew of their own accord, our side did not know about it. We came to see if they had gone or not and then we moved back." Interview with the author, Sting, 28 July 1980.

81. Two former Eastern Zone cadres in different parts of Cambodia gave consistent details of this incident. Author's interviews in Kompong Cham, 26 July 1980, and Santuk, Kompong Thom, 16 October 1980.

82. *Age*, Melbourne, 10 June 1978, quoting the U.N. High Commissioner for Refugees.

copter. "He and other Khmer Rouge defectors assembled in the former police training school at Thu Duc."[83] A new regime was in the making. But another year of violence lay ahead.

Trade and Diplomacy

China and North Korea: Weapons for Wildlife. Like the pace of other developments in Democratic Kampuchea, foreign trade picked up rapidly in early 1977. Phnom Penh signed its first contract with a Japanese firm: the purchase of ten thousand tons of rolled steel. Democratic Kampuchea also planned to buy Japanese machine tools and chemicals and to "export rice, lumber, rubber and shrimp to Japan and other foreign nations."[84]

But the China trade dominated Cambodia's economic life. Three thousand tons of yellow, black, and brown Cambodian crepe rubber fiber left Kompong Som for Shanghai on 6 February 1977. Within days, another four thousand tons was ready for loading, along with 930 tons of raw rubber and 112 tons of crepe rubber sheet. A second ship sailed for Shanghai within a week, carrying ninety-two tons of kapok, seventy-five tons of betel nut, and twelve tons of pepper in addition to the rubber.[85] Another thousand tons of crepe was exported to North Korea in late February; a repeat shipment followed a month later.[86]

On 14 March, the Chinese ship *Heng Shan* left for Whampoa with one thousand tons of Cambodian raw rubber and forty-four tons of betel, ten tons of lotus seeds, and other plant matter. But the *Heng Shan* also carried an extraordinary eighteen tons of deer horn, seven tons of pangolin scales, and two tons of tortoiseshell.[87] One hesitates to compute the number of carcasses contributing to this cargo. Many more made up a 22 May 1977 shipment to the China National Native Products and Animal By-Products Import and Export Corporation. Dispatched to Whampoa on the *Xindu* were over six tons of monkey bone, 1.5 tons of elephant bone, "24,760 pieces" of dried gecko (apparently individual animals, weighing over half a ton in all), and a ton of snake

---

83. Chanda, *Brother Enemy,* p. 255.

84. "Kyodo: Japan to Export Rolled Steel to Cambodia," 28 February 1977, *FBIS,* Asia Pacific, 2 March 1977, p. H1.

85. Cambodian National Archives, records of the Ministry of Commerce of Democratic Kampuchea (CNA, MC-DK), Box 12, Dossier 51, Fortra (Khmer Company for Foreign Trade) invoices nos. 005–7/CH/77 (5 February 1977), 013–19/CH/77 (8–10 February 1977, to China National Chemicals Import Export Corporation), and 009–012 (8 February 1977).

86. CNA, MC-DK, Box 12, Dossier 51, Fortra invoices nos. 021–22/KO/77 (18 and 19 February 1977) and 036/KO/77 (1 April 1977).

87. CNA, MC-DK, Box 12, Dossier 51, Fortra invoices nos. 025–034/CH/77(13 and 14 March 1977).

skins (mostly python), along with 145 kg of panther and tiger skins, 73 kg of black bear skins, and 128 kg of ringmark lizard.[88]

The *Xindu* also carried nearly 1,000 tons of raw rubber, plus 160 tons of green beans, 130 tons of kapok, 65 tons of strychnine, 30 tons of white sesame, 20 tons of betel, 15 tons of pepper, 5 tons of malvanut, and 2 tons of frangipani flower. Invoices for all these shipments were signed by Ngeth Hong, for the Khmer Company for Foreign Trade (Fortra). The name of the new enterprise comprised Democratic Kampuchea's first and only appropriation of the ethnic term "Khmer." This usage remained secret (just as the export trade in animal products was omitted from DK's Four-Year Economic Plan).[89] In public, Democratic Kampuchea employed the term only to describe "Khmer traitors" on the Thai border.[90] Confidential use of the term for one of its own organizations indicates its secret commitment to racial discourse.

Certificates of quality for Cambodia's animal products exports were provided by Van Rit, who had launched Democratic Kampuchea's Ren Fung trading company in Hong Kong the previous year.[91] Ren Fung was already purchasing large quantities of chemicals from Hong Kong, particularly for use in the rubber industry.[92] Incomplete statistics indicate that during 1977 Democratic Kampuchea exported about twenty-five thousand tons of rubber products to China and about four thousand tons to Korea.[93]

None of Fortra's invoices quoted any prices. Payment took several forms. The first involved book entries computed in pounds sterling. Under an agreement with North Korea signed in November 1977, for instance, Democratic Kampuchea agreed to provide 5,000 "units" of rubber, each valued at £1,000. In return, Pyongyang undertook to provide Democratic Kampuchea with goods worth £5 million. These included steel products (2,800 units), machinery and tools (1,600), chemical products and cloths (500), and minerals (100).[94] Payment on the ideological level included Pyongyang's conferring on

88. Ibid., 049–54/CH/77 (20 May 1977).

89. See Boua, Chandler, and Kiernan, eds., *Pol Pot Plans the Future*, pp. 93, 104, 149.

90. DK Ministry of Foreign Affairs statement, 7 February 1977, no. S/77/046, p. 5.

91. CNA, MC-DK, Box 12, Dossier 51, Fortra invoices nos. 039–48/CH/ 77 (19 and 20 May 1977). See also Chapter 4, above. The "Khmer Company for Foreign Trade" first emerged in November 1976.

92. One U.K. company began supplying Democratic Kampuchea in February 1977. Sales included 15 tons of citric acid (February), 40 tons of formic acid (March), 400 tons of aluminium sulphate (June–August), 80,000 liters of insecticides (May–July), 10 tons of potash alum and 10 tons of rubber processing and disease-treatment chemicals (November 1977). From the 1977–78 sales list, in the possession of the author.

93. This is based on my perusal of the relevant files of the DK ministry of commerce.

94. CNA, MC-DK, Box 9, Dossier 41, Agreement between Democratic Kampuchea and the Democratic People's Republic of Korea (24 November 1977).

Pol Pot the award of "Hero of the Democratic People's Republic of Korea."[95] Also in 1977, North Korean leader Kim Il-sung sent Khieu Samphan a personal message of congratulations on Democratic Kampuchea's rapid revolutionary achievements, asserting that though the Korean revolution advanced at the speed of a "winged horse," the Cambodian one flew "faster than the wind."[96]

China, of course, fêted Pol Pot during his October 1977 visit. Beijing had provided Cambodia with credits of 140 million *yuan* (U.S.$24.6 million) for the year 1977. By 31 October, Democratic Kampuchea had signed agreements to purchase products worth 102 million yuan, and the ministry of commerce was about to purchase diesel products worth another 36 million yuan. These arrangements were supervised by Khieu Samphan and Vorn Vet.[97]

A third form of payment was Chinese military aid. Kompong Som pilot Sok Sam says that large weapons shipments began to arrive in late 1976, "about the same time" as the arrest of the port's deputy director, Chhun Sok Nguon, on 19 October 1976. The deliveries therefore coincided with the escalation of the purges in Phnom Penh and preceded the Democratic Kampuchea attacks on Vietnam that began in March 1977. Port engineer Ung Pech agrees with Sam's chronology. He saw "tanks, armored personnel carriers, artillery, and guns" begin to arrive in Kompong Som in late 1976. Five such convoys had arrived by April 1977, the last including several ships carrying over thirty tanks and ten amphibious tanks.[98]

A CPK Central Committee member later described the Center's impatience with the rate at which China's aid arrived. "In 1977 it was said that the Chinese did not believe there was a threat to Kampuchea from Vietnam and took a complacent attitude towards the whole problem." Only in 1978, according to this claim, did China send aid to Democratic Kampuchea.[99] This is false, but China did have good reason to question Democratic Kampuchea's claim that it was a victim of aggression. On 30 July 1977, Chinese foreign minister Huang Hua conceded in a private speech to cadres of his ministry that Democratic Kampuchea had recently engaged in border conflicts with all three neighboring countries: Vietnam, Laos, and Thailand. Hua went on to say that China had already communicated its "four-point stand" to the three Indo-Chinese states. The points were (1) cease-fire and negotiations, (2) solidarity, (3) "China will

95. KCNA in English, 7 October 1977, BBC SWB, FE/5636/A3/7.

96. Author's interview with San, Paris, 29 May 1980. San, a former D.K. official in the Northwest Zone, said this message was read out at a meeting in Region Five in 1977.

97. CNA, MC-DK, Box 9, Dossier 43, "Kar prae pras ontean 140 lien yuan kit trim thngai 31 tola 1977" ("Usage of Funds of 140 Million *yuan* as of 31 October 1977").

98. Author's interviews with Sok Sam, Kompong Som, 18 July 1980, and Ung Pech, Phnom Penh, 7 September 1980.

99. Heder interview with Chap Lonh, 12 March 1980.

not take the side of any state," and (4) "We support the stand of Cambodia and her people against Soviet revisionist social-imperialism and will not watch indifferently . . . "[100] The fourth point, which contradicted the others, was China's real policy, and the Vietnamese had been made aware of this.

Pilot Sok Sam says that in 1977 and 1978 some of the Chinese weapons shipments were unloaded offshore, out of sight of dock workers. He believes that these ships had brought naval patrol vessels, which were launched directly into the water. A former staff member of the Chinese embassy in Democratic Kampuchea has confirmed that by the end of 1978, Beijing delivered to Cambodia two fast gunships of over eight hundred tons and four patrol boats, plus two hundred tanks, three hundred armored cars, three hundred artillery pieces, thirty thousand tons of ammunition, six jet fighters, and two bombers. The Chinese were also building a new railroad from Phnom Penh to Kompong Som, and a new military airport at Kompong Chhnang (70 percent completed by January 1979). Chinese technicians and advisers in Democratic Kampuchea numbered fifteen thousand.[101]

Beijing apparently expected Cambodia to become a large-scale oil exporter. In December 1977, the Design Institute of China's transport division completed a study of the specifications for the construction of auxiliary facilities for an oil refinery in Cambodia.[102] More serious, many refugees and survivors in Cambodia report that rice was being shipped to China despite the widespread starvation in the country. A CPK soldier from Region 13 in the Southwest Zone, for instance, claims that in early 1977 trucks began transporting local rice stocks to Kompong Som. Each khum (subdistrict), he reports, had to provide 5,000 thang (250 tons). The subdistrict chief and the truck drivers themselves told the soldier that the rice was to be "exchanged for Chinese equipment—for tanks, artillery, and guns."[103] Ministry of commerce records do not confirm that Cam-

100. See King C. Chen, ed., *China and the Three Worlds*, New York 1979, pp. 268–72.

101. "'Squandered Chinese aid' spelt Pol Pot's ruin," *Bangkok Post*, 1 May 1979, a report of an interview with a recent defector from the Chinese embassy to Democratic Kampuchea; and Heder interview with CPK Central Committee member Chap Lonh, 12 March 1980. Lonh underestimated the total number of Chinese advisers at 1,000.

102. CNA, Democratic Kampuchea, *Engineering for an Oil-Transfer Port for an Oil Refinery, vol. 4, Specifications* (in Chinese), December 1977. (Thanks to Valerie Hansen and Haynie Wheeler for translations.) This document is in one of thirty-six large dossiers of Chinese-language DK-period materials in the Cambodian National Archives, which should yield valuable information about China's goals in Democratic Kampuchea. On the possibility that China hoped to refine its petroleum there, see Jackson, ed., *Cambodia 1975–1978*, p. 133.

103. Author's interview with a former CPK soldier, Tram Kak, 16 July 1980. The soldier quoted the post-1975 CPK subdistrict chief of Svay Prateal (in District 106, Angkor Chey), a thirty-eight-year-old man named Ny. A peasant from another part of Region 13, Treang (District 108) in Takeo, quotes Seng, the head of his chalat regiment, as saying "hundreds of times" from 1976 to 1978 that rice was being taken away to exhange for "machinery." Author's interview, Krang Chhes, 15 July 1980.

bodian rice was being shipped to China in 1977. But in 1978 Democratic Kampuchea officials claimed to have exported 100,000 tons of rice the previous year to rice-deficit countries such as Yugoslavia, Madagascar, and Hong Kong.[104] This probably earned Democratic Kampuchea about U.S.$100 million, far below the $250 million target in the Four-Year Plan.[105]

Trade between the two countries accelerated after Democratic Kampuchea severed diplomatic relations with Vietnam on 31 December 1977. In the first six weeks of 1978, Cambodia exported to China nearly sixteen thousand tons of rubber, more than in the previous six months. Chinese *Hongqi* ("Red Flag") ships plied the South China Sea. On 3 January, one Chinese vessel left for Whampoa with a cargo of rubber plus 105 tons of sesame, 30 tons of lotus seeds, 13 tons of betel products, 12 tons of beans, and 5 tons of peanuts.[106] Nine days later, *Hongqi 162* left Kompong Som for Canton with 1,700 tons of rubber products and 13 tons of frangipani flowers. The ship quickly unloaded and returned to Kompong Som, departing again for Whampoa on 4 February with 2,000 tons of Cambodian rubber.[107]

The relationship was reinforced by the arrival of Deng Xiaoping's wife, Deng Yingchao, in mid-January. At a gathering in Phnom Penh, she met the wives of Pol Pot, Nuon Chea, Ieng Sary, Son Sen, Vorn Vet, Khieu Samphan, and Thiounn Thioeunn. Women not married to Democratic Kampuchea leaders do not seem to have attended. Deng Yingchao flew to Angkor, and was welcomed by Northern Zone CPK secretary Kang Chap. There she announced, "Democratic Kampuchea is like a pine tree standing firm on a high mountaintop which cannot be destroyed by any force. Under the correct leadership of the Communist Party of Kampuchea, the Kampuchean people are certainly moving forward toward a bright and glorious future."[108]

The movement continued to quicken. A Chinese ship leaving Kompong Som on 10 February with 140 tons of raw rubber, 450 tons of kapok, 240 tons of soya beans, and 50 tons of pepper, was followed to Whampoa the next day by another vessel carrying 4,600 tons of rubber products.[109] Over the next three months, North Korean ships sailed for Nampo with a total of 4,700 tons of

104. Malcolm Caldwell noted this claim in the diary of his December 1978 visit to Democratic Kampuchea, typescript, at p. 6.

105. *Pol Pot Plans the Future*, p. 106, table 56.

106. CNA, MC-DK, Box 12, Dossier 51, Fortra invoice nos. 123–36/CH/77 (1, 2, and 3 January 1978).

107. Ibid., Fortra invoice nos. 123–28/CH/77 (1, 2, and 3 January 1978), and Box 25, Dossier 88, Fortra invoice and delivery order nos. 001/CH/78 (11 January 1978), 005-18/CH/78 (16 January 1978), 021–27 (1 February 1978), 028-33/CH/78 (4 February 1978), and 034-45/CH/78 (11 February 1978).

108. FBIS, 24 January 1978, H6–10, Phnom Penh Radio, 19–21 January 1978.

109. CNA, MC-DK, Box 25, Dossier 88, Fortra invoices and delivery orders nos. 047–53/CH/78 (8 February 1978) and 034–45/CH/78 (11 February 1978).

crepe rubber products.[110] Another 2,100 tons of rubber was sent to China on 26 April, along with 150 tons of beans, 30 tons of sesame, 7 tons of lotus seeds, and 10 tons of strychnine.

And now, for the first time since 1975, Democratic Kampuchea began to export large quantities of timber. The 26 April shipment included 106 one-ton teak logs, 153 tons of teak bark, and 90 tons of other fine wood products.[111] A September 1978 cargo included 55 tons of woods. These two shipments also included 11 tons of deer horn. To the September cargo were added 1.6 tons of python skin, one-third of a ton of dried geckos, forty-nine tiger skins (weighing 227 kg), twenty-nine panther skins, and five black bear furs.[112]

Less exotic products also streamed out of the country. In August 1978, Cambodia sent China 5,000 tons of rice, perhaps for the first time since 1976.[113] Rice requisitions from the countryside had probably increased.[114] But most of Cambodia's rice exports went to other countries, possibly including Japan.[115] A September 1978 shipment to China included 1,600 tons of rubber products, 375 tons of kapok, 37 tons of sesame, 25 tons of lotus seeds, 10 tons of frangipani flower, 2.5 tons of strychnine, 1.5 tons of cashew nuts, and a ton of malva nuts.[116] The last recorded China-bound Cambodian cargo, which left Kompong Som for Dairen on 17 November 1978, comprised 3,250 tons of crepe rubber fiber.[117]

The military aid kept coming, notably a shipment of 1,300 tons of aviation fuel, which arrived on 17 December. Chinese ships also brought 3,000 tons of coke in March, 100 tons of sodium sulphide in April, 100 tons of wheat in

110. Ibid., Fortra invoice and delivery orders nos. 054–71/KO/78 and 104-14/KO/78.

111. Ibid., Fortra invoice and delivery orders nos. 073–100/CH/78, and Kampuchea Shipping Agency, "Manifest of Goods," *M.V. Yong Kang*, Kompong Som to Whampoa, 26 April 1978. Cambodia had exported 2,166 tons of logs to China in 1975 (Box 1, Dossier 05).

112. CNA, MC-DK, Box 25, Dossier 88, Fortra invoice no. 100/CH/78 (24 April 1978), and Kampuchea Shipping Agency, "Manifest of Goods," *M.V. Yong Kang*, Kompong Som to Whampoa, 26 April 1978 (the invoice is for 5.15 tons of deer horn, gross weight 5.63 tons); and Fortra invoice and delivery orders nos. 165, 161/CH/78 (including 5.929 tons of deer horn) and 153–158/CH/78 (22 September 1978).

113. CNA, MC-DK, Box 25, Dossier 88, Fortra invoice no. 135/CH/78 (14 August 1978). For 1976 D.K. rice exports to China, see S. Heder's interview with a former DK boat pilot, Sa Keo, 9 March 1980 (p. 236 n. 40, above).

114. Seven hundred fifty tons of rice was collected from a single subdistrict in 1978. (Author's interview with a peasant in Koh Touc subdistrict, Kampot, 29 August 1980.) Another subdistrict in the Southwest had provided only a third of this amount in 1977. See above.

115. Author's interview with Nguon Song, who worked as a Chinese-language interpreter in Phnom Penh in 1978. Song says, "My friend was an interpreter at the airport. He said Khmer rice was mostly sold to Japan" (Strasbourg, 31 October 1979).

116. CNA, MC-DK, Box 25, Dossier 88, Fortra invoice nos. 156–64/CH/78 (22 September 1978).

117. Ibid., Fortra invoice nos. 169–79/CH/78 (15, 16 November 1978).

June, and 277 tons of American DDT (for anti-malarial spraying) in December. The most important civilian import was cloth. From April to August 1978, Chinese ships brought 406 tons of clothing material to Cambodia.[118] In the same year, Democratic Kampuchea also bought 1,250 tons of DDT and 23 tons of rubber processing chemicals from a British firm in Hong Kong. As the war intensified, purchases included three tons of chloroform and quantities of other medical supplies.[119] Imports for civilian consumption were at any rate dwarfed by exports.

Cambodia's 1978 exports were again probably led by rice, but complete figures are unavailable. As in 1977, China bought about 25,000 tons of rubber products, and North Korea 5,000 more, all valued at over U.S.$15 million, precisely the 1978 target figure.[120]

Rice and rubber exports were rivaled in value by animal products. Yet the Chinese paid Cambodia very little for these rare items. Democratic Kampuchea billed China for pangolin scales at 3,582 yuan ($628) per ton.[121] Now in 1993, Chinese buyers paid 70 yuan ($12.28) per kilogram for pangolin carcasses from Laos,[122] or over $12,000 per ton. If the medicinal part of the carcass is conservatively valued at $20/kg, the March 1977 Cambodian consignment of seven tons of pangolin scales could have fetched perhaps $100,000 at 1977 prices.[123] China was billed only 25,500 yuan ($4,479). For thirty tons of Cambodian deer horn, China paid only 1,200 yuan, or $211, per ton.[124] The horns of *a single deer* would bring at least $50 on the Thai-Cambodian border in 1992.[125]

Tiger bones, to take another example, were already so scarce in China that Beijing had banned the domestic hunting of tigers in the 1960s, and in the 1970s was conducting research on developing medicinal substitutes for tiger bones. In 1993, the *New York Times* reports, "the real animal parts are so expen-

118. CNA, MC-DK, Box 23, Dossier 79.

119. List of 1977–78 sales to Cambodia of an anonymous U.K. company in Hong Kong, in the author's possession. The chloroform was supplied in May 1978.

120. *Pol Pot Plans the Future,* p. 149, gives the price of "first quality rubber" in 1976 as over $600/ton (for 1977–78 export targets, see p. 106, table 56). I use an average $500/ton for all D.K. rubber products, but on the world market, natural rubber brought 91 U.S. cents per kilogram, and crude rubber sheets, 41 cents per pound, i.e. about $910 per ton (*Commodity Year Book 1977,* New York: Commodity Research Bureau). Dollar prices quoted are all in USD.

121. CNA, MC-DK, Box 9, Dossier 43, "Pholitpol noam cenh tou prates chen men toan toutoat tomlaiy kit trim thngai 31 tola 1977" ("Produce sent to China not yet priced, as of 31 October 1977"), p. 1, item 16. The prices are still described as approximate, though the products had left in March.

122. *FEER,* 19 August 1993, p. 26.

123. Daniel P. Reid, *Chinese Herbal Medicine,* Chinese University of Hong Kong, 1987, p. 130, lists the pangolin's scales as the medicinally useful part of the animal. Thanks to Eric Taglicozzo for this reference.

124. CNA, MC-DK, Box 9, Dossier 43, "Pholitpol noam cenh . . . 31 tola 1977," p. 1, item 14.

125. "Baby tigers only worth B5,000 in Cambodia," *Bangkok Post,* 30 November 1992.

sive that often the medicines may have only trace elements."[126] The 1993 cost in China of a ten-to-twenty-gram dose of a concoction of tiger bone, tortoise-shell, and other natural products was $410.[127] Tiger bone sold in Taiwan for $500 per gram.[128] But in 1977, Democratic Kampuchea billed China only 1,400 yuan ($246) per ton for tiger, elephant, and monkey bones. Tortoiseshell fetched a mere 1,000 yuan ($175) per ton. Characteristically, Democratic Kampuchea valued these items at a price far below the price of rice. It sold Cambodian tiger skins to China for only 41 yuan ($7.19) per kilogram; the 1992 price on the Thai-Cambodian border was around $40.[129] Democratic Kampuchea billed China for dried geckoes at only 28 yuan ($4.86) per kilogram, and snake skin 7 yuan ($1.23) per kilogram.[130] The various animal products sent to China from 1976 to 1978 probably added $25 million to the real value of Cambodia's annual exports.

Cambodia's plant products were also more prized than its rice or its rubber, but again it offered bargain prices. The kapok harvest, for instance, was potentially lucrative; shipments to China quadrupled in 1978. Though Pol Pot knew the market price was $600 per ton, DK charged China a mere $175 per ton.[131] Kapok exports in 1977 and 1978 totaled 1,044 tons, at a market value of $625,000. Cambodia lost $444,000 on this deal. Such preferential sales entitled Democratic Kampuchea to its massive imports of Chinese weaponry. Cambodia's ecology carried much of the cost of Democratic Kampuchea's war against Vietnam and of its suppression of its own population.

Ideological links and the desire for Chinese weaponry may not have been the only reasons for Cambodia's fauna fire sale. Moeung Sonn, who worked in a Democratic Kampuchea fishing detail on the west coast in 1976 and 1967, suggests that self-imposed isolation from Western markets and a lack of business experience also plagued Cambodia's fish exports to Thailand. "The Thais

126. "Beijing Bans Trade in Rhino and Tiger Parts," *New York Times*, 6 June 1993.

127. *FEER*, 19 August 1993, p. 24. Reid, *Chinese Herbal Medicine*, p. 121, explains uses for "dragon bones," which apparently include tiger, elephant, and monkey bones.

128. "Medical Potions May Doom Tiger to Extinction," *New York Times*, 15 March 1994, pp. C1, 12.

129. "Baby tigers only worth B5,000 in Cambodia," *Bangkok Post*, 30 November 1992. Tiger skins were priced at 2,500 to 5,000 baht. My computation is based on an average tiger skin weighing 4.63 kgs.

130. CNA, MC-DK, Box 9, Dossier 43, "Pholitpol noam cenh . . . 31 tola 1977," 3pp.

131. *Pol Pot Plans the Future*, Document IV, p. 149, prices kapok at $600 per ton in 1976. Two 1977 shipments to Shanghai and Whampoa contained 223 tons of kapok fiber, including 150 tons of "No. 1" quality; two 1978 shipments to Whampoa of 821 tons included 558 tons of No. 1 kapok. CNA, MC-DK, Box 12, Dossier 51, Fortra invoices nos. 013 and 044/CH/77 (8 February and 20 May 1977); and Box 25, Dossier 88, Fortra invoices nos. 047-9/CH/78 and 159/CH/78 (8 February and 22 September 1978). Democratic Kampuchea billed China 1,000 yuan per ton of No. 1 kapok, 900 yuan per ton of No. 2 quality. (CNA, MC-DK, Box 9, Dossier 43, "Pholitpol noam cenh . . . 31 tola 1977," p. 3).

would come and bring fuel, diesel, spare parts for the U.S.-made machinery left in Cambodia, which the Chinese did not have. The Thais did very well out of this trade. The Khmer Rouge were so ignorant, they would sell 100 kilograms of fish for two *riels* [five cents] . . ."[132]

China's fifteen thousand technicians were working in various factories in Phnom Penh (cement, tire, electricity, and tractor works), and throughout the country in various guises, particularly at the port. They often complained privately that the regime chose illiterate youths for training, including thirteen-to-sixteen-year-old boys learning to operate tanks and armored cars, whom the Chinese refused to train.[133] They explained that "without theory nothing can be done in practice." But the directors of the factories took little notice, leaving Cambodia's Chinese-language interpreters at a loss. One recalls, "The Chinese never dared say Pol Pot was crazy. But they did secretly investigate the living conditions of the Khmer people. They got some news. We dared not tell them, for fear of death. The Chinese asked me about rations, and I replied, 'Comrades, I cannot answer. There are your own people in the countryside who could tell you.' They knew."[134]

China's interests in Democratic Kampuchea had little to do with the living conditions of Cambodians or the country's ethnic Chinese. More important even than the trade in wildlife products were the strategic opportunities Democratic Kampuchea offered China to exploit divisions in Southeast Asia and outflank Vietnam. On the very day that Phnom Penh broke off diplomatic relations with Hanoi, a special meeting of the United Nations Mekong Committee was to have raised proposals for cooperation between Vietnam and Cambodia, Laos and Thailand for joint development of the Mekong River valley. On the same day, China announced an end to its technical cooperation with the Vietnamese army.[135] China did not encourage Southeast Asian nations to cooperate without its involvement. And its ally Cambodia's war with Vietnam, despite the war's origins in Democratic Kampuchea policy, soon attracted valued adherents to China's anti-Vietnamese front.[136] President Carter's National Security Adviser, Zbigniew Brzezinski, visited China in May 1978, taking the

132. Author's interview with Moeung Sonn, Sarcelles, 25 October 1979. A lack of concern for ecological preservation was evident here, too. Sonn says the Khmer Rouge in the fishing unit "could cook and eat whatever they liked. . . . They threw away the small fish, and ate only the big ones."

133. Author's interview with Nguon Song, translator for Chinese advisers in Phnom Penh in 1978 (Strasbourg, 31 October 1979); "'Squandered Chinese aid'" *Bangkok Post*, 1 May 1979.

134. Author's interview with Nguon Song, 1979.

135. Ramesh Thakur, "Coexistence to Conflict," *Australian Outlook*, 34, 1, April 1980, p. 66.

136. For discussion see Kiernan, "ASEAN and Indochina: Asian Drama Unfolds," *Inside Asia*, 5, September-October 1985, pp. 17–19, and Kiernan, "China, Cambodia, and the UN Plan," in *The Challenge of Indochina: An Examination of the U.S. Role*, Aspen Institute (Queenstown, Md.), 1991, pp. 13–16.

first step toward a U.S. political alignment with Democratic Kampuchea that would see Brzezinski fostering international support for Pol Pot in 1979.[137] In December 1978, the United States established diplomatic relations with China, while America's regional ally, Australia, moved closer to China's protégé, Democratic Kampuchea.[138]

137. See Kiernan, ed., *Genocide and Democracy in Cambodia: The Khmer Rouge, the United Nations, and the International Community,* New Haven: Yale Southeast Asia Studies Monograph No. 41, 1993, p. 200; Becker, *When the War Was Over,* p. 440.

138. Michael Richardson, "A Softer Line on Cambodia," and "Cambodia Links Likely: Canberra," *Age* (Melbourne), 4 October and 13 December 1978. The *New York Times* published an article disputing "the genocide myth" as a "slanderous . . . lie" (Daniel Burstein, "On Cambodia: But Yet," 21 November 1978).

CHAPTER 10

"Thunder without Rain":
Race and Power in Cambodia, 1978

Escalating the War

On 31 December 1977, Democratic Kampuchea officially severed diplomatic relations with Vietnam. Four days later, Pol Pot issued secret instructions to "attack from behind the enemy's back." His orders stated, "We have to fight a guerrilla war everywhere, both outside the enemy's borders and within the enemy's borders. . . . And the guerrillas must use small forces to enter the enemy's borders everywhere. . . . In large or small spearheads, we have to intrude our guerrilla squads; one or two, two or three, six or seven squads. . . . If one spearhead has a guerrilla squad go deep within the enemy's borders, then those many squads, wherever they are, must open fire, attack the enemy, confuse the enemy and make him lose control." He ordered the deployment of up to 60 percent of Cambodia's regular and regional forces, "to go in and wage guerrilla war to tie up the enemy by the throat, shoulders and ribs on both sides, his waist, his thighs, his knees, his calves, his ankles, in order to prevent his head turning anywhere and to increase the possibility of our large or medium-sized forces smashing and breaking his head."[1]

Pol Pot then launched into arithmetic, "For example: a squad of ten marches to find, attack and smash the enemy, and kills or wounds 3 to 5 in a day and a night. If a spearhead has five squads, in a night and a day we smash 15 to 20 enemies. And if we have many spearheads sending squads to wage guerrilla warfare inside the enemy's borders on this scale, then in a day and a night we smash the enemy by the hundreds. So . . . then in ten days and ten

---

1. *Sekkedei nae noam rebos 870* ("Guidance from 870"), 3 January 1978, pp. 4–8. Similar words were soon put into the mouth of a Vietnamese "intelligence agent" captured by Democratic Kampuchea in the Gulf of Thailand. He "confessed" that it was "often said" on Phu Quoc island that "the Vietnamese party aggresses Kampuchea. Kampuchea annihilates it. It is like cutting off its legs and arms and crushing its head. We inside the country, have to cut its head off and eviscerate it." *Voice of Democratic Kampuchea* (*VODK*), 18 October 1978, translation distributed by DK embassy in Beijing, p. 4.

nights, how many thousands are killed? And how many in 20 or 30 days? And every year how many are killed?"

An idea seemed to be forming in Pol Pot's mind. The task was to "firmly stir up national hatred and class hatred for the aggressive Vietnamese enemy, in order to turn this hatred into a material hatred." He planned for Democratic Kampuchea forces to "kill the enemy at will, and the contemptible Vietnamese (a-yuon) will surely shriek like monkeys screeching all over the forest." In a reversal of Pol Pot's own youthful experience in Saigon in 1949, now it was Vietnamese who would feel like "dark monkeys from the mountains." Democratic Kampuchea would quickly move in to "smash them so that they are completely gone from our beloved land." Nothing but "piles of the enemy's bones" would be left, "thrown over our land."[2] Pol Pot did not define what he meant by "our land."

A week later, just after the Vietnamese pullback of 6 January 1978, Pol Pot arrived in the Eastern Zone. He called a public meeting at Wat Taung, beside a rubber plantation in Suong district. A large crowd of troops and civilians assembled. Also presiding were Son Sen, So Phim, and Ke Pauk. Heng Samrin attended as deputy chief of the Zone military staff. Pol Pot gave the major address. Samrin recalls hearing him start with a new arithmetical formula, "Each Cambodian is to kill thirty Vietnamese, in order to move forward to liberate, to fight strongly in order to take southern Vietnam back." Pot entrusted the armed forces with this task. "He said we would liberate it, [and] have the people of the south rebel and overthrow Vietnam and take the south. . . . He told us to encourage the Khmer people who live in southern Vietnam, the Khmer Krom, to rise up in rebellion. 'Don't be self-centered. Act in conjunction with the army's attacks.' . . . And there would be victory."[3] Meanwhile, Phnom Penh Radio made an ironic appeal to residents of the Eastern Zone to "fan the flames of national anger, class hatred and blood debts against the . . . expansionists and annexationists."[4] The intended target was Vietnam. But Phnom Penh Radio had also denounced an alleged "traitorous clique" inside Cambodia, and would soon turn on Hanoi's "clique of supporters" there.[5] Its

2. *Sekkedei nae noam rebos* 870, pp. 6, 12, 15–16.

3. Author's interview with Heng Samrin, Phnom Penh, 2 December 1991. In a second interview, I asked Samrin if Pol Pot had referred to killing Vietnamese troops only, or to civilians as well. He replied, "The whole, everyone. Both troops and civilians. Each Khmer had to kill thirty Vietnamese. Pol Pot himself said this clearly. It was certain that he was not just talking about troops" (Phnom Penh, 7 December 1992). On 10 May 1978, Phnom Penh Radio provided corroboration of this. See below.

4. U.S. Central Intelligence Agency, Foreign Broadcast Information Service (FBIS), 9 January 1978, p. H10, Phnom Penh Radio broadcast of 7 January 1978.

5. On 7 January Phnom Penh Radio denounced 'the expansionists and annexationists, and the traitorous clique,' FBIS, 9 January 1978, p. H12; another broadcast on 27 January launched the term "clique of supporters" of Hanoi; FBIS, 30 January 1978, pp. H12–13 (FBIS

5 January editorial, marking the second anniversary of the DK constitution, did not even mention Vietnam, but still called for "national and class indignation and blood rancour." [6] The Center did not confine its genocidal impulses to a single racial group. Back in the capital on 17 January, Pol Pot described Cambodia's people as an "inexaustible source of manpower for our army." He added, "We do not worry that one day our army may run out of men, for the local population from which we can recruit is unlimited."[7] Pol Pot seemed to be saying that numbers alone made a genocidal outcome unlikely. This was his reassurance. What counted, though, were "flaming national hatred, class hatred, and the seething blood debts" that Cambodians nurtured against "the Vietnamese annexationists, their lackeys, and the reactionaries of all stripes."[8]

On 5 February, Hanoi offered Democratic Kampuchea a new proposal. It called for negotiations, a mutual pullback of five kilometers on either side of the border, and international supervision of the border to prevent aggression across it. The traditional Vietnamese communists' view of themselves, as patrons of the other Indochinese revolutions,[9] had been overcome by a more urgent priority, the desire for a peaceful frontier. Had Pol Pot's regime accepted this offer, it would most likely have survived. But this also would have meant the abandonment of the aggressive CPK policies toward Vietnam developed over the previous year. With its Chinese backing, its desire to retake the Mekong Delta from Vietnam, and the instability within the CPK, the Center was not prepared to abandon those policies. It had already described the conflict with Vietnam as "not a dispute which can be resolved through compromise and negotiation."[10]

As with the evacuation of Phnom Penh in 1975, the Center prepared for war by clearing vulnerable areas of their populations. Thousands of people from Kirivong on the Southwest Zone border were evacuated north to Tram Kak district and as far as Kien Svay district, in Region 25. Another thirty thousand people from Svay Rieng province in the East were sent to Kien Svay as

employed the translation "supporting clique"; the meaning was Cambodian opponents of DK: in FBIS, 2 February 1978, p. H1–2, Phnom Penh Radio, 31 January, distinguished the term from "big imperialist powers" (the Soviet bloc) supporting Hanoi.

6. FBIS, 5 January 1978, p. H7, Phnom Penh Radio, 4 January 1978.

7. Pol Pot's speech on the "10th anniversary of the Revolutionary Army of Kampuchea," FBIS, 19 January 1978, p. H 3, Phnom Penh Radio, 17 January 1978.

8. FBIS, 30 January 1978, p. H7, Phnom Penh Radio, 21 January 1978.

9. T. Carney notes that since 1975, DK "fears of Vietnamese intentions" had been "reinforced by repeated expressions from Hanoi that a 'special relationship' existed between Cambodia and Vietnam, despite reiterations of Cambodian antipathy toward any regional grouping" (in Jackson, *Cambodia 1975–1982*, p. 96). Such a formulation does not necessarily imply domination. To take one comparison, Britain and Ireland jointly recognize "the special links and the unique relationship which exists between the peoples of Britain and Ireland." *New York Times*, "The Call for Peace in Ulster," 16 December 1993.

10. FBIS, 23 January 1978, p. H4, Phnom Penh Radio 22 January 1978.

well. Conditions there were much more severe even than in Region 13.[11] Seven coastal cooperatives in the Koh Touc subdistrict of Kampot were emptied in January and February 1978. Their thirty-seven thousand inhabitants, both new and base people, were driven north into the Elephant Mountains of the interior. Many of the new people among them soon died of starvation.[12]

Meanwhile the Center pursued its military incursions over the border. On 14 March, DK troops invaded the Vietnamese province of Ha Tien, slaughtering and disemboweling up to a hundred peasants of both Vietnamese and Khmer origin.[13] Looking back over this period several months later, Phnom Penh Radio unwittingly acknowledged Cambodia's aggression, "In March, . . . the Vietnamese did not have the strength to attack us: instead, we continued to attack them." And, "as each front involved a number of divisions, this was by no means a small war. . . . Because of their heavy defeat in March, in April the Vietnamese did not have the strength to attack us again. . . . Their April 1978 attack [sic] was also defeated. . . . We shall certainly win, even if this fight lasts 700 years or more."[14] By June 1978, three-quarters of a million Vietnamese had fled their homes near the border seeking refuge elsewhere in Vietnam.[15]

Meanwhile, DK officials had refused even to accept delivery of a copy of Hanoi's 5 February peace proposal.[16] The conflict with Vietnam became locked into Democratic Kampuchea's "continuous non-stop struggle." In late Feb-

11. Author's interviews with Ieng Thon, a former CPK soldier evacuated from Kirivong to Kien Svay in early 1978 (Prey Piey, 16 July 1980), and Muk Sim, PRK chief of Svay Rieng province, who said that around late 1977, Kompong Rou, Chantrea, and Romduol districts were emptied and their populations sent "to Kandal, Kampot, Kompong Cham, Kompong Thom, and Siemreap" (Svay Rieng, 16 January 1986).

12. Author's interviews with a former fisherman in Koh Touc, Kampot district, 29 August 1980. He said they were taken to a former CPK military school at Prey Taken, where new people received a daily ration of gruel made from 5 cans of rice for 45 people, while base people received rice rations. His child died of starvation at Prey Taken, and he saw many other bodies at Koh Sla.

13. "Vietnamese 'massacred by Khmers,'" Age (Melbourne), 3 April 1978, reporting 80–100 civilians killed; FEER, 31 March 1978, p. 12. Officials put the toll at 72 killed or wounded. Chanda's cover photo, FEER, 21 April 1978, and Brother Enemy, pp. 223–24, describe the site.

14. BBC SWB, FE/5813/A3/1–2, 15 May 1978, quoting Phnom Penh Radio, 10 May 1978. This gives weight to Hanoi's accusation that from April 22 to April 30, 1978, sixteen DK battalions invaded 16 km inside Vietnam, massacring "large numbers of civilians" and burning down 3,600 houses (Kampuchea Dossier II, p. 104).

15. U.N. High Commissioner for Refugees, Geneva, 9 June 1978, FEER, 23 June 1978, p. 7. This figure was later confirmed; see "350,000 Flee to Vietnam: UN," Age (Melbourne), 2 November 1978.

16. G. Evans and K. Rowley, Red Brotherhood at War: Vietnam, Cambodia and Laos Since 1975, London: Verso, rev. ed., 1990, pp. 106–7; N. Chanda, FEER, 17 February 1978, and Brother Enemy, p. 216.

ruary 1978, therefore, Hanoi secretly decided that Pol Pot's regime had to go.[17] Whether DK would be overthrown by internal unrest or by foreign invasion remained to be seen.

Unrest in the West

Early in 1978, a cpk meeting was convened in Kompong Speu. All members of district committees in DK's Western Zone assembled for a fifteen-day political course. Topics on the agenda included agricultural production, the international situation, the open war with Vietnam, the transfer of troops from the Zone's to the Center's armed forces, and combat readiness along the Vietnamese border.

The first major speaker was the cpk Western Zone secretary, Chou Chet. He addressed the cadres for half an hour concerning economic construction. Chai, an official from Toek Phos district who attended the meeting, recalls that Chet talked mostly about "getting people to work hard to resolve their living conditions, about building houses for them, one for each family." Chet referred only briefly to the border war, saying, "Vietnam has entered Khmer territory. So we compatriots have to be careful in order to defend our territory." He used the term "Vietnam," not the more pejorative Khmer term *yuon*. And Chet did not describe the Vietnamese as "enemies." Chai recalls, "He was just informing us. He was moderate."

Chet's deputy Sem Pal, on the other hand, was "fierce." When his turn came to speak, Pal focused on Vietnam, "The cadres of Kampuchea must all temper the people to struggle to fight the *yuon* enemy, which is a hereditary enemy of the Khmer people. Look at Kampuchea Krom, Vietnam has taken it. So we must defend the border as well as we can. We must transfer half the Zone's troops to go and guard the border." He added that Vietnam and Cambodia "could never live in peace," and that if Cambodia did not fight Vietnam, "we will end up like Kampuchea Krom."

Pal's exhortations resembled Pol Pot's aggressive instructions and his speech in the Eastern Zone at this very time. Although Pal did not go so far as to campaign for the conquest of Kampuchea Krom on this occasion, the audience immediately noticed the contrast with Chou Chet, who "did not attack Vietnam much." Chai recalls, "Afterwards, during a break, we remarked on this to one another. Usually *Angkar* was united as one, but here they were talking in opposition to one another. . . . We had never seen public differences like that before."[18]

---

17. N. Chanda, "Timetable for a Takeover," *FEER,* 23 February 1979, p. 33; *Brother Enemy,* pp. 216–7.

18. Author's interview with Chai, former CPK district chief, Kompong Chhnang, 4 September 1980.

Also in early 1978, another dispute broke out in the 1st Western Division's headquarters at Longvek. Yusof, a Cham blacksmith, says Paet Soeung and his deputy, a regimental commander named Saron, argued over living conditions in the Zone. Saron claimed that "the people in the cooperatives have no strength to work." He added, "We must let our troops eat their fill, not just gruel." Soeung retorted that that would not be "socialist revolution." It would "weaken" the regime. Yusof says Saron disregarded this and "avoided making us work at night, unlike in other organizations." Yusof, who had worked under Saron since April 1976, says he "loved me like a father." Saron told him privately that "we have to rise up, wake up from this socialism," which he described as burdened with hardships. Yusof wondered how Saron and Soeung could work together in the same division.[19]

These two confrontations in the Western Zone took place in the context of unspecified moves that the Center made in February 1978 "to strengthen the discipline of its armed forces."[20] Not long after, Saron convened a secret meeting of the battalion and company commanders of his regiment at Longvek. He told them, "Look now, what can we consider doing? Hu Nim has been killed, Hou Yuon has disappeared. Now Pol Pot is on top. We cannot survive. We have to consider secret work. . . . Pol Pot is a traitor. We cannot work with him. . . . We will suppress this Socialist Revolution." Saron tried to keep his plot secret, but his twenty-two-year-old bodyguard, who had caught some of the conversation while serving meals to the officers, quietly informed Yusof of what he had heard.

Several days later, Saron himself warned Yusof, "Whenever you hear guns firing in here, please go down to the waterside." Yusof inquired further. "He said they intended . . . to smash . . . [to] attack Ta Soeung . . . in Longvek." Saron told Yusof to head for the river, away from the Longvek base, as soon as he heard the sound of guns. The attack on Soeung's headquarters would take place in seven days' time. Chou Chet was involved in the plot, Saron said, and was to lead the rebellion. Saron's regiment of 1,200 troops would mutiny, taking advantage of the absence of many of Soeung's troops in Region 37. Saron drove off to a secret meeting with Chou Chet, presumably to arrange final details.[21]

19. Author's interview with Yusof, Kompong Tralach, 5 September 1980.
20. "Geng Biao's Report on the Situation of the Indochinese Peninsula," *Journal of Contemporary Asia*, 11, 3, 1981, p. 382.
21. Author's interview with Yusof, 1980. Around this time, Chet was indeed in Kompong Chhnang province. Chai saw him there for the last time when Chet passed through Kompong Chhnang and took district officials from the area to the Tonle Sap to supervise the planting of 1,000 hectares of dry season rice for their districts. Chet could have gone to Longvek to meet Saron before or after this journey. Author's interview with Chai, Kompong Chhnang, 4 September 1980.

Only two days before the assigned date for the uprising, the secret leaked out. Saron was arrested, along with fifty of his officers and followers in the 1st Division office. His troops were disarmed, and many were also arrested. Some managed to escape into the forest.[22] Chou Chet was arrested on 15 March. His wife, Am Nen, the CPK secretary of Oudong district, was also picked up, and taken away in a truck. Both reached Tuol Sleng on 26 March.[23]

Chet's rivals, Pal and Soeung, reigned supreme.[24] The Western Zone, secured for the Center, now joined the Southwest as a base for the further consolidation of Center control.[25]

Rebellion in the East

How widespread was the unrest? Did it extend beyond the Western Zone? Were other Zone leaders such as So Phim, in the East, or Ros Nhim, in the Northwest, involved in or aware of the plot? If Phim was involved in Chou Chet's coup, its failure and the 4 March arrest of the political commissar of the 280th Division stationed in the East[26] deterrred him from further action. A woman from the Ponhea Krek district office says that Phim called a secret meeting in Pha-Au village in March 1978. "I was serving the food for the leading cadres there, but I went in close and heard what was being said. Phim told them that the situation had now changed considerably, and the comrades should all take an interest. He reminded the regional and district cadres of this standpoint because at that time regional, district and military cadres were being taken away one after another, everywhere. When he noted this, he said that those arrested were loyal servants of the people, his friends—not traitors. He told everyone to watch out, to be careful."[27]

Though this advice was pathetically inadequate, the Center could not trust Phim—but it did have to deal with him prudently. At the end of March, Pol Pot sent Vorn Vet to the Eastern Zone to bring Phim, who was suffering from an illness, to a Phnom Penh hospital. For his part, Phim seems to have suspected treachery. Vet later wrote, "I reached Phim's house. Phim was sick and

22. Author's interview with Yusof, Kompong Tralach, 5 September 1980.
23. N. Chanda, personal communication, 13 October 1982, citing a former resident of Oudong; "Important Culprits," pp. 4–5.
24. According to a CPK insider, after Chou Chet's arrest, "the position of the Secretary of the Western Region remained open. After Soeung left the West in August 1978, Ta Pal remained behind." Phak Lim, interview with S. Heder, Sa Keo, 9 March 1980.
25. A top CPK leader in Sa Keo camp in 1980 recalled, "In the post-1975 period, politically the best Regions were the Southwest and the West. There work was carried out relatively well, and there were relatively few traitors. The Central Region was average." Heder interview with Liev, Sa Keo, 9 March 1980.
26. "Important Culprits," p. 2.
27. Author's interview with Prok Sary, Prey Veng, 12 July 1980.

lying down. A large group of family members had come to visit him. I did not say anything yet, just that *Angkar* had sent me to come and get him and take him to hospital. [I said:] Please don't fail to go. I've brought a car to pick you up. Phim kept his silence. In the afternoon, when Phim was a little better and the visitors had left, I met with him and reported to him on the situation, the arrest of Si [Chou Chet]. . . . Phim asked me about the general situation in Phnom Penh. . . . Later many visitors came, and military cadres coming to report from the front also dropped in on Phim. Phim did not want to come to Phnom Penh, but they all pushed him to come. Only in the evening did he decide to come."

After a spell in hospital in the capital, Phim took the train for the Northwest Zone, accompanied by Ros Nhim. Vorn Vet states that he went to the railway station to warn him that "the Party is now strongly tracking events in the East." Phim and Nhim should both be careful. "But we spoke only for a moment before the train left the platform. . . . when Phim returned from the Northwest, I also wanted to meet him, but I was busy elsewhere and I missed him."[28]

As Vet suggests, Phim's March-April illness and his absence from the East proved as crucial as his suspicions were justified. He returned home, not fully recovered, to find his Zone administration under withering Center attack. By 19 April, no fewer than 409 Eastern Zone cadres were being held in Tuol Sleng. The largest number from any other Zone was forty-eight, from the Northwest. The twenty-eight new prisoners who entered Tuol Sleng on 20 April were all from the East.[29] The Center was indeed "strongly tracking events in the East."

The Center linked the East with Vietnam. And it linked the 1.5 million Cambodians there with the Vietnamese enemy. On 10 May 1978, Phnom Penh Radio broadcast an appeal to "purify our armed forces, our Party, and the masses of the people." The Cambodian masses were to be "purified," ironically, in "defence of Cambodian territory and the Cambodian race."[30] Like the Khmer Krom defectors whose massacre is described in the Introduction, Democratic Kampuchea's enemy was both Cambodian and Vietnamese. But the appeal for genocide against Vietnam's population was now straightforward. Pol Pot had been working on his arithmetic: "One of us must kill thirty Vietnamese. . . . So far, we have succeeded. . . . Using these figures, one Cambodian soldier is equal to 30 Vietnamese soldiers. . . . We should have two million troops for 60 million Vietnamese. However, two million troops would be more than enough to fight the Vietnamese, because Vietnam has only 50 mil-

28. Vorn Vet's untitled confession, typed version, p. 49.

29. S-21, "Daily List of Prisoners Held 20 April 1978," in Barnett, Boua, and Kiernan, "Bureaucracy of Death: Documents from Inside Pol Pot's Torture Machine," *New Statesman* (London), 2 May 1980, p. 674.

30. BBC *SWB*, FE/5813/A3/4, 15 May 1978, Phnom Penh Radio, 10 May 1978.

lion inhabitants. . . . We need only 2 million troops to crush the 50 million Vietnamese, and we would still have six million people left. We must formulate our combat line in this manner, in order to win victory. . . . We absolutely must implement the slogan of one against thirty."[31]

At this point, however, the primary targets were Cambodians. In the first three weeks of May, Ke Pauk summoned the commanders and commissars of the three Eastern Zone divisions and five Regional brigades to "meetings" at his headquarters in Sra village, north of Highway 7. As they arrived they were disarmed and arrested. Many were executed on the spot. Ninety-two of the most important cadres were handed over to the Santebal in Phnom Penh.[32] Et Samon, commander of the 280th Division, an easterner by background, committed suicide in custody soon after his arrest. Other victims included Sarun, commander of the Region 20 regiment, his deputy, and a third member of the regimental committee; the commanders of the 3rd, 4th, and 5th Zone divisions; the secretaries of Regions 20 and 22; and the Chief of the Zone military staff, Kev Samnang.[33]

The purge struck deep. Among the seventeen ethnic Khmer "poor peasants" who arrived in Tuol Sleng from the 3rd Division were two nine-year-old boys, two ten-year-old girls, and five others, all under 16. Accused by the Santebal of association with a dissident tendency, all seventeen, the Santebal noted, were arrested because their parents or husbands had been. "Kill them all," Deuch wrote on 30 May, appending his signature.[34]

On 23 May, Pauk arrested two relatives of Heng Samrin: his younger brother, Heng Thal, commander of the Center's 290th (formerly eastern) Division, and their brother-in-law Soth, CPK secretary of Region 21. Both were taken to Tuol Sleng.[35] Heng Samrin himself was saved by the fact that on 18 May, So Phim had summoned him to Suong, relieved him of command of the 4th Division, and sent him to Prey Veng in his capacity as deputy chief of the Zone Staff. Prey Veng, on Highway 15, which links the two major east-west routes, Highways 7 and 1, was the Zone military headquarters. Samrin arrived there the same day.[36]

31. BBC SWB, FE/5813/A3/2, 15 May 1978, Phnom Penh Radio, 10 May 1978.

32. "Benchhi neak tous dael coul niw khnong khae usophea 1978" ("List of Names of Prisoners Who Entered in May 1978"), S-21, pp. 10–47.

33. For further details of these arrests, see Kiernan, "Wild Chickens," in Chandler and Kiernan, *Revolution and Its Aftermath in Kampuchea*, pp. 187–88. Several errors have been corrected here.

34. "Angkapheap kong pul lek 3: prowattarup sangkep rebos neak choap ninneakar" ("3rd Division units: short biographies of those associated with the tendency"), S-21 worksheet signed by Deuch, 30 May 1978.

35. The S-21 "confessions" of the two both give the date of their arrest as 23 May.

36. This information and the following account of Heng Samrin's activities is taken from the author's interviews with him on 2 December 1991 and 7 December 1992.

In Prey Veng, Samrin was now in direct command of the 5th, 6th, and 8th marine battalions, the latter based nearby at Neak Loeung. He could also mobilize two battalions of trainees from the Zone Armed Training School and two tanks attached to the Zone staff. The Zone artillery batteries were still stationed at Chup, and the three divisions remained at the front. "I had no command, but I could send commands by telegram to every division."

Meanwhile Pauk, having smashed Phim's Zone chain of command, now summoned him to a "meeting." Phim, ill and unaware of the full extent of the massacre, and hamstrung by a sense of party discipline, responded with little more than suspicion. "I am the president of the [Highway 7] Front. What right does the deputy president have to call me to a meeting? It should be the reverse. What does this mean?" He must have known. But the closer he came to realizing that the elements of a successful armed resistance had already been swept away, the greater his inertia. Remarking cryptically that "security" for such a meeting was better at his own headquarters than at Pauk's, he sent Mey, one of his bodyguards, to assess Pauk's activities. Mey was arrested and executed. Another message arrived, and another bodyguard set off, meeting the same fate. A third "invitation" caused Phim to send his nephew Chhoeun to investigate the disappearance of the bodyguards. Chhoeun, too, was killed. Finally, on 23 May, Phim sent the chief of his Zone office, Piem, to represent him at Pauk's headquarters. Pauk sent Piem off to Tuol Sleng with the other leading prisoners.

It took Piem's failure to return to his headquarters at Tuol Preap for Phim to finally determine that Pauk was at war. The next day, 24 May, Phim met with a deputy chief of the Zone military staff, Pol Saroeun, who ran the Zone ammunition factory in Koh Sautin district. Phim ordered Saroeun to "seek out our friends" with whom they had worked in earlier times. He warned him to rebuild bridges to the Vietnamese. But Phim issued no order to attack Pauk's forces. He merely told Saroeun that he wanted his troops on alert, to see what would happen next. On his way home from Tuol Preap, Saroeun noticed some of Pauk's troops checking the number of his motorcycle. He suspected something was up.[37]

The next day, Pauk struck. Two divisions of Central Zone troops, including an armored brigade of ten Chinese amphibious tanks, crossed the Mekong and moved swiftly east along Highway 7. Remnants of the Eastern Zone army along the way put up stiff, spontaneous resistance. Tea Sabun, secretary of Tbaung Khmum district, recalls, "I had sent my people and troops to those meetings, and they had all been arrested, and their motorcycles seized. Anyone who was a revolutionary was killed. If we wanted to survive, we had to make a revolution. I called in the militia forces from Vihear Luong, Chong Kraung, Anchaeum,

37. Author's interview with Pol Saroeun, Takeo, 27 August 1981.

Sralap, Lo Ngieng, and Kor subdistricts. There were about three to four thousand of us in the forest. We had the contents of So Phim's Eastern Zone arsenals—tens of thousands of guns including all the B-40s and B-69s. We didn't have enough trucks to cart everything away, so we had to blow up the rest.

"We hit them east of Suong at three in the morning of the 26th. There was fierce, close-in fighting for three days and three nights. We fell back and regrouped, then attacked again and drove them out of Suong. Then they recaptured it. They had two divisions to our force of approximately one regiment. We killed many of them and blew up five or six tanks and many vehicles by mining the roads. They would take a village and then we would push them out again the next day. If defeated, we would run into the jungle and then return and attack them."[38]

Meanwhile, other regional leaders joined in the resistance. The Region 21 deputy secretary, Ouch Bun Chhoeun, went to see his former superior, Phuong, DK minister of rubber plantations. Chhoeun found him fatalistic, immobilized by a combination of loyalty and despair. "You will never defeat the Party," Phuong told Chhoeun. They wished one another well, and Chhoeun slipped away to join the resistance. Phuong reached Tuol Sleng on 6 June. But Region 21 troops led by Tea Sabun, his deputy Chan Seng, and the third, Cham member of the Tbaung Khmum district committee, Mat Ly, along with Ouch Bun Chhoeun and So Phim's former courier, Mau Phok, temporarily tied down the bulk of Pauk's forces at the western end of Highway 7, giving rebels closer to the Vietnamese border valuable time to regroup and organize.

Meanwhile, Heng Samrin was at his post in Prey Veng, twenty-five kilometers to the south. He claims, "I knew as soon as the coup had taken place. I had sent telegrams to every division to report in. They reported that they had been called to a meeting by Pauk, on Highway 7. All officers of battallions, regiments and divisions at the front." After the disappearance of the officers, Samrin invited those who remained to a meeting of his own in Prey Veng. He also called in a number of Region and district officials.

But first priority went to So Phim, who was stranded in Tuol Preap, twenty kilometers northeast. When Pauk's coup got under way on 25 May, Phim radioed Heng Samrin and asked for help in getting away. Heng Samrin drove to Tuol Preap to pick him up and brought him back to Prey Veng. Samrin wanted both of them "to study the situation and events along Highway 7 and Highway 1." Phim added weight to the gathering of Eastern Zone forces. The Zone secretary and his deputy chief of staff were joined by the second deputy chief of staff, Pol Saroeun, who also came south for the conference. So did Song Neat, an officer of the 4th Division. The commanders of the 5th and 6th marine battalions also attended, as did two members of the Region 20 CPK committee, the Region secretary, Tui, and Chea Sim, secretary of Ponhea Krek district. The secretary of Komchay Meas district, Hem Bo, and his deputy, and the secretaries and deputy secretaries of Prey Veng and Peam Ro districts, were also there. In all, about twenty people gathered to decide what to do next.[39] The meeting lasted two hours. Much hinged on the position of So Phim. Heng Samrin recalls, "Phim was still ambivalent at that time. And he didn't believe me. . . . Because he still believed Pol Pot. He said the coup was the work of Son Sen, who had done it to overthrow Pol Pot. But I said that it was not [just] Son Sen, it was a policy of Pol Pot. It was very clear that Pol Pot had a policy of screening out internal agents in the Party. We had read documents talking about internal agents. So it was clear. They had already done this in every Zone but the Eastern Zone. [The East] was the last. Now the final action of Pol Pot was to use the machinery of a coup. I told Phim this. But he didn't believe me. He said he still had hope in 'Brother Number One' . . . but he did offer an opinion: 'If we fight back, the resistance has to rely on support. . . . This support is our old friends. There are only our old friends. We have to go seek out our friends for support. If we don't, we will not get any support. It is true that we have been in conflict for a short time, but we had a tradition of common resistance. The conflict is only recent. Our friends will not abandon us. If we resist, we have to run and find our friends.'" He meant Vietnam.

Most of the others preferred immediate resistance. "After the meeting we worked out a plan. . . . We declared that we would fight back." So Phim, torn between two old loyalties, arranged a compromise. It was personally courageous, but politically debilitating. "While we were fighting hard against Pol Pot at that time, he had us postpone action for a time. To hold off while he went to Phnom Penh. When he was leaving for Phnom Penh, he had a discussion with me. He said to let him go alone, with his bodyguards. If we did not see him back in three days' time, we should start to fight back again. But if he did come back in three days, we should wait to talk with him." So Phim set off for the capital with only six bodyguards.

Heng Samrin prepared a battle plan. First, having lost contact with his old 4th Division north of Highway 7, he urgently needed to reestablish a chain of command. This meant getting a message across the highway, most of which was occupied by Pauk's forces, the rest heavily contested by the Region 21 resistance. "I ordered Song Neat to take a squad to fight along Highway 15 to Chup and Peam, . . . to cross to the north of Highway 7, and make their way to Memut, in order to muster the forces of the 4th Division."

39. Author's interview with Heng Samrin, 7 December 1992. Samrin named Run and Khim Phan (minutes secretary) as two others in attendance.

Neat left immediately with seven men. After a hazardous journey, he made it through.

A larger force marched off to do battle. Pol Saroeun took command of three companies of the 75th Regiment, composed of support troops attached to the Zone artillery units. These three hundred troops set off north along Highway 15. They fought their way to Thnal Totoeng, Chup, Peam, and eventually Suong, capital of Tbaung Khmum district on Highway 7. They drove Pauk's forces from Suong, but did not try to hold it. Saroeun marched his troops through Suong and also crossed into the forest north of the highway.

A second, southern front was opened by Hem Bo, secretary of Komchay Meas district on the Vietnamese border. After the 27 May meeting, Bo left for his headquarters in Krabau subdistrict. On arrival he mobilized 150 district troops and began to launch attacks on Pauk's forces from the east.

Meanwhile, Son Sen's Center and Southwest Zone troops and Pauk's Central Zone forces were closing in on Prey Veng from the south and the north. Fierce fighting was soon raging south of the city. Son Sen's forces, moving up from Highway 1, encountered fierce resistance from the 8th marine battalion at Peam Banan. The Eastern Zone marines, dug in beside a reservoir and benefiting from a clear field of fire, opened up on the attackers crossing the plain. "We fought along Snae reservoir. They attacked and came at us, and they attacked again. . . . We destroyed many of them there," Samrin claims.[40] "My forces did not suffer many casualties. . . . We lost few." His marines held their ground for a week, before retreating in good order. As the news spread, the armed resistance seems to have encouraged local villagers to rise up in rebellion. Ten kilometers north of Peam Banan, on 2 June, the peasants of Babong village staged an uprising of their own against the village administration. The crowd, demanding food, rioted and beheaded two Khmer Rouge. Apparently without coordination, on the same day a similar uprising broke out further north, in Chamcar Kuoy village of Prey Veng district. Peasants beheaded the village chief and four others. A unit of rebel Eastern Zone forces, probably elements of the 8th marine battalion, was only thirteen kilometers from Babong village at the time. Fifty of these "So Phim troops," as the villagers called them, came straight to Babong the same day.[41] They took sanctuary in the village for three days without harming anyone. Southwest Zone troops under Son Sen's command got wind of their presence, however, and reached Babong on 5 June.

40. Heng Samrin, 1992 interview. He added, "I don't know how many we killed, but a large number. One side cannot claim to have counted! . . ."

41. Pet Theng, an elderly village woman, told the author: "So Phim was not very oppressive . . . if he was here things would not have gone as far as they did." All twelve members of her family, plus 18 other locals, were killed when Center troops reoccupied the village on 5 June. Author's interview, Babong, 12 January 1987.

Most of the rebels had left several hours before, but twenty were captured, and over eighty villagers were arrested for their part in the uprising. They were all taken to a prison north of Peam Ro, where only twelve of the one hundred survived the next ten weeks.[42]

Meanwhile, on 28 May, So Phim had driven his jeep to Arei Khsat, on the Mekong opposite Phnom Penh. He sent one of his bodyguards by boat to take a note to the office of a military commander based near Wat Unnalom in the capital. The contents of this note remain mysterious.[43] The messenger returned empty-handed, and So Phim decided to wait for a response. After an hour went by, two ferries approached, crammed with Center marines. As he later told Heng Samrin, Phim still thought they may be coming to escort him to the capital. As they drew near to the shore, the marines disembarked. They fanned out in an attempt to surround Phim. Then they opened fire, wounding him in the stomach. Surprised, and too far from his jeep, Phim had to run for his life. He reached the Arei Khsat office, commandeered the subdistrict chief's pony cart, and made off toward the west. He eventually stopped at a wat beside a banyan tree, near the village of Prek Pra, on the road from Srei Santhor to Peareang district.

Having fought off Son Sen's thrust from the south, Heng Samrin now turned his attention to Phim again. "When three days were up, I went after him," Samrin recalls. "He had disappeared, so I followed him, and found him wounded in the wat." Samrin arrived with Chhien, secretary of Region 22, and Sarun, head of the Zone commerce department, an uncle of Pol Saroeun. Phim greeted them with "Goodbye." When they questioned him, he replied, "I'm finished. I'm staying here. You friends go ahead and fight on. I can't go on."[44] Phim was bleeding from the stomach, drinking alcohol to suppress the pain. His wife, Kirou, and their children had come to join him at the wat. Samrin says, "We begged him to come along. But he insisted on staying. I arranged for the Srey Santhor district forces, 300 men in three companies, and Yi Yaun, the

42. Chanthou Boua and Ben Kiernan, "Oxfam America's Aid Program in Babong Village, Kampuchea," April 1987, p. 7. The authors, who worked in Babong for a month in December 1986 and January 1987, interviewed one hundred villagers about these and other events in the history of the village.
43. One account, by a distant relative of Heng Samrin, goes that So Phim sent a note calling for an uprising to the commander named Chey Sangkream. However, Phim's messenger did not deliver it personally but only gave it to Sangkream's courier, who then passed it on to Pol Pot. The messenger returned to Arei Khsat and reported what he had done to Phim, who immediately "knew it was all over." Interview with the author, Phnom Penh, 28 November 1991. Chey Sangkream is difficult to identify.
44. Daok Samol and Yi Yaun, chiefs of Peareang and Srey Santhor districts, later reported that Phim had told them, "You must rise up and struggle. They are traitors. You keep up the struggle. I can't solve this. We are alone. I don't know what will happen. I can't find a solution." Kiernan, "Wild Chickens," p. 191.

district secretary, to take him into the forest of Srei Santhor and guard him. He sent me away to look after the troops."

Heng Samrin left the wat at 4 P.M. on 31 May. He had deployed his marines and two tanks at Lor Khdach, on Highway 15 about ten kilometers north of Prey Veng. "Without sleeping that night, I called in all the commanders from Prey Veng and everywhere, to prepare a plan. The plan was to take Phim to the east, in order to get him out to Vietnam." But the next day, an enemy force of twelve tanks and infantry approached from the north. "They attacked early in the morning. They pounded me with artillery. . . . We blew up two of three of their tanks. Many of their forces died." But the rebels were heavily outgunned. "Many planes flew over and strafed us at Lor Khdach. They attacked and scattered my forces. I abandoned my tanks at Prey Sniet. So they fought their way into Prey Veng."[45]

Meanwhile, Center planes scattered leaflets over the Eastern Zone, proclaiming So Phim a traitor, wanted dead or alive. Some fell into the hands of members of the Srei Santhor district unit entrusted by Heng Samrin with Phim's safety. Since their commander, district chief Yi Yaun, had taken to the jungle, they took a leaflet to his deputy. Believing that the party, or its air force, could not be mistaken, the deputy district chief ordered Phim's arrest. On 3 June, as the three-hundred-strong force closed in on him and his bodyguards, Phim lost hope. Just after sunset, he drew a pistol and shot himself in the chest. A second bullet through the mouth brought an end to a thirty-year revolutionary career that had begun in the 1940s independence struggle against the French colonial regime.[46] Phim's loyal bodyguards escaped to a nearby village, drank themselves into a stupor with home-made alcohol, and then scattered. At 9 P.M., Phim's wife Kirou and their children were massacred as they prepared his body for burial.

The Center's triumph over Phim did not achieve its goal. According to Kun, interpreter for North Korean technical advisors in Regions 23 and 24, "After So Phim's death the people in Region 22 and in Komchay Meas rebelled in anger. . . . The people had long wanted the private system back again instead of the party's communitarian system, and they supported the rebellion. They stopped eating communally and were distributing oxcarts and other things among

45. Samrin adds, "They took three days to get into Prey Veng! I had no forces there, we had all left, but they dared not go in, saying that they were afraid of Prey Veng, because in Prey Veng I had killed many of them, blown up many tanks, and so on" (1991 interview).

46. In 1979 a leader of the new Vietnam-installed Cambodian government asserted that "So Phim . . . the leader of the May 1978 uprising involving a very big force . . . fell heroically in the fighting" (AFP interview with Ros Samay, *Vietnam News Bulletin,* Canberra, No. 03/79, 2 February 1979, p. 15). Stephen Heder's claims of a "myth put forward by the Vietnamese and others" that Phim's group were "internationalists" ("From Pol Pot to Pen Sovan," p. 7; *Reflections on Cambodian Political History,* p. 3) remain undocumented.

themselves. Cadres still faithful to the party line were afraid to remain in place for fear that the people would kill them, and they fled to Region 24, where I met them. The army could not go into Region 22."[47]

In early June, Pauk's units attempted to empty a village in Kanchriech district and evacuate its inhabitants across the Mekong to the Central Zone. One of the villagers, So Samnang, who had spent 1977 in jail and escaped during the Vietnamese incursion of January 1978, says that the entire village population was driven to the Mekong. Rebels shelled the ferry at Tonle Bet, however, and many of the villagers were unable to cross. They fled into Peancheang forest with the rebels and spent the next four nights sheltering from the fighting. They all managed to return to their village on 10 June. The men immediately took to the surrounding forest, seeking rebel protection. Samnang spent the rest of 1978 with the resistance.[48] An "underground opposition" that sprang up in Peareang district took the name Khmer Sor (White Khmers), used by pro-Vietnamese rebels in 1973–74. They secretly visited Maesor Prachan village and offered "to help anyone who feared for his life at the hands of the Khmer Rouge." A witness found them "very brave. . . . They had to be constantly on the move."[49]

Heng Samrin's forces, however, "scattered far and wide" by tank and aerial attack, were unable to continue resistance in Region 22. Most headed east into the forest, towards the Vietnamese border. There they found battles still raging north and south of Highway 7. In Region 20, Hem Bo's Komchay Meas district forces had been joined by militia, and the resistance there now numbered as many as three thousand guerrillas, probably not all armed.[50] Kim Y, from Ponhea Krek District, recalls, "We all fought the coup at first for two or three days, in some places two weeks. But then the fighting subsided, and airplanes dropped leaflets [signed by Seng Hong, alias Chan] which said, 'Compatriots, please put down your arms. Please pool your forces with us and participate with us. Let us exterminate the enemy together, namely So Phim, the traitor chieftain in the Eastern Zone.' Our youths and cadres thought hard. Some kept quiet; others in small squads put down their arms and went in to save their lives by confessing, and some even took their guns in with them. But most of us took our guns into the forest."[51]

Fierce fighting continued throughout June and July. The Center and

---

47. Author's interview with Kun, Montbard, 1 February 1980.
48. Author's interview with So Samnang, Prey Veng, 11 January 1987.
49. M. Stuart-Fox and Bunheang Ung, *The Murderous Revolution: Life and Death in Pol Pot's Kampuchea*, Sydney: Apcol, 1986, pp. 146–47.
50. Author's interview with Chum Sambor, former Region 20 security chief, who said he mobilized a force of three thousand in the forest of the Krabau subdistrict of Komchay Meas in this period. Prey Veng, 12 July 1980.
51. Author's interview with Kim Y, Kandol Chrum, 7 August 1980.

Southwest Zone forces had a dramatic impact on Krauchhmar district of Region 21, scene of the 1975 massacres of Chams. They began by arresting "all cadres" and decreeing "death to people who kept salt or corn in their houses." "They chased people through the jungle, hunting them down." They burnt to death two members of the district committee, including a Cham.[52] For their part, the rebels in Region 21 destroyed more than twenty military vehicles, though they took heavy casualties confronting the superior numbers of the combined forces of Pauk, Son Sen, and Mok. Song Neat, having reached Memot, contacted some of his 4th Division comrades there. A company of one hundred troops joined the rebellion under Neat's command.[53]

Across the Mekong in the Central Zone, people in Stung Trang district, fifteen kilometers west, "could hear guns firing every day."[54] In this district lived a disabled CPK soldier named Nhek Chamroeun, who had been recruited into the communist movement by former deputy information minister Tiv Ol. Chamroeun's elder brothers had worked for Tiv Ol in Phnom Penh, and had disappeared with him in 1977. In August 1978, Chamroeun discovered the Center planned to arrest him as well. "Fleeing into the jungle, he unexpectedly found . . . a person called Chem and his twelve or thirteen comrades. All had been members of the [CPK], but having become critical of the ways of the Pol Pot regime, they could not follow it. So they escaped." Chamroeun joined them, leading "a refugee life in the jungle" for the next three months.[55]

The rebellion also spread north into Kratie province. "In mid-1978 the village committee of Damrey Phong all ran into the jungle in opposition to Angkar."[56] And in neighboring Region 505, the comparatively lenient chief of Snuol district also took to the jungle in August, after being replaced by a much harsher official.[57] South of Highway 7, the 280th Division's deputy commander, Sieng Hai, defected to the rebels with two companies of troops, over two hundred men. In all, a force of around two thousand rebels was now operating in small units both north and south of Highway 7.[58] The first word of their activities reached the outside world on 13 July, when a refugee crossing into Vietnam reported that "uprisings are occurring in several areas" inside Cambodia. At the same time, Phnom Penh Radio attempted to blame the

52. Author's interview with Ieng, Koh Thom, 1 August 1980.

53. Heng Samrin, 1992 interview.

54. Author's interview with an anonymous informant from Stung Trang, Tuol, France, 28 October 1979.

55. Katuiti Honda, *Journey to Cambodia*, Tokyo, 1981, pp. 118–23.

56. Author's interview with Chandara, Phnom Penh, 21 September 1980.

57. Author's interview with Mon, Phnom Penh, 5 July 1980. She said that the former district chief of Snuol "did not kill or search out many people, and allowed us to eat in our houses. The new one did not, [and] killed more people than before. The two did not get on."

58. Heng Samrin (1992).

Eastern Zone by referring for the first time to bad cadres who have made people "work at irregular hours, day and night."[59]

The Center's losses began to mount. Its biggest blow yet was probably the defection of Pauk's own deputy. Sok, a former Southwest Zone official appointed deputy secretary of the Central Zone, fled to Vietnam after being transferred again to serve in the East.[60] On 2 August, the Santebal arrested Kang Chap, another former Southwest official now serving as secretary of the Northern Zone. Chap had helped Pauk and Sok smother the Region 106 rebellion the previous year.[61]

The CPK Standing Committee met three days later. Pol Pot and the Center concluded, "We must accept the situation we are in: the leading contingent is very small and disproportionate. . . . our tasks increase more and more. There is a major contradiction: sixty percent of our cadre have to be preoccupied with safeguarding the Organization. . . . We can hold on for a certain time, but if such a situation continues, it would become impossible for us. For we can now afford to sustain only partial losses. A prolongation of this situation would lead to the risk of collapse."[62]

But the Center still had some tricks up its sleeve. Its May 10 call for "purification" of the "masses of the people" had been no idle threat. First, the Center resorted to traditional terror tactics. The Santebal redoubled its intake. By the end of June 1978, the number of prisoners who had entered Tuol Sleng since January reached 5,675, a half-year total close to the number of prisoners registered for all of 1977 (6,330).[63] On-the-spot massacres of surrendering rebels and of the inhabitants of villages suspected of harboring "traitors," however, drove tens of thousands of peasants into the jungle during July, destroying any remaining possibility of political consolidation of the Center's hold on the Eastern Zone. Center forces totally exterminated the seven hundred people in So Phim's base village of Bos in the Ponhea Krek

59. FEER, 21 July 1978, p. 5. On 28 July, FEER reported the resistance as gaining territory. A CPK defector who reached Thailand on 2 November described Heng Samrin's revolt; see Le Point, 1 January 1979, p. 35.

60. Carney, in Jackson, Cambodia 1975–1978, p. 102.

61. Jackson, Cambodia 1975–1978, p. 101; S. Heder, interview with Phak Lim, Sa Keo, 9 March 1980; Thach Keo Dara, "Une révolte de la population," Sereika, no. 24, October 1978, p. 8.

62. République Populaire du Kampuchéa, Tribunal Populaire Révolutionnaire Siégant à Phnom Penh, August 1979, document no. 2.5.30, "Extrait du procès-verbal de la réunion de 870 (le 5 août 1978)," p. 1. Ironically, at this point Nayan Chanda reported that So Phim was "now leading the Vietnamese-backed resistance in Cambodia" (FEER, 11 August 1978, p. 10). Phim had been dead for two months.

63. Anthony Barnett, "Inside S-21," in "Bureaucracy of Death," New Statesman, 2 May 1980, p. 671.

district of Region 20.[64] In Region 22, Bunheang Ung, hiding in a grove of mango trees, watched "frozen in horror" as Southwest Zone troops committed one of the worst massacres, at a hospital in Peareang district in July-August 1978. Ung puts the total number of victims from six villages of Maesor Prachan subdistrict at fifteen hundred, all killed over five days.[65]

On 4 September, the three thousand residents of Don Sor subdistrict in Region 23 assembled at noon in their communal mess hall. The subdistrict chief, a Southwest cadre, presided. The Svay Rieng district chief, another Southwest cadre name Hong, arrived on a mototcycle with two bodyguards. Hong told the crowd he was looking for "CIA, KGB and Vietnamese" spies in the subdistrict. Twenty-seven men, three women, and two children were called from the meeting, mostly former students, officials, and police officers. At 3 P.M. they were given a meal. Two hours later, they were taken east to an uninhabited area, evacuated in early 1978. There, a subdistrict militiaman reported later, they were beaten to death with bamboo sticks and axes. The children, one of whom was two years old, were placed in a pig-cage for the night, then killed the next day. A week later, at 4 A.M., a Southwest security squad of fifteen assembled another 930 people, members of the families of people executed since 1975. At 8:00 they too were given a meal, but few could eat. Aware of the fate awaiting them, many were screaming for help. Told they were going west "to study" in Region 24, they set out along Highway 1 at 9 A.M. Two kilometers down the road, they were stopped at a wat and told to dig large pits. From 16 to 20 September, all 930 were massacred there.[66]

In 1980 I interviewed 87 people from the East, obtaining statistics on executions in 1978 in a number of individual villages in other parts of the zone. The death tolls were, according to the various informants, 100, 240, 50, 100, 600, 80, 70, 100, 23, 200, and 100 people. Further accounts reported 705 executions in 1978 among the people from one subdistrict, 1,950 from another, 400 from another. Combined with other eyewitness accounts of massacres, these figures suggest that a total death toll of 100,000 among easterners in 1978 (over one-seventeenth of the population) can safely be regarded as a conservative estimate. The real figure is probably around 250,000 dead.[67]

---

64. This information comes from many cadres and inhabitants of Ponhea Krek, particularly during a visit to Dauntey subdistrict, where Bos village is located, on 6 August 1980. Lim Thi, a native of Dauntey, says that "only one person survived" in Bos out of 700. Interview with author, Takhmau, 15 August 1980.

65. For more details see M. Stuart-Fox and Bunheang Ung, *The Murderous Revolution,* pp. 140–46. Ung himself lost thirty relatives, including 17 children, in this massacre.

66. Author's interview with Muk Sim, whose sister and niece were among the victims of the first massacre. Svay Rieng, 16 January 1986.

67. Heder describes the 1978 Eastern Zone massacres as "massive and indiscriminate purges of party, army and people alike." Vickery calls them "by far the most violent event of

Table 2. Victims of Executions in Four Communities of the Eastern Zone of Democratic Kampuchea, 1975–1978

	1975	1976	1977	1978	Total Executions
1. 120 people (Svay Rieng)	1			53 (1)	54 (1)
2. 62 people (Svay Rieng)			1 (2)	16	17 (2)
3. 11 families (Kompong Cham)		1	7 (2)	17	25 (2)
4. 15 families (Kompong Cham)			6 (2)	9	15 (2)
Total Executions	1	1	14 (6)	95 (1)	118 (7)

Katuiti Honda conducted surveys on the DK death toll among about 350 people in four small communities of eastern Cambodia. He found that nearly all of the 118 killings had occurred after "early 1978." Ninety-five executions in 1978, among a total of 350 people alive in 1975, represent a murder toll of over 27 percent in less than a year. Extrapolated to the whole Eastern Zone population, this would indicate a toll of over 400,000. Honda's data are set out in Table 2.[68]

The Evacuation of the East

In mid-June 1978, the first shipment of a new cargo arrived from China: 50 tons of blue cloth. In July, another Chinese ship brought 56 tons of blue cloth to Kompong Som. In August, three ships at weekly intervals brought cargoes of 51 tons, 56 tons, and 29 tons of blue cloth, bringing the total to 242 tons for the three-month period.[69]

Why? Blue was a new color in Democratic Kampuchea. Black cloth had been purchased from Thailand in 1976, along with black, yellow, purple, and

the entire DK period." Carney concedes that the east in 1978 "may have lost the largest number of people [of any Zone] in response to central party orders . . . a heavy toll among villagers." Heder, "From Pol Pot to Pen Sovan to the Villages," Institute of Asian Studies, Chulalongkorn University, Bangkok, May 1980, p.16; Vickery, *Cambodia 1975–1982*, p. 137; Carney, in Jackson, ed., *Cambodia 1975–1978*, pp. 93, 86. For Carney's earlier, stronger terminology, see Kiernan, *Cambodia: The Eastern Zone Massacres*, pp. 6–7.

68. Katuiti Honda, *Journey to Cambodia*, Tokyo, 1981, chs. 3 and 5. Figures in brackets represent additional deaths, caused by starvation or disease.

69. CNA, MC-DK, Box 23, Dossier 79. The first ship, the *Cheang Yin*, arrived from China on 13 June 1978 with 25.154 tons of cloth, half navy blue and half gray, and another 36.3 tons of cloth, half of it navy blue and half sea blue. The other shipments arrived on 10 July, 11 August, 18 August, and 25 August. One hundred twenty-seven tons of gray cloth arrived in the same period as the 242 tons of blue.

green (but not blue) dyes.[70] Ministry of commerce records indicate that Democratic Kampuchea imported only black cloth until June 1978. On 15 April, a Chinese vessel had brought 38 tons of black cloth, the last shipment of cloth before the blue began arriving. The first shipment of blue cloth, which arrived on 13 June, must have been ordered in May, as the Center was planning its suppression of the Eastern Zone for the end of that month.

In 1983, a Phnom Penh woman evacuated to Pursat in the Northwest, now living in the United States, described a new deportation in the second half of 1978. "Some new people came from a different part of Cambodia and they wore blue cloth instead of black. They complained that things were too hard for them here [in Pursat]. Where they came from, they had hard work, but they [had] always had enough food, and . . . more freedom to go where they wanted to. These people were blamed by the Communists in [Pursat]. They said, 'Don't listen to their stories, they are the enemies of Cambodia.' These people were killed a lot."[71] The blue-clad victims were evacuees from the East.

Chhun Vun, twenty-one, and his family of seven had been farmers by the bank of the Mekong south of Neak Leung (Region 24).[72] In 1978, all the people in that area were evacuated upriver to Pursat via Phnom Penh. On arrival by ferry at Chbar Ampeou, a southern riverside suburb of the capital, the evacuees were assembled. Cadres wearing black pajamas, rubber sandals, and red scarves, Vun recalled in a 1986 interview, distributed "clothes, medicine, blankets, mosquito nets, and scarves." Two months later, after the evacuees had arrived in Pursat, Democratic Kampuchea officials revealed the "password": "This group wearing new clothes, it's a sign for 'Vietnamese'. . . . And that's when we discovered that our new clothes and scarves were a sign of being from the Eastern Zone. . . . They accused the Eastern people of being 'Khmer bodies with Vietnamese minds.'" I enquired further:

Q. What color clothes were you wearing?

A. Men wore blue short-sleeved shirts and blue trousers, and new blue-and-white scarves. . . . The colors were mixed but the blue was more prominent than the black, and a little bit of white [i.e., a checked pattern]. . . . And when we got there they knew the sign of the Eastern Zone people. Whatever clothes they wore, they didn't use those scarves

---

70. CNA, MC-DK, Box 4, Dossier 16.

71. "Vy's Story," in Theanvy Kuoch and Mary Scully, *Cambodian Voices and Perceptions: A Collection of Materials, Experiences and Cross-Cultural Understandings*, M.A. thesis, Refugee Mental Health and Contextual Therapy, Goddard College, Plainfield, Vermont, December 1983, pp. 72–3. This was the earliest mention of the blue clothing I have been able to trace.

72. For more details see Ben Kiernan, "Genocidal Targeting: Two Groups of Victims in Pol Pot's Cambodia," in P. T. Bushnell, et al., eds., *State Organized Terror*, Boulder: Westview, 1991, pp. 207–26. The interviews recounted there were videotaped by anthropologist Dr. Gregory Stanton and Chris Munger.

in that area. . . . When we got there, there was no confusion. And if they saw us from afar they could see by our blue clothes and blue scarves that we were Eastern Zone people.

Q. Did everyone from your group wear blue scarves?

A. No other colors. Everyone was the same. One hundred percent the same.

Q. How were the people in Pursat dressed?

A. The Pursat people just wore black . . .

Q. What color scarves did they wear?

A. Their scarves were all red. . . . Noone in Pursat wore blue scarves.

Q. Did you have to wear the blue scarf?

A. We had to wear them when we went to work. If we didn't wear them, they would send us to a meeting where they would lecture us . . . They would ask me, "Why are you not wearing that scarf? These are scarves given you by *Angkar Leu*." If we didn't wear one, they would accuse us, because it was a sign for them. . . . [The Pursat people] were absolutely not allowed to wear the clothes of the Eastern Zone people . . .

All seven of Vun's family members were murdered in Pursat in 1978. He saw them arrested, accused of having "Khmer bodies with Vietnamese minds," and led away, one by one. The youngest, Vun would have been executed last, but he escaped into the forest.[73]

Sok Mat was evacuated from Region 24 to Pursat in September 1978. He recalled that when his group of one thousand arrived at Chbar Ampeou, they stayed only a morning. He too stressed that "everyone" was given new clothes, medicine, and a blue scarf. When he arrived in Pursat, Mat saw that no one besides the Eastern evacuees wore blue scarves. He claimed it was a "sign" for people to be "killed off." After a month or two, easterners realized the deadly significance of the blue scarves and stopped wearing them.[74] Huy Radi, a thirty-two-year-old Cham from the same village, told of his evacuation to Pursat in July or August 1978. Boatloads of one hundred families were taken up the Mekong from Neak Leung and disembarked at Chbar Ampeou. The three thousand deportees were then fed. Radi went on:

After we'd eaten, Angkar began to distribute clothes to us—in particular, scarves (*kromar*) and blankets. . . . The trucks came from Phnom Penh. . . . Those distributing spoke like people from the Southwest do. We didn't know them. They said, "Send someone over from your group to receive the scarves." . . . There were only blue-and-white and green-and-white scarves. . . . Everybody got a scarf. There was some shortage of blankets—one per

73. Chhun Vun, videotaped interview with the author, Peam Chor, 24 December 1986.
74. Author's interview with Sok Mat, Peam Ro, 12 January 1987.

family [only]. But as for scarves, there was one for each person. Young or old, you got a scarf. For ten people in a household there were ten scarves. . . . I saw several truckloads. A truck would come and be emptied and then another would arrive. . . . There were many scarves. . . . No one was allowed not to have one.

The wide, checkered *kromar* are popular with Khmers, who also use them as turbans, sweat bands, hand towels, and food bags. So despite the scarves' uncommon coloring and large white checks, the distribution did not strike Radi as unusual. The Eastern evacuees "were happy with the gifts Angkar had given us."

The group boarded a train for Prek Tatrau village in Maung district, near Pursat. There they joined the Northwest Zone population. But Radi noticed that locals all wore red or yellow scarves, and that "they weren't allowed to wear blue scarves" (or green ones). This fact still aroused no particular interest, beyond a recognition that Eastern deportees were being singled out. Radi had already lost an elder brother, killed for speaking the Cham language. In Pursat, "they killed people even more." Victims were regularly led away for execution, many wearing their blue scarves. Two elder sisters of Radi's were murdered in Pursat in 1978. Around December of that year, Radi saw thirty soldiers massacre twenty-four people in the hills of Pursat.

But it was not until early January 1979 that easterners in Radi's area realized the significance of the scarves they were all wearing. Locals warned them, "Don't wear that scarf if you are going far away. . . . If you keep wearing it you will be known as an Eastern Zone person, and all the Eastern Zone people are to be killed. They have been brought here to be killed. Because Eastern Zone people are Khmer bodies with Vietnamese minds." Radi only then realized that the CPK had marked the easterners with "a killing sign" to distinguish them.[75]

Lim Kuy, forty-eight, was in the Bakan district of Pursat. In front of his barber shop on the outskirts of Phnom Penh, he recalled Easterners coming to Pursat in 1978. I asked Kuy how they were dressed.

A. People from the Eastern Zone wore black clothes, except that they wore a kromar of that color. [He pointed to a blue-and-white checked scarf worn by a passerby.] That color. They were all wearing that scarf around their necks. All the same. . . . I asked them, and they said that they had arrived at Chbar Ampeou, and the Khmer Rouge had distributed them all one each. That scarf, that one over there. [He points to the blue scarf

---

75. Author's videotaped interview with Huy Radi, Kompong Trabek, 19 December 1986. The videotape, with others cited here, is in the possession of Dr. Gregory Stanton.

again, and asks the wearer to hand it to him.] Like this scarf, only the checks were a bit larger.

Q. What happened to the people from the East who arrived in Pursat?

A. I didn't see them killed but I saw them tied up. Four to ten people in a line, and they were taken to be killed. . . . While I was riding to work I saw them on the track, a small track in the forest. They tied up sometimes five people, sometimes ten people. . . . I saw it three or four times. The Khmer Rouge were riding ponies and they were tied up and being dragged, having to run along behind.[76]

Som Thon was seventeen when her family was evacuated from the East with a group of forty families in August 1978. During a two-day stay at the medicine factory at Chbar Ampeou, she said in a 1987 interview, each group of three evacuees was given medicine and a single black shirt, or (for a family), some medicine and a blue-and-white checked scarf. Thon's family received one such blue scarf. With fourteen other families, they were sent on by train to the village of Prey Khlaut in Maung district. After three months there, the local Khmer Rouge, who all wore black-and-white checked scarves, began to selectively murder the Eastern deportees. Then they would take the blue scarves from their victims and use them themselves. No other villagers were murdered while Thon was there. Of the fifteen eastern families in the village, all had blue scarves, and only seven members survived. Twelve families were wiped out. Thon's parents were both killed.[77]

Not all 1978 Eastern evacuees went via Chbar Ampeou or to the Northwest. Those from Region 21, eastern Kompong Cham, crossed the Mekong at Tonle Bet, and were sent to the Northern Zone. Many thousands of them were murdered there. In Sandan district, according to one account, 19,000 out of 20,000 deportees perished.[78] Cheav Bunleng, a former pilot, was then living in

---

76. Author's videotaped interview with Lim Kuy, Phnom Penh, 22 December 1986. Interestingly, Kuy lent credence to his evidence by stating that not only Eastern Zone people were killed. "The killings," he says, were "general." But there is no doubt from many other sources that easterners were carefully targeted in 1978. Kuy was absolutely sure that the Eastern Zone people were easily distinguishable by their unusual blue scarves. Kong Hieng, formerly from Phnom Penh, had been evacuated from Svay Rieng to Pursat in 1977. The next year he too watched the 1978 Eastern Zone evacuees arrive in Pursat, all wearing blue clothes and blue scarves. Author's interview, Phnom Penh, 13 December 1988.

77. Thon and her sister survived. "The Vietnamese saved us in time," she explained. Author's interview, Peam Ro, 12 January 1987.

78. Vickery, Cambodia 1975–1982, p. 126, citing a former naval captain. Vickery dismisses this man's figures because someone else in Sandan district considered conditions there generally "adequate." Vickery does not report having asked his second informant about the events described by the captain. A third informant remarked pertinently that widespread support for the Khmer Rouge among the peasants of Sandan in 1975–76 changed in 1977 with the arrival of new cadres who imposed considerable hardships. Author's interview with Cheav Bunleng, Creteil, 12 November 1979.

Sandan. In November 1978, trucks brought 1,000 people to his subdistrict from Region 22. Of the 110 sent to Bunleng's village, most were peasants and 16 were men. "The Khmer Rouge accused these people of being 'Vietnamese agents' but in fact they were just like the rest of us Khmers. The Khmer Rouge planned to kill them all, and then kill all the 1975 evacuees as well." By January 1979, Bunleng reports, "all 16 of the men in our village, and all of the newly arrived males in Khlaing village close by, had been executed, except for one or two who escaped."[79] In December 1978, Tep Ibrahim recalls, "boat after boat" brought evacuees across from the Eastern Zone. "Tens of thousands" of them, he claims, were landed on an island off Krauchhmar, taken by boat to Stung Trang, and then by truck to Chamcar Andong rubber plantations, where they were massacred.[80]

Survivors suggest that on their way to the Northern Zone, DK officials at Tonle Bet had apparently attempted to "mark" deportees passing through, as those passing through Chbar Ampeou had been. For instance, in June 1978, the entire Eastern village of Preal No. 1 was emptied, its people deported to the North. So Samnang, then a thirty-seven-year-old peasant, says that 70 percent of the families who passed through Tonle Bet were distributed *second-hand* scarves, either purple-and-white or black-and-white checked. He estimates that four out of five of these people later perished in the Northern Zone.[81] Uk Prathna, a rubber plantation worker in the Northern Zone from late 1976, saw "thousands" of Eastern Zone evacuees arrive in Stung Trang in 1978. "Most," he said, "wore blue-and-white checked scarves, some new, some second-hand." This distinguished them from the locals, whose scarves were red, in the case of the rubber plantation workers, and of various colors (few were blue) in the case of local peasants.[82]

79. Ibid. These killings took place, Bunleng said, "just as the Vietnamese took Kompong Thom township, and the Vietnamese forced the Khmer Rouge to retreat before they could kill the Kompong Cham people in the other five villages."

80. Author's interviews with Tep Ibrahim, Chrang Chamres, 15 September 1980 and 10 January 1986.

81. Author's interview with So Samnang, Prey Veng, 11 January 1987.

82. Nevertheless, Prathna does not believe the scarves were a "sign" of Eastern Zone origin, because the blue scarves were not all new. On this point, though, he corroborated Samnang's story. (He suggested I ask someone directly involved, not "just a witness" like himself.) One may ignore the patchy evidence from these two possibly biased State of Cambodia officials about Tonle Bet. But Prathna's scepticism about the significance of the scarves, and Samnang's recollection that their color was purple or black, rather than blue, may be authentic local or personal variations of detail that actually make the general picture look more convincing. The "identification" of victims was likely more perfunctory in a provincial center like Tonle Bet, than in the capital. But at least the systematic distribution of blue scarves in the Phnom Penh suburb of Chbar Ampeou shows that the Center planned, prepared, ordered, and executed a campaign of genocide from Phnom Penh, where the DK government was seated, and where nearly all the victims of the regime's Eastern Zone massacres

Why were Easterners given blue clothing, rather than identical clothing of some other color? Blue was an uncommon color, sure to stand out. But it may have had its own significance for the Center. It is the opposite of communist red, the color of the Khmers Rouges (*khmaer krohom*). In the 1960s, Prince Sihanouk had often distinguished the latter from the Khmers Bleus, or rightist Khmer. In the early 1970s, dissident revolutionaries active in the Southwest Zone had called themselves Blue Khmers (*khmaer khieu*), and in the East another anti-Pol Pot force, close to the Vietnamese communists, had been known as the White Khmers (*khmaer sor*). In 1978 the eastern population were also seen as dissidents. Was the CPK Center associating them with these earlier groups of traitors to the CPK cause?

A couple of details from Pol Pot's personal background may help explain the Center's choice of clothing for deportees. Each morning in Cambodia's royal palace, where Pol Pot grew up during the 1930s, prisoners were brought in on cleaning and washing detail. They wore navy blue uniforms. In the palace, a person wearing blue clothing was said to "look like a prisoner."[83] In 1950, during his studies in France, Pol Pot visited Yugoslavia and spent a summer on a work brigade in Croatia. During World War II in occupied Croatia, the Nazi puppet regime had ordered Serbs to wear blue armbands as a sign of their alien status.[84] Pol Pot was surely apprised of this.

The Massacres in the Northwest

During his evacuation from the east in 1978, Ngoy Taing Heng claims to have witnessed the murder of more than six thousand people, when Khmer Rouge deliberately blew up three large boats carrying eastern deportees off Phnom Penh. "The Mekong flowed blood-red," he says. Then, on Heng's arrival in the Northwest, "Of seven thousand people of the train, three thousand were killed there, in Pursat. Some of us were killed, some spared, selectively. I was spared because I was of Chinese origin. They did not kill Chinese, they killed the base people from Prey Veng. . . . They said they had to kill

---

passed through. The detailed evidence presented here comes from members of three different ethnic groups—Cham, Chinese, and Khmer—interviewed only several days apart in three districts (Kompong Trabek, Phnom Penh, Preah Sdach). Their evidence of events in different districts of the Northwest Zone (Maung and Bakan) is corroborated by eyewitnesses from Peam Ro district who were also evacuated via Chbar Ampeou to the Northwest.

83. Poeu Katna, interview with Eileen Blumenthal, 26 January 1991. Katna, a dancer who lived in the royal palace until 1941, said these prisoners carried water in buckets and filled people's wash basins, emptied the toilets, and did "all the dirty work." The interview went as follows: "How did these prisoners dress? Short sleeve shirt and short pants, all blue. All the same. In the palace, if someone wears blue color, they say, 'You look like a prisoner.'"

84. Mark Aarons, *Sanctuary! Nazi Fugitives in Australia*, Melbourne: Heinemann, 1989.

the Eastern base people."[85] Sah Roh, thirty-one, a Cham woman who spent the DK period in the Bakan district of Pursat, recalls:

In mid-1978, three thousand Prey Veng people came to our cooperative. At first they were put to work in the ricefields and gardens, in groups according to their ages. Two months later they were all executed. . . . None of them was spared, not even small children. . . . . At that time [the local cadres] made me a "base person," temporarily putting me aside and above the Eastern Zone people while [the latter] were being persecuted. . . . Later at a meeting of our kong [we were informed that] the Eastern Zone people were "sick" . . . ; none could be spared, they would be completely "cleaned up." . . . I was at that meeting but I didn't see the killings, which took place in the forest, where grave pits had been dug. The road in that direction was closed, we weren't allowed to go there.

I know they were killed because I lived next door to the cadres' house. . . . [One night] when they came back from killing I was still awake. They got together and were talking. They were saying, "I slashed the stomach of this one, so many months [pregnant]." They were very cruel. I lay there with no hope that I would survive . . .

A meeting was called of the elderly women from the Eastern Zone. They were divided into two kong. One was put with the base people, the second was massacred. . . . In one day over five hundred people were killed. . . . One day they killed all the girls. . . . One of the girls ran back to tell [the story, yelling]: "They didn't take us to do anything, they took us to be killed." [The cadres] were unable to make her turn back in time, and they shot her . . .

Later they collected all the youths and told them they were going to work in the gardens. . . . There were sentries guarding the place and I didn't see the killing of the youths, but I know they died. I heard [the cadres] talking about it when they got back. All gone. Of one group of Eastern Zone people, two did escape; they were smiths working with my husband [who warned them]. . . . They hid a knife under a mat and escaped after attacking their executioner. . . . At night I heard the Khmer Rouge talking about the pair's escape. They increased the sentries.

Of the Eastern Zone people in our cooperative, none of the three thousand survived except for a group of one hundred who had been selected to go and work in distant gardens. Of the ones who stayed [in the cooperative], none were left when the Vietnamese liberated us.[86]

85. Author's interview with Ngoy Taing Heng, Caen, 6 October 1979.
86. Author's interview with Sah Roh, Chrang Chamres, 10 July 1980. Her cooperative, where these 1978 events occurred, was Damnak Trap, in the Bakan district of Pursat (Region 2).

Monira, a former Lon Nol infantryman, was living in Rumlich village, also in Bakan district.[87] In 1978, over seven hundred people from Svay Rieng in the Eastern Zone arrived in his cooperative. They came in similar numbers to "every cooperative" in Bakan. Monira heard they had been moved because they were "happy to see the Vietnamese coming." These easterners were wearing "new scarves." After a period, some 1975 evacuees who were working with Khmer Rouge cadres told Monira of a document that had just arrived from the Southwest Zone. It reportedly ordered the killing of all Eastern deportees and 1975 evacuees. "We didn't know what to do," Monira says:

> The Eastern Zone people wanted to rebel and they asked the Khmer Rouge for permission to go to Phnom Penh "to fight the Vietnamese."
>
> But one day they were all shot dead by the Khmer Rouge. Then the Khmer Rouge soldiers took all the blood-soaked clothes and new scarves from the bodies, and put them aside for their own use. Then they put the bodies on carts and took them to throw into big sand-pits. Some young women who were not yet dead were buried alive. This was all done at seven or eight o'clock at night so that the people couldn't see.

Sameth, forty-five, also went to Bakan district after being evacuated from Phnom Penh in 1975. In 1978, she and many others were sent to Leach district, in the foothills of the Cardamom mountains. They walked for two days and nights, and then began clearing forest for a new cooperative. Sameth continues:

> In the first half of 1978, Eastern Zone people from Svay Rieng and Prey Veng were sent to Pursat province. They included many peasants as well as former city dwellers. A large number of them came to live in my cooperative, but the Khmer Rouge described the newcomers as "traitors" with "Vietnamese minds," and nearly every day took some of them away to be killed. About four months after their arrival they were nearly all dead; there were only a few still alive when the Pol Pot government fell. They were only women and children; all the men and many whole families had been killed. That is in my cooperative. I don't know very much about what happened in other cooperatives.
>
> The Khmer Rouge said to us that when they had finished killing the Eastern Zone people they would kill all the 1975 evacuees. We couldn't sleep at night we were so afraid.
>
> There was another group of nearly one thousand Eastern Zone people who had been sent further up in the hills, where there was no water. They

---

87. Author's interview with Monira, Chatenay-Malabry, 11 August 1979. In 1977 Rumlich had been taken over by new cadres who, unlike the previous ones, criticized Vietnam rather than the U.S.

couldn't live without water so they asked permission to move, but they were told by the Khmer Rouge to go back. However, they had all come down to our cooperative and they refused to go back. There was an argument, and the troops opened fire on them. I saw this with my own eyes. They sprayed bullets in wide arcs, and hundreds of people just fell dead on top of one another.

It took all night to drag the corpses away. Some people were not dead yet and the Khmer Rouge finished them off with knives. They were taken in ox-carts and, after being stripped of their clothes, thrown in sand ditches. There were nearly one thousand bodies in all, young and old.

Their clothes were then distributed to everyone in the cooperative, still all soaked in blood. I had to wash the set I received for weeks to get it clean. But that was how I got proper clothes to wear.[88]

Lan, evacuated to Maung district of Battambang in 1975, had settled in Thanak Run cooperative. She recalls:

In the first half of 1978, thousands of people from Svay Rieng began to arrive in Thanak Run. A group of one thousand families came, and another group of two thousand and another of three thousand.

They kept coming until after the middle of the year. Most were peasants but some were 1975 evacuees from Phnom Penh. It was said they had been deported because Vietnamese shelling along the border had made rice cultivation possible only at night. But the Khmer Rouge told us that these people were all "our enemies" and said "don't trust them." Over the next months fifty to eighty percent of these people, especially children, died or were killed. I saw a lot of the killings myself.

We 1975 evacuees were put in charge of their work and some of us, even though we now lived side by side with them, were even told to help kill some of the Svay Rieng people. In fact the Khmer Rouge stopped executing us and started executing the Svay Rieng people; they also gave us more to eat than we'd had before and gave very little to the Svay Rieng people, many of whom died from disease and starvation.

At first they would just take away the husbands "to go and help start another cooperative." But the husbands never came back and after two or three months more the Khmer Rouge would come for the man's family as well, and take them away. People were told to get their things ready to go and rejoin their husbands and father. Fifty to one hundred people would set out at night about ten o'clock, accompanied by four or five militia and two or three oxcarts. They put everything in the oxcarts.

88. Author's interview with Sameth, Melun, 17 November 1979.

But the oxcarts didn't follow the people. They went to the storehouse of the district officer. The people were all bashed to death. I know this because I asked the base people, who are a very reliable source. They trusted me with the information because they said I had a "good standpoint."

The Khmer Rouge also asked some of us 1975 evacuees to kill Svay Rieng people. They were unwilling young people between twenty and thirty years of age, threatened with death if they didn't comply with the Khmer Rouge orders. When these people came back they told me what had happened. Ten 1975 evacuees would be given axes and told to kill one hundred Svay Rieng people, who had been told to undress. They were meant to strike them on the back of the neck. They didn't want to kill them but they had no choice. They even killed young children with a single blow of an axe.

The Svay Rieng people didn't just come to my cooperative but to all the cooperatives in the area. I am just talking about what I saw with my own eyes in my cooperative.[89]

Mrs. Seng, a Phnom Penh evacuee, had gone to another village in Maung district. In 1977 the village had been taken over by cadres from the Southwest, who killed over fifty people. Then in October 1978, thousands of people from Svay Rieng and Prey Veng started arriving on foot. Twelve thousand came to Seng's cooperative in October and November. Tens of thousands of others were settled in nearby villages. Seng continues:

About a month after their arrival the Khmer Rouge started killing off those people. They killed men, women, and even little babies. I saw them call families to take them away: every night they took three to five families.

Those Eastern Zone people were extremely frightened, and didn't know what to do. When they arrived they asked me what we were getting to eat there, and I told them only a tin of rice or so per day. They became very scared. They had had enough food in the East and they thought they'd die of starvation now. Many soon became sick and some did die, but only a few; most were executed by the Khmer Rouge.

Some of them were Phnom Penh people who had gone to the East in 1975, but most were eastern peasants. A number were disarmed Khmer Rouge soldiers. My cooperative was divided into seven worksites, numbered one to seven, and each worksite contained over one hundred families. In some worksites every single Easterner died or was killed. Some newborn babies and pregnant women were also executed by the soldiers. Some people were tortured before they died and forced to tell the names of

89. Author's interview with Lan, Creteil, 18 November 1979. In 1978 she was in Sre Khnao village.

their friends, who were taken away and killed. For that reason we began to fear we would be associated with them and would be executed too, if we talked to them, so we began to keep away from them. The place where I worked milling rice was where the district officers lived. There was a rice mill and large fields, and across the oxcart track there was another worksite. One night they called sixty families, young and old, from the two worksites, to take them away and kill them all that night. They told them to get their belongings and clothes ready for a spell clearing forest. The sixty families were taken about ten kilometers away. The next day the driver of an oxcart came back from there. He told me that all those people had had their throats cut.

The Eastern Zone people were very scared the whole time. When the Vietnamese came, only eleven hundred of them were still alive, out of twelve thousand.[90]

Western Zone Cadres Take Over the Northwest

The March 1978 destruction of Chou Chet's network in the Western Zone had left the Zone in the hands of the Center and its local allies, Sem Pal and Paet Soeung. Within months they had selected and trained a new generation of cadres, chosen from among the "full rights" population. This cohort, much younger and including many females, was sent into the Northwest Zone in mid-1978. A CPK district chief from the West reports that eight thousand people, led by forty "hot and tough" cadres, were dispatched from Toek Phos district. Eighty percent of them were from the small "full rights" category, which made up only ten percent of the district's population. The rest were chosen from among the "candidates," who comprised thirty percent. The only full rights people to remain in the district were those with "important tasks." All eight thousand sent to the Northwest became village and team chiefs there.[91] Applying these figures to the other five districts of Kompong Chhnang, over forty-five thousand Westerners would have participated in this exodus.

The ground was carefully prepared. In early April, "higher authorities" ordered cooperative chiefs in the northwest to identify "suspicious elements" among their charges. "The list was to include all individuals—and their families—who were former regulars in the Lon Nol army, minor officials, school-teachers, village headmen, chiefs of ten-family units in areas under Lon Nol's

90. Author's interview with Seng, Strasbourg, 31 October 1979. In 1978 she was in Prek Chik village.
91. Author's interview with a former CPK district chief in the Western Zone. Kompong Chhnang, 4 September 1980.

control, and anyone educated or trained in Thailand or Vietnam." One Region 5 official found that seven hundred of the nine hundred families in his cooperative met one of these descriptions.[92] The crackdown came at exactly the same time as that in the East. Ros Nhim, secretary of the Northwest Zone, was arrested on 11 June 1978, eight days after So Phim's suicide. He was told he was being "transferred to Phnom Penh." Mok replaced him as Zone secretary. Two weeks later Nhim's deputy, Keu, and the secretary of Region 3, Phok Sary, met the same fate. Nhim's son, Diel, husband of So Phim's daughter, was arrested on 15 June.[93] Diel and his wife were both murdered.

Veteran revolutionary Heng Teav, then age sixty, was a member of the Zone committee and director of the state agricultural worksite in Region 3. He was arrested in June along with his entire staff of twenty-two. Troops escorted Teav by truck to Battambang, saying he was going "to meet the higher level." His bodyguards were arrested next. One escaped, but another, Teav's nephew, was imprisoned along with his child, and a brother-in-law's family of five was massacred. After four months' detention in Battambang, Teav and his wife were taken to Phnom Penh. Fortunately, they did not go to Tuol Sleng, but ended up in a Western Zone jail in Kompong Speu. Teav was suffering from fever and his wife was also ill. "In Kompong Speu they were killing people all the time, but they did not get to me. They killed the stronger people first."[94]

Region 5. In mid-1977, Ros Nhim's son Diel had briefly taken over from Hing as secretary of Region 5. He was now replaced by a Southwest Zone cadre, Heng Rin.[95] In late May 1978, Western Zone officials had already begun to take over the Sisophon district of Region 5. Refugees reported that "under the old leaders a lot were allowed to slip by. But the new leaders punished every infraction. They were unbearable." On 26 June, Western units took over the Thmar Puok district headquarters, also in Region 5. They "arrested the five-man ruling committee and disarmed the 100-man district civil militia. From there the operation fanned out to the district's 15 cooperatives." Then, on 5 July, the newcomers "officially announced that of the 70,000 citizens in the

92. *FEER,* 25 August 1978, p. 37.
93. Entry in an S-21 cadre's handwritten notebook, dated 4 July 1978 (Nhim and Diel), and author's interview with Heng Teav, Phnom Penh, 14 January 1986 (Keu). For a listing of "Northwestern Region Leadership Purges, 1977–1978," see Carney, in Jackson, ed., *Cambodia 1975–1978,* pp. 105–6.
94. Author's interview with Heng Teav, 1986.
95. S. Heder, *Reflections on Cambodian Political History,* p. 6. Heng Rin was himself arrested on 16 November 1978 (Jackson, ed., *Cambodia 1975–1978,* p. 106).

district, 40,000 were traitors who had collaborated with the U.S. Central Intelligence Agency and concealed the names of former Lon Nol soldiers and agents of Thailand and Vietnam."[96] A farmer who escaped to Thailand in late July reported being told by a relative in the Democratic Kampuchea army "that at least two-thirds of the 10,000 people in one particular area were marked for death." The leaders responsible for this plan were identified as having come from Kampot, in the Southwest Zone, as well as Kompong Chhnang in the West.[97]

In early 1978, about fifty Cambodian refugees reached Thailand each month. In April the numbers "increased sharply to more than 100 a month." But in a four-week period in July and August, no fewer than 350 Cambodians fled to Thailand from Thmar Puok and Preah Net Preah districts of Region 5 alone. The refugees now included many base people as well as Phnom Penh evacuees, and, for the first time, most were men. This was partly because of the immense dangers flight now presented. The *Guardian* reported, "Only about one in three of those who set out actually survive—the others fall victim to mines, razor sharp bamboos, and starvation or exposure, if they are not shot by military patrols. Sen said that of the 21 in his group only four survived the journey. In another group of 44 from Thmar Puok only 15 remain, in a group of 38 from Neak Ta only 16 managed to get across, and in another group of 60, just seven arrived safely."[98]

In June, airplane mechanic Van was warned by a Khmer Rouge soldier from Takeo to "watch out, something special is about to happen again" in Preah Net Preah district. It would start on 24 June and continue until 24 August, the soldier said. Van adds, "On 24 June I started to see them take away whole families." Female Southwest Zone officials led groups from three subdistricts to the district prison in Chup. At 9 P.M. each evening for a week, these women would take twenty to thirty prisoners out, kill them, and throw their bodies into pits. "Everyone was frightened. In Chakrey village we could hear the screams from the forest nearby. . . . The victims' clothes were distributed to us the next day. . . . We were all short of clothes. We knew the clothes. We could smell the bodies too." The killings devastated Chakrey's population of over 400, about 140 families. Fewer than ten adult males remained alive by 12 August. Van decided to flee.[99]

96. Richard Nations, "Another 40,000 'CIA Traitors,'" *FEER*, 25 August 1978, pp. 37–39. "Refugees from nearby cooperatives confirm this extraordinary declaration."

97. "Still More Blood-Letting?," *Asiaweek*, 25 August 1978, p. 25.

98. See Robert Whymant, "Hunger Spurs Flight of Refugees," *Guardian Weekly* (London), 6 August 1978; *FEER*, 25 August 1978, p. 37; *Asiaweek*, 25 August 1978, p. 25; "A New Surge from Cambodia," *Asiaweek*, 8 September 1978, p. 16.

99. Author's interview with Van, Strasbourg, 1 November 1979: "1978 was the real year for killings."

Ouch Sruy says that in his part of Preah Net Preah district, "murders started up again in July 1978, with the arrival of the Khmer Rouge coming from Kompong Chhnang." Sruy describes these Western Zone cadres as "veritable savages ignorant of any rule of humanity." They began murdering teachers, doctors, other intellectuals, customs officials, soldiers, and members of the police force of the old regime. Sruy made up his mind to escape. His friend, former lieutenant Chheng Leang, who accompanied him from Takeo in 1975, agreed to go along. "When the Western Zone cadres came to share power with the Southwesterners, who were mostly women, I just knew I had to leave, or I would die. . . . A week before, they had killed fifteen people. . . . Only fifty people were left in the village. All the men were gone."

Meanwhile, Western Zone cadres had arrested Seng Horl, along with another former teacher, on 23 July. Horl overheard his captors saying that "they had killed over twenty people that day, and they were so exhausted, they would put me in prison overnight and kill me off tomorrow." They tied Horl to three other prisoners in the Preah Net Preah subdistrict jail. At midnight, they took the other teacher outside and murdered him. Later Horl and another prisoner, a former army lieutenant, managed to free themselves and disappear into the night. Horl spent three days in the forest, where he met five local base people, also hiding out. He entered a village in search of food, and found that the peasants hated their new rulers. "When the Southwest and Western Zone people came and killed the Northwesterners, who were their children and relatives, the northwest base people turned to the Phnom Penh people." Horl says the 1978 killings, the worst he had known, also took the lives of ordinary base people for the first time. The villagers "cooked rice for me to eat, and gave me clothes, a knife, a scarf and some corn to get to Thailand." Eight villagers, fearing for their own lives, decided to come too.

Horl met up with Van, Sruy, and Leang and they left for Thailand with thirty other men. Eight of the escape party were shot dead en route by soldiers and five others killed by mines and bamboo stakes. Twenty-one men successfully crossed the border on 21 August 1978. For Sruy, Leang, Horl, and Van, it was the end of a long, circuitous trail that had taken them all out of Phnom Penh in 1975, first to Takeo, then to Region 5, to Thailand, and, eventually, France.[100]

In another part of Preah Net Preah district, San, the former Sisophon schoolteacher, heard in July that the authorities planned to kill thirty-five people in his village whose backgrounds were known: former police, soldiers,

100. Author's interviews with Chheng Leang and Ouch Sruy, Stains, 11 August 1979; Sruy's handwritten 4-page "Rapport sur le régime des Khmers Rouges," 1979, at p. 2; and Seng Horl, Creteil, 3 December 1979.

teachers, a female secretary. "They arrested ten people one night, twelve the next, thirteen the next, and got all thirty-five." Then they accused San of being an associate of the purged Region 5 secretary, Hing. "I had had nothing at all to eat for three days. I was swelling up, and ill. I didn't dare stay at home." San left his wife and two children and fled to Thailand. His wife died of disease two weeks later.[101]

Chnay, the former fine arts student from Phnom Penh University, had rejoined his chalat in early 1978. In April, he says, the first Western Zone cadres arrived from Kompong Chhnang. The newcomers claimed they were out to demolish the previous "regime" and "get the Khmer Rouge." They spoke reassuringly, encouraged people to air their grievances, and attempted to uncover everyone's background. Immediately, however, "people were led away by soldiers every day and night," and the Southwest cadres remained in place. In mid-1978, Chnay managed to visit his parents for the first time in two years. His father, sixty-eight, feared imminent arrest, but nevertheless advised Chnay not to attempt an escape, hoping that things might eventually improve for his son. Not long after, Chnay heard that his father had been taken away and presumably killed, along with a younger son and a daughter. Three weeks later, Chnay fled with two other brothers, their wives, a sister, and a brother-in-law. Near the Thai border the party of seven reached deep water. All three women drowned while trying to swim across. The four men arrived safely on 13 September.[102]

Twenty-four year-old peasant Sarun recalls the arrival of the Western Zone cadres in June or July. In his part of Preah Net Preah, they even arrested the Southwest Zone cadres, and also stepped up repression of the population, including members of Sarun's chalat. There were many killings. At the worksite, Sarun saw Western cadres bashing people to death. One evening they killed five of his friends, three young men and two women. Sarun feared they would come for him too, and he left for Thailand alone. After a six-day journey through the jungle, he crossed the border in early August. Later refugees brought news that Sarun's sister, who also worked in the chalat, had been executed after his escape.[103]

Former medic Kem Hong Hav agrees that in 1978, slaughter "began on a mass scale." By August, of Hav's krom of over four hundred people, only forty-nine survived. He too fled to Thailand, with thirty-six of the others. Thirteen perished during the trek, and only twelve remained in the krom. In the whole of Preah Net Preah subdistrict, he says, only two hundred men and

---

101. Author's interview with San, Paris, 29 May 1980. San said "1978 was the worst year for killings."
102. Author's interviews with Srey Pich Chnay, Surin, 5 and 15 March and 19 April 1979.
103. Author's interview with Sarun, Aranyaprathet, 1 April 1979.

twenty-two hundred women survived.[104] In the neighboring subdistrict of Phnom Liep, a village comprising five hundred families in 1975 was reduced to twenty families in late 1978.[105] Of the ninety thousand people in the whole of Preah Net Preah district at the end of 1976, just over sixty thousand survived two years later.[106]

Thmar Puok district was little better. Hong Var describes 1978 and early 1979 as by far the worst time: about five hundred people, half the population of her village, died or were killed. People caught complaining were executed. If someone accidentally broke a plowshare working in the fields, they would be accused of negligence with Angkar's property and shot. By 1978, everyone in the village hated the CPK bitterly.[107] Base person and local schoolteacher Chik adds that in his village, 1978 also saw large numbers of deaths. In late June new cadres arrived from Kompong Chhnang. The next month they executed the local Northwest cadre and his family of five. As elsewhere, Western cadres made no attempt to court the base people. "They did not trust the village militia who were the local poor and ignorant." They also targeted educated people. On 18 August, three village schoolteachers were arrested and taken away to be killed. Chik, the only surviving teacher, feared he would be next, but he decided that to flee would condemn his family to death; "they would be evacuated into the interior, with no crops to eat, and would starve." He was arrested plowing a field the same day. But in the night he managed to escape, and he made it to Thailand. In 1979 he heard his family had survived.[108]

Another base person, Savy, recalls that in late 1978, entire groups of eight to ten people had to subsist on one tin of rice per day. The Southwest cadres had accused the Northwesterners of "feeding us gruel when rice was plentiful, but they soon were giving us less than before." Savy, who recalls Ros Nhim inspecting his Sisophon worksite several times before his arrest, comments, "He and the Northwest cadres were better than the Southwest, because they did not kill their own people very much." At the end of 1978, "the Southwest cadres took away all the base people, krom chiefs and kong chiefs, to kill them. But the Vietnamese came on time."[109]

In other parts of the Northwest, the effects of the 1978 purges varied in detail, but the pattern of oppression intensified. In Region 3, cadres from

104. Author's interview with Kem Hong Hav, Stains, 13 October 1979.
105. Author's interview with Ang Ngeck Teang, Toulouse, 9 December 1979.
106. Author's interview with San, Paris, 1980. San, a Region 5 statistician in 1975–76, was given these figures by a veteran CPK official whom he had befriended in the Region statistical department.
107. Author's interviews with Hong Var, Aranyaprathet, 2 and 3 April 1979.
108. Author's interview with Chik, Strasbourg, 1 November 1979.
109. Author's interview with Savy, Toulouse, 11 December 1979.

Kampot killed over three hundred chalat workers.[110] According to an ethnic Chinese living there, in his village of forty-six hundred, ten people had been executed in 1977, but Southwest forces murdered another two hundred in three months in late 1978.[111] In Region 1, Western Zone cadres introduced a new farming technique. The sandy soil of their home province of Kompong Chhnang is best worked with small plowshares, and the Westerners brought many such implements with them. They insisted that people in Sangker district use these, even though the soil there was thicker and loamier and the small plowshares did not penetrate it effectively.[112] To Hosan, a Cham in Battambang, reported that 1978 brought less starvation than before, but a harsher work regime. A dam project on the Sangker River claimed "at least ten deaths every day" for most of the year. There were also "many secret killings." The result was that in 1979, only six hundred adults survived of the nine hundred families in the subdistrict in 1975.

Western cadres brought a song with them to teach the children of the Northwest. It highlights a brutality spawned by war and nourished by the new CPK culture:

Baribo village sheds its tears;
The enemy dropped bombs and staged a coup.
The screams of a combatant; friend, where are you ?
The hated enemy killed my friend.
When you died away, friend, you were still naked,
Chest and stomach asunder, liver and spleen gone,
You floated them away like a river's current.
Removal of liver and spleen is a cause for sadness.
The ricelands of my mother are far in the distance.
The sun slants over the green hills.
When you died away, friend, you reminded me
That the hated enemy had swallowed Kampuchea.[113]

The tables had now turned. The Northwest was not the only area of Western Zone expansion. Following the arrest of Kang Chap in early August,

110. Author's interview with Nguon Song, Strasbourg, 31 October 1979. This occurred near Thmar Koul.
111. Author's interview, Limoges, 7 December 1979. The interviewee requested anonymity. The 1978 victims included his brother, brother-in-law, and nephew. Another of the two hundred victims "was killed because he had a Citizen watch, and was called from his house and bashed to death twenty meters away. I saw the body, and many other murders. I saw over ten bodies, and fifty in another place."
112. Author's interview with Pa Iné, Melbourne, 28 August 1982. The informant lived in Sangker district.
113. Author's recording of songs learnt in Region 4 by children of the Pel family, Toul, 4 November 1979.

Western Zone military commander Paet Soeung was sent to replace him as CPK secretary of the Northern Zone.[114] Accompanied by one of his officers from Longvek, Phak Lim, Soeung spent a month in Preah Vihear province, then set up his headquarters at Angkor Wat.[115]

Meanwhile, Soeung's former deputy, Meth, who had established the Democratic Kampuchea air force in 1975,[116] was constructing a new military airport in Kompong Chhnang. Elements of Meth's 502nd Division had been sent there in February 1978 to study under about fifty Chinese technical advisors, who supervised the work and provided the machinery. The project's labor force consisted of Eastern Zone soldiers; about twenty thousand arrived at the site by July 1978. Meth's troops were forbidden to talk to them. A member of the 502nd recalls, "They worked digging the earth and leveling the land. We worked on trucks, and on the machinery. There was no contact." Meth's deputy, the northeasterner Lovei, oversaw the site.

In August, the soldier continues, groups of thirty to fifty Eastern troops began to be taken away at night. They were taken in trucks headed towards the Tonle Sap and massacred. More than five groups, totaling around six hundred dead, disappeared each month until October. "As far as I know, the orders to kill the Eastern Zone troops came from Phnom Penh. They were accused of not having fought hard on the border. . . . Those who were not killed were given the heavy and dangerous work."[117]

The Hunt for Ethnic Vietnamese and Khmer Krom Quickens

Around the time of Pol Pot's visit to Suong in early 1978, DK officials in Kratie, not far to the north, executed a number of "Chinese and part-Vietnamese."[118] In another part of Kratie, cadres announced in 1978 that Chinese, Chams, and part-Vietnamese formed an "enemy network" and were "not to be spared." A local witness reports that "from what I saw they started killing over sixty people in this way. Some Chinese were executed because they were considered lazy, even though they were just sick." The racial targeting soon spread to the Khmer population. "They started killing the part-Vietnamese first, then the people who were lazy at work, then all the new people."[119] In Region 24, a witness adds that the Center's May suppression of the Eastern Zone intensified the pogroms: "Many Khmer Rouge there were married to Vietnamese or

114. S. Heder's interview with Phak Lim, Sa Keo, 9 March 1980. Lim says Sueung arrived in the North on 9 August 1978, a week after Kang Chap's arrest.
115. Heder interview with Phak Lim, Sa Keo, 8 March 1980.
116. Heder interview with Phak Lim, Sa Keo, 9 March 1980.
117. Author's interview with Chhin Phoeun, Kong Pisei, 17 September 1980.
118. Author's interview with Mon, Phnom Penh, 5 July 1980.
119. Author's interview with Chey Sopheara, Phnom Penh, 23 September 1980.

part-Vietnamese. In 1978, new cadres came and killed these people with Vietnamese connections."[120]

Also in May 1978, Southwest cadres arriving in the Northwest Zone proclaimed Pol Pot's dictum that each Khmer had to kill thirty Vietnamese.[121] In Preah Net Preah district, San dates the first arrests of ethnic Vietnamese to March and April 1978. But here, "they had already sent all Vietnamese back home; only people with the slightest amount of Vietnamese blood remained, and Khmer Krom. . . . They arrested people with [Khmer Krom] surnames like Thach, Son, Nhoeng. They killed wives and children too; the village chief was told to present those to be killed. In my village two families of Khmer Krom were killed. . . . They executed an entire family of ten to twelve Khmer Krom behind Chakrey village. . . . I saw their bodies while grazing the cattle." In another village in Preah Net Preah, Southwest and Western forces began the new wave of purges in June. First they killed an ethnic Vietnamese couple. Then, in a nearby village, they arrested several Khmer Krom, who disappeared. Two days later the purge swept up former Lon Nol officials. In July, Western cadres in Horl's village of the same district slaughtered two families of ethnic Vietnamese and a Khmer Krom family of six. In Thmar Puok, three part-Vietnamese were executed in Chik's village in 1978.[122] In Region 3 in mid-1978, authorities "killed everyone who could speak Vietnamese," including five families of twenty people in one village.[123]

In the Southwest itself, a peasant from Region 25 reported the massacre in 1978 of over forty people in his village, "All Vietnamese and Chinese were rounded up and wiped out."[124] A CPK defector from the Central Zone has thrown light on these events. He reported that in 1978, "Angkar ordered the chiefs of Zones, Regions, districts, subdistricts, and village cooperatives to implement a screening of the population of the Vietnamese race and of the Khmer population of the Kampuchea Krom race. The government officials had to apprehend all these people and kill them, even the very small children."[125] Other sources confirm this new "nationwide campaign against the few remaining Vietnamese, their spouses, or ethnic Khmer born in Vietnam."[126] In late 1978, Southwest

120. Author's interview with Ngoy Taing Heng, Caen, 6 October 1979.

121. Author's interview with Ouch Borith, New Haven, 2 July 1992. Borith was then in Koh Kralor, south of Battambang. This coincided with Phnom Penh Radio's 10 May 1978 broadcast along these lines. See above, p. 393.

122. Author's interviews with San, Paris, 29 May 1980; Yun, Creteil, 12 November 1979; Seng Horl, Creteil, 3 December 1979; and Chik, Strasbourg, 1 November 1979.

123. Author's interview with Phi, Toulouse, 11 December 1979.

124. Author's interview with Ney, 66, a peasant in Prek Tahing, Koh Thom, 1 August 1980.

125. Lim Mean, a CPK defector interviewed by Thai officials on 15 December 1978. French translation of the Thai debriefing, provided by R.-P. Paringaux , p. 29.

126. Carney, in Jackson, ed., *Cambodia 1975–1978*, p. 83 n. 3; Vickery, *Cambodia 1975–1982*, says of the 1978 Eastern Zone massacres, "Those with Vietnamese ethnicity . . . were killed on the spot" (p. 136).

cadres stationed in the Central Zone proclaimed that "the Khmer Krom had all become Vietnamese—Khmer bodies with Vietnamese minds."[127] Like the Chams, Khmer Krom were considered contaminated by centuries of contact with Vietnamese.

Kidnapping Khmer Krom from Vietnam. Phnom Penh tailor Tam Eng escaped to Vietnam in December 1975. There she spent six months among Khmer Krom in An Giang province. She found Khmer and Vietnamese "living side by side, getting on well, doing business together." Politically, however, "Khmer were prepared to have Kampuchea Krom be part of Cambodia again, if Cambodia attacked." They often refused to speak Vietnamese. "But the Vietnamese did not worry, and allowed the Khmer to do what they liked. There was no conflict, or different status. The Khmers grew rice, and the Vietnamese bought and sold it. They were not enemies. Khmer farmers were rich, and had a lot of land."[128]

In Region 13 of the Southwest, Tram Kak district officials had explained in 1977 that "the Khmer Krom were to be brought to live in Cambodia while the Khmer were to be sent to live in Kampuchea Krom."[129] Mok and his cadres added that they wanted large numbers of Khmer Krom to come, so that DK "would have many forces" to fight Vietnam.[130] The next year, CPK officials in Kampot claimed that the Vietnamese had "killed every last Khmer Krom, and stolen their rice and cattle." They warned their subjects to "be careful" of the Vietnamese.[131]

In 1978, DK raiding parties from the Southwest kidnapped thousands of Khmer Krom from their villages inside Vietnam. In a two-week campaign in March 1978, a DK division successfully occupied the Bay Nui district of An Giang. A Khmer peasant recalls the arrival of twenty DK troops in Prey Svay village early one evening, "The Khmer Rouge came in fighting and shooting.

127. Author's interviews with locals in Santuk district, Kompong Thom, 16 October 1980.

128. Author's interview with Tam Eng, Paris, 24 January 1980. She lived in Svay Tong district. A Khmer who escaped into Vietnam and spent two years further north along the border, agrees. "The Khmer living in Vietnam live like Vietnamese, and do not talk about 'Kampuchea Krom' . . . Vietnamese girls like Khmer boys. . . . [In Vietnam] they did not teach the children to hate [Khmers] as in Kampuchea." Author's interview with Heng, 8 August 1979.

129. Author's interview with Nat, a peasant woman in Kraing Ta Chan, 16 July 1980. This policy, Nat said, was proclaimed to a meeting of thousands of village cadres and base people at Daem Beng in 1977, to explain the deportation of base people, including herself, to the border district of Kirivong.

130. Author's interview with a former DK subdistrict chief in Region 13, Kirivong, 25 August 1980. In the Tram Kak district of the same Region, it was said that Democratic Kampuchea needed "to bring our people to protect Khmer territory, not let them remain outside." Author's interview, Prey Piey, 16 July 1980.

131. Author's interview with Leng, Kampot, 29 August 1980.

First they said, 'Do not worry. . . . Eat your meal and stay here, brothers. We are going to fight on further. . . . We will all stay here together.'" Another peasant agrees, "At first they talked nicely. Some of us believed them. Their propaganda was very, very tasty. I believed them."

The DK army may have hoped to hold Bay Nui. If so, that ambition lasted only two hours. At 9 P.M., new orders came: evacuate everyone to Cambodia. Troops announced, "The Vietnamese are coming to wipe you out." The peasant from Prey Svay says, "We were not allowed to bring oxcarts, and only one or two tins of rice. They said there was plenty further up, three meals per day, trucks, everything." The Khmer Krom did not want to leave. The DK troops drove them out and burnt Prey Svay village to the ground. They evacuated seven subdistricts; only 30 percent of the population escaped evacuation to DK. The monks of twenty Buddhist wats were also kidnapped, and forcibly defrocked on the way north. The DK troops quickly returned to the offensive against Vietnam "to gather in all the others who had remained" in Bay Nui. The next month, thirty Democratic Kampuchea soldiers occupied Svay Chek village, in a neighboring district, twelve kilometers inside Vietnam. They made no attempt at spreading propaganda. Firing B-40 rockets, they immediately began to drive the village's three hundred Khmer families back into Cambodia.

A peasant woman from Tram Kak, one of many base people deported from that district to Kirivong since 1976, recalls watching Khmer Krom cross the border into Region 13. "They kept coming for seven days, driven against their will. . . . They had a harder time than even the deportees. They had nothing to eat, and could be killed. The Khmer Rouge hated them."[132] Over twenty thousand kidnapped Khmer Krom soon found themselves classed as "depositees," working twelve hours per day. The rice they produced was taken away in trucks, and the workers subsisted on gruel. "Nine months there was like nine years," a peasant remarks. Rations of a tin of rice per day were cooked privately. Husbands, wives, and teenagers were all separated. Teenagers ate communally, and some of the youths were conscripted into DK's 250th Regiment. A village of 250 families was divided into five kong ha (fifty-family groups); ten families disappeared from the village by the end of 1978. In another kong, two men were taken away, and fifty people died of starvation. In another group of two thousand Khmer Krom, which included one hundred defrocked monks, starvation wiped out a hundred families, and three families whose members stole food quickly disappeared.

One Khmer Krom recalls the captives being asked if they could speak Vietnamese, "We all said, No. If we had said Yes, we would have been killed. We all had to do family biographies. If we said we had any relatives still in Vietnam,

---

132. Author's interview with Sok, Kraing Ta Chan, 16 July 1980.

we would be killed. Or if we had been officials, not peasants."[133] Three thousand Cambodians who had fled Region 13 for Vietnam from 1972 to 1974 were carefully screened out from the native Khmer Krom. Fifty families were exterminated. The rest, including twenty families from Svay Chek village in An Giang, were taken further inside DK territory. Chip, a peasant who had fled Region 13 in 1972, was sent back there with his oxcart and two cattle. He and the other returned refugees were moved three times within Kirivong. After six months, they had to move again, leaving their carts and possessions behind.

Ninety-nine families of returnees were sent to Tram Kak district, Mok's birthplace, run by his brother-in-law San. At a meeting in Wat Chambak, the returnees were told, "You Upper Khmers who went to Lower Kampuchea, *Angkar* sends you to District 105 (Tram Kak), because you have studied well already. Don't worry about your goods. *Angkar* will look after you. There is plenty [in the Damrei Romeal mountains to the west]. We are leaving the Khmer Krom in District 109. . . . They are being observed for their thoughts, because they are from Vietnam. The Upper Khmer are to be separated from the Lower Khmer."

But the work regimen was "much harder" in Tram Kak than Kirivong. DK officials said "the rear should help the front." Every morning, each worker had to shift a cubic meter of earth by 8:30 A.M., then go to a collective worksite where targets were set for groups of thirty for the rest of the day. Like the Khmer Krom back in Kirivong, the returned refugees were classed as deportees, but they ate communally. "Anyone who broke an implement such as a plow or axe was called an 'enemy,' intent on destroying communal property." Among the ninety-nine families, four people, including a woman, were executed over the next four months, and more than ten elderly people died.[134]

Meanwhile the search continued for Khmer Krom among the general population. A former Mike Force trooper who had hid his identity for three years was arrested in mid-1978 and sent to Tram Kak district prison. He and his family were executed.[135]

The Chams in 1978

Around May 1978, a helicopter flew over Veal Andaeuk village in Region 21 and dropped propaganda leaflets. The leaflets proclaimed that the Eastern Zone CPK had to be eliminated because they were working with the Viet-

---

133. Author's interviews with four Khmers forcibly evacuated by DK troops from Vietnam into Cambodia in March-April 1978. Phnom Den, 26 August 1980.

134. Author's interview with Chip, Phnom Den, 26 August 1980.

135. Author's interview with Savann, an inmate in Kraing Ta Chan prison in Tram Kak at the time. Preah Bat Chuon Chum, 26 August 1980. The victim was Chao Kong.

namese—"helping them with medicine, cloth and hoes." Southwest forces arrived, replaced many of the local officials and militia, even schoolteachers, and executed them. A new official decreed that a Cham *hakkem* living there was defying the ban on religion and therefore should be used for "fertilizer." The hakkem and his wife were both executed.[136]

In July 1978, Sop Khatidjah, a Cham widow, and her family were moved from Veal Andaeuk to Tham Tou village. The killings continued there. Over the next six months twelve families of Chams were executed, thirty people in all. Tham Tou, a former Cham village which had been emptied, was now resettled by "maybe 2,000 families," mostly Chams, probably recent arrivals like Khatidjah. Some retained minor positions there, and those Chams who did not wish to eat pork were allowed to exchange foods with the Khmers.[137] In nearby Peuk village, on the other hand, Chams were still forced to eat pork. It remained forbidden to speak Cham or practice religion, but the Southwest forces raised food rations and also provided new clothes. Khatidjah insists, though, that 1978 was the worst year for killings of Chams, whom Southwesterners singled out for execution.[138]

Kut El, a young rubber plantation worker and base person from the east, also stayed in the Zone after the 1978 Southwest takeover. His village in Region 21 had comprised eighty families, fifty of them Cham. The Southwest forces brought a severe reduction in rations and also the worst spate of killings. Toward the end of the year, they killed thirteen families in the village. Kut El observes that the Eastern Zone forces, in his own village "and generally," had treated Chams better than the Southwest forces did.[139]

Further south, in Peareang district, Nhek Davi, a Khmer woman, recalls, "The serious killings began in 1978. In mid-year, cadres executed two families considered to be part-Vietnamese, then three families of new people were taken away, followed by three Cham families. They said the Cham nationality was 'rebellious,' and to be 'abolished.' There was more killing in nearby villages."[140] El Yusof says that on 17 August 1978, Southwest troops stationed in Peareang murdered "over one hundred families of Chams and Khmers" near his village. Yusof remarks ruefully that even Chams who had agreed to eat pork were killed in the end.

136. The hakkem's name was Haji Ismael. See Chapter 7, above, pp. 268–69.

137. Toun Ibrahim says, "After all the killing in our subdistrict in 1977, the Khmer Rouge could afford to relax things a little in 1978 as they went off to oppress other subdistricts."

138. Nate Thayer's interview with Sop Khatidjah, 58, Nong Samet, September 1984. Author's translation.

139. From 1975 to 1977, El says, six people in his village were killed by Eastern Zone cadres, mostly for allegedly failing to work hard. Nate Thayer's interview with Kut El, 25, Nong Samet, September 1984.

140. Author's interview with Nhek Davi, Melun, 20 November 1979.

Bunheang Ung, who witnessed a massacre of fifteen hundred people in Peareang in July-August 1978, says the victims fell into two categories. The first were "new people," or former city dwellers, excepting some with relatives among the base people. Second, "Chinese and Chams were preferentially selected" for execution, "though for the most part only those Chinese who were 'new people.'"[141] Thus, in the case of urban evacuees and Chinese, a connection with the bases worked in their favor. But it did not save Chams, who were targeted for destruction even though they were mostly base people. These mid-1978 massacres of Chams constituted a campaign of racial extermination.

In Kompong Trabek, Region 24, Haji Ismael recalls that in 1978 Southwest troops "killed the Cham cadres and the other Eastern Zone cadres during the time So Phim was taken away." Here the Chams of Khmaer Islam village, along with the bulk of the area's Khmer population, were evacuated to the Northwest in November 1978.[142] Ismael says the Easterners were labeled "Khmer bodies with Vietnamese minds" and that "Chams were also accused of this, there was no distinction." One of Ismael's sons was killed by Southwest troops before the evacuation. Two more were killed in Pursat in early January 1979, in Democratic Kampuchea's last days. One day they were summoned to a meeting with people from every local household.[143] They found Southwest troops waiting for them.

There were 3 or 4 soldiers standing there with 3 AK rifles. They had only said a few words when they began shooting. Many people died. Out of 150, only 3 survived to come back here. None of the over 40 Chams in that group survived. They were all children of this village, young men and women who had been cooks for the Khmer Rouge.

The Khmer Rouge said the Muslim Khmers were all enemies, recalcitrants. We did not know what that meant, just that you were killed if you were it.

Ismael and his wife survived, but three of their four children perished in Pursat. Of thirty-six Khmaer Islam villagers killed in DK, twenty-three were murdered in 1978 alone, and at least fifteen more died of other causes in the same year. Ismael estimates that of thirty entire families who perished by 1979, eighteen families were wiped out in 1978 alone.[144]

141. M. Stuart-Fox and Bunheang Ung, The Murderous Revolution, p. 146.
142. "Many thousands of people were taken. Only a few families stayed here to fish for the Khmer Rouge; three families. . . . All other Chams were evacuated. We all went together but were (again) separated when we got to Pursat." Author's interview with Haji Ismael, Kompong Trabek, 16 January 1986.
143. They had been put to work in a rice warehouse in Phnom Srap. Ibid.
144. Ibid.

Sen Osman, from Region 23, agrees that 1978 was the year the most Chams and Khmers died or disappeared. Late that year, five families were evacuated from Takeo village; three days later, six or seven families followed. They walked to Phnom Penh and then traveled by train to Maung. Osman traveled with his parents and a brother. Over the next three to four months there, he saw people being publicly bound in front of crowds, and he discovered that other victims were apprehended secretly. Osman's father, Tam Sen, recalls that "many, many people died; thirty or forty families in as many days. . . . We could get away with not eating pork. . . . But we were not allowed to practice religion." Khmer Rouge asked them, "What do you want to pray for? For the Vietnamese to come?"[145]

Him Man, a Cham youth from western Kompong Cham in the Central Zone, has recounted in detail a Khmer Rouge massacre, which he personally witnessed, of two thousand Chams there on 12 April 1978. Man and his wife were the only survivors of the DK period, out of five hundred Cham families from the village of Khsach So on the west bank of the Mekong.[146] It was one of five Cham villages totaling twelve hundred families in Kang Meas district. A 1983 official People's Republic of Kampuchea report asserts that "after having dispersed some of them, the Pol Potists massacred the remaining population on 1 August 1978. Up till now, only four have been found to have survived."[147] In Choeung Prey district, to the north, fisherman Samah Ni says 105 Muslim families from Tanup village were massacred in 1978, "No one survived. My cousins who had made the *Haj*, my aunts, etc., were all rounded up. . . . They were put on oxcarts and taken to Chamcar Loeu, . . . killed, and dropped into ditches."[148]

Nineteen seventy-eight was also the worst year in Preah Vihear, according to Yusof, a Cham trader evacuated to the North from Takeo. Large areas were flooded, and starvation peaked. "People planted potatoes and corn to eat instead of rice." In mid-1978, the local cadres were arrested and killed. Later in the year Mok arrived in the area and propagandized against Vietnam. "We never saw him, but we were afraid just when we heard his name. . . . He ordered many killings, of truckloads of people. People were afraid just at the sound of truck motors."

Back in Mok's native Southwest, 1978 saw the execution of former Cham cadres in Treang district (Region 13) who had earlier been dismissed from their posts. It was also the year of the hardest work for surviving Chams. Nao Gha, a local Cham woman, worked in the fields thirteen hours per day. Rations

145. Author's interview with Sen Osman, Romeas Hek, 16 January 1986.
146. Honda, *Journey to Cambodia*, pp. 134–39.
147. *The Destruction of Islam in Former Democratic Kampuchea*, Phnom Penh, 1983, p. 13.
148. Author's interview with Samah Ni, Chrang Chamres, 10 January 1986.

were inadequate—sweet potatoes and water vines. Yet pork was served twice a month in 1978, and it had to be eaten on pain of execution. Some Chams who did eat pork vomited it up again.[149]

The Chinese in 1978

Nao Gha also reports the murder of four Chinese families in her village in Treang in 1978.[150] We have already recounted similar anti-Chinese massacres in Region 25 and in the East and Northwest Zones. Like these areas, now under Mok's control, for most of the year the Northern Zone was run by another former Southwest official, Kang Chap. A refugee who fled Oddar Meanchey in February 1978 reported, "There were not many Chinese in my village, only three families. They were all killed in 1978. Friends from other villages told me the same thing, that many Chinese families were executed in January 1978. The Khmer Rouge said, 'the Chinese used to exploit the Cambodian people.'"[151] A second refugee, from Siem Reap, told a U.S. official in June 1978, "Early this year, I saw about thirty carts loaded with baggage pass through my village. About two hundred Chinese followed behind the carts. They had been told that they were to be resettled in Beng. . . . There were five Khmer Rouge soldiers guarding them, but the Chinese looked happy. The next day the carts came back with all the goods and luggage still loaded, but not the Chinese. A cart driver told me the Chinese had been executed. After that I saw no more Chinese."[152]

Phnom Penh itself was the site of a roundup of ethnic Chinese in March 1978. The relevant S-21 record is translated in Table 3.[153] The victims perished in Toul Sleng. At this time, Nguon Song, fluent in Chinese, was transferred from Battambang to factory work in Phnom Penh. Song also began translating Chinese technical manuals into Khmer and interpreting for Chinese advisers in his factory. He recalls an occasion on which a friend translated for visiting Chinese officials in a meeting with Pol Pot. The guests asked about the ethnic Chinese, "where they were, and how their living conditions were being taken care of." In reply, Song's friend told him, "Pol Pot lied, saying that they had been taken care of, put in comfortable places to live and work alongside the Kampuchean people. The Chinese leader then asked to meet some of the ethnic Chinese.

149. Author's interview with Nao Gha, Treang, 26 August 1980.
150. Ibid.
151. "Account of Sen Chul," Interview with Cambodian Refugee in Surin, Thailand, conducted by American embassy officer in June 1978. Report no. 18 (declassified 1978), p. 3.
152. "Account of Thu Hat," Interview with Cambodian Refugee in Surin, Thailand, conducted by American embassy officer in June 1978. Report no. 17 (declassified 1978), p. 3.
153. "Chhmou neak tous phnaek chen," D.K. Santebal document discovered in Tuol Sleng prison in 1980. Copy in possession of the author.

Table 3. "Names of Prisoners in the Chinese Section"

Original Name	Public Name	Age	Sex	From (Dept.)	Duty Before Arrest	Arrival Date
1. Khoy Chun Hiet	Hiet	35	F	Social Action	Medical Interpreter; wife of I Tong	2.3.78
2. I Tong		39	M	Commerce	Committee member of the ammunition factory, Takhmau	4.3.78
3. Phac Sat	Phing	28	M	State Agriculture	Electrical Section Leader, State Agriculture	7.3.78
4. Si Khim	Huor	37	M	Staff Office	Chairman, Workshop, Office K-65	12.3.78
5. So Thak		38	M	Industry	Interpreter for the Chinese in the Ministry	13.3.78
6. Li Lou		42	M	Industry	Old Worker, T-7 Factory	14.3.78
7. Hong			F	Industry	April 17, 1975 Hospital	14.3.78
8. Khov Hun		36	F	Industry	Wife of Li Lou	15.3.78
9. Sia Mian		48	F	Commerce	Wife of Tang Hay Hong	15.3.78
10. Seu Liang An		34	M	Staff Office	Combatant, Repair Section, Office K-65	16.3.78
11. Ung Kim Pau	Chhay	29	M	Staff Office	Combatant, Repair Section, Office K-65	16.3.78
12. Lim Hak	Vuth	32	M	Staff Office	Combatant, Office K-65	16.3.78
13. Heng Tuon	Lim	24	M	Staff Office	Combatant, Making Gunpwder, Office K-65	16.3.78
14. Chou Yin Li	Chhean	28	M	Staff Office	Deputy, Foundry Workshop, Office K-65	16.3.78
15. Mok Chiv	Cheav	42	M	Industry	Deputy Chairman, D-1 Factory	16.3.78
16. Tan Sai	Chov San	47	M	Staff Office	Interpreter for the Chinese in Office 62-B	18.3.78
17. Khou Chi Mian	Tong	41	M	Public Works	Interpreter for the Chinese in Electricity No. 2	18.3.78
18. Li Chiv Kiang		26	M	Industry	Old Worker in the D-9 Foundry Factory	19.3.78

Table 3. (continued)

Original Name	Public Age Name	Sex	From (Dept.)	Duty Before Arrest	Arrival Date
19. Lot Chu Kin	28	M	Industry	Old Worker in the D-3 Factory	19.3.78
20. Hong Sai	36	M	Energy	Interpreter for the Chinese in the Energy Ministry	19.3.78
21. Li Yu Kok	30	M	Industry	Old Worker in D-3	17.3.78
22. Mok Ming	17	M	Industry	Son of Mok Chiv	17.3.78
23. Mok Kong	18	M	Industry	Son of Mok Chiv	17.3.78
24. Li Seu Min	Tong Li 30	M	Industry	Interpreter for Chinese in the Cement Factory	21.3.78
25. Lok Bun	19	M	Kompong Som port	Interpreter for Chinese at Stung Hav, Kg Som	24.3.78
26. Lok Di	17	M	Kompong Som port	Interpreter for Chinese at Stung Hav, Kg Som	24.3.78

"Pol Pot evaded that by saying Kampuchea had just been liberated and there was still danger, inadequate security. . . . This had to be resolved first. They did not ask about the Khmer population. That they would have considered an interference in the internal affairs of Kampuchea."[154] China's officials took this issue seriously. An ethnic Chinese pleaded with Beijing's advisers in Region 4 for help in relieving the hardships of life, but they refused.[155]

The Southwest Zone in 1978

As elsewhere, the persecution of new people intensified in the Southwest in 1978. In a village in the Chhouk district of Region 35, a new hard-line subdistrict chief had thirty families of new people massacred in 1978. The victims included two doctors and their families, as well as "ordinary people, strong or weak, people who hid corn" or were accused of "spying."[156] In Kampot district another new person, a railway worker, was transferred in October 1978 "to split up our family—my uncle and aunt and grandmother

154. Author's interview with Nguon Son (pseudonym), Strasbourg, 31 October 1979.
155. Author's interview with Tae Hui Lang, Chatenay-Malabry, 10 August 1979.
156. Author's interview with Mam, a peasant woman in Koh Touc, Kampot, 29 August 1980. She said these massacres left only 18 families of new people alive in the village, Prey Ben, in Baniev subdistrict. The new subdistrict chief responsible was named Yung, from Bak Nim subdistrict.

had all been with me."[157] There is little evidence of a 1978 "amnesty" for new people.[158]

Partial statistics suggest that the Center collected more rice from the Zone in 1978: 250 tons from one subdistrict in 1977 and 750 tons from another in 1978.[159] Starvation certainly continued. In Region 13, a resident of Angkor Chey district says that rations, adequate in 1975–76, were drastically reduced in 1977–78. "We ate rice gruel and it was not enough. . . . We produced enough but the line was to economize. . . . Rice was given over to Angkar and then disappeared." Twenty to thirty percent of the population died of starvation in 1977–78.[160] Chai, a peasant from Treang, concurs. He says that when he joined the district chalat in early 1976, it comprised over five thousand male and female workers. Under the leadership of Mok's son-in-law Ren, deaths reduced this workforce to fewer than one thousand by 1979. There had been no starvation in 1975–76, but malnutrition took a heavy toll in 1977–78, mostly among city people, but many peasants starved as well. People who complained were executed. Nineteen seventy-seven and 1978 also saw the most killings.[161] Two "full rights" peasants from the "model cooperative" in Tram Kak district corroborate this general picture. One said killings intensified after 1976. "Anyone they suspected of not being happy with them, they killed. . . . There were many killings in 1977–78." The second peasant charged that in 1977–78, the authorities executed "educated or full rights people, anyone who said anything wrong," including several people in her village.[162] Also in Region 13, a CPK cadre from Kirivong estimated that two hundred people were executed and fifty died of starvation in his subdistrict from 1975 to 1978. Most killings took place in 1978, he said, when there was little starvation.[163] A base peasant couple from Kampot district in Region 35 recall many killings in 1977, but even more in 1978, including ten base people and

157. Author's interview with Muk Chot, sent to Bokor in October 1978, where "life was better," with "plenty of food. . . . but we were afraid" because of a purge in the railways department. Toul, 28 October 1979.

158. Carney, in Jackson, ed., *Cambodia 1975–1978*, p. 83 n. 3, cites the claimed July 1978 "amnesty." See below, n. 178.

159. Author's interviews with Ieng Thon, a former CPK soldier, Prey Piey, Tram Kak, 16 July 1980, citing a figure of 5,000 *thang* for 1977; and Leng, a peasant in Koh Touc subdistrict, Kampot, 29 August 1980, citing 15,000 *thang* for 1978.

160. S. Heder's interview with a CPK cadre (?) from Region 13, Mai Rut, 16 March 1980.

161. Author's interview with Chai, Krang Chhes, 15 July 1980. Ren's chalat was called the "2nd Division." A peasant woman from Krang Chhes asserted that 1978 was "no problem" as far as executions were concerned, because "everyone had already been killed." Author's interview, Krang Chhes, 15 July 1980.

162. Author's interviews at Leay Bo, Ang Tasom district, 15 July 1980.

163. Author's interview, Kirivong, 25 August 1980. The cadre said his subdistrict, Ream Andaeuk, had a population of 8,000 in the DK period.

all but two new people in their village. They lost eleven relatives, including their children.[164] One of many deported from Kirivong to Tram Kak in 1977–78 was Savann, a former Phnom Penh student. He and two others, accused of having been Lon Nol officers, were arrested in March 1978. They were all sent to Tram Kak district prison, at Kraing Ta Chan. The other two men had indeed served in the Lon Nol army. They were tortured by the prison commandant, Phen, and quickly killed. Savann was interrogated by "a torturer, a guard, and a scribe." Despite severe torture, he refused to confess, "and finally they saw I was telling the truth." After a month in jail he was put to work burying bodies near the prison. Savann buried over two hundred bodies in the next two months. In one incident, "sixty people were all brought in and killed on the spot." Nearly all prisoners were new people. Torture was administered daily. The jail always held more than thirty people. A prison document records that "from when we began smashing the enemy to now, we have got rid of 1,500 people."[165] In June 1978, Savann was released. "I was told not to dare tell anyone what I had seen there or what happened to me. I said I would be faithful till the day I died." A battalion commander cryptically concurred. An elderly base peasant accused of "resisting the cooperatives," with a son in the DK army, was released with Savann after two weeks in prison.[166]

Another new person from Kirivong, a youth named Korb, was less lucky. In July 1978, he was arrested in Tram Kak and sent to Kraing Ta Chan. The head of Korb's cooperative reported to the Tram Kak security chief: "This person formerly was normal in character. Then, over about ten days, he went crazy. He was taken to be cured in the subdistrict hospital. When he is alone he is quiet, and doesn't say a word; if many people come in, first he begins to whistle, and then he sings the following rhyme aloud:

O! Khmers with black blood
Now the eight-year Buddhist prophecy is being fulfilled.
Vietnam is the elder brother, Kampuchea is the younger.
If we do not follow the Vietnamese as our elder brothers,
There will be nothing left of the Khmer this time but ashes.

164. Author's interviews with Leng and Mai, Koh Touc, 29 August 1980.
165. Archives of the Tram Kak district prison at Kraing Ta Chan, document apparently dating from mid- to late 1978. I was permitted to photocopy these archives in July 1980. I then sent the originals back to Ang Tasom, where they have since been lost, but I also deposited a full set of copies at Tuol Sleng Museum.
166. Author's interview with Savann, 1980. Place of interview and Savann's full name withheld.

O! Khmers with black blood
Servants of the Chinese, killing your own nation.

Now you Americans have the upper hand
You must repay the Khmer quickly,
Because the Khmer have strived and struggled for a long time
Don't bring the wicked B-52s to pay us back. That's not enough.
Bring atomic bombs. That is the repayment needed.
Because the Khmers are building one hundred houses at a time.

O! Khmers with black blood
There will be nothing left of the Khmer this time but ashes.
O! Damrei Romeas mountains, The timber is all gone now.
No forest, no rocks any more. There can only be ashes left,
Because the Americans are paying Kampuchea back with blood.
Only garlic remains."[167]

By this time Savann had been released, but he recalls thirty or forty "crazy" male and female prisoners singing aloud in Kraing Ta Chan in the first half of 1978. Were such bitter verses passed on from prisoner to prisoner in conscious acts of collective resistance? The authorities certainly feared they were. Savann says, "The crazy people in the jail were killed within three to five days. They never lasted." Korb's song sealed his fate. Threatening enough to be recorded verbatim by his jailers, it provides an instructive counterpoint to the official Democratic Kampuchea song repertoire.

Savann adds that when he got back to work in the countryside, people could hear the fighting along the Vietnamese border. Confidence rose that the war with Vietnam meant the Democratic Kampuchea regime was doomed. "There is thunder but no rain," they whispered hopefully to one another.

Paranoia and Degeneration at the Center

Meanwhile, the Center started to self-destruct. The August arrest of Northern Zone secretary Kang Chap sparked a series of convulsions at the heart of the regime. The internecine purges even affected former Southwesterners like Chap, and most particularly, former Special Zone personnel. Son

---

167. "Report to Comrade Uncle An, 8 July 1978," signed by "Thuok, committee of Kronham Thom Cheung cooperative," document in the archive of the DK prison at Kraing Ta Chan. A Kirivong crk subdistrict chief identified An as security chief of Tram Kak district (author's interview, 25 August 1980), but former Kraing Ta Chan inmate Savann says that An was deputy to Phen (1980 interview).

Sen's visit to Beijing later in August, an unsuccessful attempt to commit China to DK's military defense, may have resulted in Sen's temporary removal from the Standing Committee.[168] Meanwhile, a new "special commissar for Phnom Penh" appeared. He was a former soldier named Hong, "right arm of Ieng Sary and nephew of Pol Pot." In late August, Hong told surviving returnees from abroad that "half of the country had fallen into the hands of the Vietnamese." He still predicted victory, but envisaged Vietnamese bombardment of Phnom Penh, in which case "we will be obliged to evacuate the capital and you will go live in the forest." A nephew and a daughter of Ieng Sary soon became prominent as well.[169] The Center increasingly relied on kinship rather than ideological support. Hong went to summon Thiounn Chum, a self-described "comprador capitalist" who had been evacuated into the countryside. On 28 August 1978, Chum took charge of DK's financial system, joining his brothers Thioeunn and Mumm, both cabinet ministers.[170]

Over the next few months, the Santebal arrested the ministers of industry and communications, Cheng An and Mey Prang. Cheng An was handcuffed and driven to his execution site. As the car passed the D-3 metal factory, he screamed to a crowd of workers in the yard, "I am Cheng An! Rebel, everyone! Don't follow Pol Pot, he's a traitor. He is a murderer!" The purge eventually reached An's superior, Deputy Prime Minister Vorn Vet, who was arrested in November 1978. He was taken before Pol Pot, who called him a traitor. In a rare display of a violent disposition, Pol Pot personally beat Vorn Vet so hard that he broke his leg. Vet disappeared into Tuol Sleng.[171] A former Southwest Zone official, the new Region 5 secretary, Heng Rin, was arrested on 16 November.[172] All were accused of serving Hanoi, the KGB, or the CIA.

Mey Prang, a former railway worker popular among his subordinates, may have been a genuine dissident. A female worker recalls him telling a political study meeting of fifty railway workers around 1976 that Vietnam, Cambodia, and Laos were *bang p'oun* (siblings), "a group of countries in Indochina together."[173] In March 1978, Prang made a restrained speech about Cambodian

168. *FEER*, 11 August and 8 September 1978, and January 19, 1979.

169. Y Phandara, *Retour à Phnom Penh*, Paris: Métaillé, 1982, pp. 176, 224, 226. Phandara says Hong was later given command of the army (p. 185).

170. J. Myrdal, "Why Is There Famine in Kampuchea?," *Southeast Asia Chronicle*, 77, February 1981, p. 18. A fourth brother, Thiounn Prasith, was a senior Foreign Ministry official.

171. Y Phandara, *Retour*, p. 208. Ieng Sary lied that Vorn Vet "committed suicide" on 2 November 1978 (*Monde*, 2 June 1979), but Vet's later S-21 "confessions" survive; Jackson, ed., *Cambodia 1975–1978*, p. 101.

172. Jackson, ed., *Cambodia 1975–1978*, p. 106.

173. The woman added that Prang "did not seem to be very bad to people; he resolved their living conditions, working conditions, and equipment problems" (author's interview, 2 August 1980). Surviving DK-period railway workers also offered favorable recollections of Mey Prang, a former coworker in the 1960s (author's interviews, Phnom Penh railway station, October 1981).

independence, without mentioning Vietnam or accusing it of "aggression." This resembled the fateful stance of Chou Chet in January.[174] But, beyond their "confessions" (made under torture), there is no evidence that other leaders arrested in this wave of purges were also dissidents.[175] Chasing its tail in ever-shrinking circles, the Center fell prey to its own fears. The revolution was devouring itself.

Koy Kin, forty, a former teacher who had joined the revolution in 1970, was a CPK member and a supervisor in the office of the industry ministry. Since 1975 Kin's wife, Koy La, had worked in a textile factory south of Phnom Penh. The couple would meet every ten days or so. Their five young children, including a baby, lived in special children's barracks. In May 1978, Santebal agents entered Kin's office, "accused him right, left and center," tied him up, bundled him into a car, and drove off. When workers told La two weeks later, she despaired. "I had no idea what they were talking about." She never saw Kin again.[176]

In mid-1978, La was arrested. She spent the rest of the year in a wat converted into a jail. The woman director of her textile factory and over a dozen coworkers were also arrested in 1978. La counted about one hundred people from the industry ministry. The two hundred prisoners in the wat were "mostly widows whose husbands had been taken away, and their children." Trucks brought new inmates every few weeks. At first, victims disappeared daily; motorcycles and jeeps came to the wat early each evening to take "one or two families away." None returned. After two weeks, the rate of disappearances fell. For the rest of 1978, "several trucks would take people away each month."[177]

The hunt for new people did not let up despite escalation of the intra-Party purges. A Santebal document of 21 November 1978 records that 1,824 "people from the old society" had been incarcerated in Tuol Sleng, while another "1,035" remained to be apprehended.[178] Such distinctions receded, however, as

174. Mey Prang's speech stressed "the independence, sovereignty, and territorial integrity of Democratic Kampuchea within the present borders," and did not mention Vietnam or foreign aggression. FBIS, 6 March 1978, p. H2, Phnom Penh Radio, 5 March.

175. For unsubstantiated assertions that they were dissidents, and that even Son Sen, Pauk, Mok, and Deuch "have been wrongly depicted as 'Pol Pot loyalists,'" see Heder, "Khmer Rouge Opposition to Pol Pot," p. 5.

176. Koy Kin's arrival at Tuol Sleng was recorded, but no date or other details are available.

177. Author's interview with Koy La (location withheld), August 1980. La self-consciously described her ignorance of the charges against her husband by saying, "Women have light hearts."

178. Author's notes from a 400-page S-21 ledger, perused in Tuol Sleng, 24 August 1980. (Ung Pech's name was on the list.) This document and many other sources contradict the claim that, "in July or August 1978, the Party Center sent out a circular no. 870 which was

the Santebal net was cast ever wider, and Deuch's machinery of death spun at full speed. A tiny rectangular notebook found in a house near Tuol Sleng contains five handwritten pages on "Human Experiments" (*pisaot menuh*). The notes record the results of eleven Santebal "experiments" with seventeen prisoners, living and dead. They begin, "*1*. A 17-year-old girl, with her throat cut and stomach slashed, put in water from 7:55 P.M. until 9.20 A.M., when the body begins to float slowly to the top, which it reaches by 11.00 A.M. *2*. A 17-year-old-girl bashed to death, then put in water as before, for the same period, but the body rises to the top at 1.17 P.M." Similar details were recorded for "a big woman, stabbed in the throat, her stomach slashed and removed," and "a young male bashed to death," then "four young girls stabbed in the throat," and "a young girl, still alive, hands tied, placed in water . . ."[179]

---

general amnesty [for] all people who had been engaged in CIA, KGB or Vietnamese agent activities before July 1978. . . . After this circular things were much better for us in Phnom Penh and also in some areas of the countryside" (Heder's interview with Sauv Kim Hong, Khao-I-Dang, 29 February 1980). See Carney, in Jackson, ed., *Cambodia 1975–1978*, p. 83 n. 3.

179. Author's photograph of the undated notebook, found by an informant in a house opposite S-21 in 1979.

CHAPTER ELEVEN

The End of the Pol Pot Regime

Since July 1978, Heng Samrin had been attempting to coordinate the two-thousand-strong Eastern Zone resistance. Following the paths of his officers north across Highway 7, he found Song Neat, commanding a company of 4th Division rebels in Memot, and Pol Saroeun's artillery support troops. Heng Samrin claims that fifty-strong rebel units launched about ten attacks on Center forces in this period, "especially in Damber, at Chup, and on the river bank at Krauchhmar." Once they attacked a convoy of Center trucks, destroying three and seizing another, which they drove into the forest until it ran out of fuel. In another ambush, rebels destroyed two DK tanks. Rebel Region- and district-level units, led by Mau Phok, So Nal, Ouch Bun Chhoeun, and the entire Tbaung Khmum District cPK Committee (Tea Sabun, Chan Seng, and Mat Ly), were in action elsewhere in Region 21. Having few forces and less firepower, they concentrated on small-scale guerrilla attacks. "We would attack in the morning, blow up their trucks, and escape." Samrin claims that the rebels killed about a hundred DK troops in the East. But they could not hold ground. "We did not attack and overrun their bases, but attacked on the roads and seized food supplies to eat. That's all. We did not take over anything because our forces were few and they were many."

In early August, Heng Samrin returned to the area south of the highway where his own Zone units were fighting alongside two hundred Center defectors, one hundred to two hundred Regional troops, and three hundred to four hundred district infantry, commanded by Chea Sim, Chum Sambor, Sae Chhum, and Sar Kheng. At the end of August, Samrin headed north again, for a rebel meeting in a latex factory in Memot. The main purpose of this meeting, which took place in September, was to make "a plan to unite and create a Front," a formal organization to run the resistance. Samrin says that he, Pol Saroeun, Mau Phok, and two others "made the preparations to create the

---

1. Author's interview with Heng Samrin, Phnom Penh, 7 December 1992. The others were Chhuon and Meas.

Front." More important, though, they then "went and made contact with Vietnam."[1]

By now the rebels were being driven up against the Vietnamese border. Their forces were inadequate to protect the ten thousand Cambodian civilians hiding in the forests of Ponhea Krek district, south of Highway 7.[2] The former acting secretary of Komchay Meas district, a sixty-two-year-old former Issarak named Tith Sou, was chosen to lead the first party of six hundred across the border into Vietnam. They lost twenty dead as they traversed fifty-meter-wide minefields. On arrival, Sou "smoothed things over with the Vietnamese," telling them, "If you don't help us we are finished." The Vietnamese guaranteed aid to the rebels, and Sou sent word back to Heng Samrin and Chea Sim.[3] Meanwhile, a week after the Memot meeting, Samrin met with Sim "to draw up a plan for a Front program." Sim crossed the border with a group of three hundred, mainly cadres, in late September.[4] Another group of seven hundred, mostly civilian base people, was attacked four times by Center troops on the way across. Forty people were killed.[5] Vietnamese troops then struck into Cambodia and escorted Heng Samrin and over two thousand others back across the border. As many as fourteen thousand others who had fled into Krabau forest from Komchay Meas, Ponhea Krek, and Kanchriech districts soon followed. Chum Sambor and one hundred others stayed to fight on in Krabau.

Meanwhile, north of Highway 7, most of the Region 21 rebels arrived at the border via Damber. They now numbered about three thousand. Ouch Bun Chhoeun, for one, had resisted moves to contact the Vietnamese, but Tea Sabun, who was in contact with Chea Sim, had agreed to do so. "We were out of supplies and ammunition, food, medicine, clothing. . . . We were sleeping on leaves. We had no bases to retreat to, and we realized that we could never defeat Pol Pot even if we won in the East."[6] Another ten thousand troops and civilians made the perilous frontier crossing. In all, from September to November 1978, tens of thousands of Cambodians crossed the border into Vietnam.[7] They

---

2. Author's interview with Chea Sim, Phnom Penh, 3 December 1991. Heng Samrin claims "twenty thousand people in the south," but he was north of the highway then (author's interview, 1992).

3. Author's interview with Tith Sou, Prey Veng, 12 July 1980. According to many participants' reports, the losses were far higher, around 40 percent on each crossing. Further, *Kampuchea Dossier* cites a column of 1,200 that disappeared in its entirety before reaching the frontier. "'They must have been massacred, all of them,' said old Tith Sou." (vol. 2, Hanoi: 1978, pp. 62–63.)

4. Author's interviews with various cadres (1980), and Chea Sim (1991), who put the figure at "thousands."

5. Author's interview with Tith Sou, 1980.

6. Author's interview with Tea Sabun, Phnom Penh, 23 August 1980.

7. Heng Samrin's total figure is 30–40,000 (1992 interview).

brought the total number of refugees from Democratic Kampuchea to half a million: four hundred thousand in Vietnam, one hundred thousand in Thailand.

One of those who crossed the border in October 1978 was Bou Sopha, twenty-six, who had followed his elder brother into the monkhood in Kompong Cham province in 1965. After seven years he was defrocked by the CPK and was inducted at the age of twenty into the revolutionary army. Sopha was trained as a medic by Chan Chhoeung, a Khmer doctor who had studied in Hanoi. Like most surviving Hanoi-trained former Issaraks, Chhoeung was arrested in September 1975. As the Santebal closed in on Chhoeung's "network," Sopha had fled to Vietnam in April 1977 and spent the next year in Tay Ninh. When the rebellion broke out in May 1978, Sopha returned to his home in Komchay Meas and made contact with Chea Sim. He was put in charge of a rudimentary military hospital in the forest, but after a short time returned to Vietnam.[8]

On 2 December, the United Front for the National Salvation of Kampuchea was inaugurated at a meeting of seventy rebel cadres and officers near the Snuol rubber plantation in Kratie.[9] Heng Samrin was proclaimed leader. Within weeks, the Front's impact spread inside the country. A Western intelligence source, noting its operations in Kompong Cham, commented, "Surprisingly, the Front seems to be getting popular support." Nayan Chanda reported, "After driving out the Khmer Rouge from an area the Front immediately dismantles the communal kitchen and brings in a few monks to reassure the people." In the west, Thai intelligence reported "some insurgency harassment on Route 4, linking Kompong Som to Phnom Penh," possibly by Sae Phuthang's guerrillas moving in from the Thai border.[10] Democratic Kampuchea's days were numbered.

Another Guided Tour

It was at this point that the first independent Western observers were allowed to visit Democratic Kampuchea. They were Richard Dudman of the St. Louis *Post-Dispatch*, Elizabeth Becker of the *Washington Post*, and professor Malcolm Caldwell of London University. Dudman and Becker had cov-

8. Meanwhile, his elder brother Sotha, who had studied at the Suong monastery for 12 years and then gone to Phnom Penh and on to France for four years, returned to Cambodia after 1975, and disappeared. Their younger brother became a driver for So Phim in 1976. He was killed by Center forces at the time of Phim's death in May 1978, along with their sister, a nurse who worked for Phim, her husband and their child, and the peasant father of the family, leaving alive only Sopha, his mother, and two younger sisters. Author's interview with Bou Sopha, Kompong Thom, 16 October 1980.

9. Tea Sabun, 1980 interview.

10. *Far Eastern Economic Review (FEER)*, 22 December 1978, pp. 17–18.

ered the Cambodian war in the early 1970s. Caldwell, forty-seven, an economic historian and author of such works as *The Wealth of Some Nations*, advocated autarchy and rural development to enable poor countries to feed themselves. Intrigued by Democratic Kampuchea's agrarian self-reliance, he believed the CPK had led Cambodia's peasants "to liberation," and he was writing a new book, *Kampuchea: Rationale for a Rural Policy.*[11]

In October 1978, Caldwell wrote informing me that DK had just offered him a visa. He was "really keyed up to go," and "holding" his book for his return. He added that Khmers abroad had asked him "to enquire about various Cambodians who returned after 1975; this I'm prepared to do, so if you could be thinking of a list of people you'd like me to enquire about please let me have it."[12] I replied, "Our friends Lay Roget and Ou Lam, and two others whom we didn't know well (Chu Vuth and Ku Kim Sru), went home in July 1976 from Sydney. We'd love to hear how they are." I also asked Caldwell to seek information about Hou Yuon, Phouk Chhay, and the unnamed ministers of agriculture and rubber plantations—Non Suon and Phuong. He agreed. Neither of us knew that the CPK Center had murdered all eight men over the previous two years.[13] But I suggested that Caldwell get a list, never released by the CPK, of members of its Central Committee, and asked him to enquire about the whereabouts of my Cambodian in-laws.[14]

I also mailed him my first newspaper article. It stated that Cambodian refugees reported "widespread purges," executions, and "large-scale purges throughout 1977." Strong internal opposition, the article continued, had provoked "more wide-ranging purges." Hou Yuon, Hu Nim, Phouk Chhay, and many others had disappeared, and Koy Thuon had been executed. "Nearly all public positions are now held by the Pol Pot-Ieng Sary group, their wives, or people unknown to outsiders or using aliases." I argued that "Pol Pot is after unchallenged authority," in the name of "a chauvinism that demands big continuing sacrifices from the people to build a powerful state," while "many peasants and peasant cadres have been repressed." The DK regime, I added, was "pursuing the conflict with Vietnam to galvanise internal sup-

11. Malcolm Caldwell, *The Wealth of Some Nations*, London: Zed, 1977; "The Cambodian Defence," *Guardian* (London), 6 May 1978; *Malcolm Caldwell's Southeast Asia*, Townsville, Qld.: James Cook University, 1979, which includes the Cambodia manuscript, published after Caldwell's death despite his wish to withhold it pending his on-the-spot investigation of conditions in Cambodia (*New Age*, July 1978).

12. Malcolm Caldwell, letter to the author, London, 21 October 1978.

13. Ung Pech's 1979 list of 745 "new people" sent to Tuol Sleng names the first four; S-21, "Important Culprits," names Phouk Chhay and Non Suon. Other sources reveal the fates of Hou Yuon and Phuong.

14. Author's reply to M. Caldwell, Melbourne, 27 October 1978. All nine members of my wife's family, we later discovered, had already been killed.

port."[15] Reflexively sympathetic to both Phnom Penh and Hanoi, Caldwell retained a relatively open mind. He asked that my article appear beside one of his in a forthcoming European publication, and took it to Cambodia.[16] As he left London he penned a harsh critique of China's foreign policy.[17]

On arrival in Phnom Penh in early December, the three Westerners were met by foreign ministry officials Thiounn Prasith (the fourth Thiounn brother) and Ok Sokun. They noted the guests' specific requests. Much of their visit can now be reconstructed from secret reports written by these DK officials and from Caldwell's entries in a private diary.[18] The journalists said they wanted to see Pol Pot, other CPK leaders, and Sihanouk. They also asked to meet Hou Yuon and Hu Nim, who Sokun falsely assured them were alive and well.[19] Dudman asked about "living conditions" and "the accusations about massacres." Becker hoped "to meet former city dwellers." Caldwell wanted to investigate conditions in the countryside, the border war and relations with Vietnam, and the DK education system. He also asked, "How will Kampuchea enter international commercial circles?" He foreshadowed "various other questions," which he would "mention later."[20]

After a brief tour of Phnom Penh that day, Caldwell wrote in his diary, "One girl started chatting to me in English but desisted when our guards caught up." The next evening he noted, "Factories (making clothes) still working at 7.45 P.M. on Sunday (and still at work at 11 P.M. on the Sat. night). Request to visit deflected."[21] When he did get to see a factory, he found the conditions "Dick-

15. Ben Kiernan, "Why's Kampuchea Gone to Pot?," *Nation Review* (Melbourne), 17 November 1978.

16. Letter to the author from Marcia Grandon, Transnational Institute, Amsterdam, 8 December 1978. Prof. Gavan McCormack wrote the author from Melbourne on 15 April 1979: "Elizabeth Becker, whom I met in London, mentioned that Malcolm had had a copy of your article (presumably the NR piece) on the plane en route to K[ampuchea] and had recommended it strongly to them."

17. M. Caldwell, "A Treaty That May Save Capitalism," *Nation Review*, 1 December 1978: "The Russian working classes are as far as ever from . . . a say in the governance of their lives, while it now appears that their Chinese brothers are to lay aside the indulgence of "politics" . . . to match up to the requirements of "normal" (i.e. capitalist) economic activity. . . . Moreover, . . . more tightly bound into the world economic order, Russia and China cannot avoid . . . boom and slump, inflation and unemployment. . . . Workers will . . . be forgiven for querying . . . a "socialism" which consists of scattering among them some of the durable consumer goods of the West while denying them the fruits of civil and social rights enjoyed by their counterparts in the Western labour movement."

18. I thank Lyn Caldwell for permission to read Caldwell's diary of his visit to Democratic Kampuchea, and also an anonymous Cambodian for the DK reports. See also R. Dudman, "Cambodia: A Land in Turmoil," *St. Louis Post-Dispatch*, 15 January 1979, and E. Becker, *When the War Was Over*, New York, 1986, pp. 407–36, 447–48.

19. Dudman, "A Land in Turmoil," p. 7B.

20. "Bang cheati courup snaeha" ("To Brother with Respect and Affection"), signed "Kon and Mut, 8[*sic*]-12–78," 2-page report to Ieng Sary (?).

21. Caldwell diary, typescript, pp. 1, 16.

ensian." Work practices elsewhere in the city elicited a more cryptic comment, "I have seen the past, and it works."[22]

The visitors then embarked on a journey around Cambodia with Thiounn Prasith and Ok Sakun. They set off by boat up the Mekong. On the way, Prasith decided "all of them" thought "the people are suffering because we violate their human rights."[23] He continued stalling. Caldwell requested the names of the first and second vice chairmen of the State Presidium—So Phim and Ros Nhim (both dead since June). He recorded Prasith's response, "TP has to think about [them] but will find out." When Becker asked to meet the minister of justice (Kang Chap, arrested in August), Caldwell wrote in his diary, "TP turns to OS and they chat and laugh. TP doesn't know."[24] From Kompong Cham, they traveled by car. Dudman reported, "On the road, our Mercedes-Benz was sandwiched between at least two other cars. When we walked through a factory, or a rice paddy, or temple ruins, two khaki-clad guards with pistols under their loose shirts fanned out to protect our flanks." First, they drove east on Highway 7 to Krek. They went deep into the Eastern Zone, scene of DK's worst massacres, which proceeded as they passed through. The journalists again asked about the first vice chairman of the State Presidium (So Phim), and were again met with silence.[25] Confining the visitors to the highway, Prasith prevented them from discovering or reporting the continuing slaughter in the Zone's interior. But the Westerners had read many accounts of forced labor, of Cambodians working the fields under guard. Caldwell ruminated in his diary that the "pace of work seems no different to me from the Southeast Asian norm," adding later, "I"m still struck by the leisurely tempo." But he frequently wondered if scenes were "spontaneous or staged," denouncing one as a "charade," and watched for the mechanisms of terror. "Armed guards here alright," he wrote in the East, and further on, "Teams harvesting (No armed guards ?)." He later noted that Becker "had been about to take a photo of a hut when our attention was diverted. Cadre took [the] chance to wave some armed soldiers out of sight."[26]

As the group reached Siemreap, Caldwell suspected "they've not much to show us in the way of development projects." But he refused to see Democratic Kampuchea as the "death of a civilization." He thought much remained unchanged, "and where change is underway, care is taken to make new things

22. Dudman, "A Land in Turmoil," pp. 6B, 7B.
23. *Sekkedei reaykar ompi toussenakecc sastrachar angkleh ning neak kasaet amerik* ("Report on the tour of the English professor and the American journalists"), 18 December 1978, p. 1.
24. Caldwell diary, pp. 36, 32.
25. Dudman, "A Land in Turmoil," 15 January 1979, pp. 2B, 7B.
26. Caldwell diary, pp. 41–42, 51, 62, 69; for Caldwell's term "charade," see Dudman, p. 6B.

Cambodian."[27] Yet while he praised DK's nationalism, he was saddened by its war with Vietnam, a sentiment which is unlikely to have pleased his hosts.[28] He described as "an old chestnut" the DK claim that Vietnamese soldiers fought chained to their weapons.[29] And in an exchange over the closing of Buddhist wats, when his guide claimed, "We preserve pagodas," Caldwell reminded him of "one that had been converted to rice storage." The next day Prasith admitted that "very few" monks remained. Caldwell recorded him dodging discussion of their forcible defrocking: Prasith "doesn't know if they still wear saffron but says 'that's their custom.'" That evening Caldwell wrote, "Light beginning to fade. They're keeping us close together now. If one drops back or sidesteps, a 'guide' or one of the girls is at one's shoulder politely to recall you." In Battambang the next day, the query "What happened to that pagoda?" was again "evaded."[30] Prasith called Buddhism a "reactionary faith," a category outlawed by the DK constitution.[31]

Dudman records that the three visitors then "made an urgent and rather formal request to see more homes and speak with the residents."[32] Prasith reported to Phnom Penh that they wanted to meet urban deportees. "I let them meet one in Prae Someas Cooperative but they still weren't satisfied and they requested to meet another and they wanted to choose the person themselves. We made it quite clear that they were Americans and the American imperialists had massacred very many Kampuchean people. Therefore the Kampuchean people were still very angry with the American imperialists. They stopped their requests." Caldwell wrote in his diary about "ex-clerks etc from Phnom Penh. I'm more than ever convinced they'd see rural [toil?] as

27. Caldwell diary, pp. 76, 67. More evidence of Caldwell's ambiguous view of DK is in Dudman, pp. 2B, 3B, 6B, and Chanda, *FEER*, 5 January 1979, p. 11.

28. In "China and Indochina," a paper presented at the Transnational Institute on 29 October 1978, Caldwell hoped for "disengagement" and "de-escalation" between Cambodia and Vietnam. "Both . . . exhibit an intense nationalism, rooted in long idiosyncratic histories. . . . Vietnamese and Kampucheans collaborated closely in anti-imperialist struggle, and it is false to suggest a long-standing ethnic antagonism, though recent history has conspired to prise open potentially dangerous fissures it will be hard to close again and heal. . . . The consequences have . . . been detrimental to the broader interests of Third World liberation struggles . . . forced to make choices on matters of no direct relevance to their own problems. . . . Yet at heart the Kampuchea-Vietnam dispute is about issues internal to them—notably the questions of off-shore oil and of use of the waters of the Mekong River. . . . It is hard to be optimistic. . . . But the urgency of the economic tasks facing them, and attrition along the border, may recommend to the parties a tacit *de facto* stand-off." Caldwell also foresaw the coming U.S. alignment in favor of Democratic Kampuchea (8-p. typescript, pp. 3, 6–7).

29. Dudman, "A Land in Turmoil," p. 3B.

30. Caldwell diary, pp. 63, 72, 94.

31. Becker, *When the War Was Over*, p. 429; the constitution is reproduced in Ponchaud, *Cambodia Year Zero*, p. 225.

32. Dudman, "A Land in Turmoil," p. 2B.

unbearable torture. The other side of the coin is that in Phnom Penh they ate."[33] He told Dudman, "I wonder if the cadres aren't afraid for their own safety if they go among the people."[34]

The visitors asked again "to meet people who left Phnom Penh," and also "students who came from Australia and America." These returnees had been in the care of Prasith's ministry. Knowing most were dead, he pressed for names, perhaps hoping to produce, triumphantly, a survivor. A cautious Caldwell held back. Prasith reported suspiciously to his superior, "They say they do not know the names of those students." Caldwell did ask about Chau Seng, a prominent Cambodian leftist from France, and Phouk Chhay.[35] Prasith must have known both had been murdered in 1977. He reported, "The English professor is a man with a lot of sympathy for us. He wants to find out and understand a lot. But he does not have a strong standpoint. And when he is with the American journalists he is influenced a lot by them too." And *they* were "clearly servants of the American government and the CIA." Prasith thought the three now agreed that "our system is strong," but he also feared that "this group are not yet clear on human rights. In my opinion, on that question the group will not easily become clear. Whatever way we try to explain it to them, they refuse to understand." Worse, "they will not discard their secret aim in making this visit. We must be very careful, with continued high revolutionary vigilance."[36] On the second-to-last day of their trip, the foreigners toured Leay Bo, the model cooperative in Mok's home district of the Southwest Zone. Becker later wrote, "Our visit went smoothly from start to finish. Everything was immaculate. The separate huts on stilts were furnished with fresh straw mats, cotton pillows, and solid pieces of furniture. . . . The cooperative was a showcase of the regime."[37] Some children in rags did pass by the proceedings. Caldwell surreptitiously snapped photographs of them.[38]

Dudman and Becker had an audience with Pol Pot on 22 December, the afternoon before their plane left Cambodia for Beijing. He lectured them for an hour about the Vietnamese, Becker wrote, "saying things that sounded mad."

33. "Sekkedei reaykar," p. 2; Caldwell diary, p. 95.

34. Dudman, "A Land in Turmoil," p. 2B.

35. "Sekkedei reaykar," p. 3. Chau Seng had been arrested on 18 November 1977 ("Important Culprits," p. 15). Phouk Chhay was killed on 6 July 1977 (*New Statesman*, 2 May 1980, p. 669).

36. "Sekkedei reaykar," pp. 4–5. Prasith used the insulting pronoun *via* for his guests. Earlier that year Y Phandara had heard Ieng Sary remark that "foreigners wanting to visit our country sometimes came to spy." *Retour à Phnom Penh*, p. 268.

37. Becker, *When the War Was Over*, pp. 428–29.

38. Author's interviews with two witnesses, Leay Bo, 16 July 1980. The two identified Caldwell by his beard and said he arrived with two others, including a woman (Becker). Dudman was clean-shaven.

Hanoi had "kissed the feet" of Moscow and "wants to rely on the international expansionist Soviet Union and the Warsaw Pact. But if they want to send their army to invade Kampuchea they have to send them from a long distance and they have to transport everything they need, because there is nothing in Vietnam." As Becker later wrote, these words came from someone who, "unknown to us and the rest of the world, had overseen the execution of tens of thousands of Cambodians."[39]

Caldwell's turn came immediately after that of the journalists. What happened during his solo interview with Pol Pot is not recorded in his diary. We have the word of Pot's translator, Ngo Pen, that the meeting was "friendly" and dealt with "agriculture and economics."[40] But it is clear both that Pot's major concern was Vietnam, and that Caldwell did not share his view of the war.[41] It is not known if Caldwell raised the issue or enquired after the murdered Cambodians on his list. Pol Pot likely knew that Caldwell had already asked about Chau Seng and Phouk Chhay. But if the guest displeased him further, the normally genteel Pot is unlikely to have displayed anger.[42]

Later that evening, Caldwell returned to the guest house where the three foreigners were staying, assuring the others he remained sympathetic to the revolution.[43] They were less so. Dudman, who labeled Cambodia "one huge work camp," gave DK credit for "one of the world's great housing programs." Becker, too, would soon write, "The economic system, I am forced to conclude, seems to be working," though "the human and cultural cost has been tremendous."[44] The three retired to their rooms before 11 P.M.

Another Murder

At 12:55 A.M., according to Dudman, "gunshots shattered the stillness of the almost deserted city." Bursting through the back door of the quiet

39. Becker, *When the War Was Over*, pp. 431–32.
40. Chandler, *Brother Number One*, p. 230.
41. As Becker later put it, Caldwell "regularly sided with the Khmer Rouge in arguments, accepting their revolution on a theoretical if not a human basis. At the same time, he refused to discuss Vietnam and he brushed away Khmer Rouge suggestions that he openly sided with Cambodia." *FEER*, 16 April 1982, p. 20.
42. "Not once, during a violent attack on Vietnam and the Soviet Union, did Pol Pot raise his voice or slam his fist on the arm of the chair. At the most he nodded his head slightly or flicked his dainty wrist for emphasis" (Becker, *When the War Was Over*, p. 431).
43. Dudman says that "Caldwell remained sympathetic to the Cambodian revolution, without blinding himself to its faults," a Marxist "but also a skeptical and perceptive critic." "A Land in Turmoil," 15 January 1979, pp. 6B, 2B.
44. Becker, *When the War Was Over*, p. 433, and *Australian*, 30–31 December 1978; Dudman, "A Land in Turmoil," p. 3B. Also Dudman, "Pol Pot: Brutal, Yes, But No Mass Murderer," *New York Times* 17 August 1990.

guest house, a gunman had wounded two servants. Awakened by the shooting, Becker opened the door of her room to find a man in a black T-shirt and cap, with a pistol and a submachine gun, wearing a belt of ammunition. He aimed at her. Crying "No, don't!," she fled into her room. The gunman neither fired nor followed, but climbed the stairs to the second floor. There, Dudman had also been woken by the shots. From his window he had seen "shadowy figures running back and forth outside the garden wall." Stepping into the corridor, he came across the gunman, who "seemed to motion for me to get out of the way," and then disappeared. From a front balcony, Dudman saw "several figures, apparently guards, at least one of them carrying a pistol." He went to Caldwell's room. The men conferred, and decided to wait in their dark rooms. As Dudman crossed the corridor, the gunman reappeared and fired his pistol from twenty feet away. The bullet missed. The journalist raced into his room, shut the door, and hid behind the wall. "Two more shots ripped through the wooden door. After a moment, there were three or four more shots." Malcolm Caldwell, shot in the thighs and body, lay dead on the floor of his room. His attacker, also shot, "lay sprawled across the threshhold of the open door," his weapons beside him. From his own room, Dudman recorded "a delay of 90 minutes before government forces entered the grounds to secure the house." They notified Prasith, but another seventy-five minutes passed before he arrived, at 3:45 A.M. He told Dudman that the intruder had shot himself after killing Caldwell and that another gunman had been captured and a third had escaped.[45] What had really happened?

One of the attackers took up the story very soon after, in a secret report to the Santebal.[46] The last page of this document begins, "Then the two of us, Thieun and I came to Lin's house by motor-cycle. When we arrived at the house I saw Poeurn and Khon. . . . Poeurn asked Thieun, 'What now?' Thieun replied, 'We do this. We act according to Poeurn.' First of all, the two of us, and Thuak, Chhuath and Sambath, went to instruct the contemptible Ruth to shoot the visitor because the Party's plan was to kill him." They incited Ruth's anger at some young women workers in the guest house. He went there and fired at them first, wounding two.[47] The document describes the initial intrusion, and Ruth's encounters with Becker and Dudman, and continues, "Then

45. Dudman, "A Land in Turmoil," p. 2B.

46. This document constitutes the final and sole extant page of a handwritten, unsigned, and undated report (or confession ?) by a member of the assassination squad. Wilfred Burchett, who photographed the page in Phnom Penh in early 1979, kindly provided a copy. His account and slightly incorrect translation are in Nation Review (Melbourne), 2 August 1979. The original in Tuol Sleng Museum was removed by a woman member of the museum's staff who then defected to Thailand (author's interview with Ung Pech, Tuol Sleng, 8 July 1980). It has not reappeared, but the document is also treated as authentic by S. Heder.

47. Dudman, "A Land in Turmoil," p. 2B.

the English guest stirred. He opened the door, came out and saw the contemptible Ruth, and shut it again. The contemptible Ruth ran up to crash through the door, but it did not open. He shot the lock open, then shot the guest dead. Chhuath had Sameth step forward and shoot the contemptible Ruth dead."

The killer would never reveal who had given him his orders. The Santebal now arrested Poeurn and other members of the assassination squad. Forced to "confess" to having done the deed "to ruin the party's policy," they too were executed.[48] No witnesses survived. The party Center publicly blamed Hanoi, but the "confessions" of Poeurn and others in the next two weeks show the Santebal never suspected Vietnam.[49] It most likely wanted to cover its tracks, and those of its superior, Pol Pot.[50]

Another Evacuation

On 21 December, Vietnam's defense minister, Vo Nguyen Giap, called for "an overpowering force to wipe out the enemy." Four days later, Hanoi launched a massive invasion of Cambodia from the east. Its "Blooming Lotus" strategy, devised by Vietnam's chief-of-staff, General Van Tien Dung, involved "unexpectedly striking at the centre, wiping out the enemy command there, and then fanning out to destroy perimeter outposts." One hundred fifty thousand Vietnamese troops and fifteen thousand Cambodian insurgents stormed across the border, with the "devastating" air support of forty to fifty daily sorties in the area of Kratie alone. On 30 December, they seized Kratie town, threatening to cut Cambodia in half.[51] That day, three large ships evacuated thousands of Chinese advisors from Kompong Som.[52]

48. "On the History of the Betrayal by the Contemptible Peoun from the End of 1977 On," 5 January 1979, and "Responses of the Contemptible Chhaan," S-21 documents quoted in E. Becker, "Murder with a Twist," *FEER*, 16 April 1982, pp. 20–21.

49. Dudman, "A Land in Turmoil," p. 2B; Becker, *FEER*, 16 April 1982, says the confessions "appear to rule out Vietnam as having any part in Caldwell's assassination. . . . In their private world of horror, the Khmer Rouge dropped the pretence that the Vietnamese were to blame." See also Kiernan, *FEER*, 7 May 1982.

50. S. Heder believes Pol Pot was not responsible for Caldwell's murder. He thinks Son Sen, whom he describes as a "dissident" (along with Mok, Pauk, and Deuch! [see n. 175, p. 438, above]), may have ordered the killing to embarrass Pot. The "confessions" of Poeurn and others blame Son Sen's relative Ny Kon (*FEER*, 16 April 1982), and it is possible the Santebal was preparing a case against Sen, but Heder has offered no evidence of Sen's dissidence. Sen was a close ally of Pol Pot from 1950 to at least 1992. See *Asiaweek*, 31 March 1995.

51. N. Chanda, *FEER*, 22 December 1978, p. 18, and 19 January 1979, p. 11.

52. Frances L. Starner, "Who Killed Malcolm 'C'?," unpublished report, Thailand, January 1979, p. 6; China had fifteen thousand advisors in DK (Bangkok *Post*, 1 May 1979). Chanda, *FEER*, 22 December 1978, p. 18, reported "an average of six Chinese freighters a month" still visiting Kompong Som.

But Vietnamese advances further south soon cut off the sea escape route. On 1 January, the thunder of guns rattled the windows of the Phnom Penh villa where Sihanouk lived under house arrest. The next day, in an attempt to kidnap or rescue him, a unit of Vietnamese special forces in rubber rafts crossed the Mekong and penetrated Phnom Penh, before being wiped out.[53] Democratic Kampuchea immediately advised foreigners remaining in Phnom Penh to leave "temporarily" by road or rail for Battambang. Some Chinese took ferries upriver to Siemreap. Sihanouk was also dispatched to the northwest. Pol Pot may have been hoping to hold that region. But in the northeast, Stung Treng fell on 3 January, and Vietnamese forces pushed on toward the Thai border. On 5 January, Beijing's ambassador, Sun Hao, and twenty-seven staff members left the capital by car for Thailand. Over six hundred Chinese personnel crossed the border at Aranyaprathet on 8 January.[54] Also on 5 January, Ieng Sary left Phnom Penh in a convoy of trucks and two jeeps mounted with machine guns, heading for Mt. Aural in the Cardamom ranges of the west. He reached Kompong Speu at 10 A.M. and stopped for a meal with Sem Pal at Chou Chet's former headquarters. Sary instructed Pal to evacuate the region "and meet at Mt. Aural." But the Vietnamese were moving too fast. Ieng Sary returned to Phnom Penh to leave by train for the northwest. Pal was lucky in any case. The city of Kompong Speu, a vast ammunition dump, was bombed by Vietnamese aircraft at 1 P.M. on 7 January. The town was razed in a thunder of secondary explosions.[55]

Meanwhile, Sihanouk was brought back to Phnom Penh on 5 January for a flight out to China. Pol Pot pleaded with him to put Democratic Kampuchea's case to the United Nations, and the prince agreed. He left on the last plane out of the capital, on the afternoon of 6 January.[56] Phnom Penh was surrounded by nearly five Vietnamese divisions. That day was the first anniversary of the "great victory" over the Vietnamese incursion a year earlier. In the capital's T-7 textile factory, a festival was being prepared. Ducks, chickens, pigs, and cows were slaughtered to celebrate the occasion, though one worker recalls that he "dared not ask what it was for." Rice was served, but the party was soon interrupted.[57] Workers were suddenly ordered to assemble at Phnom Penh railway station for immediate evacuation. As in 1975, the CPK was emptying the city to deny its enemy a target.[58]

53. Chandler, Brother Number One, p. 163.
54. Chanda, FEER, 19 January 1979, pp. 10–11; Starner, "Who Killed Malcolm 'C'?," pp. 4, 6.
55. Author's interviews, Samrong Tong, 12 September 1980.
56. Chandler, Brother Number One, p. 164.
57. Author's interview with Ton Bti, Toul, 4 November 1979.
58. "The departures were presented as a guerrilla tactic to dissuade the Vietnamese from bombarding the capital." Picq, Au-delà du ciel, p. 151.

Of one thousand Cambodians who had returned to DK from abroad, just over two hundred survived.[59] At 6 P.M. on 6 January, Yim Nolla, his wife Hing Sopanya, and most of the others were taken to the railway station, which was in a frenzy. Trains quickly filled up with cadres, soldiers, and workers. Returnees waited until 10 P.M. for a place, then were taken back to their camp in trucks. Their superiors warned them to be ready again at dawn.[60] Early on 7 January, under Ieng Sary's supervision, hundreds of DK officials, returnees, and wounded were crammed into railway carriages. Y Phandara was one of them: "Ieng Sary waited until the last minute to give the order to depart. He hoped that the army would succeed in holding the Vietnamese back. He took the decision when he learned that the latter had reached 5 kilometers from the town center." The train pulled out before 9 A.M. Soon after, Phandara looked overhead and saw "two helicopters coming from Phnom Penh and heading in the same direction." They disappeared over the horizon, taking Pol Pot and his aides to Thailand. The first Vietnamese troops entered the capital at 9:30. Tanks rumbled through the streets half an hour later.[61] Nolla and Sopanya's train still managed to pull away at 10:30, carrying invalids, inmates of hospitals, soldiers, and children to the west. As the train passed through Pochentong, they heard shooting in the city behind them.[62] By 11 A.M., Phnom Penh was in Vietnamese hands.

Within minutes, Pol Pot's nephew Hong slipped through the net by motorcycle. A truck carrying more foreign ministry cadres and equipment got away half an hour later.[63] But probably the last to abandon the city was Deuch, head of the Santebal. He was still in Tuol Sleng at noon, an hour after the fall. Deuch had built up such a large archive of prison records and "confessions" that he was unable to destroy much of it; he left over one hundred thousand pages of testimony to his activities since 1974. He did see to the execution of several surviving prisoners, some of them chained to their beds. Deuch only just escaped capture. By the next day he had got no further than another prison, Prey Sor, three miles away. He headed for the Cardamoms, reaching Thailand in May.[64]

59. Vandy Kaon says 85 out of 1,000 survived. ("Rapport d'enquête sur les crimes commis par la clique Pol Pot-Ieng Sary à l'encontre de la population Phnompenhoise," People's Republic of Kampuchea, *People's Revolutionary Tribunal Held in Phnom Penh for the Trial of the Genocide Crime of the Pol Pot-Ieng Sary Clique*, August 1979, Document no. 2.4.01, 28 pp., at p. 21.) Y Phandara, *Retour à Phnom Penh*, says just over 200 survived out of 1,700 returnees from abroad (pp. 163–64).

60. Author's interview with Yim Nolla and Hing Sopanya, Creteil, 14 November 1979.

61. Y Phandara, *Retour à Phnom Penh*, pp. 186, 222; Chandler, *Brother Number One*, p. 164.

62. Author's interview with Nolla and Sopanya, 1979.

63. Picq, *Au-delà du ciel*, p. 153.

64. Author's interview with Ung Pech, Tuol Sleng, 7 September 1980; Heder interview with Chap Lonh, Chanthaburi, 12 March 1980.

Vietnamese tanks, racing across northern Cambodia toward the Thai border, broke through Soeung's lines at Siemreap, killing the former Western Zone leader in battle.[65] They then ambushed Ieng Sary's train at a bridge north of Battambang. He had secretly alighted shortly beforehand.[66] But further trouble lay ahead. As early as December 24, the commander of a forced-labor camp on the far Thai border had sent a thousand surviving workers into the jungle. He advised them to "hide yourselves," because there would soon be "heavy fighting" in the area.[67] This had started a new wave of resistance to the Center in the Northwest. Another trainload of DK personnel reached the border district of Bavel, where they planned to establish a base, but Vietnamese forces caught up with them. Fleeing to Samlaut, site of the first Khmer Rouge uprising in 1967, DK officials got out of their trucks to ask locals for water. But unbeknown to the newcomers, "as soon as they had sensed the approach of the Vietnamese," the villagers had rebelled against DK, and they cut the cadres to pieces with axes. DK units were constantly on the lookout for "bandits," new people waging resistance in "large numbers" from forest hideouts, and "killing pitilessly."[68] Unknown guerrillas attacked one DK caravan; peasants pillaged another.[69] The *Far Eastern Economic Review* reported that "whole units have come over to the Salvation Front. There have been spontaneous and scattered uprisings in the northern provinces, both among civilians and army units. There are other reports of villagers cooperating with the new authorities ferreting out Khmer Rouge cadres."[70] DK cadres feared being turned in. To disguise themselves and escape popular vengeance, some in the Northwest began to wear the blue scarves of their Eastern Zone victims. They appeared to believe that wearing the victims' uniform would exonerate them.[71]

All over Cambodia, retreating DK forces set fire to granaries[72] and drove hundreds of thousands of people into the hills. A CPK subdistrict cadre from Kirivong, on the Vietnamese border, recalls, "I was ordered to send the people

65. S. Heder's interview with Phak Lim, Sakeo, 8 March 1980.
66. Y Phandara, *Retour à Phnom Penh*, p. 228.
67. Starner, "Who Killed Malcolm 'C'?," p. 2.
68. Y Phandara, *Retour à Phnom Penh*, pp. 227–28, 218–19.
69. Picq, *Au-delà du ciel*, pp. 159, 177, 181.
70. *FEER*, 26 January 1979, pp. 10 (citing "Western intelligence reports that in some areas of Cambodia the local population has been helping the PRK and Vietnamese troops"), 13.
71. Author's interview with Huy Radi, Kompong Trabek, 16 January 1986.
72. A huge rice barn at Tonle Bet on the Mekong in Kompong Cham, for instance, was burnt down by D.K. troops a few days before the Vietnamese arrived. Approximately 50 m wide by 50 m long, and at least 6 m high, it was "full of rice, taken from all over the Eastern Zone." Author's interviews with PRK officials in Tonle Bet and Ponhea Krek, 28 July and 6 August 1980.

up when the Vietnamese came. I took oxen and carts [but] met the Vietnamese, who let me survive. The people came back down. There was nothing to eat up there." But some Kirivong people were marched through the Cardamom ranges as far as Maung, in the Northwest.[73] Conditions in the hills were deplorable. Prevented from carrying much food or stopping to forage, tens of thousands of the new deportees perished from hunger and disease in early 1979. Mok drove up and down the lines in a jeep, shouting at people to keep moving. Laurence Picq recalls, "For those who were at the top of the scale, this march resembled an adventure. Those at the bottom had to hold off with each step the limit of total exhaustion." Officials and workers got priority over peasants. DK troops slaughtered "thousands" of evacuees in a single massacre at Koh Kralor in Battambang.[74] Similar incidents occurred in the Cardamoms. Heng, who spent three months with the DK forces in the mountains, at first had to dig ditches with six other Chinese families. The Khmer Rouge "said they were trenches for fighting the Vietnamese, but I saw with my own eyes that they were pits for burying Eastern Zone people, four metres long by four wide by four deep."[75] The troops also conscripted Lang, an ethnic Chinese woman, into a month-long forced march through the forests of Pursat and Battambang. During the battles that accompanied the march, she said, "the rural population would gather together and run behind the Vietnamese lines."[76] This enraged DK commanders, and massacres continued in the hills and in DK-held areas on both sides of the Thai border. The troops told civilians that after victory over Vietnam, they would "leave nothing but ashes in the Eastern Zone."[77] In Siemreap, DK forces seized Khmer peasants, labeling them "Vietnamese slaves" for reclaiming their household utensils from communal kitchens. In a macabre inversion of a Vietnamese atrocity legend from the early nineteenth century, troops buried the peasants up to their necks and set a fire between them, burning them to death while warning them "not to spill the master's tea."[78] Defiant DK soldiers captured by Hanoi troops told onlookers in Siemreap town that they would soon escape, retake Battambang, and turn the population into *prahoc* (fish paste).[79]

73. Author's interview, Kirivong, 25 August 1980.

74. Y Phandara, *Retour à Phnom Penh*, pp. 213–4, 219; Picq, *Au-delà du ciel*, p. 176.

75. Author's interview with Ngoy Taing Heng, Caen, 6 October 1979.

76. Author's interview with Lang, Chatenay-Malabry, 10 August 1979. For details see Kiernan, "Vietnam and the Governments and People of Kampuchea," *BCAS*, 11, 4, 1979, pp. 23–24. Lang's account of the DK period is in Kiernan and Boua, *Peasants and Politics*, pp. 358–62.

77. Author's interviews with two new people who were forced into the hills by retreating DK forces in early 1979. Kompong Chhnang, 5 September 1980.

78. Kiernan, in *Peasants and Politics*, pp. 376–77.

79. Author's interview with Ang Ngeck Teang, Toulouse, 9 December 1979.

In general, however, the overthrow of Democratic Kampuchea meant that Cambodians could now go home. Millions of deportees traversed the country-side in all directions, looking for lost relatives and returning to evacuated villages. Prisoners walked out of jails. In the Western Zone, former Northwest cadre Heng Teav and his wife, along with new person Moeung Sonn, all escaped from prisons in Kompong Speu when Vietnamese forces swept through.[80] In the Southwest, all one hundred local cadres fled the Chambak subdistrict of Takeo on 7 January. The base people then broke open the communal warehouse, redistributing radios, bicycles, and other goods confiscated by Democratic Kampuchea. But in mid-January, cpk forces returned to Chambak and killed ten base people and several new people in front of their homes.[81] Similar incidents and larger massacres occurred in the Northwest.[82] And in Kampot, cpk troops threw grenades into a village in Chhouk district, "killing nearly everyone."[83] In turn, people lynched isolated DK cadres. Suos, cpk chief of Kompong Trach district, in Kampot, was executed by his own troops, whose parents he had murdered. Locals also massacred three subdistrict officials who came back out of the forest.[84]

With Vietnamese support, the new People's Republic of Kampuchea gradually established its authority, and the vast majority of Cambodians applauded.[85] Heng Samrin was named president, Chea Sim became interior minister, Hun Sen, foreign minister. Sae Phuthang's ethnic Thai rebels and Bou Thong's Khmer Loeu refugees returned from the border areas to participate in the new government at levels never before reached by ethnic minorities. Surviving Eastern cadres also resumed power in their Zone. In Svay Rieng, cadres purged in 1977–78 were returned in local elections and with popular acclaim.[86] A genocidal revolution had ended. But to outside powers, it was the beginning of the "Cambodian problem."[87]

80. Author's interviews with Heng Teav, Phnom Penh, 14 January 1986, and Moeung Sonn, Sarcelles, 25 October 1979.

81. Author's interview with a former Chambak resident, Phnom Penh, 5 July 1980.

82. See Kiernan and Boua, *Peasants and Politics in Kampuchea*, pp. 343–44.

83. Author's interview with Pheap, Kampot, 29 August 1980.

84. Author's interview with Moch, Kompong Trach, 29 August 1980.

85. According to Timothy Carney, "the Cambodian people . . . welcomed the Vietnamese army . . . with applause" (Jackson, ed., *Cambodia 1975–1978*, p. 98). Earlier assessments of the first months of the prk are Kiernan, "Vietnam and the Governments and People of Kampuchea," *BCAS*, 11, 4, 1979, pp. 19–25 (and 12, 2, 1980, p. 72), and "Kampuchea 1979–81: National Rehabilitation in the Eye of an International Storm," *Southeast Asian Affairs 1982*, Singapore: Heinemann, 1982, pp. 167–195.

86. S. Heder's interview with a former Svay Rieng schoolteacher, Camp 007, Thailand, 24 March 1980, quoted in Kiernan, "Wild Chickens," in Chandler and Kiernan, *Revolution and Its Aftermath*, p. 211 n. 88.

87. Ben Kiernan, ed., *Genocide and Democracy in Cambodia: The Khmer Rouge, the United Nations, and the International Community,* New Haven: Yale Southeast Asia Council, 1993.

The Toll

I initially estimated the DK death toll at around 1.5 million people. This estimate was based on my own detailed interviews with 500 Cambodian survivors, including 100 refugees in France in 1979 and nearly 400 inside Cambodia in 1980.[88] It was also supported by a survey carried out among a different sample, the refugees on the Thai-Cambodian border. In early 1980, Milton Osborne interviewed 100 Khmer refugees in eight different camps. This group included 59 refugees of non-elite background: 42 former farmers and fishermen and 17 former low-level urban workers. Twenty-seven of these people, and 13 of the other 41 interviewees, had had close family members executed in the Pol Pot period. The 100 refugees reported a total of 88 killings of their nuclear family members. 20 of the interviewees (14 of them from the non-elite group) also reported losing forty nuclear family members to starvation and disease during the Pol Pot period. This sample of 100 families (around 500 people) thus lost 128 members, or about 25 percent.[89] Projected nationally, this points to a toll of around 1.5 million.[90] The 39 farmers had lost 25 (of, say 195) family members, suggesting a toll of 13 percent among the Cambodian peasantry.

A second survey, of 1,500 refugees on the Thai-Cambodian border in 1980–81, was carried out by Stephen Heder. It provided data on the fate of 15,000 individuals, members of the immediate families of those interviewed. Breaking down Heder's sample into categories suggests the following death tolls: 33 percent of the predominantly urban "new people,"[91] around 800,000 dead, including 50 percent of the ethnic Chinese inhabitants of Cambodia, who perished in almost even numbers from starvation, disease, and execution, and 25 percent of the Khmer "new people," in similar proportions; and 15 percent of the rural Khmer "base people," or 800,000 dead, half by execution, half of starvation and disease. The victims were thus roughly equally divided

88. For my figure of 1.5 million deaths, see Kiernan, "Kampuchea Stumbles to Its Feet" (December 1980), in *Peasants and Politics in Kampuchea*, p. 380; and Barry Wain, *The Refused: The Agony of the Indochina Refugees*, Hong Kong: Dow Jones, 1981, p. 272, n. 8.

89. M. Osborne, "Pol Pot's Terrifying Legacy," *FEER*, 6 June 1980, pp. 20–22. Thirty-three interviewees, nearly half from non-elite background, reported another 200 or more nonnuclear family members executed. Forty-two of the 100 reported having witnessed executions, particularly in the latter years of the regime.

90. If Osborne's sample were representative, the 25 percent death rate would suggest a national toll of 2 million. Despite Osborne's efforts his sample does underrepresent the peasantry, who make up 80 percent of the population (not 42 percent). But it also overrepresents Khmer Rouge supporters, as the survey was partly conducted in camps dominated by them. These data therefore point to a possible toll of around 1.5 million.

91. The terms "new people" and "base people" were used by the CPK in 1975 to describe those who had lived under enemy control until then, and those who had lived in the rural "bases."

between peasants and city dwellers. These data also point to a national toll of over 1.5 million,[92] about 20 percent of the population.

Michael Vickery favors a much lower toll: 740,000 (under 10 percent). The difference is easily explained. Vickery arrives at his figure by using a 1975 Cambodian population figure of 7.1 million, instead of the previously accepted 7.9 million. Vickery disregards the prewar population calculations of the leading demographer of Cambodia in favor of a much lower "guess" by the U.S. Central Intelligence Agency. His position is unsustainable.[93] The 1970 population was estimated at 7.363 million by demographer Jacques Migozzi.[94] A mid-1974 U.N. estimate, corroborated by an independent Western statistician then working with the Cambodian government, put the population at 7.89 million.[95] San, a former teacher who worked as a statistician for the Region 5 Committee in the Northwest Zone in 1975–76, says, "In 1975 there were about 8 million Khmers, according to what I learnt while I was doing statistics."[96] In March 1976, Democratic Kampuchea aired its own reduced count of the population, 7,735,279.[97] By August, its estimate was 7,333,000.[98] The progressively smaller figures are obviously due to the death rate after April 1975. Both remain substantially higher than Vickery's April 1975 figure of only 7.1 million, ruling it out as impossible even before considering the known intevening death toll. The number of survivors in January 1979 is thought to have been 6 to 6.7 million.[99]

92. Kiernan, "Kampuchea's Ethnic Chinese under Pol Pot: A Case of Systematic Social Discrimination," *Journal of Contemporary Asia*, 16, 1, 1986, pp. 18–29; p. 29 has the full reference.

93. See below and also Kiernan, "The Genocide in Cambodia, 1975–1979," *BCAS*, 22, 2, 1990, pp. 35–40, for the evidence for the April 1975 population figure of 7.894 million. For Vickery's 7.1 million "guess" for 1975, see his *Cambodia 1975–1982*, p. 185; Vickery, "How Many Died in Pol Pot's Kampuchea?," *BCAS*, 20, 1, pp. 70–73, and "Comments on Cham Population Figures," *BCAS*, 22, 1, pp. 31–33.

94. Jacques Migozzi, *Cambodge: Faits et problèmes de population*, Paris: CNRS, 1973, pp. 226, 212.

95. W. J. Sampson, "Cambodian Casualties," letter to the *Economist*, 26 March 1977, p. 4. Sampson gives his reasons for the figure after taking account of various demographic factors, which he specifies: "a) Natural increase, b) Higher infant mortality during war, c) Reported massacre of and emigration of Vietnamese after 1970, partly offset by some net Vietnamese immigration, d) Other net immigration, e) Armed forces deaths, both sides, f) Civilian war deaths."

96. Author's interview with San, Paris, 29 May 1980.

97. Phnom Penh Radio, 21 March 1976; see BBC *SWB*, FE/5166/B1–3.

98. "The Party's Four-Year Plan to Build Socialism in All Fields, 1977–1980," CPK Center document dated July–August 1976, in Boua, *et al., Pol Pot Plans the Future*, pp. 45–119, at p. 52, Table 1.

99. For the lower figure, see "AFP Reports Figures on Kampuchea Population," Agence France-Presse, Hong Kong, 22 January 1980, in *FBIS*, Asia Pacific, 24 January 1980, p. H4: "The Cambodian population totalled about 6 million at the end of 1979 . . . including unconfirmed information it would be 6,130,000." Higher figures are used in Vickery, *Cambodia 1975–1982*, p. 186.

Table 4. Approximate Death Tolls in Democratic Kampuchea, 1975–1979

Social group	1975 population	Number who perished	Percentage
"New People"			
urban Khmer	2,000,000	500,000	25
rural Khmer	600,000	150,000	25
Chinese (all urban)	430,000	215,000	50
Vietnamese (urban)	10,000	10,000	100
Lao (rural)	10,000	4,000	40
Total new people	3,050,000[1]	879,000	29
"Base People"			
rural Khmer	4,500,000	675,000	15
[Khmer Krom]	[5,000]	[2,000]	[40]
Cham (all rural)	250,000	90,000	36
Vietnamese (rural)	10,000	10,000	100
Thai (rural)	20,000	8,000	40
upland minorities	60,000	9,000	15
Total base people	4,840,000	792,000	16
Total Cambodia	7,890,000[2]	1,671,000	21

[1]A New Zealander carrying out a census of Phnom Penh for an international agency, whom I met there in February 1975, told me that the city's population at that time was 1.8 million. My estimate of the number of "new people" at 3,050,000 is based on this figure plus an estimate of 1.25 million for the population of other towns and rural areas then under the control of Lon Nol's Khmer Republic. This second figure is comprised as follows: Battambang province's population in 1968 was 685,000 (Migozzi, *Cambodge*, p. 228); for 1975 I have estimated 700,000, both in rural areas and in the swollen towns of Battambang, Sisophon, Nimit, Poipet, Pailin, and Maung. The twelve other Cambodian urban centers under Lon Nol control in 1975 had totaled 231,000 inhabitants in 1968 (Migozzi, p. 228), but population increase as well as rural refugee influx greatly increased thse numbers by 1975. Kompong Thom in 1968 had 14,000 inhabitatnts, but the figure rose to 60,000 in 1974 (a 76 percent increase; Donald Kirk, "The Khmer Rouge: Revolutionaries or Terrorists?," unpublished paper, p. 9); Kompong Chhnang had 19,000 in 1968, and 50,000 in 1975 (a 62 percent increase). An average increase of 50 percent for the period 1968–75 would give nearly 350,000. I have estimated the rural population controlled by Lon Nol's regime outside Battambang (mostly in Kandal) at another 200,000. (With about 400,000 rural Khmer in Battambang, there comprised the 600,000 rural Khmer "new people.")

[2]For the evidence for the national population figure of 7.894 million in April 1975, see Chapter 11, nn. 93–95, above. I have rounded this down to 7.89 million here.

All known surveys of the toll in individual communities also suggest a death rate well above 20 percent (a figure suggesting a national toll of 1.6 million). The most detailed survey is probably that of anthropologist May Ebihara, author of *Svay: A Khmer Village in Cambodia*, the only ethnographic study of a Khmer village before the Pol Pot period, based on fieldwork in a hamlet of 158 people in 1959–60. In 1990, Ebihara returned to Svay, in Kandal province south of Phnom Penh, for three weeks. She found that of the 158 people she had known in 1960, 19 had died by 1975, but no fewer than 73 (including 30 women) had died between 1975 and 1979. Thus, 53 percent of the people Ebihara had known had perished under Pol Pot. Eighteen new families had formed in the hamlet after 1960; but from 1975 to 1979, 26 of the 36 spouses and 29 of their children also perished.[100]

Similar figures were obtained from other villages in Kandal province in 1981. Honda surveyed the death toll in two communities there. In one of 168 people, the death toll was 77 (45 percent), including 20 murdered. In a village of 728, surviving families lost 35 percent of their members, or 257 dead, including 140 murdered; another 29 households were entirely exterminated, making the 1975–79 death rate in that village 41 percent.[101] This figure rivals that of an urban community in Phnom Penh. Of 100 families with a total of 1,075 members, 42 percent (456 people) were killed and 11 percent died of starvation or disease in Democratic Kampuchea, and 6 percent were missing in 1979.[102]

Honda also studied four rural communities in eastern Cambodia, comprising about 350 people in 1975. By 1979, 125 of the inhabitants (36 percent) were dead, 118 of them murdered.[103] In a Prey Veng village of 220 families where Chanthou Boua and I worked for three weeks in the mid-1980s, more than 200 people had died in the DK period, including more than a hundred murdered in 1978 alone. Among 38 families we studied, the 1975–79 toll was 45 dead, including 37 murdered.[104] Even Komchay Meas, a border district from which many thousands were able to flee to Vietnam, lost 6,000 of its 60,000 people.[105] A less fortunate border province, Svay Rieng, had a 1974 population of more than 400,000. Sixty-six thousand more were deported there from Phnom Penh in 1975. A 1982 survey of half the families in the province

100. M. Ebihara, "A Cambodian Village under the Khmer Rouge," in Kiernan, *Genocide and Democracy in Cambodia*, ch. 2.
101. Katuiti Honda, *Journey to Cambodia: Investigation into Massacre by Pol Pot Regime* (Tokyo, 1981), pp. 48–50, 56–62.
102. PRK, *People's Revolutionary Tribunal*, August 1979, Document no. 2.4.01 (c).
103. Honda, *Journey*, chs. 3, 5.
104. Chanthou Boua and Ben Kiernan, "Oxfam America's Aid Program in Babong Village, Kampuchea," unpublished consultancy report, April 1987, pp. 6, 7.
105. Author's interviews with local officials, Kranhoung, 9 August 1980.

indicated a DK-period toll of 94,500, or more than 20 percent. The victims, most of whom died in 1977 and 1978, included 19,500 Lon Nol soldiers and 54,000 peasants.[106]

In the Western Zone, the subdistrict of Chhouk Sor was largely populated by base people. From a 1970 population of 8,500, only 3,300 survived in 1979. Four thousand were killed in 1977–78 alone.[107] Of 17,000 new people who arrived in a neighboring subdistrict in 1975, 3,000 survived in 1979.[108] Another cooperative in the West counted 18,000 dead. In Koh Kralor, in the Northwest, 500 survived out of 30,000.[109] Vickery reports the testimony of two survivors regarding death tolls that surpassed 60 percent in their cooperatives in Northwest Cambodia. "They estimated that one cooperative declined from 7,000 people in 1975 to 2–3,000 in 1979, with about 15 percent executed, while another decreased from 8,500 in 1976 to 3,200 in 1979, with 25–30 percent killed."[110] In the Northern province of Kompong Thom, 60 percent of the new and base villagers of O Sala perished from 1975 to 1979. Two-thirds were murdered, mostly during Pauk's 1977 purge of the Zone. Of the 20 percent who starved to death, nearly all died in 1977–78.[111]

These figures show that the overall 1975–79 toll must have been at least 1.5 million. The DK regime was on a genocidal track. There is no reason to believe the killing would have slowed, had it not been stopped by the Vietnamese army.

Genocide Against Minority Groups

There is no question that Democratic Kampuchea waged a campaign of genocide against ethnic Vietnamese. It is not true that "virtually all" were expelled in 1975.[112] As we saw in Chapter 7, thousands remained, and they were systematically exterminated by 1979. In 1993, DK forces continued to massacre Vietnamese civilian refugees who had returned to Cambodia after 1979.[113]

---

106. Author's interview with province chief Muk Sim, Svay Rieng, 16 January 1986. Further details of this survey are in the author's possession. By December 1985, the province's population had barely recovered, numbering 324,774. Its 1968 population had been 346,000 (Migozzi, *Cambodge*, p. 228).

107. Author's interview with Ka Chu, Chhouk Sor, 5 September 1980.

108. Author's interview with Hamat, Chrang Chamres, 10 July 1980.

109. Y Phandara, *Retour à Phnom Penh*, pp. 205–9, 221.

110. Vickery notes that these two informants "had high school or university education, were accustomed to dealing with figures, and were sober and non-sensational in their accounts." *Cambodia*, pp. 118, 320 n. 195.

111. Author's interview with an anonymous O Sala resident, Kompong Svay, 16 October 1980.

112. M. Vickery, letter to author, 15 March 1990. Chandler agreed (*Tragedy of Cambodian History*, p. 285).

113. See Kiernan, *Genocide and Democracy in Cambodia*, pp. 238–39, 243–44.

The number of Chams in Cambodia fell from about 250,000 in 1975 to about 173,000 in 1979,[114] a statistical loss of 77,000. To this must be added at least another 10,000 Chams born during the DK period (at an assumed very low population growth rate of 1 percent per annum—a third of the previous normal rate), who also disappeared. More than one-third of the Chams, about 90,000 people, perished in Democratic Kampuchea. The scale of this statistical conclusion is corroborated by many individual accounts, presented in Chapter 7. The human destruction proportionally exceeded the estimated toll among all Cambodians.

Were the Chams discriminated against or persecuted *for being Chams*, that is, for racial reasons? The regime claimed to treat all its subjects, irrespective of their race, in similar fashion. And this claim was even accepted by a minority of Chams, especially those from the Northwest, the place of origin of most Chams interviewed by other researchers. Of the forty-six Cham interviewees questioned on the subject, thirty said that Democratic Kampuchea discriminated against Chams in some way, but sixteen said that it had not. Most of the latter appear to have believed that special persecution of Chams did occur, but did not consider this to constitute *discrimination*, as it was intended to make them behave exactly like Khmers.

The first point, then, is whether the Cham people were persecuted. The fact that other races were also persecuted is of no relevance. It is possible to commit multiple genocide. The Nazi crime against the Jews was no less genocidal for the fact that Gypsies also suffered Nazi genocide. When asked whether Muslim Chams had been forced to eat pork, forty-one interviewees said yes, and only six said no. Similarly, when asked whether use of the Cham language had been prohibited by the DK authorities, thirty-six said yes, and only one said no. When asked whether Cham populations had been dispersed or broken up, fifty-one interviewees said yes, and none said no. It is obvious that Chams were persecuted, and that one specific target was their cultural distinctiveness. If this was merely the application of the same regulations to all citizens of Democratic Kampuchea, it must be conceded that the all-embracing nature of these regulations and their strict enforcement represented a serious attack on minority groups.

But a strong case can be made for a second point, that the Chams were not

114. In December 1982, the Cham population in the People's Republic of Kampuchea was counted at 182,256 (*La Communauté Islamique au Kampuchéa*, pp. 17–18). Assuming a population growth rate of around 3 percent p.a. from 1979 to 1982 (Kiernan, "The Genocide in Cambodia, 1975–79"; Grant Curtis, *Cambodia: A Country Profile*, Stockholm, SIDA, 1990, pp. 6–7, suggests a range of 1.9–4 percent; Peter Hastings, *Sydney Morning Herald*, 2 October 1984, cites "2.8 percent or more"), the Cham population in January 1979 would have been 161,350, plus 11,700 abroad (Po Dharma, "Les Cam," in *Introduction à la connaissance de la péninsule indochinoise*, Paris, 1983, pp. 127–31).

only persecuted, but also discriminated against, that is, *persecuted for being Chams*. There is no record of any members of the majority group, the Khmers, being forced to eat pork. Chams were obviously specially supervised in this respect. Second, and more important, the Khmer language was not prohibited; rather, speakers of other languages, particularly Cham, were forced to communicate only in Khmer. And finally, though all Khmer urban communities were dispersed, most Khmer village populations were not. But *all Cham communities, urban or rural, "new" or "base," were dispersed*. And Cham villages were not scattered willy-nilly, but deliberately broken up into small groups of families, and it was ensured that these groups could have no contact with one another. Again discrimination is evident.[115]

We have seen that Cham new people, or deportees from the cities, were not always singled out for harsh treatment *as Chams*. Rather, they received harsh treatment due to their urban origin, apparently irrespective of their race. However, we have also seen how Cham "base people" (the vast majority of Chams) were deliberately dispersed from their villages and demoted to "depositee" status *because they were Chams*. As Heder has noted, the deportees "were last on distribution lists, first on execution lists, and had no political rights."[116] For this treatment, Cham base people were singled out because of their race, and distinguished from ethnic Khmer base people. These are strong grounds for the case that Democratic Kampuchea pursued a campaign of racial persecution against the Chams.

Under the International Genocide Convention of 1948, *genocide* is defined as various acts such as "killing members of the group" pursued with "an intent to destroy, in whole or in part, a national, ethnical, racial or religious group, as such." Now there is no doubt that the Democratic Kampuchea regime intended to destroy the Cham Muslim religious group "as such." Not only were the Chams dispersed among the Khmer, but they were also forbidden, by the threat or use of force, to practice their Islamic religion. (That Khmers were also forbidden to practice Buddhism is irrelevant to this point.) The regime's systematic extermination of Cham community and religious leaders (as shown in Chapter 7, Table 1, p. 271), let alone the massacres of tens of thousands of ordinary Chams, are further evidence of its genocidal intent.

115. Had *all* Cambodia's villages been deliberately dispersed, and had Cambodians of all races been forced to behave in ways equally unfamiliar to all, such as to eat bread and speak only English, one might then have concluded that there was no racial discrimination in D.K. policies towards the Cham. The D.K. abolition of all *religions* comes under this category of nondiscriminatory oppression.

116. S. Heder, *Kampuchean Occupation and Resistance*, Bangkok: Chulalongkorn University, 1980, p. 6.

It is similarly clear that the regime planned to destroy the ethnic Chinese community "as such," not in the sense that all Chinese were targeted for execution (though half perished), but in the sense that Democratic Kampuchea forcibly prohibited any Chinese community (as well as Chinese culture and language). The term *genocide* does not apply to the regime's treatment of all Cambodia's ethnic groups. As we saw in Chapter 7, some smaller groups remained free to speak their languages. But the repression was fierce in the case of the Cham.

That the genocide was interrupted does not invalidate the term. But it meant that the Chams survived. Like their original earth goddess, Po Ino Nagar, who has survived to the present day in the guise first of the Hindu deity Uma, then of the Muslim prophet Eve, and even of the Vietnamese "Black Virgin," the Chams and their culture in Cambodia have also survived. Haji Ismael recalls that the DK forces "were killing very strongly as the Front advanced. Phnom Penh was liberated on 7 January 1979, Pursat on 17–19 January. The Khmer Rouge had killed nearly everyone by then." By 20 January, however, Haji Ismael had made his way home to Khmaer Islam in Prey Veng. He was the first to return from the Northwest. "The place was empty. . . . I slept under a tree; there was nothing like a house left to live in." By 1980 thirty families had returned, and later others when they heard that relatives had survived and gone home. They built thatch houses and, with the new government's help, a small wooden mosque on stilts with a bamboo-slat floor. On the lintel, in Khmer, they pasted a sign testifying to their determination to remain a community. It says *Voppethoam rolum cheat roleay*—"When the culture succumbs the nation is dissolved." Haji Ismael says one hundred Cham babies were born in the village between 1979 and 1986. Of the deportees from Takeo village, in Svay Rieng province, Tam Sen and his family survived because of his skill as a blacksmith, and so did two other Cham families, including Res San's. When Vietnamese forces reached the Northwest, San made his way back to Svay Rieng. He became the new *hakkem* of the Muslim survivors of Takeo village, and he had a small wooden mosque built in 1984. Two years later, when I visited Takeo, Cham children were learning Khmer in the village school each morning, and Res San taught them Arabic in the afternoons.

Conclusion

We are also in a position to resolve a number of other contentious issues about the Pol Pot regime. Its racialist preoccupations and discourse were of primary importance, but so were totalitarian ambitions and achievements. Along with Vickery's theory of a "peasant revolution" (see Chapter 5), we can now dismiss Thion's assertion that in Democratic Kampuchea, "The state never stood on its feet."[117] Despite its underdeveloped economy, the regime probably exerted more power over its citizens than any state in world history. It controlled and directed their public and private lives more closely than government had ever done. Also untenable is the view that "certain factions won or lost in various power plays."[118] After 1975, at least, the CPK Center won every confrontation. It concentrated more and more power, progressively provoking and eliminating regional challenges as well as dissidents and rivals in the capital.

And there were CPK dissidents. Elizabeth Becker takes the contrary view, on the basis of confessions extracted by the Santebal from its prisoners under torture. She states that the Tuol Sleng archives "show" that "the entire Party was involved and implicated in 'Pol Potism.'"[119] Few confessions contain real evidence of political dissidence, which they were designed to obscure in the interrogators' cause of proving *treason*. Offering the confessions as proof of no substantial policy disagreement, however, is to ignore the limitations on human expression in a death camp.[120] One example of the problematic nature of the confessional documents is Leng Sei's complete omission of her 1976 visit to Vietnam (described in Chapter 4) from her Tuol Sleng confessions a year later.[121] Terrified, fighting for her own life after her husband Tiv Ol's execution, Sei omits the trip from her "autobiography," hoping the Santebal would not recall it. A visit to Vietnam, even an official one, was not an event that could be safely mentioned by a victim, even if likely to be publicly known. To remind her torturers would have been suicidal. Sei's only hope was to suppress the incident. Like all but seven of the twenty thousand Tuol Sleng prisoners, she was murdered anyway. But had the visit come up in her confession, the Santebal would likely have required embellishments revealing her recruitment into Hanoi's service. That would hardly constitute evidence of a lack of genuine dissidence on Sei's part. Heder asserts that "allegations that those arrested advocated that the Kampuchean revolution should imitate that of Vietnam are extremely rare. Indeed, among several dozen cadres whose 'con-

117. S. Thion, in *Revolution and Its Aftermath in Kampuchea*, p. 28.

118. E. Becker, "Cambodia Blames Ousted Leader, Not Party," *Washington Post*, 2 March 1983, p. A12.

119. Becker, *Washington Post*, 2 March 1983, p. A12.

120. For further discussion see *Revolution and Its Aftermath in Kampuchea*, pp. 231, 333 n. 11.

121. Leng Sim Hak (Leng Sei), "Ompi chhmou Leng Sim Hak hau Sei protean paet P-17" ("About Leng Sim Hak alias Sei, President of the P-17 Hospital"), dated 6 January 1978; "Chamlaiy rebos Leng Sim Hak" ("The Responses of Leng Sim Hak"), 25 January 1978; and Pon (Sei's "direct interrogator"), "Ateita lekha muntir paet P-17" ("The Former Secretary of the P-17 Hospital"). None of these versions note Sei's September 1976 Vietnam visit. A work based largely on confessions is David Chandler's *Brother Number One*. See my review in the *Journal of Asian Studies*, 52, 4, November 1993, pp. 1076–78.

fessions' I have so far examined, there seem to be only five who say they or others did this."[122] That is totally unsurprising. Such statements not only meant certain death; they were ideologically unacceptable to a Center and Santebal mindset that saw any degree of sympathy or cooperation with Vietnam as blind treason. Other sources, oral accounts and nonconfessional cPK documents, reveal the genuine opposition to Pol Pot within the Party. Chapter 3 and Part 3 of this book each describe serious anti-government uprisings. We can thus discard Heder's notion that Democratic Kampuchea faced no substantial rebellions.[123]

Of course, it has not been easy to compile an accurate account. Democratic Kampuchea was a closed regime. Its repression intensified over time. The categories into which it divided its subjects—"full rights," "candidates," and "depositees"—remained unknown to the outside world until Heng Samrin's new regime explained them in May 1979.[124] Tuol Sleng prison was first unveiled that same month.[125] Long afterwards, important information continued to slip through scholars' nets. Even today, the regime's forcing of Eastern Zone deportees in 1978 to wear distinctive blue clothing has yet to be noted in print by any other author, though a Khmer refugee in the United States wrote of it in 1983 and many witnesses confirmed it independently in 1986.[126] We will be learning about the Pol Pot revolution for many years to come. But this study has shown the dangers of not only an unbridled lust for power, but also the threat of racism, to those allegedly being protected by racialist ideology as well as to foreigners and ethnic minorities.

---

122. S. Heder, *Reflections on Cambodian Political History*, p. 6.

123. S. Heder, "Why Pol Pot?," *Indochina Issues*, 52, December 1984: "I am not convinced there was ever a major rebellion, even in the East Zone, as some people have reported" (p. 6). Becker even says "there were no reports of uprisings" by Khmers: "the few reports of rebellion were among the ethnic minorities" (*When the War Was Over*, p. 263; cf. 321 and Heder, p. 6). Heder later conceded there had been not only revolts but "pitched battles" between DK forces and Eastern Zone Khmer rebels in 1978 (*Pol Pot and Khieu Samphan*, p. 28; *Reflections*, p. 13).

124. See Carney, in Jackson, ed., *Cambodia 1975–1978*, p. 84, n. 4.

125. The first Western account was Wilfred Burchett, London *Guardian*, 11 May 1979.

126. "Vy's Story," in Theanvy Kuoch and Mary Scully, *Cambodian Voices and Perceptions: A Collection of Materials, Experiences and Cross-Cultural Understandings*, M.A. thesis, Refugee Mental Health and Contextual Therapy, Goddard College, Plainfield, Vermont, December 1983, pp. 35–85, at pp. 72–3. The first published accounts were Kiernan, "Blue Scarf/Yellow Star: A Lesson in Genocide," *Boston Globe*, 27 February 1989, and "Genocidal Targeting: Two Groups of Victims in Pol Pot's Cambodia," in *State-Organized Terror*, ed. P. Bushnell, et al., Boulder, 1991, pp. 207–26.

Select Bibliography

Ashe, Var Hong. *From Phnom Penh to Paradise: Escape from Cambodia.* London: Hodder and Stoughton, 1988.

Becker, Elizabeth. *When the War Was Over.* New York: Simon and Schuster, 1986.

Boua, Chanthou. "Genocide of a Religious Group: Pol Pot and Cambodia's Buddhist Monks." In *State-Organized Terror: The Case of Violent Internal Repression,* ed. V. Schlapentokh et al. Boulder, Colo.: Westview, 1991, pp. 227–40.

Boua, Chanthou, Ben Kiernan, and Anthony Barnett. "Bureaucracy of Death: Documents from Inside Pol Pot's Torture Machine." *New Statesman,* London, 2 May 1980, pp. 669–76.

Boua, Chanthou, David P. Chandler, and Ben Kiernan, eds. *Pol Pot Plans the Future: Confidential Leadership Documents from Democratic Kampuchea, 1976–77.* New Haven: Yale University Southeast Asia Studies Council Monograph No. 33, 1988.

Carney, Timothy M. *Communist Party Power in Kampuchea (Cambodia): Documents and Discussion,* Ithaca, N.Y.: Cornell University Southeast Asia Program Data Paper No. 106, 1977.

Chanda, Nayan. *Brother Enemy: The War after the War. A History of Indochina since the Fall of Saigon.* New York: Harcourt Brace Jovanovich, 1986.

Chandler, David P. *Brother Number One: A Political Biography of Pol Pot.* Boulder, Colo.: Westview, 1992.

———. *The Tragedy of Cambodian History: War, Politics and Revolution since 1945.* New Haven: Yale University Press, 1991.

Chandler, David P., and Ben Kiernan, eds. *Revolution and Its Aftermath in Kampuchea: Eight Essays.* New Haven: Yale University Southeast Asia Studies Council Monograph No. 25, 1983.

Criddle, Joan D., and Teeda Butt Mam. *To Destroy You Is No Loss: The Odyssey of a Cambodian Family.* New York: Atlantic Monthly Press, 1987.

Democratic Kampuchea. *Livre Noir: Faits et preuves des actes d'agression et d'annexion du Vietnam contre le Kampuchéa.* Phnom Penh: Département de la Presse et de l'Information du Ministère des Affaires Etrangères du Kampuchéa Démocratique, September 1978.

Ebihara, May Mayko. "A Khmer Village in Cambodia." Ph.D. diss., Columbia University. Ann Arbor, Mich.: University Microfilms, 1968.

Ebihara, M., Carol Mortland, and Judy Ledgerwood, eds. *Cambodian Culture Since 1975: Homeland and Exile,* Ithaca: Cornell University Press, 1994.

Elliott, David W. P., ed. *The Third Indochina Conflict*. Boulder, Colo.: Westview, 1981.

Etcheson, Craig. *The Rise and Demise of Democratic Kampuchea*. Boulder, Colo.: Westview, 1984.

Evans, Grant, and Kelvin Rowley. *Red Brotherhood at War: Vietnam, Laos and Cambodia since 1975*. Rev. ed. London: Verso, 1990.

Frieson, Kate G. "The Impact of Revolution on Cambodian Peasants, 1970–1975." Ph.D. diss., Department of Politics, Monash University, Australia, 1991.

Heder, Stephen R. *Kampuchean Occupation and Resistance*. Bangkok: Chulalongkorn University, Institute of Asian Studies, 1980.

——. *Pol Pot and Khieu Samphan*. Clayton, Victoria: Monash University Centre of Southeast Asian Studies, Working Paper No. 70. 1991.

——. *Reflections on Cambodian Political History: Backgrounder to Recent Developments*, Canberra: Australian National University, Strategic and Defence Studies Centre, Working Paper No. 239, 1991.

Honda Katuiti. *Journey to Cambodia: Investigation into Massacre by Pol Pot Regime*. Tokyo, 1981.

Jackson, Karl, ed. *Cambodia 1975–1978: Rendezvous with Death*. Princeton, N.J.: Princeton University Press, 1989.

Kiernan, Ben. "The American Bombardment of Kampuchea, 1969–1973." *Vietnam Generation* 1 (1), Winter 1989, pp. 4–41.

——. *Cambodia: The Eastern Zone Massacres*. Columbia University, Center for the Study of Human Rights, Documentation Series No. 1, 1986.

——. "Genocidal Targeting: Two Groups of Victims in Pol Pot's Cambodia." In *State-Organized Terror*, ed. V. Schlapentokh et al. Boulder, Colo.: Westview, 1991, pp. 207–26.

——. *How Pol Pot Came to Power: A History of Communism in Kampuchea, 1930–1975*. London: Verso, 1985.

——. "Kampuchea and Stalinism." In *Marxism in Asia*, ed. Colin Mackerras and Nick Knight. London, 1985, pp. 232–50.

——. "Orphans of Genocide: The Cham Muslims of Kampuchea under Pol Pot." *Bulletin of Concerned Asian Scholars* 20 (4), 1988, pp. 2–33.

——. *The Samlaut Rebellion and Its Aftermath, 1967–70: The Origins of Cambodia's Liberation Movement*. Parts 1 and 2. Clayton, Victoria: Monash University, Centre of Southeast Asian Studies, 1975.

Kiernan, Ben, ed. *Burchett: Reporting the Other Side of the World, 1939–1983*. London: Quartet, 1986.

——. *Genocide and Democracy in Cambodia: The Khmer Rouge, the United Nations, and the International Community*. New Haven: Yale Southeast Asia Studies Council Monograph No. 41, 1993.

Kiernan, Ben, and Chanthou Boua. *Peasants and Politics in Kampuchea, 1942–1981*, London: Zed Books; New York, M. E. Sharpe, 1982.

Locard, Henri, and Moeung Sonn. *Prisonnier de l'Angkar*, Paris: Fayard, 1993.

Migozzi, Jacques. *Cambodge: faits et problèmes de population*, Paris: CNRS, 1973.

Picq, Laurence. *Au-delà du ciel: cinq ans chez les Khmers Rouges*. Paris: Bernard Barrault, 1984. (English translation by Patricia Norland, *Beyond the Sky*, New York: St. Martin's, 1989.)

Pin Yathay. *L'Utopie Meurtrière*. Paris: Laffont, 1980.

Ponchaud, François. *Cambodia Year Zero*. London: Allen Lane, 1978.

Scott, James C. *Domination and the Arts of Resistance: Hidden Transcripts.* New Haven: Yale University Press, 1990.

———. *The Moral Economy of the Peasant: Rebellion and Subsistence in Southeast Asia.* New Haven: Yale University Press, 1976.

———. *Weapons of the Weak: Everyday Forms of Peasant Resistance.* New Haven: Yale University Press, 1985.

Shawcross, William. *Sideshow: Kissinger, Nixon and the Destruction of Cambodia.* London: Deutsch, 1979.

Socialist Republic of Vietnam. *Kampuchea Dossier.* Vols. 1–3. Hanoi: Foreign Languages Publishing House, 1978–89.

Someth May. *Cambodian Witness: The Autobiography of Someth May.* London: Faber and Faber, 1986.

Stuart-Fox, Martin, and Bunheang Ung. *The Murderous Revolution: Life and Death in Pol Pot's Kampuchea.* Sydney: APCOL, 1985.

Szymusiak, Molyda. *The Stones Cry Out: A Cambodian Childhood, 1975–1980.* Trans. Linda Coverdale. London: Jonathan Cape, 1987.

Vickery, Michael. *Cambodia 1975–1982.* Boston: South End, 1984.

———. *Kampuchea: Politics, Economics and Society.* London: Frances Pinter, 1986.

Werner, Jayne, and Luu Doan Huynh. *The Vietnam War: Vietnamese and American Perspectives.* New York: M. E. Sharpe, 1993.

Y Phandara. *Retour à Phnom Penh.* Paris: Métailié, 1982.

Index

Albania, 25, 118, 135, 146, 152, 155–56
Angkar Siem, 367
Angkor kingdom (medieval Cambodia), 7–8, 253
Animal parts, DK exports of, 136–38, 376–77, 381–83
Anti-French independence movement, 11–13, 150, 258
Anti-Vietnamese ideology, 10–11, 83, 101, 127, 144, 152, 194, 244, 298, 362, 366, 387–88, 394, 417, 448, 450, 454
Arabs, arrests of, 2

Bati ("District 56"), 178–80
Becker, Elizabeth, 210n115, 442–50, 464
Becker, Henri, 34ff., 51ff.
Book burning, 39, 154
Bourgeoisie, 96–97, 165
Bou Thang (Bou Thong), 82–83, 85, 372, 455
Brevié Line, 106, 111–12, 114, 118–20, 361
Brzezinski, Zbigniew, 384–85
Buddhist monks, 6, 134; war victims, 17, 20, 22; leadership, 36–37; persecution of, 55–58, 100ff., 446
Bun Mi, 82, 84–86, 372
Bun Sani, 324
Burchett, Wilfred, 7–8, 270

Caldwell, Malcolm, 442–50
Central control, 25–27; CPK Center's quest for, 62, 64, 80, 245
Central Intelligence Agency (CIA), 22, 102
Chams: persecution and suppression of, 2, 67–68, 250–52, 258–88, 407–08, 412, 427–31; genocide of, 461–63; historical role of, 6, 252–58, 260

Champa kingdom, 252–54, 259, 279–80, 283
Chan. See Seng Hong
Chan. See Mam Nay
Chan Chakrey (Mean), 32–33, 55, 67, 95, 101; 1976 coup attempt by, 320–24, 329
Chanda, Nayan, 103, 128, 442
Chandler, David P., 206, 251–52, 323
Cha Rieng, 74, 77
Chea Sim, 56–58, 60, 101, 210, 372, 397, 441–42, 455
Chen Yi, 125–26
Cheng An, 437
Chhbar Ampeou, 321, 406ff.
Chhien, 32, 41n49, 90, 399
Chho Chhan (Sreng), 91, 338
Chhouk. See Suas Nau
Chhouk district, 195–97, 199, 433, 455
China, People's Republic of: Cambodia policy of, 135; aid to CPK, 102–03, 110, 128–31, 140–41, 163, 377–85; advisers in DK, 384, 450–51; military aid to DK, 130, 132–34, 136, 138, 373, 378–79, 395; "lost territories" of, 103; imports of Cambodian rice, 235–36, 239, 379–81; CPK ideological debt to, 330; 1997 Pol Pot visit to, 354; blue cloth imports from, 405–06; and Cambodia's ethnic Chinese minority, 431, 433
Chinese minority, 70–71, 250–52; domination of cities by, 5, 10, 64, 288; persecution of, 288–96; purges of, 347, 424, 429, 431–33
Chong, 169–70, 180
Chou Chet (Sy), 78–80, 88, 89, 329, 346–47, 350, 390–92
Class ideology, 26, 210–15

Communalization, chaps. 5, 6 *passim*;
national, 101, 167; in Koh Kong, 78; in
Northeast, 83; in Tram Kak, 88, 181; in
Kratie, 308
Communist Party of Kampuchea (CPK),
passim
CPK Center, 14, 25–27, 92–96, 93*n*97,
96–101, 108, 130, 142, 147, 165, 204, 219,
235–37, 244, 320, 333; and 1975 deportations, 216–17; and dispersal of Chams,
260; and ethnic minorities, 303, 305; and
Kampuchea Krom, 364–65; and 1976
elections, 326; on Sihanouk, 326; and
1977 Siemreap repression, 340ff.; on dissent, 350, 356, 375; and attacks on
Vietnam, 360, 361, 364; and 1978 deportations, 388–89; "strengthens discipline,"
391; *1978* distribution of blue scarves,
406ff., 453, 465; paranoia of, 436–39
Communist Party of Thailand (CPT), 366–67

da Silva, Errol, 99, 140
Democratic Kampuchea (DK), *passim*; con-
stitution of, 101, 446
Democratic Party, 13
Deng Xiaoping, 127, 135, 155–56, 380
Doeun. *See* Sua Vasi
Dudman, Richard, 442–50

Eastern Zone, 89; distinctiveness of CPK
branch in 1960s, 15–16; in *1973*, 65–68;
in *1975*, 32, 35, 37, 39–43, 46–47, 52–54,
54*n*102; in *1975–77*, 205–10; *1975* military campaigns of, 31–35; ruthlessness
of, 40; conflicts with other Zones, 65–67,
313; CPK Center involvement in, 95, 207,
209, 369; Center accusations against, 96;
Center targeting of, 323–25, 336–37, 387,
393; *1977* purges of, 369–76; *1978* purges
of, 393; suppression of, in Phnom Penh,
324, 334; *1978* evacuation of, 405–11;
1978 massacres, 403–05, 411–16, 454;
repression of Cham minority in, 261–75;
Chinese, 293; Vietnamese, 298; involvement in Northern Zone, 337–38, 342–43;
rebellion in, 395–403, 440–42
Ebihara, May, 5, 459
Education: under French, 6; in DK, 98
Ethnic minority CPK cadres, 82–86, 90,
154, 302–05, 349, 357
Ethnic segregation (in 1975), 70–71, 290,
293–94

Fishing industry, 7–8, 143, 260, 383–84
Foreign Ministry of DK, 147–56, 302–05,
360
Fortra. *See* Khmer Company for Foreign
Trade
Four-Year Plan (1976–80), 245–46, 329–30,
377, 380
French colonialism, 4–6, 10, 12, 256–57,
360–61
Frieson, Kate, 166–67, 212–14

"Gang of Four," 127, 135, 155–56
Genocide, 460–63
Great Leap Forward, 126–28, 294
Great Proletarian Cultural Revolution,
126–28, 135, 147, 153, 352

Ha Thi Que, 124–25, 159–63
Heder, Stephen R., 206, 210*n*115, 252, 265,
289, 314*n*4, 316–17, 374*n*76, 456, 464–65
Hem Bo, 397–98, 401
Hem Keth Dara, 36–37
Heng Rin, 417, 437
Heng Samkai, 375–76
Heng Samrin, 31–35, 65–66, 67, 95,
206*n*97, 210, 265–66, 369, 371–72, 387,
394–401, 440–42, 455
Heng Teav, 50, 216, 417
Heng Thal, 32, 67, 95, 394
Hing. *See* Men Chun
Ho Chi Minh, 10–11
Hoang Tung, 123
Honda Katuiti, 285–86, 405, 459
Hong Kong, 145–46, 382
Hou Yuon, 11; in *1975*, 33, 59, 61; fate of,
122, 230*n*26, 231*n*27, 338, 391, 443–44
Human experimentation, 439
Hu Nim, 33, 42, 52, 59–60, 122, 132, 240,
321, 327, 336, 338, 350–52, 391, 443–44
Hun Sen, 210, 266, 370–71, 375, 455

Ieng Sary: in France, 11; and evacuation of
Phnom Penh, 48; arrival in Phnom Penh,
54, 128; and Northeast Zone, 81–82; in
October *1975*, 100; *1975* visit to Hanoi,
105; appointment as deputy prime minister, 106, 327; on Vietnam, 120–23,
152–53, 162, 323; on Cultural Revolution,
127; and China, 128, 130, 152, 155; and
Thailand, 143–44; and Yugoslavia, 146;
on "silence," 249; on minorities, 267,
302–03; visits So Phim, 354; in *1978*, 437;
flight of, 451–53

Ieng Thirith. *See* Khieu Thirith
In Tam, 144
Indians, arrests of, 2
Indochina Communist Party (1930–51), 12, 258
Intellectuals, returning from abroad, 147–56
Islam, 253–55; banning of, 2, 259, 265
Issarak (Independence) movement, 13, 15

Japan, 146–47, 376

Kaing Khek Iev (Deuch), 314–15, 322, 324, 349–50, 352, 354, 394, 439, 452
Kampuchea Krom ("Lower Cambodia"), 1, 3, 63, 104–05, 111, 114, 360–66, 370, 425; Pol Pot on, 58, 387; Sem Pal on, 390
Kang Chap, 88, 114, 116, 343–44, 403, 445
Kang Sheng, 126
Ke Vin (Pauk), 91, 260, 278, 280, 338–40, 343, 351, 369, 375, 387, 395–401
Keat Chhon, 114
Keo Meas, 331, 333
Keu, 51, 92, 417
Kham Len, 84
Khe Muth, 32, 87, 104, 169
Khek Penn (Sou), 49, 51, 96, 140–41, 143, 220, 230, 245, 326, 363
Khieu Ponnary, 11, 124, 160, 162
Khieu Samphan, DK president, 2, 52, 54, 100, 105, 123, 127, 164, 204; role in evacuation of Phnom Penh, 42–43, 49; on Kampuchea Krom, 108; and China, 128–29, 130–31, 378; and North Korea, 132, 378; on foreign policy, 148–51; and Vietnam, 162; on machinery, 320; on Sihanouk, 326–28
Khieu Thirith (Ieng Thirith), 11, 100, 160–62, 236–37
Khmer Company for Foreign Trade (Fortra), 145, 377
"Khmer bodies with Vietnamese minds," 3, 279, 406ff.
Khmer Issarak Association, 13
Khmer Krom ("Lower Khmers"), 1, 6, 12, 17; in DK, 298–300, 364–65, 387, 424–27
Khmer Loeu ("Upland Khmers"), 251; under U.S. bombardment, 24; CPK rule of, 80–86, 302–09, 446
Khmer People's Revolutionary Party (1951–60), 13
Khmer Sor ("White Khmers"), 68, 333, 411
Khmer-Vietnamese political cooperation,

12–15, 19, 68, 71, 102, 109–10, 142, 159, 270, 359, 437; Eastern Zone abandons, 16
Kinship: among DK leadership, 11, 87–88, 104–05, 338, 437, 443; in countryside, 185–86, 190, 215, 259; prohibition of family life, 154
Kirivong ("District 109"), 2, 3, 111, 122, 168–69, 189–91, 360, 388, 435, 454
Kissinger, Henry: and bombardment of Cambodia, 24; on Pol Pot in *1974*, 24–25
Koh Kong province ("Region 11"), 68–80, 372
Kola Minority, 300–01, 309
Kong Pisei ("District 54"), 172, 177–78
Korea, Democratic People's Republic of, 129–32, 135, 146, 152, 152*n*247, 377–78, 382
Kouy minority, 305
Koy Kin, 438
Koy Luon, 74
Koy Thuon, 60, 61, 91, 100, 306–07, 313ff., 319–22, 325, 338–40, 348–50, 356, 443
Kratie province, 89, 91; Chams in, 275; Vietnamese in, 298; tribal minorities in, 307–09; rebellion in, 402, 442
Kratie town: 1973 evacuation of, 62, fall of, 450
Krauchhmar district (Kompong Cham province), 255, 261–67, 270, 278, 402
Kun Deth, 266, 370

Landlessness, 6–7, 202, 212
Lao minority, 82–84, 86, 301–02, 304
Laos, 125, 135; flight to, 85–86, 307; DK designs on territory in, 368–69
Leay Bo model cooperative, 184–87, 191–92, 434, 447
Leng Sim Hak (Leng Sei), 124, 159ff., 355, 464
Lenin, V. I., 148, 309, 330
Les Kasem, 257, 266
Liberation by Vietnam, 412, 416, 421, 455, 463
Lin Biao (Lin Piao), 127
Lon Nol, 15, 31, 257–58
Lon Non, 36
Ly Phen, 324

McBeth, John, 316–18
Machinery, 97, 130–31, 134, 229, 319–20
Mam Nay, 315
Mao Zedong (Mao Tse-tung), 125–26, 131, 147, 148, 185, 330

Maoism, 27, 117, 125–28, 330, 354

Marx, Karl, 309, 330

Mat Ly, 56–57, 67, 101, 258, 263–64, 266–67, 326–27, 396, 440

Mau Khem Nuon (Phom), 150–53, 155, 350

Mayaguez incident, 103

Men Chun (Hing), 226*n*18, 227–28, 230–31, 239

Mey Mann, 10

Mey Pho, 108

Mey Prang, 437–38

"Mike Force," 1, 3, 427

Mok ("Ta" Mok), 32, 87, 169, 197, 244, 351, 353, 454; in *1973*, 22–23, 65–66, 68, 70–71, 79, 80; headquarters of, 89; on Chams, 258; on Vietnamese, 298–99; on Kampuchea Krom, 298–99, 361–62; promotion over So Phim, 326

Mok, family of, 87–88, 104–05, 169, 187–89

Money, abolition of, 47, 51, 55–57, 94, 98–99, 147, 151, 231

Moul Sambath (Ros Nhim), 90, 216, 237*n*43, 328*n*87, 351, 417, 421, 445

Neak Leung, 31, 33–34, 159, 406–07

Ney Sarann (Ya, achar Sieng), 60, 84, 86, 90, 94, 113–17, 119, 121, 307–08, 330–31, 334, 349–50

Nguyen Van Linh, 105, 114

Nhiem. *See* Prum Nhiem

Nhim (Ros Nhim or Nhim Ros). *See* Moul Sambath

1942 demonstration against French, 12

Nixon, Richard M.: invasion of Cambodia, 19; bombing of, 20, 25

Non Suon (Chey), 66, 80, 94, 95, 100, 197, 202–03, 335, 443

Northeast Zone, 80–86, 90–91, 305–09

Norodom Sihanouk: declares martial law (1953), 11; *1954–70* regime of, 6, 13, 17, 67, 69, 77, 81, 231, 257; border policy of, 112–13; CPK and, 15, 54, 100, 231; *1976* resignation of, 2, 135, 325–26, 329; "party of," 342; flight of, 451

"Northern regroupees" (Khmers trained in north Vietnam, 1954–70), 231*n*27; ethnic Thai, 69, 69*n*12, 70, 75; from Northeast Zone, 81–82; fate of families of, 107; *1975* arrests of, 108; *1976* executions of, 190; escapees to Vietnam, 442

Northern (later Central) Zone, 91; role in

1975 evacuation of Phnom Penh, 37–38, 42, 47, 51, 52–53; deportations to, 205; Chams in, 259, 276–82; Chinese in, 291; purge of, 338–39; troops of, 339; creation of Central Zone, 339, 344

Northwest Zone, 92, 130, 216–46, 460; and evacuation of cities, 49–51; in *1975*, 96, 139, 241; deportations to, 97, 171ff., 216, 225ff., 288; and foreign policy, 141–42, 144, 237, 242, 363; Center involvement in, 236–37; Chams in, 286–87; Vietnamese in, 424; Southwest Zone cadres in, 236–46, 297, 363; arrival of Eastern Zone deportees, 406–09, 411–16; arrival of Western Zone cadres and 1978 massacres, 416ff.

Nuon Chea, 33, 56–58, 100, 101, 105, 115–17, 120, 122, 132, 326–27, 347, 351

Ok Sokun, 444–45

Osborne, Milton, 456

Ouch Bun Chhoeun, 62, 265–67, 396, 440–41

Oudong, 80, 297, 392

Pa Thol (Soth), 317–19, 340–41, 344

Paet Soeung, 32, 346–48, 391–92, 416, 423, 453

Pakistanis, arrests of, 2

Palling, Bruce, 23, 134*n*147

Pauk (Ke Pauk). *See* Ke Vin

Peasant revolution, 163–68, 210–15, 463

Pech Lim Kuon, 134, 328

Phak Lim, 423

Pham Van Ba, 113–14

Phan Hien, 105, 112, 114–16, 119–22

Phan Treung, 141, 144

Phnom Penh: in 1930s, 10; CPK targets, 25; *1975* evacuation of, 31–64, 323

Phnong minority, 307–08

Phouk Chhay, 319*n*33, 320, 326, 348, 350, 352, 443, 447–48

Phuong (Ek Phon), 90, 265, 354, 443

Phu Quoc (Koh Tral), 104, 114, 153

Piem, 90, 395

Pin Yathay, 35, 37

Pol Pot (Saloth Sar): childhood, 9–10, 411; in France, 11, 411; marriage, 11; in-laws, 443; nephew Hong, 437, 452; in China, 125–27; and 1962 murder of Tou Samouth, 13*n*30; and 1967 Samlaut rebellion, 126; and evacuation of Phnom Penh, 33, 38, 55, 57; arrival in capital, 54;

at May 1975 conference, 55–58; at July 1975 meeting, 94; at October 1975 meeting, 100; becomes prime minister, 326–27; confusion over his identity, 328; at April 1977 meeting, 351; on religion, 57, 83, 266–67; on Vietnamese minority, 58; on ethnic Chinese, 431; and Northeast Zone, 81–86, 127, 302, 304, 309; on Vietnam, 101, 105, 110–11, 358, 386–87; 1975 visit to Hanoi, 105; to China, 128; and 1976 negotiations with Vietnam, 116, 118–20; and Chinese aid, 137; and Northwest Zone, 236, 238; on "silence," 246; on tractors, 320; on Sihanouk, 329; on Four-Year Plan, 329; "steps down," 330–32; on "microbes," 336; visits So Phim, 354; interview with U.S. journalists, 447–48; and murder of Malcolm Caldwell, 450

Pol Saroeun, 395–96, 398–99, 440
Ponchaud, François, 263–64, 340n147, 344
Pouvong, 96, 140, 144, 232
Pracheachon Group, 13
Prachha, 72, 75, 77
Prasath, 69ff.
Prasith (Chong), 68–72, 77, 79
Prey Krabas ("District 55"), 169–71, 172–77
Prey Veng province, 65–66, 89, 293, 398, 411, 459, 463
Prum Nhiem, 37–38, 51–53, 93, 129, 136, 335

Quinn, Kenneth K., 65ff.

Racialist ideology, chaps. 3, 7 passim; 26, 81, 279, 283, 286, 295, 305, 463, 465
Region 5 (Sisophon area), 219ff., 417ff.
Region 13 (Takeo), 87–88, 103–04, 111, 122, 169, 180–92, 195, 258, 360–61, 366, 379, 388, 425–27, 430, 434
Region 24 (Prey Veng), 65–66, 273, 293, 322, 325, 330, 337, 406–07
Region 25 (Kandal), 197–204; Chams in, 284; Chinese in, 293–94
Region 33 (Kandal-Takeo-Kompong Speu), 169–80, 221, 362–63
Region 35 (Kampot), 177–78, 192–97, 433–35, 455; Chams in, 283–84
Resistance to CPK, 465; everyday forms of, 213–15, 247–50; in Krauchhmar district, 262–67; in Siemreap, 316–18, 340–45; in Phnom Penh, 59–61, 96, 320–24, 332,

334; in Region 25, 333–34; in Eastern Zone, 369ff., 395–403, 440–42; in Western Zone, 390–92; in Northwest Zone, 239, 453
Rong Chream Kaysone, 70, 74, 77

Sae Phuthang, 69ff., 372, 442, 455
Saigon regime, military forces of, 2, 262
Saing Rin (On), 169, 180
Samlaut uprising (1967), 14, 126n102, 231, 453
Santebal (DK Special Branch), 108, 111, 244, 300, 314–16, 321, 324–25, 452, 464; use of torture, 331, 352; massacres of prisoners, 339, 354; and 1976 purges, 335–36; and 1977 purges, 350–52, 355–56; and 1978 purges, 393–94, 403, 438–39; killings of women prisoners, 335–36, 353, 439; and Caldwell murder, 450
Santesok (regional security forces), 265, 371
Sa'och minority, 301
Sa Rum (San), 230–31, 239
Sary (Region 37 secretary), 346–47
Scott, James C., 166, 213–14
Sem Pal, 88, 390, 392, 416, 451
Seng Hong (Chan), 90, 114–16, 261, 265–66, 330, 354, 370, 401
Siemreap: 1976 bombing of, 316–19; 1977 uprising in, 340–45; Southwest Zone cadres in, 363–64, 367–68; journalists' tour of, 445–46
Siet Chhe (Tum), 353
Sihanouk. See Norodom Sihanouk
Sihanoukist insurgents (1970–75), 16, 19, 42–43, 65–68, 139, 261
Sinn Sisamuth, 199
Sin Song, 55, 329, 337, 370
Soeun (son-in-law of Mok), 87–88, 104, 169, 180, 188, 283
Soeun (commander, 401st battalion), 73
Sok, 343, 403
Som Chea (Chea Sdong), 202, 203
Son Ngoc Minh, 12 16
Son Sen, 94, 95, 100, 106, 115, 117; in France, 11; and Northeast Zone, 81; capture and evacuation of Phnom Penh, 32, 51, 57; on Kampuchea Krom, 108; on Cultural Revolution, 127; and China, 132–33, 136; and Deuch, 315; and Santebal interrogations, 354; becomes deputy prime minister, 327; on CPK Standing Committee, 351, 437; replaces So Phim,

Son Sen (continued)
355; attacks Vietnam, 373; in Eastern Zone, 387, 398–99
Song Neat, 396–97, 402, 440
So Phim (Sao Phim, Yan), 14–15, 67, 89–90, 206, 398n41, 417; and Chams, 265–77, 274; omission from CPK Center, 93n97, 100, 314, 324, 326, 328, 351; target of Center, 313ff., 324ff., 352, 354–55, 369; on Chhouk, 329–30, 334; rivalry with Pauk, 338; attends April 1977 meeting, 351; demotion of, 355; heads Highway 7 Front, 369, 395; last days of, 392–400, 445
Sos Man, 67, 258, 261–62, 267
Soth. See Pa Thol
Southwest Zone, 87, 168–204 passim; 1973 bombing of, 22; 1973–75 conflict with Eastern Zone, 65ff.; with Region 11, 68–71; role in 1975 evacuation of Phnom Penh, 36, 37, 40, 43, 54n102; division of, 88–89; cooperation with CPK Center, 122; conflict with Vietnam, 240; involvement in Eastern Zone, 206, 209, 273–74, 337, 402, 413; in Northwest Zone, 237ff., 299, 418, 421–22; in Northern Zone, 278–79, 342–45, 363–64, 367–68; Chams in, 258–59, 282–86, 430–31; in 1978, 413, 433–36; killings in 1979, 455
Soviet Union, 39, 118, 140–41, 151, 152, 323, 329, 448
Special Zone CPK branch (1971–75), 53–54, 65, 66, 79, 86–87; role in 1975 evacuation of Phnom Penh, 32, 38, 42, 43; abolition of, 89, 94; creation of Santebal, 315–16
Stalinism, 164–65
Stanton, Gregory, 408n75
Stieng minority, 308–09
Suas Nau (Chhouk), 55, 59–60, 90, 321–22, 324–25, 329, 334
Sua Vasi (Doeun), 319–20, 348–50
Surin province of Thailand, 108, 363, 366–68

Takeo city, 103
Takhmau, 34, 202, 284, 316
Tea Banh, 69ff.
Tea Sabun, 395, 441
Thai minority, 68–78, 300
Thailand, trade with, 139–45, 383–84; refugee flight to, in 1960s, 69; in 1974–75, 76–77; in 1975–76, 142, 144; in 1977, 368, 370; in 1978, 418–19, 442

Thiounn Chum, 10, 327–28, 437
Thiounn Mumm, 10, 147, 327
Thiounn Prasith, 10, 327–28, 365n37, 444–49
Thiounn Thioeunn, 10, 327
Thuch Rin, 88
Timber, DK exports of, 381
Tith Nath, 32, 87
Tiv Ol, 124, 230n26, 352–53, 355–56
Tonle Sap (Freshwater River), geography of, 7
Tou Samouth, 12–14; murder of, 13n30
Touch Khamdoeun, 114
Tram Kak ("District 105"), 87–88, 169, 180–87, 191–92, 197, 362, 366, 425, 427, 434–36, 447
Tran Thanh Xuan, 122–23
Treang ("District 107"), 187–89, 258–59, 282–83, 430
Tung Padevat (Revolutionary Flags), 58, 62, 96, 123, 323, 358–59
Tuol Sleng prison, 239, 316, 335, 361, 452, 465

Um Neng (Vy), 90, 306–07, 350
United Front for National Salvation of Kampuchea (UFNSK), 442, 453
United States: intervention in Cambodia, 16–25; bombardment of Cambodia, 20–25, 43, 259, 262, 272; "secret bombing" of Cambodia, 18; imperialism, 142, 446
U.S. Special Forces, 18. See also "Mike Force"

Val ("Ta Val"), 233, 238
Vickery, Michael, 93, 164–66, 168–69, 205, 212, 219–21, 252, 256, 281, 286, 457
Vietnam, 25; DK attacks on, 3, 55, 63, 104–05, 162–63, 357–66, 370, 372, 374n76, 386–87; flight to, 2–3, 83–84, 86, 107, 107n31, 193, 195, 285, 290, 370–73, 373n72, 375, 403, 441–42
Vietnam War, impact on Cambodia, 19
Vietnamese minority, 5, 10, 55–56, 58, 64, 70, 107–09, 141, 296–98, 423–24, 460
Vietnamese troops in Cambodia, 102, 106–07, 374–75, 388, 450–55
Vinh Te canal, 360
Violence in DK, sources of, 164–65, 211–12
Vorn Vet, 22, 32, 79–80, 94, 100, 117, 197, 339, 348–49, 351, 378, 392–93, 437; and China, 138; becomes deputy prime minister, 327

Western Zone, 89, 97; Chams in, 287–88; Chinese in, 70–71, 292; Vietnamese in, 297; Khmer Krom in, 300; dissension in, 345–48, 390–92; takeover of Northwest Zone by, 416–23; toll in, 460
"White Scarves," 1–4, 190
Women's Association of Democratic Kampuchea, 124, 160–62

Yasya Asmath, 264n67, 280–81
Yin Sophi, 371, 375
Yugoslavia, 132, 146
Yun Yat, 355

Zhang Chunqiao, 127
Zhou Enlai (Chou En-lai), 135, 147, 152